OUR
PHILOSOPHICAL
HERITAGE

Fourth Edition

Andrew B. Schoedinger

Boise State University

KENDALL/HUNT PUBLISHING COMPANY
4050 Westmark Drive   Dubuque, Iowa 52002

Cover photo by: Jim Talbot

❧ C O N T E N T S ❧

PART V: METAPHYSICS

❧ P R E F A C E ❧
T O   T H E
F O U R T H
E D I T I O N

The goal of this edition is the same as to the first, second, and third, namely, an easily comprehensible introduction to a substantial range of philosophical issues within the Western tradition. It is designed to be suitable for a broad range of readers. Those who have had a long-standing curiosity concerning the nature of philosophy can educate themselves via this text. Used as a textbook for an introductory philosophy course, it possesses many advantages. The commentaries preceding the primary source material are written in a non-threatening manner thus providing the beginner the necessary background to successfully grapple with the writings of the selected philosophers. There is a page-by-page glossary for speedy and easy reference. All academic disciplines possess their own jargon and philosophy is no exception. However, this book's glossary is meant to be a general vocabulary builder as well as a philosophical lexicon. Each reading is accompanied by study questions. These questions have been crafted in such a way that they simply cannot be answered correctly unless the reader genuinely understands the material. Consequently, they ought to be viewed as friends, not enemies because they can, and should, function as very helpful learning guides. Each page of study questions is detachable in the event an instructor chooses to utilize it for submitted homework. For those interested in perusing the subject matter further, there is a comprehensive reading list at the end of each commentary.

I want to thank Beth Collier for her patience with respect to the preparation of this most recent version of *Our Philosophical Heritage.* She was of great help in that process.

Andrew B. Schoedinger
Boise, Idaho
October 2005

❧

1 *The Philosophical Act; Josef Pieper*

❧ B I O G R A P H Y ❧

Josef Pieper was born in 1904 in Elte, Germany. He studied at the University of Berlin and University of Muenster from 1923 to 1928, when he received his Ph.D. in philosophy from Muenster. His dissertation was on the ethical theory of St. Thomas Aquinas. Pieper taught at Muenster from 1928 to 1931 after which he worked as a free-lance writer for seven years. Subsequent to serving in the German Army during World War II, he taught for a brief time at Teachers College in Essen. In 1946 he returned to the University of Muenster, where he remained until his retirement from teaching in 1972. During his tenure at Muenster, he came to the United States to be a visiting professor at the University of Notre Dame (1950) and Stanford University (1956, 1962). Pieper has been awarded honorary degrees from the University of Munich (1964), the University of Muenster (1974), and the University of Eichstaett (1985).

Pieper has been a prolific writer. His books include Leisure, the Basis of Culture *(1948),* Reality and the Good *(1949),* Guide to Thomas Aquinas *(1958),* The Four Cardinal Virtues *(1964),* About Love *(1972),* The End of Time: A Meditation on the Philosophy of History *(1980), and* In Search of the Sacred *(1988).*

I

When the physicist poses the question, "What does it mean to do physics?" or "What is research in physics?"—his question is a preliminary question. Clearly, when you ask a question like that, and try to answer it, you are not "doing physics." Or, rather, you are *no longer* doing physics. But when you ask yourself, "What does it mean to do philosophy?" then you actually are "doing philosophy"—this is not at all a "preliminary" question but a truly philosophical one; you are right at the heart of the business. To go further: I can say nothing about the existence of philosophy and philosophizing without also saying something about the human being, and to do that is to enter one of the most central regions of philosophy. Our question, "What is the philosophical act?" belongs, in fact, to the field of philosophical anthropology.

Now, because it is a philosophical question, that means it cannot be answered in a permanent or conclusive way. It pertains to the very nature of a philosophical question that its answer will not be a "perfectly rounded truth" (as Parmenides said it), grasped in the hand like an apple plucked from a tree[1]. . . .

But, for a first approach, we can venture the following: a philosophical act is an act in which the work-a-day world is transcended. We must first explain what we mean by "work-a-day world," and second, what we mean by "transcending" it.

The work-a-day world is the world of the working day, the world of usefulness, of purposeful action, of accomplishment, of the exercising of functions; it is the world of supply and demand, the world of hunger and the satisfaction of hunger. It is a world dominated by one goal: the realization of the "common utility"; it is the world of work, to the extent that work is synonymous with "useful activity" (a characteristic both of activity and effort). The process of working is the process of realizing the "common utility"; this concept is not equivalent to that of the "common good" (*bonum commune*): the "common utility" is an essential component of the "common good," but the concept of the *bonum commune* is much more comprehensive. For example, as Thomas puts it[2], there are people who devote themselves to the "un-useful" life of contemplation; to philosophize belongs to the common good, whereas one could not say that contemplation, vision, or philosophizing serve the "common utility."

Of course, in the present day *bonum commune* and the "common utility" seem to be growing more identical every day; of course (it comes to the same thing) the world of work begins to become—threatens to become—our only world, to the exclusion of all else. The demands of the working world grow ever more total, grasping ever more completely the whole of human existence.

If it is correct to say that the philosophical act is one which transcends the working world, then our question, "What does it mean to philosophize?"—our so very theoretical, abstract question—becomes suddenly, and unexpectedly, a question of utmost relevance. We need only to take a single step, in our thoughts or in physical space, to find ourselves in a world in which the working process, the process of realizing the "common utility," determines the whole realm of human existence. Inwardly and outwardly, there is a boundary, very near and easy to jump across, in order to win entry into the work-a-day world, in which there is no such thing as genuine philosophy and genuine philosophizing—all this presupposes, of course, that it is correct to say that "philosophy transcends the working world" and that it pertains to the very essence of the philosophical act *not* to belong to this world of uses and efficiencies, of needs and satisfactions, this world of "useful good" (*bonum utile*), of the "common utility," but is, rather, to be incommensurable to it in principle. Indeed, the more acute the incommensurability, the more obvious the "not-belonging." It could even be said, perhaps, that this very opposition, this threat from the world of total work, is what characterizes the situation of philosophy today more than its own particular content. Philosophy increasingly adopts—necessarily, it seems—the character of the *alien*, of mere intellectual luxury, of that which seems ever more intolerable and unjustifi-

---

[1] Parmenides, fragment 1. Parmenides (born 515 B.C.) was a Greek philosopher [editor's note].

[2] Thomas Aquinas, *Commentary on the Sentences*, iv, d. 26, 1.2. Aquinas (1224 - 1274) was an influential philosopher/theologian of the Middle Ages [editor's note].

able, the more exclusively the demands of the daily world of work take over the world of man.

And yet, we have something more to say, something very concrete, about the incommensurability of the philosophical act, of this transcending the world of work, that takes place in the philosophical act.

Let's recall the things that dominate the contemporary working day; no special effort of the imagination is needed, for we all stand right in the middle of it. There is, first of all, the daily running back and forth to secure our bare physical existence, food, clothing, shelter, heat; then, the anxieties that affect, and absorb, each individual . . . Struggles for power for the exploitation of earth's commodities, conflicts of interest in matters great and small. Everywhere, tensions and burdens—only superficially eased by hastily arranged pauses and diversions: newspapers, movies, cigarettes. I do not need to paint it in any fuller detail; we all know what this world looks like. And we need not only direct our attention to the extreme instances of crisis that show themselves today: I mean simply the everyday working world, where we must go about our business, where very concrete goals are advanced and realized; goals that must be sighted with an eye fixed on the things nearest and closest at hand. Now it is not our purpose here to condemn this world, from the standpoint of some "holiday-world" of philosophy. No words need be wasted on saying that this work-a-day world is very much with us, that in it the foundations of our physical existence are secured, without which nobody can philosophize at all! Nevertheless, let us also recall, that among the voices which fill the workplace and the markets ("How do you get this or that item of daily existence?" "Where do you get that?" etc.)—in the midst of all these voices suddenly one calls out above the rest: "Why is there anything at all, and not nothing?" — asking that age-old question, which Heidegger called the basic question of all metaphysics![3] Must we explicitly state how unfathomable this Philosopher's question is, in comparison with that everyday world of needs and purposefulness? If such a question as this were asked, without introduction or interpretation, in the company of those people of efficiency and success, wouldn't the questioner be considered rather . . . mad? Through such extremely formulated contrasts, however, the real, underlying distinction comes to the fore: it becomes clear that even to ask that question constitutes taking a step toward transcending, toward leaving behind, the work-a-day world. The genuine philosophical question strikes disturbingly against the canopy that encloses the world of the citizen's work-day.

But the philosophical act is not the only way to take this "step beyond." No less incommensurable with the working-world than the philosophical question is the sound of true poetry:

In middle and ending ever stands the tree,
The birds are singing; on God's breast
The round Creation takes its holy rest . . .[4]

Such a voice sounds utterly strange in the realm of actively realized pur-

---

3   Martin Heidegger, *Was Ist Metaphysik* (Frankfurt, Germany: Klostermann, 1943), p.22. [J.P.]

4   Konrad Weiss, *In Exitu* (first verses)—which first appeared in the volume *Die cumäische Sibylle* (Munich, 1921), more readily accessible now in the collected edition: Konrad Weiss, *Gedichte*, 1914-1939 (Munich: Kösel-Verlag, 1961). Translator's note.

pose. And no differently sounds the voice of one who prays: "We praise
you, we glorify you, we give you thanks for your great glory . . ." How
can that ever be understood in the categories of rational usefulness and
efficiency? The lover, too, stands outside the tight chain of efficiency of
this working world, and whoever else approaches the margin of existence
through some deep, existential disturbance (which always brings a "shat-
tering" of one's environment as well), or through, say, the proximity of
death. In such a disturbance (for the philosophical act, genuine poetry,
musical experience in general, and prayer as well—all these depend on
some kind of disturbance) in such an experience, man senses the non-ulti-
mate nature of this daily, worrisome world: he transcends it, he takes a
step outside it.

For Plato, the laughter of the Thracian maiden, who saw Thales of
Miletus fall into a well while he was staring at the skies, is the typical
response of feet-on-the-ground, work-a-day reasoning to philosophy.[5]
And this anecdote of the Thracian maid stands at the very beginning of
Western Philosophy. "And always," as Plato says in the *Theaetetus*, the
philosopher is the butt of humor,[6] "not only for Thracian maidens, but for
most people, because one who is a stranger to the world falls into wells,
and into many other embarrassments too."[7]

And yet the incommensurability of this situation is not merely negative, for there is another side as well, known as . . . freedom. For philosophy is "useless" in the sense of immediate profit and application—that is
one thing. Another thing is, that philosophy cannot allow itself to be used,
it is not at the disposal of purposes beyond itself, for it is itself a goal. Philosophy is not functional-knowing, but rather, as John Henry Newman put
it,[8] is *gentleman's* knowledge, not "useful," but "free" knowing. But this
freedom means that philosophical knowing does not acquire its legitimacy from its utilitarian applications, not from its social function, not
from its relationship with the "common utility." Freedom in exactly this
sense is the freedom of the "liberal arts," as opposed to the "servile arts,"
which, according to Thomas "are ordered to a use, to be attained through
activity."[9] And philosophy has long been understood as the most free
among the free arts (the medieval "Arts Faculty" is the forerunner of the
"Philosophical Faculty" of today's university).

Now, this freedom of philosophy, this quality of not-being-subservi-
ent-to some purpose is intimately connected with something else (a connection which seems extremely important to point out); the theoretical
character of philosophy. Philosophy is the purest form of *theorein*, or
speculari (to observe, behold, contemplate), consisting in a purely receptive gaze on reality, whereby things alone are determinative, and the soul
is completely receptive of determination. Whenever some existent is
taken up into view in a philosophical way, the questions are asked in a
"purely theoretical" manner, and that means a manner untouched by any-

[5] This is a reference by Pieper to the legend (related by Plato) that once when the Greek
philosopher Thales (about 625-547 B.C.) was looking up to study the stars, he fell into
a cistern and was laughed at by a maid from Thrace for being so impractical [editor's
note].

[6] Plato, *Theaetetus*, Stephanus p. 174. [J.P.]

[7] Ibid.[J.P.]

[8] John Henry Newman, *The Idea of a University*, Part I, Discourse V, section 6. [J.P.]

[9] Thomas Aquinas, *Commentary on the Metaphysics*, I, 3. [J.P.]

thing practical, by any intention to change things, and thereby be raised above all serving of further purposes.

. . . our thesis (which can now be more clearly formulated), maintains that it is of the nature of the philosophical act, to transcend the world of work. This thesis, which comprehends both the freedom and theoretical character of philosophy, does not deny the world of work (in fact, it expressly presumes it as something necessary), but it maintains that true philosophy rests upon the belief that the real wealth of man lies not in the satisfaction of his necessities, nor, again, in "becoming lords and masters of nature," but rather in being able to understand *what is*—the whole of what is. Ancient philosophy says that this is the utmost fulfillment to which we can attain: that the whole order of real things be registered in our soul.[10]

II

. . . the Western philosophical tradition has understood and even defined spiritual knowing as the power to place oneself into relation with the sum-total of existing things. And this is not meant as only one characteristic among others, but as the very essence and definition of the power. By its nature, spirit (or intellection) is not so much distinguished by its immateriality, as by something more primary: its ability to be in relation to the totality of being. "Spirit" means a relating power that is so far-reaching and comprehensive, that the field of relations to which it corresponds, transcends in principle the very boundaries of its surroundings. It is the nature of spirit to have as its field of relations not just "surrounding" [*Umwelt*] but a "world" [*Welt*]. It is of the nature of the spiritual being to go past the immediate surroundings and to go beyond both its "confinement" and its "close fit" to those surroundings (and of course herein is revealed both the freedom and danger to which the spiritual being is naturally heir).

In Aristotle's treatise on the soul, the *De Anima*,[11] we can read the following: "Now, in order to sum up everything said up until this point about the soul, we can say again that, the soul, basically, is all that exists." As Thomas says in the treatise *De Veritate* ("On Truth"), the spiritual soul is essentially structured "to encounter all being" (*convenire cum omni ente*[12]), to put itself into relation with everything that has being. "Every other being possesses only a partial participation in being," whereas the being endowed with spirit "can grasp being as a whole."[13] As long as there is spirit, "it is possible for the completeness of all being to be present in a single nature."[14] And this is also the position of the Western tradition: to have spirit [*Geist*], to be a spirit, to be spiritual—all this means to be in the middle of the sum total of reality, to be in relation with the totality of being, to be *vis-à-vis de l'univers*.[15] The spirit does not live in "a" world, or in "its" world, but in *the* world: world in the sense of "everything seen and unseen" (*omnia visibilia et invisibilia*).

---

[10] Cf, Thomas Aquinas, *Disputed Questions on Truth*, Question 2, Article 2. [J.P.]

[11] Aristotle, *De anima* (*On the Soul*), Book III, Chapter 8. [J.P.]

[12] Thomas Aquinas, *Disputed Questions on Truth*, Question I, Article I. [J.P.]

[13] Thomas Aquinas, *Summa Contra Gentiles*, Book III, Chapter 112. [J.P.]

[14] Thomas Aquinas, *Disputed Questions on Truth*, Question 2, Article 2. [J.P.]

[15] *vis-à-vis de l'universe*: face-to-face with the universe (French) [editor's note].

But now, we have unwittingly taken a step closer to answering our original question: What is it to philosophize? Philosophy means just this: to experience that the nearby world, determined by the immediate demands of life, can be shaken, or indeed, must be shaken, over and over again, by the unsettling call of the "world," or by the total reality that mirrors back the eternal natures of things. To philosophize (we have already asked, What empowers the philosophical act to transcend the working-world?)—to philosophize means to take a step outside of the work-a-day world into the *vis-à-vis de l'univers*. It is a step which leads to a kind of "homeless"-ness: the stars are no roof over the head. It is a step, however, that constantly keeps open its own retreat, for the human being cannot live long in this way. He who seriously intends to wander finally and definitively outside the world of the Thracian maiden is wandering outside the realm of human reality.

III

. . . The one who philosophizes does not turn his head in a different direction, when he transcends the work-a-day world in the philosophical act; he does not take his eye off the things of the working world—away, that is, from the concrete, purposeful, manageable items of the working day— he does not need to look in a different direction in order to behold the universal world of essences.

No, it is rather this visible world, the one before our very eyes which we touch with our hands, upon which the philosopher gazes. But this world, and all these things in it, are investigated in a peculiar way; what one inquires into, in regard to them, is their ultimate nature, and the horizon of the question becomes the horizon of the sum-total of reality. The philosophical question concerns itself precisely with "this" or "that," lying before one's eyes, and not with something "outside the world," or something "in another world," outside the world of daily experience. But the philosophical question asks, "What is this, *ultimately*, and *in the last analysis*?" As Plato says, "It is not whether I am doing an injustice to you somehow, or you are doing an injustice to me: that is not what philosophy wants to get at, but rather, what is justice or injustice in itself; not, whether a king who has a lot of money is happy or not, but rather, just what kingship is, what happiness is, what misery is—what they are as such, and in the last analysis."[16]

Philosophical questioning is entirely directed toward the day-to-day world that lies before our eyes. However, what lies before our eyes becomes all at once "transparent" to the question-asker; it loses its compactness, its apparent completeness, its self-explanatory, obvious nature. Things appear, but with a strange, unfamiliar, uncertain, *deeper* appearance. When Socrates asks questions, aware that he is suddenly taking the obviousness away from things, he compares himself to a sting-ray, whose sting makes its victims numb. People are always saying, this is "my" friend, or this is "my" wife, or "my" house, that we "have" or "own" such things. But suddenly we are startled: do we really "have" all these "possessions"? Can they really be "had"? What *is* it, as such, and in the last analysis, to "have" something?

To philosophize means to remove oneself, not from the things of the everyday world, but from the usual meanings, the accustomed evaluations

---

[16]   Plato, *Theaetetus*, Stephanus p. 175. [J.P.]

of these things. And this is not motivated from some decision to think "differently" from the way most people think, but rather for the purpose of seeing everything in a new light. This is just how it is: in the everyday things (not in some separated sphere of an "essential" world, or what have you) to be able to see the deeper visage of the real so that the attention directed to the things encountered in everyday experience comes up against what is not so obvious in these things—it is exactly here, in this inner experience, that philosophy has its beginning: in the experience of *wonder*.

"Indeed, by the gods my dear Socrates, I cannot keep from being astounded at the meaning of all this, and at times I even get dizzy," exclaims the young mathematician Theaetetus after Socrates has succeeded in taking him far enough to see and accept his own ignorance— Socrates, at once so deceptive and helpful, who could make someone so confounded, even *numb*, with wonder, by his questioning. And then, in Plato's dialogue *Theaetetus*,[17] comes the ironical answer of Socrates: "Yes, this very condition is characteristic of the philosopher; this, and nothing else, is the very beginning of philosophy." Here for the first time, in the bright morning of our history, and almost in passing, with no ceremony, is the thought first expressed, which will then become almost a commonplace through the entire history of philosophy: that philosophy begins in *wonder*.

Thus the one who experiences wonder is one who realizes in an unmixed form that ancient attitude toward being, which has been called *theoria* since the time of Plato: the purely receptive stance toward reality .... *Theoria* can only exist to the extent that man has not become blind to the wondrous—the wonderful fact that something exists. No, it is not what has "never been there before," the abnormal, the sensational, that kindles philosophical wonder—the "numbing of the senses" would be a mere substitute for genuine wonder. If someone needs the "unusual" to be moved to astonishment, that person has lost the ability to respond rightly to the wondrous, the *mirandum*, of being.

---

[17] Ibid., p. 155. [J.P.]

Name_____

Date _____

1. In what sense is philosophy like poetry?

2. Why is laughter or ridicule sometimes the response which philosophy evokes?

3. Philosophical knowledge is useless. True or false? Explain.

4. Pieper says that to philosophize is "to step out of the workaday world" and yet later he says that to philosophize does *not* mean to withdraw from the things of everyday life. How can both be true?

5. What does Pieper mean when he says that from a philosophical point of view things "become all at once, transparent;...they can no longer be taken for granted"?

6. What does it mean to say that the nature of philosophy is *theoria*?

2 *What Is Philosophy?*

Perhaps the best way to go about approaching the discipline is to first understand the meaning of the word 'philosophy'. It is derived[1] from the two Greek words *philia* and *sophia*. The former means love. However, the ancient Greeks appreciated the fact that there are several different types of love.[2] Some people cater[3] to their curiosity. They want to find out what makes the world tick. Such individuals enjoy learning and acquiring knowledge. This passion for understanding the nature of the world and man's relationship to it is what the ancient Greeks meant by *philia*.[4]

Sophia means wisdom. Typically, wisdom is understood to be knowledge tempered[5] by good judgment. For example, wisdom is manifested by a person who does not immediately jump into a task without thought, but rather ascertains[6] the possible problems thereof and as a result determines the most propitious[7] manner by which to accomplish the desired goal. This, however, is a nontechnical definition of wisdom. As we will see, wisdom in the philosophical sense of the term means something quite different. To understand the study of Philosophy it is most helpful to compare the discipline with that of the sciences. I would like to do that by drawing an analogy[8] between these disciplines and a tree.

Let us imagine a tree with two major trunks. These two trunks constitute the natural sciences, the so-called "hard sciences". There are two major areas of natural science; (a) the physical sciences and (b) biological science. As the bottom of the tree demonstrates, these two areas merge manifested by the study of biochemistry and physiology. The branches of the tree represent the social sciences.[9] One thing that all of the sciences have in common is that they deal with the physical or that which can be perceived. Perception is direct acquaintance with anything through the (five) senses. More specifically, the sciences all possess as their goal the establishment of laws governing that which is physical. It is in this sense that I refer to the various studies of the tree as it exists *above the ground* as the study of Physics with a capital P.

---

[1]   *derive*: to arrive at by reasoning; deduce.

[2]   Philosophy in Western Civilization has its roots in ancient Greek culture which existed from approximately the eighth century B.C. to the birth of Christ.

[3]   *cater*: to provide anything wished for or needed.

[4]   Other Greek words for love are *eros;* that is, erotic love and *agape*, man's concern for the ultimate well-being of his neighbor.

[5]   *temper*: to modify by the addition of some moderating agent or quality; moderate.

[6]   *ascertain*: to discover through examination or experimentation; to find out.

[7]   *propitious*: favorable.

[8]   *analogy*: correspondence in some respects, especially in function or position, between things otherwise dissimilar.

[9]   It is questionable precisely where the discipline of psychology is properly represented on the tree. It possesses elements of both the natural and social sciences.

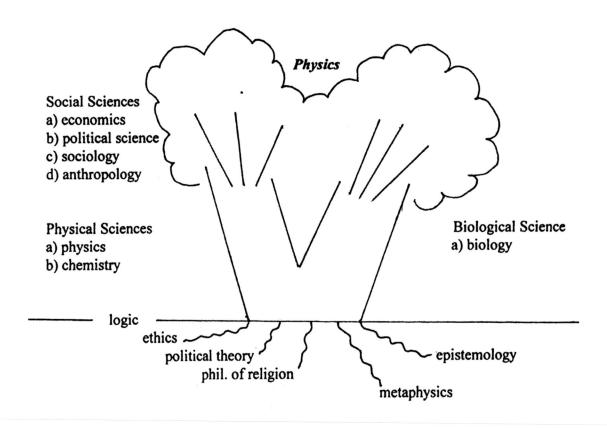

Metaphysics

We know that in addition to the visible portion of the tree it must also possess roots. A tree cannot exist without roots, otherwise it would collapse. The roots of the tree are invisible. Here we must not be too literal. Obviously, one can dislodge a tree and view its roots. But as one normally perceives a tree its roots are not in sight. We know that not only do those roots exist, but *must* exist. The tree as we perceive it cannot exist without some support structure, namely, its roots. To understand the nature of the roots we must go beyond Physics. *Meta* is the Greek word meaning beyond. In this context, *meta* is not to be construed[10] as beyond in the sense of further understanding in a visible sense, for example, examining a tree branch under a microscope. Rather, we must go beyond the Physics in order to understand the concepts that we necessarily use to explain the Physics of the tree. These concepts constitute the roots of the tree. They are not tangible[11], but are inescapably necessary.

Here an example would be helpful. I indicated that one of the goals of scientific investigation is to establish laws to which the perceptible conforms. For example, a study of physics (with a lower case p) dictates that physical bodies conform to the law of gravity. One law of economics is that of supply and demand. It is the concern of Physics (with a capital P) to establish such *specific* laws. Such laws (purport[12] to) dictate how the perceptible world functions. However, there is another way of understand-

---

[10]   *construe*: to give an explanation or translation.

[11]   *tangible*: discernible by one or more of the five senses.

[12]   *purport*: to claim or profess.

ing the laws of Physics. Such a way is not concerned with *how* the world goes round-and-round. Rather, it is more conceptual with regard to nature. If it is the case that the world functions according to laws of Physics, then it must be the case that there must be a characteristic or set of characteristics which makes a law a law. Just what is a law? Certainly, if the world functions according to laws, it should be of concern to us to understand what the nature of a law is. But the nature of a law is not within and of itself, perceptible. Rather, it is conceptual in nature. How can one possibly know in any other than a superficial way how the Physical functions without knowing what the nature of a law is? It is in this sense that one must go beyond the Physical to understand the conceptual foundations of the Physical. The study of the conceptual foundations of the Physical is called Metaphysics. Metaphysics (with a capital M) is synonymous with Philosophy.

The above example serves to point out that one cannot thoroughly understand the nature of the perceptible world without sooner or later understanding the Metaphysics of it. It is in this sense that the discipline of Philosophy constitutes[13] the original "back to basics" movement. Philosophers are always in search of an understanding of the notions they, as well as others, must employ in order to explain perceptible phenomena[14]. If notions, such as a law, are necessary to explain the tangible things of the world, then they are most certainly basic. The basic nature of the concepts which are of concern to philosophers is also demonstrated by the fact that everyone employs them. For example, one of the most commonly used words is 'good'. We speak of a good car or a good backpack. But can we honestly say that we *know* what constitutes a good automobile or backpack unless we first and foremost know what the meaning of 'good' is? It is a down to earth concern. It is Metaphysical; that is, beyond (i.e., below) the earth, right down to that which is necessary to explain that which is above ground such as cars and backpacks.

As pointed out above, we use the word 'good' on a daily basis. Unless we are to consider the use of words the meanings of which we do not understand as an acceptable practice, then it is important we get clear just exactly what we mean by such a word as 'good'. Do you know what 'good' means? Try the following test. Whenever you catch yourself using that word, stop and ask yourself what it means. Unless you can give yourself a satisfactory answer, then stop using the word. Just try to get along without it. Doing without using the word 'good' will prove difficult. That is an indication in itself as to just how basic the notion of good is in our thinking and communication process. As mentioned above, Philosophy is concerned with the basics.

The individual roots of the tree represent the various areas of Metaphysical concern. Much as zoology and botany are areas of study within the discipline of Biology, so too the discipline of Philosophy is divided into categories. There is the study of ethics, political theory, philosophy of religion, epistemology (theory of knowledge), metaphysics (with a lower case m), logic and many more.[15] The study of ethics seeks answers to such questions as what constitutes the good life and what is it to be moral? The concept of good has both moral and nonmoral uses. Non-

---

[13]   *constitute*: to be the elements or parts of; make up; compose.

[14]   *phenomenon*: any occurrence or fact that is directly perceptible by the senses. Phenomena is the plural form of the word.

[15]   Other areas of philosophical inquiry are aesthetics (philosophy of art), philosophy of science, philosophy of language, philosophy of history, philosophy of law and philosophy of mind.

moral refers to that which has absolutely nothing to do with morality. For example, under normal circumstances whether or not one eats pizza for dinner is nonmoral behavior. However, torturing one's neighbor for the fun of it does fall into the realm of moral behavior. To determine the difference between these two realms is a concern of modern and contemporary ethical theorists. They also want to know if there is a rationally derived moral principle to help resolve the moral dilemmas which are an inevitable aspect of human existence.

One of the key concepts discussed in political theory is that of a natural right. Aside from the specific natural rights of life, liberty and pursuit of happiness that we have been educated to believe we all possess, the philosopher wants to know the nature of a right. What makes a right a right as opposed to something else? It does appear reasonable that since so many people believe that there are natural rights and since governmental systems are predicated[16] on them, that we should know what the characteristics are that make a right what it is as opposed to something else. Rights are not physical in nature. They cannot be fondled as one can a piece of sculpture. Rather, they are Metaphysical. Nevertheless, natural rights are fundamental to many societies and their political systems are to a great extent designed to protect such rights. Here again is a case where the Physical can only properly be explained by relying on the Metaphysical.

Typically, a natural right has been defined as a God given right. It may appear that we have gained some ground with this definition. However, the concept of God is itself a Metaphysical notion. What characteristics does God possess? More importantly, does God exist? Unless we can demonstrate that God exists, does not the notion of a God given right become vacuous[17]?

Obviously, the notion of God is a viable[18] one. After all, the vast majority of people believe that such a being exists. But God is not a perceptible entity. Such a being is distinctly Metaphysical in nature. For example, it is often believed that God created the universe and all that therein is. This means that a Metaphysical being created the entirety of the Physical. If such is the case, then an understanding of Metaphysics is of critical importance to our understanding Physical reality. Clearly, the notion of God is as basic as one can get. Of major concern to the philosopher of religion is to determine if there are acceptable reasons and/or adequate evidence to credibly claim that God exists. If not, then obviously one should not believe that such a being created the universe.

Episteme is the Greek word for knowledge. Epistemology is the study of knowledge, namely, what is it and how do we come by it? We have knowledge *of* the Physical, but knowledge *itself* is Metaphysical. The concept of knowledge is very basic. We make knowledge claims all the time. But just what is knowledge? Surely if we claim to possess it, we ought to have some idea just what it is. What conditions must be satisfied in order for one to truly state that he *knows* something to be the case? Once again, to demonstrate the basic nature of the concept of knowledge, try eliminating it from your vocabulary. One simply cannot communicate effectively without it. Simply stated, unless we have a firm understanding of the concept of knowledge, saying we know anything is ultimately vacuous.

The concepts of belief and truth are two other epistemological notions that are just as basic as that of knowledge. Consider the number of times a

---

[16]   *predicate*: to base or establish. Used with *on* or *upon*.

[17]   *vacuous*: devoid of substance or meaning; inane.

[18]   *viable*: workable and likely to survive or to have real meaning; pertinence.

day you use those terms. Do you know what they mean? What, for example, is the difference between knowledge and belief? Furthermore, what does it mean to say, "It is *true* that it is presently warm and sunny outside."?

Just as there is a discipline of physics (with a lower case p) which is a subcategory of Physics (with a capital P), the same relationship exists between metaphysics (with a lower case m) and Metaphysics (with a capital M). There is a distinct set of issues and problems which are characterized as metaphysical in nature. Two of these are the problem of personal identity and the issue of free will versus determinism.

The problem of personal identity can be brought into focus by asking the question, "In what sense can we say that a person is the *same* person at time t_1 as he is at time t_2"? Although any given human being is constantly changing both physically and mentally from time to time, there is a sense in which it makes sense to say, "I am the same person today as I was five years ago". The philosophical issue is in just what sense does it make sense to make such a claim?

The issue of free will versus determinism boils down to whether or not human beings have any free choice regarding the daily decisions they make. It may be the case that between genetic programming and environmental conditioning we have no free will whatsoever. Certainly human beings are more than mere automatons[19]. The latter are 100% programmed. They have no choice to "behave" other than they do. But what evidence can we offer to demonstrate that human beings can do otherwise than they do, that they have free choice in their behavior?

Logic is the science of sound thinking and is as important to a proper understanding of Physics as it is to Metaphysics. Those who cannot think clearly will be successful at neither. That is why logic is depicted at the ground level of the tree. The ancient Greek philosopher Aristotle was the first person to codify[20] what are called rules of inference, the rules of sound thinking. Because of this precedence[21], logic has historically been taught as a division of philosophy although it could just as easily be taught by mathematicians since all mathematics is ultimately an extension of logic.[22]

The lion's share of people are interested only in the nature of the Physical. They take the Metaphysical for granted. I indicated above that the word 'philosophy' means love of wisdom. There is a difference between knowledge and wisdom. The ancient Greeks believed the former term to mean an understanding of the Physical. Wisdom, on the other hand, refers to an understanding of the Metaphysical. Hence, the business, if you will, of the philosopher is to accumulate as much understanding of Metaphysics as he possibly can.[23]

---

[19] *automaton*: one that behaves in an automatic or mechanical fashion.

[20] *codify*: to arrange or systematize.

[21] *precedence*: the act, right or fact or preceding in time, place, order or importance.

[22] Peano's five axioms of arithmetic are reducible to logical laws.

[23] Not surprisingly, just as people specialize within a given science, philosophers usually specialize in one of the various areas of the discipline.

Suggested Readings: What is Philosophy?

1. Danto, Arthur C., *What Philosophy Is* (New York: Harper & Row, 1968).
2. Durant, Will, *The Story of Philosophy* (N.Y.: Simon and Schuster, Inc., 1961).
3. Korner, Stephen, *What Is Philosophy?* (London: Allen Lane, 1969).
4. Newell, R.W., *The Concept of Philosophy* (London: Nethuen, 1967).
5. Wisdom, J.O., *Philosophy and Its Place in Our Culture* (London: Gordon and Breach, 1975).
6. Woodhouse, Mark B., *A Preface to Philosophy* (Belmont, Calif.: Wadsworth Publishing Co., 1984).

Name_____

Date _____

1. What is the meaning of the word "philosophy"?

2. Using the analogy of the tree, what is the function of philosophy?

3. Give at least three examples of the kinds of questions philosophy asks.

4. The concept of belief and the nature of truth are studied in the branch of philosophy known as

   _____.

5. From the ancient Greek point-of-view, what is the difference between knowledge and wisdom?

3 The Value of Philosophy; Bertrand Russell

❧ BIOGRAPHY ❧

Bertrand Russell is without doubt a pillar of 20th century philosophy. He was born at Trellect, Wales, in 1872. The death of his parents when he was young resulted in him being raised by his paternal grandmother. By age eleven Bertrand was an accomplished mathematician. The fall of 1890 saw him enrolled at Cambridge University where he studied mathematics and philosophy at Trinity College culminating in a degree after four years. He was a fellow at his college from 1895 to 1901 and a lecturer in philosophy from 1910 to 1916. From 1916 until the late 1930's Russell held no academic position supporting himself by writing and giving public lectures. Upon the death of his brother in 1931, he became Earl Russell. He moved to the United States in 1938, teaching first at the University of Chicago and then at the University of California at Los Angeles. He lectured at the Barnes Foundation in Philadelphia from 1941 to 1943. These lectures were later expanded into A History of Western Philosophy. *The following year he returned to Cambridge, having been re-elected to a fellowship at Trinity College.*

Russell was a most prolific writer. This is noteworthy considering the depth and breadth of that which he produced. His book Principia Mathematica *co-authored with Alfred North Whitehead [his mentor at Trinity College], is a three-volume landmark in which they set out to demonstrate that all of pure mathematics can be stated in [i.e., reduced to] terms of logic. Others of his works are* The Principles of Mathematics *[1903],* The Problems of Philosophy *[1912],* Our Knowledge of the External World *[1914],* On Education, Especially in Early Childhood *[1926],* Marriage and Morals *[1929],* The Conquest of Happiness *[1930],* Education and the Social Order *[1932] and* An Inquiry into Meaning and Truth *[1940]. In 1950 Russell was awarded the Nobel Prize for Literature. In making the award, the committee described him as "one of our time's most brilliant spokesmen of rationality and humanity, and a fearless champion of free speech and free thought in the West." He died in 1970 near Penrhyndeudraeth, Wales, at the age of ninety-seven.*

From *The Problems of Philosophy*, Chapter 15 (Oxford University Press, 1912).

Having now come to the end of our brief and very incomplete review of the problems of philosophy, it will be well to consider, in conclusion, what is the value of philosophy and why it ought to be studied. It is the more necessary to consider this question, in view of the fact that many men, under the influence of science or of practical affairs, are inclined to doubt whether philosophy is anything better than innocent but useless trifling, hair-splitting distinctions, and controversies on matters concerning which knowledge is impossible.

This view of philosophy appears to result, partly from a wrong conception of the ends of life, partly from a wrong conception of the kind of goods which philosophy strives to achieve. Physical science, through the medium of inventions, is useful to innumerable people who are wholly ignorant of it; thus the study of physical science is to be recommended, not only, or primarily, because of the effect on the student, but rather because of the effect on mankind in general. This utility does not belong to philosophy. If the study of philosophy has any value at all for others than students of philosophy, it must be indirectly, through its effects upon the lives of those who study it. It is in these effects, therefore, if anywhere, that the value of philosophy must be primarily sought.

But further, if we are not to fail in our endeavour to determine the value of philosophy, we must first free our minds from the prejudices of what are wrongly called "practical" men. The "practical" man, as this word is often used, is one who recognizes only material needs, who realises that men must have food for the body, but is oblivious[1] of the necessity of providing food for the mind. If all men were well off, if poverty and disease had been reduced to the lowest possible point, there would still remain much to be done to produce a valuable society; and even in the existing world the goods of the mind are at least as important as the goods of the body. It is exclusively among the goods of the mind that the value of philosophy is to be found; and only those who are not indifferent to these goods can be persuaded that the study of philosophy is not a waste of time.

Philosophy, like all other studies, aims primarily at knowledge. The knowledge it aims at is the kind of knowledge which gives unity and system to the body of the sciences, and the kind which results from a critical examination of the grounds of our convictions, prejudices, and beliefs. But it cannot be maintained that philosophy has had any very great measure of success in its attempts to provide definite answers to its questions. If you ask a mathematician, a mineralogist, a historian, or any other man of learning, what definite body of truths has been ascertained by his science, his answer will last as long as you are willing to listen. But if you put the same question to a philosopher, he will, if he is candid, have to confess that his study has not achieved positive results such as have been achieved by other sciences. It is true that this is partly accounted for by the fact that, as soon as definite knowledge concerning any subject becomes possible, this subject ceases to be called philosophy, and becomes a separate science. The whole study of the heavens, which now belongs to astronomy, was once included in philosophy; Newton's great work was called "the mathematical principles of natural philosophy." Similarly, the study of the human mind, which was, until very lately, a part of philosophy, has now been separated from philosophy and has become the science of psychology. Thus, to a great extent, the uncertainty of philosophy is more apparent than real: those questions which are already capable of definite answers are placed in the sciences, while those

---

[1]   *oblivious:* unaware, unnoticing [editor's note].

only to which, at present, no definite answer can be given, remain to form the residue which is called philosophy.

This is, however, only a part of the truth concerning the uncertainty of philosophy. There are many questions—and among them those that are of the profoundest interest to our spiritual life—which, so far as we can see, must remain insoluble to the human intellect unless its powers become of quite a different order from what they are now. Has the universe any unity of plan or purpose, or is it a fortuitous concourse of atoms? Is consciousness a permanent part of the universe, giving hope of indefinite growth in wisdom, or is it a transitory accident on a small planet of which life must ultimately become impossible? Are good and evil of importance to the universe or only to man? Such questions are asked by philosophy, and variously answered by various philosophers. But it would seem that, whether answers be otherwise discoverable or not, the answers suggested by philosophy are none of them demonstrably true. Yet, however slight may be the hope of discovering an answer, it is part of the business of philosophy to continue the consideration of such questions, to make us aware of their importance, to examine all the approaches to them, and to keep alive that speculative interest in the universe which is apt to be killed by confining ourselves to definitely ascertainable knowledge.

Many philosophers, it is true, have held that philosophy could establish the truth of certain answers to such fundamental questions. They have supposed that what is of most importance in religious beliefs could be proved by strict demonstration to be true. In order to judge of such attempts, it is necessary to take a survey of human knowledge, and to form an opinion as to its methods and its limitations. On such a subject it would be unwise to pronounce dogmatically; but if the investigations of our previous chapters have not led us astray, we shall be compelled to renounce the hope of finding philosophical proofs of religious beliefs. We cannot, therefore, include as part of the value of philosophy any definite set of answers to such questions. Hence, once more, the value of philosophy must not depend upon any supposed body of definitely ascertainable knowledge to be acquired by those who study it.

The value of philosophy is, in fact, to be sought largely in its very uncertainty. The man who has no tincture of philosophy goes through life imprisoned in the prejudices derived from common sense, from the habitual beliefs of his age or his nation, and from convictions which have grown up in his mind without the cooperation or consent of his deliberate reason. To such a man the world tends to become definite, finite, obvious; common objects rouse no questions, and unfamiliar possibilities are contemptuously rejected. As soon as we begin to philosophize, on the contrary, we find . . . that even the most everyday things lead to problems to which only incomplete answers can be given. Philosophy, though unable to tell us with certainty what is the true answer to the doubts which it raises, is able to suggest many possibilities which enlarge our thoughts and free them from the tyranny of custom. Thus, while diminishing our feeling of certainty as to what things are, it greatly increases our knowledge as to what they may be; it removes the somewhat arrogant dogmatism of those who have never travelled into the region of liberating doubt, and it keeps alive our sense of wonder by showing familiar things in an unfamiliar aspect.

Apart from its utility in showing unsuspected possibilities, philosophy has a value—perhaps its chief value—through the greatness of the objects which it contemplates, and the freedom from narrow and personal aims resulting from this contemplation. The life of the instinctive man is shut up within the circle of his private interests: family and friends may be included, but the outer world is not regarded except as it may help or hinder what comes from within the circle of instinctive wishes. In such a life there is something feverish and confined, in comparison with which the philosophical life is calm and free. The private world of instinctive interests is a small one, set in the midst of a great and powerful world which must, sooner or later, lay our private world in ruins. Unless we can so enlarge our interests as to include the whole outer world, we remain like a garrison in a beleaguered fortress, knowing that the enemy prevents escape and that ultimate surrender is inevitable. In such a life there is no peace, but a constant strife between the insistence of desire and the powerlessness of will. In one way or another, if our life is to great and free, we must escape this prison and this strife.

One way of escape is by philosophical contemplation. Philosophic contemplation does not, in its widest survey, divide the universe into two hostile camps—friends and foes, helpful and hostile, good and bad—it views the whole impartially. Philosophic contemplation, when it is unalloyed, does not aim at proving that the rest of the universe is akin to man. All acquisition of knowledge is an enlargement of the Self, but this enlargement is best attained when it is not directly sought. It is obtained when the desire for knowledge is alone operative, by a study which does not wish in advance that its objects should have this or that character, but adapts the Self to the characters which it finds in its objects. This enlargement of Self is not obtained when, taking the Self as it is, we try to show that the world is so similar to this Self that knowledge of it is possible without any admission of what seems alien. The desire to prove this is a form of self-assertion, and like all self-assertion, it is an obstacle to the growth of Self which it desires, and of which the Self knows that it is capable. Self-assertion, in philosophic speculation as elsewhere, views the world as a means to its own ends; thus it makes the world of less account than Self, and the Self sets bounds to the greatness of its goods. In contemplation, on the contrary, we start from the not-Self, and through its greatness the boundaries of Self are enlarged; through the infinity of the universe the mind which contemplates it achieves some share in infinity.

For this reason greatness of soul is not fostered by those philosophies which assimilate the universe to Man. Knowledge is a form of union of Self and not-Self; like all union, it is impaired by dominion, and therefore by any attempt to force the universe into conformity with what we find in ourselves. There is a widespread philosophical tendency towards the view which tells us that man is the measure of all things, that truth is man-made, that space and time and the world of universals[2] are properties of the mind, and that, if there be anything not created by the mind, it is unknowable and of no account for us. This view . . . is untrue; but in addition to being untrue, it has the effect of robbing philosophic contemplation of all that gives it value, since it fetters contemplation to Self. What it calls knowledge is not a union with the not-Self, but a set of prejudices, habits, and desires, making an impenetrable veil between us and the world beyond. The man who finds pleasure in such a theory of knowledge is like the man who never leaves the domestic circle for fear his word might not be law.

The true philosophic contemplation, on the contrary, finds its satisfaction in every enlargement of the not-Self, in everything that magnifies the objects contemplated, and thereby the subject contemplating. Everything, in contemplation, that is personal and private, everything that depends

---

[2]   A universal is that which two or more things, i.e., particulars have in common; that to which all common nouns refer. [editor's note].

upon habit, self-interest, or desire, distorts the object, and hence impairs the union which the intellect seeks. By thus making a barrier between subject and object, such personal and private things become a prison to the intellect. The free intellect will see as God might see, without a *here* and *now*, without hopes and fears, without the trammels of customary beliefs and traditional prejudices, calmly, dispassionately, in the sole and exclusive desire of knowledge—knowledge as impersonal, as purely contemplative, as it is possible for man to attain. Hence also the free intellect will value more the abstract and universal knowledge into which the accidents of private history do not enter, than the knowledge brought by the senses, and dependent, as such knowledge must be, upon an exclusive and personal point of view and a body whose sense-organs distort as much as they reveal.

The mind which has become accustomed to the freedom and impartiality of philosophic contemplation will preserve something of the same freedom and impartiality in the world of action and emotion. It will view its purposes and desires as parts of the whole, with the absence of insistence that results from seeing them as infinitesimal fragments in a world of which all the rest is unaffected by any one man's deeds. The impartiality which, in contemplation, is the unalloyed desire for truth, is the very same quality of mind which, in action, is justice, and in emotion is that universal love which can be given to all, and not only to those who are judged useful or admirable. Thus contemplation enlarges not only the objects of our thoughts, but also the objects of our actions and our affections: it makes us citizens of the universe, not only of one walled city at war with all the rest. In this citizenship of the universe consists man's true freedom, and his liberation from the thraldom[3] of narrow hopes and fears.

Thus, to sum up our discussion of the value of philosophy: Philosophy is to be studied, not for the sake of any definite answers to its questions, since no definite answers can, as a rule, be known to be true, but rather for the sake of the questions themselves; because these questions enlarge our conception of what is possible, enrich our intellectual imagination, and diminish the dogmatic assurance which closes the mind against speculation; but above all because, through the greatness of the universe which philosophy contemplates, the mind also is rendered great, and becomes capable of that union with the universe which constitutes its highest good.

---

[3] *thraldom:* slavery, bondage [editor's note].

Chapter 3:
The Value of Philosophy;
Bertrand Russell

Name_____

Date _____

1. According to Russell, where must the value of philosophy primarily be sought? Explain.

2. What phenomenon occurs when definite knowledge concerning any subject becomes possible?

3. Why, according to Russell, can there be no philosophical proof of religious beliefs?

4. How does the study of philosophy liberate one from common prejudices?

5. In what sense does the free intellect see as God might see?

4 *Problems of Ethics*

The study of ethics is that philosophical inquiry which attempts to determine the nature of good or moral behavior. This at the very outset entails the recognition of an all important fact concerning ethics. It is action oriented. First and foremost, one cannot be a moral agent unless one behaves in a moral fashion. A person simply cannot be moral by lounging in his living room contemplating what ought to be done without ever *doing* what ought to be done. The rational person will first attempt to determine what course of action should be taken in a moral situation, and then follow through with a rational course of action.

Once this is well understood and accepted as a fact of ethics, the problem then becomes one of determining just what *is* good or moral behavior. In order to fully appreciate the following chapters one must keep in mind that the ancient Greeks approached the issue with a completely different *gestalt*[1] than have modern and contemporary theorists.[2]

The Ancients were first and foremost concerned with the *whole* of a person's behavior. By and large the Ancients were concerned with how one can create for oneself a life of living well. The "good life" is one which is equivalent to an overall situation of living well. They are not concerned with any one particular action, but rather with an overall behavior pattern that will result in a lifestyle whereby an individual can find satisfaction. Ethics, to their way of thinking, concerns *all* human activity.

When the Greeks spoke of the good life and how it was to be attained[3], they were not specifically concerned with the distinction between moral and nonmoral behavior even though they occasionally speak of the former[4]. Care should be taken not to confuse nonmoral behavior with activity which is immoral. Nonmoral behavior refers to actions which have absolutely nothing to do with morality since, loosely speaking, morality pertains to those actions which are likely to have an effect, either in a beneficial or detrimental way, on other human beings. If in doubt as to what you ought to do in a given situation, ask yourself "Just what difference will it make to others if I do what I am contemplating doing?" If such activity makes no difference, chances are that such an activity is nonmoral in nature. However, if what you are thinking about doing has a potential effect on others, then most likely it is a moral situation, and immorality results by not taking those possibly affected individuals into account. However, the Greeks were not particularly concerned with this distinction. Good, namely ethical, behavior meant to them that which promotes an overall lifestyle of living well (whatever that ultimately means). This includes nonmoral as well as moral behavior.

This leads to an essential[5] point concerning the Greek's understanding

---

[1] *gestalt:* a mind set: a physical or psychological framework within which things, attitudes or values are construed.

[2] By 'modern and contemporary' we mean philosophy (in general) which has been produced from the time of Decartes (1596-1650 A.D.) to the present.

[3] *attain:* to gain, reach, or accomplish by mental or physical effort.

[4] This distinction is of utmost importance to modern and contemporary philosophers.

[5] *essential:* a fundamental necessary, or indispensable part, item, or principle.

of ethics. Ancient Greek ethicists were viewed by others (as well as by themselves) as fulfilling a role analogous[6] to that of a physician, namely, a psychologist.[7] When a person approaches a medical doctor he wants to find out (a) what is ailing him, and (b) precisely what to do with respect to curing the malady in question. In comparison, when it comes to such issues as what constitutes the good life, *and* how to attain it, the Greeks believed that one ought to consult a philosopher, for that was, among other things, his area of expertise. One consults a physician to diagnose a specific ailment and suggest a specific cure; whereas one seeks the advice of a philosopher to learn precisely what it is that constitutes the good life and how to attain it. While the physician offers a physical cure, the philosopher/psychologist offers behavioral guidelines for the purpose of achieving the good life.

This role of the philosopher is obscured[8] by the fact that the word 'good' is used in a rather loose way, as opposed to a medical term such as the word 'cancer'. The point is that because 'good' is commonly used people think that they know what it means, even when it is used to describe a given life style. To be sure, in most cases people do know, for example, what a good vacation or a good automobile is, but do they really know what the word 'good' means? From the ancient Greek point of view, when it comes to ascertaining[9] just exactly what 'good' means, we should seek the advice of a person who makes it his business to know about such things in the same way that one ought to seek the advice of a medical doctor to obtain information about a given disease. To determine the good life is not all that easy because it is not akin to a good vacation or a good automobile. It is more elusive than that because it is all encompassing in nature. In short, it deals with the intangibles as well as the tangibles of life.

The view of the role of the philosopher changed radically with the advent of modern philosophy. His role was no longer considered analogous to that of a physician, but rather to that of a biologist with a specialty in anatomy. How does one learn about the structure of the human body? One dissects it and analyzes which bones are which and how the muscles, nerves, and tendons connect and intertwine. In a very real sense the anatomist is not interested in the structure as a whole, but rather in the parts and how they fit together to comprise the whole. The whole is secondary; the parts are of primary importance. So too, modern and contemporary eticists by and large are not interested in the whole, namely, what constitutes an overall good life for an individual. It is as if they take a bit of behavior into the "philosophical laboratory", stick it under the "philosophical microscope", and analyze it to the nth degree. They no longer ask what constitutes the good life in general, but desire to determine the difference between moral and nonmoral behavior. Nonmoral behavior is human action which has absolutely nothing to do with morality such as eating a pizza, *ceteris paribus*[10]. Torturing a person for the fun of it, however, has moral import[11]. Once the criteria[12] that distinguish moral from

---

6   *analogy:* correspondence in some respects, especially in function or position, between things otherwise dissimilar.

7   It should be noted that it was not until the latter part of the 19th century that psychology was considered a discipline distinct from philosophy.

8   *obscure:* to make inconspicuous; unnoticed.

9   *ascertain:* to discover through examination or experimentation; find out.

10   *ceteris paribus*: all other things being equal.

11   *import*: to be of importance to; concern.

nonmoral behavior are ascertained, the central issue of ethics becomes one of deducing[13] a rule whereby one can extricate[14] oneself from moral dilemmas[15]. No one can escape moral dilemmas. They are a fact of human existence. A prerequisite of acting in a moral way is the determination of a moral guideline. This is the job of the ethicist and a service so to speak, to those who want to behave morally. A consistent application of such a rule when one is faced with a moral dilemma is the best chance one has of success at being moral.

In many moral situations it is obvious what one ought to do. One may be in a position to steal a radio. Even if there is no chance of getting caught, it is obvious that the moral thing to do is to refrain from such behavior. Unfortunately, most moral situations are not that simple. More often than not all the alternatives facing us carry with them a breach of morality. For example, truth telling is generally considered the moral thing to do. Yet, suppose that your mother needs a life-saving operation which the surgeon has confided in you will be enormously and unavoidably painful. What should you do if your mother asks you whether the doctor has clued you in concerning the potential pain of this operation due to the fact that the doctor refuses to discuss the issue with her? You have just been presented with a moral dilemma. Ought you tell the truth to your mother or lie to her realizing full well that if she understands the pain involved in this operation, she may well decide to forego it and would therefore die. Much of the moral philosophy written since the Renaissance has been concerned with trying to establish some sort of rule or set of rules for the purpose of one being able to consistently extract oneself from such difficult situations. The emphasis here is put on the specific situation, the moral situational dilemma. There is not an emphasis on an overall lifestyle. It is in short, tantamount to placing an isolated problem under the microscope and analyzing it to see what one ought to do in *that situation*. In other words, take yourself out of the picture and view the *problem* in and of itself. Be *objective* about it. Be unemotional. Don't personalize the situation. Only then can one come to a *rational* decision as to what one ought to do. This so-called objective and rational approach to ethical problem solving is characteristic of philosophers from the 17th century until the present day.

One might wonder how this change in attitude came about. The answer is not a simple one, but two factors contributed greatly to it. (1) Christianity played a major role in the decline and fall of the Roman Empire. As a result, Western Europe entered an age of spiritualism known as the Middle Ages. This period of our culture spanned a millennium[16] and began to come to an end in the mid 15th century. Not surprisingly, the major power structure at that time was the Roman Catholic Church. Consequently, the intellectual activity that took place was theologically[17] oriented, although highly philosophical in nature. The influence of the Church took its toll with respect to how people viewed the role of philosophers. They were no longer perceived as physicians to be con-

---

[12] *criterion:* a standard, rule or test on which a judgment or decision can be based. Criteria is the plural form of the word.

[13] *deduce:* to derive by reasoning.

[14] *extricate:* to release from an entanglement or difficulty; disengage.

[15] *dilemma:* a situation that requires one to choose between two equally balanced alternatives.

[16] *millennium:* 1000 years.

[17] *theology:* the study of the nature of God and religious truth; rational inquiry into religious questions.

sulted for guidance in achieving the good life. Rather, people sought the advice of the local priest. (2) The Middle Ages was brought to a close by the Renaissance. This economic rebirth of Western Europe spelled the demise[18] of spiritualism. Consequently, man's intellectual energies became focused on the here and now. There was a renewed interest in how the world ticks. Truth was no longer to be found in man's soul. Rather, the truth is objective and is demonstrated via[19] empirical[20] verification[21]. This is the essence of scientific method. Galileo is the prime example. He did not merely theorize, he *tested* his theories. He was the father of modern scientific method. This method became accepted as the only vehicle to the truth (something all philosophers are committed to attaining). Hence, scientific method which is by nature objective; that is, nonpersonal, had its influence on the philosophers of this day and age.

The loss of his role as a counselor in society in conjunction with the new respect for scientific method reshaped the image of philosophers in society. Consequently, he became a technician with respect to the problems of his trade. His business became depersonalized. To be sure, it was not entirely of his own making, but partly due to historical circumstance. Yet the fact remains to this day that, in general, philosophers are detached and attempt to be objective in their approach to problem solving. They are most comfortable observing a given problem, including ethical ones, under the philosophical "microscope" and analyzing it to the nth degree because they believe that by so doing they can discover the truth relative to the problem at hand. In other words, the individual qua[22] person is basically irrelevant except as an instrument in making the decision as to what to do. *What* one ought to do is to be arrived at in an impersonal manner. Lifestyle simply does not count. It should not count, otherwise the decision-making process would not be objective. Hence, since the Renaissance we find various attempts to establish a definitive[23] rule whereby moral dilemmas can be solved regardless of the individual involved in the decision-making process.

It is at this point that ethical relativism must be confronted. Ethical relativism is the view that there is nothing objective about moral claims or principles. Ethical relativism takes two forms: (1) individual and (2) cultural. Individual ethical relativism is the naive[24] view that moral claims are subjective value judgments made by individuals. In other words, one man's meat is another man's poison. Therefore, if Fred believes that stealing is acceptable behavior *ceteris paribus* he cannot be wrong since the content of his belief is a value judgment and therefore necessarily subjective. There are no objective standards by which to determine Fred to be wrong in his judgment. This position is naive because there are objective standards. No one is born in a vacuum. That is, everyone is born into a given society. Every society has a set of standards most fundamentally expressed by that society's moral code. Members of a given society are expected to behave in accordance with that society's moral code and in that sense the code of conduct is objective since it applies to every mem-

---

[18]   *demise:* death.

[19]   *via:* by way of.

[20]   *empirical:* relying upon or derived from observation or experiment.

[21]   *verify:* to prove the truth of by presentation of evidence; substantiate.

[22]   *qua:* in the function, character or capacity of.

[23]   *definitive:* conclusive.

[24]   *naive:* unsophisticated.

ber of that society and it is not a matter of individual opinion as to what the code of conduct is.

Cultural relativism, on the other hand, is the position that every society has its own and different set of moral standards. There is no objective set of criteria which embodies[25] the truth about morality by which one could judge that a given culture's moral code is defective or not. If the cultural relativist is correct, then ethical theory from a philosophical point of view is doomed because it would be reduced to a sociological exercise of comparing various culture's moral codes.

Fortunately for ethical theory, cultural relativism can be demonstrated untenable[26]. It is based on one formulation or another of the cultural differences argument which is

(1) Different cultures have different moral codes.
(2) Therefore, there is no objective "truth" in morality. Right and wrong are only matters of opinion, and opinions vary from culture to culture.

At the outset this argument appears acceptable. However, careful consideration of the premise,[27] i.e., (1) indicates that it is ambiguous.[28] On the one hand, it can be taken at face value to mean

(1') It is a fact that different cultures possess different moral codes.

This interpretation of (1) appears to be true and the conclusion seemingly follows from the premise in which case the cultural relativist is capable of standing his ground. It may be the case, however, that the conclusion cannot be deduced from the premise even though the premise is true. The conclusion follows from the premise only if it can be demonstrated that the fact of cultures possessing different moral codes *in and of itself* precludes[29] any one of those codes from expressing objective "truth" in morality. In other words, is there something about the quality of being different that automatically rules out objective "truth"? Is it self evidently true that the quality of being different precludes objective "truth"? Unless the cultural relativist can demonstrate that the answer to these two questions is *yes* beyond all doubt, then (2) does not follow from (1') rendering[30] the argument unacceptable. One of two possibilities does follow from the claim that different moral codes abound.[31] (a) None of the many existing codes embody the "truth" concerning morality. (Consider: all of the solutions to a given math problem may be in error. This does not preclude there being a correct solution.) (b) One culture does so possess such truth whereas the others do not. (b) means that two (or more) different moral codes cannot both (or all) be objectively true. (Consider: the astronomical theories of Copernicus and Ptolemy cannot both be true. The truth of one rules out the truth of the other.) One may wonder whether (a) is the case or (b) is the case? In pursuing the answer be aware. The answer will in no way be of help to the cultural relativist because neither precludes the objective "truth" of a given moral code. Secondly, whether or

[25] *embody:* to constitute; to consist of.
[26] *untenable:* incapable of being held, maintained or defended.
[27] *premise:* a proposition stated or assumed as leading to a conclusion.
[28] *ambiguous:* capable of being understood in two or more possible senses.
[29] *preclude:* to make impossible, especially in advance; shut out.
[30] *render:* to cause to be or become.
[31] *abound:* exist in large numbers or amounts.

not (a) or (b) is the case will only be determined by some factor other than the differentness of moral codes.

Alternatively, (1) may be understood to mean

(1")Different cultures are committed to moral codes that differ from one another.

This interpretation of the premise renders it a belief claim. We all know that beliefs do not determine what is in fact the case, otherwise the world would be flat since that was believed to be the case 500 years ago. Different moral codes entail[32] that those involved only think they know that the code to which they adhere is the true one. One thinking that he knows that p[33] is tantamount[34] to the claim that one believes that p. Accordingly, the premise ought properly to be rephrased as

(1''') It is a fact that different cultures believe in different moral codes.

This interpretation of the premise is, indeed, true and unambiguous. However, it is a factual claim about the belief profile of various cultures. Consequently, the conclusion of the argument which is a factual claim about the truth of moral codes themselves simply does not follow from the premise. Accordingly, the cultural differences argument ought to be rejected.

Furthermore, there is ample evidence that there are universal moral principles, namely principles which are held by every and all societies and for perfectly understandable reasons, most notably for the survival of society. The anthropologist Clyde Kluckholm observed that

> Every culture has a concept of murder, distinguishing this from execution, killing in war, and other "justifiable homicides." The notions of incest and other regulations upon sexual behavior, the prohibitions upon untruth under defined circumstances, of restitution and reciprocity, of mutual obligations between parents and children--these and many more moral concepts are altogether universal ["Ethical Relativity: Sic et Non," *Journal of Philosophy*, LII (1955)].

More often than not where the cultural relativist is led astray is by confusing universal moral codes within their application. Certainly there is diversity in the manner by which common moral principles are applied. For example, some cultures demonstrate their respect for human life by practicing euthanasia whereas other societies consider such activity contrary to such respect and therefore abhorent[35].

Another problem with cultural relativism is that it altogether rules out moral progress. Consider: at one stage in U.S. history slavery was perfectly acceptable. How was it that our views changed? They changed because people came to realize that there is something absolutely morally wrong about enslaving other human beings. Were it simply a matter of cultural relativism, there would be no reason for anyone to argue for emancipation[36]. It is for these reasons that cultural relativism is untenable, thus preserving the importance of ethical theory.

---

[32] *entail:* to have as a necessary consequence.

[33] Here 'p' is used as a variable for any state of affairs, i.e., fact.

[34] *tantamount:* equivalent in value, meaning or effect.

[35] *abhorent:* causing fear, disgust, detestable.

[36] *emancipation:* act or process of setting or making free; liberation.

In conclusion, the Ancients sought to discover guidelines for behavior that lead to the good life, namely, an overall lifestyle of living well. On the other hand, modern and contemporary moral philosophers are concerned with establishing principles by which to guide our moral behavior. Obviously, both approaches have merit and they need not be viewed as mutually exclusive[37]. That is, the reasoned establishment of moral guidelines can greatly contribute to one leading the good life. That is to say, there is more than a small measure of satisfaction not only behaving in a moral way in any given situation, but in knowing that one is making an honest attempt at developing for oneself moral character.

Suggested Readings: Problems of Ethics

1. Feinberg, Joel, *Moral Concepts* (Oxford University Press, 1969).
2. Frankena, William, *Ethics* (Prentice Hall, Inc., 1988).
3. Rachels, James, *The Elements of Moral Philosophy* (McGraw-Hill, Inc., 1993).
4. Sellars, W. and Hospers, J., eds., *Readings in Ethical Theory* (Appleton-Century-Crofts, Inc., 1952).
5. Taylor, Richard, *Good and Evil* (The Macmillan Co., 1970).

---

[37] *mutual exclusivity:* the cancellation of one position or alternative by the other and vice-versa.

Name_____

Date _____

1. How does the ancient Greek view of ethics differ from that of modern and contemporary ethics?

2. Explain the difference between individual and cultural ethical relativism.

3. What is the cultural differences argument? Is it sound? Explain.

4. How might one argue for the existence of universal moral principles?

5. Universal moral principles may be applied differently in different societies without entailing relativism. True or false? Give an example.

5 *Self-Actualization;*
Aristotle

Consistent with the ancient Greek approach to ethics, Aristotle was interested in determining that which constitutes the good life.[1] He understood that there are two types of good. (1) That which is *instrumentally* good is good in so far as it functions as a *means* by which some desire or goal is satisfied. For example, sunglasses are instrumentally good in that they achieve the goal of diminishing sun rays. There is nothing inherently[2] good about them. They are simply tools (instruments) which help

---

[1] See Chapter 4.

us to achieve ease of eyesight (a goal).   (2) That which is intrinsically good is essentially[3] good. The twofold goal of ethical studies, as far as the ancient Greeks were concerned, is to determine that which is intrinsically good and how to attain[4] it. It is the good life that is intrinsically good. But just what is the good life? Aristotle arrived at the conclusion that the good life is a life of happiness, since all human beings desire the good life, it follows that all people desire happiness. As he states, "Happiness then, the end to which all our conscious acts are directed, is found to be something final and self-sufficient". As so construed[5], the term 'happiness' does not refer to a momentary state of being, but rather to that which results from a way of life. Aristotle came to this conclusion by first of all observing human behavior and secondly by the way we make sense of the use of certain words in our language.

(1) Suppose I were to ask you, the student, why you are going to college. A likely response would be because you want a college degree. Why do you want a college degree? Because, say you, it will give me the opportunity to get a good job. Why do you want a good job? Well, because a good job means a better salary. But why do you want more money? Because more money means more security. So what's the big deal concerning security? You respond that without a feeling of security you can't be happy. But why do you want to be happy? How are you going to reply to that question? Here the question and answer session comes to an end. One simply wants to be happy, period. Happiness is never a means to something else. Rather, it is that toward which all other behavior is directed. It is often the case that people believe that fame, fortune or pleasure constitutes the good life and mistakenly equate them with happiness. Aristotle exposes this error by delving into semantics[6].

(2) That happiness is intrinsically good is verified by the way we use the word. Compare the following statements:

(a) John desires happiness in order to be famous.

(b) Mary desires happiness in order to be wealthy.

(c) Sam desires happiness in order to have pleasure.

These statements simply do not make sense. That is because in those statements happiness is made to function as an instrumental good; that is, as a means to something else. Furthermore, it is not by accident that Aristotle also chose fame, fortune and pleasure to play the role of intrinsic good in (a), (b) and (c). It was not uncommon, in his day, nor is it uncommon in ours, for people to believe that either fame, fortune or pleasure are what constitute the good life. But such a view is mistaken as demonstrated by the nonsense generated by the above statements. Now consider the following:

(d) John desires fame in order to be happy.

(e) Mary desires wealth in order to be happy.

---

[2]   *inherent:* existing as an essential constituent or characteristic.

[3]   *essential:* a fundamental, necessary, or indispensable part, item, or principle.

[4]   *attain:* to gain, reach, or accomplish by mental or physical effort.

[5]   *construe:* to give an explanation or translation.

[6]   *semantics:* the study or science of meaning in language forms.

(f) Sam desires pleasure in order to be happy.

These statements do make sense. They are meaningful because fame, fortune and pleasure are only instrumentally good. They are good only in so far as they are means to attaining something else.[7] Furthermore, it makes sense that happiness is precisely that which people want to achieve as a goal in life. The "sense" of this is reflected by the manner with which we properly use the word 'happiness' in a statement, namely, as that which is intrinsically good.[8]

Here one must not confuse the issue of making sense with truth or falsity. Semantics in this context pertains only to that which makes sense. Only that which makes sense can be either true or false. To ask whether the statement "The square root of chair shot the window" is either true or false itself does not make sense. Truth and falsity only apply to assertions that make sense. Aristotle's semantic argument has to do with how we use the term 'happiness' in a sensical way. And as the above argument demonstrates, it only makes sense when it is construed as an intrinsic good. Only when an assertion makes sense does the issue of truth or falsity arise. As we shall see, Aristotle most certainly argues that although (d), (e) and (f) make sense, all three are false claims.

Having demonstrated that the good life is one of happiness, Aristotle is now obligated to state how one can attain it. Here an analogy[9] can be drawn between a philosopher and a physician. In seeking a doctor's advice regarding a malady[10] one's expectations are twofold. At the outset, one wants a diagnosis of the problem. Then one wants a prescription for or a means by which to go about curing the illness. So too with the philosopher. The ancient Greeks understood the business of the philosopher to diagnose the nature of the good life and then prescribe how it is to be attained. In one sense, the problem is more complex than ascertaining[11] the nature of a physical ailment. The concept of good is on the one hand abstract in nature, something not empirically[12] verifiable. On the other hand, that which is intrinsically good is intimately concerned with the way we live our lives and therefore possesses a psychological dimension. Clearly, we cannot live the good life unless we first of all know what it is; and it will do us little benefit if we know what it is, but do not know how it is to be realized. In other words, simply because one desires happiness is no guarantee that he will achieve it. An appreciation of this fact is what gave the philosopher in ancient Greece legitimacy as a psychologist[13].

---

[7] It should be noticed that whereas fame and fortune can never meaningfully function as intrinsic goods such is not the case with pleasure. Consider the claim that "John desires fame (wealth) in order to have pleasure". That makes sense. Note, however, that pleasure here construed is an intrinsic good. Observation of this fact helped Epicurus (see Chapter 5) substantiate his claim that not only was pleasure intrinsically good but identical to happiness. The source of Aristotle's mistake lies in him concluding that pleasure cannot be intrinsically good *because* happiness does not meaningfully function as an instrumental good in statement (c).

[8] It is via this semantic argument of Aristotle's that we can understand how reality is reflected by language, namely, by the meanings we attach to words.

[9] *analogy:* correspondence in some respects, especially in function or position, between things otherwise dissimilar.

[10] *malady:* a disease, disorder or ailment.

[11] *ascertain:* to discover through examination or experimentation; to find out.

[12] *empirical:* relying upon or derived from observation or experiment.

[13] It should be noted that it was not until the latter part of the 19th century that psychology was considered a discipline distinct from philosophy.

The average person needs some guidance as to not only the nature of the good life but also how to attain it.

So it is now up to Aristotle to give us the guidance necessary to acquire the good life. In so doing, he sets forth three principles. First of all, one only achieves the good life by acting virtuously. But what is virtue? Aristotle defines virtue as a disposition. A disposition is a tendency or inclination with respect to how one acts or behaves in given situations. However, not all dispositions are admirable. Hence, a disposition, in order to qualify as virtuous, must be accompanied by some guiding principle or rule. Aristotle maintains that in the area of human conduct this rule is prudence. Prudence means being moderate in one's behavior. Aristotle recommends prudence as the rule by which we guide *all* our behavior. Consider the activity of eating. Here, Aristotle would say, one ought not overindulge or starve himself in order to achieve the good life. To be virtuous, one must eat that amount which is the mean between the extremes of excess and deficiency. One might at this stage question what eating has to do with ethical behavior. If becoming a glutton has no conceivable effect, positively or negatively, upon others, what (ethical) difference could such behavior possibly make? To Aristotle's way of thinking ethical behavior involves not only how one interacts with one's fellow human beings, but how one treats oneself as well. Self-directed behavior lies within the purview[14] of ethics just as does one's treatment of others; and one's culinary[15] patterns are certainly self-directed! In short, Aristotle takes a holistic view of ethics. His approach is holistic because the entirety of an individual's behavior he believed fell under the umbrella of ethics. All that one does, in one way or another, contributes to the quality of one's life. A quality life is the good life. Living moderately is the key to the good life.

At this point a potential problem arises. From a simplistic point of view one could apply the principle of prudence to aberrant[16] behavior. For example, one could reason that by totally avoiding rape one is going to an extreme of deficiency and, therefore, one ought to engage in this type of behavior to a moderate degree, thus rendering[17] Aristotle's ethical theory questionable indeed. However, Aristotle was aware of this possible twisting of his theory. To preclude[18] such a perverted[19] interpretation, Aristotle reasoned that on the scale of human action, rape and other forms of negative behavior (such as murder) are themselves extreme in nature, and therefore incapable of being performed in moderation. Consequently it makes no sense to speak of the mean with respect to intrinsically extreme behavior.

Second, Aristotle cites one of the virtues in particular as necessary for attaining happiness. One must live courageously. Courage is the mean between cowardice and foolhardiness. One may wonder what courage has to do with living the good life. Courage meant more to the Greeks than it does to us. To be sure, the concept was crucial to behavior in war-time situations. But in terms of overall lifestyle it has a broader application. It applies to the way we live our lives. Aristotle appreciates the fact that people can choose to be either participants or spectators in the game of life.

---

[14]   *purview:* the extent or range of function, power, or competence; scope.

[15]   *culinary:* of or pertaining to a kitchen or to cookery.

[16]   *aberrant:* deviating from the proper or expected course.

[17]   *render:* to cause to become: make

[18]   *preclude:* to make impossible, especially in advance; shut out.

[19]   *perverted:* deviating greatly from what is considered right and correct.

One can be actively involved in life, a doer. Or one can be passive and let the world go by never taking risks and thereby always playing it safe. Such is a cowardly way to live. But Aristotle understands that by taking on the challenges that life has to offer one must take risks. That takes courage. It is only by taking risks that one can reap the rewards of a full life. The good life, a life of happiness, can only be had by such involvement. This does not mean taking stupid risks. That would be foolhardy. A dead hero is nevertheless dead!

Third, due to the fact that people's needs vary, the mean course of action will vary from individual to individual depending upon the particular situation. Care must be taken at this point; Aristotle is not advocating ethical relativism[20]. Ethical relativism is the doctrine that there are no ethical guidelines or prohibitions shared by all people either individually or culturally. There is nothing relative about the principle of prudence. Aristotle meant it to be applicable to all people. To determine the mean course of action, one must possess knowledge of the situation in which one is involved. One cannot act in a virtuous manner unless one knows what the extremes of the situation are. Only then can the mean between the extremes be determined. However, there are situations which are peculiar to the individual. For example, the mean food intake will vary from person to person. What the prudent amount of food is for any given individual is unique[21]. The average person does not require the same amount of food as does the professional football player. Nevertheless, one must have knowledge of the prudent food intake before one can act in a prudent manner. Here it is important to note the importance that Aristotle, as well as all ancient Greek philosophers, put on knowledge (which includes self-knowledge). Without knowledge prudence is impossible to achieve. Therefore, without knowledge one cannot act virtuously and without virtue one cannot live the good life.

It would now appear that Aristotle has accomplished what he set out to achieve, namely to provide us with a diagnosis as to the nature of the good life and a prescription as to how to achieve it. However, it should be noted that he has not really told us what he thinks happiness is. It is clear that he does not equate it with fame, fortune or pleasure. Happiness is a very difficult concept to define because on the one hand it is a very general notion and on the other hand is very personal; that is, varies from individual to individual. Hence, happiness is both general and particular in nature. How can this be? How can one define happiness in a way that satisfies both criteria[22]? Although Aristotle never explicitly[23] defines happiness, by reading between the lines one can cogently[24] argue that he meant essentially the same as the 20th century psychologist Abraham Maslow meant by self-actualization. Self-actualization

> refers to the desire for self-fulfillment, namely, to the tendency for him to become actualized in what he is potentially. This tendency might be phrased as the desire to become more and more what one is, to become everything that one is capable of becoming.

---

[20] *relativism:* the theory that all truth is relative to the individual and to the time or place in which he acts.

[21] *unique:* being the one and only of its kind.

[22] *criterion:* a standard, rule, or test on which a judgment or decision can be based. Criteria is the plural form of the word.

[23] *explicit:* expressed with precision; clearly defined; specific.

[24] *cogent:* forcibly convincing.

The specific form that these needs will take will of course vary greatly from person to person. In one individual it may take the form of the desire to be an ideal mother, in another it may be expressed athletically, and in still another it may be expressed in painting, pictures or in inventions. It is not necessarily a creative urge although in people who have any capacities for creation it will take this form.[25]

Clearly the notion of self-actualization satisfies the criterion of being both general as well as particular. Self-actualization as well as happiness is not only difficult to define but difficult to achieve. Just as Maslow thought that relatively few people are self-actualizing, so too Aristotle did not believe that the majority of people are or will be happy. Nevertheless, happiness is precisely what all people desire.

That Aristotle meant self-actualization by the word *eudaimonia*[26] is consistent with his view that only those who commit themselves to being participants in the game of life can be happy. Self-actualization means becoming and doing what one has the potential to become and do. To actualize such potential one must take risks. To take risks one must exercise courage. Only then can one lead the good life, a life of happiness.

Suggested Readings:
Self-Actualization; Aristotle

1. Aristotle, *The Nicomachean Ethics*.
2. Blanshard, B., *Reason and Goodness* (London: Allen and Unwin, 1961).
3. Copleston, F., *A History of Philosophy*, Vol. I (N.Y.: Doubleday & Co., 1994), Chapter 31.
4. Field, G. C. *Moral Theory* (New York: Dutton), Part II.
5. Hardie, W. F. R., *Aristotle's Ethical Theory* (Oxford: Clarendon Press, 1968).
6. Huby, P., *Greek Ethics* (London: Macmillan, 1967), Chapter 5.
7. Joachim, H. H., *Aristotle: The Nicomachean Ethics* (Oxford: Clarendon Press, 1951).
8. Marshall, T., *Aristotle's Theory of Conduct* (London: T. Fisher Unwin, 1906).
9. Mure, G. R. G., *Aristotle* (New York: Oxford University Press, 1939), Chapter 7.
10. Oates, W. J., *Aristotle and the Problem of Value* (Princeton: Princeton University Press, 1963), Chapter 7, Part I.
11. Ross, W. D. *Aristotle* (5th ed. London: Methuen, 1949), Chapter 7.
12. Stewart, J. A., *Notes on the Nicomachean Ethics of Aristotle* (Oxford: The Clarendon Press, 1892).
13. Taylor, A .E., *Aristotle* (New York: Dover, 1955), Chapter 5.

---

[25]   Maslow, A.H., "A Theory of Human Motivation" in Richard J. Lowry, ed., *Dominance, Self-Esteem, Self-Actualization: Germinal Papers of A.H. Maslow* (Monterey, California: Brooks/Cole Publishing Co., 1973), p. 163.

[26]   *Eudaimonia* is the Greek word which is usually translated as happiness.

14. Veatch, Henry Babcock, *Rational Man: A Modern Interpretation of Aristotelian Ethics* (Bloomington: Indiana University Press, 1962).
15. Walsh, J.J. and Shapira, H.L., eds. *Aristotle's Ethics* (Belmont: Wadsworth Publishing Co., 1967).

Chapter 5:
Self-Actualization;
Aristotle

Name_____

Date _____

1. What did the ancient Greeks consider to be the goal of ethics?

2. Explain how courage is necessary for happiness.

3. According to Aristotle, ethics deals only with behavior that affects others. True or false? Explain.

4. Show how Aristotle's ethics might seem relativistic. Defend Aristotle against this claim.

5. Show how Aristotle's ethics could be called an ethics of self-actualization.

❦ **R E A D I N G S** ❦

Self-Actualization

Aristotle
The Nicomachean Ethics

Book I: selections
Book II: selections

From *The Nicomachean Ethics of Aristotle*, translated by D. P. Chase (London & Toronto: J. M. Dent & Sons Ltd., 1911).

Book I

And now let us revert to the Good of which we are in search: what can it be? for manifestly it is different in different actions and arts: for it is different in the healing art and in the art military, and similarly in the rest. What then is the Chief Good in each? Is it not "that for the sake of which the other things are done?" and this in the healing art is health, and in the art military victory, and in that of house-building a house, and in any other thing something else; in short, in every action and moral choice the End, because in all cases men do everything else with a view to this. So that if there is some one End of all things which are and may be done, this must be the Good proposed by doing, or if more than one, then these.

Thus our discussion after some traversing about has come to the same point which we reached before. And this we must try yet more to clear up.

Now since the ends are plainly many, and of these we choose some with a view to others (wealth, for instance, musical instruments, and, in general, all instruments), it is clear that all are not final; and so, if there is some one only which is final, this must be the object of our search: but if several, then the most final of them will be it.

Now that which is an object of pursuit in itself we call more final than that which is so with a view to something else; that again which is never an object of choice with a view to something else than those which are so both in themselves and with a view to this ulterior object: and so by the term "absolutely final," we denote that which is an object of choice always in itself, and never with a view to any other.

And of this nature Happiness is mostly thought to be, for this we choose always for its own sake, and never with a view to anything further: whereas honour, pleasure, intellect, in fact every excellence we choose for their own sakes, it is true (because we would choose each of these even if no result were to follow), but we choose them also with a view to happiness, conceiving that through their instrumentality we shall be happy: but no man chooses happiness with a view to them, nor in fact with a view to any other thing whatsoever.

The same result is seen to follow also from the notion of self-suffi-
ciency, a quality thought to belong to the final good. Now by sufficient
for Self, we mean not for a single individual living a solitary life, but for
his parents also and children and wife, and, in general, friends and countrymen; for man is by nature adapted to a social existence. But of these,
of course, some limit must be fixed: for if one extends it to parents and
descendants and friends' friends, there is no end to it. This point, however, must be left for future investigation: for the present we define that to
be self-sufficient "which taken alone makes life choice-worthy, and to be
in want of nothing;" now of such kind we think Happiness to be: and further, to be most choice-worthy of all things; not being reckoned with any
other thing, for if it were so reckoned, it is plain we must then allow it,
with the addition of ever so small a good, and of goods the greater is ever
the more choice-worthy.

So then Happiness is manifestly something final and self-sufficient,
being the end of all things which are and may be done.

The question may be determined also by a reference to our definition
of Happiness, that it is a working of the soul in the way of excellence or
virtue of a certain kind: and of the other goods, some we must have to
begin with, and those which are co-operative and useful are given by
nature as instruments.

These considerations will harmonize also with what we said at the
commencement: for we assumed the End of political science to be most
excellent: now this bestows most care on making the members of the
community of a certain character; good that is and apt to do what is
honourable.

With good reason then neither ox nor horse nor any other brute animal do we call happy, for none of them can partake in such working: and
for this same reason a child is not happy either, because by reason of his
tender age he cannot yet perform such actions: if the term is applied, it is
by way of anticipation.

For to constitute Happiness, there must be, as we have said, complete
virtue and a complete life: for many changes and chances of all kinds
arise during a life, and he who is most prosperous may become involved
in great misfortunes in his old age, as in the heroic poems the tale is told
of Priam: but the man who has experienced such fortune and died in
wretchedness, no man calls happy.

And, by the way, the question which has been here discussed, testifies
incidentally to the truth of our account of Happiness. For to nothing does
a stability of human results attach so much as it does to the workings in
the way of virtue, since these are held to be more abiding even than the
sciences: and of these last again the most precious are the most abiding,
because the blessed live in them most and most continuously, which
seems to be the reason why they are not forgotten. So then this stability
which is sought will be in the happy man, and he will be such through
life, since always, or most of all, he will be doing and contemplating the
things which are in the way of virtue: and the various chances of life he
will bear most nobly, and at all times and in all ways harmoniously, since
he is the truly good man, or in the terms of our proverb "a faultless cube."

Moreover, since Happiness is a kind of working of the soul in the way
of perfect Excellence, we must inquire concerning Excellence: for so
probably shall we have a clearer view concerning Happiness; and again,
he who is really a statesman is generally thought to have spent most pains
on this, for he wishes to make the citizens good and obedient to the laws.

But if this investigation belongs properly to political science, then clearly the inquiry will be in accordance with our original design.

Well, we are to inquire concerning Excellence, i.e. Human Excellence of course, because it was the Chief Good of Man and the Happiness of Man that we were inquiring of just now.

By Human Excellence we mean not that of man's body but that of his soul; for we call Happiness a working of the Soul.

And if this is so, it is plain that some knowledge of the nature of the Soul is necessary for the statesman, just as for the Oculist a knowledge of the whole body, and the more so in proportion as political science is more precious and higher than the healing art: and in fact physicians of the higher class do busy themselves much with the knowledge of the body.

The Excellence of Man then is divided in accordance with this difference: we make two classes, calling the one Intellectual, and the other Moral; pure science, intelligence, and practical wisdom--Intellectual: liberality, and perfected self-mastery--Moral: in speaking of a man's Moral character, we do not say he is a scientific or intelligent but a meek man, or one of perfected self-mastery: and we praise the man of science in right of his mental state; and of these such as are praiseworthy we call Excellences.

Book II

WELL: human Excellence is of two kinds, Intellectual and Moral: now the Intellectual springs originally, and is increased subsequently, from teaching (for the most part that is), and needs therefore experience and time; whereas the Moral comes from custom, and so the Greek term denoting it is but a slight deflection from the terms denoting custom in that language.

From this fact it is plain that not one of the Moral Virtues comes to be in us merely by nature: because of such things as exist by nature, none can be changed by custom: a stone, for instance, by nature gravitating downwards, could never by custom be brought to ascend, not even if one were to try and accustom it by throwing it up ten thousand times; nor could fire again be brought to descend, nor in fact could anything whose nature is in one way be brought by custom to be in another. The Virtues then come to be in us neither by nature, nor in despite of nature, but we are furnished by nature with a capacity for receiving them, and are perfected in them through custom.

Again, in whatever cases we get things by nature, we get the faculties first and perform the acts of working afterwards; an illustration of which is afforded by the case of our bodily senses, for it was not from having often seen or heard that we got these senses, but just the reverse: we had them and so exercised them, but did not have them because we had exercised them. But the Virtues we get by first performing single acts of working, which, again, is the case of other things, as the arts for instance; for what we have to make when we have learned how, these we learn how to make by making: men come to be builders, for instance, by building; harp-players, by playing on the harp: exactly so, by doing just actions we come to be just; by doing the actions of self-mastery we come to be perfected in self-mastery; and by doing brave actions brave.

And to the truth of this testimony is borne by what takes place in communities: because the law-givers make the individual members good men by habituation, and this is the intention certainly of every law-giver, and all who do not effect it will fail of their intent; and herein consists the difference between a good Constitution and a bad.

Again, every Virtue is either produced or destroyed from and by the very same circumstances: art too in like manner; I mean it is by playing the harp that both the good and the bad harp-players are formed: and similarly builders and all the rest; by building well men will become good builders; by doing it badly bad ones: in fact, if this had not been so, there would have been no need of instructors, but all men would have been at once good or bad in their several arts without them.

So too then is it with the Virtues: for by acting in the various relations in which we are thrown with our fellow men, we come to be, some just, some unjust: and by acting in dangerous positions and by habituated to feel fear or confidence, we come to be, some brave, others cowards.

Similarly is it also with respect to the occasions of lust and anger: for some men come to be perfected in self-mastery and mild, others destitute of all self-control and passionate; the one class by behaving in one way under them, the other by behaving in another. Or, in one word, the habits are produced from the acts of working like to them: and so what we have to do is to give a certain character to these particular acts, because the habits formed correspond to the differences of these.

So then, whether we are accustomed this way or that straight from childhood, makes not a small but an important difference, or rather I would say it makes all the difference.

First then this must be noted, that it is the nature of such things to be spoiled by defect and excess; as we see in the case of health and strength (since for the illustration of things which cannot be seen we must use those that can), for excessive training impairs the strength as well as deficient: meat and drink, in like manner, in too great or too small quantities, impair the health: while in due proportion they cause, increase, and preserve it.

Thus it is therefore with the habits of perfected Self-Mastery and Courage and the rest of the Virtues: for the man who flies from and fears all things, and never stands up against anything, comes to be a coward; and he who fears nothing, but goes at everything, comes to be rash. In like manner too, he that tastes of every pleasure and abstains from none comes to lose all self-control; while he who avoids all, as do the dull and clownish, comes as it were to lose his faculties of perception: that is to say, the habits of perfected Self-Mastery and Courage are spoiled by the excess and defect, but by the mean state are preserved.

Furthermore, not only do the origination, growth, and marring of the habits come from and by the same circumstances, but also the acts of working after the habits are formed will be exercised on the same: for so it is also with those other things which are more directly matters of sight, strength for instance: for this comes by taking plenty of food and doing plenty of work, and the man who has attained strength is best able to do these: and so it is with the Virtues, for not only do we by abstaining from pleasures come to be perfected in Self-Mastery, but when we have come to be so we can best abstain from them: similarly too with Courage: for it is by accustoming ourselves to despise objects of fear and stand up against them that we come to be brave; and after we have come to be so we shall be best able to stand up against such objects.

And for a test of the formation of the habits we must take the pleasure or pain which succeeds the acts; for he is perfected in Self-Mastery who not only abstains from the bodily pleasures but is glad to do so; whereas he who abstains but is sorry to do it has not Self-Mastery: he again is brave who stands up against danger, either with positive pleasure or at least without any pain; whereas he who does it with pain is not brave.

Next, we must examine what Virtue is. Well, since the things which come to be in the mind are, in all, of three kinds, Feelings, Capacities, States, Virtue of course must belong to one of the three classes.

By Feelings, I mean such as lust, anger, fear, confidence, envy, joy, friendship, hatred, longing, emulation, compassion, in short all such as are followed by pleasure or pain: by Capacities, those in right of which we are said to be capable of these feelings; as by virtue of which we are able to have been made angry, or grieved, or to have compassionated; by States, those in right of which we are in a certain relation good or bad to the aforementioned feelings; to having been made angry, for instance, we are in a wrong relation if in our anger we were too violent or too slack, but if we were in the happy medium we are in a right relation to the feeling. And so on of the rest.

Now Feelings neither the virtues nor vices are, because in right of the Feelings we are not denominated either good or bad, but in right of the virtues and vices we are.

Again, in right of the Feelings we are neither praised nor blamed (for a man is not commended for being afraid or being angry, nor blamed for being angry merely but for being so in a particular way), but in right of the virtues and vices we are.

Again, both anger and fear we feel without moral choice, whereas the virtues are acts of moral choice, or at least certainly not independent of it.

Moreover, in right of the Feelings we are said to be moved, but in right of the virtues and vices not to be moved, but disposed, in a certain way.

And for these same reasons they are not Capacities, for we are not called good or bad merely because we are able to feel, nor are we praised or blamed.

And again, Capacities we have by nature, but we do not come to be good or bad by nature, as we have said before. Since then the virtues are neither Feelings nor Capacities, it remains that they must be States.

Virtue then is "a state apt to exercise deliberate choice, being in the relative mean, determined by reason, and as the man of practical wisdom would determine."

It is a middle state between too faulty ones, in the way of excess on one side and of defect on the other: and it is so moreover, because the faulty states on one side fall short of, and those on the other exceed, what is right, both in the case of the feelings and the actions; but Virtue finds, and when found adopts, the mean.

And so, viewing it in respect of its essence and definition, Virtue is a mean state; but in reference to the chief good and to excellence it is the highest state possible.

But it must not be supposed that every action or every feeling is capable of subsisting in this mean state, because some there are which are so named as immediately to convey the notion of badness, as malevolence, shamelessness, envy; or, to instance in actions, adultery, theft, homicide; for all these and suchlike are blamed because they are in themselves bad, not the having too much or too little of them.

In these then you never can go right, but must always be wrong: nor in such does the right or wrong depend on the selection of a proper person, time, or manner (take adultery for instance), but simply doing any one so ever of those things is being wrong.

You might as well require that there should be determined a mean state, an excess and a defect in respect of acting unjustly, being cowardly, or giving up all control of the passions: for at this rate there will be of excess and defect a mean state; of excess, excess; and of defect, defect.

But just as of perfect self-mastery and courage there is no excess and defect, because the mean is in one point of view the highest possible state, so neither of those faulty states can you have a mean state, excess, or defect, but howsoever done they are wrong: you cannot, in short, have of excess and defect a mean state, nor of a mean state excess and defect.

It is not enough, however, to state this in general terms, we must also apply it to particular instances, because in treatises on moral conduct general statements have an air of vagueness, but those which go into detail one of greater reality: for the actions after all must be in detail, and the general statements, to be worth anything, must hold good here.

We must take these details then from the Table.

I. In respect of fears and confidence or boldness:

The mean state is Courage: men may exceed, of course, either in absence of fear or in positive confidence: the former has no name (which is a common case), the latter is called rash: again, the man who has too much fear and too little confidence is called a coward.

II. In respect of pleasures and pains (but not all, and perhaps fewer pains than pleasures):

The mean state here is perfected Self-Mastery, the defect total absence of Self-control. As for defect in respect of pleasure, there are really no people who are chargeable with it, so, of course, there is really no name for such characters, but, as they are conceivable, we will give them one and call them insensible.

III. In respect of giving and taking wealth (a):

The mean state is Liberality, the excess Prodigality, the defect Stinginess: here each of the extremes involves really an excess and defect contrary to each other: I mean, the prodigal gives out too much and takes in too little, while the stingy man takes in too much and gives out too little. (It must be understood that we are now giving merely an outline and summary, intentionally: and we will, in a later part of the treatise, draw out the distinctions with greater exactness.

IV. In respect of wealth (b):

There are other dispositions besides these just mentioned; a mean state called Munificence (for the munificent man differs from the liberal, the former having necessarily to do with great wealth, the latter with but small); the excess called by the names either of Want of Taste or Vulgar Profusion, and the defect Paltriness (these also differ from the extremes connected with liberality, and the manner of their difference shall also be spoken of later.)

V. In respect of honour and dishonour (a):

The mean state Greatness of Soul, the excess which may be called braggadocio, and the defect Littleness of Soul.

VI. In respect of honour and dishonour (b):

Now there is a state bearing the same relation to Greatness of Soul as we said just now Liberality does to Munificence, with the difference that is of being about a small amount of the same thing: this state having reference to small honour, as Greatness of Soul to great honour; a man may, of course, grasp at honour either more than he should or less; now he that exceeds in his grasping at it is called ambitious, he that falls short unambitious, he that is just as he should be has no proper name: nor in fact have the state, except that the disposition of the ambitious man is called ambition. For this reason those who are in either extreme lay claim to the mean as a debatable land, and we call the virtuous character sometimes by the name ambitious, sometimes by that of unambitious, and we commend sometimes the one and sometimes the other. Why we do it shall be said in the subsequent part of the treatise; but now we will go on with the rest of the virtues after the plan we have laid down.

VII. In respect of anger: Here too there is excess, defect, and a mean state; but since they may be said to have really no proper names, as we call the virtuous character Meek, we will call the mean state Meekness, and of the extremes, let the man who is excessive be denominated Passionate, and the faulty state Passionateness, and him who is deficient Angerless, and the defect Angerlessness. There are also three other mean states, having some mutual resemblance, but still with differences; they are alike in that they all have for their object-matter intercourse of words and deeds, and they differ in that one has respect to truth herein, the other two to what is pleasant; and this in two ways, the one in relaxation and amusement, the other in all things which occur in daily life. We must say a word or two about these also, that we may the better see that in all matters the mean is praiseworthy, while the extremes are neither right nor worthy of praise but of blame.

Now of these, it is true, the majority have really no proper names, but still we must try, as in the other cases, to coin some for them for the sake of clearness and intelligibleness.

I. In respect of truth:

The man who is in the mean state we will call Truthful, and his state Truthfulness, and as to the disguise of truth, if it be on the side of exaggeration, Braggadocia, and him that has it a Braggadocio; if on that of diminution, Reserve and Reserved shall be the terms.

II. In respect of what is pleasant in the way of relaxation or amusement:

The mean state shall be called Easy-pleasantry; and the character accordingly a man of Easy-pleasantry; the excess Buffoonery, and the man a Buffoon; the man deficient herein a Clown, and his state Clownishness.

III. In respect of what is pleasant in daily life:

He that is as he should be may be called Friendly, and his mean state Friendliness: he that exceeds, if it be without any interested motive, somewhat too Complaisant, if with such motive, a Flatterer: he that is deficient and in all instances unpleasant, Quarrelsome and Cross.

Now that Moral Virtue is a mean state, and how it is so, and that it lies between two faulty states, one in the way of excess and another in the way of defect, and that it is so because it has an aptitude to aim at the mean both in feelings and actions, all this has been set forth fully and sufficiently.

And so it is hard to be good: for surely hard it is in each instance to find the mean, just as to find the mean point or center of a circle is not what any man can do, but only he who knows how: just so to be angry, to give money, and be expensive, is what any man can do, and easy: but to do these to the right person, in due proportion, at the right time, with a right object, and in the right manner, this is not as before what any man can do, nor is it easy; and for this cause goodness is rare, and praiseworthy, and noble.

Therefore he who aims at the mean should make it his first care to keep away from that extreme which is more contrary than the other to the mean; just as Calypso in Homer advises Ulysses,

"Clear of this smoke and surge thy barque direct;"[1]

because of the two extremes the one is always more, and the other less, erroneous; and, therefore, since to hit exactly on the mean is difficult, one must take the least of the evils as the safest plan; and this a man will be doing, if he follows this method.

We ought also to take into consideration our own natural bias; which varies in each man's case, and will be ascertained from the pleasure and pain arising in us. Furthermore, we should force ourselves off in the contrary direction, because we shall find ourselves in the mean after we have removed ourselves far from the wrong side, exactly as men do in straightening bent timber.

But in all cases we must guard most carefully against what is pleasant, and pleasure itself, because we are not impartial judges of it.

We ought to feel in fact towards pleasure as did the old counselors towards Helen, and in all cases pronounce a similar sentence; for so by sending it away from us, we shall err the less.

Well, to speak very briefly, these are the precautions by adopting which we shall be best able to attain the mean.

Still, perhaps, after all it is a matter of difficulty, and specially in the particular instances: it is not easy, for instance, to determine exactly in what manner, with what persons, for what causes, and for what length of time, one ought to feel anger: for we ourselves sometimes praise those who are defective in this feeling, and we call them meek; at another, we term the hot-tempered manly and spirited.

Then, again, he who makes a small deflection from what is right, be it on the side of too much or too little, is not blamed, only he who makes a considerable one; for he cannot escape observation. But to what point or degree a man must err in order to incur blame, it is not easy to determine exactly in words: nor in fact any of those points which are matters of perception by the Moral Sense: such questions are matters of detail, and the decision of them rests with the Moral Sense.

At all events thus much is plain, that the mean state is in all things praiseworthy, and that practically we must deflect sometimes towards excess sometimes towards defect, because this will be the easiest method of hitting on the mean, that is, on what is right.

---

[1]   A barque is a small sailing boat. Calypso is here playing on the word 'surge' which means both a sudden increase and in nautical lingo to slacken or release (a rope or cable) suddenly. Hence, the advise is to steer clear of that by which you will get burned [editor's note].

Name_____

Date _____

1. Explain how happiness qualifies as the final good.

2. How does one acquire virtue?

3. How does Aristotle define virtue?

4. Show how virtue lies in the mean regarding Aristotle's example of Liberality.

5. Does Aristotle believe it is hard to be good? Explain.

6 *Hedonism; Epicurus*

┌───┐

❧ B I O G R A P H Y ❧

Epicurus (342/270 B.C.) was born at Samos. It was there that he became familiar with the works of Plato and Democritus. At the age of 18 he went to Athens for his military service after which he studied and taught at such diverse places as Colophon, Mitylene and Lanysacus. In 307/6 he returned to Athens where he established a school which became known as the Garden because he held his classes in that area of his confines[a]. His school was anything other than a forum[b] for exchange of ideas. Rather, Epicurus became a cult figure and his teachings were religiously followed by his students. Epicurus himself was totally intolerant of the thinkers who had gone before him. Nevertheless, his works reveal that he was heavily influenced by his predecessors[c]. Epicurus was a prolific writer. According to Diogenes Laertius he wrote approximately 300 works, most of which have since been lost. He was totally devoted to his school and it was the center of his activity until his death. It is evident that he had quite a following for his school flourished after his death. His disciples celebrated his demise[d] with a monthly feast, and his teachings became universally known throughout the Greek-speaking world.

└───┘

[a.] *confine:* a border or limit; boundary.
[b.] *forum:* a medium for open discussion.
[c.] *predecessor:* one who precedes another in time, especially in an office or position.
[d.] *demise:* death.

Hedonism is the ethical doctrine that maintains that pleasure is intrinsically good.[1] That which is intrinsically good is good in and of itself. It is essentially[2] or inherently good. Some goods, however, are instrumental in nature, namely, they are good for the purpose of achieving some goals. For example, hammers are instrumentally good because they assist one (i.e., act as instruments) in achieving the goal of driving nails. That which is intrinsically good is that goal towards which all other activity is or ought to be directed. Hence, the doctrine of hedonism maintains that the end toward which all our behavior is or ought to be directed is pleasure. At the outset, that appears rather appealing, does it not? Just imagine, without any further qualifications you need no longer feel guilty about your behavior at the last party you attended! Be it unfortunate or not, the word 'pleasure' is ambiguous[3]. It can mean either (a) short or (b) long-

---

[1] 'Hedonism' is a cognate of the Greek word *hedone* which means pleasure.

[2] *essential:* a fundamental, necessary, or indispensable part, item, or principle.

[3] *ambiguous:* susceptible of multiple interpretation.

range pleasure. Alternatively, it can be construed[4] as either (c) positive pleasure or (d) absence of pain. Normally (a) and (c) go hand in hand as do (b) and (d). The first pair constitute a crude form of hedonism expressed by the attitude of "eat, drink and be merry for tomorrow we die". We are all aware of this approach to life, one where an individual wallows in carnal[5] dissipation[6]. Long-range pleasure and absence of pain constitute a more temperate[7] approach to life. It is this form of hedonism that Epicurus advocated[8]. He construed pleasure to be absence of pain.

Philosophers of this period functioned as psychologists qua[9] physicians.[10] Just as a physician diagnoses a disease, ancient Greek ethicists diagnosed what constitutes the good life, a life of living well. Any diagnosis worth its salt must be based on evidence. Evidence takes the form of facts in conjunction with reasons. Epicurus offers (1) human observation and (2) a semantic argument to substantiate[11] his claim that the good life is one of pleasure qua absence of pain. (1) Rather than simply ask people what they want out of life, Epicurus believed that actions speak louder than words. One simply does not see (normal) folks lining up to get some unwanted, unnecessary pain. That is a matter of fact and provides good evidence for his diagnosis.

(2) Epicurus' semantic argument was offered as a response to the one supplied by his contemporary Aristotle who maintained that happiness is intrinsically good (see Chapter 4). Epicurus argued that Aristotle had mistakenly lumped pleasure together with fame and fortune whereby the statement:

(a) Max desires happiness in order to have pleasure

makes no sense because happiness in (a) functions as an instrumental good. Such statements only make sense when happiness functions as an intrinsic good, e.g.,

(b) Sally desires fame in order to be happy.

Epicurus agrees but argues that Aristotle is only half correct in his analysis as to what is intrinsically good.

(c) Mike desires wealth in order to have pleasure.

Here pleasure functions as an intrinsic good and (c) clearly makes sense. Epicurus concludes that since both (b) and (c) make sense, it must be the case that happiness and pleasure are synonymous[12].

Genuine pleasure is absence of pain. Upon observing human behavior Epicurus concluded that there are two varieties of pain, namely, phys-

---

[4]   *construe:* to give an explanation or translation.

[5]   *carnal:* pertaining to the flesh or body.

[6]   *dissipate:* to exhaust or expend intemperately; to waste; squander.

[7]   *temperate:* moderate in degree or quality.

[8]   *advocate:* to speak in favor of; recommend.

[9]   *qua:* in the function or capacity of.

[10]   Keep in mind that the discipline of psychology as we know it today grew out of philosophy. It was not until 1879 that the former was recognized as a separate field of study due to the work of Wilhelm Wundt.

[11]   *substantiate:* to show to be true or real by giving evidence.

[12]   *synonymous:* equivalent or similar in meaning.

ical and psychological. The latter is anxiety qua fear. People neither like to physically hurt nor to be "up-tight". Epicurus tailors his prescription to thwart[13] both physical and psychological pain.

Just as a medical doctor properly diagnoses an illness and determines its cure; so, too, the ancient Greek ethicists thought it their business to determine what the good life is and then provide guidance as to how to attain[14] it. If we can avoid pain and fear, we will achieve a life of living well, and this is what Epicurus meant by living a life of pleasure. But how is this pleasurable way of life to be attained? First of all, one cannot be free of pain unless one has a *healthy body*. This is to be attained by living moderately. You simply must take care of the physical aspect of your being. This cannot be done if you do not live moderately. "It is not possible to live pleasantly without living prudently, and honorably, and justly; nor to live prudently, and honorably, and justly, without living pleasantly. But he to whom it does not happen to live prudently, honorably, and justly, cannot possibly live pleasantly."

Second, one must care for his soul. Here the term 'soul' refers to the psychological aspect of our being.[15] Epicurus was far ahead of his time for he maintained that it is important for one to be concerned about mental health. He expressed this by stating that we can only live a life of pleasure if we have tranquility of the soul, namely, if we rid ourselves of anxiety. Tranquility of the soul means that *(a) one must be secure in the knowledge that he has a healthy body, (b) that he minimize his enemies, and (c) that he does not fear the gods or afterlife.*

It may appear redundant[16] that the issue of health of the body should reappear. But one cannot rest easy if he is not secure in the knowledge that he has such stature[17]. One may indeed be physically fit, but we all know the psychosomatic[18] problems that result from not being convinced of that fact. One's state of health and relevant knowledge thereof are immanently[19] tied to one another. And this is especially true if one is not in the best of health. Even if you *are* healthy, if you *think* you are ill, no doubt you will eventually experience some physical manifestation to prove it. Here we see Epicurus being far ahead of his time by appreciating what we now refer to as holism. Holism is the theory that a high percentage of one's physical condition is mentally caused. This works both negatively and positively. One can will themselves into physical sickness. Alternatively, a positive mental attitude can have curative powers. The best way to curb any *concern* about one's physical well-being is to live in a prudent[20] manner, for it is well established now, as it was then, that a moderate life style is the best way to guarantee a life free of pain.

In addition, one must be free of the fear of enemies. The notion of an enemy involves more than a foe on a battlefield. There are (potential)

---

[13] *thwart:* to prevent from taking place; frustrate; block.

[14] *attain:* to gain, reach, or accomplish by mental or physical effort.

[15] Epicurus is ambiguous in his use of the term 'soul'. On the one hand, he clearly means it to refer to the psychological side of being. On the other hand, he claims that the soul is the principal cause of sensation with respect to a living human being.

[16] *redundant:* needlessly repetitive; verbose.

[17] *stature:* a level achieved; status, caliber.

[18] *psychosomatic:* of/or pertaining to a partially or wholly psychogenic disease or physiological disorder.

[19] *immanent:* remaining or operating within the subject considered; indwelling, inherent.

[20] *prudent:* capable of directing or conducting oneself wisely and judiciously.

enemies around us all the time. There are people who simply cannot be trusted. They are unscrupulous[21] and use other human beings for their own gain. Enemies cause pain. Hence, one should try to minimize them for the purpose of living as pain-free an existence as possible. One means by which we can minimize our enemies is to have a lot of friends. But keep in mind that having friends is only *instrumental* to minimizing enemies. They are not identical. Epicurus, although he refers to the value of friendship, is somewhat reserved with respect to it, noting all the time that a reclusive[22] life is the best means by which one can avoid anxiety in this area of his life. And he was true to his teachings. He lived a very quiet and removed existence.

It is imperative[23] that if one is to achieve tranquility of the soul one must not fear the gods or afterlife. This involves the most complex aspect of Epicurus' theory. First of all, one must understand that the Greeks had a totally different concept of religion from those subscribing to the Judeo-Christian tradition. They were polytheists, which means that they believed in many gods. And they attributed[24] human characteristics to their gods, otherwise known as anthropomorphism. Aphrodite, for example, was the goddess of love, love in its purest and most perfect form. The love she represented was meant to be construed as the ultimate standard of that quality. They also believed that their deities possessed super-human virtues as well as vices. The majority of Greeks at the time believed that the gods and goddesses had powers that influenced human destiny[25]. For example, they believed that Hades was the god of the underworld and that when one died his soul resided in a never-never land below the sea. Epicurus, on the other hand, maintained that the gods and goddesses were considered to possess super-human virtues and vices for the purpose of bringing into focus what human beings ought and ought not do in *this* life. He argued that the gods and goddesses ought to be viewed as role models of behavior. By way of example, Zeus was a philanderer[26]. His wife, Hera, was fully aware of his aberrant[27] behavior. Every time he attempted to commit adultery she would thwart his plans and make him pay dearly for it. Now, what is the moral of this scenario[28]? The message has nothing to do with an afterlife; rather, it is an example of how human beings ought not behave in this life. The extremity of Zeus' behavior functions as a method of demonstrating what is not morally acceptable so far as human behavior is concerned. That is also why the Greek gods and goddesses are anthropomorphic in nature so far as Epicurus is concerned. The fundamental point is that the value of believing in the gods is not for rewards or punishment upon death but for moral guidance in the present. In other words, the god's proper function is that of role models for us in the here and now *sans*[29] any judgment on their behalf.

---

[21] *unscrupulous:* without scruples; contemptuous of what is right or honorable.

[22] *recluse:* one who withdraws from the world to live in solitude and seclusion, as a hermit.

[23] *imperative:* expressing a command or plea; peremptory.

[24] *attribute:* to regard or assign as belonging to.

[25] *destiny:* the predetermined course of events often conceived as a resistless power or agency; fate.

[26] *philander:* to engage in love affairs frivolously or casually.

[27] *aberrant:* deviating from the proper or expected course.

[28] *scenario:* an outline of a hypothesized chain of events.

[29] *sans:* without.

If one did believe that the gods influence an afterlife, then he would be anxiety-ridden and could not, therefore, live a life of pleasure. Why? Because if you feel worried about what is going to happen to you when you die, and if you believe in an afterlife determined by your earthly deeds, there is no way you can avoid anxiety because no person is perfect in his dealings with other human beings. The proper way to avoid this type of anxiety is to understand that the notion of an afterlife is a self-contradiction. An essential characteristic of life is sensation. Death entails a cessation[30] of sensation. Death is the absence of life; so, for Epicurus, it is totally *meaningless* to speak of, not to mention believe in, life after death. When you die, that's it. You, qua you, the person you are becomes nothing upon death; absolutely nothing so far as your personal identity is concerned. This leads us to Epicurus' theory of the universe.

He believed that there are only two things that constitute the universe, atoms and space. The only things that exist are particles, called atoms[31] and conglomerates[32] thereof, which occupy a void called space. Space is the absence of atoms. Nothing else exists. Conglomerates of atoms may change their form, but the constituents always remain the same. Upon death a human being disintegrates according to the law of conservation of energy. The soul being the principal cause of sensation "is dispersed and no longer has the same powers nor performs its movements so that it does not possess sensation either." Once one realizes this, there is no need to be anxiety-ridden about a personalized soul surviving bodily death or any possible consequences thereof. Materially there is no difference between the soul and the body. By so understanding, a person can undermine one of the greatest sources of human anxiety. One can thus take a giant step towards achieving tranquility of the soul and without that no one can live a pleasurable existence, namely, the good life.[33]

Suggested Readings: Hedonism; Epicurus

1. Baily, C., *The Greek Atomists and Epicurus* (Oxford: The Clarendon Press, 1928), Chapter 10.
2. Copleston, F., *A History of Philosophy*, Vol. I (Baltimore: Newman Press, 1994), I, Chapter 37.
3 DeWitt, N.W., *Epicurus and His Philosophy* (Minneapolis: University of Minnesota Press, 1954).
4. Hicks, R.D., *Stoic and Epicurean* (New York: Russell and Russell, 1962), Chapter 5.
5. Lucretius., *On the Nature of the Universe.*
6. Reanney, Darryl, *After Death: A New Future for Human Consciousness* (N.Y.: Wm Morrow & Co., Inc., 1991).
7. Rist J.M., *Epicurus* (London: Cambridge University Press, 1972)
8. Strodach, G.K., *The Philosophy of Epicurus* (Evanston: Northwestern University Press, 1963), Introduction.

---

[30] *cessation:* a ceasing of or discontinuance, as of action; a stop.

[31] *atom:* an irreducible, indestructible unit.

[32] *conglomerate:* a collection of parts that form a coherent whole.

[33] For a thorough discussion of Epicurus' atomic theory see Lucretius, *On the Nature of the Universe.*

9. Taylor, A. E., *Epicurus* (London: Constable, 1911).
10. Taylor, P. (ed.), *Problems of Moral Philosophy: An Introduction to Ethics* (Belmont, Calif.: Dickenson, 1967), Chapter 3.
11. Watson, J., *Hedonistic Theories from Aristippus to Spencer* (New York: Macmillan, 1895), Chapter 3.
12. Zeller, E., *The Stoics, Epicureans, and Sceptics*, trans. by O.J. Reichel (London: Longmans, 1880) ,Chapters 19-20.

STUDY

QUESTIONS

Name_____

Date _____

Chapter 6:
Hedonism;
Epicurus

1. What is hedonism? Does Epicurus advocate an "eat, drink and be merry" philosophy? Explain.

2. How does one achieve "tranquility of soul"?

3. How does Epicurus' view of the gods further tranquility of the soul?

4. Briefly explain Epicurus' theory of the universe.

5. What does Epicurus mean when he speaks of the soul? (Remember he uses the term ambiguously.)

Epicurus, *The Extant Remains*, translated by Cyril Bailey (Oxford: The Clarendon Press, 1926). Permission granted by Oxford University Press.

Letter to Menoeceus

Let no one when young delay to study philosophy, nor when he is old grow weary of his study. For no one can come too early or too late to secure the health of his soul. And the man who says that the age for philosophy has either not yet come or has gone by is like the man who says that the age for happiness is not yet come to him, or has passed away. Wherefore both when young and old a man must study philosophy, that as he grows old he may be young in blessings through the grateful recollection of what has been, and that in youth he may be old as well, since he will know no fear of what is to come. We must then meditate on the things that make our happiness, seeing that when that is with us we have all, but when it is absent we do all to win it.

The things which I used unceasingly to commend to you, these do and practice, considering them to be the first principles of the good life.

First of all believe that god is a being immortal and blessed, even as the common idea of a god is engraved on men's minds, and do not assign to him anything alien to his immortality or ill-suited to his blessedness: but believe about him everything that can uphold his blessedness and immortality. For gods there are, since the knowledge of them is by clear vision. But they are not such as the many believe them to be: for indeed they do not consistently represent them as they believe them to be. And the impious man is not he who denies the gods of the many, but he who attaches to the gods the beliefs of the many. For the statements of the many about the gods are not conceptions derived from sensation, but false suppositions, according to which the greatest misfortunes befall the wicked and the greatest blessings the good by the gift of the gods. For men being accustomed always to their own virtues welcome those like themselves, but regard all that is not of their nature as alien.

Become accustomed to the belief that death is nothing to us. For all good and evil consists in sensation, but death is deprivation of sensation. And therefore a right understanding that death is nothing to us makes the mortality of life enjoyable, not because it adds to it an infinite span of time, but because it takes away the craving for immortality. For there is nothing terrible in life for the man who has truly comprehended that there is nothing terrible in not living. So that the man speaks but idly who says that he fears death not because it will be painful when it comes, but because it is painful in anticipation. For that which gives no trouble when it comes, is but an empty pain in anticipation. So death, the most terrifying of ills, is nothing to us, since so long as we exist, death is not with us; but when death comes, then we do not exist. It does not then concern either the living or the dead, since for the former it is not, and the latter are no more.

But the many at one moment shun death as the greatest of evils, at another yearn for it as a respite from the evils in life. But the wise man neither seeks to escape life nor fears the cessation of life, for neither does life offend him nor does the absence of life seem to be any evil. And just as with food he does not seek simply the larger share and nothing else, but rather the most pleasant, so he seeks to enjoy not the longest period of time, but the most pleasant.

And he who counsels the young man to live well, but the old man to make a good end, is foolish, not merely because of the desirability of life, but also because it is the same training which teaches to live well and to die well. Yet much worse still is the man who says it is good not to be born, but

> 'once born make haste to pass the gates of Death'.
> [Theognis, 427]

For if he says this from conviction why does he not pass away out of life? For it is open to him to do so, if he had firmly made up his mind to this. But if he speaks in jest, his words are idle among men who cannot receive them.

We must then bear in mind that the future is neither ours, nor yet wholly not ours, so that we may not altogether expect it as sure to come, nor abandon hope of it, as if it will certainly not come.

We must consider that of desires some are natural, others vain, and of the natural some are necessary and others merely natural; and of the necessary some are necessary for happiness, others for the repose of the body, and others for very life. The right understanding of these facts enables us to refer all choice and avoidance to the health of the body and the soul's freedom from disturbance, since this is the aim of the life of blessedness. For it is to obtain this end that we always act, namely, to avoid pain and fear. And when this is once secured for us, all the tempest of the soul is dispersed, since the living creature has not to wander as though in search of something that is missing, and to look for some other thing by which he can fulfill the good of the soul and the good of the body. For it is then that we have need of pleasure, when we feel pain owing to the absence of pleasure; but when we do not feel pain, we no longer need pleasure. And for this cause we call pleasure the beginning and end of the blessed life. For we recognize pleasure as the first good innate in us, and from pleasure we begin every act of choice and avoidance, and to pleasure we return again, using the feeling as the standard by which we judge every good.

And since pleasure is the first good and natural to us, for this very reason we do not choose every pleasure, but sometimes we pass over many pleasures, when greater discomfort accrues to us as the result of them: and similarly we think many pains better than pleasures, since a greater pleasure comes to us when we have endured pains for a long time. Every pleasure then because of its natural kinship to us is good, yet not every pleasure is to be chosen: even as every pain also is an evil, yet not all are always of a nature to be avoided. Yet by a scale of comparison and by the consideration of advantages and disadvantages we must form our judgement on all these matters. For the good on certain occasions we treat as bad, and conversely the bad as good.

And again independence of desire we think a great good--not that we may at all times enjoy but a few things, but that, if we do not possess many, we may enjoy the few in the genuine persuasion that those have the sweetest pleasure in luxury who least need it, and that all that is natural is easy to be obtained, but that which is superfluous is hard. And so plain savours bring us a pleasure equal to a luxurious diet, when all the pain due to want is removed; and bread and water produce the highest pleasure, when one who needs them puts them to his lips. To grow accustomed therefore to simple and not luxurious diet gives us health to the full, and makes a man alert for the needful employments of life, and when after long intervals we approach luxuries disposes us better towards them, and fits us to be fearless of fortune.

When, therefore, we maintain that pleasure is the end, we do not mean the pleasures of profligates and those that consist in sensuality, as is supposed by some who are either ignorant or disagree with us or do not understand, but freedom from pain in the body and from trouble in the mind. For it is not continuous drinkings and revellings, nor the satisfaction of lusts, nor the enjoyment of fish and other luxuries of the wealthy table, which produce a pleasant life, but sober reasoning, searching out the motives for all choice and avoidance, and banishing mere opinions, to which are due the greatest disturbance of the spirit.

Of all this the beginning and the greatest good is prudence. Wherefore prudence is a more precious thing even than philosophy: for from prudence are sprung all the other virtues, and it teaches us that it is not possible to live pleasantly without living prudently and honourably and justly, nor, again, to live a life of prudence, honour, and justice without living pleasantly. For the virtues are by nature bound up with the pleasant life, and the pleasant life is inseparable from them. For indeed who, think you, is a better man than he who holds reverent opinions concerning the gods, and is at all times free from fear of death, and has reasoned out the end ordained by nature? He understands that the limit of good things is easy to fulfil and easy to attain, whereas the course of ills is either short in time or slight in pain: he laughs at destiny, whom some have introduced as the mistress of all things. He thinks that with us lies the chief power in determining events, some of which happen by necessity and some by chance, and some are within our control; for while necessity cannot be called to account, he sees that chance is inconstant, but that which is in our control is subject to no master, and to it are naturally attached praise and blame. For, indeed, it were better to follow the myths about the gods than to become a slave to the destiny of the natural philosophers: for the former suggests a hope of placating the gods by worship, whereas the later involves a necessity which knows no placation. As to chance, he does not regard it as a god as most men do (for in a god's acts there is no disorder), nor as an uncertain cause of all things: for he does not believe that good and evil are given by chance to man for the framing of a blessed life, but that opportunities for great good and great evil are afforded by it. He therefore thinks it better to be unfortunate in reasonable action than to prosper in unreason. For it is better in a man's actions that what is well chosen should fail, rather than that what is ill chosen should be successful owing to chance.

Meditate therefore on these things and things akin to them night and day by yourself, and with a companion like to yourself, and never shall you be disturbed waking or asleep, but you shall live like a god among men. For a man who lives among immortal blessings is not like to a mortal being.

Letter to Herodotus

First of all, Herodotus, we must grasp the ideas attached to words, in order that we may be able to refer to them and so to judge the inferences of opinion or problems of investigation or reflection, so that we may not either leave everything uncertain and go on explaining to infinity or use words devoid of meaning. For this purpose it is essential that the first mental image associated with each word should be regarded, and that there should be no need of explanation, if we are really to have a standard to which to refer a problem of investigation or reflection or a mental inference. And besides we must keep all our investigations in accord with our sensations, and in particular with the immediate apprehensions whether of the mind or of any one of the instruments of judgment, and likewise in accord with the feelings existing in us, in order that we may have indications whereby we may judge both the problem of sense-perception and the unseen.

Having made these points clear, we must now consider things imperceptible to the senses. First of all, that nothing is created out of that which does not exist: for if it were, everything would be created out of everything with no need of seeds. And again, if that which disappears were destroyed into that which did not exist, all things would have perished, since that into which they were dissolved would not exist. Furthermore, the universe always was such as it is now, and always will be the same. For there is nothing into which it changes: for outside the universe there is nothing which could come into it and bring about the change.

Moreover, the universe is (bodies and space): for that bodies exist sense itself witnesses in the experience of all men, and in accordance with the evidence of sense we must of necessity judge of the imperceptible by reasoning, as I have already said. And if there were not that which we term void and place and intangible existence, bodies would have nowhere to exist and nothing through which to move, as they are seen to move. And besides these two nothing can even be thought of either by conception or on the analogy of things conceivable such as could be grasped as whole existences and not spoken of as the accidents or properties of such existences. Furthermore, among bodies some are compounds, and others those of which compounds are formed. And these latter are indivisible and unalterable (if, that is, all things are not to be destroyed into the nonexistent, but something permanent is to remain behind at the dissolution of compounds): they are completely solid in nature, and can by no means be dissolved in any part. So it must needs be that the first-beginnings are indivisible corporeal existences.

Moreover, the universe is boundless. For that which is bounded has an extreme point: and the extreme point is seen against something else. So that as it has no extreme point, it has no limit; and as it has no limit, it must be boundless and not bounded. Furthermore, the infinite is boundless both in the number of the bodies and in the extent of the void. For if on the one hand the void were boundless, and the bodies limited in number, the bodies could not stay anywhere, but would be carried about and scattered through the infinite void, not having other bodies to support them and keep them in place by means of collisions. But if, on the other hand, the void were limited, the infinite bodies would not have room wherein to take their place.

Besides this the indivisible and solid bodies, out of which too the compounds are created and into which they are dissolved, have an incomprehensible number of varieties in shape: for it is not possible that such great varieties of things should arise from the same (atomic) shapes, if they are limited in number. And so in each shape the atoms are quite infinite in number, but their differences of shape are not quite infinite, but only incomprehensible in number.

And the atoms move continuously for all time, some of them falling straight down, others swerving, and others recoiling from their collisions. And of the latter, some are borne on separating to a long distance from one another, while others again recoil and recoil, whenever they chance to be checked by the interlacing with others, or else shut in by atoms interlaced around them. For on the one hand the nature of the void which separates each atom by itself brings this about, as it is not able to afford resistance, and on the other hand the hardness which belongs to the atoms makes them recoil after collision to as great a distance as the interlacing permits separation after the collision. And these motions have no beginning, since the atoms and the void are the cause.

These brief sayings, if all these points are borne in mind, afford a sufficient outline for our understanding of the nature of existing things.

Moreover, we must suppose that the atoms do not possess any of the qualities belonging to perceptible things, except shape, weight, and size, and all that necessarily goes with shape. For every quality changes; but the atoms do not change at all, since there must needs be something which remains solid and indissoluble at the dissolution of compounds, which can cause changes; not changes into the non-existent or from the non-existent, but changes effected by the shifting of position of some particles, and by the addition or departure of others. For this reason it is essential that the bodies which shift their position should be imperishable and should not possess the nature of what changes, but parts and configuration of their own. For thus much must needs remain constant. For even in things perceptible to us which change their shape by the withdrawal of matter it is seen that shape remains to them, whereas the qualities do not remain in the changing object, in the way in which shape is left behind, but are lost from the entire body. Now these particles which are left behind are sufficient to cause the differences in compound bodies, since it is essential that some things should be left behind and not be destroyed into the non-existent.

Moreover, we must not either suppose that every size exists among the atoms, in order that the evidence of phenomena may not contradict us, but we must suppose that there are some variations of size. For if this be the case, we can give a better account of what occurs in our feelings and sensations. But the existence of atoms of every size is not required to explain the differences of qualities in things, and at the same time some atoms would be bound to come within our ken and be visible; but this is never seen to be the case, nor is it possible to imagine how an atom could become visible.

Besides this we must not suppose that in a limited body there can be infinite parts or parts of every degree of smallness. Therefore, we must not only do away with division into smaller and smaller parts to infinity, in order that we may not make all things weak, and so in the composition of aggregate bodies be compelled to crush and squander the things that exist into the non-existent, but we must not either suppose that in limited bodies there is a possibility of continuing to infinity in passing even to smaller and smaller parts. For if once one says that there are infinite parts in a body or parts of any degree of smallness, it is not possible to conceive how this should be, and indeed how could the body any longer be limited in size? (For it is obvious that these infinite particles must be of some size or other; and however small they may be, the size of the body too would be infinite.) And again, since the limited body has an extreme point, which is distinguishable, even though not perceptible by itself, you cannot conceive that the succeeding point to it is not similar in character, or that if you go on in this way from one point to another, it should be possible for you to proceed to infinity marking such points in your mind...

Next, referring always to the sensations and the feelings for in this way you will obtain the most trustworthy ground of belief, you must consider that the soul is a body of fine particles distributed throughout the whole structure, and most resembling wind with a certain admixture of heat, and in some respects like to one of these and in some to the other. There is also the part which is many degrees more advanced even than these in fineness of composition, and for this reason is more capable of feeling in harmony with the rest of the structure as well. Now all this is made manifest by the activities of the soul and the feelings and the readiness of its movements and its processes of thought and by what we lose at the moment of death. Further, you must grasp that the soul possesses the chief cause of sensation: yet it could not have acquired sensation, unless it were in some way enclosed by the rest of the structure. And this in its turn having afforded the soul this cause of sensation acquires itself too a share in this contingent capacity from the soul. Yet it does not acquire all the capacities which the soul possesses: and therefore when the soul is released from the body, the body no longer has sensation. For it never possessed this power in itself, but used to afford opportunity for it to another existence, brought into being at the same time with itself: and this existence, owing to the power now consummated within itself as a result of motion, used spontaneously to produce for itself the capacity of sensation and then to communicate it to the body as well, in virtue of its contact and correspondence of movement, as I have already said. Therefore, so long as the soul remains in the body, even though some other part of the body be lost, it will never lose sensation; nay more, whatever portions of the soul may perish too, when that which enclosed it is removed either in whole or in part, if the soul continues to exist at all, it will retain sensation. On the other hand the rest of the structure, though it continues to exist either as a whole or in part, does not retain sensation, if it has once lost that sum of atoms, however small it be, which together goes to produce the nature of the soul. Moreover, if the whole structure is dissolved, the soul is dispersed and no longer has the same powers nor performs its movements, so that it does not possess sensation either. For it is impossible to imagine it with sensation, if it is not in this organism and cannot effect these movements, when what encloses and surrounds it is no longer the same as the surroundings in which it now exists and performs these movements. Furthermore, we must clearly comprehend as well, that the incorporeal in the general acceptation of the term is applied to that which could be thought of as an independent existence. Now it is impossible to conceive the incorporeal as a separate existence, except the void: and the void can neither act nor be acted upon, but only provides opportunity of motion through itself to bodies. So that those who say that the soul is incorporeal are talking idly. For it would not be able to act or be acted on in any respect, if it were of this nature. But as it is, both these occurrences are clearly distinguished in respect of the soul. . . .

Principal Doctrines

I. The blessed and immortal nature knows no trouble itself nor causes trouble to any other, so that it is never constrained by anger or favour. For all such things exist only in the weak.

II. Death is nothing to us: for that which is dissolved is without sensation; and that which lacks sensation is nothing to us.

III. The limit of quantity in pleasures is the removal of all that is painful. Wherever pleasure is present, as long as it is there, there is neither pain of body nor of mind, nor of both at once.

IV. Pain does not last continuously in the flesh, but the acutest pain is there for a very short time, and even that which just exceeds the pleasure in the flesh does not continue for many days at once. But chronic illnesses permit a predominance of pleasure over pain in the flesh.

V. It is not possible to live pleasantly without living prudently and honourably and justly, [nor again to live a life of prudence, honour, and justice] without living pleasantly. And the man who does not possess the pleasant life, is not living prudently and honourably and justly, [and the man who does not possess the virtuous life], cannot possibly live pleasantly.

VI. To secure protection from men anything is a natural good, by which you may be able to attain this end.

VII. Some men wished to become famous and conspicuous, thinking that they would thus win for themselves safety from other men. Wherefore if the life of such men is safe, they have obtained the good which nature craves; but if it is not safe, they do not possess that for which they strove at first by the instinct of nature.

VIII. No pleasure is a bad thing in itself: but the means which produce some pleasures bring with them disturbances many times greater than the pleasures.

IX. If every pleasure could be intensified so that it lasted and influenced the whole organism or the most essential parts of our nature, pleasures would never differ from one another.

X. If the things that produce the pleasures of profligates could dispel the fears of the mind about the phenomena of the sky and death and its pains, and also teach the limits of desires (and of pains), we should never have cause to blame them: for they would be filling themselves full with pleasures from every source and never have pain of body or mind, which is the evil of life.

XI. If we were not troubled by our suspicions of the phenomena of the sky and about death, fearing that it concerns us, and also by our failure to grasp the limits of pains and desires, we should have no need of natural science.

XII. A man cannot dispel his fear about the most important matters if he does not know what is the nature of the universe but suspects the truth of some mythical story. So that without natural science it is not possible to attain our pleasures unalloyed.

XIII. There is no profit in securing protection in relation to men, if things above and things beneath the earth and indeed all in the boundless universe remain matters of suspicion.

XIV. The most unalloyed source of protection from men, which is secured to some extent by a certain force from expulsion, is in fact the immunity which results from a quiet life and the retirement from the world.

XV. The wealth demanded by nature is both limited and easily procured; that demanded by idle imaginings stretches on to infinity.

XVI. In but few things chance hinders a wise man, but the greatest and most important matters reason has ordained and throughout the whole period of life does and will ordain.

XVII. The just man is most free from trouble, the unjust most full of trouble.

XVIII. The pleasure in the flesh is not increased, when once the pain due to want is removed, but is only varied: and the limit as regards pleasure in the mind is begotten by the reasoned understanding of these very pleasures and of the emotions akin to them, which used to cause the greatest fear to the mind.

XIX. Infinite time contains no greater pleasure than limited time, if one measures by reason the limits of pleasure.

XX. The flesh perceives the limits of pleasure as unlimited and unlimited time is required to supply it. But the mind, having attained a reasoned understanding of the ultimate good of the flesh and its limits and having dissipated the fears concerning the time to come, supplies us with the complete life, and we have no further need of infinite time: but neither does the mind shun pleasure, nor, when circumstances begin to bring about the departure from life, does it approach its end as though it fell short in any way of the best life.

XXI. He who has learned the limits of life knows that that which removes the pain due to want and makes the whole of life complete is easy to obtain; so that there is no need of actions which involve competition.

XXII. We must consider both the real purpose and all the evidence of direct perception, to which we always refer the conclusions of opinion; otherwise, all will be full of doubt and confusion.

XXIII. If you fight against all sensations, you will have no standard by which to judge even those of them which you say are false.

XXIV. If you reject any single sensation and fail to distinguish between the conclusion of opinion as to the appearance awaiting confirmation and that which is actually given by the sensation or feeling, or each intuitive apprehension of the mind, you will confound all other sensations as well with the same groundless opinion, so that you will reject every standard of judgment. And if among the mental images created by your opinion you affirm both that which awaits confirmation and that which does not, you will not escape error, since you will have preserved the whole cause of doubt in every judgment between what is right and what is wrong.

XXV. If on each occasion instead of referring your actions to the end of nature, you turn to some other nearer standard when you are making a choice or an avoidance, your actions will not be consistent with your principles

XXVI.Of desires, all that do not lead to a sense of pain, if they are not satisfied, are not necessary, but involve a craving which is easily dispelled, when the object is hard to procure or they seem likely to produce harm.

XXVII.Of all the things which wisdom acquires to produce the blessedness of the complete life, far the greatest is the possession of friendship.

XXVIII.The same conviction which has given us confidence that there is nothing terrible that lasts for ever or even for long, has also seen the protection of friendship most fully completed in the limited evils of this life.

XXIX. Among desires some are natural (and necessary, some natural) but not necessary, and others neither natural nor necessary, but due to idle imagination.

XXX. Wherever in the case of desires which are physical, but do not lead to a sense of pain, if they are not fulfilled, the effort is intense, such pleasures are due to idle imagination, and it is not owing to their own nature that they fail to be dispelled, but owing to the empty imaginings of the man.

XXXI. The justice which arises from nature is a pledge of mutual advantage to restrain men from harming one another and save them from being harmed.

XXXII. For all living things which have not been able to make compacts not to harm one another or be harmed, nothing ever is either just or unjust; and likewise too for all tribes of men which have been unable or unwilling to make compacts not to harm or be harmed.

XXXIII. Justice never is anything in itself, but in the dealings of men with one another in any place whatever and at any time it is a kind of compact not to harm or be harmed.

XXXIV. Injustice is not an evil in itself, but only in consequence of the fear which attaches to the apprehension of being unable to escape those appointed to punish such actions.

XXXV. It is not possible for one who acts in secret contravention of the terms of the compact not to harm or be harmed, to be confident that he will escape detection, even if at present he escapes a thousand times. For up to the time of death it cannot be certain that he will indeed escape.

XXXVI. In its general aspect justice is the same for all, for it is a kind of mutual advantage in the dealings of men with one another: but with reference to the individual peculiarities of a country or any other circumstances the same thing does not turn out to be just for all.

XXXVII. Among actions which are sanctioned as just by law, that which is proved on examination to be of advantage in the requirements of men's dealings with one another, has the guarantee of justice, whether it is the same for all or not. But if a man makes a law and it does not turn out to lead to advantage in men's dealings with each other, then it no longer has the essential nature of justice. And even if the advantage in the matter of justice shifts from one side to the other, but for a while accords with the general concept, it is none the less just for that period in the eyes of those who do not confound themselves with empty sounds but look to the actual facts.

XXXVIII.Where, provided the circumstances have not been altered, actions which were considered just, have been shown not to accord with the general concept in actual practice, then they are not just. But where, when circumstances have changed, the same actions which were sanctioned as just no longer lead to advantage, there they were just at the time when they were of advantage for the dealings of fellow-citizens with one another; but subsequently they are no longer just, when no longer of advantage.

XXXIX. The man who has best ordered the element of disquiet arising from external circumstances has made those things that he could akin to himself and the rest at least not alien: but with all to which he could not do even this, he has refrained from mixing, and has expelled from his life all which it was of advantage to treat thus.

XL. As many as possess the power to procure complete immunity from their neighbours, these also live most pleasantly with one another, since they have the most certain pledge of security, and after they have enjoyed the fullest intimacy, they do not lament the previous departure of a dead friend, as though he were to be pitied.

1. Explain Epicurus' argument for why we should not fear death.

2. What is the motivating factor in all of our actions according to Epicurus?

3. Every pleasure is good, says Epicurus, therefore every pleasure is to be chosen. True or false? Explain.

4. Give at least two reasons why Epicurus believes we should eat a simple diet.

5. According to his "Letter to Menoeceus", Epicurus maintained that the beginning and the greatest good is

    _____.

6. In his "Letter to Herodotus", Epicurus says that "those who say that the soul is incorporeal are talking idly". What does he mean by 'incorporeal', and why cannot this term be applied to the soul?

7 The Categorical Imperative; Immanuel Kant

❧ BIOGRAPHY ❧

Immanuel Kant (1724-1804) was born of humble origins in Konigsberg, a town in East Prussia. His father was a saddler and according to his own account was the grandson of a Scottish immigrant. Kant studied at the local high school, the Collegium Fridericianun, after which he attended the University of Konigsberg. His first academic employment consisted of being tutor to several families in the vicinity. His devotion to academia led to the achievement of his masters degree in 1755 at which time he became an instructor at the university from which he had graduated. At this time in his life, he was primarily interested in the sciences. He lectured on a wide variety of subjects including physics, mathematics, and physical geography as well as philosophy. He held this post for fifteen years at which time he was promoted to the rank of professor. Although he had published several treatises at this point in his life, his major philosophical ideas were still in the germination[a] process. During the ensuing eleven years he not only lectured but formulated the basis of a systematic philosophy which was detailed in his famous Critique of Pure Reason. *This was followed by his publication of the* Prolegomena to any Future Metaphysics *in 1783 and the* Fundamental Principles of the Metaphysics of Morals *in 1785.*

Kant is often portrayed as an austere person. There is no doubt that he was a man who adhered to a strict schedule. This does not mean, however, that he was asocial. He very much enjoyed the company of others. This is verified[b] by the rather lengthy lunch hours he took with colleagues and friends. He was also known for his rather witty lectures during which he often cracked jokes.

During his early years as a tutor, Kant was poor but as his reputation grew he became not only well respected but economically comfortable. He remained intellectually acute until the time of his death, committed to demonstrating that his critics did not fully understand his philosophical positions.

[a.] *germinate:* to start developing or growing.

[b.] *verify:* to prove the truth by presentation of evidence or testimony; substantiate.

Central to Kant's ethics is the determination of a rule by which one can extricate[1] oneself from moral dilemmas[2]. A solution to this problem should be of interest not only to philosophers but to anyone concerned about living a morally upright life.   Everyone is faced with a moral dilemma from time to time. For example, ought one engage in the practice of telling white lies, not outright lying, but bending the truth a little? We have all been in that position and it creates for us, at the very least, a mini moral crisis. Consistent with the ancient Greek belief that consistency in thought, as well as behavior, is better than inconsistency, Kant wants to deduce[3] some formula (i.e., rule) that we can utilize when we find ourselves in such situations. If we cannot discover some such rule, we will be destined to go about the process of moral decision-making in a hit and miss manner and the result will not be consistent and, therefore, we will not be as successful moral agents as possible. (Consistency is the key to success in all of our behavior.)

As a general observation, ethical theory pertains[4] to moral principles. A moral principle is a directive and entails[5] the notion of ought. It tells someone what he ought to do given certain circumstances such as when he is faced with a moral dilemma. Part of the logic of the concept ought is free will. Just think about that for a moment. If human beings had no free will, it would be utterly meaningless to tell them what they ought to do. Suppose my leg is paralyzed. It makes no sense for someone to say to me that I ought to move my leg out of the way. To suggest that one ought to move his leg implies[6] that it is within his power to move his leg which, in turn, means that he is free to choose to move his leg.

The assumption fundamental to Kant's ethical theory is that all human beings possess free will with respect to one's decisions regardless of circumstance. Just what exactly does he mean by this claim? Clearly, we human beings are limited in our choices by a number of factors. We have genetic limiations, e.g., we do not have wings so we for all intents and purposes do not have the free will to fly. Our choices are limited by the environment into which we were born, e.g., our socio-economic status greatly determines the scope of our choices. All this is true. However, according to Kant, it is reasonable to *assume* that we are always free to choose the manner by which to deal with any and all situations in which we find ourselves or by which we are confronted. Nevertheless, Kant realizes that it is impossible to *prove* that human beings possess free will. Since there is, however, no contradiction generated by assuming that our choices are free, that alone is sufficient to justify the supposition.[7] It is free will that makes a human being autonomous. Being autonomous means existing and functioning independently as a self-contained perfect whole in the sense of complete self-regulation. This autonomy is the cornerstone of Kant's ethics.

Part of the logic of the concept freedom is responsibility. That is the essential[8] difference between freedom and license. A state of license is one defined by a total absence of law and, therefore, order. In a state of lawlessness it is impossible for one to break any rules. It's open season whereby anything goes; any and all behavior is permissible. Such a state

---

[1]   *extricate:* to release from an entanglement or difficulty; disengage.

[2]   *dilemma:* a situation that requires one to choose between two equally balanced alternatives.

[3]   *deduce:* to infer by logical reasoning.

[4]   *pertain:* involve, concern, have to do with.

[5]   *entail:* to cause or require as a necessary consequence; necessitate.

[6]   *imply:* to have as a necessary part, condition, or effect.

[7]   *supposition:* assumption.

[8]   *essential:* a fundamental, necessary or indispensable part, item or principle,

of existence is not free for no other reason than that license breeds fear; all kinds of fear, most especially fear of harm being done to oneself and family. A state of freedom, on the other hand, requires that individuals exercise responsibility with respect to their behavior. Responsibility entails obligation or duty. Kant's ethics is duty or deontologically oriented. (*Deon* is the Greek word for duty).

Kant maintains that people can act out of duty in one of two ways.

(1) One can act for the sake of duty or,

(2) one can act in accordance with duty.

When one acts in the latter manner, he performs his duty teleologically[9]; that is, doing one's duty in order to accomplish a goal which is other than the performance of the duty in question. For example, if someone does his duty in order to avoid being punished (or alternatively to be rewarded), then he is acting in accordance with duty. Here the motivation behind the behavior is one of consequences. In such a case, the aspect of duty is strictly secondary. Acting in accordance with duty is nonmoral in nature and provides the basis for hypotheticas imperatives. An imperative is a command, an order. A hypothetical situation is iffy in nature, e.g., *if* it sunshines this coming Saturday, *then* I will go skiing. Hypothetical imperatives tell you what you *must* do *in order to* achieve certain goals. That is why such imperatives are teleological in nature. Hypothetical imperatives pertain only to nonmoral behavior. Nonmoral behavior is that type of behavior that carries with it no moral implications whatsoever *ceteris paribus*[10]. For example, under normal conditions the dilemma as to whether or not to go skiing has not the slightest thing to do with morality. Furthermore, the activity of skiing has nothing whatsoever to do with any given hypothetical imperative. However, if one wants to go skiing, one or more hypothetical imperatives demand satisfaction. For example, *if* you want to go skiing *then* you *must* purchase a lift ticket.

However, when one acts for the sake of duty, he acts out of duty simply because it *is* his duty. For example, if someone keeps a promise because he realizes he has a duty to do so and not because of the possible adverse[11] consequences of not so honoring his word, then he is acting for the sake of duty. Here the consequences of one's action are secondary whereas the obligation is of central importance. Autonomy of will is achieved by choosing to act for the sake of duty because by so acting one performs his duty for *no other reason* than it is his duty to so act. Since ethics presupposes free will and human beings are autonomous by being in possession of 100% free choice, one becomes the ultimate moral agent by exercising his autonomy which he manifests by acting for the sake of duty. When one acts for the sake of duty the behavior in question must be consistent with the moral law otherwise known as the Categorical Imperative. There is nothing iffy at stake here. Duties of a categorical nature command that one perform them without exception. Kant maintains that moral duties are categorical.

When one acts for the sake of duty he has a good will which is the *summum bonum* or the perfect good. The perfect good is that will (the guiding force behind all action) which strives after complete accordance with the moral law or Categorical Imperative. However, the nature of the

---

[9] *teleological:* means satisfying end results.

[10] *ceteris paribus:* all other things being equal; given normal or standard conditions.

[11] *adverse:* contrary to one's interests or welfare; unfavorable; unpropitious.

good will is slightly more complicated than meets the eye. In order for one's will to qualify as being good, it must do two distinct things. (1) It must first of all figure out (postulate) just exactly what the Categorical Imperative (moral law) is and, (2) act according to the Categorical Imperative. It is clear that one cannot act in accordance with the moral law unless he knows what it is. But how is one to figure out what it is? One does so by the use of reason.

What Kant is looking for is a rule of consistency that applies to human behavior. Consistency is the essence of logic. If he can determine that the bottom line of ethical behavior is logical in nature, then ethics is objective. There is nothing subjective about the rules of logic (and consequently of sound thinking) any more so than the rules of mathematics.[12] Now the rule of consistency that pertains to human action is the principle of universalizability. In this context to universalize means pertaining to all human beings. The first formulation of the Categorical Imperative is Kant's expression of the principle of universalizability. He says,

> Act only according to that maxim by which you can at the same time will that it should become a universal law.

There are several important aspects concerning this moral dictate[13].

(1) A maxim is defined as a subjective principle of action. (a) Moral decisions should be predicated on the principle of action involved in the dilemma. For example, let us suppose that you are at a grocery checkout stand and you receive back in change from a twenty dollar bill five dollars more than is your due. It would not be uncommon for you to struggle with the dilemma as to whether or not to return the five dollars. In order to follow the Categorical Imperative one must consider not the peculiarities of the situation, i.e., "Nobody will be hurt if I keep the five dollars. After all, grocery stores provide for a certain amount of slack in the system." Rather, one must address the principle of action involved in the dilemma which in this case is theft. Yes, keeping the five dollars not due you is a form of theft. Theft is theft regardless of the peculiarities of the situation. In principle keeping the five dollars is no different than robbing a bank. (b) A maxim is subjective because one has the free will to choose to act according to the principle of action in question or choose not to so act.

(2) The Categorical Imperative can be understood as asking if you possessed the power to make the principle of action in question a universally accepted practice, would you so command. For example, if you were king of the world, would you decree that theft become the law of the land? The reason, says Kant, that no reasonable person would so decree is because by imagining the scenario of universally accepted theft the logical inconsistency of that behavior is exposed. Consider the purpose of stealing. It is to acquire something you don't possess. However, if everybody engaged in that practice, people would steal from you which is self-defeating since others stealing from you would leave you with less than with which you started. Similarly, if the breaking of promises became a universally accepted behavior it would not be long before the very practice of promise-making would be rendered[14] vacuous[15]. In other words, the process of universalizing upon a given principle of action will expose its logical character. If the universalizing process reveals logical inconsis-

---

[12] Note that Peano's five axioms of arithmetic are reducible to logical laws.

[13] *dictate:* a directive or command.

[14] *render:* to cause to become; make.

[15] *vacuous:* empty.

tency, then reason dictates that one ought to reject that principle of action and act only on *that* principle whereby one could in good faith will that it become a universally accepted form of behavior.

(3) If you cannot so will that the maxim in question should become a universal law, then you ought not engage in that type of behavior otherwise you would be doubly illogical by making an exception for yourself. The making of exceptions is itself a form of inconsistency. It ought to be noticed that the principle of universalizability is strictly a rule of consistency. However, there is nothing inherently[16] moral about consistency. Kant needs a statement of the Categorical Imperative that is distinctly moral in character. This would be a directive that pertains to the autonomy of individuals since it is precisely our autonomy which provides the basis for us being moral agents. The second formulation of the Categorical Imperative commands us to:

> Act so that you treat humanity, whether in your own person or in that of another, always as an end and never as a means only.

This means is that it is immoral to use people. Now Kant is fully aware that we cannot avoid using people in the sense of, say, employing their services. He means using people in the strict sense of the term (e.g., taking advantage of them). Kant argues, quite correctly, that when a person is used his autonomy is violated. Such violation is immoral. In other words, we are moral creatures by virtue of our autonomy. Any action that detracts from that autonomy lessens the moral dimension of the individual, be it oneself or someone else. The act of using a person is, in essence, an act of detracting from the "wholeness" of that person's autonomy, namely, the very essence of his moral nature. It should be noted that Kant instructs us not to use ourselves as well as others. Two classic examples of using oneself are prostitution and suicide. In the former case, one detracts from one's autonomy by freely choosing to sell one's body. Such an act is morally offensive for such self-use is degrading. Alternatively suicide can be understood as the total negation of one's autonomy and therefore the epitome[17] of moral corruption.

It should also be appreciated how the directive of not using oneself links the second formulation to the first one. Were the prohibition solely other directed it would be possible to consistently make an exception for the way one treats oneself which would admit of inconsistency. By commanding that one not use oneself simply as a means, the second formulation is tied to the first one by virtue of universalizability.

Furthermore, it so happens that the second formulation can function to undermine counter-examples[18] to the first formulation. For example, Adolf Hitler might have reasoned, in all seriousness and good faith, that if he were Jewish he would will that he himself ought to be exterminated. By so willing, he would not be making an exception for himself and hence he would satisfy the above formulation of the Categorical Imperative and at the same time remain true to the ideology[19] that all Jews should

---

[16]   *inherent:* existing as an essential constituent or characteristic; intrinsic.

[17]   *epitome:* embodiment.

[18]   *counter-example:* an instance of the kind of thing over which a generalization or universal statement has been made which lacks the property said to be possessed by all things of that kind; an example that refutes a claim about some subject matter.

[19]   *ideology:* the body of ideas reflecting the social needs and aspirations of an individual, group, class or culture.

be exterminated[20]. In other words, Hitler's position would have been consistent with one willing that his maxim become a universal law. Such consistency can obviously result in an aberration[21] of morality. However, the second formulation of the Categorical Imperative renders such counterexamples immoral.

Kant reasons that there is a grand payoff for those who strive after complete adherence to the moral law. The payoff is happiness. But note: one can never find happiness by having it as a goal of his behavior. One will only attain[22] a state of happiness by committing himself to live by the moral law; that is, by following the two formulations of the Categorical Imperative. Happiness comes as a coincidental result of doing one's duty for its own sake.

At some point or other, theory must make contact with reality. Just how well does Kant's moral theory guide us in the nitty-gritty moral decision-making process? Suppose that one has promised to meet someone for lunch, a definite obligation in Kant's lexicon[23]. Furthermore, let us assume that on the way to honoring that commitment one drives over a canal and sees a child in the middle of it flailing away for his life. What ought one to do? If he stops to save the child's life he will not be able to keep his *promised* luncheon appointment. If he keeps on traveling the child most likely will drown. Just what is he to do from a moral point of view? Common sense tells us that one ought to break the promise and attempt to save the drowning youngster. But given Kant's theory one would be immoral by breaking the promise to meet his friend for lunch. Why? The answer lies in the principle of action involved here. *In principle* one would not (reasonably) will that promise breaking become a universal law. Hence, one has a duty to keep the promises that he makes. If it is one's duty to keep his promise, then extenuating circumstances are irrelevant, including the intervening situation of a drowning child. On the other hand, ignoring the drowning child is tantamount[24] to murdering him by omission[25]. One would not (reasonably) will that murder become a universal law. The point here is that Kant's ethical theory is too rigid. It does not take into account legitimate moral exceptions to the rule. Basically, what Kant's theory lacks is some method to help one determine what to do in *complex* moral dilemmas. As it stands, one is damned if he does and damned if he doesn't. If he keeps his promise to meet his friend for lunch, then the child most likely will drown. If he stops to save the child, then he will have to break his promise of meeting his friend for lunch, which is a categorical no-no to Kant's way of thinking.

In principle Kant is correct. If one strips away the peculiarities of a moral situation and contemplates only the principles of action involved, one finds that they all are of equal value. Considered by itself and out of context, it is categorically immoral to break promises just as it is categorically immoral to condone murder. The problem is that the moral dilemmas we find ourselves in necessarily occur within some context and hence it is inevitable that conflicts between the principles of action associated with that context will arise. Kant was unwilling to argue for a hierarchy[26]

---

[20]   *exterminate:* to get rid of by destroying completely.

[21]   *aberrant:* deviating from the proper or expected course; straying from the right way.

[22]   *attain:* to achieve or accomplish.

[23]   *lexicon:* a dictionary.

[24]   *tantamount:* equivalent in effect or value.

[25]   *omission:* failure to do as one should.

[26]   *hierarchy:* a body of entities arranged in graded series.

of values to resolve such conflicts. One might wonder why Kant is so inflexible in his moral theory. He is rightfully suspicious of extenuating circumstances concerning moral situations. If it is morally acceptable to hedge on the Categorical Imperative, just what are the limits going to be? One can always claim that the moral situation at hand is unique, and hence justify any sort of aberrant behavior. Basically, Kant sacrifices the uniqueness of a moral situation in the face of moral principle. It boils down to a conflict between what is theoretically the moral thing to do *sans*[27] complications and the grubby moral reality of conflicting moral principles.

Note should also be made that the inclusion of a hierarchy of values to the theory to resolve complex moral dilemmas will not salvage[28] it because any such hierarchy will be incomplete due to an infinite variety of possible complex moral dilemmas. In other words, there would always be the possibility of an exception to the hierarchy arising sometime in the future.

Just what went wrong with Kant's theory? In essence, he made universalizability a criterion of morality. Suppose, for example, one's child is disciplined at school for throwing rocks at the girls during recess. Upon asking for a justification of such behavior he replies: "Well, John and Jim were throwing rocks at the girls." [Note the shabby attempt to universalize the behavior.] You reply: "That's interesting. Suppose you were on a bridge and John and Jim jumped to their death. Would you follow them?" "Of course not," says the child. "Well, why not?" you ask. "Because that would be a stupid thing to do," the child says in reply. "That's absolutely correct. Jumping off a bridge is a stupid thing to do and has nothing whatsoever to do with what other people do. And throwing rocks at the girls is a morally wrong thing to do and has nothing whatsoever to do with what other people do." The point here is that a given action is not moral because it is universalizable. Rather a given action is universalizable because it is moral to begin with. This is to say that what makes a given action moral is independent of its universalizability. That some action is moral *justifies* it being universalized. So understood, universalizability plays an important role in ethics. It is simply not the litmus test as to whether a given action is moral.

Suggested Readings: The Categorical Imperative; Kant

1. Acton, H. B., *Kant's Moral Philosophy* (London: Macmillan, 1970).
2. Bradley, F. H., *Ethical Studies*, 2nd ed. (Oxford: The Clarendon Press, 1972), Essay 4.
3. Broad, C. D., *Five Types of Ethical Theory* (London: Routledge, 1930), Chapter 5.
4. Copleston, F., *A History of Philosophy*, Vol. VI (N.Y.: Doubleday & Co., 1994), Chapter 14.
5. Duncan, A. R. C., *Practical Reason and Morality* (London: Nelson, 1957).
6. Field, G. C., *Moral Theory* (New York: Dutton), Part I.

---

[27] *sans:* without.

[28] *salvage:* the saving or rescue of any goods, property, etc. from destruction, damage or waste.

7. Ewing, A. C., *Ethics* (N.Y.: Free Press, 1953), Chapter 4.

8. Jones, W.T., *Morality and Freedom in the Philosophy of Immanuel Kant* (London: Oxford University Press, 1940).

9. Korner, S., *Kant* (Baltimore: Penguin, 1955), Chapters 6 and 7.

10. Murphy, J. G., *Kant: The Philosophy of Right* (New York: St. Martin's, 1970), Chapters 2 and 3.

11. Paton, H. J., *The Categorical Imperative: A Study in Kant's Moral Philosophy* (London: Hutchinson's University Library, 1946).

12. Radshall, H., *The Theory of Good and Evil* (Oxford: Clarendon Press, 1907), Vol. I, Chapter 5.

13. Ross, W.D., *Kant's Ethical Theory* (London: Oxford University Press, 1954).

14. Scott, J. W., *Kant on the Moral Life* (London: A. and C. Black, 1924).

15. Teale, H. E., *Kantian Ethics* (London: Oxford University Press, 1951).

16. Werkmeister, W. H., *Theories of Ethics: A Study in Moral Obligation* (Lincoln, Neb.: Johnsen, 1961), Chapter 8-9.

17. Williams, T. C., *The Concept of the Categorical Imperative* (Oxford: Clarendon Press, 1968).

Name_____

Date _____

1. What is the fundamental assumption about human nature which underlies Kant's theory for solving moral dilemmas? How does Kant argue for (i.e., support) this assumption?

2. To have a good will means to act for the sake of duty. True or false? Explain.

3. What is a hypothetical imperative? What is its relation to a good will?

4. State and explain the first formulation of the Categorical Imperative.

5. State and explain the second formulation of the Categorical Imperative.

6. Explain one problem that arises in applying Kant's theory to moral situations.

Taken from *Fundamental Principles of the Metaphysics of Ethics* by Immanual Kant, translated by Otto Manthey-Zorn. Published by Irvington Publishers. Reprinted by permission of the publisher.

Chapter II

Each thing in nature works according to laws. Only a rational being has the faculty to act *according to the conception* of laws, that is according to principles, in other words has a will. Since the deduction of actions from laws requires *reason* the will is nothing but practical reason. If reason invariably determines the will then the actions which such a being recognizes as objectively necessary are subjectively necessary as well, that is to say, the will is the faculty to choose *that only* which reason, independent of inclination, recognizes as practically necessary, that is, good. But if reason of itself alone does not sufficiently determine the will, if the latter is dependent also on subjective conditions (certain impulses) which do not always correspond with the objective conditions; in a word, if the will is not *in itself* in full accord with reason (as is actually the case with men) then the actions which objectively are recognized as necessary are subjectively contingent, and the determination of such a will according to objective laws is *obligation*. By this we mean, the relation of the objective laws to a will which is not good throughout is conceived as the determination of the will of a rational being by principles of reason which, however, this will does not by virtue of its nature necessarily follow.

The conception of an objective principle in so far as it is obligatory for the will, is called a command (of reason), and the formula of the command is called an *imperative*.

All imperatives are expressed by a "Thou Shalt" and thereby indicate the relation of an objective law of reason to a will which is not by virtue of its subjective constitution necessarily determined by it (an obligation).

These imperatives say that something would be good to do or to omit, but they say it to a will which does not always do a thing merely because it is presented to it as being good to do. That, however, is practically good which determines the will by means of the conception of reason, accordingly not from subjective causes, but from objective ones, that is to say on principles which are valid for every rational being as such. It is distinguished from the *pleasant* as that which influences the will only by means of sensations from merely subjective causes which apply only to the feeling of this or that person, and not as principles of reason valid for everyone.[1]

Now all imperatives command either *hypothetically* or *categorically*. The former represents the practical necessity of a possible action as a means to arrive at something else that is willed (or may be willed). The categorical imperative would then be that which represented an action as objectively necessary of itself without relation to another end.

Since every practical law represents a possible action as good and consequently as necessary for a subject who can be determined practically by reason, therefore all imperatives are formulae for actions which are necessary according to the principle of a will that in some manner or other is good. Now, if the action is meant to be good merely as a means to *something else*, then the imperative is *hypothetical*; but if it is represented as good of itself and thus necessary as a principle of a will which is of itself in accord with reason, then it is *categorical*.

The imperative then tells me which of my possible actions would be good, and presents the practical rule in relation to a will which, however, does not at once perform an act because it is good, partly because the object does not always know that it is good, partly, even though it knows it, because its maxims may still be opposed to the objective principles of practical reason.

The hypothetical imperative accordingly tells only that an action is good for this or that possible or actual purpose. In the first case it is a *problematic* principle, in the second case an assertorial practical principle. The categorical imperative, which declares that the action is of itself objectively necessary without relation to any purpose and therefore also without any other end than itself, has the nature of a (practical) APODIC-TIC[2] principle.

That which is possible only by virtue of some rational being may also be conceived as a possible purpose of some will; and therefore the principles of action are indeed infinitely numerous in so far as they are considered necessary for the realization of a possible purpose. All sciences have

---

[1]   The dependence of the desire on sensations is called inclination and this accordingly always indicates a *want*. But the dependence of a will which may be determined by chance on the principles of reason is called an *interest*. The latter therefore arises only with a dependent will which is not of itself at all times in accord with reason. Within the Divine Will an interest is inconceivable. But also the human will can *take an interest* in something without therefore *acting out of interest*. The former denotes *practical* interest in an action, the latter *pathological* interest in the object of the action. The first shows merely the dependence of the will on principles of reason as such, the second on principles of reason on behalf of inclination, inasmuch as reason merely supplies the practical rules by which the wants of inclination may be met. In the first case the actions themselves interest me, in the second the object of the action (inasmuch as it is pleasant to me). In the first section we have seen that in an action done from duty the interest to be regarded must not be in the object, but in the action itself and in its principle of reason (the law).

[2]   *apodictic:* absolutely certain or necessarily true [editor's note].

a practical part consisting of problems stating the possibility of some purpose, and of imperatives that direct how to realize the purpose. The latter
may therefore be called in general imperatives of *skill*. Whether the end is
reasonable and good is of no concern here at all; but only what must be
done to attain it. The prescription given by a physician in order to effect
the thorough cure of his patient, and that prepared by a poisoner to bring
about certain death, are both of equal value in so far as each serves to realize its purpose perfectly. Because it is unknown what purposes life may
later present to youth, parents seek above all to have their children learn *a
great many things* and encourage the development of *skill* in the use of the
means to *all sorts* of ends, of none of which they are able to determine
that it will really become in the future a purpose for the child, though it
possibly may. This concern is so great that parents commonly neglect
because of it to form and set aright in their children the judgments on the
value of the things that may be chosen as ends.

There is nevertheless *one* end that may be assumed as being present in
all rational beings (in so far as they are dependent beings and imperatives
apply to them) and therefore one purpose of which they not only are
capable, but of which it may safely be assumed that each and every one
must by a natural necessity *possess* it. This purpose is *happiness*. The
hypothetical imperative, which represents the practical necessity of an
action as means to the advancement of happiness, is ASSERTORIAL[3].
This must be explained as necessary not only, to an uncertain and merely
possible purpose, but also to a purpose that can be assumed in each person
with certainty and *a priori*,[4] because it is part of his being. Now skill in
the choice of the means to one's own greatest well-being may be called
prudence,[5] in the narrowest sense of the word. Therefore the imperative
which refers to the choice of the means to one's own happiness, the precept of prudence, is still hypothetical; the action is not commanded absolutely, but only as a means to another purpose.

Finally, there is an imperative which commands a certain conduct
directly and which is not based on the condition of attaining any other
purpose by it. This imperative is categorical. It has nothing to do with the
matter of the action or with that which results from it, but with the form
and the principle from which it itself proceeds; and its essential good consists of the state of mind irrespective of what may result from it. This
imperative may be called the *IMPERATIVE OF MORALITY.*

In accordance with these three kinds of principles volition is clearly
differentiated also by the *dissimilarity* of the will. To make these differences clear it would seem best to describe them in their order as existing
either as *rules* of skill, or *counsels* of prudence, or *commands (laws)* of
morality. For the law alone involves an unconditional and, moreover,
objective and, therefore, universally valid necessity; and commands are
laws that must be obeyed, that is, must be followed even against the incli-

---

[3] *assertorial:* adjectival form of assertoric. *assertoric:* of or relating to assertion, namely,
    a positive declaration [editor's note].

[4] *a priori*: that (e.g., a proposition) which is a result of pure reason, and no (sense) expe-
    rience is sufficient to determine anything about it.

[5] The word *prudence* is taken in two senses. In the one it may be called worldly pru-
    dence, in the other private prudence. The first is the skill of a person to influence others
    so as to use them for his own purposes. The second is the ability to see how to unite all
    these purposes for one's own lasting benefit. The latter is really the one to which even
    the value of the former is traced; and when a person is prudent in the first sense, but not
    in the second, we might better say of him that he is clever and cunning, but, on the
    whole, imprudent.

nations. Counsels, to be sure, also involve necessity, but this can be valid only under the subjective contingent, whether this or that person considers this or that part of his happiness. The categorical imperative, however, is limited by no condition and may with complete propriety be called a command as being absolutely, though practically, necessary. The first imperatives may also be called *technical* (belonging to art) the second *pragmatic*[6] (to welfare), the third *moral* (belonging to free conduct generally, that is, to *morals*).

Now the question arises: how are all these imperatives possible? This question does not demand to know how the execution of an action which the imperative demands is possible, but merely how the obligation of the will can be conceived, the problem of which the imperative expresses. How an imperative of skill is possible probably needs no special explanation. Whoever wills the end, also (in so far as reason has a decisive influence upon his actions) wills the indispensably necessary means at his disposal. As regards volition this proposition is analytical. For in willing an object as my effect there is already implied the causality of myself as acting cause, that is, the employment of the means, and the imperatives already derive the conception of actions necessary to this end from the conception of the willing of the end. (To determine the means to a chosen end there is need, to be sure, of synthetical propositions, which, however, do not concern the principle, the act of the will, but the realization of the object.) To be sure, mathematics uses only synthetical propositions to teach that in order to bisect a line I must draw two intersecting arcs from its extremities; but it is an analytical proposition to say, when I know that by a certain act alone the intended effect can be reached, that I also will the action that accomplishes the effect. For it is one and the same thing to conceive an effect as possible of attainment in a certain manner by me and to conceive myself as acting in this same manner in respect to it.

If it were as easy to make a definite concept of happiness, the imperative of prudence would in every way be similar to those of skill and likewise analytical. For here as well the proposition would read: Whoever wills the end also wills (necessarily according to reason) the indispensable means that are in his power. However, it is unfortunate that the concept of happiness is so indefinite that, although everybody desires to attain it, he can never say definitely and consistently what he really desires and wills. The reason for this is that the elements belonging to the concept of happiness are altogether empirical, that they must all be taken from experience, but at the same time require an absolute whole, a maximum of well-being in the present and every future state. However, it is impossible that the human being who is most penetrating and also most capable, but nevertheless limited, should construct for himself a definite conception of what he really wants. If he wills riches, with what worry, envy and persecution is he not apt to burden himself because of it? If he wills knowledge and insight, that may merely make his eyes sharper to see as the more terrible the unavoidable evils which are still hidden from him, or else burden his avidity that already troubles him enough with further desires. If he desires a long life, what guarantee is there that it will not be a long misery? If he at least wants health, how often has not the

---

[6]   It seems to me that this is the most accurate determination of the real meaning of the word *pragmatic*. For those *sanctions* are called pragmatic which do not really proceed from the rights of the states as necessary laws, but from the provision for the general welfare. A *history* is pragmatic when it makes men *prudent*, that is, when it teaches the world how to foster its advantages better than in the past, or at least as well.

discomfort of the body prevented dissipations to which an unimpaired health may have tempted him, and so forth. In short he is unable to determine with complete certainty, according to any principle, what will make him truly happy because it would take omniscience to do so. It is therefore impossible to act according to definite principles in order to be happy, but one must act in accordance with empirical counsels, for example, of diet, economy, courtesy, restraint and the like, of which experience teaches that they on the average best promote well-being. It follows from this that the imperatives of prudence cannot command at all in the strict sense of the word, that is, that they cannot present actions objectively as practically *necessary*; that they are to be considered counsels (*consilia*) rather than precepts (*praecepta*) of reason; that the problem how to determine surely and absolutely what action will promote the happiness of a rational being is wholly insoluble; that therefore there can be no imperative which in a strict sense would command to do that which makes happy, because happiness is not an ideal of reason but of the imagination and therefore rests on empirical grounds only, of which it is vain to expect that they should determine an action whereby the totality of an actually endless series of effects would be attained. However, if it is assumed that the means to happiness can be definitely described, then this imperative of prudence would be an analytical practical proposition, for it differs from the imperative of skill only in this, that in the latter the end is merely possible, but in the former it is given. But since both ordain merely the means to that which is assumed as being willed as an end, therefore the imperative which commands the willing of the means for him who wills the end is in both cases analytical. Consequently there is no difficulty in regard to the possibility of an imperative of this kind either.

The only question in need of a solution is how an imperative of *morality* is possible, since it is in no sense hypothetical and the objective necessity which it presents is consequently based on no assumption as is the case with a hypothetical imperative. However, one must always be mindful that *by no example*, that is empirically, can it be discovered whether there is such an imperative at all; but one must apprehend that all imperatives that seem to be categorical may in some hidden way still be hypothetical. For example when it says: You shall not make a false promise, and one answers that the necessity of this prohibition is not a mere counsel to avoid some other evil, so that it would perhaps say: You shall not make a lying promise lest you be discredited when the lie is detected; rather when an action of this sort must be considered evil in itself and the imperative of the prohibition consequently is categorical, even then one cannot show with certainty in any example that the will was determined by no other impulse than the law, even though that may appear to be the case. For it is always possible that fear of humiliation or perhaps some hidden worry of other dangers may have a secret influence upon the will. How can the non-existence of a cause be proven by experience when the latter teaches only that we do not observe it? But in such a case the so-called moral imperative which, being moral, appears to be categorical and unconditional would in fact be a mere pragmatic precept which makes us attentive to our advantage and merely teaches us to observe it.

We shall then have to investigate wholly *a priori* the possibility of a *categorical* imperative, since we do not have the advantage in the case of this imperative that its actuality is given in experience and that therefore the possibility of its being is not necessary to establish it but merely to explain it. To begin with we must understand, however, that the categorical imperative alone has the form of a practical *law*, while all the other imperatives may indeed be called *principles* of the will, but not laws. For whatever is necessary to do merely to attain some intention or other may be considered as in itself contingent and we can always free ourselves from the precept by giving up the intention; while, on the other hand, the absolute command leaves the will no choice to go contrary to it, and therefore it alone carries with it that necessity which we require in a law.

In the second place, the difficulty of understanding the possibility of this categorical imperative or law of morality is indeed very great. It is an *a priori* synthetical practical proposition.[7] And inasmuch as it is so difficult to understand the possibility of a proposition of this kind in speculative knowledge it easily follows that the difficulty will be no less in practical knowledge.

In attacking this problem we shall investigate first whether perhaps the mere concept of a categorical imperative will not supply also the formula which contains the proposition that alone can be a categorical imperative. To comprehend how such an absolute command is possible, even when we know its formula, will require further special and difficult study which we shall reserve for the last section.

When I conceive a *hypothetical* imperative in general I do not know what it will contain until the condition is supplied. But when I conceive a *categorical* imperative I know at once what it contains. For, since besides the law the imperative contains only the maxim[8] to accord with this law, the law however contains no condition which limits it; therefore nothing remains but the universality of the law in general with which the maxim of action shall conform, and this conformity alone the imperative really represents as necessary.

Consequently there is only one categorical imperative and it is this: *Act only on that maxim which will enable you at the same time to will that it be a universal law.*

Now if all imperatives of duty can be deduced from this single imperative as from their principle, then, although we here refrain from stating whether what one calls duty may be an empty notion, we shall at least be able to indicate what we understand by it and what the concept means.

The will then is conceived as a faculty of determining oneself to action *in accordance with the conception of certain laws*. Such a faculty can be found in rational beings only. That which serves the will as the objective ground of its self-determination is the *end*, and if this is given by reason alone it must be valid equally for all rational beings. What, on the other hand, contains merely the ground for the possibility of the action, the effect of which is the end, is called *means*. The subjective ground of desiring is the *impulsion*, the objective ground of volition is the *motive*; hence the distinction between subjective ends based on impulsions and objective ends dependent on motives is valid for all rational beings. Practical principles are *formal* when they disregard all subjective ends; but

---

[7]   I connect the act with the will without implying the condition of any inclination, but *a priori* and consequently necessarily (though only objectively, that is under the idea of a reason which would have full power over all objective motives). This is consequently a practical proposition which does not deduce the willing of an action analytically from another already presupposed (for we have no such perfect will); but rather connects it immediately with the concept of a rational being, as something not contained in it.

[8]   A maxim is the subjective principle to act and must be distinguished from the *objective principle*, the practical law. The former contains the practical rule which reason determines according to the conditions of the subject (often its ignorance or its inclinations), and it is therefore the principle by which the subject *acts*. On the other hand, the law is the objective principle valid for every being, and the principle by which it *shall* act, that is, an imperative.

they are *material* when they are based on subjective ends and consequently on impulses. The ends which a rational being selects arbitrarily as *effects* of his action (material ends) are throughout relative only; for their value lies wholly in their relation to a specifically constituted desire of the subject, and this value can therefore afford no principles universal for all rational beings and valid and necessary for every volition, that is to say, no practical laws. Hence these relative ends are the basis of hypothetical imperatives only.

Assuming, however, that there is something, the *existence of which of itself* has an absolute value which, *as end in itself*, could be the basis of definite laws; then the basis of a possible categorical imperative or practical law would lie in it and in it alone.

Now I say: Man and every rational being anywhere *exists* as end in itself, *not merely as means* for the arbitrary use by this or that will; but in all his actions, whether they are directed upon himself or upon other rational beings, he must at all times be looked upon as *end*. All objects of the inclinations have merely a conditional value. For if the inclinations and the needs based upon them did not exist, then their object would have no value. But the inclinations themselves as source of the needs are so far from having an absolute value that makes them desirable that, on the contrary, it must be the universal wish of every rational being to be wholly free of them. Consequently the value of all objects *to be acquired* by our actions is always conditional. The creatures, the existence of which depends perhaps not on our will but on nature's, if they are non-rational, have merely a relative value as means and therefore are called *things*. On the other hand, rational beings are called *persons* because their very nature distinguishes them as ends in themselves, that is as something that must not be employed as mere means and which consequently limits arbitrary action to this extent (and is an object of respect). Therefore these are not mere subjective ends the existence of which possesses a value *for us* as effects of our actions, but *objective ends*, that is to say, things whose existence is an end in itself, and moreover an end that cannot be replaced by any other end for which they would serve as means *only*, because that would make it impossible to find anything of *absolute value* anywhere. But if all value were conditional and consequently contingent, then nowhere could there be found a supreme practical principle of reason.

If then there is to be a supreme practical principle and in respect to the human will a categorical imperative, then it must be one which, when we conceive what is necessarily an end for everybody because it is the *end in itself*, must constitute an *objective* principle of the will and therefore be able to serve as universal practical law. The basis of this principle is: *Rational nature exists as end in itself*. Man necessarily conceives his own being in this way, and therefore it is thus far a *subjective* principle of human actions. But every other rational being conceives his existence in the same way and on rational grounds identical with my own[9]; therefore it is at the same time an *objective principle* from which as the supreme practical basis all laws of the will must be capable of being deduced. The practical imperative will then read as follows: *Act so that in your own person as well as in the person of every other you are treating mankind also as an end, never merely as a means.*

The principle that humanity and every rational nature generally is an *end in itself* (which is the supreme limiting condition of the freedom of

---

[9] This statement I here set up as a postulate. The argument for it will be found in the last section.

the action of every single person) is not derived from experience, firstly, because of its universality, inasmuch as it applies to all rational beings and no experience is sufficient to determine anything about it; secondly, because with it mankind is not conceived as an end of men (subjectively), that is as a thing which one actually makes an end of and for oneself, but as an objective end which, whatever ends we may have, is meant to constitute as a law the supreme limiting condition of all subjective ends. It must therefore arise from pure reason. The basis moreover of all practical legislation lies (according to the first principle) *objectively in the rule* and the form of universality which enables it to be a law (perhaps a law of nature), but *subjectively* it lies in the end. The subject of all ends, however, (according to the second principle) is each rational being as end in himself. From this follows the third practical principle of the will as supreme condition of its agreement with the universal practical reason: the idea of *the will of every rational being as a universally legislative* will.

In accord with this principle all maxims are rejected that are inconsistent with the universal legislation of the will itself. Thus the will is not simply subjected to the law, but subjected in such way that it must be looked upon also *as giving itself the law*, and for that reason really subject to the law (of which it can regard itself the author).

In the presentation which we have made of imperatives thus far, in the general lawfulness of actions similar to a *system of natural laws*, or in the general *prerogative* of rational beings *as ends in themselves*, these imperatives, for the very reason that they were taken as categorical, excluded from their high claim to authority every admixture of any interest whatever as impulsions to action. However, they were merely *assumed* to be categorical because this assumption was necessary to explain the concept of duty. But that there are practical propositions that command categorically could not be proved of itself, nor can it be done in this section. However, we might have done one thing, namely shown that the denial of all interest in volition from duty indicates in the imperative itself, by some distinction which it contains, the specific character that differentiates the categorical from the hypothetical imperative. This is done in the present third formula of the principle, in the idea of the will of every rational being as a *universally legislative will*.

Although a will *which is subject to law*s may be bound to the law by means of some interest, a will which is itself a supreme lawgiver cannot possibly as such be dependent on some interest. For such a dependent will would itself need some other law to restrict the interest of its self-love to the condition that it must be valid as universal law.

The *principle* then that every human will is a will which *gives universal laws in all its maxims*[10] would, granted that it exists at all, be very *well adapted* to be the categorical imperative because it *is based on no interest* by virtue of the very idea of universal legislation, and thus among all possible imperatives it alone can be unconditional. Or better still, let us convert the proposition. If there is a categorical imperative (a law for the will of every rational being), then it can only command that everything be done from the maxim of a will that could also have itself as universal lawgiver as its object. For then alone the practical principle and the imperative which it obeys are unconditional because they simply cannot be based on any interest.

Now as we look back upon all attempts that have been made in the past to discover the principle of morality, we can see why they had to fail.

---

[10]   I may be excused from elucidating this principle by examples that were used to elucidate the categorical imperative and its formula may be used here as well.

They saw man bound by his duties to laws, but it never occurred to anyone to see that man is subject *only to his own* and yet to *universal legislation*, and that he is obligated to act only in accordance with his own will which, however, in view of the end of nature is a universally legislating will. For when man was thought of as subject to a law (whatever it may be), some interest as impulse or coercion had to be implied because it did not arise as a law from *his* will, but this will was by rule obliged by something else to act in a certain way. But because of this necessary consequence all the labor to find a supreme basis of duty was irretrievably lost. For the result was never duty, but the necessity of the action from a certain interest. This may have been a private interest or a remote one. The imperative, however, always had to prove to be conditional and could not possibly serve as moral law. I shall therefore speak of the principle of the *autonomy* of the will in contrast with every other which I shall reckon as *HETERONOMY*[11].

It is now possible to end with what we started out, namely with the conception of an unconditionally good will. *That will is absolutely good* which cannot be evil, that is, whose maxim, if made a universal law, can never contradict itself. This principle then is also its highest law: Always act on that maxim, the universality of which you can also will to be that of the law. This is the only condition under which a will can never contradict itself, and such an imperative is categorical. Because the validity of the will as a universal law for possible actions is analogous to the universal interconnection of the existence of things according to universal laws, which constitute the formal in nature generally, the categorical imperative may also be expressed thus: *Act on maxims that can also have for their object themselves as universal laws of nature*. This then is the formula of an absolutely good will.

Rational nature is distinguished from the rest of nature in that it sets itself an end. This end would constitute the matter of every good will. But since in the idea of an absolutely good will, free from every limiting condition (the attainment of this or that end), we must wholly disregard every end *to be effected* (since that would make every will merely relative), the end in this case must not be conceived as one to be effected, but as a *independent* end. Consequently it is conceived merely negatively, that is as an end contrary to which there should be no action, and which in every volition must not be considered merely as means, but always also as end. Now this must necessarily be the subject of all possible ends, because this is at the same time subject of a possible absolutely good will, and the latter cannot without contradiction be rated less than some other thing. The principle: In relation to every rational being, yourself and others, act so that in your maxim he can also be considered end in itself, is basically the same as the principle: Act on a maxim which also contains within itself its own universal validity for every rational being. For saying, that in the employment of means to every end I should restrict my maxim to the condition of its universal validity as law for every subject, is identical with saying, that the subject of ends, namely the rational being himself, must be made the basis of all maxims of action, and never merely as means, but as the supreme restricting condition in the use of all means, that is always as end.

---

[11]   *heteronomy:* the condition of lacking moral freedom or self-determination [editor's note].

From what has just been said it is easy to understand why, although with the concept of duty we imply a subjection to the law, we still attribute a certain nobility and *dignity* to a person who fulfils all his duties. For though he possesses no nobility in so far as he is *subject* to the moral law, he is indeed noble in so far as, in regard to the very same law, he also *makes the law* and is subject to it for that reason only. We have also shown above that the impulsion which gives moral worth to an action is neither fear nor inclination, but solely respect for the law. Our own will, conceived as acting under the sole condition of a possible universal legislation by means of its maxims, this ideal will of which we are capable, is the real object of respect; and the dignity of mankind consists in this very capacity of making universal laws, though with the condition that it is itself subject to this same legislation.

Name_____

Date _____

1. What is a maxim? What relationship does it have to the Categorical Imperative?

2. What is an end or purpose which every human being has by nature?

3. In Kant's view could we hold that whatever actions lead to happiness are commands of reason and therefore the moral thing to do? Why not?

4. Why did Kant believe that all previous efforts to discover the principle of morality were bound to fail? (Hint: connected to the formula of autonomy)

5. In the end, what is it that ultimately gives dignity to the person who acts for duty's sake?

8 Classical Utilitarianism; Jeremy Bentham

❧ BIOGRAPHY ❧

Jeremy Bentham (1748-1832) was an Englishman who was concerned not only with philosophical ideas, but with their application as well. He followed in the footsteps of his father, who was a lawyer. Although he never practiced that profession, he was appalled by the behavior of the members of it as well as by the cumbersome manner in which the legal machinery at that time in England functioned. He noted that it was not only sluggish, but brutal in its meeting out of justice. He was an interesting figure in the history of Western Philosophy for he understood that the ethics of the marketplace is not, nor cannot, function according to an ethical theory which is philosophically pure. Purity, in the sense of total (theoretical) consistency, is not compatible with human behavior. People must be met on their own ground and that means that any ethical theory which will work for the benefit of society must be "down to earth". He was indeed concerned about the health of society and as such his writings manifest a curious intertwine of political theory with principles of ethics. This is no more evident than as expressed by the title of his major work, The Principles of Morals and Legislation. *He was a political activist manifested by the fact that he founded and was editor of the* Westminster Review, *a publication dedicated to offering an alternative point of view to the already existing Whig oriented* Edinburgh *and* Tory Quarterly. *Whether we like it or not, his ethico-political views have had a tremendous effect upon the continually developing political and social scene of American Society. We are, in fact, a utilitarian-oriented group of people and not completely by our own design.*

Bentham was a rather shy individual who chose to write more than be a public figure. He produced "tons" of literature, most of which was never published. But he could not escape notoriety. The movement he initiated via[a] his journal ultimately resulted in the founding of a university, University College, London, located in his home town.

---

a. *via:* by way of.

Jeremy Bentham in a very real sense reversed the theory held by the Greeks that the principles of politics are an outgrowth of the (rational) behavior of individuals, namely, ethical behavior. As a result of observing human behavior, Bentham concluded that people are generally selfish. More specifically, he believed that the motivation underlying all human action is the attainment of one's own pleasure. Such egocentric[1] behavior is not conducive[2] to morality. Left on their own people simply will not act in an altruistic[3] manner. Hence, he believed that people will not be moral agents unless they are forced to act that way. In short, morality must be legislated. Interestingly enough, Bentham developed this attitude not by observing the man in the street, but on the basis of the behavior of his peers[4]. He had been formally trained in the legal profession, and he observed a considerable amount of mendacity[5] functioning within its ranks. He observed a great deal of slack in the English legal system, namely, precedent[6] predicated[7] on influence peddling rather than on principle. In short, he viewed his legal peers as unprincipled as the masses, and it was from this standpoint that he developed his theory of ethics. After all, if tutored[8] individuals are corrupt, then it is imperative[9] that some moral code be imposed. That is to say, if the educated; that is, those who presumably know better, do not behave in a moral fashion, what can be expected of the average (relatively uneducated) person?

Here Bentham is faced with a problem. On the one hand, people are motivated to seek their own pleasure. On the other hand, we are social creatures which means we are dependent upon our group (i.e., society). How can the needs of the individual and the needs of the group be satisfied simultaneously? Since all people do in fact strive to obtain their own pleasure, and because the group is essential to the well-being of the individual, Bentham reasoned that one *ought* to strive to obtain the greatest amount of pleasure for the greatest number of people. This is the basic principle of Classical Utilitarianism. Hence, one ought not consider his pleasure superior to the pleasure of others if the latter is equal to a greater amount of pleasure for a greater number of people. The problem is that people do not always do what they ought to do. For Bentham this was not a philosophical problem, but rather a political one. Given his pessimistic view of human nature, that people only seek their own pleasure because they are basically selfish, he further reasoned that the only way people will do what they ought to do is through force. Coercion[10] via negative reinforcement is the only way to successfully encourage people to act in a moral fashion.

There are four general ways to make people conform to the principle of utility. (1) A person can be *physically* punished. Whipping is a good example of this method. Granted, it's a rather crude way of getting people to "see the light", but then again some people are rather thick-headed. (2) There are *political* means by which the members of a society can be forced to behave morally. The threat of going to jail functions as an adequate deterrent for some people. (3) *Moral* or social sanctions[11] function in a very powerful way. The possibility of social ostracism[12] does won-

---

[1]   *egocentric:* thinking or acting with the view that oneself is the center, object, and norm of all experience.

[2]   *conducive:* promoting; leading; contributive.

[3]   *altruism:* concern for the welfare of others.

[4]   *peer:* a person who has equal standing with another, as in rank, class or age.

[5]   *mendacious:* lying, untruthful.

[6]   *precedent:* convention or custom.

[7]   *predicate:* to base or establish (a concept, statement, or action).

[8]   *tutored:* educated or informed.

[9]   *imperative:* obligatory: mandatory.

[10]   *coerce:* to force to act or think in a given manner; to compel by pressure or threat.

[11]   *sanction:* a law or decree.

ders for keeping people in line. (4) Last, but far from least, is the power of *religion.* People will walk the "straight and narrow" here on earth if they believe that if they don't, their souls will burn in hell for eternity.

Having established the means by which society can coerce people into becoming moral agents, the issue still remains as to how a person can ascertain[13] which of his (possible) actions in a given situation will produce the greatest pleasure for the greatest number of people. To help one resolve a moral dilemma, namely, to determine which of two mutually exclusive courses of action one ought to pursue, Bentham devised what is known as the hedonic[14] calculus. It is a method whereby one assigns a unit value to various courses of action that constitute a moral dilemma. Why, pray tell, would anyone try to computerize such a decision-making process? This quantitative approach to ethical decision-making is a manifestation of the scientific mind set of philosophy of the modern and contemporary periods of our culture (see Chapter 3).

In order to achieve an appreciation of his pleasure calculus as a means of determining what one ought to do given a moral dilemma[15] from a utilitarian standpoint, some examples are in order. Let us suppose that an individual must decide to either visit an ailing relative or stay home and watch T.V. He knows, due to previous visits, that seeing this relative will thoroughly depress him. Hence, he may estimate his depression at, say, 6 units of pain (i.e., -6 units of pleasure). On the other hand, he knows that he will get a certain amount of pleasure from pleasing his hospitalized kin, perhaps 3 units worth; obviously not enough to compensate for his depression. But, in order to be a good Benthamite, he must also attempt to calculate the amount of pleasure that his sick relative would obtain as a result of his visit. Knowing that this person has few visitors, he may ascertain that his relative will receive 10 units of pleasure. Now all he has to do is to compute the above units of pleasure and pain, i.e., $(10 + 3) - 6 = 7$ units of pleasure.

The alternative is to remain at home to watch television. The pleasure he derives from this activity he may evaluate at 7 units. This pleasure, however, will probably be reduced by realizing that his ailing relative will be disappointed if he does not pay a visit resulting in, say, 3 units of pain (i.e., -3 units of pleasure). He must also take into account the feelings of his kin and the consequent sadness resulting from the lack of (momentary) companionship to the tune of, say, 8 units of pain (i.e., -8 units of pleasure). The computation of seven minus three minus eight equals minus four establishes that this alternative course of action results in 4 units of pain.

Now what ought our ideal Benthamite do? Ought he visit his bedridden relative or stay home and watch T.V.? The answer is easily determined. The first course of action he calculated was estimated at 7 units of pleasure, whereas the alternative he projects to yield 4 units of pain. At this point his decision as to what to do should already have been made. The answer to his dilemma is in the numbers. Obviously, he should visit his relative since that course of action in this situation has been calculated to produce the greatest amount of pleasure for the greatest number of people.

---

[12] *ostracize:* to banish or exclude from a group; shut out; shun.

[13] *ascertain:* to discover through examination or experimentation; find out.

[14] *hedonism:* the ethical doctrine that only that which is pleasant or has pleasant consequences is intrinsically good.

[15] *dilemma:* a predicament

Believe it or not, the above situation is a relatively uncomplicated one. There are seven aspects of pleasure as Bentham sees it. (1) The *intensity* of the pleasure must be taken into account and calculated. For example, romantic love would rate a high point average in this category. (2) Some pleasures carry with them a greater *duration* than others. Here the study of philosophy would likely qualify! (3) There are those pleasures which are *certain* as opposed to *uncertain*. It should be well understood that this aspect of pleasure has no necessary temporal[16] element attached to it. It may be the case that one only gets the opportunity to play a slot machine once every five years. Nevertheless, the individual in question may know full well that when the opportunity presents itself, he will certainly derive[17] a great amount of pleasure from pulling the "one-armed bandit". (4) On the other hand, the *propinquity* aspect of pleasure deserves its fair share, namely, how soon the pleasure! For example, the person cited above may be certain of the pleasure derived from playing a slot machine, but he may wait a very long time before the opportunity presents itself. The point is that some pleasures are nearer at hand than others and, therefore, a legitimate aspect of the hedonic calculus. (5) One must not forget the aspect of *fecundity*, namely, the likelihood of the pleasure in question being followed by some of the same kind. This type of pleasure is not quite the same as (1)-(4). Here we are not speaking of a given pleasure *per se*[18] but rather of pleasures which result from the pleasurable activity in question. Will such-and-such a pleasure produce even more pleasure of its own kind, or otherwise? The pleasure one derives from a stock purchase that appreciates in value is an example of the fecundity aspect of pleasure. (6) The *purity* of any given pleasure is equally important; to wit, the possibility of the pleasure in question being followed by a price tag, namely, pain. Most people have had the (apparent) enjoyment of imbibing[19] in liquor. If overdone, however, one realizes the consequences the following morning. Such excessive behavior rates very low with respect to the purity aspect of the hedonic calculus. (7) The *extent* of the pleasure is purely quantitative in nature. It pertains to the number of individuals who may be affected by the decision one makes with respect to a dilemma. And part of this factor entails determining as best as one can whether those other individuals affected by the proposed courses of action will net pleasure or pain relative to factors 1-6 in the calculus. What one ends up with is something like the following.[20]

	Action A		Action B
intensity	9	3
duration	6	1
certainty or uncertainty	6	5
propinquity or remoteness	2	7
fecundity	4	4
purity	–5	8
TOTAL	22	28

---

[16] *temporal:* of or relating to time.

[17] *derive:* to obtain or receive from a source.

[18] *per se:* in or by itself; intrinsically.

[19] *imbibe:* to drink.

This procedure is to be performed relative to each person presumed to be affected by action A and action B after which the total units of pleasure and pain are to be calculated. The action garnering the greatest number of positive points is what the person doing the calculating, i.e., the one faced with the moral dilemma ought to do. If the sum total of pleasure vs. pain units of action A is calculated to be the same as those of action B, then the two actions are of equal moral value so far as Bentham is concerned and therefore it makes no difference which course of action the agent chooses to pursue.

The seventh criterion[21] of pleasure brings into focus the potential conflict between the individual vs. the group with respect to the pleasure domain. There are many situations which not only involve one's own pleasure, but the pleasure of others. The principle of utility maintains that one ought to do that which (he believes) will produce the greatest amount of pleasure for the greatest number of people. Obviously the element of extent, namely, the number of people who will be affected by a given course of action, is relevant at this point. The problem is that one may calculate that of his alternative courses of action the one which he believes will produce the greatest amount of pleasure over all, namely, for the group (which includes himself, since he is a member of it) will either not (specifically) give *him* any pleasure at all or result in some pain for him. It is obvious that the moral thing to do, so far as the utilitarians are concerned, is to act with respect to that course of action which will, in such a case, presumably result in no pleasure for the person making the decision. In so doing, the individual sacrifices his pleasure for the sake of the whole, namely, those who will be affected by his decision as to how to act in that situation. That is not a very comfortable realization. Sometimes we must sacrifice our own pleasure for the overall pleasure of the group. Bentham, true to his pessimistic attitude toward the individual in society, said "tough luck" in such situations, and if you don't opt for that course of action which will contribute to the overall pleasure of the group, then we will punish you via one or more of the four sanctions described above. One may wonder how it is possible to successfully calculate the anticipated pleasure or pain of other people affected in the moral decision-making process. Bentham argues that you do the best you can based on your (past) experience. Such a procedure may not be perfect but its really the only tool we have at our disposal.

There are some distinct philosophical problems with Bentham's utilitarian theory. (1) How can one quantify qualities? This is a rock-bottom theoretical issue. Pleasure has to do with the quality of the activity in question. A quality is an attribute, property or characteristic of something. For example, one characteristic of many automobiles is that they are red. Now how is it possible when viewing a red car to calculate its degree of redness? For sure, one can ascertain that the vehicle in question is blue-red as opposed to yellow-red, but those themselves are qualities. The car is one shade of red or another. That is a simple fact. Considered in and of itself, blue-red has no value at all, it simply stands (valueless) on its own as a matter of fact. It is no different where intensity of a given pleasure is taken into account. How is it possible to rationally determine units of intensity of pleasure when pleasure is itself a quality of a given action? The point is that pleasure is not the type of thing that can be

---

[20] It makes no difference what scale one uses in the calculus, e.g. o to +/– 10 or 0 to +/– 100 just as long as one maintains consistency throughout the various categories of pleasure, otherwise the procedure will end up skewed and therefore grossly inaccurate.

[21] *criterion:* a standard, rule, or test on which a judgement or decision can be based.

stuffed into a (human) computer for the purpose of obtaining some consistent formula by which one can guide his actions. There doesn't seem to be any definitive basis of comparison and, therefore, no way to consistently apply Bentham's computerized approach to extracting oneself from the dilemma presented by two or more alternative courses of action.

(2) Not only that, but how is someone able to accurately determine the relative value of pleasure vs. pain? Is one unit of pain equal to one unit of pleasure? Such is a tough question, if not impossible to answer. Why? Because pleasure and pain do not, as it were, constitute two sides of the same coin. They are not comparable qualities.

(3) Finally, the principle of utility, if left unqualified, can lead to situations which offend common-sense morality. Let us suppose that there are 100 individuals in a so-called free society each of whom derives one unit of pleasure and hence 100 units of pleasure overall. It could be the case that they conclude that by enslaving 10 of their ilk, the units of pleasure for the whole will be increased by a factor of 5, namely, to 450 units of pleasure. According to the principle of utility they ought to engage in the practice of slavery for, whereas the unfortunate 10 probably will derive 0 units of pleasure, the other 90% will radically increase their pleasure. But even gut-level morality is offended by such a possible situation.

Enough has been said about the negative aspects of Classical Utilitarianism. There are indeed some positive things that can be said about it. It should be noted that the principle of majority rule is predicated on the utilitarian ethic. Basically, a democratic system of government is utilitarian in nature. To be sure, we place a great deal of emphasis on individual rights to prevent such aberrant[22] situations as pointed out in (3) above from occurring. But once such rights are taken into account, then the principle of utility qua[23] majority rule takes over. You may find yourself in the minority with respect to some situations, but that's "tough luck". The object of desire (pleasure) of the greatest number of people in a given situation is what we believe ought to be obtained. Once individual rights are protected, the principle of utility turns out to be a quite satisfactory one upon which to build a system of government.

Suggested Readings: Utilitarianism; Bentham

1. Albee, E., *A History of English Utilitarianism* (London: Swan Sonnenschein, 1902), Chapter 9.
2. Baumgardt, D., *Bentham and the Ethics of Today* (Princeton, N.J.: Princeton University Press, 1952).
3. Bayles, M. D. (ed.), *Contemporary Utilitarianism* (Garden City, N.Y.: Ancho Books, 1968).
4. Bradley, F. H., *Ethical Studies*, 2nd ed. (Oxford: The Clarendon Press, 1927), Essay 3.
5. Brandt, R. B., *Ethical Theory: The Problems of Normative and Critical Ethics* (Englewood Cliffs, N.J.: Prentice-Hall, 1959), Chapter 15.
6. Carritt, E. F., *The Theoy of Morals* (London: Oxford University Press, 1928), Chapters 2 and 4.

---

[22] *aberrant:* deviating from the proper or expected course.
[23] *qua:* in the function or capacity of.

7. Copleston, F., *A History of Philosophy*, Vol. VIII (Baltimore: Newman Press, 1994), Chapters 1-2.

8. Ewing, A. C., *Ethics* (N.Y.: Free Press, 1953). Chapter 3. An introductory and unsympathetic treatment of "The Pursuit of General Happiness."

9. Lundin, H. G., *The Influence of Jeremy Bentham on English Democratic Development*. (Iowa City, 1920).

10. Moore, G.E. *Ethics* (London: Oxford University Press, 1912), Chapters 1 and 2.

11. Plamenatz, J., *The English Utilitarians* (Oxford: Blackwell, 1966), Chapter 4.

12. Rashdall, H., *The Theory of Good and Evil* (Oxford: The Clarendon Press, 1907), Vol. I, Chapters 2 and 3.

13. Sidgwick, H., *The Method of Ethics* (London: Macmillan, 1874), Book IV.

14. Smart, J. J., and B. Williams, *Utilitarianism: For and Against* (Cambridge, England: Cambridge University Press, 1973).

15. Stephen, L., *The English Utilitarians* (London: Duckworth, 1900), Vol. I, Chapters 5 and 6.

Name_____

Date _____

1. What is the basic principle of Classical Utilitarianism?

2. What is Bentham's view of human nature?

3. What does Bentham mean by "fecundity" and "purity" of pleasures? Why are these important?

4. What are some problems with Bentham's utilitarian theory?

5. A democratic system of government is utilitarian in nature. True or false? Explain.

⋙ **R E A D I N G S** ⋘

Utilitarianism

Jeremy Bentham
*The Principles of Morals and
Legislation*

CHAPTERS I, III and IV

Chapter I

Of the Principle of Utility

Nature has placed mankind under the governance of two sovereign masters, *pain* and *pleasure*. It is for them alone to point out what we ought to do, as well as to determine what we shall do. On the one hand the standard of right and wrong, on the other the chain of causes and effects, are fastened to their throne. They govern us in all we do, in all we say, in all we think: every effort we can make to throw off our subjection, will serve but to demonstrate and confirm it. In words a man may pretend to abjure[1] their empire: but in reality he will remain subject to it all the while. The *principle of utility* recognizes this subjection, and assumes it for the foundation of that system, the object of which is to rear the fabric of felicity[2] by the hands of reason and of law. Systems which attempt to question it, deal in sounds instead of sense, in caprice instead of reason, in darkness instead of light.

But enough of metaphor and declaration: it is not by such means that moral science is to be improved.

ii. The principle of utility is the foundation of the present work: it will be proper therefore at the outset to give an explicit and determinate account of what is meant by it. By the principle of utility is meant that principle which approves or disapproves of every action whatsoever, according to the tendency which it appears to have to augment or diminish the happiness of the party whose interest is in question: or, what is the same thing in other words, to promote or to oppose that happiness. I say of every action whatsoever; and therefore not only of every action of a private individual, but of every measure of government.

iii. By utility is meant that property in any object, whereby it tends to produce benefit, advantage, pleasure, good, or happiness, (all this in the present case comes to the same thing) or (what comes again to the same thing) to prevent the happening of mischief, pain, evil, or unhappiness to the party whose interest is considered: if that party be the community in

---

[1]   To give up [editor's note].
[2]   Happiness [editor's note].

general, then the happiness of the community: if a particular individual, then the happiness of that individual.

iv. The interest of the community is one of the most general expressions that can occur in the phraseology of morals: no wonder that the meaning of it is often lost. When it has a meaning, it is this. The community is a fictitious *body*, composed of the individual persons who are considered as constituting as it were its *members*. The interest of the community then is, what?--the sum of the interests of the several members who compose it.

v. It is in vain to talk of the interest of the community, without understanding what is the interest of the individual. A thing is said to promote the interest, or to be *for* the interest, of an individual, when it tends to add to the sum total of his pleasures: or, what comes to the same thing, to diminish the sum total of his pains.

vi. An action then may be said to be conformable to the principle of utility, or, for shortness sake, to utility, (meaning with respect to the community at large) when the tendency it has to augment the happiness of the community is greater than any it has to diminish it.

vii. A measure of government (which is but a particular kind of action, performed by a particular person or persons) may be said to be conformable to or dictated by the principle of utility, when in like manner the tendency which it has to augment the happiness of the community is greater than any which it has to diminish it.

viii. When an action, or in particular a measure of government, is supposed by a man to be conformable to the principle of utility, it may be convenient, for the purposes of discourse, to imagine a kind of law or dictate, called a law or dictate of utility: and to speak of the action in question, as being conformable to such law or dictate.

ix. A man may be said to be a partisan of the principle of utility, when the approbation or disapprobation he annexes to any action, or to any measure, is determined by and proportioned to the tendency which he conceives it to have to augment or to diminish the happiness of the community: or in other words, to its conformity or unconformity to the laws or dictates of utility.

x. Of an action that is conformable to the principle of utility one may always say either that it is one that ought to be done, or at least that it is not one that ought not to be done. One may say also, that it is right it should be done; at least that it is not wrong it should be done: that it is a right action; at least that it is not a wrong action. When thus interpreted, the words *ought*, and *right* and *wrong*, and others of that stamp, have a meaning: when otherwise, they have none.

xi. Has the rectitude of this principle been ever formally contested? It should seem that it had, by those who have not known what they have been meaning. Is it susceptible of any direct proof? It should seem not: for that which is used to prove every thing else, cannot itself be proved: a chain of proofs must have their commencement somewhere. To give such proof is as impossible as it is needless.

xii. Not that there is or ever has been that human creature breathing, however stupid or perverse, who has not on many, perhaps on most occasions of his life, deferred to it. By the natural constitution of the human frame, on most occasions of their lives men in general embrace this principle, without thinking of it: if not for the ordering of their own actions, yet for the trying of their own actions, as well as of those of other men. There have been, at the same time, not many, perhaps, even of the most intelligent, who have been disposed to embrace it purely and without reserve. There are even few who have not taken some occasion or other to quarrel with it, either on account of their not understanding always how to apply it, or on account of some prejudice or other which they were afraid to examine into, or could not bear to part with. For such is the stuff that man is made of: in principle and in practice, in a right track and in a wrong one, the rarest of all human qualities is consistency.

xiii. When a man attempts to combat the principle of utility, it is with reasons drawn, without his being aware of it, from that very principle itself. His arguments, if they prove any thing, prove not that the principle is *wrong*, but that, according to the applications he supposes to be made of it, it is *misapplied*. Is it possible for a man to move the earth? Yes; but he must first find out another earth to stand upon.

xiv. To disprove the propriety of it by arguments is impossible; but, from the causes that have been mentioned, or from some confused or partial view of it, a man may happen to be disposed not to relish it. Where this is the case, if he thinks the settling of his opinions on such a subject worth the trouble, let him take the following steps, and at length, perhaps, he may come to reconcile himself to it.

(1) Let him settle with himself, whether he would wish to discard this principle altogether; if so, let him consider what it is that all his reasonings (in matters of politics especially) can amount to?

(2) If he would, let him settle with himself, whether he would judge an act without any principle, or whether there is any other he would judge and act by?

(3) If there be, let him examine and satisfy himself whether the principle he thinks he has found is really any separate intelligible principle; or whether it be not a mere principle in words, a kind of phrase, which at bottom expresses neither more nor less than the mere averment of his own unfounded sentiments; that is, what in another person he might be apt to call caprice?

(4) If he is inclined to think that his own approbation or disapprobation, annexed to the idea of an act, without any regard to its consequences, is a sufficient foundation for him to judge and act upon, let him ask himself whether his sentiment is to be a standard of right and wrong, with respect to every other man, or whether every man's sentiment has the same privilege of being a standard to itself?

(5) In the first case, let him ask himself whether his principle is not despotical, and hostile to all the rest of human race?

(6) In the second case, whether it is not anarchial, and whether at this rate there are not as many different standards of right and wrong as there are men? and whether even to the same man, the same thing, which is right today may not (without the least change in its nature) be wrong tomorrow? and whether the same thing is not right and wrong in the same place at the same time? and in either case, whether all argument is not at an end? and whether, when two men have said, 'I like this,' and 'I don't like it,' they can (upon such a principle) have any thing more to say?

(7) If he should have said to himself, No: for that the sentiment which he proposes as a standard must be grounded on reflection, let him say on what particulars the reflection is to turn? If on particulars having relation to the utility of the act, then let him say whether this is not deserting his own principle, and borrowing assistance from that very one in opposition to which he sets it up: or if not on those particulars, on what other particulars?

(8) If he should be for compounding the matter, and adopting his own principle in part, and the principle of utility in part, let him say how far he will adopt it?

(9) When he has settled with himself where he will stop, then let him ask himself how he justifies to himself the adopting it so far? and why he will not adopt it any farther?

(10) Admitting any other principle than the principle of utility to be a right principle, a principle that it is right for a man to pursue; admitting (what is not true) that the word right can have a meaning without reference to utility, let him say whether there is any such thing as a motive that a man can have to pursue the dictates of it: if there is, let him say what that motive is, and how it is to be distinguished from those which enforce the dictates of utility: if not, then lastly let him say what it is this other principle can be good for?

Chapter III

Of the Four Sanctions or Sources of Pain and Pleasure

It has been shown that the happiness of the individuals, of whom a community is composed--that is, their pleasures and their security--is the end and the sole end which the legislator ought to have in view: the sole standard, in conformity to which each individual ought, as far as depends upon the legislator, to be *made* to fashion his behavior. But whether it be this or anything else that is to be done, there is nothing by which a man can ultimately be *made* to do it, but either pain or pleasure. Having taken a general view of these two grand objects (viz. pleasure, and what comes to the same thing, immunity from pain) in the character of final causes; it will be necessary to take a view of pleasure and pain itself, in the character of *efficient*[3] causes or means.

ii. There are four distinguishable sources from which pleasure and pain are in use to flow: considered separately, they may be termed the *physical*, the *political*, the *moral*, and the *religious*: and inasmuch as the pleasures and pains belonging to each of them are capable of giving a binding force to any law or rule of conduct, they may all of them be termed *sanctions*.

iii. If it be in the present life, and from the ordinary course of nature, not purposely modified by the interposition of the will of any human being, nor by any extraordinary interposition of any superior invisible being, that the pleasure or the pain takes place or is expected, it may be said to issue from or to belong to the *physical sanction*.

iv. If at the hands of a *particular* person or set of persons in the community, who under names correspondent to that of *judge*, are chosen for the particular purpose of dispensing it, according to the will of the sovereign or supreme ruling power in the state, it may be said to issue from the *political sanction*.

v. If at the hands of such *chance* persons in the community, as the party in question may happen in the course of his life to have concerns with, according to each man's spontaneous disposition, and not according to any settled or concerted rule, it may be said to issue from the *moral* or *popular sanction*.

---

[3] Directly producing an effect or result [editor's note].

vi. If from the immediate hand of a superior invisible being, either in the present life, or in a future, it may be said to issue from the *religious sanction*.

vii. Pleasures or pains which may be expected to issue from the *physical, political*, or *moral* sanctions, must all of them be expected to be experienced, if ever, in the present life: those which may be expected to issue from the *religious* sanction, may be expected to be experienced either in the present life or in a future.

viii. Those which can be experienced in the present life, can of course be no others than such as human nature in the course of the present life is susceptible of: and from each of these sources may flow all the pleasures or pains of which, in the course of the present life, human nature is susceptible. With regard to these then (with which alone we have in this place any concern) those of them which belong to any one of those sanctions, differ not ultimately in kind from those which belong to any one of the other three: the only difference there is among them lies in the circumstances that accompany their production. A suffering which befalls a man in the natural and spontaneous course of things, shall be styled, for instance, a *calamity*; in which case, if it be supposed to befall him through an imprudence of his, it may be styled a punishment issuing from the physical sanction. Now this same suffering, if inflicted by the law, will be what is commonly called a *punishment*; if incurred for want of any friendly assistance, which the misconduct, or supposed misconduct, of the sufferer has occasioned to be withholden, a punishment issuing from the *moral* sanction; if through the immediate interposition of a particular providence, a punishment issuing from the religious sanction.

ix. A man's goods, or his person, are consumed by fire. If this happened to him by what is called an accident, it was a calamity: if by reason of his own imprudence (for instance, from his neglecting to put his candle out) it may be styled a punishment of the physical sanction: if it happened to him by the sentence of the political magistrate, a punishment belonging to the political sanction; that is, what is commonly called a punishment: if for want of any assistance which his *neighbour* withheld from him out of some dislike to his moral character, a punishment of the *moral* sanction: if by an immediate act of *God's* displeasure, manifested on account of some *sin* committed by him, or through any distraction of mind, occasioned by the dread of such displeasure, a punishment of the *religious* sanction.

x. As to such of the pleasures and pains belonging to the religious sanction, as regard a future life, of what kind these may be we cannot know. These lie not open to our observation. During the present life they are matter only of expectation; and, whether that expectation be derived from natural or revealed religion, the particular kind of pleasure or pain, if it be different from all those which lie open to our observation, is what we can have no idea of. The best ideas we can obtain of such pains and pleasures are altogether unliquidated in point of quality. In what other respects our ideas of them *may* be liquidated will be considered in another place.

xi. Of these four sanctions the physical is altogether, we may observe, the ground work of the political and the moral; so is it also of the religious, in as far as the latter bears relation to the present life. It is included in each of those other three. This may operate in any case, (that is, any of the pains or pleasures belonging to it may operate) independently of *them*; none of *them* can operate but by means of this. In a word, the powers of nature may operate of themselves; but neither the magistrate, nor men at large, *can* operate, nor is God in the case in question *supposed* to operate, but through the powers of nature.

xii. For these four objects, which in their nature have so much in common, it seemed of use to find a common name. It seemed of use, in the first place, for the convenience of giving a name to certain pleasures and pains, for which a name equally characteristic could hardly otherwise have been found; in the second place, for the sake of holding up the efficacy of certain moral forces, the influence of which is apt not to be sufficiently attended to. Does the political sanction exert an influence over the conduct of mankind? The moral, the religious sanctions do so too. In every inch of his career are the operations of the political magistrate liable to be aided or impeded by these two foreign powers; who, one or other of them, or both, are sure to be either his rivals or his allies. Does it happen to him to leave them out in his calculations? He will be sure almost to find himself mistaken in the result. Of all this we shall find abundant proofs in the sequel of this work. It behoves him, therefore, to have them continually before his eyes; and that under such a name as exhibits the relation they bear to his own purposes and designs.

Chapter IV

Value of a Lot of Pleasure or Pain, How to Be Measured.

Pleasures then, and the avoidance of pains, are the *ends* which the legislator has in view: it behoves him therefore to understand their *value*. Pleasures and pains are the *instruments* he has to work with: it behoves him therefore to understand their force, which is again, in other words, their value.

ii. To a person considered *by himself*, the value of a pleasure or pain considered *by itself*, will be greater or less, according to the four following circumstances:

(1) Its *intensity*.

(2) Its *duration*.

(3) Its *certainty* or *uncertainty*.

(4) Its *propinquity* or *remoteness*.

iii. These are the circumstances which are to be considered in estimating a pleasure or a pain considered each of them by itself. But when the value of any pleasure or pain is considered for the purpose of estimating the tendency of any act by which it is produced, there are two other circumstances to be taken into account. These are:

(5) Its *fecundity*, or the chance it has of being followed by sensations of the *same* kind: that is, pleasures, if it be a pleasure: pains, if it be a pain.

(6) Its *purity*, or the chance it has of *not* being followed by sensations of the *opposite* kind: that is, pains, if it be a pleasure; pleasures, if it be a pain.

These two last, however, are in strictness scarcely to be deemed properties of the pleasure or the pain itself; they are not, therefore, in strictness to be taken into the account of the value of that pleasure or that pain. They are in strictness to be deemed properties only of the act, or other event, by which such pleasure or pain has been produced; and accordingly are only to be taken into the account of the tendency of such act or such event.

iv. To a *number* of persons, with reference to each of whom the value of a pleasure or a pain is considered, it will be greater or less, according to seven circumstances: to wit, the six preceding ones; viz.

(1) Its *intensity.*

(2) Its *duration.*

(3) Its *certainty* or *uncertainty.*

(4) Its *propinquity* or *remoteness.*

(5) Its *fecundity.*

(6) Its *purity.*

And one other; to wit:

(7) Its *extent*; that is, the number of persons to whom it *extends*; or (in other words) who are affected by it.

v. To take an exact account then of the general tendency of any act, by which the interests of a community are affected, proceed as follows. Begin with any one person of those whose interests seem most immediately to be affected by it, and take an account:

(1) Of the value of each distinguishable *pleasure* which appears to be produced by it in the first instance.

(2) Of the value of each *pain* which appears to be produced by it in the first instance.

(3) Of the value of each pleasure which appears to be produced by it *after* the first. This constitutes the *fecundity* of the first *pleasure* and the *impurity* of the first *pain*.

(4) Of the value of each *pain* which appears to be produced by it after the first. This constitutes the *fecundity* of the first *pain*, and the *impurity* of the first pleasure.

(5) Sum up all the values of all the *pleasures* on the one side, and those of all the pains on the other. The balance, if it be on the side of pleasure, will give the *good* tendency of the act upon the whole, with respect to the interests of that *individual* person; if on the side of pain, the *bad* tendency of it upon the whole.

(6) Take an account of the *number* of persons whose interests appear to be concerned; and repeat the above process with respect to each. *Sum up* the numbers expressive of the degrees of *good* tendency which the act has, with respect to each individual in regard to whom the tendency of it is good upon the whole; do this again with respect to each individual, in regard to whom the tendency of it is *good* upon the whole; do this again with respect to each individual in regard to whom the tendency of it is *bad* upon the whole. Take the *balance*; which, if on the side of *pleasure*, will give the general *good tendency* of the act, with respect to the total number or community of individuals concerned; if on the side of pain, the general *evil tendency*, with respect to the same community.

vi. It is not to be expected that this process should be strictly pursued previously to every moral judgment, or to every legislative or judicial operation. It may, however, be always kept in view; and as near as the process actually pursued on these occasions approaches to it, so near will such process approach to the character of an exact one.

vii. The same process is alike applicable to pleasure and pain, in whatever shape they appear, and by whatever denomination they are distinguished: to pleasure, whether it be called *good* (which is properly the cause or instrument of pleasure) or *profit* (which is distant pleasure, or the cause or instrument of distant pleasure), or *convenience*, or *advantage benefit, emolument, happiness,* and so forth; to pain, whether it be called *evil*, (which corresponds to *good*) or *mischief*, or *inconvenience*, or *disadvantage*, or *loss*, or *unhappiness*, and so forth.

viii. Nor is this a novel and unwarranted, any more than it is a useless theory. In all this there is nothing but what the practice of mankind wheresoever they have a clear view of their own interest is perfectly conformable to. An article of property, an estate in land, for instance, is valuable on what account? On account of the pleasures of all kinds which it enables a man to produce, and (what comes to the same thing) the pains of all kinds which it enables him to avert. But the value of such an article of property is universally understood to rise or fall according to the length or shortness of the time which a man has in it: the certainty or uncertainty of its coming into possession, and the nearness or remoteness of the time at which, if at all, it is to come into possession. As to the *intensity* of the pleasures which a man may derive from it, this is never thought of, because it depends upon the use which each particular person may come to make of it; which cannot be estimated till the particular pleasures he may come to derive from it, or the particular pains he may come to exclude by means of it, are brought to view. For the same reason, neither does he think of the *fecundity* or *purity* of these pleasures....

Name_____

Date _____

1. What does Bentham mean by "utility"?

2. Explain Bentham's claim that the physical sanction may operate independently of political, moral and religious sanctions, but the latter three always involve the physical sanction.

3. What does Bentham mean by the extent value of an action?

4. Bentham expects that a good moral person would always strictly pursue his method of calculating pleasure and pain before every moral judgment. True or false? Explain.

5. How does Bentham finally argue for the plausibility of his theory?

9 *Problems of Political Theory*

Part II
&
Political Theory

There is little disagreement among philosophers and social scientists that human beings are primarily social creatures. In other words, the survival of the species depends upon its members banding together in groups. That creates a problem because individuals have needs and desires which often do not coincide with the needs of the group with which they are associated. Any given political theory is a comprehensive recommendation for resolving that conflict. Any reasonable resolution of this conflict must involve the element of compromise. Man realizes that he must accept a communal environment in order to best survive. In so doing, certain sacrifices must be made. He cannot pursue his every whim such as abducting his neighbor's wife or for that matter torching the house of someone he intensely dislikes. Man must exercise a certain degree of control of himself when living with others even though he occasionally may not feel like it. Political theory, in part, concerns itself with the limitations with respect to human conduct necessary to create and continue a viable[1] society. It also attempts to establish reasonable safeguards for the individuals living within a given society. Let's face it, the situation is a two-way street. A group is a composition of individuals. If individual's needs are not satisfied, there is little reason for being associated with any given group. However, being social creatures, we have group needs as well. For example, the group needs to be protected from individual crazies such as serial killers. A political philosopher is much like an architect. Rather than designing buildings, the former's goal is to design a society with the express purpose of creating a structure that satisfies as much as possible both individual and group needs. This is a difficult task because these two types of need often times conflict with one another.

It is at this point that a fundamental question arises. If it is indeed the case that people have needs, where do those needs come from? They are the result of human nature. But what is human nature? The answer to this question will, in part, determine the type of governmental system recommended by a given political theorist. For example, if one argues that man is fundamentally greedy, then chances are that he will recommend a strict law and order form of government to protect the individuals in society from the avarice[2] of others and thereby insure the survival of the group. Such a law and order type of government may take the form of obedience to a dictator or it may entail[3] submission to religious law.[4] On the other hand, if one argues that human beings are by nature cooperative, then an alternative governmental system will be more conducive[5] to the well-being of the group. Such a form of government would emphasize individual responsibility and decision-making. It should be well understood, however, that in order for one's beliefs about human nature to qualify as

---

[1] *viable:* capable of being put into practice; workable.

[2] *avarice:* greed.

[3] *entail:* to have as a necessary accompaniment or consequence: "they did eat in disobedience; and disobedience to God entails death."

[4] Consider, for example, early American communities such as the Puritans in New England.

[5] *conducive*: contributive.

119

philosophically credible, evidence for that point of view must be offered. It is not simply a guessing game as to what human nature is. To so determine it, one must observe human behavior in a variety of contexts[6]. One might reasonably conclude that the theory best suited to man's nature will be the most successful in meeting both his group and individual needs and therefore constitute[7] a good, if not the best, conceivable society.

Unfortunately, the situation is not that simple. Merely determining the nature of human beings is not the only issue at stake since construed[8] in such a manner it does not take into account the origin of mankind. Many people believe that man was created by God for the purpose of doing His work on earth. This carries with it implications[9] as to what a good society ought to be regardless of the status of human nature. Most people who believe in the Judeo-Christian God argue that each individual is created equal and independent (i.e., free) by Him. This, of course, does not mean that God created each person with equal physical and mental capacities. Rather, it means that He created individuals equal in terms of God-given rights. A violation of such rights constitutes a violation against God Himself. Such rights are often referred to as natural rights or inalienable rights. A natural right is a God-given right which each person possesses regardless of race, religion, ethnic origin, gender, or time and place of birth. Here a clarification must be made. The word 'posses' as used in the preceding sentence is ambiguous[10]. On the one hand, it could mean that individuals possess such rights only if they are respected by others. Construed in such a manner, it would be evident that some, if not many, people have no such rights for no matter what a natural right specifically is, there can always be found a violation of it. Rather, what the word 'possess' means in this context is that people possess natural rights regardless of whether or not anyone respects them. And this certainly makes sense since if such rights are God-given, then only He could take them away. One must not confuse the *possession* of rights with the abuse of them. History amply demonstrates that there is no shortage of abuse of people's natural rights. Hence, some governmental systems are designed for the protection of rights.

So far we have only a *definition* of a natural right. Definitions, however, are general in nature. The issue now becomes, just what are those God-given rights specifically? The United States Declaration of Independence assures us that they are the rights to life, liberty and the pursuit of happiness. But why these (so-called) rights and *only* these rights? To be, sure, if anything is a natural right it is the right to life, for without human life the concept of right would be rendered[11] vacuous[12]. That is, taken to its logical extreme, if we killed each other off there would be no one, at least on earth, even to discuss the issue of rights much less attempt to respect them. The claim that we have a right to life is, however, more complex than meets the eye. Take, for example, the abortion issue. To a great extent the clash concerning abortion is one of conflicting criteria[13]

---

[6] *context:* the circumstances in which a particular event occurs; a situation.

[7] *constitute:* to be the elements or parts of; make up; compose.

[8] *construe:* to interpret.

[9] *implication:* something implied, from which an inference may be drawn.

[10] *ambiguous:* susceptible to multiple interpretation.

[11] *render:* to give or make available.

[12] *vacuous:* empty.

[13] *criterion:* a standard rule or test on which a judgment or decision can be based. Criteria is the plural form of the word.

as to what constitutes human life. Once we go beyond the right to life, the situation becomes progressively vague. Just what does the right to liberty mean? It certainly does not mean the right to do whatever you want when you want. If it did, it would in many cases cancel out the right to life as murder amply demonstrates. Here we can help clarify the nature of liberty by drawing a distinction between liberty (or freedom) and license. A state of license is one without any restraints on human behavior whatsoever. In other words, in a state of license any and all types of behavior are permissible. However, a state of liberty is one which demands individual responsibility. Only in such a case can genuine freedom obtain[14]. Consider the events of September 11, 2001 when terrorists attacked the United States. Huge numbers of people developed a fear of flying. Consequently, their freedom of movement was severely restricted. When some individuals act in a lawless manner the freedom of those affected is diminished. The point is that there can be no state of liberty without people controlling themselves in a responsible way.

Unfortunately, from both a theoretical as well as practical point of view the situation gets progressively nebulous[15]. In the United States part of what constitutes the right to liberty is that of free speech. Does that mean that you can say or write anything you desire at any time? Simply stated, the right to free speech would seem to indicate yes. But again, qualifications must be made due to the fact that the overall well-being of the group, namely, society, must be taken into account as much as individual freedom. Hence, a person is not free to scream "fire" in a crowded theater that is not ablaze. The reason for such a prohibition should be obvious. But what about pornography? Does not that come under the freedom of expression? Some people say "yes", others say "no". Those who would prohibit the dissemination[16] of pornography argue that such literature is detrimental[17] to the long range well-being of society for it contributes to the breakdown of morality. All societies are founded on taboos or morés which are simply expressions of values. One basic value is, of course, that of survival. Everyone will agree that survival is valuable, for without it nothing else *can* be of value. This, of course, means survival of the group or society as well as the individuals that constitute that unit since, as pointed out above, survival of the individual is dependent upon survival of the group. Hence, anything that threatens that survival will be considered immoral (or antimoral). Most people would agree that the family unit is essential to both the physical and psychological well-being of an individual. Hence, anything that is believed to threaten it will be deemed immoral. Pornography, it is argued, has an insidious[18] denigrating[19] effect with respect to sex and therefore ultimately with respect to the family and therefore ultimately with respect to society itself. As such, it is immoral and therefore should be prohibited. People should not have the freedom to disseminate pornography since it ultimately contributes to the breakdown of society.

---

[14] *obtain:* to become actualized; to become a reality; fact.

[15] *nebulous:* unclear; vague; indefinite.

[16] *disseminate:* to scatter widely; distribute; disperse.

[17] *detrimental:* causing damage or harm; injurious.

[18] *insidious:* working or spreading harmfully in a subtle or stealthy manner.

[19] *denigrate:* to belittle the character or reputation of; defame.

There are those, however, that maintain that pornography should be protected by the right of free speech. Proponents of this point of view argue that first of all, no one has yet been successful in defining the word 'pornography'. How can something that has not been defined be outlawed? Second, they point out that no one forces another to look at or purchase pornography so that (a) those who feel that it has a corrupting influence need not view it and (b) those who desire to satisfy their prurient[20] interests are already corrupted. Furthermore, there has yet to be produced a definitive[21] empirical[22] study demonstrating that pornography has a detrimental effect on the family unit. And so the battle over pornography and its relationship to the right of liberty qua[23] free speech goes on. The major point of the above bit of analysis is to demonstrate the vagueness of a natural right such as that of liberty. If you are not convinced, ponder the ambiguity of the inalienable right to happiness. Just what does happiness mean? Obviously, it means many things to many people. And that's okay except when one person's happiness gets in the way of someone else's. Is not your right to happiness compromised if what makes me happy impedes[24] your happiness and vice-versa (even if each of our happinesses do not infringe upon our respective rights to life and liberty)?

There is another monumental problem concerning natural rights. That is, just who is to determine what they are even in the most general of terms? We have been informed by the Declaration of Independence that man's natural rights are ones to life, liberty and the pursuit of happiness. But that declaration was written by a human being. Conceivably someone else could claim that not those (save for life) but others are natural rights. If so, which opinion is the correct one? In order to settle such a difference of opinion an independent source must be consulted; someone who *knows* what set of rights are inalienable. Now the problem becomes, is there a higher authority than man? Well, what do you think? Remember what the definition of a natural right is. It is a God-given right. If God does exist and bestows upon us inalienable rights, He obviously knows what they are.

Now what do you suppose the problem is? Since God does not write documents, at least not earthly ones, He must somehow communicate to human beings the nature of the natural rights He has given to mankind. Divine communication is carried out by means of revelation; that is, the direct "speaking" to human beings regardless of the medium. Here the problem is twofold. (a) If one has such a revelation there is essentially no way to challenge it. That is because revelation is direct and therefore non-derivative. Consequently, revelation is not a function of reason, viz. logical deduction. Furthermore, the content of revelation is private in the sense that it is not objectively verifiable. This reduces the subject matter of any and all revelations to the status of unsubstantiated personal opinion. At that level there is no objective truth to be had.

(b) How is the issue to be resolved if two or more people have divine revelations and receive different information from God as to just what our inalienable rights are? That possibility is not inconceivable. Who is then to judge which recipient is really in the know? That remains an unresolved problem. There are only two possibilities. Either somebody must

---

[20] *prurient:* obsessively interested in improper matters, especially of a sexual nature.

[21] *definitive:* precisely defining or outlining; explicit.

[22] *empirical:* relying on or derived from observation or experiment.

[23] *qua:* taken as; considered as, e.g., an automobile qua racing machine.

[24] *impede:* to bar or hinder the progress of; obstruct or delay.

be shown to have been dishonest with respect to his report of his revelation or there must be an appeal to yet a higher authority, higher than God Himself, a Super God. This latter approach is ridiculous, for, with a little thought, it would ultimately lead to an appeal to a Super-Super God *ad infinitum*[25] with the result that no solution to the problem would ever be reached. The other alternative is just as frustrating for how can one prove that another is lying with respect to a revelation from God?

By exposing the above problems with respect to God-given rights it is not suggested that we abandon the notion. What such an analysis should do is to help us focus more clearly on the concept of *human* rights. Regardless of one's views concerning God, we know that we must live in a communal atmosphere if we are to survive. This at the very least involves some compromises on behalf of the individuals living within a given society. We simply cannot survive without respecting the rights of others, be they considered inalienable or of a different nature. A society simply cannot survive unless certain forms of behavior are prohibited such as murder, theft and assault. To be sure, a society can survive occasional abuses with respect to such forms of activity, but if the practice becomes widespread, that society will literally come apart at the seams. Here the issue is twofold. Not only is it a pragmatic[26] issue concerning the survival of society itself, but again, it is human beings that constitute society. Do not the individuals who (voluntarily) agree to make communal existence a way of life deserve consideration for the sake of the whole? Such consideration is the only way that the whole, the unit called society can survive. The concept of human rights is an outgrowth of that concern. What human rights boils down to is a respect for other human beings within a society for the sake of the common good which ultimately reduces to the survival of that group and therefore to the survival of the individuals that comprise that group.[27]

At this point the issue of human nature once again raises its ugly head. One could take the position that human beings are the way they are and open the arena to anyone who can best survive in it. If those who have a concern for their fellow man survive, fine. If not, then the greedier and more ruthless of the species are properly the representatives of the group. Such an approach to existence may work well when it comes to cockfights, but it fails to take into account an important characteristic of human beings. Such creatures have a degree of self-awareness, namely, consciousness, that no other living creatures possess. Because of this factor, human beings not only desire life, but they have been able to formulate the *concepts* of liberty and happiness. And this applies to the individuals in a ghetto as well as to those who have status as a result of an accident of birth. The point is that people regardless of their status in life can *think*. They can reflect upon their desires beyond mere survival. And it is this factor that drives individuals regardless of their initial status to seek out something better not only for themselves, but for the group as well. Hence, a survival of the fittest attitude will always have opposition due to the fact that human beings are self-reflective creatures who are capable of understanding what survival of the fittest means in the first place. They are beings who are capable of realizing that not every specimen of the species is equal in physical or mental capabilities. It is this *awareness* that provides the basis of understanding that we are reliant

---

[25]   *ad infinitum:* to infinity; without end.

[26]   *pragmatic:* practical.

[27]   Keep in mind that the term 'society' is an ambiguous one. It can mean either a tribe, a nation or the world community at large.

upon one another for our survival, our liberty, our happiness. Such an understanding is the bedrock of the concept of human rights.

Now it may be the case, as Henry David Thoreau observed, that government, namely, civil[28] society is a necessary evil. It is evil in the sense that by living in groups individuals must exercise some restraint concerning their behavior and in *that* sense abrogate[29] a portion of their liberty. Any abrogation of one's freedom is evil. That, however, is the price one must pay for survival. Thus, government is necessary. The only alternative is to acquiesce[30] to a state of anarchy; a state in which the only law is the law of survival of the fittest. For those who do survive in such a state, it is a very mean one indeed. It is one in which life is, as Thomas Hobbes put it, "solitary, poor, nasty, brutish and short".

Suggested Readings: Problems in Political Theory

1. Beck, Robert, N., ed., *Perspectives in Social Philosophy* (N.Y.: Holt, Rinehart and Winston, Inc., 1967)
2. Benn, S. I., and R. S. Peters, *The Principles of Political Thought* (New York: The Free Press, 1965).
3. Diggs, B. J., ed., *The State, Justice, and the Common Good* (Glenview, Illinois and Brighton, England: Scott, Foresman and Co., 1974).
4. Morris, H., ed., *Freedom and Responsibility* (Stanford, California: Stanford University Press, 1961).
5. Taylor, R., *Freedom, Anarchy, and the Law* (Englewood Cliffs, New Jersey: Prentice-Hall, 1973).

---

[28] *civil:* of a community of citizens, their government, or their interrelations.

[29] *abrogate:* cancel or annul.

[30] *acquiesce:* consent.

Name_____

Date _____

1. How does the need for political theory arise?

2. How does one's theory of human nature play a role in the adoption of a political theory?

3. What is meant by a natural right?

4. To what problems does the theory of natural rights give rise?

5. Is government, namely, civil society a necessary evil? Why or why not?

6. What problems arise in a state of anarchy?

10 *Authoritarianism; Thomas Hobbes*

---

* B I O G R A P H Y *

Thomas Hobbes was born at Malmesbury, Wiltshire, England in 1588. His mother, out of shock upon hearing of the approach of the Spanish Armada, gave premature birth to a son who was to live to the age of ninety-one (1679) in a time when it was not unusual to die at half that age.

Young Hobbes was brought up by a wealthy uncle, under whose auspices[a] he received a rigorous education. At fourteen he went to Oxford University where he spent the next five years. Such training led him to the position of tutor to the young son of William Cavendish, then the Earl of Devonshire. Hobbes used this opportunity to tutor himself as much as the Earl's son. Over the next twenty years Hobbes developed the foundation of his views of human nature. He became a student of the ancient historian, Thucydides, and by translating his works into English hoped to demonstrate to his countrymen the dangers of civil war, of which England was on the brink.

King Charles I (1625-1649) faced religious and political dissidents[b] who ultimately overwhelmed him and sent him to the block. It was another eleven years before England had a monarch. For the majority of the interim[c] the motherland had as her head of state, Oliver Cromwell. England was in the midst of a religious civil war. It was as a result of the brutality of this war that Hobbes formed his attitudes concerning human nature. He was a royalist, which means that he supported the office of the monarchy regardless of who filled the office. As a result, he was forced to spend a good deal of time on the Continent; for royalists at this period in English history were out of favor more than in. However, such a political position paid off in the end. Due to his loyalty to the crown, when Charles II was restored to the throne in 1660, Hobbes was in his good graces and as a result received a pension[d]. He did not treat this as retirement, but remained active in philosophical debate throughout his eighties.

---

a. *auspices:* protection or support; patronage.
b. *dissident:* a dissenter.
c. *interim:* a intervening period of time.
d. *pension:* a sum of money paid regularly, especially as a retirement benefit.

Thomas Hobbes lived in an extremely turbulent era. During his lifetime England was torn apart by a religious civil war. It was indeed a

grisly[1] period in English history. Bands of Roman Catholics would literally rape, pillage[2] and burn Protestant villages and vice-versa. In 1649
King Charles I, a Roman Catholic, was trapped in a hamlet[3] in the English
countryside by the leader of the Protestant forces, Oliver Cromwell. The
king was beheaded within hours of his capture, an indication of the
extremity of the violence of the day. Cromwell became Protectorate of
the Realm. (He could not become king since he was a commoner.) He
died in 1658. It was not until 1660 that England had a king again.
Charles II, son of Charles I, returned from the Continent, a traditional
haven[4] for the English in times of instability. It was from this setting that
Hobbes formulated his views with respect to human nature. He maintained that all human action springs from two fundamental sources. First
of all, man is motivated out of greed. The three dimensions of greed are
competition, thus motivating men to "invade for gain", diffidence which
motivates men to seek safety, and glory which drives men to acquire reputation. Hence, first and foremost, Hobbes believed that man is an animal
functioning primarily out of self-interest. Second, man has a fear of
death, especially violent death. These two elements of human nature balance each other so that man can survive in this world. The foundation of
Hobbes' political theory is therefore that of self-preservation.

   Men, due to their desire for power, go to war. What saves them from
total destruction is the fear of violent death. It is this fear of violent death
which leads men to band together to form a civil[5] society. The rational
man will harness his lust for power for he realizes that the indiscriminate[6]
grasp for power will ultimately lead to war; and war leads to death, which
any rational man abhors[7]. The rational man is a reasonable man. It is by
his own reason that man figures out that the only way to achieve self-preservation is to enter into contracts with other men to form a civil society
whereby men can live in peace. Without such a civil society, man will be
in a state of nature (that is, a precivil state of existence) which means for
Hobbes, a state of war. By a state of war, Hobbes means either out and
out daily battle or the potential that war might break out at any moment.
Existence in the state of nature is "solitary, poor, nasty, brutish and short".
Given the events of the times, he thought England was essentially in a
state of nature. It is upon such an analysis of human behavior that leads
Hobbes to state the laws of nature, or natural law. The notion of a law of
nature in this context is not the same as a physical law, the purpose of
which is to explain how the world or universe functions. A law of nature
is, for Hobbes, a dictate of reason. Man via[8] his innate[9] ability to reason
can ascertain[10] the rules (i.e., laws) necessary for his survival. The first
law of nature is "that every man, ought to endeavour peace, as far as he
has hope of obtaining it; and when he cannot obtain it, that he may seek,
and use, all helps and advantages of war". There are two parts of this first

---

[1]   *grisly:* horrifying; repugnant; gruesome.

[2]   *pillage:* to rob of goods by violent seizure: plunder.

[3]   *hamlet:* a very small village.

[4]   *haven:* a place of refuge; sanctuary.

[5]   The word 'civil' is a cognate of 'civilized' and civilization'. Civil behavior is charac-
      terized as orderly. Civil society is characterized by law and order.

[6]   *indiscriminate:* not discriminating; not making careful choices or distinctions.

[7]   *abhor:* to dislike intensely; loathe.

[8]   *via:* by way of.

[9]   *innate:* possessed at birth; inborn.

[10] *ascertain:* to discover through examination or experimentation; find out.

law of nature. Both parts are perfectly consistent with Hobbes' analysis of human nature, namely, that first and foremost, man fears death; and secondly, that man has the desire for power. The first part of the first law of nature says that the *best* way to avoid death is to seek peace. Peace is established only by banding together with others to form a civil society. But it just might be that the others around you do not want to form a civil society. What should you do then? Hobbes tells us what to do in the second part of his first law. When you are forced to remain in the state of nature; that is, a state of war, the best method of self-preservation is to take every advantage of war that you can which means that there are no rules of the game. It's a free-for-all, the primary goal of which is self-preservation. Anything goes in a state of war, and you had better be more cunning[11] than the next guy because if you are not, you won't survive. This does not mean, however, that one should go looking for a fight. That would most definitely be irrational. Reason dictates that you do not go looking for a fight. Rather, you ought to prepare yourself for the worst by becoming the most proficient warrior possible.

Hobbes' second law of nature presupposes that those in the state of nature want peace and it is a means of formalizing that desire. It says, "that a man be willing, when others are so too, as far-forth, as for peace, and defense of himself he shall think it necessary, to lay down his right to all things; and be contented with so much liberty against other men, as he would allow other men against himself". This law simply says that, again, the best way to survive is to band together with others to form a civil society. In such a civil society, one person has no more rights than another person. It is clear that Hobbes is here thinking in terms of the Golden Rule. That is, life in a civil society entails not doing anything to your neighbor which you would not want him to do to you.

How do people formalize this banding together to form a civil society? Hobbes says that it is done by entering into a contract with each of your neighbors. In other words, social contracts are made one-to-one; that is, between each and every one of your neighbors. Furthermore, a contract is the mutual transferring of a right; a right in this instance being the right to hinder your neighbor's well-being to ensure your own safety and survival. In a contract, one gives up such rights. The whole point of the contract is that everyone gives up such rights so that no one has an advantage over another person. When such a contract is made, whereby trust in keeping the contract over an extended period of time is invested in the other party, then the contract is called a covenant. This leads Hobbes to state the third law of nature which is, "that men perform their covenants made". When men make covenants they should keep them. Why? The answer is simple. By keeping such covenants man prevents himself from slipping back into a state of war. It was his desire for self-preservation which led him to understand that his chances for self-survival were best secured by forming a civil society, a prerequisite of which is entering into covenants with one's neighbors. Hence, it is in one's self-interest to perform covenants made.[12] Nevertheless, reason dictates that once covenants are made there will be conflicts of interest. To resolve these conflicts by way of the sword would result in a return to the state of nature. The alternative is for those in conflict to submit to arbitration. Hobbes says, "And therefore it is of the law of nature, that they that are at controvery, submit their right to the judgement of an arbitrator." It is of utmost importance to

---

[11] *cunning:* shrewd; crafty.

[12] Hobbes maintains that there are nineteen laws of nature. See his *Leviathan*, Part I.

understand that submission to arbitration provides the theoretical foundation for authoritarian rule.

Hobbes realized that man's greed is great. It is so great, in fact, that a mere verbal commitment in the form of a covenant is not enough to curb his greed. That is, covenants not backed by the sword are but mere words. Hence, the next step in the formation of a civil society is the establishment of a power structure to ensure that men will perform their covenants made. There are two important points concerning the establishment of a power structure. First of all, the man or assembly of men endowed[13] with the power to rule the commonwealth, are given *total* power. When a group of men make a covenant with each other, they say, "I authorize and give up my right of governing myself to this man, or to this assembly of men, on this condition that thou give up thy right to him, and authorize all his actions in a like manner". Hobbes believes that it is only by giving the sovereign complete and total power that a commonwealth can be held together and prevented from returning to a state of nature. Hobbes' insistence that the sovereign must be given complete and total authority over his subjects borders on being paranoid[14]. Why is this so? As was mentioned at the beginning of this chapter, Hobbes lived in a very politically turbulent time. He thought that England was literally returning to the state of nature and that Her destruction was near at hand. It is understandable, therefore, that he thought that the only way a commonwealth could survive was if the sovereign was handed complete and total power to rule the commonwealth. Once again, however, it is important to note that by handing over such unlimited power to a sovereign, the people do so out of self-interest. From a 20th century point of view, this would seem to be a contradiction. How could one give, on the basis of self-interest, someone else unlimited power to rule? Given 17th century England, however, man's greed was destroying man himself. The only way of curbing this greed was, Hobbes believed, in the office of a sovereign endowed with such total power that anarchy[15] could never get a start. If man could only realize that anarchy contains the seeds of his own destruction, he would willingly give total power to a sovereign, so that such anarchy could be prevented. It is out of man's fear of extinction[16] that he willingly hands over unlimited power to a sovereign.

There is a second important point concerning the establishment of a power structure. Covenants are made between men who desire to leave the state of nature and form a civil society. These men then appoint a sovereign or an assembly of men to rule. There is no covenant made between the men and the sovereign. Covenants are made only by men of the commonwealth. These men hand over the power to a sovereign. In so handing over complete and total power to a sovereign, they do *not* thereby make a covenant with him. The sovereign, to be sure, has a responsibility to the people who gave him total power to rule, but that responsibility does not constitute a covenant between the members of the commonwealth and the sovereign. That is because Hobbes defines a covenant as something which can only be made between individuals; consequently, they are made one-to-one only. By definition, then, a sovereign cannot make a covenant with the members of a commonwealth, for the members

---

[13]   *endow:* to furnish, as with some gift, faculty, or quality.

[14]   *paranoia:* a chronic mental disorder characterized by systematized delusions of persecution.

[15]   *anarchy:* the state of society where there is no law or supreme power; the state of political disorder.

[16]   *extinction:* destruction or annihilation.

of a commonwealth constitute not an individual, but a body of men. The only other alternative, then, would be for the sovereign to make a covenant between each and every member of the commonwealth. What then is the result when there is a dispute between two men? Whose side will the sovereign then be on? Given the condition under which the covenant was made, the sovereign is to look out for the self-interest of each and every man of the commonwealth. But in a dispute, two men's self-interests run counter. Whose side will the sovereign take? He can take neither side without violating one covenant, for in taking a side, he goes against the opposite party's self-interest. Hobbes reasons that such a situation would result in a return to the sword; that is, to the state of nature. The conclusion Hobbes draws is that it simply cannot be the case that the sovereign make a covenant with the members of a commonwealth. Since it is a law of nature that conflicting parties submit to arbitration, this process is only successful if the arbitrator is an objective third party. Given that covenants are one-to-one contracts, it follows that the arbitrator must be outside the contract. Reason dictates this and thus men are willing to submit themselves to the authority of one with whom they have made no covenant. Thus, the members of a commonwealth freely endow a sovereign with power in the hope, so to speak, that he will be benevolent as well as stern. A reading of Hobbes indicates that when Hobbes said that the sovereign was to have unlimited power, he meant just that.

At this point a reasonable question arises. Where does the sovereign come from? The members of the commonwealth have two options. They can either choose an outsider, i.e., a person from a different country or they can choose one of their own. Hobbes believes that the latter is preferable because outsiders are not as likely to be trusted. This, however, raises a very thorny problem for Hobbes. If the sovereign is of the commonwealth, then he would have had to be chosen before covenants were made because there can be no covenant between the sovereign and the members of the commonwealth. But this puts the cart before the horse. Clearly, the choosing of a sovereign comes after covenants are made which means that the future sovereign was a member of the commonwealth and had made covenants as did the other members of the commonwealth.

The sovereign does have a responsibility to the members of a commonwealth. He is a virtual dictator to be sure, but he must be benevolent for two reasons: one theoretical and one practical. The theoretical reason why the sovereign must be benevolent; that is, fulfill his responsibility to the members of a commonwealth, is once again directly related to the reason why men banded together in the first place to form a commonwealth. The sovereign accepts the position of unlimited power in full knowledge that he is given this power for the purpose of preventing the members of the commonwealth from slipping back into a state of nature due to unchecked greed. The whole point of establishing a commonwealth is to insure a better chance of self-survival. The sovereign knows this when he is endowed with total power. Obviously, if the sovereign directly threatens the survival of the members of the commonwealth, those members are no better off than when they were in a state of nature.

This leads to the practical reason for benevolence on behalf of the sovereign. The sovereign is a man just as are the members of the commonwealth. As such, he has as much interest in self-survival as do they. It is obvious that if the sovereign cannot maintain a commonwealth in which the survival of its members is imminent[17], the survival of the sovereign will be in jeopardy. If it becomes obvious to the members of a com-

---

[17] *imminent:* about to occur; impending.

monwealth that their well-being is tenuous[18] due to the incompetence[19] of the sovereign, then the sovereign has got to go. So the sovereign has his own self-survival to worry about. The best way he can guarantee his own survival is to rule the commonwealth in such a fashion that its member's survival is assured. "The obligation of subjects to the sovereign, is understood to last as long, and no longer, than the power lasteth by which he is able to protect them."

Hobbes argues that there are two, and only two, conditions under which a person is justified in refusing a directive issued by the sovereign. He says, "If a sovereign commands a man, though justly condemned, to kill, wound, or maim himself; or not to resist those that assault him; or to abstain from the use of food, air, medicine, or any other thing without which he cannot live; yet hath that man the liberty to disobey". In other words, any command issued by the sovereign that is immediately life-threatening can reasonably be disobeyed. (This includes self-incrimination.) The other condition pertains[20] to war. On the one hand, one is not justified in dodging the draft if such military duty is in defense of one's country. If, however, the sovereign wishes to wage an aggressive war, namely, an unnecessary one, then avoidance of the draft is acceptable. The reason for this is straightforward. War is not conducive[21] to one's survival. However, if one opts not to fight on foreign soil, he is obligated to hire someone to take his place, i.e., a mercenary.

Hobbes' view of human nature is rather pessimistic[22]. Consequently, he recommends a political system of severity[23] to accommodate it. One gets the feeling, on the one hand, that Hobbes is correct in his assessment of human beings, and on the other hand, that something is missing. People, to be sure, are egocentric but they are also capable of genuine acts of altruism[24]. It is as if Hobbes believes that the only needs we have are physiological and safety ones. Whereas these needs are real they are not the only ones we have. In essence,[25] Hobbes' view of human nature is incomplete. As a result, his political system is inadequate. In all fairness, however, it should be noted that when societies become chaotic[26] the only reasonable solution is that of Hobbes. Note, for example, how the student riots of the 1960's in this country were countered by a strong law and order reaction. No society can be viable[27] when anarchy prevails. There must be law and order. The crucial[28] issue is one of balance. How much law and order is necessary for people to be able to satisfy their need to be free?

---

[18] *tenuous:* of little significance; weak; unsubstantial; flimsy.

[19] *incompetent:* without adequate ability, knowledge, fitness, etc.; failing to meet requirements; incapable; unskillful.

[20] *pertain:* to have reference or relevance.

[21] *conducive:* contributive, favorable.

[22] *pessimism:* a tendency to take the gloomiest view of a situation.

[23] *severe:* unsparing and harsh in treating others; stern; strict.

[24] *altruism:* concern for the welfare of others as opposed to egoism; selflessness.

[25] *essence:* the quality or qualities of a thing that give it its identity; the intrinsic or indispensable properties of a thing.

[26] *chaos:* any condition or place of total disorder or confusion.

[27] *viable:* capable of living or developing under normal or favorable conditions.

[28] *crucial:* of supreme importance; critical; decisive.

Suggested Readings: Authoritarianism; Hobbes

1. Copleston, F., *A History of Philosophy*, Vol. V (N.Y.: Doubleday & Col, 1994), Chapter 2.
2. Laird, John, *Hobbes* (New York and London, 1934).
3. Peters, Richard S., *Hobbes* (Harmondsworth, England, 1956).
4. Robertson, G. C., *Hobbes* (London and and Edinburgh, 1886).
5. Stephen, Leslie, *Hobbes* (London, 1904).
6. Strauss, Leo, *The Political Philosophy of Thomas Hobbes* (New York and London, 1936; Chicago, 1963).
7. Warrender, J. H., *The Political Philosophy of Thomas Hobbes* (New York and London, 1957).

Chapter 10:
Authoritarianism;
Hobbes

Name_____

Date _____

1. What does Hobbes mean by the state of nature?

2. How is it possible to form a civil society?

3. Explain the notion of covenant and how it works.

4. Is the power of the sovereign absolute? Is there any justification for overthrowing the sovereign?

5. What correlations might be drawn between Hobbes' view of human nature and society, and the political conditions existing in England at the time he lived?

Part I: Of Man; Chapter XIII

Of the Natural Condition of Mankind as Concerning their Felicity, and Misery

Nature hath made men so equal, in the faculties of the body and mind; as that, though there be found one man sometimes manifestly stronger in body or of quicker mind than another, yet when all is reckoned together, the difference between man and man is not so considerable, as that one man can thereupon claim to himself any benefit, to which another may not pretend as well as he. For as to the strength of body, the weakest has strength enough to kill the strongest, either by secret machination, or by confederacy with others that are in the same danger with himself.

And as to the faculties of the mind--setting aside the arts grounded upon words, and especially that skill of proceeding upon general and infallible rules, called science; which very few have, and but in few things; as being not a native faculty, born with us; nor attained, as prudence, while we look after somewhat else--I find yet a greater equality amongst men, than that of strength. For prudence is but experience, which equal time equally bestows on all men, in those things they equally apply themselves unto. That which may perhaps make such equality incredible, is but a vain conceit of one's own wisdom, which almost all men think they have in a greater degree than the vulgar; that is, than all men but themselves, and a few others, whom by fame, or for concurring with themselves, they approve. For such is the nature of men, that howsoever they may acknowledge many others to be more witty, or more eloquent, or more learned, yet they will hardly believe there be many so wise as themselves; for they see their own wit at hand, and other men's at a distance. But this proveth rather that men are in that point equal, than unequal. For there is not ordinarily a greater sign of the equal distribution of anything, than that every man is contented with his share.

From this equality of ability, ariseth equality of hope in the attaining of our ends. And therefore if any two men desire the same thing, which nevertheless they cannot both enjoy, they become enemies; and in the way to their end, which is principally their own conservation, and sometimes their delectation only, endeavor to destroy, or subdue one another. And from hence it comes to pass that where an invader hath no more to fear than another man's single power; if one plant, sow, build, or possess a convenient seat, others may probably be expected to come prepared with forces united, to dispossess and deprive him, not only of the fruit of his labor, but also of his life or liberty. And the invader again is in the like danger of another.

And from this diffidence of one another, there is no way for any man to secure himself so reasonable as anticipation; that is, by force or wiles to master the persons of all men he can, so long, till he see no other power great enough to endanger him: and this is no more than his own conservation requireth, and is generally allowed. Also because there be some, that taking pleasure in contemplating their own power in the acts of conquest, which they pursue farther than their security requires; if others, that otherwise would be glad to be at ease within modest bounds, should not by invasion increase their power, they would not be able long time, by standing only on their defense, to subsist. And by consequence, such augmentation of dominion over men being necessary to a man's conservation, it ought to be allowed him.

Again, men have no pleasure, but on the contrary a great deal of grief, in keeping company, where there is no power able to overawe them all. For every man looketh that his companion should value him at the same rate he sets upon himself; and upon all signs of contempt, or undervaluing, naturally endeavors, as far as he dares (which amongst them that have no common power to keep them in quiet, is far enough to make them destroy each other), to extort a greater value from his condemners by damage, and from others by the example.

So that in the nature of man, we find three principal causes of quarrel. First, competition; second, diffidence; thirdly, glory.

The first maketh men invade for gain; the second, for safety; and the third, for reputation. The first use violence to make themselves masters of other men's persons, wives, children, and cattle; the second, to defend them; the third, for trifles, as a word, a smile, a different opinion, and any other sign of undervalue, either direct in their persons, or by reflection in their kindred, their friends, their nation, their profession, or their name.

Hereby it is manifest that during the time men live without a common power to keep them all in awe, they are in that condition which is called war; and such a war as is of every man against every man. For *war* consisteth not in battle only, or the act of fighting, but in a tract of time wherein the will to contend by battle is sufficiently known, and therefore the notion of *time* is to be considered in the nature of war, as it is in the nature of weather. For as the nature of foul weather lieth not in a shower or two of rain, but in an inclination thereto of many days together; so the nature of war consisteth not in actual fighting, but in the known disposition thereto, during all the time there is no assurance to the contrary. All other time is *peace*.

Whatsoever therefore is consequent to a time of war, where every man is enemy to every man; the same is consequent to the time, wherein men live without other security than what their own strength and their own invention shall furnish them withal. In such condition there is no place for industry, because the fruit thereof is uncertain: and consequently no culture of the earth; no navigation, nor use of the commodities that may be imported by sea; no commodious building; no instruments of moving, and removing, such things as require much force; no knowledge of the face of the earth; no account of time; no arts; no letters; no society; and which is worst of all, continual fear, and danger of violent death; and the life of man, solitary, poor, nasty, brutish, and short.

It may seem strange to some man that has not well weighed these things, that nature should thus dissociate, and render men apt to invade and destroy one another; and he may therefore, not trusting to this inference, made from the passions, desire perhaps to have the same confirmed by experience. Let him therefore consider with himself, when taking a journey, he arms himself and seeks to go well accompanied; when going to sleep, he locks his doors; when even in his house he locks his chests; and this when he knows there be laws, and public officers, armed, to revenge all injuries shall be done him: what opinion he has of his fellow-subjects, when he rides armed; of his fellow-citizens, when he locks his doors; and of his children, and servants, when he locks his chests. Does he not there as much accuse mankind by his actions, as I do by my words? But neither of us accuse man's nature in it. The desires, and other passions of man, are in themselves no sin. No more are the actions that proceed from those passions, till they know a law that forbids them: which till laws be made they cannot know; nor can any law be made, till they have agreed upon the person that shall make it.

It may peradventure be thought, there was never such a time nor condition of war as this; and I believe it was never generally so, over all the world: but there are many places where they live so now. For the savage people in many places of America, except the government of small families, the concord whereof dependeth on natural lust, have no government at all; and live at this day in that brutish manner, as I said before. Howsoever, it may be perceived what manner of life there would be, where there were no common power to fear; by the manner of life which men that have formerly lived under a peaceful government, use to degenerate into in a civil war.

But though there had never been any time wherein particular men were in a condition of war one against another; yet in all times, kings, and persons of sovereign authority, because of their independency, are in continual jealousies, and in the state and posture of gladiators; having their weapons pointing, and their eyes fixed on one another; that is, their forts, garrisons, and guns upon the frontiers of their kingdoms; and continual spies upon their neighbors; which is a posture of war. But because they uphold thereby the industry of their subjects, there does not follow from it that misery which accompanies the liberty of particular men.

To this war of every man against every man, this also is consequent: *that nothing can be unjust*. The notions of right and wrong, justice and injustice, have there no place. Where there is no common power, there is no law; where no law, no injustice. Force and fraud are in war the two cardinal virtues. Justice and injustice are none of the faculties neither of the body nor mind. If they were, they might be in a man that were alone in the world, as well as his senses and passions. They are qualities that relate to men in society, not in solitude. It is consequent also to the same condition, that there be no propriety, no dominion, no *mine* and *thine* distinct; but only that to be every man's, that he can get; and for so long as he can keep it. And thus much for the ill condition which man by mere nature is actually placed in; though with a possibility to come out of it, consisting partly in the passions, partly in his reason.

The passions that incline men to peace are fear of death, desire of such things as are necessary to commodious living, and a hope by their industry to obtain them. And reason suggesteth convenient articles of peace, upon which men may be drawn to agreement. These articles are they which otherwise are called the Laws of Nature whereof I shall speak more particularly in the two following chapters.

Chapter XIV; Of the First and Second Natural Laws, and of Contracts

The right of nature, which writers commonly class *jus naturale,* is the liberty each man hath to use his own power, as he will himself, for the preservation of his own nature; that is to say, of his own judgment and reason, he shall conceive to be the aptest means thereunto.

By *liberty,* is understood, according to the proper signification of the word, the absence of external impediments: which impediments, may oft take away part of a man's power to do what he would; but cannot hinder him from using the power left him, according as his judgment and reason shall dictate to him.

A *law of nature, lex naturalis,* is a precept or general rule, found out by reason, by which a man is forbidden to do that which is destructive of his life, or taketh away the means of preserving the same; and to omit that by which he thinketh it may be best preserved. For though they that speak of this subject, use to confound *jus* and *lex, right* and *law*; yet they ought to be distinguished: because *right* consisteth in liberty to do or to forbear, whereas *law* determineth and bindeth to one of them; so that law, and right differ as much as obligation and liberty; which in one and the same matter are inconsistent.

And because the condition of man, as hath been declared in the precedent chapter, is a condition of war of everyone against everyone; in which case everyone is governed by his own reason, and there is nothing he can make use of that may not be a help unto him in preserving his life against his enemies: it followeth, that in such a condition every man has a right to everything; even to one another's body. And therefore, as long as this natural right of every man to everything endureth, there can be no security to any man, how strong or wise soever he be, of living out the time which nature ordinarily alloweth men to live, and consequently it is a precept, or general rule of reason, *that every man ought to endeavor peace, as far as he has hope of obtaining it; and when he cannot obtain it, that he may seek and use all helps and advantages of war.* The first branch of which rule containeth the first and fundamental law of nature; which is, *to seek peace and follow it.* The second, the sum of the right of nature; which is, *by all means we can, to defend ourselves.*

From this fundamental law of nature, by which men are commanded to endeavor peace, is derived this second law: *that a man be willing, when others are so too, as far forth as for peace and defense of himself he shall think it necessary, to lay down this right to all things; and be contented with so much liberty against other men, as he would allow other men against himself.* For as long as every man holdeth this right, of doing anything he liketh, so long are all men in the condition of war. But if other men will not lay down their right, as well as he, then there is no reason for anyone to divest himself of his; for that were to expose himself to prey, which no man is bound to, rather than to dispose himself to peace. This is the law of the Gospel: whatsoever you require that others should do to you, that do ye to them....

To *lay down* a man's *right* to anything, is to divest himself of the *liberty*, of hindering another of the benefit of his own right to the same....

Right is laid aside, either by simply renouncing it, or by transferring it to another. By *simply renouncing*, when he cares not to whom the benefit thereof reboundeth. By *transferring*, when he intendeth the benefit thereof to some certain person or persons. And when a man hath in either manner abandoned or granted away his right; then is he said to be *obliged*, or bound not to hinder those to whom such right is granted or abandoned, from the benefit of it; and that he ought, and it is his duty, not to make void that voluntary act of his own; and that such hindrance is *injustice*, and *injury*, as being *sine jure*; the right being before renounced, or transferred. So that injury, or injustice, in the controversies of the world, is somewhat like to that, which in the disputations of scholars is called *absurdity*. For as it is there called an absurdity to contradict what one maintained in the beginning; so in the world, it is called injustice, and injury, voluntarily to undo that which from the beginning he had voluntarily done. The way by which a man either simply renounceth, or transferreth his right, is a declaration, or signification, by some voluntary and sufficient sign or signs, that he doth so renounce or transfer, or hath so renounced or transferred the same, to him that accepteth it....

Whensoever a man transferreth his right, or renounceth it; it is either in consideration of some right reciprocally transferred to himself, or for some other good he hopeth for thereby. For it is a voluntary act; and of the voluntary acts of every man, the object is some *good to himself*. And therefore there be some rights which no man can be understood by any words, or other signs, to have abandoned or transferred. As first a man cannot lay down the right of resisting them that assault him by force, to take away his life; because he cannot be understood to aim thereby, at any good to himself. The same may be said of wounds, and chains, and imprisonment....

The mutual transferring of right, is that which men call *contract*.

Again, one of the contractors may deliver the thing contracted for on his part, and leave the other to perform his part at some determinate time after, and in the meantime be trusted; and then the contract on his part is called *pact*, or *covenant*: or both parts may contract now to perform hereafter; in which cases, he that is to perform in time to come, being trusted, his performance is called *keeping of promise*, or faith; and the failing of performance, if it be voluntary, *violation of faith*.

Chapter XV; Of Other Laws of Nature

From that law of nature by which we are obliged to transfer to another such rights as, being retained, hinder the peace of mankind, there followeth a third; which is this, *that men perform their covenants made*: without which, covenants are in vain, and but empty words; and the right of all things remaining, we are still in the condition of war.

And in this law of nature, consisteth the fountain and original of *justice*. For where no covenant hath preceded, there hath no right been transferred, and every man has right to everything; and consequently, no action can be unjust. But when a covenant is made, then to break it is *unjust* and the definition of *injustice* is no other than *the not performance of covenant*. And whatsoever is not unjust, is *just*.

But because covenants of mutual trust, where there is a fear of not performance on either part, as hath been said in the former chapter, are invalid; through the original[1] of justice be the making of covenants; yet injustice actually there can be none, till the cause of such fear be taken away; which while men are in the natural condition of war, cannot be done. Therefore before the names of just and unjust can have place, there must be coercive power, to compel men equally to the performance of their covenants, by the terror of some punishment greater than the benefit they expect by the breach of their covenant; and to make good that propriety which by mutual contract men acquire, in recompense of the universal right they abandon: and such power there is none before the erection of a commonwealth....

And because, though men be never so willing to observe these laws, there may nevertheless arise questions concerning a man's action; first, whether it were done, or not done; secondly, if done, whether against the law, or not against the law; the former whereof is called a question of *fact*, the latter a question of *right*: therefore unless the parties to the question covenant mutually to stand to the sentence of another, they are as far from peace as ever. This other to whose sentence they submit is called an *arbitrator*. And therefore it is of the law of nature, *that they that are at controversy, submit their right to the judgment of an arbitrator.*

Part II: Of Commonwealth; Chapter XVII; Of the Causes, Generation, and Definition of a Commonwealth

The only way to erect such a common power, as may be able to defend them from the invasion of foreigners, and the injuries of one another, and thereby to secure them in such sort as that, by their own industry and by the fruits of the earth, they may nourish themselves and live contentedly; is, to confer all their power and strength upon one man, or upon one assembly of men, that may reduce all their wills, by plurality of voices, unto one will: which is as much as to say, to appoint one man, or assembly of men, to bear their person; and everyone to own and acknowledge himself to be author of whatsoever he that so beareth their person, shall act or cause to be acted in those things which concern the common peace and safety; and therein to submit their wills, everyone to his will, and their judgments, to his judgment. This is more than consent, or concord; it is a real unity of them all, in one and the same person, made by covenant of every man with every man, in such manner as if every man should say to every man, "*I authorize and give up my right of governing myself to this man, or to this assembly of men, on this condition, that thou give up thy right to him, and authorize all his actions in like manner.*" This done, the multitude so united in one person, is called a *commonwealth*,...

And in him consisteth the essence of the commonwealth; which, to define it, is *one person, of whose acts a great multitude, by mutual covenants one with another, have made themselves every one the author, to the end he may use the strength and means of them all, as he shall think expedient, for their peace and common defense.*

[1]   The source or cause from which something arises [editor's note].

And he that carrieth this person, is called *sovereign*, and said to have sovereign power; and everyone besides, his *subject*.

The attaining to this sovereign power is by two ways. One, by natural force; as when a man maketh his children to submit themselves and their children to his government, as being able to destroy them if they refuse; or by war subdueth his enemies to his will, giving them their lives on that condition. The other, is when men agree amongst themselves to submit to some man, or assembly of men, voluntarily, on confidence to be protected by him against all others. This latter, may be called a political commonwealth, or commonwealth by *institution*, and the former, a commonwealth by *acquisition*. And first, I shall speak of a commonwealth by institution.

Chapter XVIII; Of the Rights of Sovereigns by Institution

From this institution of a commonwealth are derived all the *rights* and *faculties* of him, or them, on whom sovereign power is conferred by the consent of the people assembled.

First, because they covenant, it is to be understood they are not obliged by former covenant to anything repugnant hereunto. And consequently they that have already instituted a commonwealth, being thereby bound by covenant to own the actions and judgments of one, cannot lawfully make a new covenant amongst themselves to be obedient to any other, in anything whatsoever, without his permission. And therefore, they that are subject to a monarch, cannot without his leave cast off monarchy, and return to the confusion of a disunited multitude; nor transfer their person from him that beareth it, to another man, or other assembly of men: for they are bound, every man to every man, to own, and be reputed author of all, that he that already is their sovereign shall do and judge fit to be done; so that any one man dissenting, all the rest should break their covenant made to that man, which is injustice: and they have also every man given the sovereignty to him that beareth their person; and therefore if they depose him, they take from him that which is his own, and so again it is injustice.

Secondly, because the right of bearing the person of them all, is given to him they make sovereign, by covenant only of one to another, and not of him to any of them; there can happen no breach of covenant on the part of the sovereign; and consequently none of his subjects, by any pretense of forfeiture, can be freed from his subjection. That he which is made sovereign maketh no covenant with his subjects beforehand, is manifest; because either he must make it with the whole multitude, as one party to the covenant, or he must make a several covenant with every man. With the whole, as one party, it is impossible, because as yet they are not one person: and if he make so many several covenants as there be men, those covenants after he hath the sovereignty are void; because what act soever can be pretended by any one of them for breach thereof, is the act both of himself and of all the rest because done in the person, and by the right of every one of them in particular. Besides, if any one, or more of them, pretend a breach of the covenant made by the sovereign at his institution; and others, as one other of his subjects, or himself alone, pretend there was no such breach: there is in this case, no judge to decide the controversy; it returns therefore to the sword again; and every man recovereth the right of protecting himself by his own strength, contrary to the design they had in the institution. It is therefore in vain to grant sovereignty by way of precedent covenant...

Thirdly, because the major part hath by consenting voices declared a sovereign, he that dissented must now consent with the rest; that is, be contented to avow all the actions he shall do, or else justly be destroyed by the rest. For if he voluntarily entered into the congregation of them that were assembled, he sufficiently declared thereby his will, and therefore tacitly covenanted to stand to what the major part should ordain; and therefore if he refuse to stand thereto, or make protestation against any of their decrees, he does contrary to his covenant, and therefore unjustly. And whether he be of the congregation or not, and whether his consent be asked or not, he must either submit to their decrees, or be left in the condition of war he was in before; wherein he might without injustice be destroyed by any man whatsoever.

Fourthly, because every subject is by this institution author of all the actions and judgments of the sovereign instituted; it follows that whatsoever he doth, it can be no injury to any of his subjects, nor ought he to be by any of them accused of injustice. For he that doth anything by authority from another, doth therein no injury to him by whose authority he acteth: but by this institution of a commonwealth, every particular man is author of all the sovereign doth: and consequently he that complaineth of injury from his sovereign, complaineth of that whereof he himself is author; and therefore ought not to accuse any man but himself; no nor himself of injury, because to do injury to one's self, is impossible. It is true that they that have sovereign power may commit iniquity, but not injustice, or injury, in the proper signification.

Fifthly, and consequently to that which was said last, no man that hath sovereign power can justly be put to death, or otherwise in any manner by his subjects punished. For seeing every subject is author of the actions of his sovereign, he punisheth another for the actions committed by himself.

Sixthly, it is annexed to the sovereignty, to be judge of what opinions and doctrines are averse, and what conducing to peace; and consequently, on what occasions, how far, and what men are to be trusted withal, in speaking to multitudes of people; and who shall examine the doctrines of all books before they be published. For the actions of men proceed from their opinions; and in the well-governing of opinions consisteth the well-governing of men's actions, in order to their peace and concord. And though in matter of doctrine nothing ought to be regarded but the truth, yet this is not repugnant to regulating the same by peace. For doctrine repugnant to peace can no more be true, than peace and concord can be against the law of nature. It is true that in a commonwealth, where, by the negligence or unskillfulness of governors and teachers, false doctrines are by time generally received; the contrary truths may be generally offensive. Yet the most sudden and rough bursting in of a new truth that can be, does never break the peace, but only sometimes awake the war. For those men that are so remissly governed, that they dare take up arms to defend or introduce an opinion, are still in war; and their condition not peace, but only a cessation of arms for fear of one another; and they live, as it were, in the precincts of battle continually. It belongeth therefore to him that hath the sovereign power, to be judge, or constitute all judges of opinions and doctrines, as a thing necessary to peace; thereby to prevent discord and civil war.

Seventhly, is annexed to the sovereignty, the whole power of prescribing the rules, whereby every man may know what goods he may enjoy, and what actions he may do, without being molested by any of his fellow-subjects; and this is it men call *propriety*....

Eighthly, is annexed to the sovereignty, the right of judicature; that is to say, of hearing and deciding all controversies which may arise concerning law, either civil or natural, or concerning fact. For without the decision of controversies, there is no protection of one subject against the injuries of another; the laws concerning *meum*[2] and *tuum*[3] are in vain; and to every man remaineth, from the natural and necessary appetite of his own conservation, the right of protecting himself by his private strength, which is the condition of war, and contrary to the end for which every commonwealth is instituted.

Ninthly, is annexed to the sovereignty, the right of making war and peace with other nations and commonwealths; that is to say, of judging when it is for the public good, and how great forces are to be assembled, armed, and paid for that end; and to levy money upon the subjects, to defray the expenses thereof. For the power by which the people are to be defended, consisteth in their armies; and the strength of an army, in the union of their strength under one command: which command the sovereign instituted, therefore hath; because the command of the militia, without other institution, maketh him that hath it sovereign. And therefore whosoever is made general of an army, he that hath the sovereign power is always generalissimo.

Tenthly, is annexed to the sovereignty, the choosing of all counselors, ministers, magistrates, and offices, both in peace and war. For seeing the sovereign is charged with the end, which is the common peace and defense, he is understood to have power to use such means as he shall think most fit for his discharge.

Eleventhly, to the sovereign is committed the power of rewarding with riches, or honor, and of punishing with corporal or pecuniary punishment, or with ignominy,[4] every subject according to the law he hath formerly made; or if there be no law made, according as he shall judge most to conduce to the encouraging of men to serve the commonwealth, or deterring of them from doing disservice to the same.

Chapter XXI; Of the Liberty of Subjects

Fear and liberty are consistent; as when a man throweth his goods into the sea for *fear* the ship should sink, he doth it nevertheless very willingly, and may refuse to do it if he will; it is therefore the action of one that was *free*: so a man sometimes pays his debt, only for fear of imprisonment, which because nobody hindered him from detaining, was the action of a man at *liberty*. And generally all actions which men do in commonwealths, for fear of the law, are actions which the doers had liberty to omit.

...The liberty of a subject lieth therefore only on those things which in regulating their actions, the sovereign hath pretermitted: such as is the liberty to buy, and sell, and otherwise contract with one another; to choose their own abode, their own diet, their own trade of life, and institute their children as they themselves think fit; and the like.

---

[2] My own [editor's note].

[3] Yours [editor's note].

[4] *ignominy*: loss of one's reputation; shame and dishonor [editor's note].

Nevertheless we are not to understand that by such liberty, the sovereign power of life and death is either abolished or limited. For it has been already shown that nothing the sovereign representative can do to a subject, on what pretense soever, can properly be called injustice, or injury; because every subject is author of every act the sovereign doth; so that he never wanteth right to anything, otherwise than as he himself is the subject of God, and bound thereby to observe the laws of nature. And therefore it may, and doth often happen in commonwealths, that a subject may be put to death, by the command of the sovereign power, and yet neither do the other wrong....

To come now to the particulars of the true liberty of a subject--that is to say, what are the things which, though commanded--we are to consider, what rights we pass away when we make a commonwealth; or, which is all one, what liberty we deny ourselves by owning all the actions, without exception, of the man, or assembly, we make our sovereign. For in the act of our *submission* consisteth both our *obligation* and our *liberty*; which must therefore by inferred by arguments taken from thence: there being no obligation on any man which ariseth not from some act of his own; for all men equally are by nature free. And because such arguments must either be drawn from the express words, "I authorize all his actions," or from the intention of him that submitteth himself to his power, which intention is to be understood by the end for which he so submitteth; the obligation, and liberty of the subject, is to be derived either from those works or others equivalent, or else from the end of the institution of sovereignty, namely, the peace of the subjects within themselves and their defense against a common enemy.

First therefore, seeing sovereignty by institution is by covenant of everyone to everyone; and sovereignty by acquisition, by covenants of the vanquished to the victor, or child to the parent, it is manifest that every subject has liberty in all those things, the right whereof cannot by covenant be transferred. I have shown before, in the fourteenth chapter, that covenants not to defend a man's own body are void. Therefore:

If the sovereign command a man, though justly condemned to kill, wound, or maim himself; or not to resist those that assault him; or to abstain from the use of food, air, medicine, or any other thing, without which he cannot live; yet hath that man the liberty to disobey.

If a man be interrogated by the sovereign, or his authority concerning a crime done by himself, he is not bound, without assurance of pardon, to confess it; because no man, as I have shown in the same chapter, can be obliged by covenant to accuse himself.

Again, the consent of a subject to sovereign power is contained in these words, "I authorize, or take upon me, all his actions;" in which there is no restriction at all of his own former natural liberty: for by allowing him to kill me, I am not bound to kill myself when he commands me. It is one thing to say "Kill me, or my fellow, if you please;" another thing to say, "I will kill myself, or my fellow." It followeth therefore that:

No man is bound by the words themselves, either to kill himself or any other man, and consequently, that the obligation a man may sometimes have, upon the command of the sovereign to execute any dangerous or dishonorable office, dependeth not on the words of our submission, but on the intention, which is to be understood by the end thereof. When therefore our refusal to obey, frustrates the end for which the sovereignty was ordained, then there is no liberty to refuse, otherwise there is.

Upon this ground, a man that is commanded as a soldier to fight against the enemy, though his sovereign have right enough to punish his refusal with death, may nevertheless in many cases refuse, without injustice; as when he substituteth a sufficient soldier in his place: for in this case he deserteth not the service of the commonwealth. And there is allowance to be made for natural timorousness, not only to women, of whom no such dangerous duty is expected, but also to men of feminine courage. When armies fight, there is on one side, or both, a running away, yet when they do it not out of treachery, but fear, they are not esteemed to do it unjustly, but dishonorably. For the same reason, to avoid battle is not injustice, but cowardice. But he that enrolleth himself a soldier, or taketh imprest money, taketh away the excuse of a timorous nature; and is obligated not only to go to the battle, but also not run from it, without his captains leave. And when the defense of the commonwealth requireth at once the help of all that are able to bear arms, everyone is obligated; because otherwise the institution of the commonwealth, which they have not the purpose or courage to preserve, was in vain.

To resist the sword of the commonwealth in defense of another man, guilty or innocent, no man hath liberty, because such liberty takes away from the sovereign the means of protecting us, and is therefore destructive of the very essence of government. But in case a great many men together have already resisted the sovereign power unjustly, or committed some capital crime, for which every one of them expecteth death, whether have they not the liberty then to join together and assist and defend one another? Certainly they have; for they but defend their lives, which the guilty man may as well do as the innocent. There was indeed injustice in the first breach of their duty; their bearing of arms subsequent to it, though it be to maintain what they have done, is no new unjust act. And if it be only to defend their persons, it is not unjust at all. But the offer of pardon taketh from them, to whom it is offered, the plea of self-defense, and maketh their perseverance in assisting, or defending the rest, unlawful.

As for other liberties, they depend on the silence of the law. In cases where the sovereign has prescribed no rule, there the subject hath the liberty to do, or forbear, according to his own discretion. And therefore such liberty is in some places more, in other places less, according as they that have the sovereignty shall think most convenient.

If a monarch, or sovereign assembly, grant a liberty to all or any of his subjects, which grant standing, he is disabled to provide for their safety, the grant is void; unless he directly renounce, or transfer the sovereignty to another....

The obligation of subjects to the sovereign, is understood to last as long, and no longer, than the power lasteth by which he is able to protect them. For the right men have by nature to protect themselves, when none else can protect them, can by no covenant be relinquished. The sovereignty is the soul of the commonwealth; which once departed from the body, the members do no more receive their motion from it. The end of obedience is protection; which, wheresoever a man seeth it, either in his own or in another's sword, nature applieth his obedience to it, and his endeavor to maintain it. And though sovereignty, in the intention of them that make it, be immortal; yet it is in its own nature, not only subject to violent death, by foreign war; but also through the ignorance, and passions of men, it hath in it, from the very institution, many seeds of a natural mortality, by intestine discord.

STUDY
❧ QUESTIONS ❧

Chapter 10:
Readings; Hobbes

Name_____

Date _____

1. In what aspects of human life are all persons equal according to Hobbes? How does he argue for this?

2. Show how the propensity to prey on one another arises out of equality.

3. What is justice according to Hobbes? Why does it not apply to existence in the state of nature?

4. Regarding the liberty of subjects, Hobbes says that nothing a sovereign does to a subject can be considered unjust. Why?

5. Does a subject have liberty to disobey any commands of a sovereign? Explain.

11 *Republicanism; John Locke*

❧ B I O G R A P H Y ❧

John Locke was born at Wrington, Somerset, England in 1632 to a liberal Puritan family. His early years were relatively uneventful and devoted to studying the classics. In 1652 he entered Oxford University where he remained until he received his master's degree. Locke's academic interests were not confined to philosophy. He was interested in chemistry and physics as well. This led him to pursue studies in medicine. He obtained a license to practice and much later (1674) the medical degree, a requirement to teach the profession. However, Locke never made medicine a career.

Upon the death of his father in 1661, Locke received a modest inheritance which allowed him some independence. During subsequent years he became acquainted with numerous men of stature. In 1666 he met Lord Ashley, later the first Earl of Shaftesbury, an acquaintance that blossomed into a lifelong friendship and association which changed the course of Locke's life. The following year Locke entered the service of Ashley, functioning as his medical advisor and as tutor to his son. Ashley saw great potential in Locke and when the former became Lord Chancellor in 1672 he appointed his friend to several political posts. However, in 1675 ill health forced Locke to leave Ashley's employment and he took up residence in France for four years during which time he spent studying and writing. Upon his return to England Locke re-entered Shaftesbury's service. In 1683 Ashley was forced to flee to Holland due to his involvement in an aborted attempt to assassinate James, then Duke of York and brother of King Charles II. Fearing for his own safety, Locke fled to Holland in the autumn of the same year. There he remained until the rebellion of 1688, the culmination[a] of a religious civil war, the seeds of which were planted by King Henry VII (1485-1509) in his determination to bring the religious establishment under the power of the crown.

[a.] *culmination:* the attainment of full development.

> *There were two very important outcomes of the Glorious Revolu-*
> *tion of 1688 (the name given it, incidentally, by Locke). This upheaval*
> *sent King James II into exile and placed William of Orange on the*
> *throne of England. (The line of succession was justified by the fact that*
> *William's mother was Mary, daughter of King Charles I. William was*
> *also the husband of Mary II, daughter of King James II. William and*
> *Mary ruled as joint sovereign from 1689 to 1702.) (1) There was a*
> *final resolution to the religious issue. The official state religion was to*
> *be forevermore Anglicanism (vs. Catholicism). (2) England became a*
> *constitutional monarchy. Locke exerted a vast influence in this change*
> *via his* Two Treatises of Government.
>
> *From 1689 to 1700 Locke served as a commissioner on the Board*
> *of Trade and Plantations. In 1691 at the request of Sir Francis and*
> *Lady Masham he took up residence at their country estate at Oates.*
> *After years of ill health he died on October 28, 1704 while Lady*
> *Masham was reading the Psalms to him.*

The political events of the time very much influenced Locke. He
lived during that turbulent time when England was in the midst of a prolonged religious civil war. Although England was in a state of chaos,
Locke was optimistic that when the smoke finally cleared a better form of
government would prevail and he did everything in his power to that end.
Locke was very much opposed to the notion of a sovereign endowed[1]
with dictatorial power. He was, in short, a proponent of representative
government. In the end his views prevailed, for once the dust settled after
the (so-called) revolution of 1688, the notion of the divine right of kings
was discarded.[2] From that point on, the government of England functioned as a constitutional monarchy.

Locke postulated[3] that mankind lived in a state of nature before people joined together to form a civil[4] society. For Locke, "Men living
together according to reason, without a common superior on earth with
authority to judge between them, is properly the state of nature". This is
very significant for it implies that Locke believes that there is an unearthly
superior, namely, God. By definition, a state of nature is a pre-civil state
of existence. That means that there are no formalized laws to follow.
Without formal or civil law there can be no authority to adjudicate[5] conflicts among men. Yet men can, in fact, live quite peacefully in a state of
nature because they are reasonable creatures and it is by reason that men
come to understand that "The State of Nature has a law of nature to govern it, which obliges everyone; and reason...teaches all mankind who will
but consult it that, being all equal and independent, no one ought to harm
another in his life, health, liberty, or possessions".

There is a certain logical thought pattern hidden in these two quotes
from Locke. By claiming at the outset that there is an unearthly superior,

---

[1]   *endow:* to provide or equip gratuitously; enhance.

[2]   The divine right of kings is a medieval notion meaning that the king is literally God's
chosen representative on earth in charge of secular affairs.

[3]   *postulate:* something assumed without proof as being self-evident or generally
accepted.

[4]   *civil:* of a community of citizens relative to government.

[5]   *adjudicate:* to serve as a judge (in or on a dispute or problem).

Locke intends us to understand that God is the creator of the universe and all that therein is. He created human beings equal and independent. This is very important because it is the basis of natural rights. Equality and independence constitute the bridge between being created by God and God-given rights. A natural right is a God-given right which all people possess by virtue of being human regardless of race, religion, ethnic origin, sex or time and place of birth.[6] Consequently, the state of nature is a state of liberty, not one of license.[7]

Locke took it as fairly obvious that each and every man has the natural rights of self-preservation and freedom. What is not so obvious is man's natural right of possessions, i.e., to own property. One might reasonably ask, "Why did Locke think ownership of property a natural right?" That is a good question. To answer it, we must again look at Locke's background. Recall that Locke was in the service of Lord Ashley who was, as his title makes obvious, a member of the landed gentry. Locke was not merely in Lord Ashley's service as a tutor to his son, but as confidant[8] and political sidekick. From this rapport[9] with such Whig[10] landowners, it is easily understandable why Locke thought the possession of private property to be a natural right. His views were Whig views.

Remember though, that Locke was a philosopher, and it was therefore incumbent upon him not merely to state his views, but to offer cogent[11] arguments in support of them. That leads us to Locke's justification of private property. He says,

> Though the earth and all inferior creatures be common to all men, yet every man has a property in his own person; this nobody has any right to but himself. The labor of his body and the work of his hands, we may say, are properly his. Whatsoever then he removes out of the state that nature has provided and left it in, he has mixed his labor with, and joined to it something that is his own, and thereby makes it his property. It being by him removed from the common state nature has placed it in, it has by this labor something annexed to it that excludes the common right of other men. For this labor being the unquestionable property of the laborer, no man but he can have a right to what that is once joined to, at least where there is enough and as good left in common for others.

> As much as any one can make use of to any advantage of life before it spoils, so much he may by his labor fix a property in; whatever is beyond this is more than his share and belongs to others. Nothing was made by God for man to spoil or destroy.

---

6   Here one must not confuse abuse of rights with the possession of them. It stands to reason that if natural rights are God-given, then only God can take them away. No human being can take away another person's natural rights. This does not preclude the abuse of a person's rights by another. There is ample evidence of this throughout history. The point is that abuse of rights does not constitute the negation of them.

7   In order for a state of liberty to obtain, people must exercise self-control. Without exercising self-control a situation is created whereby "anything goes". For example, if my neighbor, or anyone else for that matter, follows his urge to shoot at me while I'm driving to work, my freedom of mobility is severely curtailed. A state of license is a state in which there are no rules of any kind. A state of license is a free-for-all in which anyone can do whatever their urges dictate.

8   *confidant:* one to whom secrets are confided.

9   *rapport:* a close or sympathetic relationship; agreement; harmony.

10   *Whig:* in England, a political party (1697-c. 1832) which championed popular rights and change in the direction of democracy; it later became the Liberal Party opposed to Tory.

11   *cogent:* having a powerful appeal to the mind; compelling; convincing.

Here Locke is claiming that in a state of nature no one is born with any more rights than any other person. You are autonomous.[12] In that sense, you own yourself, at least here on earth. This follows from God creating all men independent from one another.[13] If you own yourself, you therefore own not only your body, but whatever results from the use of that body, namely, the labor produced by your body. The whole objective in labor is to get some return from it. Hence, Locke reasons that one not only owns his own labor, but also whatever is obtained as a result of that labor. Mother Nature does not own herself. She is just "out there" waiting to become the servant of someone. So when a man, who in a state of nature owns his own labor, channels this labor toward nature by mixing his labor with the land, whatever the land produces as a result of his labor is properly said to be his own. The fruits of man's labor are his property.

However, you will note from the above citation that the natural right of ownership of property does not mean that one has the right to accumulate goods beyond his needs and to such an extent that the needs of his fellow man cannot be satisfied.

But Locke was no naive[14] man. It was obvious to him that in a state of nature, even though every man has the right to life, health, liberty, and property, oftentimes these rights are not respected. Men are reasonable in the state of nature and generally respect the rights of other men. However, there are occasional abuses. The abuses are frequent enough to lead men to form a civil society. It is important at this point to note that a state of nature for Locke is a state of liberty which ultimately becomes a state of inconvenience due to the abuses of people's natural rights.

Man in a state of nature must function as his own legislator, judge, and executioner of the law of nature. As such, he dispenses[15] justice to those who abuse his person, freedom, and property. That man must so function in the state of nature is inconvenient from both a theoretical and practical point of view. Theoretically, justice is not best served in the state of nature since a wronged person cannot function as an objective arbitrator. Practically, the righting of wrongs done to one is simply too time consuming. When man by social contract enters into a civil society, he hands over legislative, adjudicative, and executive powers for the commonwealth or general welfare which takes the form of an organized community. Man gives up these powers as a matter of self-interest for he realizes that his *own* life, liberty, and possessions are more secure in a commonwealth than in a state of nature.

Men form a commonwealth by common consent. Locke thinks of a group of men coming together to form a civil society; and by agreement, they decide either to govern themselves by direct majority rule or to put themselves under the auspices[16] of a sovereign or an assembly of men. However, it is crucial to an adequate understanding of Locke that embedded in the social contract between men is the assumption that the majority opinion will always rule. It should be clear, however, that the main objective of civil society, which results from the formation of social contracts, is the protection of rights. There is no "right" of the majority to infringe on an individual's natural rights. Men, in forming a commonwealth, might choose to entrust a sovereign or an assembly of men with the lead-

---

[12] *autonomous:* independent in government; having the right of self-government.

[13] In a different sense, however, you are the property of God.

[14] *naive:* having unaffected simplicity; ingenuous; artless; unsophisticated.

[15] *dispense:* distribute.

[16] *auspices:* patronage; protection.

ership of that commonwealth. But Locke is anxious to make clear what counts as leadership.

As was Hobbes, Locke is careful to exclude chosen leaders from the social contract but for different reasons. Were a social contract to be made between leaders and the members of society obligations would be created on both sides. Locke wants the duties to rest with the political leaders only. Consequently, a trust is created between the chosen leaders and the electorate.[17]

Contracts create two way obligations; that is, obligations between both parties to the contract. Trusts, on the other hand, are one way with the obligations residing only with the trustees. The trustees in this case are the chosen political leaders. The beneficiary of the trust, i.e., the community has no obligations to those it has elected as its sovereign or assembly of representatives.

For Locke, the formation of a civil society is different from the formation of a government whose job it is to execute and protect the natural rights of the people. Men first come together and by social contract formed a civil society. This social contract is a contract between each and every man. In other words, it is a one-to-one contract. Implicit[18] in making a social contract is the acceptance of majority rule. After men by social contract form a civil society, they, by majority rule, decide either to run the society by themselves; that is, by direct majority rule or they may elect by majority rule an oligarchy[19] or monarchy as representative of the majority. A sovereign is a leader in the sense that he is the one whose job it is to see that the majority opinion is respected and heeded. So far as Locke is concerned, the concept of a sovereign endowed with complete and total power is contrary to the very purpose of the social contract. Locke says, no doubt with respect to Hobbes' theory, that "absolute monarchy, which by some men is counted the only government in the world, is indeed inconsistent with civil society, and so can be no form of civil government at all". Locke's analysis of the relationship between society and the sovereign obviously gives the individual in society a considerable amount of leeway. This can be partially explained by again taking Locke's background into consideration. His political dealings affirm that he was strongly against a ruler endowed with unlimited power. He went so far as to plot against James II before he became king, and harbored a strong distaste for Charles II while he was king. Locke, in short, thought the concept of the possession of unlimited power by one man to be untenable.[20] Why? Simply because an individual's life, liberty, health and property have greater protection via[21] rule by the majority than by a dictator. The reason man enters into a civil society in the first place is to create a situation for himself whereby his life, liberty and property are more secure than in a state of nature. Man wants from society the best possible guarantees for his life, liberty and property. The guarantees are not as great under the rule of a dictator as they are under majority rule. Locke is anxious to establish the extent of legislative power whereby the individual can gain the most security regarding his natural rights. (1) The legislative branch of govern-

---

[17] *electorate:* the body of persons entitled to vote in an election.

[18] *implicit:* involved in the nature or being of something, though not shown, expressed, or realized.

[19] *oligarchy:* a form of government in which the power is vested in a few, or a state so governed; also, those who form the ruling few.

[20] *untenable:* incapable of being held, maintained, or defended.

[21] *via:* by way of.

ment must govern by promulgated[22] laws which treat every member of society, including the members of the legislature, as equal before the eyes of the law. (2) There must be one, and only one, purpose behind such promulgated laws, namely, the good of the people. (3) The legislature may not levy taxes without consent of the majority of the people, given either by themselves via a plebiscite[23] or by their duly elected representatives. Taxation is a necessary evil because governments cannot function without money. For example, it takes money to support a military for the defense of the country. Here Locke demonstrates his concern that the power of taxation not rest in the hands of a single person with absolute power to rule, e.g., the king. (4) The power of the legislature is nontransferable unless by specific consent of the majority of the people.

If these limits of government are exceeded, the dissolution[24] of that government is justified. Locke supported the dissolution of government both in theory and practice. He strongly supported the rebellion of 1688 whereby King James II was exiled.[25] More importantly, England terminated[26] its commitment to the concept of Divine Right of Kings in preference to a more liberal and representative form of government, namely, a constitutional monarchy. Locke even goes so far as to refer to that rebellion as the "glorious" revolution. One should keep in mind, however, that no responsible person, including Locke, advocates revolution at the drop of a hat.

There is a potential problem with Locke's theory. It concerns the (supposed) natural right of property. The fundamental purpose of forming a civil society is the protection of our natural rights. The legislature or the people via majority rule are empowered to levy taxes. In other words, the majority can legislate with respect to one of our natural rights. Taxes take away property in one form or another. Nevertheless, Locke says

> ... it is fit to consider that every man, when he at first incorporates himself into any commonwealth, he, by his uniting himself thereunto, annexes also, and submits to the community, those possessions which he has or shall acquire that do not already belong to any other government; for it would be a direct contradiction for anyone to enter into society with others for the securing and regulating of property, and yet to suppose his land, whose property is to be regulated by the laws of the society, should be exempt from the jurisdiction of that government to which he himself, the proprietor of the land, is a subject.

The issue at stake here is whether an individual is free to abridge[27] one or any of his natural rights. One could reasonably argue that if there are natural, i.e., God-given rights, only God can modify them. If such is the case and given the necessity of taxation, this inconsistency can only be avoided by not construing[28] property as a natural right.[29]

---

[22]   *promulgate:* to make known or public the terms of (a proposed law).

[23]   *plebiscite:* an expression of the people's will by direct ballot on a political issue.

[24]   *dissolution:* formal dismissal of an assembly.

[25]   *exile:* to banish or expel from one's own country.

[26]   *terminate:* to put an end to; to end.

[27]   *abridge:* to diminish.

[28]   *construe:* to explain or deduce the meaning of.

[29]   It is noteworthy that Locke's justification of property ownership is fallacious. It is one thing to justify ownership of what the land produces via mixing one's labor with it. It is altogether different to argue that one can properly own the land itself. His argument rests on the claim that longevity of use of a piece of land ultimately carries title to it. Given the difficulties associated with property being construed as a natural right, it is noteworthy that the fabricators of the Constitution of the United States did not include it as such.

Suggested Readings: Republicanism; Locke

1. Copleston, F., *A History of Philosophy*, Vol. 5 (N.Y.: Doubleday & Co., 1994), Chapter 7.
2. Czaijkowski, C.J., *The Theory of Private Property in Locke's Political Philosophy* (Notre Dame, Indiana, 1941).
3. Gough, J.W., *John Locke's Political Philosophy.* Eight Studies (Oxford, 1950).
4. Medina, Vincente, *Social Contract Theory* (Md: Rowman & Littlefield, 1990)
5. von Leyden, W., "John Locke and Natural Law," *Philosophy*, vol. 31 (1956).
6. Yolton, J.W., "Locke on the Law of Nature," *Philosophical Review*, Vol. 67 (1958), pp. 477-98

Name_____

Date _____

1. Name two facts from Locke's background or from events of his time which may have influenced his views.

2. What is the natural law according to Locke? What is its source?

3. Explain why the abuse of natural rights does not constitute the negation of them.

4. Explain the difference between a contract and a trust.

5. How does Locke differ from Hobbes regarding sovereign power? Explain.

Chapter I

The Introduction

3. Political Power then I take to be a right of making laws with penalties of death, and consequently all less penalties, for the regulating and preserving of property, and of employing the force of the community, in the execution of such laws, and in the defense of the commonwealth from foreign injury, and all this only for the public good.

Chapter II

Of the State of Nature

4. To understand political power aright, and derive it from its original,[1] we must consider what state all men are naturally in, and that is, a state of perfect freedom to order their actions, and dispose of their possessions, and persons as they think fit, within the bounds of the law of nature, without asking leave, or depending upon the will of any other man.

A state also of equality, wherein all the power and jurisdiction is reciprocal, no one having more than another: there being nothing more evident, than that creatures of the same species and rank promiscuously born to all the same advantages of nature, and the use of the same faculties, should also be equal one amongst another without subordination or subjection, unless the Lord and Master of them all, should by any manifest declaration of his will set one above another, and confer on him by an

---

[1]   The source or cause from which something arises [editor's note].

evident and clear appointment an undoubted right to dominion and sovereignty.

6. But though this be a state of liberty, yet it is not a state of license, though man in that state have an uncontrollable liberty, to dispose of his person or possessions, yet he has not liberty to destroy himself, or so much as any creature in his possession, but where some nobler use, than its bare preservation calls for it. The state of nature has a law of nature to govern it, which obliges every one: and reason, which is that law, teaches all mankind, who will but consult it, that being all equal and independent, no one ought to harm another in his life, health, liberty, or possessions. For men being all the workmanship of one omnipotent, and infinitely wise Maker--all the servants of one sovereign Master, sent into the world by His order and about His business--they are His property, whose workmanship they are, made to last during His, not one another's pleasure; and being furnished with like faculties, sharing all in one community of nature, there cannot be supposed any such subordination among us, that may authorize us to destroy one another, as if we were made for one another's uses, as the inferior ranks of creatures are for ours. Everyone as he is bound to preserve himself, and not to quit his station wilfully; so by the like reason when his own preservation comes not in competition, ought he, as much as he can, to preserve the rest of mankind, and may not unless it be to do justice on an offender, take away, or impair the life, or what tends to the preservation of the life, liberty, health, limb or goods of another.

7. And that all men may be restrained from invading others' rights, and from doing hurt to one another, and the law of nature be observed, which willeth the peace and preservation of all mankind, the execution of the law of nature is in that state, put into every man's hands, whereby every one has a right to punish the transgressors of that law to such a degree, as may hinder its violation. For the law of nature would, as all other laws that concern men in this world, be in vain, if there were nobody that, in the state of nature, had a power to execute that law, and thereby preserve the innocent and restrain offenders. And if anyone in the state of nature may punish another, for any evil he has done, every one may do so. For in that state of perfect equality, where naturally there is no superiority or jurisdiction of one, over another, what any may do in persecution of that law, every one must needs have a right to do.

8. And thus in the state of nature, one man comes by a power over another; but yet no absolute or arbitrary power, to use a criminal when he has got him in his hands, according to the passionate heats, or boundless extravagancy of his own will, but only to retribute to him, so far as calm reason and conscience dictates, what is proportionate to his transgression, which is so much as may serve for reparation and restraint. For these two are the only reasons, why one man may lawfully do harm to another, which is that we call punishment. In transgressing the law of nature, the offender declares himself to live by another rule, than that of reason and common equity, which is that measure God has set to the actions of men, for their mutual security; and so he becomes dangerous to mankind, the tie which is to secure them from injury and violence, being slighted and broken by him. Which, being a trespass against the whole species, and the peace and safety of it, provided for by the law of nature, every man upon this score, by the right he hath to preserve mankind in general, may restrain, or, where it is necessary, destroy things noxious to them, and so may bring such evil on any one, who hath transgressed that law, as may make him repent the doing of it, and thereby deter him, and by his

example others, from doing the like mischief. And in this case, and upon this ground, every man hath a right to punish the offender, and be executioner of the law of nature.

13. To this strange doctrine--viz., that in the state of nature every one has the executive power of the law of nature--I doubt not but it will be objected that it is unreasonable for men to be judges in their own cases, that self-love will make men partial to themselves and their friends. And on the other side, that ill-nature, passion and revenge will carry them too far in punishing others; and hence nothing but confusion and disorder will follow, and that therefore God hath certainly appointed government to restrain the partiality and violence of men. I easily grant that civil government is the proper remedy for the inconveniences of the state of nature, which must certainly be great, where men may be judges in their own case, since 'tis easily to be imagined that he who was so unjust as to do his brother an injury, will scarce be so just as to condemn himself for it. But I shall desire those who make this objection, to remember that absolute monarchs are but men, and if government is to be the remedy of those evils, which necessarily follow from men's being judges in their own cases, and the state of nature is therefore not to be endured, I desire to know what kind of government that is, and how much better it is than the state of nature, where one man commanding a multitude, has the liberty to be judge in his own case, and may do to all his subjects whatever he pleases, without the least question or control of those who execute his pleasure; and in whatsoever he doth, whether led by reason, mistake or passion, must be submitted to, which men in the state of nature are not bound to do one to another? And if he that judges, judges amiss in his own, or any other case, he is answerable for it to the rest of mankind.

Chapter IV

Of Slavery

22. The natural liberty of man is to be free from any superior power on earth, and not to be under the will or legislative authority of man, but to have only the law of nature for his rule. The liberty of man, in society, is to be under no other legislative power but that established by consent in the commonwealth; nor under the dominion of any will, or restraint of any law, but what the legislative shall enact, according to the trust put in it. Freedom then is not what Sir Robert Filmer tells us, (O.A. 55).[2] "A liberty for everyone to do what he pleases, and not to be tied by any laws". But freedom of men under government is to have a standing rule to live by, common to every one of that society, and made by the legislative power erected in it; a liberty to follow my own will in all things, where the rule prescribes not; and not to be subject to the inconstant, uncertain, unknown, arbitrary will of another man: as freedom of nature is to be under no other restraint but the law of nature.

---

[2]   The reference is to *Filmer's Observations upon Aristotle's Politiques, Touching Forms of Government*, published in 1679 [editor's note].

Chapter V

Of Property

25.   Whether we consider natural reason, which tells us that men being once born have a right to their preservation, and consequently to meat and drink, and such other things, as nature affords for their subsistence: or revelation, which gives us an account of those grants God made of the world to Adam, and to Noah and his sons, 'tis very clear that God, as King David says, Psalm cxv. 16, "has given the earth to the children of men," given it to mankind in common. But this being supposed, it seems to some a very great difficulty, how any one should ever come to have a property in anything. I will not content myself to answer that if it be difficult to make out property upon a supposition that God gave the world to Adam and his posterity in common, it is impossible that any man but one universal monarch should have any property upon a supposition that God gave the world to Adam, and his heirs in succession, exclusive of all the rest of his posterity. But I shall endeavor to show how men might come to have a property in several parts of that which God gave to mankind in common, and that without any express compact of all the commoners.

26.   God, who hath given the world to men in common, hath also given them reason to make use of it to the best advantage of life, and convenience. The earth, and all that is therein is given to men for the support and comfort of their being. And though all the fruits it naturally produces, and beasts it feeds, belong to mankind in common, as they are produced by the spontaneous hand of nature; and nobody has originally a private dominion, exclusive of the rest of mankind, in any of them, as they are thus in their natural state; yet being given for the use of men, there must of necessity be a means to appropriate them some way or other before they can be of any use, or at all beneficial to any particular man. The fruit, or venison, which nourishes the wild Indian, who knows no inclosure, and is still a tenant in common, must be his, and so his, i.e., a part of him, that another can no longer have any right to it, before it can do him any good for the support of his life.

27.   Though the earth and all inferior creatures be common to all men, yet every man has a property in his own person. This no body has any right to but himself. The labor of his body and the work of his hands we may say are properly his. Whatsoever, then, he removes out of the state that nature hath provided and left it in, he hath mixed his labor with, and joined to it something that is his own, and thereby makes it his property. It being by him removed from the common state nature placed it in, hath by this labor something annexed to it, that excludes the common right of other men. For this labor being the unquestionable property of the laborer, no man but he can have a right to what that is once joined to, at least where there is enough, and as good left in common for others.

31.   It will perhaps be objected to this, that if gathering the acorns, or other fruits of the earth, makes a right to them, then anyone may engross as much as he will. To which I answer, not so. The same law of nature that does by this means give us property, does also bound that property too. "God has given us all things richly" (1 Tim. vi. 17) is the voice of reason confirmed by inspiration. But how far has he given it us? To enjoy. As much as any one can make use of to any advantage of like before it spoils, so much he may by his labor fix a property in; whatever is beyond this, is more than his share, and belongs to others. Nothing was made by

God for man to spoil or destroy. And thus considering the plenty of natural provisions there was a long time in the world, and the few spenders, and to how small a part of that provision the industry of one man could extend itself, and engross it to the prejudice of others--especially keeping within the bounds, set by reason of what might serve for his use--there could be then little room for quarrels or contentions about property so established.

38. The same measures governed the possessions of land, too. Whatsoever he tilled and reaped, laid up, and made use of before it spoiled, that was his peculiar right; whatsoever he enclosed and could feed and make use of, the cattle and product was also his. But if either the grass of his enclosure rotted on the ground, or the fruit of his planting perished without gathering and laying up, this part of the earth, notwithstanding his enclosure, was still to be looked on as waste, and might be the possession of any other. . . .

46. . . .Now, of those good things which nature hath provided in common, everyone hath a right, as hath been said, to as much as he could use, and had a property in all he could effect with his labor--all that his industry could extend to, to alter from the state nature had put it in, was his. He that gathered a hundred bushels of acorns or apples had thereby a property in them; they were his goods as soon as gathered. He was only to look that he used them before they spoiled, else he took more than his share, and robbed others; and, indeed, it was a foolish thing, as well as dishonest, to hoard up more than he could make use of. If he gave away a part to anybody else, so that it perished not uselessly in his possession, these he also made use of; and if he also bartered away plums that would have rotted in a week, for nuts that would last good for his eating a whole year, he did no injury; he wasted not the common stock, destroyed no part of the portion of goods that belonged to others, so long as nothing perished uselessly in his hands. Again, if he would give his nuts for a piece of metal, pleased with its color, or exchange his sheep for shells, or wool for a sparkling pebble or a diamond, and keep those by him all his life, he invaded not the right of others; he might heap up as much of these durable things as he pleased, the exceeding of the bounds of his just property not lying in the largeness of his possessions, but the perishing of anything uselessly in it.

47. And thus came in the use of money--some lasting thing that men might keep without spoiling, and that, by mutual consent, men would take in exchange for the truly useful but perishable supports of life.

49. Thus in the beginning all the world was America, and more so than that is now, for no such thing as money was any where known. Find out something that hath the use and value of money amongst his neighbours, you shall see the same man will begin presently to enlarge his possessions.

50. But since gold and silver, being little useful to the life of man in proportion to food, raiment, and carriage, has its value only from the consent of men, whereof labor yet makes, in great part, the measure, it is plain that men have agreed to disproportionate and unequal possession of the earth--I mean out of the bounds of society and compact; for in governments the laws regulate it; they having, by consent, found out and agreed in a way how a man may rightfully and without injury possess more than he himself can make use of by receiving gold and silver, which may

continue long in a man's possession, without decaying for the overplus, and agreeing those metals should have a value.

51. And thus, I think, it is very easy to conceive how labor could at first begin a title of property in the common things of nature, and how the spending it upon our uses bounded it: so that there could then be no reason of quarreling about title, nor any doubt about the largeness of possession it gave. Right and conveniency went together; for as a man had a right to all he could employ his labor upon, so he had no temptation to labor for more than he could make use of. This left no room for controversy about the title, nor for encroachment on the right of others; what portion a man carved to himself was easily seen, and it was useless, as well as dishonest, to carve himself too much, or take more than he needed.

Chapter VIII

Of the Beginning of Political Societies

95. Men being, as has been said, by nature all free, equal and independent, no one can be put out of this estate, and subjected to the political power of another, without his own consent. The only way whereby any one divests himself of his natural liberty, and puts on the bands of civil society is by agreeing with other men to join and unite into a community for their comfortable, safe, and peaceable living one amongst another, in a secure enjoyment of their properties, and a greater security against any that are not of it. This any number of men may do, because it injures not the freedom of the rest; they are left as they were in the liberty of the state of nature. When any number of men have so consented to make one community or government, they are thereby presently incorporated, and make one body politic, wherein the majority have a right to act and conclude the rest.

96. For when any number of men have, by the consent of every individual, made a community, they have thereby made the community one body, with a power to act as one body, which is only by the will and determination of the majority. For that which acts any community being only the consent of the individuals of it, and it being necessary to that which is one body to move one way, it is necessary the body should move that way whither the greater force carries it, which is the consent of the majority; or else it is impossible it should act or continue one body, one community which the consent of every individual that united into it, agreed that it should; and so everyone is bound by that consent to be concluded by the majority. And therefore we see that in assemblies empowered to act by positive laws where no number is set by that positive law which empowers them, the act of the majority passes for the act of the whole, and of course determines, as having by the law of nature and reason, the power of the whole.

99. Whosoever therefore out of a state of nature unite into a community must be understood to give up all the power necessary to the ends for which they unite into society, to the majority of the community, unless they expressly agreed in any number greater than the majority. And this is done by barely agreeing to unite into one political society, which is all the compact that is, or needs be, between the individuals, that enter into, or make up a commonwealth. And thus that which begins and actually

constitutes any political society is nothing but the consent of any number of freemen capable of a majority to unite and incorporate into such a society. And this is that, and that only, which did or could give beginning to any lawful government in the world.

100. To this I find two objections made.

First: That there are no instances to be found in story of a company of men independent, and equal one amongst another, that met together and in this way began and set up a government.

Secondly: 'Tis impossible of right that men should do so, because all men being born under government, they are to submit to that, and are not at liberty to begin a new one.

101. To the first there is this to answer--That it is not at all to be wondered that history gives us but a very little account of men that lived together in the state of nature. The inconveniences of that condition, and the love and want of society, no sooner brought any number of them together, but they presently united and incorporated if they designed to continue together. And if we may not suppose men ever to have been in the state of nature, because we hear not much of them in such a state, we may as well suppose the armies of Salmanasser, or Xerxes were never children, because we hear little of them, till they were men, and embodied in armies. Government is everywhere antecedent to records, . . .

Chapter X

Of the Forms of a Commonwealth

132. The majority having, as has been shown, upon men's first uniting into society, the whole power of the community, naturally in them, may employ all that power in making laws for the community from time to time, and executing those laws by officers of their own appointing: and then the form of the government is a perfect democracy; or else may put the power of making laws into the hands of a few select men, and their heirs or successors, and then it is an oligarchy; or else into the hands of one man and then it is a monarchy; if to him and his heirs, it is an hereditary monarchy; if to him only for life, but upon his death the power only of nominating a successor to return to them, an elective monarchy. And so accordingly of these, the community may make compounded and mixed forms of government, as they think good. And if the legislative power be at first given by the majority to one or more persons only for their lives, or any limited time, and then the supreme power to revert to them again; when it is so reverted, the community may dispose of it again anew into what hands they please, and so constitute a new form of government. For the form of government depending upon the placing of the supreme power, which is the legislative, it being impossible to conceive that an inferior power should prescribe to a superior, or any but the supreme make laws, according as the power of making laws is placed, such is the form of the commonwealth.

Chapter XI

Of the Extent of the Legislative Power

134. The great end of men's entering into society being the enjoyment of their properties in peace and safety, and the great instrument and means of that being the laws established in that society: the first and fundamental positive law of all commonwealths, is the establishing of the legislative power; as the first and fundamental natural law, which is to govern even the legislative itself, is the preservation of the society, and (as far as will consist with the public good) of every person in it. This legislative is not only the supreme power of the commonwealth, but sacred and unalterable in the hands where the community have once placed it; nor can any edict of anybody else, in what form soever conceived, or by what power soever backed, have the force and obligation of a law, which has not its sanction from that legislative which the public has chosen and appointed. For without this the law could not have that, which is absolutely necessary to its being a law, the consent of the society over whom nobody can have a power to make laws; but by their own consent, and by authority received from them; and therefore all the obedience, which by the most solemn ties anyone can be obliged to pay, ultimately terminates in this supreme power, and is directed by those laws which it enacts; nor can any oaths to any foreign power whatsoever, or any domestic subordinate power discharge any member of the society from his obedience to the legislative, acting pursuant to their trust; nor oblige him to any obedience contrary to the laws so enacted, or farther than they do allow; it being ridiculous to imagine one can be tied ultimately to obey any power in the society which is not the supreme.

135. Though the legislative, whether placed in one or more, whether it be always in being, or only by intervals, though it be the supreme power in every commonwealth, yet,

First, It is not nor can possibly be absolutely arbitrary over the lives and fortunes of the people. For it being but the joint power of every member of the society given up to that person, or assembly, which is legislator; it can be no more than those persons had in a state of nature before they entered into society, and gave it up to the community. For nobody can transfer to another more power than he has in himself; and nobody has an absolute arbitrary power over himself, or over any other to destroy his own life, or take away the life or property of another. A man as has been proved cannot subject himself to the arbitrary power of another; and having in the state of nature no arbitrary power over the life, liberty, or possession of another, but only so much as the law of nature gave him for the preservation of himself, and the rest of mankind; this is all he doth, or can give up to the commonwealth, and by it to the legislative power, so that the legislative can have no more than this. Their power in the utmost bounds of it, is limited to the public good of the society. It is a power that hath no other end but preservation, and therefore can never have a right to destroy, enslave, or designedly to impoverish the subjects. The obligations of the law of nature cease not in society, but only in many cases are drawn closer, and have by laws known penalties annexed to them to enforce their observation. Thus the law of nature stands as an eternal rule to all men, legislators as well as others. The rules that they make for other men's actions must, as well as their own, and other men's actions be conformable to the law of nature, i.e., to the will of God, of which that is a declaration, and the fundamental law of nature being the preservation of mankind, no human sanction can be good or valid against it.

136. Secondly, The legislative, or supreme authority, cannot assume to itself a power to rule by extemporary arbitrary decrees, but is bound to dispense justice, and decide the rights of the subject by promulgated standing laws, and known authorized judges. For the law of nature being unwritten, and so nowhere to be found but in the minds of men, they who through passion or interest shall miscite or misapply it, cannot so easily be convinced of their mistake where there is no established judge. And so it serves not, as it ought, to determine the rights, and fence the properties of those that live under it, especially where everyone is judge, interpreter, and executioner of it too, and that in his own case; and he that has right on his side, having ordinarily but his own single strength hath not force enough to defend himself from injuries, or punish delinquents. To avoid these inconveniences, which disorder men's properties in the state of nature, men unite into societies that they may have the united strength of the whole society to secure and defend their properties, and may have standing rules to bound it, by which everyone may know what is his. To this end it is that men give up all their natural power to the society which they enter into, and the community put the legislative power into such hands as they think fit, with this trust, that they shall be governed by declared laws, or else their peace, quiet, and property, will still be at the same uncertainty as it was in the state of nature.

137. Absolute arbitrary power, or governing without settled standing laws, can neither of them consist with the ends of society and government, which men would not quit the freedom of the state of nature for, and tie themselves up under, were it not to preserve their lives, liberties, and fortunes; and by stated rules of right and property to secure their peace and quiet. It cannot be supposed that they should intend, had they a power so to do, to give to anyone, or more, an absolute arbitrary power over their persons and estates, and put a force into the magistrate's hand to execute his unlimited will arbitrarily upon them. This were to put themselves into a worse condition than the state of nature, wherein they had a liberty to defend their right against the injuries of others, and were upon equal terms of force to maintain it, whether invaded by a single man or many in combination. Whereas, by supposing they have given up themselves to the absolute arbitrary power and will of a legislator, they have disarmed themselves, and armed him, to make prey of them when he pleases. He being in a much worse condition that is exposed to the arbitrary power of one man who has the command of 100,000, than he that is exposed to the arbitrary power of 100,000 single men; nobody being secure that his will, who hath such a command, is better than that of other men, though his force be 100,000 times stronger. And, therefore, whatever form the commonwealth is under, the ruling power ought to govern by declared and received laws, and not by extemporary dictates and undetermined resolutions. For then mankind will be in a far worse condition than in the state of nature, if they shall have armed one, or a few men, with the joint power of a multitude to force them to obey at pleasure the exorbitant and unlimited decrees of their sudden thoughts, or unrestrained, and, till that moment, unknown wills, without having any measures set down which may guide and justify their actions. For all the power the government has, being only for the good of the society, as it ought not to be arbitrary and at pleasure, so it ought to be exercised by established and promulgated laws; that both the people may know their duty and be safe and secure within the limits of the law; and the rulers too kept within their due bounds, and not be tempted by the power they have

in their hands to employ it to such purposes, and by such measures, as they would not have known, and own not willingly.

138. Thirdly, the supreme power cannot take from any man any part of his property without his own consent. For the preservation of property being the end of government, and that for which men enter into society, it necessarily supposes and requires that the people should have property, without which they must be supposed to lose that by entering into society, which was the end for which they entered into it, too gross an absurdity for any man to own. Men, therefore, in society having property, they have such a right to the goods which by the law of the community are theirs, that nobody hath a right to take them or any part of them from them, without their own consent; without this they have no property at all. For I have truly no property in that which another can by right take from me when he pleases, against my consent. Hence it is a mistake to think that the supreme or legislative power of any commonwealth can do what it will, and dispose of the estates of the subjects arbitrarily, or take any part of them at pleasure. This is not much to be feared in governments where the legislative consists wholly, or in part, in assemblies which are variable, whose members, upon the dissolution of the assembly, are subjects under the common laws of their country, equally with the rest. But in governments where the legislative is in one lasting assembly, always in being, or in one man, as in absolute monarchies, there is danger still, that they will think themselves to have a distinct interest from the rest of the community, and so will be apt to increase their own riches and power by taking what they think fit from the people. For a man's property is not at all secure, though there be good and equitable laws to set the bounds of it between him and his fellow subjects, if he who commands those subjects have power to take from any private man what part he pleases of his property, and use and dispose of it as he thinks good.

139. But government, into whosesoever hands it is put, being, as I have before shown, entrusted with this condition, and for this end, that men might have and secure their properties, the prince, or senate, however it may have power to make laws for the regulating of property between the subjects one amongst another, yet can never have a power to take to themselves the whole or any part of the subject's property without their own consent. For this would be in effect to leave them no property at all. And to let us see that even absolute power, where it is necessary, is not arbitrary by being absolute, but is still limited by that reason, and confined to those ends which required it in some cases to be absolute, we need look no farther than the common practice of martial discipline. For the preservation of the army, and in it the whole commonwealth, requires an absolute obedience to the command of every superior officer, and it is justly death to disobey or dispute the most dangerous or unreasonable of them; but yet we see that neither the sergeant, that could command a soldier to march up to the mouth of a cannon, or stand in a breach, where he is almost sure to perish, can command that soldier to give him one penny of his money; nor the general, that can condemn him to death for deserting his post, or not obeying the most desperate orders, cannot yet, with all his absolute power of life and death, dispose of one farthing of that soldier's estate, or seize one jot of his goods, whom yet he can command anything, and hang for the least disobedience. Because such a blind obedience is necessary to that end for which the commander has his power, viz., the preservation of the rest; but the disposing of his goods has nothing to do with it.

140. 'Tis true governments cannot be supported without great charge, and it is fit everyone who enjoys a share of the protection should pay out

of his estate his proportion for the maintenance of it. But still it must be with his own consent, i.e., the consent of the majority giving it either by themselves or their representatives chosen by them. For if anyone shall claim a power to lay and levy taxes on the people, by his own authority, and without such consent of the people, he thereby invades the fundamental law of property, and subverts the end of government. For what property have I in that which another may by right take, when he pleases, to himself?

141. Fourthly, The legislative cannot transfer the power of making laws to any other hands; for it being but a delegated power from the people, they who have it cannot pass it over to others. The people alone can appoint the form of the commonwealth, which is by constituting the legislative, and appointing in whose hands that shall be. And when the people have said we will submit to rules, and be governed by laws made by such men, and in such forms, nobody else can say other men shall make laws for them; nor can the people be bound by any laws but such as are enacted by those whom they have chosen and authorized to make laws for them.

142. These are the bounds which the trust that is put in them by the society, and the law of God and Nature, have set to the legislative power of every commonwealth, in all forms of government.

First, They are to govern by promulgated established laws, not to be varied in particular cases, but to have one rule for rich and poor, for the favorite at court and the countryman at plough.

Secondly, these laws also ought to be designed for no other end ultimately but the good of the people.

Thirdly, they must not raise taxes on the property of the people without the consent of the people, given by themselves or their deputies. And this properly concerns only such governments where the legislative is always in being, or at least where the people have not reserved any part of the legislative to deputies, to be from time to time chosen by themselves.

Fourthly, The legislative neither must nor can transfer the power of making laws to anybody else, or place it anywhere but where the people have.

Name_____

Date _____

1. Explain Locke's state of nature.

2. How are all persons equal? How does Locke account for equality?

3. Why is government necessary (in light of Locke's view that every individual possesses reason, knows the law of nature and has the right to punish breaches of this law)?

4. How does Locke argue for the right to property? What limitation does he put on ownership? Could one amass any amount of durable goods that he wished?

5. Why can not the commonwealth have absolute arbitrary power over persons? What limits are placed on the power of government?

6. Is the power of the government to levy taxes inconsistent with the right to property? Explain.

12 Conservatism; Edmund Burke

❧ BIOGRAPHY ❧

Edmund Burke (1729-1797) was born in Dublin, Ireland to a middle-class family. His mother was a Catholic and his father a Protestant. As was the custom at that time in mixed marriages, the sons were raised with respect to the convictions of the father and the daughters in the religious persuasion of the mother. Following this tradition, Burke was educated at a Quaker school in Ballitore. At the age of fifteen he entered Trinity College, Dublin. It was there that he achieved a first class honors degree in classics.

At the insistence of his father he enrolled at the Middle Temple, London to study law. He soon discovered that the law held few attractions for him. He far preferred literature. This caused his father to cease supporting him. As a consequence, Burke, at the age of twenty-seven, was forced to support himself. That year (1757) he published his first book, The Vindication of Natural Society. *This earned Burke something of a reputation although no financial stability. The same year he published* A Philosophical Inquiry into the Origin of our Ideas of the Sublime and Beautiful. *His reputation was now on the increase and his circle of influential friends began to widen. In 1765 he was introduced to the Marquis of Rockingham, who made him his private secretary. On July 13, 1765, Rockingham became Prime Minister.*

It was during this period of his life that Burke became the champion of political conservatism. In November 1774 he was elected to a seat in the House of Commons. He remained in that capacity for twenty years. His reputation as a great orator was so widespread that it was said in jest that once Burke began a monologue on the floor of the House one could leave for and return from lunch without him ever noticing the occurrence.

Throughout his political career Burke was a controversial figure. His convictions on a variety of political issues were unwavering. His last appearance in the House of Commons was on June 20, 1794. He died three years later.

First and foremost, conservatism is a political ideology which shuns[1] the notion of utopia[2] and embraces pragmatism[3] in politics. That is to say, people of this persuasion do not believe that perfection in politics can ever

---

[1] *shun:* to keep away from; avoid scrupulously or consistently.

[2] *utopia:* any perfect political or social system.

[3] *pragmatic:* concerned with actual practice, everyday affairs, etc., not with theory or speculation; practical.

be achieved. Conservatives are not ones to chase after rainbows. Rather, they believe in and rely on what works. What works is normally the tried and therefore true, namely, the traditional way of going about life; and this applies no less to politics.

Conservatism tends to be elitist[4] in nature for two related reasons. (1) To Edmund Burke's way of thinking, the overall political stance of a society is vastly more important than the needs of any given individual or individuals within it. Notwithstanding the truth or falsity of such a claim, it quickly becomes of central importance as to what group (i.e., class) within a society is the most adequate representative and protector of it. So far as Burke is concerned, the class in question is the one the members of which are educated and own property. (2) Those who are uneducated ought not have a place in the political decision-making process simply because they are not well versed in such matters.

In order to understand Burke's point of view, it is necessary to appreciate his historical circumstance. He was a member of the British House of Commons for twenty years during the 18th century. He, to a great extent, represents the tenor[5] of the democratic heritage of representative government. This legacy[6] has its roots long in the past and has evolved slowly albeit[7] with mistakes and pain. Although Britain underwent periodic turmoils[8] which produced change, it is nevertheless the case that there was always a thrust toward stability even in the midst of the most revolutionary of times. The nature of that stability has always been conceived to be that of stable government.

Burke was no exception. He did not abhor[9] change. He did believe, however, that such change, if it was warranted[10] at all, could come about constructively only if it was initiated by men who were educated and, therefore, knowledgeable in the affairs of state. In this sense, he was not insensitive to the needs of the average person, but realized that people of such a status needed guidance, not in terms of their everyday judgments, but rather in decisions which have the potential to affect an entire nation. In this regard, Burke should not be construed[11] so much as an elitist, but as paternalistic[12] in nature.

It simply boils down to the fact, as he saw it, that some people are better at masonry and others better at politics. Hence, masons ought not meddle[13] in politics! But since an involvement in politics requires a greater scope of the world than does such pursuits as masonry, one can easily understand how such an attitude does lead to elitism. It is important here to keep in mind that Burke's elitism is founded on what he considered the facts of any society. Except in an ultimate moral sense, people are unequal. This fact provides the basis for the inevitability of the development of classes in every society. Such is not only a fact, but one which

---

[4]   *elite:* the group or part of a group selected or regarded as the finest, best, most distinguished, most powerful, etc.

[5]   *tenor:* general course or tendency.

[6]   *legacy:* anything handed down from , or as from, an ancestor.

[7]   *albeit:* although; even though.

[8]   *turmoil:* tremulant; commotion; uproar; confusion.

[9]   *abhor:* to shrink from in fear, disgust, or hatred; detest.

[10] *warrant:* to serve as justification or reasonable grounds for.

[11] *construe:* to explain or deduce the meaning of; interpret.

[12] *paternalism:* the principle or system of governing or controlling a country, group of employees, etc. in a manner suggesting a father's relationship with his children.

[13] *meddle:* to tamper with.

carries with it a beneficial result, namely, the dominance of one class over another. Without this, leadership would not be possible. And in turn, without leadership any given society is doomed.

Although Burke was primarily a politician, he did have a philosophical side to him. In many ways he was ahead of his times given his analysis of what motivates human beings. It is no doubt the case that the element of reason separates man from beast. However, most people do not function primarily in a rational manner. Wants play the dominant role in the causal process of their behavior. Here Burke departs from the time-honored belief that because man is a rational animal he, therefore, acts primarily in a rational manner. All human beings have wants, needs which are natural and must be satisfied. Many of these needs have nothing whatsoever to do with rationality. The most basic ones, such as the needs for food and water, do not. People also need to love and be loved. Contemplate, for instance, the crazy (i.e., irrational) things people often do when they are "in love".

Once again, Burke is not being critical. He only wants to point out the facts as he sees them. Once such facts are exposed, then, and only then, can one set about developing a political theory which will be realistic, namely, one which works. Due to the fact that human needs and wants are not always rational; that is, that many of them come from the gut *and* because it is a fact that they demand satisfaction, one would be mistaken to suppose that any sort of political, i.e., societal stability could be predicated[14] on them. Burke concluded that although the behavior of any given individual is unreliable, when one takes into account the activity of people in general, one can detect a thread of consistency with respect to human behavior. Given the overall picture of human behavior, rationality does manifest[15] itself. But how? It does so via[16] the perpetuation[17] of social institutions. The pillars of a society are its religious, educational and political institutions.

There are two important points with respect to any and all institutions as far as Burke is concerned. (1) They are organic manifestations of individual qua[18] group efforts. That is, institutions are living entities because they are composed of living, breathing human beings. However, institutions survive longer than any of the individuals associated with them. Furthermore, institutions have the unique[19] ability to sift out and discard the irrationality manifested by the membership. At the same time institutions preserve and propagate[20] any bits of rationality generated by the members of them. (2) Consequently, it is institutions that embody[21] time-honored truths.

Burke's reasoning here is rather simple as well as fallacious[22]. Institutions are lasting entities[23]. Truth itself is not something momentary, but

---

[14] *predicate:* to affirm or base something on or upon given facts, arguments, conditions, etc.

[15] *manifest:* palpable, evident, apparent to the senses, especially that of sight, or to the mind; obvious; clear; plain.

[16] *via:* by way of.

[17] *perpetuate:* cause to continue or be remembered; preserve from oblivion.

[18] *qua:* in the function, character, or capacity of; as.

[19] *unique:* one and only; single, sole.

[20] *propagate:* to cause to spread out and affect a greater number or greater area; foster the spread of.

[21] *embody:* to bring together into an organized whole.

[22] *fallacy:* an error in reasoning; flow or defect in argument.

lasting. He concluded that the products of institutions are the embodiment of truth. Here the logical foundation of conservatism exposes itself, namely, that if we are interested in truth, we ought go to every extreme to preserve our institutions. This does not mean, however, that Burke was unaware of the benefits of change within any given institutional structure.

Change is inevitable because institutions are organic, alive. Change is not only good, but necessary due to the fact that changing times require new approaches to problem solving. He is simply opposed to *radical* change. It is the old conservative bit that it is unwise policy to heave over the apple cart because it contains some rotten apples unless one has at his disposal a supply of fruit which is not equally decayed[24]. In short, he condones[25] evolutionary change as opposed to change by revolution. The latter, so far as he is concerned, can yield nothing but the destruction of whatever good has been built up over the generations. Sticking by the tried and (therefore) true is the only way by which utter[26] societal chaos can be avoided. There is nothing wrong with change as long as it is plotted against the good which man has realized through the past.

It is at this point that the three institutions mentioned above come to play an important role in Burke's political philosophy.

(a) First and foremost, man is a religious animal. This is a fact. If one considers the history of the world, one will discover that religion provides the cornerstone of all societies. Religion, regardless of its content, is, in fact, a universal societal institution. This fact leads Burke to conclude that the institution of religion is not only divinely inspired, but that it offers an indication that institutionalism is good. Hence, we ought to preserve this (as well as other) institutions.

(b) The educational institution is important to Burke in light of his belief that human beings are not born equal except in an ultimate moral sense. Given his religious attitude, he cannot help but accept the notion that God created all men equal in the sense that they have the same natural rights. Aside from this conviction, he understood it to be a fact that people are not born equal either in mental or physical capacities. And he was right. This fact, however, plays an exceedingly important role with respect to the educational institution of a given society. Since people are not born equal, they ought not be educated in an egalitarian[27] manner. The educational system of his day suited him just fine. Keep in mind that traditional British education is very selective. It has only been until recent years that the English have approximated what Americans call public education. The former are highly selective in choosing those individuals who ultimately make it to the university. Those who make the grade are the ones traditionally believed to be "cut out" for such professions as clergymen, university professors, lawyers and statesmen.[28] The traditional mind-set is that one ought not waste university time on an individual who, because of his intellectual endowments[29], is most likely to

---

[23]   *entity:* something that has independent or separate existence.

[24]   *decay:* to rot or decompose.

[25]   *condone:* to accept as inevitable.

[26]   *utter:* carried to the utmost point or highest degree; absolute, complete, entire, total.

[27]   *egalitarian:* of, advocating, or characterized by the belief that all men should have equal political, social, and economic rights.

[28]   Note that these professions parallel the three major institutions whereby a society derives its stability. Indeed, the members of these professions are the leaders of society's institutions and hence the leaders of society.

[29]   *endowment:* a gift of nature; inherent talent, ability.

become a tradesman. Again, this was a method which appeared to Burke as tried and true and, therefore, it would be a drastic mistake to change the existing policy. The most equitable situation to his way of thinking was not only to support the existing educational system, but to instill in those who attain the heights of a university education an obligation to serve and guide those poor souls who are not, because of an accident of birth, so fortunate.

(c) His commitment to the *status quo*[30] with respect to this issue runs even more deeply. As is indicated above, Burke was a strong believer in what he took to be a fact of all societies, namely, that classes within any given society are inevitable. The inequities that are the result of an act of birth are reinforced by the educational system and produce an aristocracy which is essential to the success of any society, for such a class provides the leadership for that society. This is precisely the group which tends to own property which is a key factor in Burke's philosophy. The ownership of property economically frees the possessors of it so that they have the leisure time to be concerned about the well-being of others. If they are properly educated, they will understand that concern for others is their obligation. In other words, those who have the economic means and, therefore, status to have their children educated are those with property. But how does one acquire property? By being born to the "right" family.

Burke takes one more step in furthering his nonegalitarian approach to political theory by reintroducing his prior stated emphasis upon man being a religious creature. His argument "boils down" to this:

(a) It is a fact that man is a *universally* religious as well as social being.
(b) Therefore, it must be the case that there is a God.
(c) It is a fact that there are classes constituting every society, some of which have demonstrated a capacity to rule over other classes of men.
(d) Therefore, God has ordained that group of individuals in question to rule over the remainder of society.

Given this line of reasoning, it seemed reasonable to Burke that those who are not members of the divinely chosen few (due to an accident of birth) *ought* to accept their status in society and wholeheartedly put their faith and trust in those who were born to lead; that is, head the institutions of society. Hence, the well established institutions within a given society ought not to be tampered[31] with. They stand as the stable and divinely inspired backbone of any society.

It is also evident that Burke does not agree with the state of nature theorists who preceded him. They construed human beings as ones who initially found themselves in a prepolitical state. As a result of the use of reason, people decided to get together and form social contracts, thereby creating a civil society and ultimately a form of government. Burke, on the other hand, is not so naive[32]. Chances are that man, including his anthropological ancestors, were always social creatures, namely, ones who lived in groups. The question is, how can the needs of the individuals of the group be satisfied in the most practical way possible? Burke understands that some members of the group are superior to others. They will be the leaders. Established ways of satisfying the needs of the individuals, and ultimately the group, will be recognized and accepted by that

---

[30]   *status quo:* the existing state of affairs.

[31]   *tamper:* to interfere with or meddle with.

[32]   *naive:* unsophisticated.

social entity. Thereafter, the leaders will dictate what sorts of behavior are acceptable and which are not. This line of thought applies to the most complicated forms of society. In the end what is of utmost importance is the survival of the society, not the satisfaction of the needs of any given individual within it. The stability of the society is of primary importance for without such stability no individual can survive. In a weird sort of way, any given individual becomes expendable for the sake of the society at large.

This leads naturally to Burke's concept of natural rights. Since he rejected the notion of a state of nature, it follows that the notion of natural rights is only meaningful within the context of the structure of society. To conceive of them isolated from or independent of such a structure is pointless. Burke was not only a political theorist, but a pragmatist as well. In essence,[33] natural rights are a function of what a society can afford its citizens. Consistent with what has already been stated about his attitudes, he maintained that the best way of protecting the so-called natural rights of an individual is by incorporating them into the framework of a traditional political institution and hence one which is tried and true.

The issue may arise as to what an individual can and ought to do if the existing political institution in which he lives does not respect his (so-called) natural rights. Ought he rebel? Burke argues that governments can be legitimately overthrown, but he does not believe that the masses ought to have an active hand in the process. Basically, the man in the street does not know what is beneficial to him from a political point of view. Therefore, it is incumbent upon[34] legislators to decide whether or not the existing power structure functions at any given time for the benefit of the masses. If a political upheaval is warranted, it is only within the purview[35] of the ruling elite to make such a determination. Obviously, this will almost never happen since those in power are not likely to vote themselves out of power. Such a fact is perfectly okay with Burke for it contributes to the long range stability of a society; that is, radical change is not likely to occur.

Finally, in those cases where national security is at stake, the individual ought to be considered last, as far as Burke is concerned. This point of view is perfectly consistent with his commitment to the overriding importance of political institutions. Without them, individuals cannot survive. Hence, it is better that the group survive at the expense of any given individual. This attitude, to Burke's way of thinking, nets out to the belief that political institutions are more valuable than singular persons.

In conclusion, the maintenance of such institutions is of central importance to Burke's political philosophy. This is the essence of a conservative attitude towards society at large. It is not a rejection of change. Rather conservatives believe that change within the context of any institution, be it religious, educational or political, is only constructive when it occurs in an evolutionary way. Revolution entails a complete destruction of institutions which have by their very nature, i.e., their longevity, demonstrated their value. To destroy them would be the ultimate act of irrationality.

---

[33] *essence:* that which makes something what it is; intrinsic, fundamental nature or most important quality.

[34] *incumbent upon:* resting upon as a duty or obligation.

[35] *purview:* the extent or range of control, activity or concern.

Suggested Readings: Conservatism; Burke

1. Cobban, A., *Edmund Burke and the Revolt Against the Eighteenth Century* (London and New York, 1929).
2. Cone, C.B., *Burke and the Nature of Politics* (Lexington, Ky., 1957).
3. Copeland, T.W., *Our Eminent Friend, Edmund Burke: Six Essays* (New Haven, 1949).
4. MacCunn, J., *The Political Philosophy of Burke* (London and New York, 1913)
5. Magnus, P., *Edmund Burke* (London, 1939).
6. Parkin, C., *The Moral Basis of Burke's Political Thought* (London and New York, (1956).

STUDY QUESTIONS

Chapter 12:
Conservatism;
Burke

Name_____

Date _____

1. Why does conservatism tend to be elitist?

2. A possible objection to elitist conservatism is that all human beings are rational by nature and therefore capable of self-government. What is Burke's position on this?

3. What are the major institutions of a society?

4. In Burke's view, what is the importance of a society's institutions?

5. According to Burke, which is more important, the individual or society? Why?

6. How can change come about in a conservative political system?

Reflections on the Revolution in France

Our oldest reformation is that of Magna Charta. You will see that Sir Edward Coke, that great oracle of our law, and indeed all the great men who follow him, to Blackstone (See Blackstone's Magna Charta, printed at Oxford, 1759), are industrious to prove the pedigree of our liberties. They endeavor to prove that the ancient charter, the Magna Charta of King John, was connected with another positive charter from Henry I., and that both the one and the other were nothing more than a reaffirmance of the still more ancient standing law of the kingdom. In the matter of fact, for the greater part, these authors appear to be in the right; perhaps not always; but if the lawyers mistake in some particulars, it proves my position still the more strongly; because it demonstrates the powerful pre-possession towards antiquity, with which the minds of all our lawyers and legislators, and of all the people whom they wish to influence, have been always filled; and the stationary policy of this kingdom in considering their most sacred rights and franchises as an *inheritance*.

In the famous law of the 3rd of Charles I. called the *Petition of Right*, the parliament says to the king, "Your subjects have *inherited* this free-dom," claiming their franchises not on abstract principles "as the rights of men," but as the rights of Englishmen, and as a patrimony derived from their forefathers. Selden, and the other profoundly learned men, who drew this Petition of Right, were as well acquainted, at least, with all the general theories concerning the "rights of men," as any of the discoursers in our pulpits, or on your tribune; full as well as Dr. Price, or as the Abbe Sieyes. But, for reasons worthy of that practical wisdom which super-seded their theoretic science, they preferred this positive, recorded, hered-itary title to all which can be dear to the man and the citizen, to that vague speculative right, which exposed their sure inheritance to be scrambled for and torn to pieces by every wild, litigious spirit.

The same policy pervades all the laws which have since been made for the preservation of our liberties. In the 1st of William and Mary, in the famous statute, called the Declaration of Right, the two Houses utter not a syllable of "a right to frame a government for themselves." You will see, that their whole care was to secure the religion, laws, and liberties, that had been long possessed, and had been lately endangered. "Taking into their most serious consideration the *best* means for making such an estab-lishment, that their religion, laws, and liberties might not be in danger of being again subverted," they auspicate[1] all their proceedings, by stating as some of those *best* means, "in the *first place*" to do "as their *ancestors in like cases have usually done* for vindicating their *ancient* rights and liberties, to *declare*";--and then they pray the king and queen, "that it may be *declared* and enacted, that *all and singular* the rights and liberties *asserted and declared*, are the true *ancient* and indubitable rights and liberties of the people of this kingdom."

You will observe, that from Magna Charta to the Declaration of Right, it has been the uniform policy of our constitution to claim and assert our liberties, as an *entailed inheritance* derived to us from our forefathers, and to be transmitted to our posterity; as an estate specially belonging to the people of this kingdom, without any reference whatever to any other more general or prior right. By this means our constitution preserves a unity in so great a diversity of its parts. We have an inheritable crown; an inheritable peerage; and a House of Commons and a people inheriting privileges, franchises, and liberties, from a long line of ancestors.

This policy appears to me to be the result of profound reflection; or rather the happy effect of following nature, which is wisdom without reflection, and above it. A spirit of innovation is generally the result of a selfish temper and confined views. People will not look forward to posterity, who never look backward to their ancestors. Besides, the people of England well know, that the idea of inheritance furnishes a sure principle of conservation and a sure principle of transmission; without at all excluding a principle of improvement. It leaves acquisition free; but it secures what it acquires. Whatever advantages are obtained by a state proceeding on these maxims, are locked fast as in a sort of family settlement; grasped as in a kind of mortmain[2] for ever. By a constitutional policy, working after the pattern of nature, we receive, we hold, we transmit our government and our privileges, in the same manner in which we enjoy and transmit our property and our lives. The institutions of policy, the goods of fortune, the gifts of providence, are handed down to us, and from us, in the same course and order. Our political system is placed in a just correspondence and symmetry with the order of the world, and with the mode of existence decreed to a permanent body composed of transitory parts; wherein, by the disposition of a stupendous wisdom, moulding together the great mysterious incorporation of the human race, the whole, at one time, is never old, or middle-aged, or young, but, in a condition of unchangeable constancy, moves on through the varied tenor of perpetual decay, fall, renovation, and progression. Thus, by preserving the method of nature in the conduct of the state, in what we improve, we are never new; in what we retain, we are never wholly obsolete. By adhering in this manner and on those principles to our forefathers, we are guided not by the superstition of antiquarians, but by the spirit of philosophic analogy. In this choice of inheritance we have given to our frame of polity the image of a relation in blood; binding up the constitution of our country with our dearest domestic ties; adopting our fundamental laws into the bosom of our family affections; keeping inseparable, and cherishing with the warmth of all their combined and mutually reflected charities, our state, our hearths, our sepulchers,[3] and our altars.

---

[1]   'Auspicate' means to begin formally as with a ceremony invoking good fortune [editor's note].

[2]   'Mortmain' literally means dead hand [editor's note].

[3]   A sepulcher is a vault for burial [editor's note].

Through the same plan of a conformity to nature in our artificial institutions, and by calling in the aid of her unerring and powerful instincts, to fortify the fallible and feeble contrivances of our reason, we have derived several other, and those no small benefits, from considering our liberties in the light of an inheritance. Always acting as if in the presence of canonized forefathers, the spirit of freedom, leading in itself to misrule and excess, is tempered with an awful gravity. This idea of a liberal descent inspires us with a sense of habitual native dignity, which prevents that upstart insolence almost inevitably adhering to and disgracing those who are the first acquirers of any distinction. By this means our liberty becomes a noble freedom. It carries an imposing and majestic aspect. It has a pedigree and illustrating ancestors. It has its bearings, and its ensigns armorial. It has its gallery of portraits; its monumental inscriptions; its records, evidences, and titles. We procure reverence to our civil institutions on the principle upon which nature teaches us to revere individual men; on account of their age, and on account of those from whom they are descended. All your sophisters cannot produce anything better adapted to preserve a rational and manly freedom than the course that we have pursued, who have chosen our nature rather than our speculations, our breasts rather than our inventions, for the great conservatories and magazines of our rights and privileges.

The Chancellor of France at the opening of the States, said, in a tone of oratorical flourish, that all occupations were honourable. If he meant only, that no honest employment was disgraceful, he would not have gone beyond the truth. But in asserting that anything is honourable, we imply some distinction in its favour. The occupation of a hair-dresser, or of a working tallow-chandler, cannot be a matter of honour to any person--to say nothing of a number of other more servile employments. Such descriptions of men ought not to suffer oppression from the state; but the state suffers oppression, if such as they, either individually or collectively, are permitted to rule. In this you think you are combating prejudice, but you are at war with nature.

Nothing is a due and adequate representation of a state, that does not represent its ability, as well as its property. But as ability is a vigorous and active principle, and as property is sluggish, inert, and timid, it never can be safe from the invasions of ability, unless it be, out of all proportion, predominant in the representation. It must be represented too in great masses of accumulation, or it is not rightly protected. The characteristic essence of property, formed out of the combined principles of its acquisition and conservation, is to be unequal. The great masses therefore which excite envy, and tempt rapacity, must be put out of the possibility of danger. Then they form a natural rampart about the lesser properties in all their gradations. The same quantity of property, which is by the natural course of things divided among many, has not the same operation. Its defensive power is weakened as it is diffused. In this diffusion each man's portion is less than what, in the eagerness of his desires, he may flatter himself to obtain by dissipating the accumulations of others. The plunder of the few would indeed give but a share inconceivably small in the distribution to the many. But the many are not capable of making this calculation; and those who lead them to rapine[4] never intend this distribution.

---

[4] *rapine:* the act of seizing and carrying off by force other's property [editor's note].

The power of perpetuating our property in our families is one of the most valuable and interesting circumstances belonging to it, and that which tends the most to the perpetuation of society itself. It makes our weakness subservient to our virtue; it grafts benevolence even upon avarice. The possessors of family wealth, and of the distinction which attends hereditary possession (as most concerned in it), are the natural securities for this transmission. With us the House of Peers is formed upon this principle. It is wholly composed of hereditary property and hereditary distinction; and made therefore the third of the legislature; and, in the last event, the sole judge of all property in all its subdivisions. The House of Commons too, though not necessarily, yet in fact, is always so composed, in the far greater part. Let those large proprietors be what they will, and they have their chance of being amongst the best, they are, at the very worst, the ballast in the vessel of the commonwealth. For though hereditary wealth, and the rank which goes with it, are too much idolized by creeping sycophants, and the blind, abject admirers of power, they are too rashly slighted in shallow speculations of the petulant, assuming, shortsighted coxcombs[5] of philosophy. Some decent, regulated pre-eminence, some preference (not exclusive appropriation) given to birth, is neither unnatural, nor unjust, nor impolitic.

It is said, that twenty-four millions ought to prevail over two hundred thousand. True; if the constitution of a kingdom be a problem of arithmetic. This sort of discourse does well enough with the lamp-post for its second: to men who may reason calmly, it is ridiculous. The will of the many and their interest must very often differ; and great will be the difference when they make an evil choice. A government of five hundred country attorneys and obscure curates is not good for twenty-four millions of men, though it were chosen by eight-and-forty millions; nor is it the better for being guided by a dozen of persons of quality, who have betrayed their trust in order to obtain that power. . . .

Far am I from denying in theory, full as far is my heart from withholding in practice (if I were of power to give or to withhold), the real rights of men. In denying their false claims of right, I do not mean to injure those which are real and are such as their pretended rights would totally destroy. If civil society be made for the advantage of man, all the advantages for which it is made become his right. It is an institution of beneficence; and law itself is only beneficence acting by a rule. Men have a right to live by that rule; they have a right to do justice, as between their fellows, whether their fellows are in public function or in ordinary occupation. They have a right to the fruits of their industry; and to the means of making their industry fruitful. They have a right to the acquisitions of their parents; to the nourishment and improvement of their parents; to the nourishment and improvement of their offspring; to instruction in life, and to consolation in death. Whatever each man can separately do, without trespassing upon others, he has a right to do for himself; and he has a right to a fair portion of all which society, with all its combinations of skill and force, can do in his favour. In this partnership all men have equal rights; but not to equal things. He that has but five shillings in the partnership, has as good a right to it, as he that has five hundred pounds has to his larger proportion. But he has not a right to an equal dividend in the product of the joint stock; and as to the share of power, authority and direction which each individual ought to have in the management of the state, that I must deny to be amongst the direct original rights of man in civil society; for I

---

[5]   In this context Burke means silliness [editor's note].

have in my contemplation the civil social man, and no other. It is a thing to be settled by convention.

If civil society be the offspring of convention, that convention must be its law. That convention must limit and modify all the descriptions of constitution which are formed under it. Every sort of legislative, judicial, or executory power are its creatures. They can have no being in any other state of things; and how can any man claim under the conventions of civil society, rights which do not so much as suppose its existence? rights which are absolutely repugnant to it? One of the first motives to civil society, and which becomes one of its fundamental rules, is, *that no man should be judge in his own cause*. By this each person has at once divested himself of the first fundamental right of uncovenanted man, that is, to judge for himself, and to assert his own cause. He abdicates all right to be his own governor. He inclusively, in a great measure, abandons the right of self-defense, the first law of nature. Men cannot enjoy the rights of an uncivil and of a civil state together. That he may obtain justice, he gives up his right of determining what it is in points the most essential to him. That he may secure some liberty, he makes a surrender in trust of the whole of it.

Government is not made in virtue of natural rights, which may and do exist in total independence of it; and exist in much greater clearness, and in a much greater degree of abstract perfection; but their abstract perfection is their practical defect. By having a right to everything they want everything. Government is a contrivance of human wisdom to provide for human wants. Men have a right that these wants should be provided for by this wisdom. Among these wants is to be reckoned the want, out of civil society, of a sufficient restraint upon their passions. Society requires not only that the passions of individuals should be subjected, but that even in the mass and body, as well as in the individuals, the inclinations of men should frequently be thwarted, their will controlled, and their passions brought into subjection. This can only be done *by a power out of themselves*; and not, in the exercise of its functions, subject to that will and to those passions which it is its office to bridle and subdue. In this sense the restraints on men, as well as their liberties, are to be reckoned among their rights. But as the liberties and the restrictions vary with times and circumstances, and admit of infinite modifications, they cannot be settled upon any abstract rule; and nothing is so foolish as to discuss them upon that principle.

We know, and what is better, we feel inwardly, that religion is the basis of civil society, and the source of all good and of all comfort. In England we are so convinced of this, that there is no rust of superstition, with which the accumulated absurdity of the human mind might have crusted it over in the course of ages, that ninety-nine in a hundred of the people of England would not prefer to impiety. We shall never be such fools as to call in an enemy to the substance of any system to remove its corruptions, to supply its defects, or to perfect its construction. If our religious tenets should ever want a further elucidation, we shall not call on atheism to explain them. We shall not light up our temple from that unhallowed fire. It will be illuminated with other lights. It will be perfumed with other incense, than the infectious stuff which is imported by the smugglers of adulterated metaphysics. If our ecclesiastical establishment should want a revision, it is not avarice or rapacity, public or private, that we shall employ for the audit, or receipt, or application of its consecrated revenue. Violently condemning neither the Greek nor the Armenian, nor, since heats are subsided, the Roman system of religion, we prefer the Protestant; not because we think it has less of the Christian religion in it, but because, in our judgment, it has more. We are Protestants, not from indifference, but from zeal.

Society is indeed a contract. Subordinate contracts for objects of mere occasional interest may be dissolved at pleasure--but the state ought not to be considered as nothing better than a partnership agreement in a trade of pepper and coffee, calico or tobacco, or some other such low concern, to be taken up for a little temporary interest, and to be dissolved by the fancy of the parties. It is to be looked on with other reverence; because it is not a partnership in things subservient only to the gross animal existence of a temporary and perishable nature. It is a partnership in all science; a partnership in all art; a partnership in every virtue, and in all perfection. As the ends of such a partnership cannot be obtained in many generations, it becomes a partnership not only between those who are living, but between those who are living, those who are dead, and those who are to be born. Each contract of each particular state is but a clause in the great primaeval contract of eternal society, linking the lower with the higher natures, connecting the visible and invisible world, according to a fixed compact sanctioned by the inviolable oath which holds all physical and all moral natures, each in their appointed place. This law is not subject to the will of those, who by an obligation above them, and infinitely superior, are bound to submit their will to that law. The municipal corporations of that universal kingdom are not morally at liberty at their pleasure, and on their speculations of a contingent improvement, wholly to separate and tear asunder the bands of their subordinate community, and to dissolve it into an unsocial, uncivil, unconnected chaos of elementary principles. It is the first and supreme necessity only, a necessity that is not chosen, but chooses, a necessity paramount to deliberation, that admits no discussion, and demands no evidence, which alone can justify a resort to anarchy. This necessity is no exception to the rule; because this necessity itself is a part too of that moral and physical disposition of things, to which man must be obedient by consent or force: but if that which is only submission to necessity should be made the object of choice, the law is broken, nature is disobeyed, and the rebellious are outlawed, cast forth, and exiled, from this world of reason, and order, and peace, and virtue, and fruitful penitence, into the antagonist world of madness, discord, vice, confusion, and unavailing sorrow.

At once to preserve and to reform is quite another thing. When the useful parts of an old establishment are kept, and what is superadded is to be fitted to what is retained, a vigorous mind, steady, persevering attention, various powers of comparison and combination, and the resources of an understanding fruitful in expedients, are to be exercised; they are to be exercised in a continued conflict with the combined force of opposite vices, with the obstinacy that rejects all improvement, and the levity that is fatigued and disgusted with everything of which it is in possession. But you may object--"A process of this kind is slow. It is not fit for an assembly, which glories in performing in a few months the work of ages. Such a mode of reforming, possibly, might take up many years." Without question it might; and it ought. It is one of the excellencies of a method in which time is amongst the assistant, that its operation is slow, and in some cases almost imperceptible. If circumspection and caution are a part of wisdom, when we work only upon inanimate matter, surely they become a part of duty too, when the subject of our demolition and construction is not brick and timber but sentient beings, by the sudden alteration of whose state, condition, and habits, multitudes may be rendered miserable. But it seems as if it were the prevalent opinion in Paris, that an unfeeling heart, and an undoubting confidence, are the sole qualifications for a perfect legislator. Far different are my ideas of that high office. The true lawgiver ought to have a heart full of sensibility. He ought to love and respect his kind, and to fear himself. It may be allowed to his temperament to catch his ultimate object with an intuitive glance; but his movements towards it ought to be deliberate. Political arrangement, as it is a work for social ends, is to be only wrought by social means. There mind must conspire with mind. Time is required to produce that union of minds which alone can produce all the good we aim at. Our patience will achieve more than our force. If I might venture to appeal to what is so much out of fashion in Paris, I mean to experience, I should tell you, that in my course I have known, and, according to my measure, have co-operated with great men; and I have never yet seen any plan which has not been mended by the observations of those who were much inferior in understanding to the person who took the lead in the business. By a slow but well-sustained progress, the effect of each step is watched; the good or ill success of the first gives light to us in the second; and so, from light to light, we are conducted with safety through the whole series. We see that the parts of the system do not clash. The evils latent in the most promising contrivances are provided for as they arise. One advantage is as little as possible sacrificed to another. We compensate, we reconcile, we balance. We are enabled to unite into a consistent whole the various anomalies and contending principles that are found in the minds and affairs of men. From hence arises, not an excellence in simplicity, but one far superior, an excellence in composition. Where the great interests of mankind are concerned through a long succession of generations, that succession ought to be admitted into some share in the councils which are so deeply to affect them. If justice requires this, the work itself requires the aid of more minds than one age can furnish. It is from this view of things that the best legislators have been often satisfied with the establishment of some sure, solid, and ruling principle in government; a power like that which some of the philosophers have called a plastic nature; and having fixed the principle, they have left it afterwards to its own operation.

STUDY
❧ QUESTIONS ❧

Chapter 12:
Readings; Burke

Name_____

Date _____

1. Burke puts considerable emphasis on the concept of "inheritance". What are the various meanings he gives to "inheritance"?

2. Why is the concept of inheritance important to conservatism? Is Burke convincing?

3. Burke disagrees with the Chancellor of France who claimed that all occupations are honorable. Explain.

4. Why does Burke frown on "rule by the many"?

5. What does Burke mean when he says, "Society is indeed a contract"?

13 Communism; Karl Marx

<hr>

❧ BIOGRAPHY ❧

Karl Marx was born in 1818 at Treves in the Rhineland of present day Germany. Although he received his doctoral degree (from the University of Jena in 1841) in philosophy, he was basically an economic and social theorist. He was a follower of Hegel's analysis of historical process which is a theory that history, be it on a societal or cultural level, only progresses via[a] the tension of conflicting forces. Marx tried to apply Hegel's theory to the socio-economic situation of his time. This had both practical and theoretical consequences. His radical viewpoints concerning the inevitability of class conflicts within society made it impossible for him to follow an academic career under the repressive Prussian government of his day. As an alternative he became editor of a liberal businessmen's newspaper, the Rheinische Zeitung, located at Cologne, which was suppressed in 1843. As a result of this Prussian autocracy, Marx decided to move to Paris, France to continue his struggle against oppressionistic Prussia. During this period of his life he developed a lifelong friendship with Friedrick Engels, the son of a prosperous English manufacturer who supported him financially in his later years.

Marx was expelled from France in 1845 for his radical viewpoints and moved to Brussels, Belgium. It was there that he wrote the Communist Manifesto, a semi-philosophical work that depicted an inevitable economic class struggle.

It came to pass that Marx was forced to leave Brussels and he ultimately found his way to Cologne and became editor of the new Rheinische Zeitung. In his abortive attempt to promote a parliamentary democracy, he was arrested and tried for sedition[b]. Upon his acquittal, he was booted out of the area. This occurred in 1849.

The writings of Marx fall into two categories: (a) the philosophical and (b) the emotive[c]. The latter took the form of pamphleteering, a style deliberately written to insight riot. Such is The Communist Manifesto. An example of the former is Das Kapital, the first volume of which was published in 1867. The remainder of it was gathered together by Engels and published posthumously.

Personal tragedy and lack of a general acceptance of his ideas during his time led Marx to die a poverty-ridden and frustrated man in 1883.

<hr>

[a] *via:* by way of.

[b] *sedition:* the stirring up of discontent, resistance or rebellion against the government in power.

[c] *emotive:* attended by or having the character of, emotion; expressing emotion.

The political theory of Karl Marx is a consequence of an economic interpretation of Hegel's philosophy of history in conjunction with his moral outrage over the slave labor conditions produced by the Industrial Revolution of the 19th century. Therefore, a brief understanding of issues central to the philosophy of history is required as a starting point.

There are two central questions that concern philosophers who specialize in this area. (1) At the outset they want to know if historical events follow any given pattern. If so, what is it? Some people claim, for example, that history repeats itself, that it functions in a cyclical manner. We have all heard at some time or another someone rave that American society is immoral and corrupt in the same way Rome was and, furthermore, that we are going to crash and burn just like Rome, if not literally, then figuratively. Such a claim is based on a cyclical view of history. Others argue that there is no such repetition, but rather that historical process is linear in nature, namely, it proceeds without regard or relationship to the past save for the immediate cause of present and past situations and events.

(2) If it is successfully argued that there is some historical process, the issue then becomes whether or not there is any purpose or meaning which underlies that process. If there is, what is it? For example, perhaps the underlying purpose of historical process is a continued betterment in the overall human condition here on earth. Keep in mind at this stage that philosophers do not pretend to be magicians, namely, practicing the art of pulling (theoretical) rabbits out of a hat. Philosophers, regardless of their specialty, must not simply make claims with respect to what they conceive to be the case, but offer arguments[1] in support of their viewpoints. In order to do this, they must support their respective positions with evidence.

Georg Wilhelm Friedrich Hegel (1770 - 1831) argued that there was a recognizable historical process that manifested itself as a combination of the cyclical and linear models mentioned above. Although there is a recurring theoretical pattern to history, situations and values do not repeat themselves in the manner claimed above by the comparison of American society with Ancient Rome. Rather, Hegel argued that world history proceeded according to what he called the Dialectical Method. The term 'dialectic' is derived from dialogue. From a literary point of view a dialogue consists of protagonist, namely an advocate for an idea or action and an antagonist or opponent. In a dialogue the protagonist advances a thesis, e.g., an idea. The antagonist proceeds to demonstrate one or more weaknesses in the thesis. The thesis is then revised to account for the weaknesses and the process continues until both the protagonist and antagonist agree on a final modification of the thesis. From this notion Hegel reasoned that historical events occurred as a result of opposing forces. His model of historical process includes three elements:

(a) thesis
(b) antithesis
(c) synthesis[2]

What complicates Hegel's theory is that these three elements are defined differently with respect to the historical level to which they are applied. He argued that the Dialectical Method functions on three levels:

---

[1]   *argument:* a reason or reasons offered in proof; reasoning.

[2]   *synthesis:* a composition or combination of parts or elements so as to form a whole.

cultural, group (e.g., groups within a society) and individual (i.e., human creativity). However, we will explore the mechanism of the Dialectical Method only as it functions on the group level since that is what is applicable to the political theory of Marx. His definition of the thesis as applied to the group level is the attitudes and consequent behavior of the dominant socio-economic group in any given society.

Fundamental to Hegel's theory is that the thesis will inevitably sow the seeds of its own destruction. It will always give rise to an antithesis, a movement fundamentally opposed to the thesis. Hegel maintained that because no thesis is perfect, it will invariably generate its own destruction from within much as the human body generates a cancerous entity which increases to such proportions that it eventually becomes a question as to which is most viable[3], the healthy portion of the body or that which is prone to the destruction of it. When the antithesis reaches a strength comparable to that of the thesis, the two destroy each other. The result is a synthesis. Every synthesis manifests a greater degree of human freedom than the thesis preceding it. Consequently, there is human progress throughout history in a linear fashion. The synthesis then becomes the thesis of the next cycle which in turn sows the seeds of its own destruction. This process continues until humanity reaches the Ideal State, the ultimate state of human freedom.

During the 19th century, an industrial revolution transpired[4] in England, France and the United States. Industrialization was genuinely revolutionary for it replaced the rural agricultural economics of these countries with factory-based urban economies. Industry created many large cities by drawing people from the rural environment of farms. Along with this shift came the celebrated book *The Wealth of Nations* by the Scottish philosopher Adam Smith in which he detailed how industrial economies function according to the principle of supply and demand. This principle states that the price of a given product is inversely proportional to its supply relative to the demand for it. As the availability of a desired product increases, the price will decrease and vice-versa. It is the marketplace that determines the price of a product. There need not, nor ought not, be any government interference [i.e., regulations] regarding this process because it is self-regulating. Consequently the governments of counties with industrial economies ought properly treat them with a hands-off or *laissez-faire* posture[5]. Accordingly, industrialization flourishes as a function of free enterprise.

Prior to industrialization products of design [e.g., clocks] were hand-made by craftsmen. To become a qualified craftsman, one had to become skilled in the art of a given craft. That meant the design, creation of parts from scratch and completion of the product of that craft. Whereas this process generated quality, it was most time consuming. As a consequence, the availability of such products was limited and they were expensive. Industrialization replaced the guild system via[6] "mass production" otherwise known as the assembly line approach to production. Such a method is highly efficient since laborers specialize in a single aspect of the production process with the result that a great deal of product can be manufactured at a relatively low cost which translates to a lower price per unit to the customer than would be the case for a hand-made item. So

---

[3]   *viable:* able to live or likely to survive.

[4]   *transpired:* to come to pass; happen; occur.

[5]   *posture:* state of mind; attitude.

[6]   *via:* by way of.

with industrialization more people can have more "stuff" which in economic terms means that on balance the society increases its standard of living. Sounds great. However, with government taking a *laissez-faire* approach to the economy, the law of supply and demand applied to labor as well as product. This Marx termed the labor theory of value. He observed that free enterprise is based on competition between manufacturers. The most efficient competitors win the free enterprise game by staying in business. They stay in business because they are able to manufacture their products at a lower cost than the competition and pass those savings onto customers. The largest fixed cost of production is labor. So it stands to reason that manufacturers are motivated to acquire labor at the lowest possible cost. Since there is typically more labor than jobs available, a *laissez-faire* system permits those in control of production to negotiate the lowest possible wage for labor. The effect is the creation of a slave labor class of people. In the final analysis, the labor theory of value entails[7] that a man's labor is worth precisely what it takes him to live, namely, a subsistence wage. In other words, management can succeed by only paying a subsistence wage on the basis of supply and demand within the labor force. From this Marx concluded that one's freedom is a direct correlation of one's economic status. That is, the only meaningful sense of freedom has dollar signs attached to it. This is not an outrageous claim. Just think about it for a minute. For example, if you can't afford a car you're limited to the use of public transportation. If you don't have much money, you can't vacation or travel very far. And without economic independence you're not free to tell your boss at work to "take a hike." *Freedom, so far as Marx is concerned, means economic freedom.* This is an important qualification of freedom as the role it plays in Marx's interpretation of Hegel's Dialectical Method.

While living in France, Marx observed the conditions confronting the labor force generated by industrialization. Because wages were subsistent, the elder children of laborers were forced to quit school and go to work to help support the family thus creating a vicious cycle of economic entrapment. Furthermore, because of government's commitment to *laissez-faire* there were no safety standards for labor[8]. It is fair to say that Marx was repulsed[9] by what he saw. This turned to moral outrage evidence of which is his highly emotive[10] work titled *The Communist Manifesto*. Man is primarily an economic animal ultimately interested in bettering his economic status. Consequently, history is properly the study of how groups of individuals organize in order to realize this goal. Specifically, history is the study of the social organization of economic production. He observed that the organization of production involved two concepts: (a) surplus and (b) status or class within that society. The group of individuals within a society which is privy[11] to the surplus of the production of it determines that society's notion of class. This principle is not to be taken lightly; control over production, according to Marx, actually determines the economic status of any given individual. The notion of class is defined in terms of how we organize for the purpose of that

---

[7]   *entail:* to have as a necessary accompaniment or consequence.

[8]   *labor:* To appreciate the environment within which Marx formed his theory read *Germinal* by the French author Emile Zola. This is an exposé of the coal mining industry in France during the 19th century. *The Jungle* by the American author Upton Sinclair is an eye-opener to the labor conditions pertaining to the U.S. meat packing industry.

[9]   *repulsion:* a feeling of aversion or disgust.

[10]   *emotive:* attended by or having the character of, emotion; expressing emotion.

[11]   *privy:* for private use or personal service; not public.

production. Such organization can vary, but once the organizational structure is determined, so too is the class concept within that society. Inevitably, it all boils down to that sector of the society which has control over the production of goods within it, namely, its economy. Classes are determined by production as opposed to consumption. Obviously, one cannot consume unless one has the economic means by which to do it. How does one get those means? Ultimately, by controlling the forces of production. This does not mean that one must necessarily be the president of an oil corporation, but it does mean that one must have more than a consumer's stake within the economic machinery of a given society. What Marx means is that one cannot achieve economic clout[12] simply by being an employee. One may survive with such a status, but he will never gain any significant measure of economic influence within his milieu[13].

Marx analyses history using Hegel's Dialectical Method within an economic framework. Consequently, Marx's theory is called Dialectical Materialism. He justifies his prediction concerning the demise[14] of capitalism and it being succeeded by communism via Dialectical Materialism. Communism, Marx believed, is an inevitable outcome of historical process and constitutes what Hegel called the Ideal State, a state Marx believed to be one in which there are no class distinctions. Without classes, there can be no economic tyranny of one class over another and therefore people under communism are as free as humanly possible. Given that Marx formulated his theory during the height of the Industrial Revolution, his views about the rise of communism were strictly predictive made plausible as a consequence of his analysis of historical process.

Marx began his historical analysis with the Middle Ages. As a timeline, the sacking of Rome by the Vandals in 455 A.D. signified the termination[15] of the Roman Empire. Barbarian invasions into the Roman Empire had had the effect of isolating Western Europe from the Middle East both of which were part of that empire. The only political entity[16] remaining was that of the Roman Catholic Church. As a result, Western Europe as we know it today, entered a prolonged period of spiritualism otherwise known as the Middle Ages. It is of utmost importance to realize that an attitude of "other-wordliness" was the accepted value of the period. That is to say, life on earth was understood to be merely a preparatory[17] state to life everlasting. Consequently, creature comforts and the economics attendant[18] to them were of no value during the Middle Ages. Obviously, this world-view had a great deal to do with the one institution that survived the collapse of Rome, namely the Church. A secular[19] influence, however, eventually emerged[20]. There was a succession of conquerors, namely, Charles Martel [c. 688-741], Pippin III [d. 768] and Charlemagne [c. 742-814] who contributed to the reconstitution[21] of the previous empire as the Holy Roman Empire. It was Charles Martel who

---

[12] *clout:* influence; force.

[13] *milieu:* environment; setting.

[14] *demise:* death.

[15] *termination:* end.

[16] *entity:* something that exists independently; not relative to other things.

[17] *preparatory:* preparing, or serving to prepare, for something.

[18] *attendant:* accompanying; following as a consequence.

[19] *secular:* of, or pertaining to the worldly or temporal as distinguished from the spiritual or eternal.

[20] *emerge:* to come into being through evolution.

[21] *reconstitution:* reconstruction.

established the economy of the Middle Ages by instituting the horse as a modern means of warfare[22]. That is, he created a cavalry. Since this was an age of spiritualism worldly goods were essentially[23] of no value. However, it was necessary to support livestock and in particular horses for the purpose of greater conquests. Land provided this support. Military leaders such as Martel rewarded their generals with land grants known as fiefs. And thus the aristocracy, as we know it, was born. Fiefs were the basis of feudalism, the economic system of the Middle Ages. In Marx Dialectical Materialism feudalism constitutes the thesis. With land goes title [e.g., the Duke of Bedford]. It didn't take long for the aristocracy to realize that equal inheritance by offspring would undermine the power that went with land ownership. Consequently, the law of primogeniture was established. This law dictated that the oldest son inherit title to the family estate. This creates a problem for second and third sons. During The Middle Ages there were only two viable[24] options for such individuals, namely the military or the clergy.

The law primogeniture was a seed of destruction sowed by the dominate socio-economic group [viz.[25] the aristocracy] because it contributed to an ever expanding military. This was not a problem while Western Europe was undergoing approximately 100 years of reconsolidation after which it settled into a period of stability lasting some 250 years. Then, factionalism[26] began to occur and local conflicts became relatively common. A very astute[27] pope named Urban II [1088-1099] understood that people trained in the discipline of military arts love war and the only way to satisfy such individuals was to provide them with a source of conflict. This Pope was committed to stability within Western Europe and realizing that "tigers do not change their stripes" he called for a holy war whereby anyone who ventured[28] on a crusade to the Holy Land to wrest[29] that property from the Muslim infidel[30] would be forgiven all past, present and future sins. Given that this was a Christian/Spiritual Age, the mere thought of being guaranteed a place in Heaven by virtue of going on a crusade made that extended military campaign plausible. There were eight crusades, from 1096 to 1268. Eventually, and after numerous debacles[31] the West secured the Middle East from the Arabs. This eventually included Northern Africa and control of the Mediterranean Sea. This latter development was pivotal[32] regarding the demise of the Middle Ages. In conforming to the Dialectical Method, the Crusades were a seed of destruction to the thesis of feudalism and along with the law of primogeniture played the role of antithesis. An aftereffect of the Crusades was the settling in the Middle East by many of the victors. That area, known as Byzantium, never experienced an age of spiritualism. It had always been materialistic. Those Western conquerors carved out for themselves not only land but established trade contacts with Middle Eastern merchants

---

[22] Note that the Chinese had done this for centuries.

[23] *essentially:* that which is fundamental to the basic nature of a given type of thing.

[24] *viable:* capable of growing and developing.

[25] *viz.:* namely.

[26] *factionalism:* a state of dissention or conflict between various groups within society.

[27] *astute:* shrewd.

[28] *venture:* to undertake the risk of, to brave, dare.

[29] *wrest:* to snatch or wrench forcibly, especially by usurpation or extortion.

[30] *infidel:* not holding to the faith; especially non-Christian.

[31] *debacles:* a sudden breakdown; collapse.

[32] *pivotal:* central in importance, function, influence or effect.

and began exporting Middle Eastern goods to Western Europe via the Mediterranean Sea. This influx of material goods occurred first in Italy. As the Italians satiated[33] themselves, they began to distribute the goods to which they had become accustomed out along the rivers of Western Europe. This necessitated the development of distributors, otherwise known as merchants. And thus was born capitalism as an economic system comprised of three classes of people: (1) an aristocracy, (2) a middle class qua[34] merchants and (3) peasants. It is important to understand that as far as Marx is concerned, there is nothing wrong with capitalism. Its occurrence is an inevitability of historical evolution. In fact, capitalism conforms to the Hegelian Dialectical Method in that initially, at least, there is an increase of human [economic] freedom because there is an additional class of people sharing in the wealth, namely, the middle class comprised of merchants whose goal it is to accumulate wealth via the distribution and sale of goods. Capitalism functions as the synthesis in this cycle of the Dialectical Method. In turn, it becomes the thesis of the next cycle.

It is important to realize, however, that regardless of the specific seeds of destruction regarding a given thesis that they take a great deal of time to flourish[35] and are never singular[36]. Seeds of destruction contribute to [i.e., germinate[37]] other seeds of destruction which manifest themselves in historical developments ultimately contrary to the very values of the thesis. For example, it would be a mistake to think that there were only two seeds of destruction of the Middle Ages, namely, the law of primogeniture and the Crusades. To be sure, there were other causes of its demise.

So far as Marx was concerned all went well from the end of the Middle Ages until the Industrial Revolution. During this period consumer products were created by craftsmen. This all changed with industrialization. Marx observed that those countries affected by industrialization underwent a bifurcation[38] of two classes; to wit, the middle and peasant classes. Schematically, what occurred was thus:

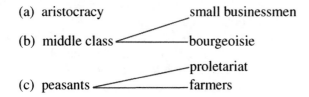

    (a) aristocracy   small businessmen

    (b) middle class   bourgeoisie

                           proletariat

    (c) peasants   farmers

With industrialization certain individuals demonstrated adeptness[39] at what is today known as big business and became barons of industry. These were the bourgeoisie. The proletariat were comprised of individuals who migrated from rural areas to centers of industry [which for the most part, became present day U.S. cities]. And from there on out you know the story. The proletariat became economic slaves.

The seeds of destruction of capitalism are directly related to the Industrial Revolution because it was that which created the bourgeoisie

---

[33] *satiated:* to glut.

[34] *qua:* in so far as; in the capacity or character of.

[35] *flourish:* to thrive.

[36] *singular:* of or pertaining to a single unit.

[37] *germinate:* to begin to grow or develop.

[38] *bifurcation:* the division into two branches.

[39] *adeptness:* thoroughly proficient; expert.

which could not exist without the proletariat, the economic slaves of industrialism. Marx believed that the proletariat would eventually become so fed up and dissatisfied that they would successfully organize a worldwide workers revolution. This constitutes another seed of destruction to the thesis of capitalism and together with the Industrial Revolution itself provide the antithesis to capitalism. The synthesis will be the economic system of communism, namely an agrarian[40] quasi-industrial economy centered around communes. This would entail the termination of private property and of all right of inheritance. Agriculture and manufacturing would be combined resulting in the "gradual abolition[41] of the distinction between town and country, by a more equitable distribution of the population over the country". This expectation of Marx is somewhat based on his view of human nature. He believed that people were fundamentally cooperative; that human nature was devoid[42] of competition. Therefore, people would naturally gravitate to and be happy with living in communes whereby people gave and accepted according to their abilities and needs. Furthermore, Marx believed that industrialization stripped workers of their innate[43] sense of creativity. An assembly line is inhumane because it negates human creativity. Return to the commune is most admirable because it promotes human creativity. Communism constitutes the Ideal State so far as Marx is concerned because people are as free as they possibly can be. This does not mean that everyone receives the same wage. Marx understands that the commune constitutes the Ideal State because there is shared wealth "from each according to his ability, to each according to his need".

As historical events developed the proletariat of Western Europe never consolidated with the laborers of America. There was no worldwide workers revolution. What occurred was evolution, not revolution. In America, laborers were encouraged to organize by a few enlightened individuals and, although there were some brutal confrontations, a compromise of interest was eventually established. As a result, management and labor negotiate when one or the other believe that their needs are not being met. We call this collective bargaining. Collective bargaining became successful via the creation of labor unions.

There is no doubt that Marx has had a tremendous effect upon the world as it exists today. Vladimir Lenin (of Russia) and Mao Tse-Tung (of China) have obviously made their mark on the events of world history. They were undoubtedly successful in their aspirations[44] to turn their respective societies into ones which became economically better off than before the revolutions they created. Keep in mind, however, that they were successful because they were working within essentially feudal societies, namely, ones with no middle class to speak of. Had such societies possessed such an element, revolution may not have been the result of their efforts. That such is the case is born out by the fact that no such revolution was encouraged in Western Europe or America save for Marx himself.

---

[40] *agrarian:* organized or designed to promote agricultural interests.

[41] *abolition:* termination.

[42] *devoid:* without; empty of.

[43] *innate:* to be born in; originate in.

[44] *aspiration:* the thing so desired.

Suggested Readings: Communism; Marx

1. Avineri, Shlomo, *The Social and Political Thought of Karl Marx* (London: Cambridge University Press, 1969).
2. Buber, Martin, *Paths in Utopia* (Boston: Beacon Press, 1958).
3. Cohen, G. A., *Karl Marx's Theory of History: A Defense* (Princeton, N.J.: Princeton University Press, 1978).
4. Evans, Michael, *Karl Marx* (Bloomington: Indiana University Press, 1975).
5. Fromm, Erich, *Marx's Concept of Man* (New York: Ungar, 1961).
6. Gregor, A. James, *A Survey of Marxism* (New York: Random House, 1965).
7. Heiss, Robert, *Hegel, Kierkegaard, Marx* (New York: Delacorte Press, 1975).
8. Hoffman, J., *Marxism and the Theory of Praxis: A Critique of Some New Versions of Old Fallacies* (London: Lawrence & Wishart, 1975).
9. Hook, Sidney, *From Hegel to Marx* (New York: Reynal and Hitchcock, 1963).
10. Kamenka, Eugene, *The Ethical Foundations of Marxism* (London: Routledge and K. Paul, 1962).
11. Lefebvre, Henri, *The Sociology of Marx* (New York: Random House, 1969).
12. Lichtheim, George, *Marxism* (New York: Praeger, 1961).
13. Marcuse, Herbert, *Reason and Revolution*, 2nd ed. (New York: Humanities Press, 1954).
14. McLellan, David, *Karl Marx: His Life and Thought* (New York: Harper and Row, 1973).
15. _____, *The Thought of Karl Marx* (New York: Harper and Row, 1971).
16. Ollman, Bertell, *Alienation: Marx's Conception of Man in Capitalist Society* (Cambridge University Press, 1971).
17. Popper, Karl R., *The Open Society and Its Enemies*. 4th ed. (Princeton, N.J.: Princeton University Press, 1963)
19. Venable, Vernon, *Human Nature: The Marxian View* (New York: Knopf, 1945)

┌─────────────────────────────────┐
│   S T U D Y   │
│   ✣ Q U E S T I O N S ✣   │
│   ─────────────────────────   │
│   Chapter 13:   │
│   Communism;   │
│   Marx   │
└─────────────────────────────────┘

Name_____

Date _____

1. What is the basic idea from Hegel's philosophy which Marx applied to his own work?

2. Show how Hegel's view of the historical process is both cyclical and linear.

3. To what aspect of human life did Marx apply Hegel's method?

4. According to Marx, what determines status or class within a society?

5. How did Marx envision the dialectical process working out in the aftermath of industrialization and the rise of communism?

Communism

Karl Marx
The Communist Manifesto

(Selections)

Marx, K. and Engels, F., *Manifesto of the Communist Party*, translated by Samuel Moore.

I

Bourgeois and Proletarians

The history of all hitherto existing society is the history of class struggles.

Freeman and slave, patrician and plebeian, lord and serf, guild-master and journeyman, in a word, oppressor and oppressed, stood in constant opposition to one another, carried on an uninterrupted, now hidden, now open fight, a fight that each time ended, either in a revolutionary reconstitution of society at large, or in the common ruin of the contending classes.

In the earlier epochs of history, we find almost everywhere a complicated arrangement of society into various orders, a manifold gradation of social rank. In ancient Rome we have patricians, knights, plebeians, slaves; the Middle Ages, feudal lords, vassals, guild-masters, journeymen, apprentices, serfs; in almost all of these classes, again, subordinate gradations.

The modern bourgeois society that has sprouted from the ruins of feudal society, has not done away with class antagonisms. It has but established new classes, new conditions of oppression, new forms of struggle in place of the old ones.

Our epoch, the epoch of the bourgeoisie, possesses, however, this distinctive feature: It has simplified the class antagonisms. Society as a whole is more and more splitting up into two great hostile camps, into two great classes directly facing each other--bourgeoisie and proletariat.

Each step in the development of the bourgeoisie was accompanied by a corresponding political advance of that class. An oppressed class under the sway of the feudal nobility, it became an armed and self-governing association in the medieval commune; here independent urban republic (as in Italy and Germany), there taxable "third estate" of the monarchy (as in France); afterwards, in the period of manufacture proper, serving either the semi-feudal or the absolute monarchy as a counterpoise against the nobility, and, in fact, cornerstone of the great monarchies in general--the bourgeoisie has at last, since the establishment of modern industry and of the world market, conquered for itself, in the modern representative state, exclusive political sway. The executive of the modern state is but a committee for managing the common affairs of the whole bourgeoisie.

The bourgeoisie has played a most revolutionary role in history.

The bourgeoisie, wherever it has got the upper hand, has put an end to all feudal, patriarchal, idyllic relations. It has pitilessly torn asunder the motley feudal ties that bound man to his "natural superiors," and has left no other bond between man and man than naked self-interest, than callous "cash payment." It has drowned the most heavenly ecstasies of religious fervor, of chivalrous enthusiasm, of philistine sentimentalism, in the icy water of egotistical calculation. It has resolved personal worth into exchange value, and in place of the numberless indefeasible chartered freedoms, has set up that single, unconscionable freedom--Free Trade. In one word, for exploitation, veiled by religious and political illusions, it has substituted naked, shameless, direct, brutal exploitation.

The bourgeoisie has stripped of its halo every occupation hitherto honored and looked up to with reverent awe. It has converted the physician, the lawyer, the priest, the poet, the man of science, into its paid wage-laborers.

The bourgeoisie has torn away from the family its sentimental veil, and has reduced the family relation to a mere money relation.

The bourgeoisie has disclosed how it came to pass that the brutal display of vigor in the Middle Ages, which reactionaries so much admire, found its fitting complement in the most slothful indolence. It has been the first to show what man's activity can bring about. It has accomplished wonders far surpassing Egyptian pyramids, Roman aqueducts, and Gothic cathedrals, it has conducted expeditions that put in the shade all former migrations of nations and crusades.

The bourgeoisie cannot exist without constantly revolutionizing the instruments of production, and thereby the relations of production, and with them in the whole relations of society. Conservation of the old modes of production in unaltered form, was, on the contrary, the first condition of existence for all earlier industrial classes. Constant revolutionizing of production, uninterrupted disturbance of all social conditions, everlasting uncertainty and agitation distinguish the bourgeois epoch from all earlier ones. All fixed, fast-frozen relations, with their train of ancient and venerable prejudices and opinions, are swept away, all new-formed ones become antiquated before they can ossify. All that is solid melts into air, all that is holy is profaned, and man is at last compelled to face with sober senses his real conditions of life and his relations with his kind.

The need of a constantly expanding market for its products chases the bourgeoisie over the whole surface of the globe. It must nestle everywhere, settle everywhere, establish connections everywhere.

The bourgeoisie, during its rule of scarce one hundred years, has created more massive and more colossal productive forces than have all preceding generations together. Subjection of nature's forces to man, machinery, application of chemistry to industry and agriculture, steam-navigation, railways, electric telegraphs, clearing of whole continents for cultivation, canalization of rivers, whole populations conjured out of the ground--what earlier century had even a presentiment that such productive forces slumbered in the lap of social labor?

We see then that the means of production and of exchange, which served as the foundation for the growth of the bourgeoisie, were generated in feudal society. At a certain stage in the development of these means of production and of exchange, the conditions under which feudal society produced and exchanged, the feudal organization of agriculture and manufacturing industry, in a word, the feudal relations of property became no longer compatible with the already developed productive forces; they became so many fetters. They had to be burst asunder; they were burst asunder.

Into their place stepped free competition, accompanied by a social and political constitution adapted to it, and by the economic and political sway of the bourgeois class.

A similar movement is going on before our own eyes. Modern bourgeois society with its relations of production, of exchange and of property, a society that has conjured up such gigantic means of production and of exchange, is like the sorcerer who is no longer able to control the powers of the nether world whom he has called up by his spells. For many a decade past the history of industry and commerce is but the history of the revolt of modern productive forces against modern conditions of production, against the property relations that are the conditions for the existence of the bourgeoisie and of its rule. It is enough to mention the commercial crises that by their periodical return put the existence of the entire bourgeois society on trial, each time more threateningly. In these crises a great part not only of the existing products, but also of the previously created productive forces, are periodically destroyed. In these crises there breaks out an epidemic that, in all earlier epochs, would have seemed an absurdity--the epidemic of over-production. Society suddenly finds itself put back into a state of momentary barbarism; it appears as if a famine , a universal war of devastation had cut off the supply of every means of subsistence; industry and commerce seem to be destroyed. And why? Because there is too much civilization, too much means of subsistence, too much industry, too much commerce. The productive forces at the disposal of society no longer tend to further the development of the conditions of bourgeois property; on the contrary, they have become too powerful for these conditions, by which they are fettered, and no sooner do they overcome these fetters than they bring disorder into the whole of bourgeois society, endanger the existence of bourgeois property. The conditions of bourgeois society are too narrow to comprise the wealth created by them. And how does the bourgeoisie get over these crises? On the one hand, by enforced destruction of a mass of productive forces; on the other, by the conquest of new markets, and by the more thorough exploitation of the old ones. That is to say, by paving the way for more extensive and more destructive crises, and by diminishing the means whereby crises are prevented.

The weapons with which the bourgeoisie felled feudalism to the ground are now turned against the bourgeoisie itself.

But not only has the bourgeoisie forged the weapons that bring death to itself; it has also called into existence the men who are to wield those weapons--the modern working class--the proletarians.

In proportion as the bourgeoisie, i.e., capital, is developed, in the same proportion is the proletariat, the modern working class, developed-- a class of laborers, who live only so long as they find work, and who find work only so long as their labor increases capital. These laborers, who must sell themselves piecemeal, are a commodity, like every other article of commerce, and are consequently exposed to all the vicissitudes of competition, to all the fluctuations of the market.

Owing to the extensive use of machinery and to division of labor, the work of the proletarians has lost all individual character, and, consequently, all charm for the workman. He becomes an appendage of the machine, and it is only the most simple, most monotonous, and most easily acquired knack, that is required of him. Hence, the cost of production of a workman is restricted, almost entirely, to the means of subsistence that he requires for his maintenance, and for the propagation of his race. But the price of a commodity, and therefore also of labor, is equal to its cost of production. In proportion, therefore, as the repulsiveness of the work increases, the wage decreases. Nay more, in proportion as the use of machinery and division of labor increases, in the same proportion the burden of toil also increases, whether by prolongation of the working hours, by increase of the work exacted in a given time, or by increased speed of the machinery, etc.

Modern industry has converted the little workshop of the patriarchal master into the great factory of the industrial capitalist. Masses of laborers, crowded into the factory, are organized like soldiers. As privates of the industrial army they are placed under the command of a perfect hierarchy of officers and sergeants. Not only are they slaves of the bourgeois class, and of the bourgeois state, they are daily and hourly enslaved by the machine, by the over-looker, and, above all, by the individual bourgeois manufacturer himself. The more openly this despotism proclaims gain to be its end and aim, the more petty, the more hateful and the more embittering it is.

The proletariat goes through various stages of development. With its birth begins its struggle with the bourgeoisie. At first the contest is carried on by individual laborers, then by the work people of a factory, then by the operatives of one trade, in one locality, against the individual bourgeois who directly exploits them. They direct their attacks not against the bourgeois conditions of production, but against the instruments of production themselves; they destroy imported wares that compete with their labor, they smash machinery to pieces, they set factories ablaze, they seek to restore by force the vanished status of the workman of the Middle Ages.

At this stage the laborers still form an incoherent mass scattered over the whole country, and broken up by their mutual competition. If anywhere they unite to form more compact bodies, this is not yet the consequence of their own active union, but of the union of the bourgeoisie, which class, in order to attain its own political ends, is compelled to set the whole proletariat in motion, and is moreover still able to do so for a time. At this stage, therefore, the proletarians do not fight their enemies, but the enemies of their enemies, the remnants of absolute monarchy, the landowners, the non-industrial bourgeois, the petty bourgeoisie. Thus the whole historical movement is concentrated in the hands of the bourgeoisie; every victory so obtained is a victory for the bourgeoisie.

But with the development of industry the proletariat not only increases in number; it becomes concentrated in greater masses, its strength grows, and it feels that strength more. The various interests and conditions of life within the ranks of the proletariat are more and more equalized, in proportion as machinery obliterates all distinctions of labor and nearly everywhere reduces wages to the same low level. The growing competition among the bourgeois, and the resulting commercial crises, make the wages of the workers ever more fluctuating. The unceasing improvement of machinery, ever more rapidly developing, makes their livelihood more and more precarious; the collisions between individual workmen and individual bourgeois take more and more the character of collisions between two classes. Thereupon the workers begin to form combinations (trade unions) against the bourgeoisie; they club together in order to keep up the rate of wages; they found permanent associations in order to make provision beforehand for these occasional revolts. Here and there the contest breaks out into riots.

Now and then the workers are victorious, but only for a time. The real fruit of their battles lies, not in the immediate result, but in the ever expanding union of the workers. This union is furthered by the improved means of communication which are created by modern industry, and which place the workers of different localities in contact with one another. It was just this contact that was needed to centralize the numerous local struggles, all of the same character, into one national struggle between classes. But every class struggle is a political struggle. At that union, to attain which the burghers of the Middle Ages, with their miserable highways, required centuries, the modern proletarians, thanks to railways, achieve in a few years.

This organization of the proletarians into a class, and consequently into a political party, is continually being upset again by the competition between the workers themselves. But it ever rises up again, stronger, firmer, mightier. It compels legislative recognition of particular interests of the workers, by taking advantage of the divisions among the bourgeoisie itself. Thus the ten-hour bill in England was carried.

Altogether, collisions between the classes of the old society further the course of development of the proletariat in many ways. The bourgeoisie finds itself involved in a constant battle. At first with the aristocracy; later on, with those portions of the bourgeoisie itself whose interests have become antagonistic to the progress of industry; at all times with the bourgeoisie of foreign countries. In all these battles it sees itself compelled to appeal to the proletariat, to ask for its help, and thus, to drag it into the political arena. The bourgeoisie itself, therefore, supplies the proletariat with its own elements of political and general education, in other words, it furnishes the proletariat with weapons for fighting the bourgeoisie.

Further, as we have already seen, entire sections of the ruling classes are, by the advance of industry, precipitated into the proletariat, or are at least threatened in their conditions of existence. These also supply the proletariat with fresh elements of enlightenment and progress.

Finally, in times when the class struggle nears the decisive hour, the process of dissolution going on within the ruling class, in fact within the whole range of old society, assumes such a violent, glaring character, that a small section of the ruling class cuts itself adrift, and joins the revolutionary class, the class that holds the future in its hands. Just as, therefore, at an earlier period, a section of the nobility went over to the bourgeoisie, so now a portion of the bourgeoisie goes over to the proletariat, and in particular, a portion of the bourgeois ideologists, who have raised themselves to the level of comprehending theoretically the historical movement as a whole.

Of all the classes that stand face to face with the bourgeoisie today the proletariat alone is a really revolutionary class. The other classes decay and finally disappear in the face of modern industry; the proletariat is its special and essential product.

The lower middle class, the small manufacturer, the shopkeeper, the artisan, the peasant, all these fight against the bourgeoisie, to save from extinction their existence as fractions of the middle class. They are therefore not revolutionary, but conservative. Nay more, they are reactionary, for they try to roll back the wheel of history. If by chance they are revolutionary, they are so only in view of their impending transfer into the proletariat; they thus defend not their present, but their future interests; they desert their own standpoint to adopt that of the proletariat.

The "dangerous class," the social scum, that passively rotting mass thrown off by the lowest layers of old society, may, here and there, be swept into the movement by a proletarian revolution; its conditions of life, however, prepare it far more for the part of a bribed tool of reactionary intrigue.

The social conditions of the old society no longer exist for the proletariat. The proletarian is without property; his relation to his wife and children has no longer anything in common with bourgeois family relations; modern industrial labor, modern subjection to capital, the same in England as in France, in America as in Germany, has stripped him of every trace of national character. Law, morality, religion, are to him so many bourgeois prejudices, behind which lurk in ambush just as many bourgeois interests.

All the preceding classes that got the upper hand, sought to fortify their already acquired status by subjecting society at large to their conditions of appropriation. The proletarians cannot become masters of the productive forces of society, except by abolishing their own previous mode of appropriation, and thereby also every other previous mode of appropriation. They have nothing of their own to secure and to fortify; their mission is to destroy all previous securities for, and insurances of, individual property.

All previous historical movements were movements of minorities, or in the interest of minorities. The proletarian movement is the self-conscious, independent movement of the immense majority, in the interest of the immense majority. The proletariat, the lowest stratum of our present society, cannot stir, cannot raise itself up, without the whole superincumbent strata of official society being sprung into the air.

Though not in substance, yet in form, the struggle of the proletariat with the bourgeoisie is at first a national struggle. The proletariat of each country must, of course, first of all settle matters with its own bourgeoisie.

In depicting the most general phases of the development of the proletariat, we traced the more or less veiled civil war, raging within existing society, up to the point where that war breaks out into open revolution, and where the violent overthrow of the bourgeoisie lays the foundation for the sway of the proletariat.

Hitherto, every form of society has been based, as we have already seen, on the antagonism of oppressing and oppressed classes. But in order to oppress a class, certain conditions must be assured to it under which it can, at least, continue its slavish existence. The serf, in the period of serfdom, raised himself to membership in the commune, just as the petty bourgeois, under the yoke of feudal absolutism, managed to develop into a bourgeois. The modern laborer, on the contrary, instead of rising with the progress of industry, sinks deeper and deeper below the conditions of existence of his own class. He becomes a pauper and pauperism develops more rapidly than population and wealth. And here it becomes evident, that the bourgeoisie is unfit any longer to be the ruling class in society, and to impose its conditions of existence upon society as an overriding law. It is unfit to rule because it is incompetent to assure an existence to its slave within his slavery, because it cannot help letting him sink into such a state, that it has to feed him, instead of being fed by him. Society can no longer live under this bourgeoisie, in other words, its existence is no longer compatible with society.

The essential condition for the existence and sway of the bourgeois class, is the formation and augmentation of capital; the condition for capital is wage-labor. Wage-labor rests exclusively on competition between the laborers. The advance of industry, whose involuntary promoter is the bourgeoisie, replaces the isolation of the laborers, due to competition, by their revolutionary combination, due to association. The development of modern industry, therefore, cuts from under its feet the very foundation on which the bourgeoisie produces and appropriates products. What the bourgeoisie therefore produces, above all, are its own grave-diggers. Its fall and the victory of the proletariat are equally inevitable.

II

Proletarians and Communists

The Communists are distinguished from the other working class parties by this only: (1) In the national struggles of the proletarians of the different countries, they point out and bring to the front the common interests of the entire proletariat, independently of all nationality. (2) In the various stages of development which the struggle of the working class against the bourgeoisie has to pass through, they always and everywhere represent the interests of the movement as a whole.

The immediate aim of the Communists is the same as that of all the other proletarian parties: Formation of the proletariat into a class, overthrow of bourgeois supremacy, conquest of political power by the proletariat.

The distinguishing feature of Communism is not the abolition of property generally, but the abolition of bourgeois property. But modern bourgeois private property is the final and most complete expression of the system of producing and appropriating products that is based on class antagonisms, on the exploitation of the many by the few.

In this sense, the theory of the Communists may be summed up in the single sentence: Abolition of private property.

We Communists have been reproached with the desire of abolishing the right of personally acquiring property as the fruit of a man's own labour, which property is alleged to be the groundwork of all personal freedom, activity and independence.

Hard-won, self-acquired, self-earned property! Do you mean the property of the petty artisan and of the small peasant, a form of property that preceded the bourgeois form? There is no need to abolish that; the development of industry has to a great extent already destroyed it, and is still destroying it daily.

Or do you mean modern bourgeois private property?

But does wage-labour create any property for the labourer? Not a bit. It creates capital, i.e., that kind of property which exploits wage-labour, and which cannot increase except upon condition of begetting a new supply of wage-labour for fresh exploitation. Property, in its present form, is based on the antagonism of capital and wage-labour. Let us examine both sides of this antagonism.

To be a capitalist, is to have not only a purely personal, but a social *status* in production. Capital is a collective product, and only by the united action of many members, nay, in the last resort, only by the united action of all members of society, can it be set in motion.

Capital is therefore not a personal, it is a social, power.

When, therefore, capital is converted into common property, into the property of all members of society, personal property is not thereby transformed into social property. It is only the social character of the property that is changed. It loses its class character.

Let us now take wage-labour.

The average price of wage-labour is the minimum wage, i.e., that quantum of the means of subsistence which is absolutely requisite to keep the labourer in bare existence as a labourer. What, therefore, the wage-labourer appropriates by means of his labour, merely suffices to prolong and reproduce a bare existence. We by no means intend to abolish this personal appropriation of the products of labour, an appropriation that is made for the maintenance and reproduction of human life, and that leaves no surplus wherewith to command the labour of others. All that we want to do away with is the miserable character of this appropriation, under which the labourer lives merely to increase capital, and is allowed to live only insofar as the interest of the ruling class requires it.

In bourgeois society, living labour is but a means to increase accumulated labour. In Communist society, accumulated labour is but a means to widen, to enrich, to promote the existence of the labourer.

In bourgeois society, therefore, the past dominates the present; in Communist society, the present dominates the past. In bourgeois society capital is independent and has individuality, while the living person is dependent and has no individuality.

And the abolition of this state of things is called by the bourgeois, abolition of individuality and freedom! And rightly so. The abolition of bourgeois individuality, bourgeois independence, and bourgeois freedom is undoubtedly aimed at.

By freedom is meant, under the present bourgeois conditions of production, free trade, free selling and buying.

But if selling and buying disappears, free selling and buying disappears also. This talk about free selling and buying, and all the other "brave words" of our bourgeoisie about freedom in general, have a meaning, if any, only in contrast with restricted selling and buying, with the fettered traders of the Middle Ages, but have no meaning when opposed to the Communist abolition of buying and selling, of the bourgeois conditions of production, and of the bourgeoisie itself.

We have seen above, that the first step in the revolution by the working class, is to raise the proletariat to the position of ruling class, to establish democracy.

The proletariat will use its political supremacy to wrest, by degrees, all capital from the bourgeoisie, to centralize all instruments of production in the hands of the state, i.e., of the proletariat organized as the ruling class; and to increase the total of productive forces as rapidly as possible.

Of course, in the beginning, this cannot be effected except by means of despotic inroads on the rights of property, and on the conditions of bourgeois production; by means of measures, therefore, which appear economically insufficient and untenable, but which, in the course of the movement, outstrip themselves, necessitate further inroads upon the old social order, and are unavoidable as a means of entirely revolutionizing the mode of production.

These measures will of course be different in different countries.

Nevertheless in the most advanced countries, the following will be pretty generally applicable.

(1) Abolition of property in land and application of all rents of land to public purposes.
(2) A heavy progressive or graduated income tax.
(3) Abolition of all right of inheritance.
(4) Confiscation of the property of all emigrants and rebels.
(5) Centralization of credit in the hands of the state, by means of a national bank with state capital and an exclusive monopoly.
(6) Centralization of the means of communication and transport in the hands of the state.
(7) Extension of factories and instruments of production owned by the state; the bringing into cultivation of waste lands, and the improvement of the soil generally in accordance with a common plan.
(8) Equal obligation of all to work. Establishment of industrial armies, especially for agriculture.
(9) Combination of agriculture with manufacturing industries; gradual abolition of the distinction between town and country, by a more equable distribution of the population over the country.
(10) Free education for all children in public schools. Abolition of child factory labour in its present form. Combination of education with industrial production, etc.

When, in the course of development, class distinctions have disappeared, and all production has been concentrated in the hands of a vast association of the whole nation, the public power will lose its political character. Political power, properly so called, is merely the organized power of one class for oppressing another. If the proletariat during its contest with the bourgeoisie is compelled, by the force of circumstances, to organize itself as a class; if, by means of a revolution, it makes itself the ruling class, and, as such sweeps away by force the old conditions of production, then it will, along with these conditions, have swept away the conditions for the existence of class antagonisms, and of classes generally, and will thereby have abolished its own supremacy as a class.

In place of the old bourgeois society, with its classes and class antagonisms, we shall have an association, in which the free development of each is the condition for the free development of all.

Name _____

Date _____

1. Marx believes that the history of society can be viewed as the history of _____.

2. How does the modern form of class division compare to earlier epochs?

3. How does Marx depict the plight of the proletarians?

4. How does the bourgeoisie gradually undermine its own existence according to Marx?

5. Why is it the case that in the beginning of the proletarian revolution resort to despotism is necessary?

14 *Problems of the Philosophy of Religion*

The central question in the philosophy of religion is whether or not God exists. For our purposes 'God' refers to the Judeo-Christian concept of that being. These religious traditions are monotheistic[1] wherein God is understood to be infinite in nature. This infinity is expressed by Him being omnipotent[2], omniscient[3], omnipresent[4], and omnibeneficent[5]. The issue of God's existence is precisely what separates the philosopher of religion from the theologian. The latter, by definition, assumes at the outset that God does exist. That, in fact, is how he gets his name for *theo* is the Greek word for god. The philosopher, on the other hand, is not willing to make that assumption. Rather, he wants to construct a logically sound argument[6] which proves that God exists. The difference between the two approaches can be represented in the following manner.

I   Argument approach on behalf of the philosopher of religion:

1. Premises[7] the content of which consists of reasons and/or data in support of God's existence.
2. A conclusion that God exists based on the evidence presented in the premises.

II   Argument approach on behalf of the theologian:

1. A premise assuming the existence of God.
2. Premises the content of which consists of reasons and/or data that God possesses X characteristic (e.g., that God is incorporeal[8]).
3. A conclusion that God possesses X characteristic based on the evidence presented in the premises under II,2.

One might reasonably ask, why does the philosopher desire proof that God exists? After all, most of us have been raised to take His existence for granted. The philosopher can begin to answer that question by posing another one. Why do scientists desire proof that there is a potential for life on the planet Mars? The answer is that philosophers as well as scientists are interested in the way the world (universe) actually is. Alterna-

---

[1]   *monotheistic:* the doctrine or belief that there is but one God.

[2]   *omnipotent:* having unlimited or universal power, authority, or force; all-powerful.

[3]   *omniscient:* having total knowledge, knowing everything.

[4]   *omnipresence:* the fact of being present everywhere.

[5]   *omnibeneficent:* all-good.

[6]   *argument:* a course of reasoning aimed at demonstrating the truth or falsehood of something.

[7]   *premise:* a proposition upon which an argument is based or from which a conclusion is drawn.

[8]   incorporeal: having no material body or form.

tively, we are not prone to accept ghosts simply because someone is afraid of the dark. If someone maintains that ghosts exist, then it is perfectly natural to require that individual to furnish evidence to support his belief. In the same way, it is natural for the philosopher to request evidence supporting someone's belief in God. The type of evidence that is offered in support of God's existence determines the nature of a given argument for His existence. Evidence is a generic term and can mean data and/or reasons offered as support for the conclusion that God exists. Given the fact that all philosophical concerns are metaphysical in nature (see Chapter 2), it ought not be surprising that all arguments for the existence of God utilize reasons. In this context reasons involve conceptual analysis. Concepts are most often quite complex and the point of analyzing them is to remove any and all confusion resulting from such complexity. Data is physical evidence gathered from the world around us. Some of these arguments consist solely of conceptual analysis whereas others utilize a mix of reasons and data. It is the nature (i.e., kind) of data or reasons (conceptual analysis) which determine the *type* of argument for the existence of God. To prevent a mishmash of an argument the evidence so presented must be of the same variety within that argument. In other words, one must not mix apples and oranges. Traditionally there are four kinds of argument for the existence of God: (1) ontological, (2) cosmological, (3) teleological and (4) moral.

(1) The ontological argument: this type of argument is derived from the Greek word *onto* which means being. Being, of course, involves existence. There are two types of existence, unexemplified and exemplified. Unexemplified existence is that type of existence the object of which is dependent upon an act of thought. For example, unicorns and mermaids only exist as objects or things resulting from an act of thought. In other words, such creatures do not "make it" on their own. Someone must conjure up the thought of a unicorn or mermaid for them to exist. Make no mistake. Obviously pictures of them exist. We can find them in any number of books and tapestries. But such are only pictures, not the real beast. There is no such thing as a real, live unicorn or mermaid. Someone might ask, how do you know that there are no living unicorns or mermaids? The answer is that we can empirically[9] verify[10] that there are none.

Exemplified existence is that type of existence the object of which is not dependent upon an act of thought. For example, there are tennis courts regardless of whether anyone is thinking about them. It may be the case that for tennis courts to exist on their own they must first have existed in an unexemplified way; that is, as the object of someone's thought. But people built them and as such they now exist on their own. They possess exemplified existence. Furthermore, not all things require an act of thought (on behalf of human beings) to achieve a status of exemplified existence. After all, the brontosaurus existed on its own long before *homo sapiens*[11] appeared on the scene. It definitely possessed exemplified existence. These examples should make it clear that migration between these two types of existence is possible with respect to some types of things. However, some things are such that there is no (physical) possibility of any such migration, e.g., mermaids.

This distinction between unexemplified and exemplified existence constitutes the key to understanding any ontological argument for the

[9]   *empirical:* relying upon or derived from observation or experimentation.

[10]   *verify:* to prove the truth of by the presentation of evidence or testimony; substantiate.

[11]   *homo sapiens:* the biological classification of human beings.

existence of God. There is no doubt that God exists in an unexemplified way. If He did not exist in such a manner it would be impossible to talk about Him in the first place. Think about that. Obviously, those so-called things that do not even exist as the result of an act of thought (imagination) are members of the null set. In other words, they are nothing at all. But we do talk about God and, therefore, He must at the very least possess unexemplified existence. However, that is not enough. If God only exists in an unexemplified way, then by definition His existence is dependent upon someone's act of thought. That would put God in a very weak position. In such a case He would not be omnipotent, omniscient, omnipresent and omnibeneficent. Certainly an all-powerful being cannot be dependent upon anything, least of all an act of human thought! So the problem becomes one of developing an argument which makes the transition from God's unexemplified existence to a conclusion that He exists in an exemplified manner, namely, a conclusion that God exists on His own, independent of any act of thought. Now we can see why such arguments are ontological ones. Their subject matter solely concerns the nature of God's existence. All ontological arguments consist of only conceptual analysis, namely, they involve reasoning concerning the different types of possible existence. This type of argument utilizes no empirical data.

(2) The cosmological argument: this type of argument is derived from the Greek word *cosmos* which means world order. Recall that the type of evidence that is offered in support of God's existence determines the nature of a given argument for His existence. Any given cosmological argument is composed of premises which offer evidence of the most fundamental aspect of order, namely, that of cause and effect. This world (universe) functions according to the principle of cause and effect. Every occurrence has a cause. Such occurrences need not be orderly in their own right. Random as well as chaotic occurrences have causes. Furthermore, we need not know what the cause of a given occurrence is. Often times we are ignorant as to what *the* cause of a specific event is, but that does not prevent us from knowing that a given occurrence had *a* cause. Each occurrence *is* an effect, and part of the very *meaning* of the word 'effect' is that every effect is caused. Can you imagine *anything* happening without a cause? If so, what sort of thing would that be? More importantly, where would such a thing have come from? If it did not have a cause, a genesis[12], then it must have come from nothing whatsoever. But it is logically impossible for something to come or begin from nothing. Just think about that. If in the beginning of time there was absolutely nothing whatsoever, nothing could possibly happen. Hence, if there is something, and we know that there is, e.g., you are something reading this book, then there must have been a first cause. If there *must have been* a first cause, then there *is* a first cause. Once we get this far in our reasoning process, would it not be reasonable to think of this first cause of the universe as God?

This brings us to the second characteristic of cosmological arguments, namely, the necessary existence of the first cause. The statement was just made that if there must have been a first cause, then there is a first cause. If something *must* be, then it exists necessarily. That which necessarily exists, is such that it cannot possibly cease to exist. And if it cannot possibly cease to exist, then it exists. Therefore, if God is the first cause, He cannot possibly cease to exist and, therefore, He does exist. With that we have reached the conclusion we desired, namely, that God exists. The vast majority of things in the universe exist only contingently. That is, it

---

[12] *genesis:* the coming into being of anything; origin; creation.

is possible for them to cease to exist in an exemplified way. But as just argued, God exists and necessarily so. If He does not exist necessarily, then it would be possible for the first cause not to exist, in which case the door is open to the possibility that the first cause *did not exist* in the first place. Hence, we would be faced with our original problem of explaining how the world (universe) came from nothing.

In conclusion, we see that cosmological arguments differ from ontological ones in that they do not attempt to prove the exemplified existence of God from an analysis of His essential[13] nature alone. Rather, they arrive at His existence via[14] an analysis of the way the world (universe) functions, namely, on the basis of cause and effect.

(3) The teleological argument: this type of argument is derived from the Greek word *telos* which means purpose or goal. Once again, keep in mind that the type of evidence that is offered in support of God's existence determines the nature of a given argument for His existence. Any given teleological argument is composed of premises which offer evidence of design throughout the universe, including *the* universe itself. Things that are created are designed for a purpose. For example, when Henry Ford created automobiles, he designed them to carry out some function. The purpose or goal of automobiles is efficient transportation. People simply do not design and create things without some purpose in mind. Even a Rube Goldberg machine has a purpose, namely, to do nothing; nothing constructive at any rate. The purpose or goal of a do-nothing machine is precisely that, to do nothing. Therefore, those things which are created have a purpose according to their design. It follows that if something is created with design, there must be a designer and creator who did the designing and creating. The human being itself is a beautiful example of a superbly designed machine. Consider how intricate a machine the human body is and how well it functions under normal circumstances. So we know that within this world not only do human beings design and create other things, but that they themselves are exquisite examples of design. Hence, we know that many things are designed and created *in* this world. But what about the world (universe) itself? If it was created, then it must have some designer and creator. Is it not at this stage of the game reasonable to conclude that that designer and creator is God since the universe is infinite and would, therefore, require an infinite creator?

(4) The moral argument: this type of argument is based on the fact that throughout the history of mankind there has always existed some sort of moral structure consisting of moral rules. One can argue that, in fact, a human society cannot exist without such guidelines. After all, consider what state of affairs would exist if murder and theft were widely accepted *within* a given society; eventually, there would be no such society at all. I say *within* because history has demonstrated that societies can survive by warring against one another. Furthermore, it should be clearly understood that prohibitions against such acts as murder and theft are fundamentally moral rules, and only after a tribe or society develops some degree of sophistication does it transform those rules into statute[15] law. In other words, moral rules or laws are absolutely necessary for the survival of the human species.

The issue now turns on the nature of a rule or law. If a rule or law is understood to be a command, then there must be a commander. If it is the

---

[13]   *essential:* constituting or part of the essence of something, basic or indispensable.

[14]   *via:* by way of.

[15]   *statute:* a law enacted by the legislative body of a representative government.

case that moral laws are universal; that is, common to all mankind, then there must be a universal commander. The judgments of human beings are obviously not universal demonstrated by the fact that humans disagree among themselves save for agreement on the rules that are necessary for them to survive as a society. Simply put, people are finite creatures, but they can come to understand that certain patterns of behavior are necessary if they are to survive as a unit. The agreement is with respect to a universal form of behavior. Since no one human individual is the source of such laws of behavior, it is not unreasonable to conclude that there must be some higher being who is. That higher being we call God.

It should be noted that each of the four types of arguments presented above attempt to demonstrate that God exists on the basis of evidence. Again, the philosopher wants evidence to justify a belief in the existence of God.

It would be advisable at this point to discuss the nature of an argument. From a logical point of view, an argument is not a verbal fight as one might have with one's spouse. Rather, an argument is a [self-contained] unit of reasoning. Arguments are comprised of 1-n premises and a conclusion. 1-n premises indicates that there is no restriction on the number of premises in any given argument. Premises offer justification for the conclusion. Premises and conclusions are statements. Statements are either true or false. Now the whole point of this reasoning process [the argument] is to produce a true conclusion. That makes sense. Suppose you are discussing with a friend a given subject. Your friend presents you with an argument relevant to the subject at hand. You think his argument over and realize that the conclusion of his argument is clearly false. How would you react upon confronting him with your insight if he said, "Oh, I know that."? At the very least, it would be reasonable to respond, "Well, why are we even discussing this issue?" The point is that if we engage in argumentation we expect the final result to be true; that is, that the conclusion of the argument at hand is true. Otherwise there is simply no point to the process.

Pointed out above are two distinct features of an argument; the reasoning process and truth vs. falsity. These two aspects of an argument reflect one of the most basic of philosophical distinctions, namely the form/content distinction. Everything that exists possesses both form and context. Form pertains to structure whereas content has to do with the stuff [material] of some thing. Loosely speaking, form has to do with the shape of a thing. A chair, for example, has a definite shape [structure]. What the chair is made of is entirely different than its shape. Two chairs can possess the same shape and be made of different materials, i.e., metal and wood. Alternatively, two chairs may be made of the same material but possess different shapes, i.e., a study chair and a lounge chair, both made of wood. But remember, *every* thing must possess both. There is no such thing as pure form or pure content even though we can make an intellectual distinction between the two.

Arguments are no different. They possess both form and content. Form pertains to the reasoning process and content has to do with the truth or falsity of the premises/conclusion. Furthermore, we can concentrate on one or the other. For example, we can strip an argument of its content for the purpose of more easily understanding its form. To wit:

          A.   1] All X are Y
                 2] all Y are Z
     Therefore   3] All X are Z

A. is an argument, a unit of reasoning. 1] and 2] are the premises. 3] is the conclusion indicated by the word "therefore." By stripping this argument of its content we can more easily determine whether the reasoning of it is acceptable. Upon determining that the reasoning is acceptable we properly say that the argument is valid. If the reasoning is unacceptable we say that the argument is invalid. *Validity and invalidity pertain only to the form of the argument.* So now, is A. valid or invalid? Premise 1] asserts that anything that is X is also a Y; that is, all X are a subclass of Y. Premise 2] claims that anything that is a Y is also a Z; that is, all Y are a subset of Z. The conclusion that follows is that anything that is an X is also a Z; that is, all X are a subclass of Z. A. is valid demonstrated by the following diagram.

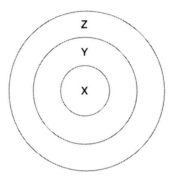

From this we can see that the conclusion does indeed legitimately follow from the premises for it demonstrates that X is a subclass of Z. Now consider

B.   1] All X are Z
        2] all Y are Z
Therefore 3] All X are Y

This line of reasoning is invalid. This is, the conclusion does not legitimately follow from the premises *regardless of what the content of the premises claim.* The invalidity of the above form can be demonstrated thusly:

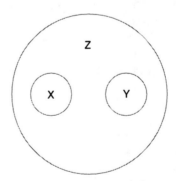

This diagram expresses exactly what the argument claims. It is evident from the diagram that nothing that the premises state warrant the conclusion that all X are Y. Hence, the argument is invalid. Validity and invalidity apply *only* to the form of an argument. And remember, an argument is a unit of reasoning. A unit reasoning is just that, a unit, not a part thereof.

Alternatively, the issue of truth and falsity pertain to statements. It is statements that comprise arguments. Truth and falsity are notions that characterize the parts of arguments, namely statements whereas validity or invalidity pertain to the argument as a whole. Recall that truth and falsity are characteristics of statements. Statements are those units of language [as opposed to questions or imperatives] that are either true or false. *It is statements that are either true or false.* The business of statements is to linguistically reflect facts. Facts are the way the world is at any given point in space/time. That is, when you ask me what I am observing out my window, I say, "The cat is on the mat." This is a statement and as such it is a linguistic picture of what I perceive.[16] The reason that the statement is a linguistic picture of the fact is because it has a point-to-point correspondence with the fact. Suppose the following is that which I perceive, namely the fact that the cat is on the mat.

I linguistically represent this fact by the utterance, "The cat is on the mat." Note the point-to-point correspondence.

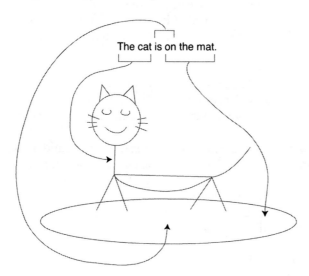

The phrase "The cat" refers to that thing we call a cat. "The mat" refers to that thing we call a mat. And the phrase "is on" refers to the relationship of the cat to the mat. It is in such a way that a statement is a "picutre" of the fact that it claims to represent. When that linguist representation [i.e., statement] is accurate, it is true. When a statement is an inaccurate representation of the fact it purports[17] to represent, then that statement is false. Hence, truth and falsity are a function of statements and only statements. Arguments are neither true nor false because arguments pertain only to the reasoning aspect of an argument. Truth and falsity apply only to statements. Statements are the elements of an argument. As such, truth and falsity do not pertain to facts. Facts simply are. What we say about the facts [by way of statements] is either true or false. Were it

---

[16] *perceive:* to become aware of through the senses.

[17] *purport:* to convey, imply, or profess outwardly (as meaning, intention, or true character).

the case that there are true facts, then it would be possible that there be false facts. The notion of a false fact is absurd.

Now, given the argument from A. above, are the premises true? The answer is, "Who knows?" That is because the form of an argument gives no indication as to the *content* of any given statement. And truth and falsity are functions of the content of a statement. This means that with respect to argument A. we cannot determine that the conclusion is true or false although we do know that the reasoning process is valid. In order to ascertain that the conclusion is true we need to add content to the argument. For example:

> C. 1] All canines are mammals.
>   2] All mammals are warm-blooded.
> Therefore 3] All canines are warm-blooded.

This argument is identical in form to A. above. By adding content to the form we can determine whether or not the conclusion is true. [Remember, the whole point of an argument is to yield a true conclusion.]

We can see that C. yields a true conclusion. That is because A. is a valid form and the content of the premises in C. are true. So, to be *guaranteed* a true conclusion the argument must be *both* valid and possess all true premises. So when analyzing any given argument one must be sure that the argument [form] is valid and the premises [content] are true.

Form and content are separate issues with respect to an argument. That is to say, an argument may be valid and possess one or more false premises. Alternatively, an argument may be invalid and possess all true premises. Consider D. and E.

> D. 1] All canines are mammals.
>   2] All mammals are fierce animals.
> Therefore 3] All canines are fierce animals.

The form of D. is the same as A. Hence D. is a valid argument. However, premise 2 is false. As a result the conclusion is false.

> E. 1] All canines are mammals.
>   2] All felines are mammals.
> Therefore 3] All canines are felines.

The premises of E. are true. However, the conclusion is false. That is because the argument form is invalid. [Compare B. and E.]

There is another issue in the philosophy of religion that deserves recognition, namely, the problem of evil. If God exists, how can one account for the existence of evil given that He is omnibeneficent and omnipotent? How can an all-good God permit all the pain and suffering that exists in the world?[18] It would not appear that God either cannot (indicating that He is not omnipotent) or will not (indicating that He is not omnibeneficent) prevent evil. It should be noted, however, that it is simply not legitimate to solve the problem by whittling away at God's attributes,[19] namely, by concluding that in the face of all the evil that exists in the world it must be the case that He is either not omnibeneficent or not

---

[18] It should be noted that there are two kinds of evil. There is natural evil such as that wrought by earthquakes and volcanos, and there is moral evil which is the result of man's inhumanity to man.

[19] *attributes:* a quality, character or characteristic ascribed to something.

omnipotent, or both. The reason such a solution is not viable[20] is because it results in a God other than the one with which we began, namely, the Judeo-Christian concept of that Being. There are, however, at least three solutions to the problem of evil with which one should be familiar.

(1) One solution is to argue that there is no such thing as evil. There is only apparent evil. Since God is conceived to be all-good, anything less than Him is less good in comparison. The lesser the good the more it appears to be its opposite in comparison to the greatest good, namely, God. But such lesser goods only *appear* to be evil. In reality, they are simply lesser goods. Given such an analysis, the problem of evil dissolves into thin air. The problem with this solution is that it is not very convincing. It is fairly difficult to persuade a victim of rape that such an act was simply a lesser good. This leads naturally to a second solution.

(2) The eschatological[21] solution has the advantage of accepting as a fact the existence of evil. There are two forms of it, philosophical and theological. One can think of the philosophical form of the solution as the tossed salad approach for it is based on the model that a little bit of good plus a little bit of evil results in a greater degree of good. When that greater degree of good is mixed with some more evil even greater good results. In this way the existence of evil can be justified since it is necessary for the creation of greater and greater good. One can think of the theological form of the solution as the "thanks, I needed that" approach for it is based on the model that those human attributes which are good, namely, humility, kindness and justice are only achieved through adversity.

(3) One of the most popular solutions to the problem of evil employs[22] the notion of free will. Simply stated, God created human beings with the capacity to freely choose between good and evil. Only by having free will would it be meaningful for people to carry out God's work on earth. Otherwise, individuals would simply be robots always functioning according to their computer program. But it is meaningless to talk about computers choosing between good and evil. Only by having free will is such a choice a meaningful one.

However, by introducing the notion of free will to solve the problem of evil an additional problem is created. If God is omniscient, then He knows what happened in the past, knows what occurs in the present, and knows what will happen in the future. There is no problem with respect to the former two types of knowledge. The problem of human free will concerns God's knowledge of the future. If He knows everything that will happen, what room does that leave for human beings freely choosing what to do? In other words, if God knows everything that will occur in the future, He therefore knows what you will do this coming weekend, e.g., go skiing. If He knows that, then you *will* go skiing with no ifs, ands, or buts about the matter. In other words, you can do nothing other than go skiing. If you can do nothing other than go skiing, then you have no choice in the matter. That you have no such choice means that you have no free will. And if you have no free will, then free will cannot be offered as a solution to the problem of evil. Some individuals will undoubtedly protest by maintaining that in their past experience when a given weekend came along they deliberated as to whether or not to go skiing. Such deliberation is offered as evidence for the existence of free will.

---

[20] *viable:* capable of being put into practice; workable.

[21] *eschatology:* the branch of theology that is concerned with the ultimate or last things, such as death, judgement, heaven, and hell.

[22] *employ:* to make use of; use.

However, if God knows everything, then He knows when you will deliberate over a given course of action as well as the outcome of your deliberation, the outcome being what He knows will happen from the very beginning. Think about that! The problem of evil is a very sticky one indeed.

Suggested Readings: Problems of the Philosophy of Religion

The Problem of the Existence of God

1. Abernathy, G., and Langford, T. (eds), *Philosophy of Religion* (N.Y.: The Macmillan Co., 1968).
2. Brody, B. (ed.), *Readings in the Philosophy of Religion* (Englewood Cliffs, N.J. Prentice-Hall, Inc., 1974).
3. Cushman, Robert E., and Egil Grislis, (eds.), *The Heritage of Christian Thought* (New York: Harper & Row, 1965).
4. Edwards, Rem B., *Reason and Religion: An Introduction to the Philosophy of Religion* (N.Y.: Harcourt Brace Jovanovich, Inc., 1972).
5. Hartshorne, Charles and William L. Reese, *Philosophers Speak of God* (Chicago: University of Chicago Press, 1953).
6. Hick, John (ed.), *Philosophy of Religion* (Englewood Cliffs, N.J.: Prentice-Hall, Inc., 1964).
7. Hume, David, *Dialogues Concerning Natural Religion*.
8. Rowe, W., and Wainwright, W. (eds), *Philosophy of Religion* (N.Y.: Harcourt, Brace, Jovanovich, Inc., 1973).
9. Scheller, N. (ed.), *Philosophy of Religion* (N.Y.: Macmillan Publishing Co., 1974).
10. Taylor, A.E., *Does God Exist?* (New York: The Macmillan Company, 1947).

The Problem of Evil

1. Hick, John, *Evil and the God of Love* (New York: Harper & Row, 1966).
2. Laird, John, *Mind and Deity* (New York: Philosophical Library, 1941).
3. Lewis, C.S., *The Problem of Pain* (New York: The Macmillan Company, 1950).
4. Lewis, Edwin, *The Creator and the Adversary* (New York: Abingdon-Cokesbury Press, 1948).
5. Mill, John Stuart, *Three Essays on Religion* (New York: Holt, Rinehart & Winston, 1884).
6. Petit, Francois, *The Problem of Evil*. trans., Christopher Williams (New York: Hawthorn Books, 1959).
7. Rashdall, Hastings, *The Theory of Good and Evil*, Vol. II. (London: Oxford University Press, 1924).
8. Weiss, Paul, "Good and Evil," *Review of Metaphysics* (September 1949), III, 1, no. 9, pp. 81-94.

STUDY
QUESTIONS

Name_____

Date _____

Chapter 14:
Problems of the Philosophy
of Religion

1. What distinguishes the philosophy of religion from theology?

2. What is the fundamental difference between an ontological argument for God's existence and a cosmo-logical one?

3. In general, what determines the nature of a given argument for God's existence?

4. The problem of evil results when God is believed to have two characteristics which seem incompatible with the existence of evil. What are these characteristics? Explain the problem.

5. Explain the form/content distinction. How does this distinction pertain to arguments?

6. What is the difference between validity and truth?

15 *The Ontological Argument; St. Anselm*

St. Anselm (1033-1109) was born of a noble family in Piedmont, England. After preliminary studies, he entered the Benedictine Order. In 1063 he became Prior of Bec. He was appointed to the position of abbot of that institution in 1078. It was upon the death of his teacher and friend, Lanfranc, that Anselm succeeded him as the Archbishop of Canterbury in 1093.

Of critical importance is Anselm's conception of the relationship between reason and faith. He said in the Proslogium that "I do not attempt, O Lord, to penetrate Thy profundity, for I deem my intellect in no way sufficient thereunto, but I desire to understand in some degree Thy truth, which my heart believes and loves. For I do not seek to understand, in order that I may believe; but I believe, that I may understand. For I believe this too, that unless I believed, I should not understand". By such a statement we can see that there was at this point in our culture no clear-cut distinction between philosophy and theology. His attempt at proving the existence of a (Judeo-Christian) God is one which is without doubt very rigorous from a philosophical point of view, but one which also demonstrates a deep seated belief that such a being does exist in the first place. However, those individuals who possess rigorous minds by nature do not rest easy on their beliefs (or intuitions) and, therefore, feel compelled to offer other grounds which support their beliefs. It was his powers of reasoning for the purpose of supporting his already existing belief in the existence of God that led him to (attempt to) demonstrate the existence of God from a philosophical (i.e., logical) point of view. As a result, he formulated his (ontological) argument for that Being. The argument is best understood as a demonstration of God's existence rather than a proof of it; if by proof one means the creation of God's existence. Clearly, if God is infinite, no argument will bring Him into existence although it may force upon us an awareness of His existence.

It is in this respect, given Anselm's point of view, that philosophy and theology are not altogether separate bedfellows. In short, the use of reason (philosophy) can be utilized to explain (i.e., justify) that which we believe to be the case, namely, the existence of the Judeo-Christian God.

The root of the word ontology is onto. *Onto* is the Greek word for being. So it is no surprise that a study of ontology involves delving into the various types of being. Being has to do with existence. The "things" of the world can exist in different ways. At the very least there are two varieties of existence, unexemplified and exemplified. Unexemplified existence is that type of existence the object of which is *dependent* upon an act of thought. Consider, for example, unicorns. Such beasts are dependent upon an act of thought for their existence. They are simply *objects of though*t. One may argue that pictures of unicorns exist and therefore they have an independent existential status. But there is a huge difference between a *picture* of a unicorn and a living, breathing horse with a horn projecting from its forehead. Such creatures simply do not "make it" on their own. They are thought dependent. On the other hand, exemplified existence is that type of existence the object of which *is* independent of an act of thought. Telephones, for example, fall into this category. The telephone in front of me exists whether or not I am thinking of it. It *does* "make it" on its own.

Care must be taken at this point. It should be noted that some things have always been relegated[1] to the realm of unexemplified existence, others not. Mermaids have always been unexemplified. However, we do know that dinosaurs at one stage in world history were exemplified, but are no longer so. They have become extinct as seen by their remains and therefore presently exist only in the minds of men. On the other hand, some things which were once only unexemplified have made the transition to exemplified status. There was at one point only the thought of a tennis court in someone's mind. With some ingenuity, a means of establishing their independent existence was contrived and now such recreational areas exist on their own independent of anyone's thought about them.

It is at this point that the nature of an ontological argument for the existence of God begins to make some sense. It is obvious that God at the very least exists in an unexemplified way. This is verified by the fact that people do, in fact, think, not to mention talk, about such an entity[2]. He does exist as an object of thought. For the philosopher, however, this is not enough. After all, what sort of degenerate God would we have on our hands if He were capable of going out of existence due to the lack of thought about Him? No; what is demanded is a deomonstration that God exists in an exemplified manner, namely existence *independent* of the thoughts of man. Only then will He be the meaningful entity he is believed to be in the Judeo-Christian tradition, namely a being who is omnipotent (all-powerful), omniscient (all-knowing), omnipresent (ever-present) and omnibeneficent (all-good). A being possessing these attributes[3] would qualify as perfect or one with all perfections. The philosophical problem is one of developing an argument whereby one can deomonstrate God's exemplified existence by starting out with *only* what is known for sure, namely that He exists in an unexemplified way. St. Anselm, the foremost philosopher-theologian[4] of the 11th century, attempted to do precisely that.

---

[1]   *relegate:* to assign to a particular class or category; classify.

[2]   *entity:* a particular and discreet unit.

[3]   *attribute:* a quality or characteristic belonging to a person or thing; a distinctive feature.

[4]   *theology:* the study of the nature of God and religious truth. Derived from the Greek word *theo* which means god.

Before we look at the content of this argument it is advisable to determine whether or not it is valid. It takes the form of a very common type of reasoning called *modus ponens*.

1] If A, then B.
2] A
Therefore 3] B

Premise 1] is what we call a conditional statement. It does not assert what is the case. Rather it indicates a relationship between A and B. It states that B will obtain [come to be] if A obtains. In other words, B's coming to be is guaranteed by the coming to be of A. 1] makes no claim that either A or B obtains. Premise 2] claims that A does, in fact, obtain. Consequently, it must be the case that B obtains. That is why the *modus ponens* form is valid.

Two important points:

1] In any given argument the order of the premises is irrelevant to the validity or invalidity of it.

2] The number of variables in an argument is irrelevant to the validity or invalidity of it. Both of these points are demonstrated in St. Anselm's argument. When we substitute variables for the content of the premises his argument is as follows:

1] A
2] B
3] If [A and B], then C
Therefore 4] C

This is a *modus ponens* form.

Hence, we know that St. Anselm's argument is valid. Let us now turn to the content of his argument. At this stage we want to determine that all of the premises are true.

He begins his ontological argument with what he understood to be an incontestable[5] truth that:

(1) God is something nothing greater than which can be conceived.

By this he means that God is the most perfect of possible conceptions. Here there are three important points. (a) Anselm is clearly beginning his argument with a statement of God's unexemplified existence. (b) He is perfectly consistent with the Judeo-Christian view that God has all perfections, namely, that He is *conceived* as the ultimate perfect being. Here it is important to note that this is a factual claim. To verify the Judeo-Christian conception of God one need only to peruse[6] the Old Testament of the Bible where this conception is stated in black and white. (c) It matters not whether any mortal can, in fact, conjure[7] up the image of such perfection. It is simply a matter of whether *if* one could so imagine God, He would manifest Himself as the ultimate in perfection. This latter point nips in the bud the retort[8] of the antagonist[9] that he simply is incapable of imagining a being with all perfections. Anselm proceeds to reason that:

---

[5]   *incontestable:* incapable of being contested; unquestionable.

[6]   *peruse:* to examine in detail; scrutinize.

[7]   *conjure:* to bring to the mind's eye; evoke.

[8]   *retort:* to present a counter argument.

[9]   *antagonist:* one who opposes and actively competes with another; adversary.

(2) An entity possesses a greater degree of perfection by being exempli-
     fied than merely existing in an unexemplified manner.

This claim involves both a conceptual and a practical truth. The conceptual truth hinges on the notion of dependence. By (2) Anselm observes
that that which is dependent is not as perfect as that which is independent.
Dependency is an inferior state of existence compared to independent
existence. Think about that. For something, anything, to have to rely on
something else for its existence or anything else is in one sense incomplete. It is not whole. It is not independent and therefore not as perfect as
that which is independent.

The practical truth contained in the above claim is seen by the following example. Suppose that you get lost on a hunting trip and are without
food. Chances are that at some point you'll get hungry. As that hunger
progresses, it would not be surprising that you conjure up some delectable[10] item to eat. But would it not be a more perfect state of affairs if that
succulent[11] dish were exemplified, namely, right before your very eyes so
you could, in fact, eat it rather than merely think about it? The answer is
obvious, namely, exemplified food is more perfect in nature than unexemplified sustenance[12]. In opposition to Anselm's claim, one can argue that
the exemplified version of that which is conceived is oftentimes inferior to
its imagined counterpart. For example, rarely does one's conception of
the perfect mate coincide with the realities thereof. True, but such a
rejoinder is not detrimental to Anselm's point. Such is merely a "mechanical" problem. If it *were* possible for a spouse to match one's "dream" of
the ultimate partner, then it would, in fact, be the case that that person's
exemplified existence would manifest a greater degree of perfection than
his/hers unexemplified status.

The third premise in Anselm's argument is the conditional (i.e., if
___, then...) statement.

(3) If God is something nothing greater than which can be conceived, and
     exemplified existence is more perfect than unexemplified existence,
     then He must exist in an exemplified manner.

Anselm has asserted the quite reasonable Judeo-Christian belief that God
is the most perfect being imaginable. And since an exemplified state of
existence is more perfect than an unexemplified one, then it logically follows that God exists independently of the thoughts of man. Hence,

(4) God exists (in an exemplified manner).

This is precisely what Anselm set out to prove. Not so bad for openers,
wouldn't you say? But Anselm has only begun to fight! He has only
demonstrated that God exists in an exemplified way. He has not by the
aforesaid reasoning demonstrated that God exists necessarily. In other
words, Anselm has only shown that God exists in the same way that dinosaurs once existed. He has not thus argued that God is incapable of going
out of existence and, therefore, capable of assuming an unexemplified status. If such were possible, that would really be "bad news" for those
believers within the Judeo-Christian tradition. Hence, Anselm must

---

[10] *delectable:* greatly pleasing; enjoyable; delightful.

[11] *succulent:* full of juice or sap; juicy.

[12] *sustenance:* the supporting of life or health; maintenance.

develop an addendum[13] to the above argument to demonstrate that God in no way can make the transition from exemplified to unexemplified existence.[14] Realizing this he offers the following for our consideration.

(5) That which cannot be conceived not to exist manifests a more perfect state of being than that which can be conceived not to exist.

This claim appears to be more difficult in content than it really is. To bring the point into focus, let us imagine the following situation. If one were to roll a "live" grenade under a chair one could well imagine that the chair would soon go out of (exemplified) existence. We can, in fact, imagine innumerable things which have the potential of going out of exemplified existence. All Anselm is saying is that if something can in no way be conceived of going out of (exemplified) existence, then it is more perfect than if it can be so conceived. In other words, eternal exemplified existence is more perfect than (momentary) exemplified existence. Eternal exemplified existence is synonymous[15] with necessary existence.[16] Hence,

(6) If God is something nothing greater than which can be conceived, and that which cannot be conceived not to exist is more perfect than that which can be conceived not to exist, then it must be the case that God cannot be conceived not to exist.

This leads to the conclusion that God's existence is not only exemplified but eternally exemplified at that. And this leads Anselm to finally conclude that:

(7) God *must* (i.e., necessarily) exist,

which is to say that it is impossible for God to exist in any manner other than in an eternal exemplified way. And that is precisely what Anselm set out to demonstrate.

Anselm's argument has not gone without criticism. A contemporary of his, a monk named Gaunilon, suggested that if Anselm's argument was logically sound, then it would follow that if one were to conceive of the most perfect island, then it must exist in an exemplified way. But, of course, the mere thought of such an island does not guarantee its exemplified existence. By parallel reasoning, God's exemplified existence does not follow from one's conception of Him. There are actually two criticisms hidden in Gaunilon's perfect island objection. (1) He is correct in his claim that the mere thought of something does not guarantee its exemplified existence. For example, exemplified existence does not follow from the mere conception of a unicorn. However, this point only applies to the first formulation of Anselm's argument (i.e., steps 1-4), the part

---

[13] *addendum:* something added or to be added.

[14] Here one should not fall into the trap that such a limitation is a breach of God's omnipotence. In a similar vein, it has been argued that God is indeed not all-powerful for if He were He would be capable of creating a rock so heavy that He could not lift it. That is, in fact, no threat to God's omnipotence for the problem is an example of a (logical) contradiction. Namely, it can be reduced to the symbolic statement that "S can do X and cannot do X" which has nothing to do with God's powers. It simply does not make any sense.

[15] *synonymous:* equivalent or similar in meaning.

where he attempts to prove that God exists in an exemplified manner, but not necessarily so. Gaunilon's objection, however, does not damage the second formulation of the argument (i.e., steps 5-7). If part of the nature of perfection is *necessary* (exemplified) existence, then it matters not whether any mortal conceives of God in the first place. He simply *must* exist. Looking at it this way, Anselm avoids the criticism of making an illegitimate shift from unexemplified to exemplified existence. (2) That we can conceive of the most perfect island does not guarantee its exemplified existence since islands are the type of things which can indeed be conceived not to exist. Islands do not exist necessarily. This demonstrates that the most perfect island does not possess all perfections, otherwise, it would exist necessarily, namely, we could not imagine it going out of exemplified existence. That we can so imagine, indicates that such an island does not have all perfections. And that is reasonable so far as Anselm is concerned, for only *one* thing has all perfections which entails necessary existence and that is God. Hence, he claims that his ontological proof only properly applies to God and not to other beings, i.e., "things". Again, Anselm holds his own. An alternative way of grasping this point is to understand that in the case of Gaunilon's island example, perfection modifies (i.e., characterizes) an object the nature of which can be fully understood without any reference to perfection. Not so with the Judeo-Christian god. This god is conceived to *be* perfection; that is, He is one and the same with perfection. Here perfection does not modify (i.e., characterize) God. Perfection *is* God.

There is an objection which does harm Anselm's argument. It concerns the first premise[17]

(1) God is something nothing greater than which can be conceived.

The problem involves the word 'is'. It is ambiguous and can be interpreted in two ways:

(1') God exists as something nothing greater than which can be conceived, or

(1") God = something nothing greater than which can be conceived.

---

[16] Premise five pertains to the distinction between contingent and necessary existence. Contingent existence is that type of existence the object of which can cease to exist in an exemplified way. This means that anything that so exists is such that one can imagine that that thing can cease to exist in an exemplified manner. We know that there are things that exist in a contingent way. E.g., you can imagine an animal dying or a building burning down. From this fact one can understand what it would be like for an object to be indestructible; that is, could not cease to exist. In other words, from the fact that one knows what it would be like for something to be destructible, it follows that one can understand the negation of destructible existence. The negation of destructible existence is indestructible existence. Indestructible existence is otherwise known as necessary existence and is defined as that type of existence the object of which cannot cease to exist in an exemplified way. Here's the rub. Since we know (a) things exist contingently and (b) contingency entails the possibility of negation (i.e., the cesation of existence), the negation of contingency (as a type of existence) follows as a *possibility*. The negation of contingent existence is necessary existence. Realize that it makes no difference whether you or I can "imagine" something existing neccessarily. All we need to know is that something existing necessarily is at least a possibility.

[17] *premise:* a proposition upon which an argument is based or from which a conclusion is drawn.

If we choose (1') as the proper interpretation of 'is', then it is possible that Anselm has committed the fallacy[18] of begging the question which means that he has assumed at the outset precisely what he wanted to prove. (1') is a statement that God *exists*. But God's existence is precisely what Anselm wants to *prove*. Merely claiming that something exists does not constitute[19] evidence that it exists. Construed[20] in such a way (1') is merely a dogmatic[21] claim. In Anselm's defense, however, one can argue that the first premise is clearly not a claim that God simply exists, but that He at the very least exists in an unexemplified way. He explicitly states that God is something nothing greater than which can be *conceived*. Such is not a claim of God's exemplified existence and therefore Anselm has not begged the question (unless there is no essential[22] difference between exemplified and unexemplified existence).

If we choose (1") as the proper interpretation of 'is', then the statement is tantamount[23] to a definition.[24] Nothing of an exemplified sort logically follows from a definition because definitions pertain[25] only to the meanings of words. For example, from the definition that bachelors are (=) unmarried men exceeding the age of 21 years, the exemplified existence of such creatures simply does not follow. Look at it this way; it happens to be the case that bachelors do exist in an exemplified manner. However, it is possible that we could gather up all the bachelors in the world and exterminate[26] them. Such a state of affairs, namely, a world void of exemplified bachelors would in no way affect the definition of a bachelor. The point is that definitions simply have no *logical* connection with exemplified existence. Hence, if we construe the first premise of Anselm's argument as one of definition, then it will not be logically possible to derive God's exemplified existence which, of course, is his goal.

In conclusion, the question arises, is premise (1), *in fact,* a definition? If it is, it would seem that Anselm has not derived God's exemplified existence. If it is not, then perhaps Anselm has accomplished what he set out to prove.

Suggested Readings: The Ontological Argument; Anselm

1. Copleston, F., *A History of Philosophy*, Vol. II (N.Y.: Doubleday & Co., 1994) Chapter 15.
2. Edwards, Rem B., *Reason and Religion: An Introduction to the Philosophy of Religion* (N.Y.: Harcourt Brace Jovanovich, Inc., 1972), Chapter 9.

[18] *fallacy:* a statement or thesis that is inconsistent with logic or fact and thus renders the conclusion invalid.
[19] *constitute:* to make up; be the components or elements of.
[20] *construe:* to interpret.
[21] *dogmatic:* characterized by an authoritative, arrogant assertion of unproven or unprovable principles.
[22] *essential:* of or constituting the intrinsic, fundamental nature of something.
[23] *tantamount:* equivalent in effect or value.
[24] One rule of thumb for testing for a definition is to switch the subject and predicate terms and if the resulting statement means the same as the original one, then it is a definition. That is the fundamental point behind the use of the equals sign.
[25] *pertain:* involve, concern, have to do with.
[26] *exterminate:* to get rid of by destroying completely.

3. Flew, Anthony, and MacIntyre, Alasdair, (eds.), *New Essays in Philosophical Theology* (New York, Macmillan, 1955), pp. 31-41 and Chapter 4.

4. Hartshorne, Charles, *Anselm's Discovery* (LaSalle, Ill., Open Court, 1962).

5. _____, *Man's Vision of God* (Hamden, Conn., Archon Books, 1964), Chapter 9.

6. _____, *The Logic of Perfection* (LaSalle, Ill., Open Court, 1962), Chapters 1-2.

7. Hick, John, *Philosophy of Religion* (Englewood Cliffs, N.J., Prentice-Hall, 1963), pp. 15-20.

8. Mackie, J. L., *The Miracle of Theism: Arguments For and Against the Existence of God* (Oxford: The Clarendon Press, 1982), Chapter 3.

9. Malcolm, Norman, "Anselm's Ontological Arguments," *The Philosophical Review*, Vol. LXIX (January 1960).

10. Miller, Ed., *God and Reason: An Invitation to Philosophical Theology*, 2nd edition (Englewood Cliffs, N.J.: Prentice-Hall, 1995), Chapter 2.

11. Plantinga, Alvin, *The Ontological Argument: From St. Anselm to Contemporary Philosophers* (Garden City, N.J., Doubleday, 1965).

12. Shaffer, Jerome, "Existence, Predication, and the Ontological Argument," *Mind*, Vol. LXXI (July, 1962), pp. 307-25.

Chapter 15:
The Ontological Argument;
Anselm

Name_____

Date _____

1. How does Anselm view the relation between reason and faith regarding God's existence?

2. Explain the difference between exemplified and unexemplified existence.

3. What is Anselm's concept of God?

4. What is meant by "necessary existence"?

5. Why is the concept of necessary existence critical to Anselm's argument?

6. Explain in detail the form of reasoning Anselm uses in his ontological argument.

❧ READINGS ❧

The Ontological Argument

Anselm
Proslogium; In Behalf of the Fool; Anselm's Apologetic
(selections)

From *St. Anselm: Basic Writings*, translated by S. N. Deane (La Salle, Ill.: Open Court Publishing Co., 1962), pp. 1-2, 6-9, 149-152 and 158-159.

Anselm's Proslogium; *Or Discourse on The Existence of God*

Preface

. . . I began to ask myself whether there might be found a single argument which would require no other for its proof than itself alone: and alone would suffice to demonstrate that God truly exists, and that there is a supreme good requiring nothing else, which all other things require for their existence and well-being; and whatever we believe regarding the divine Being.

Although I often and earnestly directed my thought to this end, and at some times that which I sought seemed to be just within my reach, while again it wholly evaded my mental vision, at last in despair I was about to cease, as if from the search for a thing which could not be found. But when I wished to exclude this thought altogether, lest, by busying my mind to no purpose, it should keep me from other thoughts, in which I might be successful; then more and more, though I was unwilling and shunned it, it began to force itself upon me, with a kind of importunity. So, one day, when I was exceedingly wearied with resisting its importunity, in the very conflict of my thoughts, the proof of which I had despaired offered itself, so that I eagerly embraced the thoughts which I was strenuously repelling.

Chapter I

. . . I do not endeavor, O Lord, to penetrate thy sublimity, for in no wise do I compare my understanding with that; but I long to understand in some degree thy truth, which my heart believes and loves. For I do not seek to understand that I may believe, but I believe in order to understand. For this also I believe,--that unless I believed, I should not understand.

Chapter II

Truly there is a God, although the fool hath said in his heart, There is no God.

And so, Lord, do thou, who dost give understanding to faith, give me, so far as thou knowest it to be profitable, to understand that thou art as we believe; and that thou art that which we believe. And, indeed, we believe that thou art a being than which nothing greater can be conceived. Or is there no such nature, since the fool hath said in his heart there is no God? (Psalms xiv. 1). But, at any rate, this very fool, when he hears of this being of which I speak--a being than which nothing greater can be conceived--understands what he hears, and what he understands is in his understanding; although he does not understand it to exist.

For, it is one thing for an object to be in the understanding, and another to understand that the object exists. When a painter first conceives of what he will afterwards perform, he has it in his understanding, but he does not yet understand it to be, because he has not yet performed it. But after he has made the painting, he both has it in his understanding, and he understands that it exists, because he has made it.

Hence, even the fool is convinced that something exists in the understanding, at least, than which nothing greater can be conceived. For, when he hears of this, he understands it. And whatever is understood, exists in the understanding. And assuredly that, than which nothing greater can be conceived, cannot exist in the understanding alone. For, suppose it exists in the understanding alone: then it can be conceived to exist in reality; which is greater.

Therefore, if that, than which nothing greater can be conceived, exists in the understanding alone, the very being, than which nothing greater can be conceived, is one, than which a greater can be conceived. But obviously this is impossible. Hence, there is no doubt that there exists a being, than which nothing greater can be conceived, and it exists both in the understanding and in reality.

Chapter III

God cannot be conceived not to exist.--God is that, than which nothing greater can be conceived.--That which can be conceived not to exist is not God.

And it assuredly exists so truly, that it cannot be conceived not to exist. For, it is possible to conceive of a being which cannot be conceived not to exist; and this is greater than one which can be conceived not to exist. Hence, if that, than which nothing greater can be conceived, can be conceived not to exist, it is not that, than which nothing greater can be conceived. But this is an irreconcilable contradiction. There is, then, so truly a being than which nothing greater can be conceived to exist, that it cannot even be conceived not to exist; and this being thou art, O Lord, our God.

So truly, therefore, dost thou exist, O Lord, my God, that thou canst not be conceived not to exist; and rightly. For, if a mind could conceive of a being better than thee, the creature would rise above the Creator; and this is most absurd. And, indeed, whatever else there is, except thee alone, can be conceived not to exist. To thee alone, therefore, it belongs to exist more truly than all other beings, and hence in a higher degree than all others. For, whatever else exists does not exist so truly, and hence in a less degree it belongs to it to exist. Why, then, has the fool said in his heart, there is no God (Psalms xiv. 1), since it is so evident, to a rational mind, that thou dost exist in the highest degree of all? Why, except that he is dull and a fool?

In Behalf of The Fool *by Gaunilon, monk of Marmoutier*

5. . . . if it should be said that a being which cannot be even conceived in terms of any fact, is in the understanding, I do not deny that this being is, accordingly, in my understanding. But since through this fact it can in no wise attain to real existence also, I do not yet concede to it that existence at all, until some certain proof of it shall be given.

For he who says that this being exists, because otherwise the being which is greater than all will not be greater than all, does not attend strictly enough to what he is saying. For I do not yet say, no, I even deny or doubt that this being is greater than any real object. Nor do I concede to it any other existence than this (if it should be called existence) which it has when the mind, according to a word merely heard, tries to form the image of an object absolutely unknown to it.

How, then, is the veritable existence of that being proved to me from the assumption, by hypothesis, that it is greater than all other beings? For I should still deny this, or doubt your demonstration of it, to this extent, that I should not admit that this being is in my understanding and concept even in the way in which many objects whose real existence is uncertain and doubtful, are in my understanding and concept. For it should be proved first that this being itself really exists somewhere; and then, from the fact that it is greater than all, we shall not hesitate to infer that it also subsists in itself.

6. For example: it is said that somewhere in the ocean is an island, which, because of the difficulty, or rather the impossibility, of discovering what does not exist, is called the lost island. And they say that this island has an inestimable wealth of all manner of riches and delicacies in greater abundance than is told of the Islands of the Blest; and that having no owner or inhabitant, it is more excellent than all other countries, which are inhabited by mankind, in the abundance with which it is stored.

Now if some one should tell me that there is such an island, I should easily understand his words, in which there is no difficulty. But suppose that he went on to say, as if by a logical inference: "You can no longer doubt that this island which is more excellent than all lands exist, somewhere, since you have no doubt that it is in your understanding. And since it is more excellent not to be in the understanding alone, but to exist both in the understanding and in reality, for this reason it must exist. For if it does not exist, any land which really exists will be more excellent than it; and so the island already understood by you to be more excellent will not be more excellent."

If a man should try to prove to me by such reasoning that this island truly exists, and that its existence should no longer be doubted, either I should believe that he was jesting, or I know not which I ought to regard as the greater fool: myself, supposing that I should allow this proof; or him, if he should suppose that he had established with any certainty the existence of this island. For he ought to show first that the hypothetical excellence of this island exists as a real and indubitable fact, and in no wise as any unreal object, or one whose existence is uncertain, in my understanding.

7. This, in the mean time, is the answer the fool could make to the arguments urged against him. When he is assured in the first place that this being is so great that its nonexistence is not even conceivable, and that this in turn is proved on no other ground than the fact that otherwise it will not be greater than all things, the fool may make the same answer, and say: When did I say that any such being exists in reality, that is, a being greater than all others?--that on this ground it should be proved to me that it also exists in reality to such a degree that it cannot even be conceived not to exist? Whereas in the first place it should be in some way proved that a nature which is higher, that is, greater and better, than all other natures, exists; in order that from this we may then be able to prove all attributes which necessarily the being that is greater and better than all possesses.

Moreover, it is said that the nonexistence of this being is inconceivable. It might better be said, perhaps, that its nonexistence, or the possibility of its nonexistence, is unintelligible. For according to the true meaning of the word, unreal objects are unintelligible. Yet their existence is conceivable in the way in which the fool conceived of the nonexistence of God. I am most certainly aware of my own existence; but I know, nevertheless, that my nonexistence is possible. As to that supreme being, moreover, which God is, I understand without any doubt both his existence, and the impossibility of his nonexistence. Whether, however so long as I am most positively aware of my existence, I can conceive of my nonexistence, I am not sure. But if I can, why can I not conceive of the nonexistence of whatever else I know with the same certainty? If, however, I cannot, God will not be the only being of which it can be said, it is impossible to conceive of his nonexistence.

Anselm's Apologetic[1]

Chapter III

But, you say, it is as if one should suppose an island in the ocean, which surpasses all lands in its fertility, and which, because of the difficulty, or rather the impossibility, of discovering what does not exist, is called a lost island; and should say that there can be no doubt that this island truly exists in reality, for this reason, that one who hears it described easily understands what he hears.

Now I promise confidently that if any man shall devise anything existing either in reality or in concept alone (except that than which a greater cannot be conceived) to which he can adapt the sequence of my reasoning, I will discover that thing, and will give him his lost island, not to be lost again.

But it now appears that this being than which a greater is inconceivable cannot be conceived not to be, because it exists on so assured a ground of truth; for otherwise it would not exist at all.

Hence, if any one says that he conceives this being not to exist, I say that at the time when he conceives of this either he conceives of a being than which a greater is inconceivable, or he does not conceive at all. If he does not conceive, he does not conceive of the nonexistence of that of which he does not conceive. But if he does conceive, he certainly conceives of a being which cannot be even conceived not to exist. For if it

---

[1]   *apologetic:* defending in writing or speech; vindicating [editor's note].

could be conceived not to exist, it could be conceived to have a beginning and an end. But this is impossible.

He, then, who conceives of this being conceives of a being which cannot be even conceived not to exist; but he who conceives of this being does not conceive that it does not exist; else he conceives what is inconceivable. The nonexistence, then, of that than which a greater cannot be conceived is inconceivable.

Name_____

Date _____

1. What is the significance of Anselm opening his argument with a prayer?

2. What example does Anselm use to demonstrate the difference between existing "in the understanding" (unexemplified being) and existing "in reality" (exemplified being)?

3. What example does Gaunilon use to discredit Anselm's argument and how does he use it?

4. How does Anselm respond to Gaunilon's argument?

5. What does the word 'apologetic' mean?

16 The Cosmological Argument; St. Thomas Aquinas

❧ B I O G R A P H Y ❧

St. Thomas Aquinas was born in 1224 not far from Naples, Italy. He was a product of a rather wealthy background, his father being the Count of Aquino. When young Thomas reached the age of five his parents placed him in the Benedictine Abbey of Montecassino where he remained until 1239. At the age of fourteen he went to the University of Naples where there was a convent of Dominican friars, a lifestyle to which Thomas was attracted. This greatly disturbed his family who by all accounts would have preferred that he remain in the Benedictine order at Montecassino, one believed by them to be of greater prestige. Such opposition on behalf of his family led them to kidnap Thomas while he was on his way to Paris by way of Bologna. He was subsequently held captive in Aquino for approximately one year. Only by his determination to remain loyal to his Order was he able to eventually make his way to Paris.

It is probably the case that Aquinas remained at Paris until 1248 when he accompanied St. Albert the Great to Cologne (Germany) where the latter founded a "chapter" of the Dominican Order. Albert the Great was indeed a genuine mentor to Thomas. Albert was open-minded. His student, Thomas, was one who was capable of synthesizing the rather "free-wheeling" notions of his teacher into the joint framework of philosophy and theology. In a real sense, they were an unbeatable team. On the one hand, Albert provided the ideas and on the other hand, Thomas possessed the intellectual powers to systematize them. In his Summa Theologica Aquinas maintained that the existence of God can be demonstrated in five ways, the first three of which are cosmological proofs. The fourth way is based on the reasoning that the degrees of perfection necessarily imply the existence of a best, i.e., a supreme being. His fifth proof is a teleological argument.

In 1252 Aquinas returned to Paris from Cologne where he continued his studies and lectured at the University of Paris. It was in 1256 that he was awarded the equivalent of a doctoral degree in theology. He continued to teach at this institution as Dominican professor until 1259. Because of an internal political struggle between the Dominican and Franciscan factions at the University, Aquinas returned to Italy where he taught theology at the Stadium Curial.

> *In 1268 he returned to Paris where he remained for four years, after which it was requested of him to direct a Dominican center of study in Naples. Illness forced him to discontinue his teaching and writing toward the end of 1273. Then Pope Gregory X summoned Aquinas to accompany him to the Council of Lyon. It was on that trip to Lyon that he fell ill and died near his hometown on March 7, 1274.*

How a given argument for the existence of God is categorized is determined by the type of evidence and/or reasons that are offered in support of His existence. The cosmological argument is derived from the Greek word *cosmos* which means world order. By orderliness in this case philosophers do not mean how the world functions in a manner which suggests some sort of plan like a patch-work quilt, namely, something well designed. Rather, they are here concerned with the nature of the conceptual underpinnings of the functioning of the world (universe). Simply stated, how does the world go round and round? It does so by means of cause and effect. We know as a matter of common sense that every effect has a cause. We know also that there is a universe. Hence, *it* must have had a cause otherwise it would not be here. Just what is the nature of the cause of the universe? That is a question which is of just as much interest to the philosopher as it is to the physicist. Some physicists have proposed the "big-bang" theory by which the creation of the universe was the result of a unique combination of atoms. Suddenly, and in some mysterious manner, the world (universe) simply appeared. The theory has some credibility[1] if all that is being considered is the earth or our solar system. It is indeed possible that by some unique combination of already existing elements there all of a sudden occurred the creation of the aforementioned celestial[2] bodies. But keep in mind that in order for such a happening to take place one must *presuppose* some preexisting elements in the universe. Why? Because it is illogical to argue that something, in this case the solar system, can come from nothing. To so suppose simply does not make sense. Now if we push the process back a step, the creation of the universe at large becomes the central issue. Just how did it come about? Here we are faced with a double headed problem. (1) Either there must have been some existing elements prior to the beginning of the universe which via[3] an accident of fate combined bringing the world into existence as we now know it, or (2) the universe simply came into existence out of nothing. If (1) is the case, then we are faced with an infinite regress for it is then legitimate to ask where those preexisting elements came from. If such elements derived their existence from pre-preexisting elements, then where did they come from and so on *ad infinitum*[4]? If (2) is the case, then the above illogical result once again manifests itself, namely, that the universe was "born" out of nothingness.

Thomas Aquinas, in light of the above dilemma[5], argued that the only plausible cause of the universe was God. He did this by three cosmological proofs.[6] The first two arguments are of the same form and therefore differ only in content. They are what is known as disjunctive syllogisms.

---

[1] *credible:* worthy of belief.

[2] *celestial:* of or pertaining to the sky or visible heavens.

[3] *via:* by way of.

[4] *ad infinitum:* without limit.

[5] *dilemma:* a situation involving choice between equally unsatisfactory alternatives.

[6] Aquinas formulated five arguments for the existence of God, the first three of which are cosmological in nature.

> 1] A or B
>
> 2] not A
>
> Therefore   3] B

A disjunctive claim states that either A obtains [is the case] or B obtains or both A and B obtain. What a disjunctive statement rules out is that neither A nor B obtains. In other words, at the very least one of the disjuncts [in this case A or B] must obtain. The second premise states that A does not obtain. Therefore, it must be the case that B obtains. Such is a valid form of reasoning.

Let us examine the first two arguments.

I.

1. Some things are in motion (verified by sense experience[7]).
2. If anything is in motion, it is moved by another mover.
3. If there is another mover, then there is a first mover (since it is impossible to regress to infinity in the order of movers and things moved at least from an ontological as opposed to a temporal point of view). Therefore,
4. There is a first mover.
5. This first mover we call God.

II.

1. Something is changing (verified by sense experience).
2. If anything is changing, there is at least one cause of that change.
3. If there is at least one cause of change, then there is a first cause of change (since it is impossible to regress to infinity in the order of such causes at least from an ontological as opposed to a temporal point of view). Therefore,
4. There is a first cause.
5. This first cause of change we call God.

First of all, it should be noted that these two arguments basically make the same claim. The first premise[8] of each pertains to the fact that causation exists in the universe. The difference is one of emphasis, namely, between motion and change. Aquinas says, "By 'motion' we mean nothing else than the change of something from a state of potentiality into a state of actuality". A state of potentiality is one of possibility for developing into a state of reality. Change means to be altered (i.e., modified) in some way or other.

The second premise of both arguments states that there can be no effect without a cause; that is to say, nothing can be moved or changed without something to move or change it. Nothing merely potential has the power to actualize itself. Changes of any type must be initiated by something already actualized.[9] Sense experience verifies[10] that this is

---

[7] *sense experience:* that which is provided by the five senses.

[8] *premise:* a previous statement or assertion that serves as the basis for an argument.

[9] It is interesting to note that the renowned physicist Isaac Newton (1642-1727 A.D.) concluded the same, namely, that a body at rest remains at rest unless acted upon by an equal and opposite force.

[10] *verify:* to prove the truth of by the presentation of evidence or testimony; substantiate.

true. Can you think of any motions or changes that are *self-initiated*? Perhaps one could argue that human beings possess free will which provides the basis for self-initiated activity. For example, if I freely choose to raise my arm, then I cause my arm to rise. The causal activity of me raising my arm begins with me. Nothing caused me to raise my arm otherwise it would not have been an act of free will. This may be true but it does not undermine the truth of the second premises of Aquinas' first two arguments. We as creatures (supposedly) endowed with free will did not create ourselves, nor did we create the world in which we live.

The rub comes with the third premise of both arguments. They appear to contradict the second premise of each. On the one hand, Aquinas claims that every effect has a cause *ad infinitum*. On the other hand, he states that if we push the causal sequences back far enough, there must be a first uncaused cause which started the whole ball rolling, namely, the universe at large. In order to dispel the apparent contradiction some explanation is necessary. He makes a distinction between temporal[11] and ontological[12] infinity. In order to understand the difference it is best to think of the fact that every cause has an effect in terms of the Great Chain of Being. The term 'Great' refers to the universe at large. And according to the second premise of each argument the Chain is continuous in the following pictorial manner:

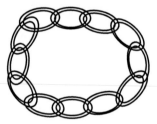

Given this view of causation it appears that there is no end to the causal process. And that is true from a temporal point of view as Aquinas sees it. It is indeed the case that one event causes another *ad infinitum* through time. However, if one looks at the *overall* chain of causal events, it becomes important to question how the chain *itself* came into being. Granted, the chain of causal events may go on through temporal infinity, but *how* did the chain at the outset come to be? This issue is analogous[13] to looking at a perpetual motion machine and asking who built it. This is an ontological question. Now in order to avoid an infinite regress of causes which precludes[14] ever getting to the beginning and therefore origin of the universe, Aquinas reasons that there must be a first cause which is itself uncaused. Although the notion of an uncaused cause runs counter to our understanding of the concept of a cause always being itself caused, Aquinas argues that we simply have no choice but to accept it. Concluding that there must be an uncaused cause is the lesser of two evils, as it were. Given such a viewpoint the apparent contradiction between the 2nd and 3rd premises of the first two arguments is resolved.

The disjunctive nature of the second argument can be seen by restating it in the following manner.

---

[11]   *temporal:* of or pertaining to, or limited by time.

[12]   *ontology:* the branch of metaphysics dealing with the nature of being, reality or ultimate substance.

[13]   *analogous:* similarity, correspondence, parallelism.

[14]   *preclude:* to make impossible, especially in advance.

> 1] Either [A] you can go on to infinity in the order of
>   causes and things caused or [B] you cannot.
>
> 2] Not [A].
>
> Therefore   3] [B] You cannot go on to infinity in the order of
>   causes and things caused.

This means that there must be a first cause which is itself uncaused. Aquinas thinks it is reasonable that this uncaused cause is God.

This leads naturally to Aquinas' third cosmological argument. The third argument is an example of the form *reductio ad absurdum* which means to reduce to absurdity. If an assumption leads to a conclusion that is either contradictory or just plain false, one must reject the assumption. Logically speaking, such rejection means negating the assumption. In Aquinas' third argument we see the assumption being stated in premise 3 manifested by the word "if." If means an assumption is being made. This is a very common way of reasoning and you do it frequently in your decision-making process. Let's say that you want to go party and you have an exam the following day. Furthermore, you want to do well on the exam. You think, "*If* I go party tonight, *then* there is a high degree of likelihood that I will not do well on the exam." So what do you decide to do given that you want to do well on the exam? You reject going out and partying because that is contrary to what you want most which is to do well on the exam. Such rejection is the equivalent of negating the assumption that led to the unacceptable conclusion, namely not doing well on the exam.

III.

1. Some things come into being and go out of being.
2. It follows that for such things, it is possible for them to exist or not exist. They do not exist necessarily.
3. If time is infinite, and if all things are capable of not existing, then the potentiality of not existing would eventually be actualized. There would then be nothing.
4. But something cannot come from nothing.
5. There are things (verified by our sense experience). Therefore,
6. It is false to say that there ever was literally nothing. Therefore,
7. It is impossible that *all* things should be capable of existing or not existing. Therefore,
8. There must be a necessary being.

Let us consider this argument step by step. The first premise is obviously true not from a micro but a macro point of view. That is, such things as chairs and human beings do, in fact, come into and go out of existence as the things they are, notwithstanding their molecular makeup in terms of the law of conservation of energy. Second, given this macro view of such entities, it follows that they can either exist or not exist. In other words, such things can be conceived not to exist given the fact that they do occasionally cease to exist. This is what it means for something to exist in a contingent manner. The existence of such things is not necessary.

The third premise is the assumption needed for a *reductio ad absurdum* argument. He asks us to suppose (a) that time is infinite (which is not altogether outrageous either from a physical or philosophical point of view) and (b) that all things in the universe are by their very nature contingent. Given such a supposition what would happen? He reasons that if such were the case the universe and all that therein is would eventually cease to exist and there would then be nothing, a total void. Let us view the situation from the point of view of the here and now. We know that there are things, otherwise we would not be here discussing the issue in the first place. Now let us suppose that everything that exists is capable of going out of existence. It follows that eventually everything *would* go out of existence. Why? Because, all possibilities are realized over an infinite amount of time. Minute as the possibility is that everything in the universe would cease to exist at the same instant, it is nevertheless a possibility and would eventually come to pass. There would be nothing; absolutely nothing, which entails[15] the nothingness of the universe itself. Such would be the logical conclusion following the assumption that the universe and all that there is is contingent in nature.

However, such a dismal picture has only been painted with respect to the future, predicated on the assumption that all things are contingent. What gives Aquinas' argument the ultimate muscle is that the same pattern of reasoning applies to the past. Given the above reasoning, let us begin again. Let us assume that time is infinite, only now that it is that way with respect to the past. Furthermore, let us assume that the universe and all that therein is is contingent, namely, that it is capable of going out of existence. Now, if all things are contingent, then given the fact that all possibilities no matter how minute, are realized over an infinite amount of time, then there would have come a time in the past when everything ceased to exist at precisely the same instant. At that point in time there would have been nothing. According to the reasoning of Aquinas such a result would have been inevitable and subsequently there would presently be nothing. But there is something, namely, you and me discussing the issue. Hence, so far as he is concerned, the only reasonable conclusion to draw is that not everything in the cosmos is contingent. The initial assumption that everything is contingent results in the conclusion that even before we could discuss the matter there would have been nothing. But since we are, in fact, here discussing the issue, it cannot be the case that *everything* is contingent (namely, capable of ceasing to exist). There simply must be something that must be, that exists necessarily, otherwise the whole ball game of existence would have long ago been over. And we know that we cannot get something from nothing. Hence, there must be something that exists in a manner other than in a contingent fashion.

Now since we know that individual things within the cosmos do in fact come and go out of existence, it must be the case that something greater exists for ever and ever. What could that something be? Here the 1st and 2nd proofs come into play. Recall that an analysis of those proofs construed God as the causal basis of the universe, namely, the Great Chain of Being. The third argument demonstrates that God is the *necessary* uncaused cause. The point is that there *must* be at least one "thing" that exists necessarily, namely something that *cannot* possibly go out of existence. After that, it is purely a semantic[16] issue. You may choose to call (that is, name) this necessary "force" or "entity" God or whatever. The point is that one cannot escape the necessity of such a necessary whatever!

---

[15]   *entail:* to have as a necessary consequence.

[16]   *semantics:* the study of the meanings of words.

Aquinas appears to have a convincing argument. But being consistent with philosophical tradition it is not without criticism. One such criticism concerns not the fact that all possibilities are realized (i.e., come to be) over an infinite amount of time, but whether the possibility of total (i.e., universal) nonexistence has yet to be actualized with respect to all things being contingent. The point is that perhaps that instant of total nonexistence has not yet occurred. In other words, we may be living on borrowed time. If such is the case, then one might reasonably argue that there is not necessarily a necessary "force" or "entity" which sustains the cosmos. Unfortunately, there is no way to resolve the issue. It turns on one's interpretation of infinity with respect to past time, namely, whether one emphasizes the past nature of past time or the future nature of past time. If one opts for the former then it would seem reasonable that all probabilities have indeed been realized. In other words, if time is infinite with respect to the past *ad infinitum*, then all such probabilities would have been realized. But if one interprets the situation in terms of infinite past time in an ongoing nature (i.e., with respect to the future), then perhaps not all the possibilities have been realized in which case the end of the universe would not have yet occurred in light of its (possible) contingent nature.

Aquinas has argued that the universe and all that therein is is contingent because *all* of our sense experience indicates that it is. God provides the necessity and is a being separate from the universe. During Aquinas' lifetime a group known as naturalists took issue with him. The naturalists argued that whereas something is necessary, we need not (nor should not) identify that necessary something as God. Why not dispense with God altogether and maintain that it is the universe itself that is the necessary being. The necessity of the universe is manifested through the law of conservation of energy. The necessary elements of the universe are its basic elements. They are neither created nor destroyed. All that is contingent are the various and sundry arrangements of the basic elements. The arrangements come and go but the basic elements remain the same. God playing a role in all of this simply constitutes ontological extra baggage.

This led Aquinas to identify; that is, equate the universe and all that therein is with God. This is known as pantheism and eventually got him in hot water because pantheism is inconsistent with established Roman Catholic theology. After charges of heresy were brought against Thomas, he abandoned this position. That, however, does not undermine the possibility of God being dispensible[17] from a cosmological point of view.

Suggested Readings: The Cosmological Argument; St. Thomas Aquinas

1. Burrill, Donald R., (ed.), *The Cosmological Arguments* (Garden City, N.Y., Doubleday, 1967).
2. Copleston, F., *A History of Philosophy,* Vol. II (N.Y.: Doubleday & Co., 1994), Chapter 34.
3. Craig, William L., *The Kalam Cosmological Argument* (N.Y.: Barnes and Noble, 1977).
4. Edwards, Rem B., *Reason and Religion: An Introduction to the Philosophy of Religion* (N.Y.: Harcourt Brace Jovanovich, Inc., 1972), Chapter 10.

---

[17] *dispense:* to get rid of; do away with.

5. Kenny, Anthony, *Five Ways: St. Thomas' Proofs of God's Existence* (London: Routledge and Kegan Paul, 1969).
6. Martin, C. B., *Religion Belief* (Ithaca, N.Y.:, Cornell University Press, 1959), Chapter 9.
7. Meynell, Hugo A., *The Intelligible Universe: A Cosmological Argument* (N.Y.: Barnes and Noble, 1982).
8. Miller, E. L., *God and Reason: An Invitation to Philosophical Theology*, 2nd ed. (Englewood Cliffs, N.J.: Prentice-Hall, 1995) Chapters 1 and 3.
9. Munitz, Milton K., *The Mystery of Existence* (New York, Appleton-Century-Crofts, 1965), Part III.
10. Swineburne, R., *The Existence of God* (Oxford: The Clarendon Press, 1979) Chapter 7 and 8.

STUDY
QUESTIONS

Name_____

Date _____

Chapter 16:
The Cosmological
Argument;
Aquinas

1. What concept does Aquinas use as the starting point for each of the three cosmological proofs?

2. What is the dilemma Aquinas faces in the first two cosmological arguments?

3. What is the difference between temporal and ontological infinity?

4. What is the value of Aquinas' third argument?

5. What point does the naturalist make with respect to the third argument?

❧ R E A D I N G S ❧

The Cosmological Arguments

St. Thomas Aquinas
Summa Theologica
Part I
Question II
Third Article (selections)

The *"Summa Theologica" of St. Thomas Aquinas*, translated by Fathers of the English Dominican Province (London: R. and T. Washbourne, Ltd., 1911), pp. 24-26.

Third Article

Whether God Exists?

We proceed thus to the Third Article

Objection 1. It seems that God does not exist; because if one of two contraries be infinite, the other would be altogether destroyed. But the word 'God' means that He is infinite goodness. If, therefore, God existed, there would be no evil discoverable: but there is evil in the world. Therefore God does not exist.

Obj. 2. Further, it is superfluous to suppose that, what can be accounted for by a few principles has been produced by many. But it seems that everything that appears in the world can be accounted for by other principles, supposing God did not exist. For all natural things can be reduced to one principle, which is nature; and all things that happen intentionally can be reduced to one principle, which is human reason, or will. Therefore there is no need to suppose God's existence.

On the contrary, It is said in the person of God: *I am Who am* (Exod. iii. 14).

I answer that, The existence of God can be proved in five ways. The first and more manifest way is the argument from motion. It is certain, and evident to our senses some things are in motion. Whatever is in motion is moved by another, for nothing can be in motion except it have a potentiality for that towards which it is being moved; whereas a thing moves inasmuch as it is in act. By 'motion' we mean nothing else than the reduction of something from a state of potentiality into a state of actuality. Nothing, however, can be reduced from a state of potentiality into a state of actuality, unless by something already in a state of actuality. Thus that which is actually hot as fire, makes wood, which is potentially hot, to be actually hot, and thereby moves and changes it. Now it is not possible that the same thing should be at once in a state of actuality and potentiality from the same point of view, but only from different points of view.

What is actually hot cannot simultaneously be only potentially hot; still, it is simultaneously potentially cold. It is therefore impossible that from the same point of view and in the same way anything should be both mover and moved, or that it should move itself. Therefore, whatever is in motion must be put in motion by another. If that by which it is put in motion be itself put in motion, then this also must needs be put in motion by another, and that by another again. This cannot go on to infinity, because then there would be no first mover, and consequently, no other mover--seeing that subsequent movers only move inasmuch as they are put in motion by the first mover; as the staff only moves because it is put in motion by the hand. Therefore it is necessary to arrive at a First Mover, put in motion by no other; and this everyone understands to be God.

The second way is from the formality of efficient[1] causation. In the world of sense we find there is an order of efficient causation. There is no case known (neither is it, indeed, possible) in which a thing is found to be the efficient cause of itself; for so it would be prior to itself, which is impossible. In efficient causes it is not possible to go on to infinity, because in all efficient causes following in order, the first is the cause of the intermediate cause, and the intermediate is the cause of the ultimate cause, whether the intermediate cause be several, or one only. To take away the cause is to take away the effect. Therefore, if there be no first cause among efficient causes, there will be no ultimate, nor any intermediate, cause. If in efficient causes it is possible to go on to infinity, there will be no first efficient cause, neither will there be an ultimate effect, nor any intermediate efficient causes; all of which is plainly false. Therefore it is necessary to put forward a First Efficient Cause, to which everyone gives the name of God.

The third way is taken from possibility and necessity, and runs thus. We find in nature things that could either exist or not exist, since they are found to be generated, and to corrupt; and, consequently, they can exist, and then not exist. It is impossible for these always to exist, for that which can one day cease to exist must be at some time have not existed. Therefore, if everything could cease to exist, then at one time there could have been nothing in existence. If this were true, even now there would be nothing in existence, because that which does not exist only begins to exist by something already existing. Therefore, if at one time nothing was in existence, it would have been impossible for anything to have begun to exist; and thus even now nothing would be in existence--which is absurd. Therefore, not all beings are merely possible, but there must exist something the existence of which is necessary. But every necessary thing either has its necessity caused by another, or not. It is impossible to go on to infinity in necessary things which have their necessity caused by another, as has been already proved in regard to efficient causes. Therefore we cannot but postulate the existence of some being having of itself its own necessity, and not receiving it from another, but rather causing in others their necessity. This all men speak of as God.

.   .   .

Reply Obj. 1. As Augustine says: *Since God is wholly good, He would not allow any evil to exist in His works, unless His omnipotence and goodness were such as to bring good even out of evil.* This is part of the infinite goodness of God, that He should allow evil to exist, and out of it produce good.

---

[1]   *efficient:* directly producing an effect or result [editor's note].

Reply Obj. 2. Since nature works out its determinate end under the direction of a higher agent, whatever is done by nature must needs be traced back to God, as to its first cause. So also whatever is done designedly must also be traced back to some higher cause other than human reason or will, for these can suffer change and are defective; whereas things capable of motion and of defect must be traced back to an immovable and self-necessary first principle.

1. What does Aquinas mean by "motion"?

2. Why cannot something be both "moved" and "mover"?

3. With regard to the past, why is it impossible to proceed to infinity in the order of causes and things caused?

4. Why does Aquinas think that there is no incompatibility between an omnipotent, omnibeneficent being and the existence of evil?

5. Explain in detail the form of reasoning Aquinas uses in his first two cosmological arguments.

6. Explain in detail the form of reasoning Aquinas uses in his third cosmological argument.

17

The Teleological Argument; William Paley

The term 'teleological' is derived from the Greek word *telos* which means purpose, goal or end. Although such notions are not synonymous[1], they entail[2] the same sphere of activity. That is, there is no purpose without some goal or end to be achieved. Just think about it. It would be rather absurd for someone to claim that they had some purpose in mind without at the same time having something they wanted to accomplish. The two concepts go hand in hand. Such notions are said to be correlative; that is, although they are not synonymous, they are nevertheless defined in terms of one another.

Furthermore, the notion of a purpose and, therefore, some goal entails that there is someone who has a purpose and a goal. Purposes just do not exist in an unattached fashion. This is born out by imagining someone going into a store and asking for a dozen purposes. That simply does not

---

[1] *synonymous:* having the character of a synonym; alike or nearly alike in meaning or significance.

[2] *entail:* to have as a necessary accompaniment or consequence.

make sense. Purposes are attached to creatures that have the capacity to possess them.

In addition, the goal towards which the purpose is directed usually involves some game plan, some plan of attack whereby the goal can be achieved. This can be readily seen with respect to the process of playing a game. Usually, there is some sort of strategy, a master plan, a strategic design if you will. Here the crucial point is that if some sort of design can be detected, then one can be sure that there is a "master-mind" behind it. To be sure, goals can be achieved without some plan or design, but if such can be isolated, one can be confident that there is a creature capable of such design behind the scenes. Why? Because plans or designs simply do not exist (i.e., they do not make sense) without the presupposition of some such being for the same reason that purposes do not exist unattached.

A teleological argument is one which offers evidence indicative[3] of some sort of purposeful design and/or activity within the universe by which one can reasonably conclude that there must be a designer of such a cosmos[4] which would fit the Judeo-Christian concept of God. Keep in mind that such a being is conceived to be one which is omnipotent (all-powerful), omniscient (all-knowing), omnipresent (ever-present) and omnibeneficient (all-good). The issue now becomes whether or not the universe manifests some sort of design. If so, then it would appear reasonable that there must *be* a master mind as the creator of it all. So the task of a teleological argument lies in providing cold, hard evidence of design throughout the universe; not just evidence of occasional design, but overall design. But is there such evidence? Here we come down to the nitty-gritty of the matter. The central issue with respect to any teleological argument for the existence of God is whether or not it is reasonable to conclude that the universe is an example of design and, therefore, the product of some divine designer. What sort of evidence could one compile to reasonably conclude that such a designer exists?

It just so happens that there is a great deal of such evidence. Let us consider, for example, the entire phylogenetic scale. One can argue that the process of evolution, the phenomenon[5] of species within the biosphere[6] changing in those ways necessary in order to survive, indicates some sort of design, namely, a design that was not static at the initial point of creation, but a design that permitted such species the potential for change. Such a potential for change was *out of their control. They* had no choice in the matter. Such potential was there at the outset. But where did such a potential come from? Would it not be reasonable to conclude that such a phenomenon when applied to the entire biosphere came from a higher source, namely, God? That *some* species were not capable of adapting to their environment and, therefore, became extinct is no detriment[7] to such a conclusion. So long as the *potential* was there, the point stands. It is obvious that the environment can change so rapidly that the evolutionary process can be, and is occasionally, "nipped in the bud". For example, dinosaurs became extinct because they could not adapt to a rapidly changing environment. But the potential for adaptation was there.

---

3   *indicative:* pointing out; giving intimation or knowledge (of something not visible or obvious); suggestive.

4   *cosmos:* the universe conceived of as an orderly and harmonious system.

5   *phenomenon:* any fact, circumstance or experience that is apparent to the senses and that can be scientifically described or appraised.

6   *biosphere:* the sphere of living organisms.

7   *detriment:* injury or damage, or that which causes it.

Furthermore, it could be argued that some species had to become extinct *in order for* (a sign of purpose) other species to come to be and hence not only to survive, but to achieve some greater accomplishment. Here we are discussing the evolution of mentality. Dinosaurs could not think, but *homo sapiens*[8] can. Perhaps the entire process was *designed* for the purpose of one species to realize that there is some sort of design manifested by the very fact of evolution itself! That is a consideration at least worth thinking about. So long as the theory of evolution is a viable[9] one, such a consideration is worth taking into account.

There is another salient[10] example that the universe functions as a result of some overall design. It is twofold in nature. Consider the manner in which autonomous organisms function as constituents[11] of the biosphere. Not only do they (a) operate internally from a teleological point of view but, (b) externally as well. 'Internal' here means that over which an organism has no control. For example, in organisms with a central nervous system, the phenomenon of shivering serves the purpose of generating body heat. We have all had this experience, namely, convulsions of the body including rattling teeth. It serves a purpose; that is, to get us warm. We have no control over such situations. It simply happens. But what makes it happen? There are only two alternative explanations. Either that's just the way it is, or there must be some design of the organism that makes it possible to shiver so that it can get warm. Obviously, the organism did not design itself in such a manner.

Organisms manifest external purposeful behavior by way of overt[12] behavior. When one decides that pizza would be "just the ticket" for dinner, and there are no intervening circumstances, what happens? That's right--he goes to a pizza parlor and satisfies his desire. What better example could there be of purposeful activity? There is a goal to be had and, all other things being equal, it is achieved. Given such a case, it can be argued that no higher (i.e., divine) purpose is involved. To be sure, no reasonable divine being would have planned to have any given individual eat pizza of a given evening, but that is irrelevant. The central issue is whether or not such a finite creature could have such a goal in the first place if it were not for the fact that there was some higher being around who could create such a pizza-eating oriented creature. After all, it is not just a situation of an individual attempting to eat pizza. What about that creature (who appears autonomous[13]) that wants to eat that type of food. Does not that person fit into an overall game plan? The point is that there is no human activity that is totally autonomous and independent. But, once we get beyond autonomy from an organic point of view, then it becomes a real possibility that a greater sense of wholeness exists. This we can verify from our own experience. This world, not to mention the universe, does not function on the basis of the things within it operating in a manner unrelated to other "things". Does not the interrelatedness of the operation of all the aspects of the cosmos indicate that there is some Designer of the entire apparatus[14]? This brings us to the second point that the universe functions as a result of some overall design.

---

[8]   *homo sapiens:* The biological classification of human beings.

[9]   *viable:* workable and likely to survive or to have real meaning, pertinence, etc.

[10]   *salient:* standing out from the rest; noticeable; conspicuous; prominent.

[11]   *constituent:* component.

[12]   *overt:* open to view, public; apparent.

[13]   *autonomous:* functioning independently without control by others.

[14]   *apparatus:* any complex instrument, appliance or piece of machinery.

How can one explain the predictable behavior of molecules? We know that the constituents of the earth are not only limited in number, but that each such molecule has a given valency. Valency concerns the number of atoms surrounding any given molecule. Compatible valencies between molecules is the systematic basis of compound formation which constitutes[15] the foundation of the material objects we perceive, such as tables and chairs. Such is an eloquent[16] example of design, and one over which human beings have limited control. Here we are getting right down to the basic design of the world, if not the universe. Unless there were chemical bondings, in the sense of valencies "agreeing" with one another, we simply would not have the earth as we know it. It matters not if the earth was of a *different* form; that is, an organization of different basic component parts. A different organization nevertheless entails organization of some sort or other. At this point it is reasonable to ask whether or not such a phenomenon could conceivably happen by chance. Given the overwhelming amount of evidence that bespeaks design, what do you think?

The form of argumentation that William Paley uses is called an analogy. This is a very common sort of reasoning. It is based on a comparison between two things for the purpose of demonstrating shared characteristics. An analogy works in the following manner:

Object A	Object B

Characteristics

m	m
n	n
o	o
p	p
q	q
"	"
"	"
z	

Therefore Z

If in comparing two objects we determine many similar characteristics and eventually discover a characteristic in one object that we do not find in the other object, the method of analogy allows one to conclude that the second object must have the characteristic in question. The strength of the analogy typically [but not always] depends on the number of shared related characteristics. The more shared related characteristics the stronger the analogy. In practical everyday life arguing by analogy can be very effective. Philosophically speaking, however, arguing by analogy is very dangerous.

Paley's teleological argument proceeds in the following manner. Let us suppose that you were walking along a pathway and came upon a rock. Such an experience would not force you to conclude anything other than that a rock was a rock. But, if you were to happen onto a watch, even though you had never seen such a device, you would be led to conclude that it could not have just happened there in the same manner as did the rock. Such a conclusion would be verified by examining the watch. Upon observing its internal workings, it would be natural to conclude that such a mechanism did not come about by chance, but that it was the prod-

[15]   *constitute:* to make up; compose.

[16]   *eloquent:* vividly or movingly expressive or revealing.

uct of some intelligent design. After all, such an eloquent piece of machinery could not just happen. That it could is unreasonable. Now if you observe the world, not to mention the universe, it is obvious that it is equally as intricate in terms of its design from a mechanistic point of view. Consider, for example, an eye, any eye be it human or otherwise. It is a consummate[17] example of design. Is it not reasonable, therefore, to conclude that there must be a divine cosmic maker analogous[18] to a watchmaker, namely, one who not only constructed the universe and all that therein is, but who also makes it "tick"?

In reaction to such an argument it will do no good to claim that ignorance as to how such a machine works or its purpose is a justification that there is no aspect of design and, therefore, no designer. Merely by examining the watch (or world) one can ascertain[19] that what one is viewing is highly complicated and organized. That being the case, one is forced to conclude the existence of a designer.

Nor can one reasonably argue that because the machine (watch or world) has periodic breakdowns, namely, that it does not function in a perfect fashion, that it has no designer. The mere fact that there can be breakdowns indicates that there is some organized, namely, designed machine which is capable of breaking down. Without some sort of design, the concept of breaking down would be rendered[20] vacuous[21].

The element of chance has often been used as an attack on the teleological argument. What evidence is there that all the design manifested by the universe did not come about as a result of chance? As Paley astutely[22] observes, unless there is some *evidence* that the order we perceive[23] with respect to the universe is a result of chance, then such a criticism is clearly unfounded. The criticism lacks substance because without sufficient evidence to the contrary, it is simply more logical to conclude that what we perceive is, in fact, the result of design and therefore of a designer.

Furthermore, Paley argues that the substitution of a principle of order for God as the cause of the order that exists in the universe is unacceptable. If one looks at the interlocking nature of Nature, namely the ecosystem, it is clearly the result of design. Substitution of a principle of order for a creator is simply a semantic[24] move at best and not a very good one at that, as he poignantly[25] observed by his question, "Was a watch or an eye ever produced by a principle of order"?

Paley's argument seems rather convincing. But, there are some problems confronting it. If one conceives of God as one with the attributes pointed out above, (in this case, omnibeneficient) then it becomes questionable why He would create a world that is imperfect, namely, a mechanism that permits suffering and injustice. Injustice is prevalent worldwide. Consider, for example, the suffering as a result of man's inhuman-

---

[17] *consummate:* complete or perfect in every way; supreme.

[18] *analogy:* a relation of likeness between two things or of one thing to or with another.

[19] *ascertain:* to find out or learn for a certainty, by trial, examination, or experiment; to get to know.

[20] *render:* to cause to become.

[21] *vacuous:* empty.

[22] *astute:* having or displaying shrewd discernment and sagacity.

[23] *perceive:* to become aware of through sight, hearing, touch, taste or smell.

[24] *semantic:* of or relating to meaning in language.

[25] *poignant:* incisive, penetrating.

ity to man. How, given any sort of complimentary view of a deity, can such occurrences be accounted for as part of a well-designed machine?

There is an even more philosophically damaging criticism of Paley's argument. It has been observed that if one were to extend his argument by analogy to its fullest, one achieves a result that is totally unacceptable from a Judeo-Christian point of view. He argues that the universe is analogous to a watch, namely, a highly complex and organized machine. Given the facts, it must follow *by analogy* that since reason dictates that the watch had a designer, then the universe must also have had a designer. The difficulty with this line of reasoning lies in the fact that we know that if there was a designer of the watch, he must be a finite creature. If Paley's argument is to remain true to the analogical form of reasoning, then it must be the case that the creator of the universe must also be finite. But the Judeo-Christian concept of God is that he is infinite in nature. Hence, by basing his teleological argument on an analogical form of reasoning, Paley undercut his own position. However, one ought to understand that one need not approach the data from an analogical point of view. It may not be feasible[26] to argue for the existence of God by virtue of analogy. That does not entail that the evidence that constitutes the content of the argument does not establish in its own right teleological evidence for the existence of God.

There is another factor that needs to be taken into account. As sentient[27] beings we may only feel comfortable, while coping with this experience called life, only if we impose some order on the myriad[28] of experiences we have. We may in fact *impose* order on that which we perceive by formulating so-called laws of nature and, thereby, make some momentary sense out of the chaos, i.e., the universe at large in which we find ourselves. After all, what is a law of nature without a human being to formulate it? The point is that it may very well be the case that underneath it all the universe is not very well ordered, and that the order that we make out of it is self-imposed out of a matter of necessity in terms of our needs. Given this possibility, there is one issue that remains, namely how is it the case that human beings have the capacity and desire to organize in the *first* place? The issue as to whether this is a matter of divine design or not remains an open question.

Suggested Readings: The Teleological Argument; William Paley

1. Dawkins, Richard, *The Blind Watchmaker: Why the Evidence of Evolution Reveals a Universe without Design* (N.Y.: Norton, 1986).
2. Edwards, Rem B., *Reason and Religion: An Introduction to the Philosophy of Religion* (N.Y.: Harcourt Brace Jovanovich, Inc., 1972), Chapter 11.
3. Flew, Antony, *God and Philosophy* (New York, Dell, 1966), Chapter 3.
4. Hick, John, *Philosophy of Religion* (Englewood Cliffs, N.J., Prentice-Hall, 1963), pp. 23-26.

---

[26] *feasible:* capable of being done, executed, or effected; possible of realization.

[27] *sentient:* capable of sensation and consciousness.

[28] *myriad:* an indefinitely large number.

5. Matson, Wallace I., *The Existence of God* (Ithaca, N.Y., Cornell University Press, 1955), pp. 87-131.

6. Miller, Ed., *God and Reason: An Invitation to Philosophical Theology*, 2nd edition (Englewood Cliffs, N.J.: Prentice Hall, 1995), Chapters 1 and 4.

7. du Noiiys, Lecomte, *Human Destiny* (N.Y.: Longmans, Green & Co., 1947).

8. Taylor, A. E., *Does God Exist* (London, Macmillan, 1945), Chapter 4.

9. Taylor, Richard, *Metaphysics* (Englewood Cliffs, N.J: Prentice Hall, 1992), pp. 109-10.

10. Tennant, F. R., *Philosophical Theology*, Vol. II (New York, Cambridge University Press, 1969), Chapter 4.

Name_____

Date _____

1. What is the meaning of the term 'teleological'?

2. List three different *kinds* of teleological data.

3. Briefly explain the teleological argument (not Paley's).

4. Could one argue that because watches occasionally break down, they do not show design? Why or why
    not?

5. What do you think is the most convincing objection to the teleological argument?

6. Explain in detail the form of reasoning Paley uses in his teological argument.

The Analogy of the Watch

Chapter One

In crossing a heath[1], suppose I pitched my foot against a *stone* and were asked how the stone came to be there, I might possibly answer that for anything I knew to the contrary it had lain there forever; nor would it, perhaps, be very easy to show the absurdity of this answer. But suppose I had found a *watch* upon the ground, and it should be inquired how the watch happened to be in that place, I should hardly think of the answer which I had before given, that for anything I knew the watch might have always been there. Yet why should not this answer serve for the watch as well as for the stone; why is it not as admissible in the second case as in the first? For this reason, and for no other, namely, that when we come to inspect the watch, we perceive--what we could not discover in the stone--that its several parts are framed and put together for a purpose, e.g., that they are so formed and adjusted as to produce a motion, and that motion so regulated as to point out the hour of the day; that if the different parts had been differently shaped from what they are, or placed after any other manner or in any other order than that in which they are placed, either no motion at all would have been carried on in the machine, or none which would have answered the use that is now served by it. To reckon up a few of the plainest of these parts and of their offices[2], all tending to one result: we see a cylindrical box containing a coiled elastic spring, which, by its endeavor to relax itself, turns round the box. We next observe a flexible chain--artificially wrought for the sake of flexure--communicating the action of the spring from the box to the fusee. We then find a series of wheels, the teeth of which catch in and apply to each other, conducting the motion from the fusee to the balance and shape of those wheels, so regulating that motion as to terminate in causing an index, by an equable and measured progression, to pass over a given space in a given time. We take notice that the wheels are made of brass, in order to keep them from rust; the springs of steel, no other metal being so elastic; that over the face of the watch there is placed a glass, a material employed in no other part of the work, but in the room of which, if there had been any other than a transparent substance, the hour could not be seen without opening the

---

[1] *heath:* a track of open wasteland, esp. in the British Isles, covered with heather, low shrubs, etc.; a moor [editor's note].

[2] *office:* special, proper or assigned service or function [editor's note].

case. This mechanism being observed--it requires indeed an examination of the instrument, and perhaps some previous knowledge of the subject, to perceive and understand it; but being once, as we have said, observed and understood the inference we think is inevitable, that the watch must have had a maker--that there must have existed, at some time and at some place or other, an artificer or artificers who formed it for the purpose which we find it actually to answer, who completely comprehended its construction and designed its use.

I. Nor would it, I apprehend, weaken the conclusion, that we had never seen a watch made--that we had never known an artist capable of making one--that we were altogether incapable of executing such a piece of workmanship ourselves, or of understanding in what manner it was performed; all this being no more than what is true of some exquisite remains of ancient art, of some lost arts, and, to the generality of mankind, of the more curious productions of modern manufacture. Does one man in a million know how oval frames are turned? Ignorance of this kind exalts our opinion of the unseen and unknown artist's skill, if he be unseen and unknown, but raises no doubt in our minds of the existence and agency of such an artist, at some former time and in some place or other. Nor can I perceive that it varies at all the inference, whether the question arise concerning a human agent or concerning an agent of a different species, or an agent possessing in some respects a different nature.

II. Neither, secondly, would it invalidate our conclusion, that the watch sometimes went wrong or that it seldom went exactly right. The purpose of the machinery, the design, and the designer might be evident, and in the case supposed, would be evident, in whatever way we accounted for the irregularity of the movement, or whether we could account for it or not. It is not necessary that a machine be perfect in order to show with what design it was made: still less necessary, where the only question is whether it were made with any design at all.

III. Nor, thirdly, would it bring any uncertainty into the argument, if there were a few parts of the watch, concerning which we could not discover or had not yet discovered in what manner they conduced to the general effect; or even some parts, concerning which we could not ascertain whether they conduced to that effect in any manner whatever. For, as to the first branch of the case, if by the loss, or disorder, or decay of the parts in question, the movement of the watch were found in fact to be stopped, or disturbed, or retarded, no doubt would remain in our minds as to the utility or intention of these parts, although we would be unable to investigate the manner according to which, or the connection by which, the ultimate effect depended upon their action or assistance; and the more complex the machine, the more likely is this obscurity to arise. Then, as to the second thing supposed, namely, that there were parts which might be spared without prejudice to the movement of the watch, and that we had proved this by experiment, these superfluous parts, even if we were completely assured that they were such, would not vacate the reasoning which we had instituted concerning other parts. The indication of contrivance remained, with respect to them, nearly as it was before.

IV. Nor, fourthly, would any man in his senses think the existence of the watch with its various machinery accounted for, by being told that it was one out of possible combinations of material forms; that whatever he had found in the place where he found the watch, must have contained some internal configuration or other; and that this configuration might be the structure now exhibited, namely, of the works of a watch, as well as different structure.

V. Nor, fifthly, would it yield his inquiry more satisfaction, to be answered that there existed in things a principle of order, which had disposed the parts of the watch into their present form and situation. He never knew a watch made by the principle of order; nor can he even form to himself an idea of what is meant by a principle of order distinct from the intelligence of the watchmaker.

VI. Sixthly, he would be surprised to hear that the mechanism of the watch was no proof of contrivance, only a motive to induce the mind to think so:

VII. And not less surprised to be informed, that the watch in his hand was nothing more than the result of the laws of *metallic* nature. It is a perversion of language to assign any law as the efficient, operative cause of any thing. A law presupposes an agent, for it is only the mode according to which an agent proceeds: it implies a power, for it is the order according to which that power acts. Without this agent, without this power, which are both distinct from itself, the *law* does nothing, is nothing. The expression, "the law of metallic nature," may sound strange and harsh to a philosophic ear; but it seems quite as justifiable as some others which are more familiar to him, such as "the law of vegetable nature," "the law of animal nature," or, indeed, as "the law of nature" in general, when assigned as the cause of phenomena, in exclusion of agency and power, or when it is substituted into the place of these.

VIII. Neither, lastly, would our observer be driven out of his conclusion or from his confidence in its truth by being told that he knew nothing at all about the matter. He knows enough for his argument; he knows the utility of the end; he knows the subserviency and adaptation of the means to the end. These points being known, his ignorance of other points, his doubts concerning other points affect not the certainty of his reasoning. The consciousness of knowing little need not beget a distrust of that which he does know.

Chapter Two

Suppose, in the next place, that the person who found the watch should after some time discover that, in addition to all the properties which he had hitherto observed in it, it possessed the unexpected property of producing in the course of its movement another watch like itself--the thing is conceivable; that it contained within it a mechanism, a system of parts--a mold, for instance, or a complex adjustment of lathes, files, and other tools--evidently and separately calculated for this purpose; let us inquire what effect ought such a discovery to have upon his former conclusion.

I. The first effect would be to increase his admiration of the contrivance, and his conviction of the consummate skill of the contriver. Whether he regarded the object of the contrivance, the distinct apparatus, the intricate, yet in many parts intelligible mechanism by which it was carried on, he would perceive in this new observation nothing but an additional reason for doing what he had already done--for referring the construction of the watch to design and to supreme art. If that construction *without* this property, or, which is the same thing, before this property had been noticed, proved intention and art to have been employed about it, still more strong would the proof appear when he came to the knowledge of this further property, the crown and perfection of all the rest.

II. He would reflect that, though the watch before him were *in some sense* the maker of the watch which was fabricated in the course of its movements, yet it was in a very different sense from that in which a carpenter, for instance, is the maker of a chair--the author of its contrivance, the cause of the relation of its parts to their use. With respect to these, the first watch was no cause at all to the second; in no such sense as this was it the author of the constitution and order, either of the parts which the new watch contained, or of the parts by the aid and instrumentality of which it was produced. We might possibly say, but with great latitude of expression, that a stream of water ground corn; but no latitude of expression would allow us to say, no stretch of conjecture could lead us to think that the stream of water built the mill, though it were too ancient for us to know who the builder was. What the stream of water does in the affair is neither more nor less than this: by the application of an unintelligent impulse to a mechanism previously arranged, arranged independently of it and arranged by intelligence, an effect is produced, namely, the corn is ground. But the effect results from the arrangement. The force of the stream cannot be said to be the cause or the author of the effect, still less of the arrangement. Understanding and planning in the formation of the mill were not the less necessary for any share which the water has in grinding the corn; yet is this share the same as that which the watch would have contributed to the production of the new watch, upon the supposition assumed in the last section. Therefore,

III. Though it be now no longer probable that the individual watch which our observer had found was made immediately by the hand of an artificer, yet this alteration does not in anywise affect the inference that an artificer had been originally employed and concerned in the production. The argument from design remains as it was. Marks of design and contrivance are no more accounted for now than they were before. In the same thing, we may ask for the cause of different properties. We may ask for the cause of the color of a body, of its hardness, of its heat; and these causes may be all different. We are now asking for the cause of that subserviency to a use, that relation to an end, which we have remarked in the watch before us. No answer is given to this question by telling us that a preceding watch produced it. There cannot be design without a designer; contrivance without a contriver; order without choice; arrangement without anything capable of arranging; subserviency and relation to a purpose without that which could intend a purpose; means suitable to an end, and executing their office in accomplishing that end, without the end ever having been contemplated or the means accommodated to it. Arrangement, disposition of parts, subserviency of means to an end, relation of instruments to a use imply the presence of intelligence and mind. No one, therefore, can rationally believe that the insensible, inanimate watch, from which the watch before us issued, was the proper cause of the mechanism we so much admire in it--could be truly said to have constructed the instrument, disposed its parts, assigned their office, determined their order, action, and mutual dependency, combined their several motions into one result, and that also a result connected with the utilities of other beings. All these properties, therefore, are as much unaccounted for as they were before.

IV. Nor is anything gained by running the difficulty farther back, that is, by supposing the watch before us to have been produced from another watch, that from a former, and so on indefinitely. Our going back ever so far brings us no nearer to the least degree of satisfaction upon the subject. Contrivance is still unaccounted for. We still want a contriver. A designing mind is neither supplied by this supposition nor dispensed with. If the difficulty were diminished the farther we went back, by going back indefinitely we might exhaust it. And this is the only case to which this sort of reasoning applies. Where there is a tendency, or, as we increase the number of terms, a continual approach toward a limit, there, by supposing the number of terms to be what is called infinite, we may conceive the limit to be attained; but where there is no such tendency or approach, nothing is effected by lengthening the series. There is no difference as to the point in question, whatever there may be as to many points, between one series and another--between a series which is finite and a series which is infinite. A chain composed of an infinite number of links can no more support itself than a chain composed of a finite number of links. And of this we are assured, though we never *can* have tried the experiment; because, by increasing the number of links, from ten, for instance, to a hundred, from a hundred to a thousand, etc., we make not the smallest approach, we observe not the smallest tendency toward self-support. There is no difference in this respect--yet there may be a great difference in several respects--between a chain of a greater or less length, between one chain and another, between one that is finite and one that is infinite. This very much resembles the case before us. The machine which we are inspecting demonstrates, by its construction, contrivance and design. Contrivance must have had a contriver, design a designer, whether the machine immediately proceeded from another machine or not. That circumstance alters not the case. That other machine may, in like manner, have proceeded from a former machine: nor does that alter the case; the contrivance must have had a contriver. That former one from one preceding it: no alteration still; a contriver is still necessary. No tendency is perceived, no approach toward a diminution of this necessity. It is the same with any and every succession of these machines--a succession of ten, of a hundred, of a thousand; with one series, as with another--a series which is finite, as with a series which is infinite. In whatever other respects they may differ, in this they do not. In all equally, contrivance and design are unaccounted for.

The question is not simply, how came the first watch into existence? which question, it may be pretended, is done away by supposing the series of watches thus produced from one another to have been infinite, and consequently to have had no such *first* for which it was necessary to provide a cause. This, perhaps, would have been nearly the state of the question, if nothing had been before us but an unorganized, unmechanized substance, without mark or indication of contrivance. It might be difficult to show that such substance could not have existed from eternity, either in succession--if it were possible, which I think it is not, for unorganized bodies to spring from one another--or by individual perpetuity. But that is not the question now. To suppose it to be so is to suppose that it made no difference whether he had found a watch or a stone. As it is, the metaphysics of that question have no place; for, in the watch which we are examining are seen contrivance, design, and end, a purpose, means for the end, adaptation to the purpose. And the question which irresistibly presses upon our thoughts is, whence this contrivance and design? The thing required is the intending mind, the adapted hand, the intelligence by which that hand was directed. This question, this demand is not shaken off by increasing a number or succession of substances destitute of these properties; nor the more, by increasing that number to infinity. If it be said that, upon the supposition of one watch being produced from another in the course of that other's movements and by means of the mechanism within it, we have a cause for the watch in my hand, namely, the watch from which it proceeded--I deny that for the design, the contrivance, the suitableness of means to an end, the adaptation of instruments to a use, all of which we discover in the watch, we have any cause whatever. It is in vain, therefore, to assign a series of such causes or to allege that a series may be carried back to infinity; for I do not admit that we have yet any cause at all for the phenomena, still less any series of causes either finite or infinite. Here is contrivance but no contriver; proofs of design, but no designer.

V. Our observer would further also reflect that the maker of the watch before him was in truth and reality the maker of every watch produced from it: there being no difference, except that the latter manifests a more exquisite skill, between the making of another watch with his own hands, by the mediation of files, lathes, chisels, etc., and the disposing, fixing, and inserting of these instruments, or of others equivalent to them, in the body of the watch already made, in such a manner as to form a new watch in the course of the movements which he had given to the old one. It is only working by one set of tools instead of another.

The conclusion which the *first* examination of the watch, of its works, construction, and movement, suggested, was that it must have had, for cause and author of that construction, an artificer who understood its mechanism and designed its use. This conclusion is invincible. A *second* examination presents us with a new discovery. The watch is found, in the course of its movement, to produce another watch similar to itself; and not only so, but we perceive in it a system or organization separately calculated for that purpose. What effect would this discovery have or ought it to have upon our former inference? What, as has already been said, but to increase beyond measure our admiration of the skill which had been employed in the formation of such a machine? Or shall it, instead of this, all at once turn us round to an opposite conclusion, namely, that no art or skill whatever has been concerned in the business, although all other evidences of art and skill remain as they were, and this last and supreme piece of art be now added to the rest? Can this be maintained without absurdity? Yet this is atheism.

Chapter Five

Every observation which was made in our first chapter concerning the watch may be repeated with strict propriety concerning the eye, concerning animals, concerning plants, concerning, indeed, all the organized parts of the works of nature. As,

I. When we are inquiring simply after the *existence* of an intelligent Creator, imperfection, inaccuracy, liability to disorder, occasional irregularities may subsist in a considerable degree without inducing any doubt into the question; just as a watch may frequently go wrong, seldom perhaps exactly right, may be faulty in some parts, defective in some, without the smallest ground of suspicion from thence arising that it was not a watch, or not made for the purpose ascribed to it. When faults are pointed out, and when a question is started concerning the skill of the artist or the dexterity with which the work is executed, then, indeed, in order to defend these qualities from accusation, we must be able either to expose some intractableness and imperfection in the materials or point out some invincible difficulty in the execution, into which imperfection and difficulty the matter of complaint may be resolved; or, if we cannot do this, we must adduce such specimens of consummate art and contrivance proceeding from the same hand as may convince the inquirer of the existence, in the case before him, of impediments like those which we have mentioned, although, what from the nature of the case is very likely to happen, they be unknown and unperceived by him. This we must do in order to vindicate the artist's skill, or at least the perfection of it; as we must also judge of his intention and of the provisions employed in fulfilling that intention, not from an instance in which they fail but from the great plurality of instances in which they succeed. But, after all, these are different questions from the question of the artist's existence; or, which is the same, whether the thing before us be a work of art or not; and the questions ought always to be kept separate in the mind. So likewise it is in the works of nature. Irregularities and imperfections are of little or no weight in the consideration when that consideration relates simply to the existence of a Creator. When the argument respects his attributes, they are of weight; but are then to be taken in conjunction--the attention is not to rest upon them, but they are to be taken in conjunction with the unexceptional evidences which we possess of skill, power, and benevolence displayed in other instances; which evidences may, in strength, number, and variety, be such and may so overpower apparent blemishes as to induce us, upon the most reasonable ground, to believe that these last ought to be referred to some cause, though we be ignorant of it, other than defect of knowledge or of benevolence in the author.

II. There may be also parts of plants and animals, as there were supposed to be of the watch, of which in some instances the operation, in others the use, in unknown. These form different cases; for the operation may be unknown, yet the use be certain. Thus it is with the lungs of animals. It does not, I think, appear that we are acquainted with the action of the air upon the blood, or in what manner that action is communicated by the lungs; yet we find that a very short suspension of their office destroys the life of the animal. In this case, therefore, we may be said to know the use, nay, we experience the necessity of the organ though we be ignorant of its operation. Nearly the same thing may be observed of what is called the lymphatic system. We suffer grievous inconveniences from its disorder, without being informed of the office which it sustains in the economy of our bodies. There may possibly also be some few examples of the second class in which not only the operation is unknown, but in which experiments may seem to prove that the part is not necessary; or may leave a doubt how far it is even useful to the plant or animal in which it is found. This is said to be the case with the spleen, which has been extracted from dogs without any sensible injury to their vital functions. Instances of the former kind, namely, in which we cannot explain the operation, may be numerous, for they will be so in proportion to our ignorance. They will be more or fewer to different persons, and in different stages of science. Every improvement of knowledge diminishes their number. There is hardly, perhaps, a year passes that does not in the works of nature bring some operation or some mode of operation to light, which was before undiscovered--probably unsuspected. Instances of the second kind, namely, where the part appears to be totally useless, I believe to be extremely rare; compared with the number of those of which the use is evident, they are beneath any assignable proportion and perhaps have been never submitted to trial and examination sufficiently accurate, long enough continued, or often enough repeated. No accounts which I have seen are satisfactory. The mutilated animal may live and grow fat--as was the case of the dog deprived of its spleen--yet may be defective in some other of its functions, which, whether they can all, or in what degree of vigor and perfection be performed or how long preserved without the extirpated organ, does not seem to be ascertained by experiment. But to this case, even were it fully made out, may be applied the consideration which we suggested concerning the watch, namely, that these superfluous parts do not negate the reasoning which we instituted concerning those parts which are useful, and of which we know the use; the indication of contrivance, with respect to them, remains as it was before.

III. One atheistic way of replying to our observations upon the works of nature, and to the proofs of a Deity which we think that we perceive in them, is to tell us that all which we see must necessarily have had some form, and that it might as well be its present form as any other. Let us now apply this answer to the eye, as we did before to the watch. Something or other must have occupied that place in the animal's head, must have filled up, as we say, the socket; we will say, also, that it must have been of that sort of substance which we call animal substance, as flesh, bone, membrane, or cartilage, etc. But that it should have been an *eye*, knowing as we do what an eye comprehends, namely, that it should have consisted, first, of a series of transparent lenses--very different, by the by, even in their substance, from the opaque materials of which the rest of the body is, in general at least, composed, and with which the whole of its surface, this single portion of it excepted, is covered: secondly, of a black cloth or canvas--the only membrane in the body which is black--spread out behind these lenses, so as to receive the image formed by pencils of light transmitted through them, and at which alone a distinct image could be formed, namely, at the concourse of the refracted rays: thirdly, of a large nerve communicating between this membrance and the brain; without which the action of light upon the membrane, however modified by the organ, would be lost to the purposes of sensation that this fortunate conformation of parts should have been the lot not of one individual out of many thousand individuals, like the great prize in a lottery or like some singularity in nature, but the happy chance of a whole species; nor of one species out of many thousand species with which we are acquainted, but of by far the greatest number of all that exist, and that under varieties not causal or capricious, but bearing marks of being suited to their respective exigencies that all this should have taken place merely because something must have occupied these points on every animal's forehead, or that all this should be thought to be accounted for by the short answer that "whatever was there must have had some form or other" is too absurd to be made more so by any argumentation. We are not contented with this answer; we find no satisfaction in it, by way of accounting for appearances of organization far short of those of the eye, such as we observe in fossil shells, petrified bones, or other substances which bear the vestiges of animal or vegetable recrements, but which, either in respect to utility or of the situation in which they are discovered, may seem accidental enough. It is no way of accounting even for these things, to say that the stone, for instance, which is shown to us--supposing the question to be concerning a petrifaction--must have contained some internal conformation or other. Nor does it mend the answer to add, with respect to the singularity of the conformation, that after the event it is no longer to be computed what the chances were against it. This is always to be computed when the question is whether a useful or imitative conformation be the product of chance or not: I desire no greater certainty in reasoning than that by which chance is excluded from the present disposition of the natural world. Universal experience is against it. What does chance ever do for us? In the human body, for instance, chance, that is, the operation of causes without design, may produce a wen, a wart, a mole, a pimple, but never an eye. Among inanimate substances, a clod, a pebble, a liquid drop might be; but never was a watch, a telescope, an organized body of any kind, answering a valuable purpose by a complicated mechanism, the effect of chance. In no assignable instance has such a thing existed without intention somewhere.

Name_____

Date _____

1. What is the important difference between the watch and the stone which forms the basis of Paley's argument?

2. Suppose you found a "super-watch" (a device that produces watches), and therefore you have accounted for the coming into existence of the watch found on the ground. Would this nullify the teleological argument? Explain.

3. How does Paley argue against the objection that the workings of nature could simply be chance?

4. Why does the eye refute the atheist's thesis concerning the works of nature?

5. Speculate as to what the relationship is between chance and causation.

18

The Problem of Evil; David Hume

❧ B I O G R A P H Y ❧

David Hume was born at Edinburgh, Scotland, on April 26, 1711. Although his father was a member of the landed gentry, the estate was rather small and his family was not well to do. His mother came from a family of lawyers and since David was a younger son and therefore ineligible to inherit the family estate, he was encouraged to pursue the law. He did so after attending the University of Edinburgh but soon developed an intense dislike for the law. He then tried his hand at a merchant's career. This too David found "unsuitable" to his tastes and interests. Eventually he headed for France determined to seek the life of a man of letters having acquired "an insurmountable aversion to everything but the pursuit of philosophy and general learning". Within three years of his arrival there, at the age of twenty-six, his monumental work A Treatise of Human Nature *was published. This is especially impressive since in philosophy he was almost completely self-educated. To his chagrin[a] his book was not well received. This was most probably because Thomas Reid and Immanuel Kant were Hume's only contemporaries capable of understanding the complete philosophical system detailed in the* Treatise. *In 1740 he published* An Abstract of a Treatise of Human Nature *and in 1748 and 1751 respectively* Philosophical Essays concerning the Human Understanding *and* An Enquiry concerning the Principles of Morals. *His other major work, the* Dialogues concerning Natural Religion *was published posthumously.[b]*

Interestingly, Hume never held a professorship, though he applied unsuccessfully for chairs of philosophy at Edinburgh and Glasgow. However, in 1752 he was elected librarian of the Advocates' Library in Edinburgh, a post he held for five years. It was during this period that he began work on his History of England, *a project which took nearly ten years to complete. It was this book that brought Hume both fame and fortune. Personable and witty, he was a most popular figure in the literary world of the period. His French friends referred to him as "le bon David". In Scotland he was known as "Saint David". He died of cancer on August 25, 1776.*

[a.] *chagrin:* distress caused by humbling of pride, by failure or disappointment.

[b.] *posthumous:* following or occurring after one's death.

There are two kinds of evil. [1] Natural evil is the evil that befalls[1] individuals as a result of natural occurrences. Great misfortune comes to those via[2] floods, earthquakes, tornados and other natural events. Such misfortune is harmful to those who experience it and is therefore considered evil. [2] Moral evil is man's inhumanity to man. People do bad things to other human beings. They steal, cheat, lie, rape and murder. When someone intentionally or unnecessarily harms another person they do evil. One need only to read the daily newspaper to determine that there is no shortage of moral evil in the world. The problem of evil from the standpoint of the philosophy of religion is this: if God is omnipotent[3] and omnibeneficent[4], how can He permit evil to exist? After all, if He is omnipotent, He has the power to prevent it. If He is omnibeneficent, He would exempt[5] people from evil. If He doesn't exercise His power, then it would appear that He is not genuinely omnibeneficent. If His goodness cannot save people from evil, then He is not omnipotent. Something seemingly must give. If He is not omnipotent on the one hand or not omnibeneficent on the other hand, then He is not the Judeo-Christian God He is conceived to be. And it is naive to think that there is no evil. The problem of evil boils down to preserving God's attributes[6] of omnipotence and omnibeneficence *and* recognizing that evil is for real. How can one account for evil in light of God's omnipotence and omnibeneficence? Since the Middle Ages a considerable amount of energy has been expended[7] on behalf of philosophers of religion to solve this problem. Others, on the other hand, have argued that there is no solution to the problem of evil, thus casting doubt on the existence of the Judeo-Christian god. The renowned[8] Scottish philosopher David Hume took this position.

Hume first deals with the issue of natural evil. He observes that the lion's share of natural evil depends on four circumstances. [1] Pain is evil. Animals possess the capacity to feel pain. That they are so able does not mean that they experience pain all the time. "Why then is any animal ever rendered[9] susceptible[10] of such a sensation?" asks Hume. "If animals can be free from it an hour, they might enjoy a perpetual exemption from it; ..." The essence[11] of this point is that since animals [of which human beings are a subgroup] do not feel pain some of the time, they need not feel pain at any time. Since animals do feel pain some of the time, such pain is unnecessary. If pain is unnecessary, why does God permit it to exist if He has the power to prevent it and is an all-loving, all-good being?

[2] The capacity to feel pain as evil hinges on the second circumstance. Some argue that the pain people experience as a result of natural occurrences can be explained away by noting that the world functions in

---

[1]   *befall:* to come to pass; to happen [to].

[2]   *via:* by way of.

[3]   *omnipotent:* all-powerful.

[4]   *omnibeneficent:* all-loving, all-good.

[5]   *exempt:* set apart; cut off; exclude.

[6]   *attribute:* any quality or characteristic that may be predicated of some subject.

[7]   *expend:* to consume by use in any way; to spend.

[8]   *renown:* illustrious reputation; exalted fame; celebrity.

[9]   *render:* to cause to become; make.

[10]   *susceptible:* having such a constitution or temperament as to be open, subject or unresistant to some stimulus, influence or agency.

[11]   *essence:* the quality or qualities of a thing that give it its identity; the intrinsic or indispensable properties of a thing.

accordance with laws of nature. Phenomena that are the result of laws of nature are impersonal. Volcanos and floods are not out to "get" people. People are adversely[12] affected by natural occurrences simply by being in the wrong place at the wrong time; that is, by getting in the way of the natural functioning of the planet upon which they live. As such, God's omnipotence and omnibeneficence simply play no role relative to natural evil. In response to this Hume admits that were the Deity to intervene to thwart[13] the laws of nature from causing animals pain, the course of nature as we know it would be completely unpredictable, but so what? The issue here is whether or not the Deity could prevent pain caused by natural occurrences. If the Deity cannot break the laws of nature, then He is not omnipotent. If He chooses not to break them to save us from pain, then He is not omnibeneficent.

[3] The third circumstance addresses the pain and therefore suffering animals experience due to "the great frugality with which all powers and faculties are distributed to every particular being". For example, some animals endowed[14] with great strength possess poor eyesight. Others are swift but not strong. Hume argues that there is no good reason for such economy; that is, limitation of such powers or endowments. Such limitations result in much pain which would otherwise not be the case. It is those limitations that more often than not put animals at peril.[15] If God is the benevolent being He is conceived to be, why did He not [a] create the various species of animals in such a way to effectively guard against accidents or [b] create "fewer animals, and to have endowed these with more faculties for their happiness and preservation?"

[4] The fourth circumstance that undermines God's [supposed] omnipotence and omnibeneficence pertains to the disastrous effects resulting from the inaccuracies of the great machine of nature. Such disastrous effects are evil because they are the source of much pain and suffering. "Rains are necessary to nourish all the plants and animals of the earth: But how often are they defective? How often excessive? Heat is requisite to all life and vegetation; but it is not always found in due proportion." This is the case with practically all natural phenomena.

Now unless *a priori* reasons; that is, self-evident reasons can be offered that mitigate[16] circumstances [1] through [4], then all we have at our disposal to make a judgement concerning God's [supposed] omnipotence and omnibeneficence is empirical[17] data. That data is the subject of circumstances [1] through [4] and it would suggest that God is not omnipotent or omnibeneficent [or both].

The situation is no better when we consider moral evil. How can one effectively explain away the horrid things people do to one another? If person A tortured; that is, caused person B grievous[18] and unnecessary pain, what caused person A to engage in that heinous[19] activity? All actions have a cause and that cause must be caused. One cannot adequately explain the situation by claiming that person A tortured person B

---

[12] *adverse:* in hostile opposition to one's interests.

[13] *thwart:* to prevent from taking place; frustrate; block.

[14] *endow:* to furnish, as with some gift, quality or faculty.

[15] *peril:* exposure to the risk of being injured or destroyed.

[16] *mitigate:* to make or become less severe or harsh.

[17] *empirical:* capable of being confirmed, verified or disproved by observation or experiment.

[18] *grievous:* severe; intense.

[19] *heinous:* hateful; atrocious; give great offense.

as an act of free will thus stopping the causal chain. We may hold person A responsible for his behavior. That, however, does not entail[20] that person A's behavior had no cause or was uncaused. That every cause is itself caused creates two, and only two, options. Either [a] one goes on to infinity in the sequence of causes or [b] one maintains that there is a first cause. This first cause must be the cause of all subsequent causes and hence their effects manifested throughout the universe. For the theist,[21] this first cause is God. Since God is the ultimate cause of all things, He is the cause of all the evil that exists. If this is the case, He is most certainly not the benevolent being people believe Him to be and therefore not the Judeo-Christian god.

The problem of evil has created consternation[22] among many people who otherwise have no problem believing in the existence of the Judeo-Christian god. And this is most understandable. When one considers the pain and suffering that exist in the world it becomes difficult to understand why an omnipotent, omnibeneficent being would allow it. Be aware that appeal to ignorance constitutes[23] no good solution to the problem. That is, to maintain that the solution to this problem is beyond the [intellectual] grasp of humans but that God nevertheless exists as an omnipotent, omnibeneficent being is fallacious[24] reasoning. No legitimate belief ever follows from ignorance, viz.[25] what we do not know or understand.

There is, however, no good reason to give up on a philosophical problem. To be sure, there have been numerous proposed solutions to the problem of evil. St. Augustine argued that since God is omnibeneficent and the creator of the universe there is no genuine evil. What appears to us humans as evil is simply lesser[26] good. Others have argued that the very concept of good would be meaningless were it not for evil. Since the concept of good is meaningful, evil must exist. This is the same as observing that there cannot be mountains without valleys. In other words, the two are inseparable. And some have maintained the position that when all is said and done, ultimate good cannot be achieved without evil. In other words, when a lesser good is "mixed" with some evil a greater good results. And when that good is "mixed" with some more evil even greater good results until we reach a state of final or ultimate good.

Suggested Readings: The Problem of Evil; Hume

1. Hick, John, *Evil and the God of Love* (New York: Harper & Row, 1966).
2. Laird, John, *Mind and Deity* (New York: Philosophical Library, 1941).
3. Lewis, C.S., *The Problem of Pain* (New York: The Macmillan Company, 1950).

---

[20] *entail:* to cause or require as a necessary consequence; necessitate.

[21] *theist:* one who believes in the existence of a god or gods.

[22] *consternation:* dismay that hinders or throws one into confusion.

[23] *constitute:* to be the elements or parts of; make up; compose.

[24] *fallacious:* manifesting an error in reasoning.

[25] *viz:* namely.

[26] *lesser:* less, smaller; inferior.

4. Lewis, Edwin, *The Creator and the Adversary* (New York: Abingdon-Cokesbury Press, 1948).

5. Mill, John Stuart, *Three Essays on Religion* (New York: Holt, Rinehart & Winston, 1884).

6. Petit, Francois, *The Problem of Evil*. trans., Christopher Williams (New York: Hawthorn Books, 1959).

7. Rashdall, Hastings, *The Theory of Good and Evil*, Vol. II. (London: Oxford University Press, 1924).

8. Weiss, Paul, "Good and Evil," *Review of Metaphysics* (September 1949), III, 1, no. 9, pp. 81-94.

STUDY
  QUESTIONS

Name_____

Chapter 18:
The Problem of Evil; Hume

Date _____

1. Briefly describe the two types of evil.

2. What two of God's attributes play a role in the problem of evil?

3. Briefly describe the problem of evil.

4. Why is appeal to ignorance an unacceptable solution to the problem of evil?

5. Cite one possible solution to the problem of evil.

The Problem of Evil

David Hume
*Dialogues Concerning Natural
Religion*
Part XI (selections)

Part XI

I SCRUPLE not to allow, said Cleanthes, that I have been apt to suspect the frequent repetition of the word, *infinite*, which we meet with in
all theological writers, to savour more of panegyric[1] than of philosophy,
and that any purposes of reasoning, and even of religion, would be better
served, were we to rest contented with more accurate and more moderate
expressions. The terms, *admirable, excellent, superlatively great, wise,*
and *holy*; these sufficiently fill the imaginations of men; and any thing
beyond, besides that it leads into absurdities, has no influence on the
affections or sentiments. Thus, in the present subject, if we abandon all
human analogy, as seems your intention, Demea, I am afraid we abandon
all religion, and retain no conception of the great object of our adoration.
If we preserve human analogy, we must for ever find it impossible to reconcile any mixture of evil in the universe with infinite attributes; much
less, can we ever prove the latter from the former. But supposing the
Author of nature to be finitely perfect, though far exceeding mankind; a
satisfactory account may then be given of natural and moral evil, and
every untoward phenomenon be explained and adjusted. A less evil may
then be chosen, in order to avoid a greater: Inconveniences be submitted
to, in order to reach a desirable end: And in a word, benevolence, regulated by wisdom, and limited by necessity, may produce just such a world
as the present. You, Philo, who are so prompt at starting views, and reflections, and analogies; I would gladly hear, at length, without interruption,
your opinion of this new theory; and if it deserve our attention, we may
afterwards, at more leisure, reduce it into form.

My sentiments, replied Philo, are not worth being made a mystery of;
and therefore, without any ceremony, I shall deliver what occurs to me
with regard to the present subject. It must, I think, be allowed, that, if a
very limited intelligence, whom we shall suppose utterly unacquainted
with the universe, were assured, that it were the production of a very
good, wise, and powerful Being, however finite, he would, from his conjectures, form *beforehand* a different notion of it from what we find it to
be by experience; nor would he ever imagine, merely from these attributes
of the cause, of which he is informed, that the effect could be so full of
vice and misery and disorder, as it appears in this life. Supposing now,
that this person were brought into the world, still assured, that it was the
workmanship of such a sublime and benevolent Being; he might, perhaps,

---

[1] *panegyric:* a eulogistic oration or writing [editor's note].

be surprised at the disappointment; but would never retract his former belief, if founded on any very solid argument; since such a limited intelligence must be sensible of his own blindness and ignorance, and must allow, that there may be many solutions of those phenomena, which will for ever escape his comprehension. But supposing, which is the real case with regard to man, that this creature is not antecedently[2] convinced of a supreme intelligence, benevolent, and powerful, but is left to gather such a belief from the appearances of things; this entirely alters the case, nor will he ever find any reason for such a conclusion. He may be fully convinced of the narrow limits of his understanding; but this will not help him in forming an inference concerning the goodness of superior powers, since he must form that inference from what he knows, not from what he is ignorant of. The more you exaggerate his weakness and ignorance, the more diffident you render him, and give him the greater suspicion, that such subjects are beyond the reach of his faculties. You are obliged, therefore, to reason with him merely from the known phenomena, and to drop every arbitrary supposition or conjecture.

Did I show you a house or palace, where there was not one apartment convenient or agreeable; where the windows, doors, fires, passages, stairs, and the whole œconomy of the building were the source of noise, confusion, fatigue, darkness, and the extremes of heat and cold; you would certainly blame the contrivance, without any farther examination. The architect would in vain display his subtilty, and prove to you, that if this door or that window were altered, greater ills would ensue. What he says, may be strictly true: The alteration of one particular, while the other parts of the building remain, may only augment the inconveniences. But still you would assert in general, that, if the architect had had skill and good intentions, he might have formed such a plan of the whole, and might have adjusted the parts in such a manner, as would have remedied all or most of these inconveniences. His ignorance, or even your own ignorance of such a plan, will never convince you of the impossibility of it. If you find many inconveniences and deformities in the building, you will always, without entering into any detail, condemn the architect.

In short, I repeat the question: Is the world considered in general, and as it appears to us in this life, different from what a man or such a limited being would, *beforehand*, expect from a very powerful, wise, and benevolent Deity? It must be strange prejudice to assert the contrary. And from thence I conclude, that, however consistent the world may be, allowing certain suppositions and conjectures, with the idea of such a Deity, it can never afford us an inference concerning his existence. The consistence is not absolutely denied, only the inference. Conjectures, especially where infinity is excluded from the divine attributes, may, perhaps, be sufficient to prove a consistence; but can never be foundations for any inference.

There seem to be *four* circumstances, on which depend all, or the greatest part of the ills, that molest sensible creatures; and it is not impossible but all these circumstances may be necessary and unavoidable. We know so little beyond common life, or even of common life, that, with regard to the œconomy of a universe, there is no conjecture, however wild, which may not be just; nor any one, however plausible, which may not be erroneous. All that belongs to human understanding, in this deep ignorance and obscurity, is to be sceptical, or at least cautious; and not to admit of any hypothesis, whatever; much less, of any which is supported by no appearance of probability. Now this I assert to be the case with regard to all the causes of evil, and the circumstances on which it

---

[2]   *antecedent:* going before in time; prior; preceding [editor's note].

depends. None of them appear to human reason, in the least degree, necessary or unavoidable; nor can we suppose them such, without the utmost licence of imagination.

The *first* circumstance which introduces evil, is that contrivance or œconomy of the animal creation, by which pains, as well as pleasures, are employed to excite all creatures to action, and make them vigilant in the great work of self-preservation. Now pleasure alone, in its various degrees, seems to human understanding sufficient for this purpose. All animals might be constantly in a state of enjoyment; but when urged by any of the necessities of nature, such as thirst, hunger, weariness; instead of pain, they might feel a diminution of pleasure, by which they might be prompted to seek that object, which is necessary to their subsistence. Men pursue pleasure as eagerly as they avoid pain; at least, might have been so constituted. It seems, therefore, plainly possible to carry on the business of life without any pain. Why then is any animal ever rendered susceptible of such a sensation? If animals can be free from it an hour, they might enjoy a perpetual exemption from it; and it required as particular a contrivance of their organs to produce that feeling, as to endow them with sight, hearing, or any of the senses. Shall we conjecture, that such a contrivance was necessary, without any appearance of reason? And shall we build on that conjecture as on the most certain truth?

But a capacity of pain would not alone produce pain, were it not for the *second* circumstance, viz. the conducting of the world by general laws; and this seems nowise necessary to a very perfect Being. It is true; if every thing were conducted by particular volitions, the course of nature would be perpetually broken, and no man could employ his reason in the conduct of life. But might not other particular volitions remedy this inconvenience? In short, might not the Deity exterminate all ill, wherever it were to be found; and produce all good, without any preparation or long progress of causes and effects?

Besides, we must consider, that, according to the present œconomy of the world, the course of nature, though supposed exactly regular, yet to us appears not so, and many events are uncertain, and many disappoint our expectations. Health and sickness, calm and tempest, with an infinite number of other accidents, whose causes are unknown and variable, have a great influence both on the fortunes of particular persons and on the prosperity of public societies: And indeed all human life, in a manner, depends on such accidents. . . .

. . .

If every thing in the universe be conducted by general laws, and if animals be rendered susceptible of pain, it scarcely seems possible but some ill must arise in the various shocks of matter, and the various concurrence and opposition of general laws: But this ill would be very rare, were it not for the *third* circumstances, which I proposed to mention, viz. the great frugality with which all powers and faculties are distributed to every particular being. So well adjusted are the organs and capacities of all animals, and so well fitted to their preservation, that, as far as history or tradition reaches, there appears not to be any single species which has yet been extinguished in the universe. Every animal has the requisite endowments; but these endowments are bestowed with so scrupulous an œconomy, that any considerable diminution must entirely destroy the creature. Wherever one power is increased, there is a proportional abatement in the others. Animals, which excel in swiftness, are commonly defective in force. Those, which possess both, are either imperfect in some of their senses, or are oppressed with the most craving wants. The human species, whose chief excellency is reason and sagacity[3], is of all others the most necessitous, and the most deficient in bodily advantages; without clothes, without arms, without food, without lodging, without any convenience of life, except what they owe to their own skill and industry. In short, nature seems to have formed an exact calculation of the necessities of her creatures; and like a *rigid master*, has afforded them little[4] more powers or endowments, than what are strictly sufficient to supply those necessities. An indulgent parent would have bestowed a large stock, in order to guard against accidents, and secure the happiness and welfare of the creature, in the most unfortunate concurrence of circumstances. Every course of life would not have been so surrounded[5] with precipices, that the least departure from the true path, by mistake or necessity, must involve us in misery and ruin. Some reserve, some fund would have been provided to ensure happiness; nor would the powers and the necessities have been adjusted with so rigid an œconomy. The Author of nature is inconceivably powerful: His force is supposed great, if not altogether inexhaustible: Nor is there any reason, as far as we can judge, to make him observe this strict frugality in his dealings with his creatures. It would have been better, were his power extremely limited, to have created fewer animals, and to have endowed these with more faculties for their happiness and preservation. A builder is never esteemed prudent, who undertakes a plan, beyond what his stock will enable him to finish.

. . .

The *fourth* circumstance, whence arises the misery and ill of the universe, is the inaccurate workmanship of all the springs and principles of the great machine of nature. It must be acknowledged, that there are few parts of the universe, which seem not to serve some purpose, and whose removal would not produce a visible defect and disorder in the whole. The parts hang all together; nor can one be touched without affecting the rest, in a greater or less degree. But at the same time, it must be observed, that none of these parts or principles, however useful, are so accurately adjusted, as to keep precisely within those bounds in which their utility consists; but they are, all of them, apt, on every occasion, to run into the one extreme or the other. One would imagine, that this grand production has not received the last hand of the maker; so little finished is every part, and so coarse are the strokes, with which it is executed. Thus, the winds are requisite to convey the vapours along the surface of the globe, and to assist men in navigation: But how oft, rising up to tempests and hurricanes, do they become pernicious?[6] Rains are necessary to nourish all the plants and animals of the earth: But how often are they defective? how often excessive? Heat is requisite to all life and vegetation; but is not always found in the due proportion. On the mixture and secretion of the humours and juices of the body depend the health and prosperity of the animal: But the parts perform not regularly their proper function. What more useful than all the passions of the mind, ambition, vanity, love, anger? But how oft do they break their bounds, and cause the greatest convulsions in society? There is nothing so advantageous in the universe, but what frequently becomes pernicious, by its excess or defect; nor has nature guarded, with the requisite accuracy, against all disorder or confu-

---

[3]   *sagacity:* keennest of discernment or judgement [editor's note].

[4]   *Read* no *for* little [editor's note].

[5]   *Read* bordered *for* surrounded [editor's note].

[6]   *pernicious:* highly injurious or destructive in character; deadly [editor's note].

sion. The irregularity is never, perhaps, so great as to destroy any species; but is often sufficient to involve the individuals in ruin and misery.

On the concurrence, then, of these *four* circumstances does all or the greatest part of natural evil depend. Were all living creatures incapable of pain, or were the world administered by particular volitions, evil never could have found access into the universe: And were animals endowed with a large stock of powers and faculties, beyond what strict necessity requires; or were the several springs and principles of the universe so accurately framed as to preserve always the just temperament and medium; there must have been very little ill in comparison of what we feel at present. What then shall we pronounce on this occasion? Shall we say, that these circumstances are not necessary, and that they might easily have been altered in the contrivance of the universe? This decision seems too presumptuous for creatures so blind and ignorant. Let us be more modest in our conclusions. Let us allow, that, if the goodness of the Deity (I mean a goodness like the human) could be established on any tolerable reasons *a priori*, these phenomena, however untoward, would not be sufficient to subvert that principle; but might easily, in some unknown manner, be reconcilable to it. But let us still assert, that as this goodness is not antecedently established, but must be inferred from the phenomena, there can be no grounds for such an inference, while there are so many ills in the universe, and while these ills might so easily have been remedied, as far as human understanding can be allowed to judge on such a subject. I am sceptic enough to allow, that the bad appearances, notwithstanding all my reasonings, may be compatible with such attributes as you suppose: But surely they can never prove these attributes. Such a conclusion cannot result from scepticism; but must arise from the phenomena, and from our confidence in the reasonings which we deduce from these phenomena.

Look round this universe. What an immense profusion of beings, animated and organized, sensible and active! You admire this prodigious variety and fecundity[7]. But inspect a little more narrowly these living existences, the only beings worth regarding. How hostile and destructive to each other! How insufficient all of them for their own happiness! How contemptible or odious to the spectator! The whole presents nothing but the idea of a blind nature, impregnated by a great[8] vivifying principle, and pouring forth from her lap, without discernment or parental care, her maimed and abortive children.

. . .

There may *four* hypotheses be framed concerning the first[9] causes of the universe: *that* they are endowed with perfect goodness, *that* they have perfect malice, *that* they are opposite and have both goodness and malice, *that* they have neither goodness nor malice. Mixed phenomena can never prove the two former unmixed principles. And the uniformity and steadiness of general laws seem to oppose the third. The fourth, therefore, seems by far the most probable.

What I have said concerning natural evil will apply to moral, with little or no variation; and we have no more[10] reason to infer, that the rectitude of the supreme Being resembles human rectitude than that his benevolence resembles the human. Nay, it will be thought, that we have still greater cause to exclude from him moral sentiments, such as we feel

[7] *fecundity:* quality or power of producing offspring or fruit; fertility, hence productiveness [editor's note].

[8] *Read* an infinity *for* great [editor's note].

[9] *Read* original *for* first [editor's note].

[10] *Read* the same *for* no more [editor's note].

them; since moral evil, in the opinion of many, is much more predominant above moral good than natural evil above natural good.

But even though this should not be allowed, and though the virtue, which is in mankind, should be acknowledged much superior to the vice; yet so long as there is any vice at all in the universe, it will very much puzzle you anthropomorphites[11], how to account for it. You must assign a cause for it, without having recourse to the first cause. But as every effect must have a cause, and that cause another; you must either carry on the progression *in infinitum*, or rest on[12] that original principle, who is the ultimate cause of all things. . . .

Hold! Hold! cried Demea: Whither does your imagination hurry you? I joined in alliance with you, in order to prove the incomprehensible nature of the divine Being, and refute the principles of Cleanthes, who would measure every thing by a human rule and standard. But I now find you running into all the topics of the greatest libertines[13] and infidels[14], and betraying that holy cause, which you seemingly espoused. Are you secretly, then, a more dangerous enemy than Cleanthes himself?

And are you so late in perceiving it? replied Cleanthes. Believe me, Demea; your friend Philo, from the beginning, has been amusing himself at both our expence; and it must be confessed, that the injudicious reasoning of our vulgar theology has given him but too just a handle of ridicule. The total infirmity of human reason, the absolute incomprehensibility of the divine nature, the great and universal misery and still greater wickedness of men; these are strange topics surely to be so fondly cherished by orthodox divines and doctors. In ages of stupidity and ignorance, indeed, these principles may safely be espoused; and perhaps, no views of things are more proper to promote superstition, than such as encourage the blind amazement, the diffidence, and melancholy of mankind. . . .

. . .

Thus Philo continued to the last his spirit of opposition, and his censure of established opinion. But I could observe, that Demea did not at all relish the latter part of the discourse; and he took occasion soon after, on some pretence or other, to leave the company.

---

[11] *anthropomorphite:* one who ascribes human characteristics to God [editor's note].

[12] *Read* stop at *for* rest on [editor's note].

[13] *libertine:* freethinking in religion—used derogatorily [editor's note].

[14] *Read* sceptics *for* infidels [editor's note].

Name_____

Date _____

1. Hume introduces the problem of evil by drawing an analogy to an architect who designs a faulty building. Explain the analogy.

2. Explain the first circumstance which, according to Hume, establishes the existence of evil.

3. Explain the second circumstance which, according to Hume, establishes the existence of evil.

4. Explain the third circumstance which, according to Hume, establishes the existence of evil.

5. Explain the fourth circumstance, which according to Hume, establishes the existence of evil.

19 *Problems of Epistemology*

Epistemology is derived from the Greek word *episteme* which means knowledge. The word 'ology', of course, means the study of. Hence epistemology is the study of knowledge, namely, what it is and how we come by it. "What is knowledge?" is a very basic question manifested by how often we use the verb to know. We make knowledge claims all the time. That fact, in itself, is enough to make some people curious as to just what knowledge is. After all, if we use such a word as often as we do, it only seems reasonable that we know what we mean when we use it!

There are several other epistemological notions that are of interest to philosophers; to wit, we often make claims concerning our beliefs. What is the difference between knowledge and belief? Certainly they are not the same. It is perfectly plausible for one to believe that a certain state of affairs[1] is the case without at the same time knowing that state of affairs to be the case. For example, 400 years ago it was not uncommon for Western Europeans to claim that the earth was flat. They thought they knew that the world was flat but they were mistaken. They falsely believed that the world was flat because the earth was and is not, in fact, flat. Just what is the difference between knowledge and belief? One of the differences between knowledge and belief involves the concept of truth. Whereas it makes perfect sense to speak of false belief, it is nonsense to characterize a bit of knowledge as false. To fully appreciate this point let us examine the three traditional criteria[2] that must obtain[3] in order for one to make a genuine knowledge claim. Consider, for example, the proposition

$$S \text{ knows that } p$$

where S functions as a variable for some person, say, Mary and p functions as a variable for some state of affairs, say, the refrigerator is white. Hence, S knows that p means, in this case, that Mary knows that the refrigerator is white. In order for it to be true to say that S knows that p, it must be the case that (i) S believes that p. Now just think about that. It would certainly be odd to claim that Mary knows that the refrigerator is white but that she earnestly does not believe it to be white. The reason for this lies in the second criterion for making a genuine knowledge claim, namely, (ii) p is the case. To say that p is the case is to make an assertion that it is a fact[4] that p. If S knows that p, then it is a fact that p. However, if S believes that p, it does not necessarily follow that it is a fact that p, as demonstrated by the above example of the belief that the earth is flat. The very foundation of knowledge is that of facts.

At this point it is absolutely necessary to understand the connection between facts and the notions of truth and falsity. Since facts are simply the state of things as they are at a given time, it follows that there can be great disparity[5] between the facts and what is said about them. It is what

---

[1] *state of affairs:* fact; the state of things as they are.

[2] *criterion:* a standard, rule or test on which a judgement or decision can be based. Criteria is the plural form of the word.

[3] *obtain:* to be established.

[4] *fact:* the state of things as they are.

[5] *disparity:* inequality or difference.

is claimed (said) to be factual that is either true or false. If what one says about some particular fact is accurate, then his statement is true. If what one says about a given fact is inaccurate, then his statement is false. It is of crucial importance to understand that truth and falsity are functions of statements (about facts).

That knowledge entails[6] facts leads naturally to how we know what we know as opposed to what we merely believe to be the case. This involves the third criterion of knowledge. (iii) *S* must have adequate evidence that *p*. Just what constitutes adequate evidence is of great philosophical importance. And in many day-to-day cases it is equally important. For example, our legal system presupposes a person innocent until proven guilty. In order for one to be proven guilty it must be demonstrated beyond a shadow of a doubt that he committed the crime for which he is being tried. In other words, in our legal system we strive not to convict someone unless we know that he committed the evil deed. In this context adequacy of evidence is considered to be that which is beyond a shadow of a doubt.

If one thinks about everyday circumstances it is clear that one is often asked to "back up" his knowledge claim with evidence. The important philosophical question at hand is just how much evidence must one have in order for it to be considered adequate? This leads to the distinction between two different types of knowledge, namely (a) knowledge of inner states and (b) knowledge of the external world.

(a) Knowledge of inner states is the type of knowledge we have when we know, for example, that we are in pain. In such a case, the mere experiencing of the pain constitutes adequate evidence that we are, in fact, in pain. This holds true for all of our perceptions. A perception is what we experience by one or more of our five senses. The mere fact of one having some perception or other is, in itself, adequate evidence that he is having that perception. For example, the experience of perceiving a mermaid (such as in a dream) is, in and of itself, adequate evidence that one has had the *perception* of a mermaid. The perception verifies itself as it were. It is in this sense that one cannot be mistaken about one's perceptions.

(b) On the other hand, there is knowledge of the external world. The external world is that which exists independently of our perceiving it. For example, one's automobile (supposedly) exists when it is out of one's perceptual field, i.e., when one is not looking at it. Here the criterion of adequate evidence for one's knowledge takes on a greater significance than that of knowledge of inner states. Knowledge of the external world is objective, that is, it is knowledge of the facts of the world. Consequently, there is room for disagreement among perceivers as to just exactly what the facts are. Clearly, one can be mistaken about the nature of the world around him via[7] his perceptions of it. We are all aware of the situation of a parched traveler in the desert who, on the basis of his perceptions, believes that he sees an oasis when, in fact, that which he perceives is only a mirage. Ordinarily, the discrepancies[8] between the facts and one's perceptions of them can be explained by some law of physics or abnormality on behalf of the perceiver. However, from a philosophical point of view a problem nevertheless remains. Consider, for example, the following claims:

---

[6]   *entail:* to have as a necessary accompaniment or consequence.

[7]   *via:* by way of.

[8]   *discrepancy:* lack of agreement.

(1) I am having an apple-like perception and

(2) There is an apple that I am perceiving.

(1) is a statement of knowledge of an inner state whereas (2) is a statement of knowledge of the external world, namely, that there really is an apple that exists independently of my perceiving it. I cannot be mistaken about the truth of (1). However, I can be mistaken about the truth of (2). Can one legitimately make the inference[9] from (1) to (2)? One can only do so with adequate evidence. The philosophical issue at stake is whether or not there can ever be evidence adequate enough for one to be absolutely *certain* that there really is an apple based on my apple-like perception. This example may appear trivial[10]. However, consider making the inference from (3) I am having a flying saucer-like perception to (4) There is a flying saucer that I am perceiving. Clearly, there is a good deal of slack between these two knowledge claims.

This issue of knowledge of the external world and in particular certain knowledge of it leads philosophers to develop theories centered on how we attain such knowledge. During the modern period of philosophy in Western Culture (approximately 1650-1850 A.D.) theories of knowledge dominated the discussion. There were two primary schools of thought, empiricism and rationalism. The former is more narrow-minded than the latter. Empiricism is that doctrine which maintains that *all* of our knowledge of the world around us is derived solely from sense experience. Sense experience pertains to the information one acquires by one or more of the five senses. This position is rooted in the belief that the use of reason cannot yield knowledge which is new or unique when applied in conjunction with sense experience. To be sure, reason plays a vital role in our lives. It simply does not, via its application provide any new or unique knowledge of the external world. For example, if one burns oneself on a hot stove, the knowledge gained has nothing to do with the use of reason. Presumably, one would use that bit of sense experience to reason that if one in the future plants one's hand on a red-hot range, a burn will result. Here the application of reason with respect to the experience will not deliver any unique knowledge which is unrelated to the experience.

But our experiences with the world are not always so simple. Suppose you conjure[11] up the notion of a mermaid. Since there are no such things that exist in the world, how could one have such an "idea"? The empiricist would typically claim that one's (sense) experience with female *homo sapiens*[12] and fish provide the basis of putting the two experiences together in a rather bizarre[13] manner. Although it is the use of reason which makes such a combination possible, the empiricist would maintain that nothing really new has been created for the elements that compose a mermaid are rooted in the (sense) experiences of the two aforementioned creatures.

Up to this point the rationalist would heartily agree with the empiricist. But the issue at hand is not nearly so simple. Rationalism is that epistemological school of thought which maintains that knowledge *can be* attained primarily by the use of reason after a modicum[14] of sense experi-

---

[9] *inference:* the deriving of a conclusion.

[10] *trivial:* unimportant; insignificant.

[11] *conjure:* to call to mind.

[12] *homo sapiens:* modern man; human being.

[13] *bizarre:* odd in manner or appearance.

[14] *modicum:* a small or moderate amount or quantity.

ence. There are two significant points here. (1) The rationalist is in total agreement with the empiricist that knowledge cannot be obtained without *some* sense experience. Sense experience provides the springboard for all knowledge. (2) The disagreement between the rationalist and empiricist concerns the issue as to whether the application of reason to sense experience can ever result in knowledge which is new and unique; that is, knowledge which is rooted in sense experience, but which concerns truths of the world which could never be ascertained[15] without the use of reason.

Consider the following situation. Suppose that you were sitting beneath an apple tree and an apple which happened to be red all over fell beside you. You know that by sense experience. However, you might after examining this object, come to the realization that it cannot be both red all over and not red all over at one and the same time. That realization constitutes a bit of knowledge. The question is whether or not it, the knowledge, is unique or simply an extension of your experience.

Here the empiricist is put on the defensive for it is not at all clear that such a case is analogous[16] to the mermaid example cited above. To be sure, the knowledge that was attained concerned an insight on behalf of the perceiver of the law of noncontradiction which is that an object cannot both possess a given property and not possess that property at one and the same time. It is a fact that everything we perceive must conform to that dictum whether we perceive any given thing or not. We may not, even could not, come to a knowledge of the law of noncontradiction without some sort of sense experience analogous to the apple example. On the other hand, (a) the power of reasoning was absolutely essential in order to figure out the law as a result of the experience and, (b) the reason that the apple cannot be both red all over and not red all over at one and the same time is because *all* things *must* conform to the law of noncontradiction in much the same way that the fallen apple conformed to the law of gravity within the context of the above example.

This latter point is significant with respect to the epistemological battle between the rationalists and empiricists. It is the issue of whether or not the world (i.e., universe) functions according to laws which are certain or not. The rationalist says "yes", the empiricist says "no". By a certain law we mean in this context laws which can be known for certain. If so, once we attain a knowledge of such laws, then they will provide a "backdrop" for what is possible within the world (i.e., universe). That is, if we attain a knowledge of the law of noncontradiction or the law of gravity, then we will know that not just one thing, but everything conceivable must conform to them. The object of any sense experience (i.e., an apple) which gave rise to such knowledge becomes inconsequential. Individual examples of such laws turn out to be confirmatory instances[17] of the laws themselves *not* something basic or essential to the laws. If, however, such aforementioned laws are not capable of being known for certain, as the empiricist maintains, then all one can do is to claim that it would *appear* that nothing can both possess and not possess the same property at one and the same time as a result of one's sense experience with the apple.

It follows from this that it would be possible, albeit[18] conceivable, for one to have a sense experience in the future which defied our prior sense experience. By such reasoning, it is easy to understand the basis of the

---

[15]   *ascertain:* to find out with certainty.

[16]   *analogous:* similar or comparable in certain respects.

[17]   *confirmatory instance:* an occurrence that demonstrates and therefore proves the authenticity of a hypothesis or law.

[18]   *albeit:* although, even though.

empiricist's claim that all knowledge of the external world results from sense experience and that reason cannot produce with the aid of experience any knowledge that is conclusive with respect to the nature of the world (i.e., universe).

Thus, we have the basis of an epistemological conflict that extended over a couple of centuries, roughly between 1650 and 1850. It would certainly be intellectually dishonest to leave the dispute at this stage. Hence, we must proceed to a more esoteric[19] level. This dispute between the rationalist and empiricist boils down to whether or not there is *a priori* knowledge of the external world. Such a term is not meant to frighten one off. *A priori* knowledge is simply new and/or unique knowledge which is gained primarily by the use of reason after a modicum of sense experience. Given the prior discussion, it should be clear that the rationalist firmly believes that such knowledge of the external world exists.

A posteriori knowledge, on the other hand, is knowledge which is achieved solely as a result of sense experience. The empiricist maintains that this type of knowledge is the only kind one can have of the external world.

It is at this point that the plot begins to thicken with respect to the two adversaries[20]. Knowledge is one thing. How we express it is another. The expression of knowledge necessarily entails the use of language. *If* there are two different types of knowledge, then it follows that there will be two different kinds of statements which express them. This does not mean that these differing statements will vary notably from a syntaxical[21] point of view. Rather, they will vary with respect to their truth conditions. Statements are either true or false. For example, the statement that you, the reader, are six feet tall is either true or false. Or the statement that it is presently raining is either true or false. The truth or falsity with respect to statements is what truth conditions are all about. In this regard, the truth conditions of statements expressing *a priori* and *a posteriori* knowledge differ.

A priori statements are universally true which means that in no way can they be false. Can you imagine the statement, "This apple cannot be both red and not red all over at the same time" being false? Of course not. It is universally true in the sense that even a Martian who understood the manner in which we Earthlings use language, i.e., what we meant by the use of the words we employ, would agree *without doubt* that the aforesaid statement was true. It is not only true, but true *beyond all doubt*. For a statement to be true beyond all doubt is what philosophers mean by universal truth, namely, true even for a Martian.

A posteriori statements are ones which are theoretically capable of being demonstrated (i.e., proven) false. That does not mean that they must have been so proven at some time or other. It simply means that with respect to *a posteriori* statements there is no certainty that they are absolutely true. The statement, "All crows are black" does not rule out the possibility that one might some day happen on a crow that is not black. Past experience tells us that such a case is highly unlikely, but the denial of the aforesaid claim is not contradictory.

This is a very important point with respect to the distinction at hand. If one denies an *a priori* statement, then a contradiction results. A contradiction is a statement or thought which both affirms[22] and denies the attri-

---

[19] *esoteric:* difficult to understand; obtuse.

[20] *adversary:* an opponent; enemy.

[21] *syntax:* the way in which words are put together to form phrases and sentences.

bution of a given property to some object. The denial of an *a posteriori* statement, on the other hand, does not create a contradiction. To say that "All crows are not black" may indeed be false (given the knowledge we have at our disposal), but it is nevertheless *conceivable* that there may presently exist (unbeknownst to us) a nonblack crow or that such a hybrid bird may turn up in the future. The point is that the thought or the expression of a nonblack crow does not manifest a contradiction, namely, a logical impossibility.

In order to fully appreciate the debate between the rationalist and empiricist, we must explore another distinction. Again, keep in mind that communication is carried on by the use of language. The following distinction is linguistic in nature. It involves that aspect of language known as semantics. Semantics pertains to reference and meaning. Reference in language is tantamount[23] to a pin the tail on the donkey game only one pins a word on a thing. The word 'table' is employed as a linguistic tool for the purpose of labeling a particular type of thing, a thing in the world external to us. That which is referred to is called the referent and the process of pinning the word on the thing is known as referring. Aside from any particular instance of using a word to refer to some thing, that word *also* has meaning. It has meaning in the sense that one can use it without at the same time referring to any specific object. Not only that, some words have meaning, but at the same time have no referent. Take for example, the word 'unicorn'. There exists no such creature, yet the word nevertheless has meaning. The point is that there is a radical difference between reference and meaning. If there is any doubt about this, consider the following two phrases;

(a) the morning star and
(b) the evening star.

There is no doubt of the fact that they carry with them different meanings for the words 'morning' and 'evening' connote[24] something different. Yet they refer to the same thing, namely, the planet Venus. It is at this point that the scenery becomes a bit more complicated. We do not communicate by means of singular words. Rather, we engage in the process of communication by the use of entire sentences (statements). In other words, we do not normally say, "table" but rather, "There is a table".

Not surprisingly, there are two types of statements, one whose main purpose is to tell us something about the world, and the other to define the meanings of words. The difference between the two types of statements provides the basis of the analytic/synthetic distinction. Let us begin with an analysis of synthetic statements by considering the statement, "The cat is on the mat". (1) First of all, such a statement tells us something about the world. It is a (linguistic) claim that there is an object, a cat, "out there" which has a given spatio-temporal relationship with another thing (out there), namely, a mat. (2) Such an utterance *refers* to a fact, namely, that the cat (so viewed) is on the mat. (3) Another way of looking at the nature of synthetic statements is that their subject does not refer to the same class of things as does the predicate term. That is to say, the class of things referred to by the word 'cat' is not identical to the class of things referred to by the word 'mat'. Simply stated, cats are not mats. (4) Such

---

[22] *affirm:* to declare positively or firmly; maintain to be true.

[23] *tantamount:* equivalent in effect or value.

[24] *connote:* indicate

a statement as "The cat is on the mat" may be true or it may be false. It always has the potential of being false because it refers to the external world and the uttering of such a statement may be the result of an hallucination tantamount to the perception of the oasis example cited above.

Let us turn now to the nature of analytic statements. (1) First of all, they tell us nothing about the world. For example, the statement "All bachelors are unmarried men", makes no claim about the actual existence of bachelors. That is to say, the word 'bachelor' has meaning regardless of the existence of them. We could, for example, gather up all the existing bachelors and annihilate[25] them in which case there would no longer be any bachelors to which to refer. In such a case, the word 'bachelor' would nevertheless retain its meaning. The point is that analytic statements tell us about the *meanings of words, not about facts*. Whether or not any bachelors exist does not alter the meaning of the word 'bachelor', namely, an unmarried man. (2) Analytic statements are self-referential which is to say that the subject and predicate terms refer to each other. Such statements are self-contained in that they do not refer to facts as do synthetic statements. The word 'bachelor' refers to the phrase 'unmarried man' and vice-versa. The vice-versa referring aspect of such statements is precisely what makes them *self*-referential. Perhaps this point can be best explained by exploring the third characteristic of analytic statements. (3) The subject and predicate terms of such statements refer to the same (i.e., identical) class of objects, which is to say that the word 'bachelor' refers to the same class of objects as does the phrase 'unmarried man' whether or not that class of objects exists in the "real" world. (4) Because the subject and predicate terms refer to each other, analytic statements are always (i.e., universally) true. The denial of such a statement results in a contradiction. Can you imagine the possibility of the statement, "Bachelors are not unmarried men" being true? Of course not. That is because the class of things to which the word 'bachelor' refers is identical to the class of things to which the phrase 'unmarried man' refers. To deny the identity results in a contradiction.

This foray[26] into the nature of synthetic and analytic statements is not without a purpose. It began with a dispute over the possibility of certain knowledge of the external world. Empiricists do, in fact, accede[27] to *a priori* knowledge and therefore to *a priori* statements. But they do so with stipulation[28]. They maintain that all *a priori* statements are analytic in nature.[29] Furthermore, the empiricist will claim that all synthetic statements are *a posteriori* because statements about the world are grounded in sense experience. Since sense experience is never 100% reliable, no synthetic statement is beyond doubt. The point is that the empiricist categorically denies the possibility of a synthetic *a priori* statement, namely, one which tells us something about the world that is universally true. No statement, as far as he is concerned, which linguistically portrays a fact external to a human being is beyond doubt and, therefore, can in no way be *a priori* in nature.

The rationalist, on the other hand, is not quite so rigid. It appears to him that there is the possibility of a synthetic *a priori* statement, namely,

---

[25] *annihilate:* to destroy completely; wipe out; reduce to nonexistence.

[26] *foray:* to make a raid or brief invasion.

[27] *accede:* to give assent; give in; agree.

[28] *stipulate:* to specify as a condition of an agreement; require by contract.

[29] Hence, the empiricist understands that knowledge of mathematics is *a priori*. Such knowledge is certain. However, it tells us nothing about the world.

one which tells us something about the world which is universally true. Take, for example, the statement, "Red is a color". Such a statement conforms to the aforesaid criterion of a synthetic statement, namely, that the subject and predicate terms do not refer to the same class of things. After all, there are many colored things that are not red. Therefore, the term 'color' is not equivalent to the term 'red'. Hence, the aforementioned statement must be a synthetic one. On the other hand, can you imagine that statement to be false? The denial of it is not false, but contradictory. If so, it must be universally true. It would be absurd to claim that red is not a color because part of the very *meaning* of red is that it is a color. Hence, it appears that the rationalist has somewhat of an edge on the empiricist. Nevertheless, the debate has continued into the 20th century.

Suggested Readings: Problems of Epistemology

Problems of Perception:

1. Armstrong, D. M., *Perception and the Physical World*, 1961.
2. Austin, J. L., *Sense and Sensibilia*, 1962.
3. Ayer, A. J., *Foundations of Empirical Knowledge*, 1947.
4. Broad, C. D., *The Mind and Its Place in Nature*, 1929, Chapter 4.
5. ____, *Scientific Thought*, 1927, Part II.
6. Chisholm R. M., *Perceiving: A Philosophical Study*, 1957.
7. Hirst, R. J., *The Problems of Perception*, 1959.
8. Hirst, R. J., Wyburn, G. M., and Pickford, R. W., *Human Senses and Perception*, 1964, Part III.
9. Lovejoy, A. O., *The Revolt Against Dualism*, 1930.
10. Price, H. H., *Perception*, 1933.
11. Russell, Bertrand, *The Problems of Philosophy*, 1912, Chapters 1-3.
12. Sellars, Wilfred, *Science, Perception, and Reality*, 1963, Chapter 3.
13. Stace, W.T., *Theory of Knowledge and Existence*, 1932, Chapter 6.

Criteria of Meaning:

14. Alston, William P., *Philosophy of Language*, 1964, Chapter 4.
15. Ayer, A. J., *Language, Truth, and Logic*, 2nd ed., 1950, Introduction and Chapter 1.
16. Bridgman, P. W., *The Logic of Modern Physics*, 1927, Chapter 1.
17. Carnap, Rudolf, "Testability and Meaning," *Philosophy of Science*, Vol. 3 (1936) and Vol. 4 (1937); reprinted with omissions in Feigl, H., and Brodbeck, M. (eds.), *Readings in the Philosophy of Science*, 1953.
18. Cohen, L. Jonathan, *The Diversity of Meaning*, 1962, Chapter 6.
19. Lewis, C. I., "Experience and Meaning," in Feigl, H., and Sellars, W. (eds.), *Readings in Philosophical Analysis*, 1949.
20. Mehlberg, Henry, *The Reach of Science*, 1958, Part III.

Meaning and Reference:

21. Austin, J. L., *Philosophical Papers*, 1961, Chapters 2 and 10.

22. Brown, Roger, *Words and Things*, 1958, Chapter 3.
23. Carnap, Rudolf, *Meaning and Necessity*, 2nd ed., 1955, Chapter 1 and Supplement.
24. Meinong, Alexius von, "The Theory of Objects," in Chisholm, *Realism and the Background of Phenomenology*, Chapter 4.
25 Morris, Charles, *Signs, Language, and Behavior*, 1946, Chapter 1.
26 Ryle, Gilbert, "The Theory of Meaning," in Mace, C.E. (ed.), *British Philosophy in the Mid-Century*, 1957.
27. Waismann, Friedrich, "Language Strata," In Flew, A. G. N. (ed.), *Logic and Language*, 2nd Series, 1953, Chapter 1.

Analytic and Synthetic Propositions:

28. Austin, J. L., *Philosophical Papers*, 1961, Chapter 1.
29. Ayer, A. J., *Language, Truth and Logic*, 2nd ed., 1950, Chapter 4.
30. Coffey, Peter, *Epistemology*, 1917, Vol. 1, Chapter 8.
31. Cohen, L. Jonathan, *The Diversity of Meaning*, 1962, Chapter 6.
32. Cohen, Morris R., *Reason and Nature*, 1931, Chapter 3, Section V.
33. Dewey, John, *Logic*, 1938, Chapters 1, 14, and 20.
34. James, William, *The Principles of Psychology*, 1890, Vol. 2, Chapter 28.
35. Kemeny, J. G., "Analyticity versus Fuzziness," in Gregg, J. R., and Harris, F. T. (eds.), *Form and Strategy in Science*, 1964.
36. Laird, John, *Knowledge, Belief, and Opinion*, 1930, Chapters 8, 9, and 10.
37. Lewis, C. I., *Mind and the World Order*, 1929, Chapters 7-9.
38. Mates, Benson, "Synonymy," in Linsky, L. (ed.), *Semantics and the Philosophy of Language*, 1952, Chapter 7.
39. Pap, Arthur, *Semantics and Necessary Truth*, 1958, Chapters 5 and 7.
40. Sellars, Wilfrid, "Is There A Synthetic A Priori?" *Science, Perception, and Reality*,1963, Chapter 10.
41. White, Morton, "The Analytic and the Synthetic: An Untenable Dualism," in Hook, S. (ed.), *John Dewey: Philosopher of Science and Freedom*, 1950.

The Nature of Truth:

42. Black, Max, "The Semantic Definition of Truth," *Language and Philosophy* 1949, Chapter 4.
43. Bradley, F. H., *Essays on Truth and Reality*, 1914, Chapters 5, 7, and 8.
44. Coffey, Peter, *Epistemology*, 1917, Vol. 2, Chapter 23.
45. Hobhouse, L. T., *The Theory of Knowledge*, 3rd ed., 1921, Part III, Chapters 1, 2, and 8.
46. James, William, "A Word More About Truth," *The Meaning of Truth*, 1909.
47. Royce, Josiah, "The Nature of Truth," in Ewing, A.C. (ed.), *The Idealist Tradition*, 1957.
48. Russell, Bertrand, *Human Knowledge*, 1948, Part II, Chapter 11.
49. Wilson, John, *Language and the Pursuit of Truth*, 1956, Chapter 3.

50. Wood, Ledger, *The Analysis of Knowledge*, 1941, Chapter 11.
51. Woozley, A.D., *Theory of Knowledge*, 1949, Chapters 6-7.

Chapter 19:
Problems of Epistemology

Name_____

Date _____

1. What is the difference between knowledge and belief?

2. I cannot be mistaken about the fact that I perceive a mermaid. True or false? Explain.

3. The two schools of thought regarding how we acquire knowledge are _____ and _____.

4. Empiricists believe we can never have certain knowledge of the external world. True or false? Explain.

5. What is the difference between *a priori* and *a posteriori* knowledge?

6. Analytic statements are always true. True or false? Explain.

7. What is meant by synthetic *a priori* statements? How do empiricists and rationalists differ regarding them?

20 Rationalism; René Descartes

❧ BIOGRAPHY ❧

René Descartes (1596-1650), one of the founders of modern philosophy, was born in the small French town of Touraine. His father sent him to the college of La Flèche which was under the direction of the Jesuits. It is clear from all accounts that he was considered by his instructors to be not only an ardent student, but a gifted one as well. During his latter years at this institution he gravitated toward the study of logic, philosophy and mathematics.

In an effort to learn more about the world, he joined the army of Prince Maurice of Nassau. He viewed the experience as somewhat of a sabbatical for he did not accept pay and took his enlisted time to think. This experience culminated academically in his treatise on music, Conpenduim Musical. In 1619 Descartes left the service of Maurice of Nassau and joined the army of Maximilian of Barvia. It was during this time that he experienced several dreams that subsequently motivated him to seek truth by reason and reason alone. This happenstance provided the historical basis of rationalism, the epistemological point of view that the fundamental truths of the world can be ascertained[a] by the use of reason.

It is no doubt the case that Descartes' mathematical background played a role in his philosophical viewpoints. He was a mathematician par excellence. The truths of math are ascertained via[b] the use of reason. His philosophical goal became to demonstrate that the truths of the world are determined accordingly. After all, the functions of the world are explained through physics and physics is nothing other than applied math! Hence, one can understand the functioning of the world and all that therein is by the use of reason. However, there must be some game rules with respect to such a pursuit, namely, the rules which are necessary in order to establish what one can first of all claim to know before one can determine how the world does, in fact, function. This led Descartes to write and publish his Discourse on Method which was dedicated to establishing the criteria[c] of knowledge about anything, especially the external world, the world that exists around us which we perceive.

In 1649 he accepted an invitation from Queen Christina of Sweden to become her tutor. However, it proved to be his ultimate undoing. It was his custom to lie in bed during the morning hours for the purpose of contemplation. Her program entailed[d] 5 AM tutorials. This was simply too much for Descartes. He contracted pneumonia from the severe climatic conditions and died on February 11, 1650.

a. *ascertain:* to get to know.
b. *via*: by way of.
c. *criterion:* a standard, rule, or test on which a judgement or decision can be based. Criteria is the plural form of the word.
d. *entail*: to cause or require as a necessary consequence; involve.

As an epistemologist, Descartes did not begin by committing himself to rationalism (see Chapter 18). Rather, he brought to his search for knowledge a set of expectations which, when developed, became known as rationalism. It is in this sense that Descartes was a pioneer of modern philosophy, that period from approximately 1650 to 1850 and dominated by a prolonged epistemological debate between rationalists and empiricists. The expectations Descartes had for epistemology were determined by the enormous influence mathematics had on his life.[1] He was a superb mathematician most notably demonstrated by having invented analytic geometry. Mathematical knowledge is *a priori*; that is, it is principally a product of reason. Such knowledge is beyond doubt; it is indubitable. Mathematical knowledge, however, does not tell us anything about the external world, the world that (presumably) exists external to our perceiving[2] it. In other words, all mathematical claims are analytic as well as *a priori*. Mathematics is, if you will, a game of pure reason. If you are good enough at it, you don't even need a blackboard. You do it in your head! With the understanding that certain knowledge is better than that which is uncertain, Descartes wondered whether or not he could establish any *a priori* knowledge of the external world. Is there any such knowledge that is beyond all doubt? And if there is, how are we to know it to be such? In other words, a test for certainty of knowledge must be determined at the outset of our epistemological quest. And if you think about it, this test must itself be *a priori* else it will not be beyond doubt. This led Descartes to postulate his four rules of methodic doubt:

> The first rule was never to accept anything for true which I did not clearly know to be such; that is to say, carefully to avoid precipitancy and prejudice, and to comprise nothing more in my judgment than what was presented to my mind so clearly and distinctly as to exclude all ground of doubt.

Such an approach to one's knowledge of the external world, namely, the world about us, is admirable indeed. But we must be somewhat scrutinizing[3] at this point. Just what does he mean by not accepting as absolutely certain that which does not present itself to him so clearly and distinctly as to exclude all ground of doubt? He is maintaining that a criterion for certainty (indubitability) of a claim to knowledge is clearness and distinctness.

Now, the philosophical question is, just what constitutes clearness and distinctness? It would do Descartes absolutely no good to say that the measure of clearness and distinctness is certainty for that would fall subject to the fallacy[4] of arguing in a circle, namely, to define one term by another and then define the latter by the former term. Descartes is not so unskilled as to fall into such a trap. Rather, he introduces an interesting

---

[1] Here it is most helpful to understand that one's epistemological expectations determine to a great extent where one is going to end up; that is, what results will be produced.
[2] *perceive:* to become aware of through sight, hearing, touch, taste or smell.
[3] *scrutinize:* to examine or observe with great care, inspect minutely or critically.
[4] *fallacy:* the quality of being in error; incorrectness of reasoning or belief.

notion to clarify his criterion of clearness and distinctness for indubitability. It is the notion of an innate idea. The word 'innate' means inborn. Here there are two possible sources of confusion. (1) Descartes does not mean that human beings are born with a bunch of ideas rattling about in their heads as marbles in a sack. Rather, our minds are innately constructed in such a manner that when stimulated by sense experience we can (and do) produce indubitable intuitions which he calls innate ideas. Care should be taken in understanding that only *some* of our ideas are of this variety.

(2) A careful reading of Descartes' first rule of methodic doubt reveals the crafting of judgments with regard to that which is presented to his mind, namely, ideas. Clear and distinct presentations are innate ideas. Judgments of clear and distinct ideas when linguistically expressed are *a priori* statements.

Here the germane[5] question is, "What is an example of an innate idea?" Descartes argued that we all first and foremost have the intuition *Cogito, ergo sum.* This Latin expression means "I think, therefore I exist". This claim is *a priori*; that is, it is universally true, which is to say that it cannot be false, which, in turn, is to say that it is indubitable. And the idea expressed by it is clear and distinct. The *cogito* is indubitable because the denial of it makes absolutely no sense at all. But why? Because the very *act* of denying it proves the truth of the assertion. Clearly, one cannot think unless he exists. To doubt is itself an act of cognition (i.e., thinking). So, in doubting the above claim one, in essence, verifies its truth. Furthermore, the *cogito* is the most fundamental of intuitions.

> There can be no other truth to take off from than this: *I think; therefore, I exist.* There we have the absolute truth of consciousness becoming aware of itself. Every theory which takes man out of the moment in which he becomes aware of himself is, at its very beginning, a theory which confounds truth, for outside the Cartesian *cogito*, all views are only probable, and a doctrine of probability which is not bound to a truth dissolves into thin air. In order to describe the probable, you must have a firm hold on the true. Therefore, before there can be any truth whatsoever, there must be absolute truth; and this one is simple and easily arrived at; it's on everyone's doorstep; it's a matter of grasping it directly.[6]

With the *cogito* we have the "absolute truth of consciousness becoming aware of itself". However, the indubitable existence established by an act of self-awareness is not objective, but completely subjective in nature. It is a truth of something internal, namely consciousness and therefore makes no claim concerning the external world. The goal of an epistemologist is to analyze our knowledge of the external world. Does such knowledge follow from the *cogito*? No. Because consciousness can never get outside of itself. And as far as Descartes is concerned, consciousness is a mental, as opposed to a physical, activity. His position is persuasive. You and I may well believe that consciousness is a function of brain activity. We are able to so believe by first of all *assuming* that there are human beings similar to ourselves. We demonstrate the relationship between brains and consciousness by tampering with other people's brains in varied and sundry ways. Our findings, however, are all based on

5 *germane:* truly relevant; pertinent.
6 Sartre, Jean-Paul, *Existentialism and Human Emotion* (N.Y.: Philosophical Library, Inc., 1957). pp. 36-37.

the assumption that there are other people with minds (qua[7] consciousness)! Common sense tells us that that assumption is warranted. The
problem is that no act of consciousness can have as its object of awareness the process of consciousness itself, namely the electrochemical reac-
tions that give rise to consciousness. Consequently, an act of
consciousness can never verify the (presumed) relationship between itself
and the physical process of brain activity that gives rise to consciousness.
In other words, there is an inevitable chasm between the mental and the
physical. As such, it does not look too good for Descartes for establishing
certain knowledge of the external world. Help for him is on the way,
however.

Descartes reasons that the second most fundamental idea we have is
that God exists. Although the intuition that God exists is an innate one,
the proposition that he does so is not *a priori* and therefore requires proof.
Since the God of the Judeo-Christian tradition is conceived to be infinite,
if such a being does, in fact, exist, that being must exist independently of
our conception of Him; that is, He must exist external to us.[8] Having
driven a wedge between the mental and the physical, Descartes realizes he
cannot (attempt to) prove the existence of God by any argument that relies
on empirical[9] data (such as do cosmological and teleological ones; see
Chapters 15 and 16). He must get the job done by pure reason. He needs
an *a priori* argument for the existence of God. In other words, Descartes
must prove God's existence by means of an ontological argument.[10] He
realizes this and so provides. Now, given that the Judeo-Christian God is
also conceived to be omnibeneficient[11], it follows that He would not
deceive us in believing in either (a) the existence of the external world qua
physical things or (b) the indubitability of such straightforward analytic
propositions as those of mathematics. Both (a) and (b) are two radically
different epistemological kettles of fish. Belief concerning (a) involves
synthetic propositions. In either case, Descartes' conviction that he has
proved the existence of God ontologically prohibits the possibility that we
are or can be systematically duped into thinking (1) that there is no material (i.e., physical) world, or (2) that the propositions of mathematics are
false as could be the case if there existed an evil genius "out there" whose
sole purpose in existence was to make us falsely believe that (1) and (2)
are the case. It is very important to understand that if one starts from the
cogito as did Descartes, one snares oneself at the outset in a phenomenological trap[12] whereby something like an ontological argument for the
existence of God is necessary to get out of the trap. If the ontological
argument provided is fallacious, then one is left caught in the trap which
entails at best that there can be no knowledge of the external world and at
worst that there is no external world at all, namely, that the only thing that
exists is my stream of consciousness.

From the *cogito* and God's existence Descartes argues that we have
other innate ideas. These are expressed as (a) logical laws and (b) physi-

---

7   *qua:* in the function or capacity of.

8   The Judeo-Christian God cannot exist as an infinite being and be dependent upon the
thoughts of finite creatures (i.e., human beings).

9   *empirical:* originating in or relying or based on factual information, observation or
direct sense experience.

10   Ontological arguments are purely conceptual in nature. That is, they do not rely on any
empirical data.

11   *omnibeneficient:* all-good.

12   A situation whereby one can never get beyond phenomena; that is, objects of sense perception as distinguished from ultimate reality.

cal laws of nature. Keep in mind that sense experience provides the occasion upon which innate ideas are formed. With regard to (a), suppose you were sitting under an apple tree and one of its fruits dropped by your side. Upon examining the apple you notice it to be red all over. From that sense experience you can reason that that apple cannot be both red all over and not red all over at one and the same time. As such, your powers of reasoning have produced a tautology.[13] By generalizing the realization that the apple cannot be both red all over and not red all over at one and the same time, one would formulate the proposition that nothing can both possess and not possess a given property at one and the same time. That is a statement of the logical law of noncontradiction. It is *a priori*. Note, however, that it, the law, does not tell you what is; that is, what exists. It only tells you what cannot be.

(b) Descartes argued that the laws of physics are innate ideas because physics is, in essence[14], applied math. Mathematical knowledge is *a priori* because all math propositions are instantiations of the logical law of identity. Consequently, if you had the proper math background, you could by way of the aforesaid apple falling by your side figure out the law of gravity. Were such the case, reason would be able to provide you with *a priori* knowledge of the way the world functions. How the world functions according to physical laws does not, however, give us any clue as to what is functioning according to them. Such requires sense experience which provides instances of those laws so functioning. And here's the rub. Because our senses do not provide us with infallible[15] data, we may have an *a priori* knowledge of the framework within which and by which the world can and must function, but such never leads to an infallible knowledge of what is specifically and how it specifically is functioning as the content (viz. object) of any given sense experience.

Even though in Descartes' system God prevents an evil genius from "conning" us into falsely believing in that which common sense dictates is the case, namely, that an external world full of physical objects exists; his theory nevertheless makes certain knowledge of the external world out of the question. This is so because the proof of God does not remove the wedge between the mental and the physical. The existence of God makes our belief in the existence of the external world reasonable. God's existence cannot make any knowledge of the external world indubitable. So, as I indicated at the beginning of this chapter, where one begins determines to a great extent where one ends up. In the case of Descartes, he begins with the *cogito* and goes full circle whereby he ends with the *cogito* leaving a chasm between the mental and the physical which he was never able to successfully bridge. He left the philosophical world with the very difficult mind-body problem, namely, how does one's mind interact with one's body? Suppose, for example, you decide at three o'clock in the afternoon to have pizza for dinner. What is the nature of the process whereby your mental act of decision-making directs your body to physically go to the pizza parlor and physically eat a pizza?

---

[13] A tautology is the instantiation of a logical law. To instantiate means to substitute a value for a variable. Hence 2 + 2 = 4 is an instantiation of the logical law of identity symbolized as X = X.

[14] *essence:* that which makes something what it is; intrinsic, fundamental nature or most important quality (of something).

[15] *infallible:* incapable of error; never wrong.

Suggested Readings: Rationalism; Descartes

1. Beck, Leslie J., *The Method of Descartes*, (Oxford: Clarendon Press, 1952).
2. _____, *The Metaphysics of Descartes*, (Oxford: Clarendon Press, 1965).
3. Caton, Hiram, *The Origin of Subjectivity: An Essay on Descartes* (New Haven: Yale University Press, 1973).
4. Copleston, F., *A History of Philosophy*: vol. 4 (N.Y.: Doubleday & Co., 1994), Chapters II, III & IV.
5. Doney, Willis (ed.), *Descartes* (New York: Doubleday, 1968).
6. Joachim, H.H., *Descartes' Rules for the Direction of the Mind* (London: Allen and Unwin, 1957).
7. Keeling, Stanley V., *Descartes*, 2nd ed. (New York: Oxford University Press, 1968).
8. Kenny, Anthony, *Descartes* (New York: Random House, 1968).
9. Malcolm, Norman, *Problems of Mind: Descartes to Wittgenstein* (New York: Harper & Row, 1971).
10. Roth, L., *Descartes' Discourse on Method* (Oxford: Clarendon Press, 1937).
11. Sesonske, Alexander and Fleming, Noel (eds.), *Meta-Meditations* (Belmont, Cal.: Wadsworth, 1965).
12. Smith, Norman Kemp, *New Studies in the Philosophy of Descartes* (London: Macmillan, 1952).
13. Vrooman, Jack Rochford, *Rene Descartes: A Biography* (New York: Putnum, 1970).

1. How might one arrive at rationalism from mathematics?

2. What is Descartes' criterion for certainty? What role do innate ideas play?

3. Why is an ontological argument for God's existence necessary in Descartes' system?

4. To what conclusion about the certainty of our knowledge of the external world does Descartes' theory lead? Why?

5. What is the mind/body problem and how does it arise in Descartes' theory?

> ## ❧ R E A D I N G S ❧
>
> ### *Rationalism*
>
> ### René Descartes
> #### *Discourse on Method*
> #### PART I (selections)
> #### PART IV (complete)

Descartes, René, *Discourse on Method*, translated by John Veitch (La Salle, Ill.: The Open Court Publishing Co., 1962), pp. 13-19 and 34-43.

Part I

It is true, however, that it is not customary to pull down all the houses of a town with the single design of rebuilding them differently, and thereby rendering the streets more handsome; but it often happens that a private individual takes down his own with the view of erecting it anew, and that people are even sometimes constrained to this when their houses are in danger of falling from age, or when the foundations are insecure. With this before me by way of example, I was persuaded that it would indeed be preposterous for a private individual to think of reforming a state by fundamentally changing it throughout, and overturning it in order to set it up amended; and the same I thought was true of any similar project for reforming the body of the Sciences, or the order of teaching them established in the Schools: but as for the opinions which up to that time I had embraced, I thought that I could not do better than resolve at once to sweep them wholly away, that I might afterwards be in a position to admit either others more correct, or even perhaps the same when they had undergone the scrutiny of Reason. I firmly believed that in this way I should much better succeed in the conduct of my life, than if I built only upon old foundations, and leant upon principles which, in my youth, I had taken upon trust. For although I recognized various difficulties in this undertaking, these were not, however, without remedy, nor once to be compared with such as attend the slightest reformation in public affairs. Large bodies, if once overthrown, are with great difficulty set up again, or even kept erect when once seriously shaken, and the fall of such is always disastrous. Then if there are any imperfections in the constitutions of states, (and that many such exist the diversity of constitutions is alone sufficient to assure us), custom has without doubt materially smoothed their inconveniences, and has even managed to steer altogether clear of, or insensibly corrected a number which sagacity could not have provided against with equal effect; and, in fine, the defects are almost always more tolerable than the change necessary for their removal in the same manner that highways which wind among mountains, by being much frequented, become gradually so smooth and commodious, that it is much better to follow them than to seek a straighter path by climbing over the tops of rocks and descending to the bottoms of precipices.

Hence it is that I cannot in any degree approve of those restless and busy meddlers who, called neither by birth nor fortune to take part in the management of public affairs, are yet always projecting reforms; and if I thought that this Tract contained aught which might justify the suspicion that I was a victim of such folly, I would by no means permit its publication. I have never contemplated anything higher than the reformation of my own opinions, and basing them on a foundation wholly my own. And although my own satisfaction with my work has led me to present here a draft of it, I do not by any means therefore recommend to every one else to make a similar attempt. Those whom God has endowed with a larger measure of genius will entertain, perhaps, designs still more exalted; but for the many I am much afraid lest even the present undertaking be more than they can safely venture to imitate. The single design to strip one's self of all past beliefs is one that ought not to be taken by every one. The majority of men is composed of two classes, for neither of which would this be at all a befitting resolution: in the *first* place, of those who with more than a due confidence in their own powers, are precipitate in their judgments and want the patience requisite for orderly and circumspect thinking; whence it happens, that if men of this class once take the liberty to doubt of their accustomed opinions, and quit the beaten highway, they will never be able to thread by a way that would lead them by a shorter course, and will lose themselves and continue to wander for life; in the *second* place, of those who, possessed of sufficient sense or modesty to determine that there are others who excel them in the power of discriminating between truth and error, and by whom they may be instructed, ought rather to content themselves with the opinions of such than trust for more correct to their own Reason.

For my own part, I should doubtless have belonged to the latter class, had I received instruction from but one master, or had I never known the diversities of opinion that from time immemorial have prevailed among men of the greatest learning. But I had become aware, even so early as during my college life, that no opinion, however absurd and incredible, can be imagined, which has not been maintained by some one of the philosophers; and afterwards in the course of my travels I remarked that all those whose opinions are decidedly repugnant to ours are not on that account barbarians and savages, but on the contrary that many of these nations make an equally good, if not a better, use of their Reason than we do. I took into account also the very different character which a person brought up from infancy in France or Germany exhibits, from that which, with the same mind originally, this individual would have possessed had he lived always among the Chinese or with savages, and the circumstance that in dress itself the fashion which pleased us ten years ago, and which may again, perhaps, be received into favor before ten years have gone, appears to us at this moment extravagant and ridiculous. I was thus led to infer that the ground of our opinions, I remarked that a plurality of suffrages is no guarantee of truth where it is at all of difficult discovery, as in such cases it is much more likely that it will be found by one than by many. I could, however, select from the crowd no one whose opinions seemed worthy of preference, and thus I found myself constrained, as it were, to use my own Reason in the conduct of my life.

But like one walking alone and in the dark, I resolved to proceed so slowly and with such circumspection, that if I did not advance far, I would at least guard against falling. I did not even choose to dismiss summarily any of the opinions that had crept into my belief without having been introduced by Reason, but first of all took sufficient time carefully to satisfy myself of the general nature of the task I was setting myself, and ascertain the true Method by which to arrive at the knowledge of whatever lay within the compass of my powers.

Among the branches of Philosophy, I had, at an earlier period, given some attention to Logic, and among those of the Mathematics to Geometrical Analysis and Algebra,--three arts or Sciences which ought, as I conceived, to contribute something to my design. But, on examination, I found that, as for Logic, its syllogisms and the majority of its other precepts are of avail rather in the communication of what we already know, or even as the Art of Lully, in speaking without judgement of things of which we are ignorant, than in the investigation of the unknown; and although this Science contains indeed a number of correct and very excellent precepts, there are, nevertheless, so many others, and these either injurious or superfluous, mingled with the former, that it is almost quite as difficult to effect a severance of the true from the false as it is to extract a Diana or a Minerva from a rough block of marble. Then as to the Analysis of the ancients and the Algebra of the moderns, besides that they embrace only matters highly abstract, and, to appearance, of no use, the former is so exclusively restricted to the consideration of figures, that it can exercise the Understanding only on condition of greatly fatiguing the Imagination; and, in the latter, there is so complete a subjection to certain rules and formulas, that there results an art full of confusion and obscurity calculated to embarrass, instead of a science fitted to cultivate the mind. By these considerations I was induced to seek some other Method which would comprise the advantages of the three and be exempt from their defects. And as a multitude of laws often only hampers justice, so that a state is best governed when, with few laws, these are rigidly administered; in like manner, instead of the great number of precepts of which Logic is composed, I believed that the four following would prove perfectly sufficient for me, provided I took the firm and unwavering resolution never in a single instance to fail in observing them.

The *first* was never to accept anything for true which I did not clearly know to be such; that is to say, carefully to avoid precipitancy and prejudice, and to comprise nothing more in my judgement than what was presented to my mind so clearly and distinctly as to exclude all ground of doubt.

The *second*, to divide each of the difficulties under examination into as many parts as possible, and as might be necessary for its adequate solution.

The *third*, to conduct my thoughts in such order that, by commencing with objects the simplest and easiest to know, I might ascend by little and little, and, as it were, step by step, to the knowledge of the more complex; assigning in thought a certain order even to those objects which in their own nature do not stand in a relation of antecedence and sequence.

And the *last*, in every case to make enumerations so complete, and reviews so general, that I might be assured that nothing was omitted.

Part IV

. . .but as I then desired to give my attention solely to the search after truth, I thought that a procedure exactly the opposite was called for, and that I ought to reject as absolutely false all opinions in regard to which I could suppose the least ground for doubt, in order to ascertain whether after that there remained aught in my belief that was wholly indubitable. Accordingly, seeing that our senses sometimes deceive us, I was willing

324 Part IV: Epistemology

to suppose that there existed nothing really such as they presented to us; and because some men err in reasoning, and fall into paralogisms, even on the simplest matters of Geometry, I, convinced that I was as open to error as any other, rejected as false all the reasonings I had hitherto taken for demonstrations; and finally, when I considered that the very same thoughts (presentations) which we experience when awake may also be experienced when we are asleep, while there is at that time not one of them true, I supposed that all the objects (presentations) that had ever entered into my mind when awake, had in them no more truth than the illusions of my dreams. But immediately upon this I observed that, whilst I thus wished to think that all was false, it was absolutely necessary that I, who thus thought, should be somewhat; and as I observed that this truth, *I think, hence I am*, was SO certain and of such evidence, that no ground of doubt, however extravagant, could be alleged by the Sceptics capable of shaking it, I concluded that I might, without scruple, accept it as the first principle of the Philosophy of which I was in search.

In the next place, I attentively examined what I was, and as I observed that I could suppose that I had no body, and that there was no world nor any place in which I might be; but that I could not therefore suppose that I was not; and that, on the contrary, from the very circumstance that I thought to doubt of the truth of other things, it most clearly and certainly followed that I was; while, on the other hand, if I had only ceased to think, although all the other objects which I had ever imagined had been in reality existent, I would have had no reason to believe that I existed; I thence concluded that I was a substance whose whole essence or nature consists only in thinking, and which, that it may exist, has need of no place, nor is dependent on any material thing; so that "I," that is to say, the mind by which I am what I am, is wholly distinct from the body, and is even more easily known that the latter, and is such, that although the latter were not, it would still continue to be all that it is.

After this I inquired in general into what is essential to the truth and certainty of a proposition; for since I had discovered one which I knew to be true, I thought that I must likewise be able to discover the ground of this certitude. And as I observed that in the words I *think*, hence I am, there is nothing at all which gives me assurance of their truth beyond this, that I see very clearly that in order to think it is necessary to exist, I concluded that I might take, as a general rule, the principle, that all the things which we very clearly and distinctly conceive are true, only observing, however, that there is some difficulty in rightly determining the objects which we distinctly conceive.

In the next place, from reflecting on the circumstance that I doubted, and that consequently my being was not wholly perfect, (for I clearly saw that it was a greater perfection to know than to doubt), I was led to inquire whence I had learned to think of something more perfect than myself; and I clearly recognized that I must hold this notion from some Nature which in reality was more perfect. As for the thoughts of many other objects external to me, as of the sky, the earth, light, heat, and a thousand more, I was less at a loss to know whence these came; for since I remarked in them nothing which seemed to render them superior to myself, I could believe that, if these were true, they were dependencies on my own nature, in so far as it possessed a certain perfection, and, if they were false, that I held them from nothing, that is to say, that they were in me because of a certain imperfection of my nature. But this could not be the case with the idea of a Nature more perfect than myself; for to receive it from nothing was a thing manifestly impossible; and, because it is not less repugnant that the more perfect should be an effect of, and dependence on the less perfect, than that something should proceed from nothing, it was equally impossible that I could hold it from myself: accordingly, it but remained that it had been placed in me by a Nature which was in reality more perfect than mine, and which even possessed within itself all the perfections of which I could form any idea; that is to say, in a single word, which was God. And to this I added that, since I knew some perfections which I did not possess, I was not the only being in existence, (I will here, with your permission, freely use the terms of the schools); but, on the contrary, that there was of necessity some other more perfect Being upon whom I was dependent, and from whom I had received all that I possessed; for if I had existed alone, and independently of every other being, so as to have had from myself all the perfection, however little, which I actually possessed, I should have been able, for the same reason, to have had from myself the whole remainder of perfection, of the want of which I was conscious, and thus could of myself have become infinite, eternal, immutable, omniscient, all-powerful, and, in fine, have possessed all the perfections which I could recognize in God. For in order to know the nature of God, (whose existence has been established by the preceding reasonings), as far as my own nature permitted, I had only to consider in reference to all the properties of which I found in my mind some idea, whether their possession was a mark of perfection; and I was assured that no one which indicated any imperfection was in him, and that none of the rest was wanting. Thus I perceived that doubt, inconstancy, sadness, and such like, could not be found in God, since I myself would have been happy to be free from them. Besides, I had ideas of many sensible and corporeal things; for although I might suppose that I was dreaming, and that all which I saw or imagined was false, I could not, nevertheless, deny that the ideas were in reality in my thoughts. But, because I had already very clearly recognized in myself that the intelligent nature is distinct from the corporeal, and as I observed that all composition is an evidence of dependency, and that a state of dependency is manifestly a state of imperfection, I therefore determined that it could not be a perfection in God to be compounded of these two natures, and that consequently he was not so compounded; but that if there were any bodies in the world, or even any intelligences, or other natures that were not wholly perfect, their existence depended on his power in such a way that they could not subsist without him for a single moment.

I was disposed straightway to search for other truths; and when I had represented to myself the object of the geometers, which I conceived to be a continuous body, or a space indefinitely extended in length, breadth, and height or depth, divisible into diverse parts which admit of different figures and sizes, and of being moved or transposed in all manner of ways, (for all this the geometers suppose to be in the object they contemplate), I went over some of their simplest demonstrations. And, in the first place, I observed, that the great certitude which by common consent is accorded to these demonstrations, is founded solely upon this, that they are clearly conceived in accordance with the rules I have already laid down. In the next place, I perceived that there was nothing at all in these demonstrations which could assure me of the existence of their object: thus, for example, supposing a triangle to be given, I distinctly perceived that its three angles were necessarily equal to two right angles, but I did not on that account perceive anything which could assure me that any triangle existed: while, on the contrary, recurring to the examination of the idea of a Perfect Being, I found that the existence of the Being was comprised in the idea in the same way that the equality of its three angles to two right angles is comprised in the idea of a triangle, or as in the idea of a sphere, the equidistance of all points on its surface from the centre, or even still more clearly; and that consequently it is at least as certain that God, who is this Perfect Being, is, or exists, as any demonstration of Geometry can be.

But the reason which leads many to persuade themselves that there is a difficulty in knowing this truth, and even also in knowing what their mind really is, is that they never raise their thoughts above sensible objects, and are so accustomed to consider nothing except by way of imagination, which is a mode of thinking limited to material objects, that all that is not imaginable seems to them not intelligible. The truth of this is sufficiently manifest from the single circumstance, that the philosophers of the Schools accept as a maxim that there is nothing in the Understanding which was not previously in the Senses, in which however it is certain that the ideas of God and of the soul have never been; and it appears to me that they who make use of their imagination to comprehend these ideas do exactly the same thing as if, in order to hear sounds or smell odors, they strove to avail themselves of their eyes; unless indeed that there is this difference, that the sense of sight does not afford us an inferior assurance to those of smell or hearing; in place of which, neither our imagination nor our senses can give us assurance of anything unless our Understanding intervene.

Finally, if there be still persons who are not sufficiently persuaded of the existence of God and of the soul, by the reasons I have adduced, I am desirous that they should know that all the other propositions, of the truth of which they deem themselves perhaps more assured, as that we have a body, and that there exist stars and an earth, and such like, are less certain; for, although we have a moral assurance of these things, which is so strong that there is an appearance of extravagance in doubting of their existence, yet at the same time no one, unless his intellect is impaired, can deny, when the question relates to a metaphysical certitude, that there is sufficient reason to exclude entire assurance, in the observation that when asleep we can in the same way imagine ourselves possessed of another body and that we see other stars and another earth, when there is nothing of the kind. For how do we know that the thoughts which occur in dreaming are false rather than those other which we experience when awake, since the former are often not less vivid and distinct than the latter? And though men of the highest genius study this question as long as they please, I do not believe that they will be able to give any reason which can be sufficient to remove this doubt, unless they presuppose the existence of God. For, in the first place, even the principle which I have already taken as a rule, viz., that all the things which we clearly and distinctly conceive are true, is certain only because God is or exists, and because he is a Perfect Being, and because all that we possess is derived from him: whence it follows that our ideas or notions, which to the extent of their clearness and distinctness are real, and proceed from God, must to that extent be true. Accordingly, whereas we not unfrequently have ideas or notions in which some falsity is contained, this can only be the case with such as are to some extent confused and obscure, and in this proceed from nothing, (participate of negation), that is, exist in us thus confused because we are not wholly perfect. And it is evident that it is not less repugnant that falsity or imperfection, in so far as it is imperfection, should proceed from God, than that truth or perfection should proceed from nothing. But if we did not know that all which we possess of real and true proceeds from a Perfect and Infinite Being, however clear and distinct our ideas might be, we should have no ground on that account for the assurance that they possessed the perfection of being true.

But after the knowledge of God and of the soul has rendered us certain of this rule, we can easily understand that the truth of the thoughts we experience when awake, ought not in the slightest degree to be called in question on account of the illusions of our dreams. For if it happened that an individual, even when asleep, had some very distinct idea, as, for example, if a geometer should discover some new demonstration, the circumstance of his being asleep would not militate against its truth; and as for the most ordinary error of our dreams, which consists in their representing various objects in the same way as our external senses, this is not prejudicial, since it leads us very properly to suspect the truth of the ideas of sense; for we are not unfrequently deceived in the same manner when awake; as when persons in the jaundice see all objects yellow, or when the stars or bodies at a great distance appear to us much smaller than they are. For, in fine, whether awake or asleep, we ought never to allow ourselves to be persuaded of the truth of anything unless on the evidence of our Reason. And it must be noted that I say of our *Reason*, and not of our imagination or of our senses: thus, for example, although we very clearly see the sun, we ought not therefore to determine that it is only of the size which our sense of sight presents; and we may very distinctly imagine the head of a lion joined to the body of a goat, without being therefore shut up to the conclusion that a chimæra exists; for it is not a dictate of Reason that what we thus see or imagine is in reality existent; but it plainly tells us that all our ideas or notions contain in them some truth; for otherwise it could not be that God, who is wholly perfect and veracious[1], should have placed them in us. And because our reasonings are never so clear or so complete during sleep as when we are awake, although sometimes the acts of our imagination are then as lively and distinct, if not more so than in our waking moments, Reason further dictates that, since all our thoughts cannot be true because of our partial imperfection, those possessing truth must infallibly be found in the experience of our waking moments rather than in that of our dreams.

---

[1] truthful [editor's note].

Name_____

Date _____

1. Why does Descartes decide to use his own Reason in his pursuit of truth?

2. Briefly state the four laws Descartes will follow in his method of seeking knowledge.

3. What reasons does Descartes find for doubting his sense knowledge?

4. What does Descartes discover that he cannot doubt?

5. How does Descartes argue from his *idea* of God to the *existence* of God?

21 Empiricism; John Locke

Empiricism was one of the two dominant epistemological[1] schools of thought between the 17th and early twentieth centuries. One of the best ways to understand empiricism *in general* is to think of it as the philosophical equivalent of the scientific method. Fundamental to the latter is a commitment to gathering data[2] regarding the external world before one formulates any theory(ies) about it. The point is that before one can reason out a theory about how the world functions, one must first of all have experienced it. Experiencing the world entails[3] either casually or rigorously gathering data about it. This is done by means of one or more of the five senses otherwise known as sense experience. From a scientific point of view it would be illogical to attempt to build a theory without such data. To do so would simply be putting the cart before the horse. In a parallel fashion, empiricism is that epistemological school of thought that maintains that *all* of our knowledge of the world around us; that is, the external world is derived solely from sense experience.

This does not mean that the use of reason is useless or plays no role whatsoever regarding human beings as the creative thinking individuals that we are. It means, rather, that the use of reason will not result in knowledge of the external world that is (really) new or unique when applied to what we experience regarding it. Take, for example, a child who is bitten by a dog. That is certainly a direct confrontation with the external world and constitutes for that individual a bit of datum. Hopefully, it is a learning experience and reason will instruct the child in the future to approach canines with caution. His use of reason is instrumental[4] in guiding his future behavior, but is, nevertheless, directly related to the initial experience and in that sense carries with it nothing essentially[5] new so far as the child is concerned.

The aforesaid example is, however, slightly elemental. Let us consider a more complex one. We all know what one means when he speaks of a unicorn. Such creatures we know for a fact do not exist in the external world. Nevertheless, we know that the word refers to a (white) horse possessing a curled conical horn projecting from its forehead. How did

---

[1] *epistemology:* the division of philosophy that investigates the nature and origin of knowledge.

[2] *datum:* something that is given from being experimentally encountered; a fact. Data is the plural form of the word.

[3] *entail:* to have as a necessary accompaniment or consequence.

[4] *instrumental:* serving as an instrument; helpful.

[5] *essential:* constituting or part of the essence of something; basic or indispensable.

the first person who thought of such a beast ever have that idea? Since unicorns do not exist, he could not have experienced it by one or more of his five senses. Here let us make no mistake. Many of us have had the (sense) experience of seeing a picture of a unicorn. But pictures are different than the real thing which does not exist independently of our idea of it. So how did the first person arrive at his idea of this hybrid[6] equine[7] having never had the experience of sensing one? The typical response on behalf of the empiricist is that he had had the sense experiences of horses and horns and then by his creative powers switched and matched them; the result being such a mythical horse-like being. The use of thinking or reasoning, if you will, in such a case does not result in something more or unique so far as the empiricist is concerned. Such powers only produce variations on a theme or themes, namely, prior sense experiences with the external world. There is nothing really unique about the intellectual conception of a unicorn. Its component parts can be directly related to some sense experience with the external world. It is at this point, however, that the waters get somewhat muddied. It concerns the issue of (a) what we know we experience as opposed to (b) what we know of the external world. Although not apparent to most people, this distinction is a rock-bottom one so far as epistemologists are concerned. (a) pertains[8] to knowledge of inner states whereas the domain of (b) is a knowledge claim concerning the world around us. Consider, for example, the following two statements:

(1) I have an apple-like perception[9] and
(2) There is an apple.

Statement (1) is an expression of an inner state. Such states pertain to the actual and immediate sense experiences one has. Such states do not *necessarily* have any reference to what, in fact, is for "real". The point is that one could be hallucinating whereby the content of the illusionary experience was apples (or pink alligators). Given such circumstances, one could in no way deny having apple-like perceptions, although given such circumstances there are no genuine apples which are being perceived that exist external to the perceiving agent. To make the point more blunt, the child referred to above cannot be mistaken about the pain he suffered as a result of the dog bite. The point is that that which is registered by one or more of the five senses cannot be doubted. If it cannot be doubted, then one has certain knowledge of it.

Statement (2), on the other hand, makes a claim about the external world, namely, that there *is* an apple out there that (supposedly) gives rise to our apple-like sense perception of it. But can we be absolutely *certain* about such a claim? Given "normal circumstances" we have little hesitation answering yes, and rightly so. However, from a philosophical point of view the qualifier "normal circumstances" raises difficulties. Just what does that mean? From a technical point of view, it may be the case that we are hallucinating 100% of the time in which case there would be no logical basis to claim that there really is an apple "out there" that we per-

---

[6]   *hybrid:* something of mixed origin or composition.

[7]   *equine:* of, pertaining to, or characteristic of a horse.

[8]   *pertain:* to have reference; relate.

[9]   *perception:* sense experience.

ceive. Such a (logical) possibility does not preclude[10] our having such an apple-like perception.

So how does one *know* that there *is* an apple that one is perceiving? The only criterion[11] we have to go on at this point is everyday experience along with common sense. However, common sense has its limits. At the risk of whipping a dead horse, consider the lost traveler on a desert who thinks he perceives an oasis. Upon walking endlessly he finds to his chagrin[12] that what he thought he perceived as a water hole was an illusion. The philosophical issue at this point is, how can anyone be *sure* that there is *anything* "out there" backing up his perception of it or them? One cannot consult a second party for assurance for how can one, namely, you the perceiver, be absolutely certain that the second party is not also an illusion? After all, you and only you can be certain of your perceptions. But you cannot be *sure* that your perceptions coincide with what really exists in the external world.

Empiricists in general concede[13] this point. As a result they normally adhere to a causal theory of perception. This is a theory that is predicated[14] upon common sense. Epistemologists of this bent are caught between the theoretical difficulties cited above and what simply makes sense, and in this case the two are not easy to reconcile[15]. On the one hand, it does not make a great deal of sense if one falls down a flight of stairs and proclaims that there were no stairs and that he is merely experiencing pain. It appears most reasonable, on the other hand, that there was something external to the agent that he failed to negotiate whereby he incurred a fractured leg. Even though the agent cannot be absolutely certain from a philosophical point of view that there were stairs that he fell down, it nevertheless is imminently[16] reasonable that such a structure existed independently of him and contributed to his present painful state.

Given this dilemma[17], most empiricists opt for the alternative that there *is* an external world which provides a causal basis for our absolutely certain perceptions of it. This is to say that they sacrifice the somewhat bizarre[18] philosophical possibility that everything we perceive is a figment[19] of our imagination and that we ought to cater[20] to the common sense side of the dilemma. Here, once again, we can see the scientific leanings of the empiricist school of thought. To be sure, there may never be absolute certainty of our knowledge of the external world. On the other hand, what will we achieve regarding our knowledge of it if we

---

[10] *preclude:* to make impossible or impractical by previous action; prevent.

[11] *criterion:* a standard rule, or test on which a judgement or decision can be based.

[12] *chagrin:* a feeling of embarrassment or humiliation caused by failure or disappointment.

[13] *concede:* to admit as true or valid; acknowledge.

[14] *predicate:* to base or establish.

[15] *reconcile:* to settle or resolve, as a dispute.

[16] *imminent:* about to occur; impending.

[17] *dilemma:* a situation that requires one to choose between two equally balanced alternative.

[18] *bizarre:* striking unconventional and far-fetched in style or appearance; odd; grotesque.

[19] *figment:* a fabrication.

[20] *cater:* to supply what is required or desired.

"write it all off" to subjectivism[21]? After all, there is nothing heinous[22] about the use of common sense!

John Locke felt the same way. He was willing to concede two points at the outset, namely, that (a) we do not know *how* we come to perceive the things that we do so perceive and (b) that we cannot have certain knowledge of the things that we do perceive. Nevertheless, given the (normal) state of our perceiving capabilities, everything is in our favor that there is an external world which has the potential of being perceived by us. So far as he is concerned, the common sense assumption that there is an external world would not be warranted if one could conjure up[23] the taste of a pineapple without ever having eaten and experientially tasted one. But alas, any given individual could not bring to mind the taste of such a fruit unless one *had actually* plopped a piece of the delectable[24] item on his tongue. Such evidence is enough to satisfy Locke's common sense point of view that there really do exist objects external to our perceptions of them. One cannot reasonably request or demand of a second party who has never tasted the ambrosia[25] of pineapple to offer a description of that taste for no other reason than that he has never experienced it. That he cannot is evidence that there is something external and independent of him.

Such an argument is enough, so far as Locke is concerned, to establish the existence of an external world and all that therein is. In addition, common sense demands that we recognize that there is a world independent of our own existence which provides or sets the stage, if you will, for the causal basis of the perceptions we have of it. As the pineapple example points out above, were it not for things in the external world which existed independently of us we would never be able to formulate an *idea* of what pineapple tastes like. If such things exist external to us, then it must be the case that they provide an independent basis whereby they *cause* in us the perceptions we have regarding them.

This issue of the production of ideas is crucial[26] to Locke's epistemology. At the outset, he maintains that intuition provides for us the idea of self, namely, our own being. This is the starting point. After this we develop ideas by experiencing the world around us. This seemingly poses no problem when it comes to our sense experiences regarding hot stoves, canines and pineapples. At a more sophisticated level, however, some individuals begin to wonder about that which ontologically [27] supports such *particular* items. If one "pushes" the issue back far enough it appears, by the application of common sense, that there must be some *common* ground from which spring all the individual items that exist in the world. This common ground Locke refers to as substance. Something cannot come from nothing. There simply must be some "base line" substance of which the parts of dogs and pineapples are composed. We can figure this out by the use of reason; and, if so, we must have an *idea* of this fundamental substance. And indeed we do.

---

[21] *subjectivism:* the doctrine that all knowledge is restricted to the conscious self and sensory states.

[22] *heinous:* grossly wicked or reprehensible; adominable; odious; vile.

[23] *conjure:* to bring to the mind's eye; evoke.

[24] *delectable:* greatly pleasing; enjoyable; delightful.

[25] *ambrosia:* anything with an especially delicious flavor or fragrance.

[26] *crucial:* of supreme importance; critical; decisive.

[27] *ontology:* that branch of philosophy that deals with the nature of being.

It is at this point that Locke faces a split-level trap. On the one hand, we can determine that there must be this aforesaid, but non-defined substance. The use of reason leads us to such a conclusion. On the other hand, we have never directly experienced *pure* substance. We have only perceived such things as dogs and pineapples. If we have never directly "experienced" this fundamental "stuff", then how on earth can we have an idea of it? The only answer that Locke can provide is that logic and reason lead us to this conclusion. Once again, common sense asserts itself.

As the readings of Locke make evident, he willingly admits that although substance is necessary for particulars (e.g., canines) to exist, it is something the composition of which he "knows not what". Although he has no idea of what the constituents of substance are, he does "know" via[28] the use of reason that the primal notion of substance is necessary in order to explain the identifiable things we know exist in the external world.[29] Substance is the ground of being necessary for the independent existence of physical objects. Such a concession is important from an epistemological point of view for it provides the theoretical groundwork for a causal theory of perception.

What Locke ends up maintaining is that common sense forces us to believe that there is an external world full of physical objects which provide the basis of our perceptions. In essence, common sense leads us to *believe* that these individual objects "out there" provide the ontological basis of causing within us the perceptions we have of them. Locke and many other empiricists are convinced that such is a perfectly justifiable belief due to the fact that it has its roots in common sense.

Having once established this (supposedly) justifiable belief in the existence of physical objects in an external world, Locke proceeds to analyze the source and nature of our knowledge. He rejects Descartes' notion of innate[30] ideas by arguing that children and idiots do not possess them, which would needs be the case if such ideas come about due to the innate construction of human mentality. Rather, we are all born *tabula rasas*, or blank slates by which he means we have no knowledge to begin with. All of our knowledge comes from experience. Sense experience produces in us ideas. All ideas come from either sensation or reflection. "*External objects* furnish the mind with the ideas of sensible qualities, ...and *the mind* furnishes the understanding with ideas of its own operations...and such are perception, thinking, doubting, believing, reasoning, knowing, and all the different actings of our own minds; ...Whosoever the mind perceives in itself, or is the immediate object of perception, thought or understanding, that I call *idea*; and the power to produce any idea in our mind, I call quality of the subject wherein that power is." It is at this point that Locke proposes the distinction between primary and secondary qualities. The former are qualities which are inherent in a given object, namely, solidity, extension, figure, motion or rest and number. These are constant qualities no matter what one does regarding any perceivable object. If one divides, even smashes, a table to bits the resulting parts will still possess the same qualities of solidarity, extension, etc. These quali-

---

[28] *via:* by way of.

[29] Locke also has another logical point on his side. If it were the case that we could break everything that we perceive down into its component parts indefinitely, namely, *ad infinitum*, we would never be able to possess an idea of the composite entity external to us. Why? Because there must be some starting point without which no complex thing would be possible. In other words, some things must be unbreakable; that is, atomic in nature, otherwise no composite thing would have a basis (i.e., ground) for *being*.

[30] *innate:* to be born in; originate in.

ties remain as part of any given entity whether or not a given individual perceives them or not. In that sense, they are constant; which does not mean that they cannot change but rather that such change is not dependent upon our perceptions of them.

Consider this point. From Locke's point of view there exist in the external world objects external to any given perceiver; such entities must possess solidity, extension, figure, and the capability of motion, otherwise they simply could not exist. However, there are qualities which do not exist on their own, but which nevertheless appear to be real. These qualities Locke refers to as secondary qualities, ones which are produced or are capable of being produced, namely, *caused* by primary qualities. These are qualities such as colors, sounds and tastes. Consider, for example, viewing a range of mountains. Within a close proximity it may appear to be somewhat green due to the fact that it is covered with trees. Forty miles off, however, the mountain range may appear to be somewhat hazy or purple in color. Now we know that the mountain range did not change its fundamental composition. Therefore, it must be the case that its color is not a quality possessed by it that is constant, namely, unchanging. Such an observation provides the basis for Locke's distinction between primary and secondary qualities. Common sense tells us that the mountain range does not change in solidity or figure, but our senses regarding other qualities pertaining to it do, in fact, change, namely, its color. Hence, primary qualities of any given object are an inherent part of the object itself. Secondary qualities derive their existence from the primary qualities of the object, namely, the object itself. And the primary qualities have the power to produce in the perceiver sensations characterized as secondary qualities.

Such a distinction provides the basis for (a) maintaining that there is a "real" world "out there" for people to agree upon and, at the same time, (b) to admit that there is a difference of opinion as to just how that world is perceived. At the outset, common sense tells us that there is an external world with a multitude of objects in it which possess solidity, extension, bulk, figure, and motion. We also know that not only are there disagreements among perceivers regarding their perceptions of such entities, but also that our own perceptions of the same object at different times do not coincide. These variations of perceptions are accounted for by Locke's notion of secondary qualities.

On the face of it, Locke's theory seems quite sound especially when it comes to explaining individuals' different perceptions of (supposedly) the same thing. There are some fundamental philosophical problems with it, however. (1) There still remains the element of faith involved in believing that there is an external world with objects in it which provide the causal basis of our perceptions of such *entia*[31]. Given Locke's epistemology, we can never be certain that there really *is* something "out there" which we perceive. At the most fundamental level we must accept the existence of the external world and everything in it as a matter of faith. He realizes this point and credit ought to be given to him for it. (2) The distinction between primary and secondary qualities has been called into question. It has been argued that one cannot separate the two. How can one, for example, separate the color of an object from its shape?   Nothing extended is *colorless* and color makes no sense unless it is attached to some *thing*. Even the mental picture of say, the color blue adheres to some *thing* albeit[32] an amorphous[33] patch in a dream. The point is that

---

[31]   *entia:* (Latin) entities.

[32]   *albeit:* although, even though.

Locke's distinction between primary and secondary qualities ultimately breaks down, if you will. Sooner or later, from an epistemological standpoint, one either (a) makes a leap of that there is an external world with objects in it that ultimately cause the perceptions we have of them or, (b) that we individually exist alone in a world of our own, perceiving things with no substantive foundation, and that the active perceiving process is all that there really *is*. (a) is the epistemological approach whereby one under "normal circumstances" feels comfortable making the transition from the certain sensation of something apple-like to the commitment (belief) that there is an apple that he is perceiving. (b) is an example of a more skeptical viewpoint. Since we can only be sure of our perceptions, which may not reflect the real world, we are not justified in believing in an external world independent of our perceptions of it. As we know nothing of the world aside from such perceptions, we are not logically justified in believing that anything is real other than our perceptions.

In summation, the result of Locke's theory is that we do not, even cannot, view the external world *directly*, considering the varied perceptions of it. We can and do agree (as an act of faith) that there is such an independent sphere as a result of the similarity of our perceptions of it. But again, we do not view the world directly. There is a *tertium quid*, a third whatness, which stands between us, the perceiving beings that we are, and the world "out there". Secondary qualities play the role of this *tertium quid*. It is as if each and every one of us views the world through rose-colored lenses. These lenses are the secondary qualities whereby we can never perceive the objects of the world in precisely the same way as they "really" are. But common sense, in conjunction with the similar perceptions of other individuals, leads us to believe that there is an external world without which we would not have those perceptions or such agreements.

Suggested Readings: Empiricism; Locke

1. Aaron, R.I. *John Locke*, 3rd ed. (Oxford: Clarendon Press, 1971).
2. Copleston, F., *A History of Philosophy*, Vol. V (N.Y.: Doubleday & Co., 1994) Chapters 5 and 6.
3. Gibson, James, *Locke's Theory of Knowledge* (Cambridge University Press, 1917).
4. Mabbott, J.D., *John Locke* (London: Macmillan, 1973).
5. O'Connor, D.J., *John Locke* (Harmondsworth: Penguin, 1952).
6. Smith, Norman Kemp, *John Locke* (Manchester University Press, 1933).
7. Woolhouse, R.S., *Locke's Philosophy of Science and Knowledge* (New York: Barnes & Noble, 1971).
8. Yolton, John W., *Locke and the Compass of Human Understanding* (Cambridge University Press, 1970).
9. _____, *Locke and the Way of Ideas* (Oxford: Clarendon Press, 1956).

---

[33] *amorphous:* without definite form; lacking a specific shape.

┌─────────────────────────────────┐
│   **S T U D Y**   │
│   ‰ **Q U E S T I O N S** ‰   │
│   ─────────────────────   │
│   *Chapter 21:*   │
│   *Empiricism; John Locke*   │
└─────────────────────────────────┘

Name_____

Date _____

1. As an epistemological position, what does empiricism hold regarding our knowledge of the external world?

2. What do empiricists believe about the use of reason in knowledge?

3. What is a causal theory of perception?

4. What are primary qualities? Secondary qualities? How do they differ?

5. What is one criticism of Locke's theory?

Book I.   Neither Principles nor Ideas are Innate

Chapter 1: *No Innate Speculative Principles*

1. It is an established opinion among some men that there are in the understanding certain *innate principles*; some primary notions, *koinai ennoiai*[1], characters, as it were, stamped upon the mind of man, which the soul receives in its very first being and brings into the world with it. It would be sufficient to convince unprejudiced readers of the falseness of this supposition, if I should only show (as I hope I shall in the following parts of this discourse) how men, barely by the use of their natural faculties, may attain to all the knowledge they have, without the help of any innate impressions; and may arrive at certainty, without any such original notions or principles. For I imagine anyone will easily grant that it would be impertinent to suppose the ideas of colours innate in a creature to whom God has given sight and a power to receive them by the eyes from external objects: and no less unreasonable would it be to attribute several truths to the impressions of nature, and innate characters, when we may observe in ourselves faculties fit to attain as easy and certain knowledge of them as if they were originally imprinted on the mind.

But because a man is not permitted without censure to follow his own thoughts in the search of truth when they lead him ever so little out of the common road, I shall set down the reasons that made me doubt of the truth of that opinion, as an excuse for my mistake, if I be in one; which I leave to be considered by those who, with me, dispose themselves to embrace truth wherever they find it.

2. There is nothing more commonly taken for granted than that there are certain *principles*, both *speculative* and *practical* (for they speak of both), universally agreed upon by all mankind: which therefore, they argue, must needs be the constant impressions which the souls of men receive in their first beings, and which they bring into the world with them, as necessarily and really as they do any of their inherent faculties.

3. This argument, drawn from universal consent, has this misfortune in it, that if it were true in matter of fact, that there were certain truths wherein all mankind agreed, it would not prove them innate, if there can

---

[1]   *koinai ennoiai:* common conceptions (Greek) [editor's note].

be any other way shown how men may come to that universal agreement in the things they do consent in, which I presume may be done.

4. But, which is worse, this argument of universal consent, which is made use of to prove innate principles, seems to me a demonstration that there are none such: because there are none to which all mankind give an universal assent. I shall begin with the speculative, and instance in those magnified principles of demonstration, "Whatsoever is, is" and "It is impossible for the same thing to be and not to be"; which, of all others, I think have the most allowed title to innate. These have so settled a reputation of maxims universally received, that it will no doubt be thought strange if anyone should seem to question it. But yet I take liberty to say that these propositions are so far from having an universal assent, that there are a great part of mankind to whom they are not so much as known.

5. For, first, it is evident that all children and idiots have not the least apprehension or thought of them. And the want of that is enough to destroy that universal assent which must needs be the necessary concomitant of all innate truths: It seeming to me near a contradiction to say that there are truths imprinted on the soul, which it perceives or understands not: imprinting, if it signify anything, being nothing else but the making certain truths to be perceived. For to imprint anything on the mind without the mind's perceiving it, seems to me hardly intelligible. If therefore children and idiots have souls, have minds, with those impressions upon them, *they* must unavoidably perceive them, and necessarily know and assent to these truths; which since they do not, it is evident that there are no such impressions. For if they are not notions naturally imprinted, how can they be innate? And if they are notions imprinted, how can they be unknown? To say a notion is imprinted on the mind, and yet at the same time to say that the mind is ignorant of it and never yet took notice of it, is to make this impression nothing. No proposition can be said to be in the mind which it never yet knew, which it was never yet conscious of. For if any one [proposition] may, then, by the same reason, all propositions that are true and the mind is capable ever of assenting to, may be said to be in the mind, and to be imprinted: since, if any one can be said to be in the mind, which it never yet knew, it must be only because it is capable of knowing it; and so the mind is of all truths it every shall know. Nay, thus truths may be imprinted on the mind which it never did, nor ever shall know; for a man may live long, and die at last in ignorance of many truths which his mind was capable of knowing, and that with certainty. So that if the capacity of knowing be the natural impression contended for, all the truths a man ever comes to know will, by this account, be every one of them innate; and this great point will amount to no more, but only to a very improper way of speaking; which, while it pretends to assert the contrary, says nothing different from those who deny innate principles. For nobody, I think, ever denied that the mind was capable of knowing several truths. The capacity, they say, is innate; the knowledge acquired. But then to what end such contest for certain innate maxims? If truths can be imprinted on the understanding without being perceived, I can see no difference there can be between any truths the mind is *capable* of knowing in respect of their original:[2] they must all be innate or all adventitious:[3] in vain shall a man go about to distinguish them. He therefore that talks of innate notions in the understanding cannot (if he intend thereby any distinct sort of truths) mean such truths to be in the understanding as it never perceived, and is yet wholly ignorant of. For if these words "to be in the

---

[2]   *original:* origin [editor's note].

[3]   *adventitious:* coming from an external source [editor's note].

understanding" have any propriety, they signify to be understood. So that to be in the understanding and not to be understood, to be in the mind and never to be perceived, is all one has to say anything is and is not in the mind or understanding. If therefore these two propositions, "Whatsoever is, is" and "It is impossible for the same thing to be and not to be," are by nature imprinted, children cannot be ignorant of them: infants, and all that have souls, must necessarily have them in their understandings, know the truth of them, and assent to [them].

Book II. Of Ideas

Chapter 1. Of Ideas in general, and their Original

1. Every man being conscious to himself that he thinks; and that which his mind is applied about whilst thinking being the *ideas* that are there, it is past doubt that men have in their minds several ideas-- such as are those expressed by the words whiteness, *hardness, sweetness, thinking, motion, man, elephant, army, drunkenness*, and others: it is in the first place then to be inquired, *How he comes by them?*

I know it is a received doctrine, that men have native ideas, and original characters, stamped upon their minds in their very first being. This opinion I have at large examined already; and, I suppose what I have said in the foregoing Book will be much more easily admitted, when I have shown whence the understanding may get all the ideas it has; and by what ways and degrees they may come into the mind--for which I shall appeal to every one's own observation and experience.

2. Let us then suppose the mind to be, as we say, white paper, void of all characters, without any ideas. How comes it to be furnished? Whence comes it by that vast store which the busy and boundless fancy of man has painted on it with an almost endless variety? Whence has it all the *materials* of reason and knowledge? To this I answer, in one word, *experience*. In that all our knowledge is founded; and from that it ultimately derives itself. Our observation, employed either about external sensible[4] objects or about the internal operations of our minds perceived and reflected on by ourselves, is that which supplies our understandings with all the *materials* of thinking. These two are the fountains of knowledge from whence all the ideas we have, or can naturally have, do spring.

3. First, our senses, conversant about particular sensible objects, do convey into the mind several distinct perceptions of things, according to those various ways wherein those objects do affect them. And thus we come by those *ideas* we have of *yellow, white, heat, cold, soft, hard, bitter, sweet*, and all those which we call sensible qualities; which when I say the senses convey into the mind, I mean, they from external objects convey into the mind what produces there those perceptions. This great source of most of the ideas we have, depending wholly upon our senses, and derived by them to the understanding, I call *sensation*.

4. Secondly, the other fountain from which experience furnishes the understanding with ideas is the perception of the operations of our own mind within us, as it is employed about the ideas it has got--which operations, when the soul comes to reflect on and consider, do furnish the understanding with another set of ideas, which could not be had from

---

[4] *sensible*: able to be sensed [editor's note].

things without. And such are *perception, thinking, doubting, believing, reasoning, knowing, willing*, and all the different actings of our own minds--which we being conscious of, and observing in ourselves, do from these receive into our understandings as distinct ideas as we do from bodies affecting our senses. This source of ideas every man has wholly in himself; and though it be not sense, as having nothing to do with external objects, yet it is very like it, and might properly enough be called *internal sense*. But as I call the other *sensation*, so I call this *reflection*, the ideas it affords being such only as the mind gets by reflecting on its own operations within itself. By reflection, then, in the following part of this discourse, I would be understood to mean, that notice which the mind takes of its own operations, and the manner of them, by reason whereof there come to be ideas of these operations in the understanding. These two, I say, namely, external material things, as the objects of *sensation*, and the operations of our own minds within, as the objects of *reflection*, are to me the only originals from whence all our ideas take their beginnings. The term *operations* here I use in a large sense, as comprehending not barely the actions of the mind about its ideas, but some sort of passions[5] arising sometimes from them, such as is the satisfaction or uneasiness arising from any thought.

5. The understanding seems to me not to have the least glimmering of any ideas which it does not receive from one of these two. *External objects* furnish the mind with the ideas of sensible qualities, which are all those different perceptions they produce in us; and the *mind* furnishes the understanding with ideas of its own operations.

These, when we have taken a full survey of them, and their several modes, combinations, and relations, we shall find to contain all our whole stock of ideas; and that we have nothing in our minds which did not come in one of these two ways. Let any one examine his own thoughts and thoroughly search into his understanding; and then let him tell me, whether all the original ideas he has there, are any other than of the objects of his reflection. And how great a mass of knowledge soever he imagines to be lodged there, he will, upon taking a strict view, see that he has not any idea in his mind but what one of these have imprinted--though perhaps, with infinite variety compounded and enlarged by the understanding, as we shall see hereafter.

6. He that attentively considers the state of a child as his first coming into the world, will have little reason to think him stored with plenty of ideas that are to be the matter of his future knowledge. It is *by degrees* he comes to be furnished with them. And though the ideas of obvious and familiar qualities imprint themselves before the memory begins to keep a register of time or order, yet it is often so late before some unusual qualities come in the way, that there are few men that cannot recollect the beginning of their acquaintance with them. And if it were worthwhile, no doubt a child might be so ordered as to have but a very few, even of the ordinary ideas, till he were grown up to a man. But all that are born into the world, being surrounded with bodies that perpetually and diversely affect them, variety of ideas, whether care be taken of it or not, are imprinted on the minds of children. Light and colours are busy at hand everywhere, when the eye is but open; sounds and some tangible qualities fail not to solicit their proper senses, and force an entrance to the mind-- but yet, I think, it will be granted easily that if a child were kept in a place where he never saw any other but black and white till he were a man, he would have no more ideas of scarlet or green, than he that from his child-

---

5   *passions:* states of being acted upon (viz. being passive) [editor's note].

hood never tasted an oyster, or a pineapple, has of those particular rel-
ishes.

7. Men then come to be furnished with fewer or more simple ideas
from without, according as the objects they converse with afford greater
or less variety; and from the operations of their minds within, according
as they more or less reflect on them. For, though he that contemplates the
operations of his mind cannot but have plain and clear ideas of them; yet,
unless he turn his thoughts that way and considers them attentively, he
will no more have clear and distinct ideas of all the operations of his
mind, and all that may be observed therein, than he will have all the particular ideas of any landscape, or of the parts and motions of a clock, who
will not turn his eyes to it and with attention heed all the parts of it. The
picture or clock may be so placed that they may come in his way every
day; but yet he will have but a confused idea of all the parts they are made
up of, till he applies himself with attention to consider them each in particular.

8. And hence we see the reason why it is pretty late before most children get ideas of the operations of their own minds; and some have not
any very clear or perfect ideas of the greatest part of them all their lives.
Because, though they pass there continually, yet, like floating visions,
they make not deep impressions enough to leave in their mind clear, distinct, lasting ideas, till the understanding turns inward upon itself, reflects
on its own operations, and makes them the objects of its own contemplation. Children, when they come first into it, are surrounded with a world
of new things, which, by a constant solicitation of their senses, draw the
mind constantly to them; forward to take notice of new, and apt to be
delighted with the variety of changing objects. Thus the first years are
usually employed and diverted in looking abroad. Men's business in them
is to acquaint themselves with what is to be found without; and so growing up in a constant attention to outward sensations, seldom make any
considerable reflection on what passes within them, till they come to be of
riper years; and some scarce ever at all.

Chapter II. Of Simple Ideas

1. The better to understand the nature, manner, and extent of our
knowledge, one thing is carefully to be observed concerning the ideas we
have; and that is, that some of them are *simple* and some *complex*.

Though the qualities that affect our senses are, in the things themselves, so united and blended that there is no separation, no distance
between them; yet it is plain, the ideas they produce in the mind enter by
the senses simple and unmixed. For, though the sight and touch often take
in from the same object, at the same time, different ideas--as a man sees at
once motion and colour; the hand feels softness and warmth in the same
piece of wax: yet the simple ideas thus united in the same subject are as
perfectly distinct as those that come in by different senses. The coldness
and hardness which a man feels in a piece of ice [are] as distinct ideas in
the mind as the smell and whiteness of a lily; or as the taste of sugar, and
smell of a rose. And there is nothing can be plainer to a man than the
clear and distinct perception he has of those simple ideas; which, being
each in itself uncompounded, contains in it nothing but *one uniform
appearance, or conception in the mind*, and is not distinguishable into different ideas.

2. These simple ideas, the materials of all our knowledge, are suggested and furnished to the mind only by those two ways above men-

tioned, namely, sensation and reflection. When the understanding is once stored with these simple ideas, it has the power to repeat, compare, and unite them, even to an almost infinite variety, and so can make at pleasure new complex ideas. But it is not in the power of the most exalted wit or enlarged understanding, by any quickness or variety of thought, to *invent* or *frame* one new simple idea in the mind, not taken in by the ways before mentioned: nor can any force of the understanding *destroy* those that are there. The dominion of man in this little world of his own understanding [is] much the same as it is in the great world of visible things; wherein his power, however managed by art and skill, reaches no farther than to compound and divide the materials that are made to his hand; but can do nothing towards the making the least particle of new matter, or destroying one atom of what is already in being. The same inability will every one find in himself, who shall go about to fashion in his understanding one simple idea, not received in by his senses from external objects, or by reflection from the operations of his own mind about them. I would have anyone try to fancy any taste which had never affected his palate; or frame the idea of a scent he had never smelled, and when he can do this, I will also conclude that a blind man has ideas of colours, and a deaf man true distinct notions of sounds.

Chapter VIII: *Some Further Considerations Concerning Our Simple Ideas of Sensation*

1. Concerning the simple ideas of Sensation, it is to be considered--that whatsoever is so constituted in nature as to be able, by affecting our senses, to cause any perception in the mind, does thereby produce in the understanding a simple idea; which, whatever be the external cause of it, when it comes to be taken notice of by our discerning faculty, it is by the mind looked on and considered there to be a real positive idea in the understanding, as much as any other whatsoever; though, perhaps, the cause of it be but a privation[6] of the subject.

2. Thus the ideas of heat and cold, light and darkness, white and black, motion and rest, are equally clear and positive ideas in the mind; though, perhaps, some of the causes which produce them are barely privations in those subjects from whence our senses derive those ideas. These the understanding, in its view of them, considers all as distinct positive ideas, without taking notice of the causes that produce them: which is an inquiry not belonging to the idea, as it is in the understanding, but to the nature of the things existing without us. These are two very different things, and carefully to be distinguished; it being one thing to perceive and know the idea of white or black, and quite another to examine what kind of particles they must be, and how ranged in the superficies[7], to make any object appear white or black.

7. To discover the nature of our ideas the better, and to discourse of them intelligibly, it will be convenient to distinguish them *as they are ideas or perceptions in our minds*; and *as they are modifications of matter in the bodies that cause such perceptions in us*: that so we may not think (as perhaps usually is done) that they are exactly the images and resemblances of something inherent in the subject; most of those of sensation being in the mind no more the likeness of something existing without us,

---

[6]   *privation:* the absence of positive character or existence [editor's note].

[7]   *superficies:* a surface; outer area [editor's note].

than the names that stand for them are the likeness of our ideas, which yet upon hearing they are apt to excite in us.

8. Whatsoever the mind perceives *in itself*, or is the immediate object of perception, thought, or understanding, that I call *idea*; and the power to produce any idea in our mind, I call *quality* of the subject wherein that power is. Thus a snowball having the power to produce in us the ideas of white, cold, and round, the power to produce those ideas in us as they are in the snowball, I call qualities; and as they are sensations or perceptions in our understandings, I call them ideas; which *ideas*, if I speak of sometimes as in the things themselves, I would be understood to mean those qualities in the objects which produce them in us.

9. Qualities thus considered in bodies are:

First, such as are utterly inseparable from the body, in what state soever it be; and such as in all the alterations and changes it suffers, all the force can be used upon it, it constantly keeps; and such as sense constantly finds in every particle of matter which has bulk enough to be perceived; and the mind finds inseparable from every particle of matter, though less than to make itself singly be perceived by our senses. For example, take a grain of wheat, divide it into two parts; each part has still solidity, extension, figure, and mobility: divide it again, and it retains still the same qualities; and so divide it on, till the parts become insensible[8]; they must retain still each of them all those qualities. For division (which is all that a mill, or pestle, or any other body, does upon another, in reducing it to insensible parts) can never take away either solidity, extension, figure, or mobility from any body, but only makes two or more distinct separate masses of matter, of that which was but one before; all which distinct masses, reckoned as so many distinct bodies, after division, make a certain number. These I call *original* or *primary qualities* of body, which I think we may observe to produce simple ideas in us, namely solidity, extension, figure, motion or rest, and number.

10. *Secondly*, such qualities which in truth are nothing in the objects themselves but powers to produce various sensations in us by their primary qualities, i.e., by the bulk, figure, texture, and motion of their insensible parts, as colours, sounds, tastes, etc. These I call *secondary qualities*. To these might be added a *third* sort, which are allowed to be barely powers; though they are as much real qualities in the subject as those which I, to comply with the common way of speaking, call qualities, but for distinction, secondary qualities. For the power in fire to produce a new colour, or consistency, in *wax* or *clay*--by its primary qualities, is as much a quality in fire as the power it has to produce in *me* a new idea or sensation of warmth or burning, which I felt not before--by the same primary qualities, namely, the bulk, texture, and motion of its insensible parts.

11. The next thing to be considered is how bodies produce ideas in us; and that is manifestly by impulse, the only way which we can conceive bodies to operate in.

12. If then external objects be not united to our minds when they produce ideas therein; and yet we perceive these *original* qualities in such of them as singly fall under our senses, it is evident that some motion must be thence continued by our nerves or animal spirits, by some parts of our bodies, to the brains or the seat of sensation, there to produce in our minds the particular ideas we have of them. And since the extension, figure, number, and motion of bodies of an observable bigness may be perceived at a distance by the sight, it is evident some singly imperceptible bodies

---

[8] *insensible:* not able to be sensed [editor's note].

must come from them to the eyes, and thereby convey to the brain some motion; which produces these ideas which we have of them in us.

13. After the same manner that the ideas of these original qualities are produced in us, we may conceive that the ideas of *secondary* qualities are also produced, namely, by the operation of insensible particles on our senses. For, it being manifest that there are bodies and good store of bodies, each [of which] are so small that we cannot by any of our senses discover either their bulk, figure, or motion--as is evident in the particles of the air and water, and others extremely smaller than those; perhaps as much smaller than the particles of air and water, as the particles of air and water are smaller than peas or hail-stones--let us suppose at present that the different motions and figures, bulk and number, of such particles, affecting the several organs of our senses, produce in us those different sensations which we have from the colours and smells of bodies; e.g., that a violet, by the impulse of such insensible particles of matter, of peculiar figures and bulks, and in different degrees and modifications of their motions, causes the ideas of the blue colour and sweet scent of that flower to be produced in our minds. It [is] no more impossible to conceive that God should annex such ideas to such motions, with which they have no similitude, than that he should annex the idea of pain to the motion of a piece of steel dividing our flesh, with which that idea has no resemblance.

14. What I have said concerning colours and smells may be understood also of tastes and sounds, and other the like sensible equalities; which, whatever reality we by mistake attribute to them, are in truth nothing in the objects themselves, but powers to produce various sensations in us; and depend on those primary qualities, namely, bulk, figure, texture, and motion of parts, as I have said.

15. From whence I think it easy to draw this observation--that the ideas of primary qualities of bodies are resemblances of them, and their patterns do really exist in the bodies themselves, but the ideas produced in us by these secondary qualities have no resemblance of them at all. There is nothing like our ideas, existing in the bodies themselves. They are, in the bodies we denominate from them, only a power to produce those sensations in us: and what is sweet, blue, or warm in idea, is but the certain bulk, figure, and motion of the insensible parts in the bodies themselves, which we call so.

16. Flame is denominated hot and light; snow, white and cold; and manna, white and sweet, from the ideas they produce in us. Which qualities are commonly thought to be the same in those bodies that those ideas are in us, the one the perfect resemblance of the other, as they are in a mirror, and it would by most men be judged very extravagant if one should say otherwise. And yet he that will consider that the same fire that at one distance produces in us the sensation of warmth, does, at a nearer approach, produce in us the far different sensation of pain, ought to bethink himself what reason he has to say--that this idea of warmth, which was produced in him by the fire, is *actually in the fire*; and his idea of pain, which the same fire produced in him the same way, is *not* in the fire. Why are whiteness and coldness in snow, and pain not, when it produces the one and the other idea in us; and can do neither, but by the bulk, figure, number, and motion of its solid parts?

17. The particular bulk, number, figure, and motion of the parts of fire or snow are really in them--whether anyone's senses perceive them or no: and therefore they may be called real qualities, because they really exist in those bodies. But light, heat, whiteness, or coldness are no more really in them than sickness or pain is in manna. Take away the sensation of them; let not the eyes see light or colours, nor the ears hear sounds; let

the palate not taste, nor the nose smell, and all colours, tastes, odours, and sounds, *as they are such particular ideas*, vanish and cease and are reduced to their causes, i.e., bulk, figure, and motion of parts.

26. To conclude. Beside those before-mentioned primary qualities in bodies, namely, bulk, figure, extension, number, and motion of their solid parts; all the rest, whereby we take notice of bodies and distinguish them one from another, are nothing else but several powers in them, depending on those primary qualities; whereby they are fitted, either by immediately operating on our bodies to produce several different ideas in us; or else, by operating on other bodies, so to change their primary qualities as to render them capable of producing ideas in us different from what before they did. The former of these, I think, may be called secondary qualities *immediately perceivable*; the latter, secondary qualities *mediately perceivable*.

Chapter XII. *Of Complex Ideas*

We have hitherto considered those ideas, in the reception whereof the mind is only passive, which are those simple ones received from sensation and reflection before mentioned, whereof the mind cannot make one to itself, nor have any idea which does not wholly consist of them. But as the mind is wholly passive in the reception of all its simple ideas, so it exerts several acts of its own, whereby out of its simple ideas, as the materials and foundations of the rest, the others are framed. The acts of the mind, wherein it exerts its power over its simple ideas, are chiefly these three: (1) Combining several simple ideas into one compound one; and thus all *complex ideas* are made. (2) The second is bringing two ideas, whether simple or complex, together, and setting them by one another, so as to take a view of them at once, without uniting them into one; by which way it gets all its *ideas of relations*. (3) The third is separating them from all other ideas that accompany them in their real existence: this is called abstraction: and thus all its *general ideas* are made. This shows man's power, and its ways of operation, to be much the same in the material and intellectual world. For the materials in both being such as he has no power over, either to make or destroy, all that man can do is either to unite them together, or to set them by one another, or wholly separate them. I shall here begin with the first of these in the consideration of complex ideas, and come to the other two in their due places.[9] As simple ideas are observed to exist in several combinations united together, so the mind has a power to consider several of them united together as one idea; and that not only as they are united in external objects, but as itself has joined them together. Ideas thus made up of several simple ones put together, I call *complex*--such as are beauty, gratitude, a man, an army, the universe; which though complicated of various simple ideas, or complex ideas made up of simple ones, yet are, when the mind pleases, considered each by itself, as one entire thing, and signified by one name.

2. In this faculty of repeating and joining together its ideas, the mind has great power in varying and multiplying the objects of its thoughts, infinitely beyond what sensation or reflection furnished it with: but all this still confined to those simple ideas which it received from those two sources, and which are the ultimate materials of all its compositions. For simple ideas are all from things themselves, and of these the mind *can* have no more, nor other than what are suggested to it. It can have no

---

[9] For Locke's analysis of general ideas see below Part V, Chapter 25 [editor's note].

other ideas of sensible qualities than what come from without by the senses; nor any ideas of other kind of operations of a thinking substance, than what it finds in itself. But when it has once got these simple ideas, it is not confined barely to observation, and what offers itself from without; it can, by its own power, put together those ideas it has, and make new complex ones, which it never received so united.

3. Complex ideas, however compounded and decompounded, though their number be infinite, and the variety endless, wherewith they fill and entertain the thoughts of men; yet I think they may be all reduced under these three heads--

(1) Modes.
(2) Substances.
(3) Relations.

4. First, *Modes* I call such complex ideas which, however compounded, contain not in them the supposition of subsisting by themselves, but are considered as dependencies on, or affections of substances--such as are the ideas signified by the words triangle, gratitude, murder, etc. And if in this I use the word mode in somewhat a different sense from its ordinary signification, I beg pardon; it being unavoidable in discourses, differing from the ordinary received notions, either to make new words, or to use old words in somewhat a new signification; the later whereof, in our present case, is perhaps the more tolerable of the two.

6. Secondly, the ideas of *Substances* are such combinations of simple ideas as are taken to represent distinct *particular* things subsisting by themselves; in which the supposed or confused idea of substance, such as it is, is always the first and chief. Thus if to substance be joined the simple idea of a certain dull whitish colour, with certain degrees of weight, hardness, ductility, and fusibility, we have the idea of lead; and a combination of the ideas of a certain sort of figure, with the powers of motion, thought and reasoning, joined to substance, make the ordinary idea of a man. Now of substances also, there are two sorts of ideas--one of *single* substances, as they exist separately, as of a man or a sheep; the other of several of those put together, as an army of men, or flock of sheep--which *collective* ideas of several substances thus put together are as much each of them one single idea as that of a man or an unit.

7. Thirdly, the last sort of complex ideas is that we call *Relation*, which consists in the consideration and comparing one idea with another.

Chapter XIII. *Complex Ideas of Simple Modes*

18. I endeavour as much as I can to deliver myself from those fallacies which we are apt to put upon ourselves, by taking words for things. It helps not our ignorance to feign a knowledge where we have none, by making a noise with sounds, without clear and distinct significations. Names made at pleasure, neither alter the nature of things, nor make us understand them, but as they are signs of and stand for determined ideas. And I desire those who lay so much stress on the sound of these two syllables, *substance*, to consider whether applying it, as they do, to the infinite, incomprehensible God, to finite spirits, and to body, it be in the same sense; and whether it stands for the same idea, when each of those three so different beings are called substances. If so, whether it will thence fol-

low--that God, spirits, and body, agreeing in the same common nature of substance, differ not any otherwise than in a bare different *modification* of that substance; as a tree and a pebble, being in the same sense body, and agreeing in the common nature of body, differ only in a bare modification of that common matter, which will be a very harsh doctrine. If they say, that they apply it to God, finite spirit, and matter, in three different significations and that it stands for one idea when God is said to be a substance; for another when the soul is called substance; and for a third when body is called so--if the name substance stands for three several distinct ideas, they would do well to make known those distinct ideas, or at least to give three distinct names to them, to prevent in so important a notion the confusion and errors that will naturally follow from the promiscuous use of so doubtful a term; which is so far from being suspected to have three distinct, that in ordinary use it has scarce one clear distinct signification. And if they can thus make three distinct ideas of substance, what hinders why another may not make a fourth?

19. They who first ran into the notion of *accidents*, as a sort of real beings that needed something to inhere in, were forced to find out the word *substance* to support them. Had the poor Indian philosopher (who imagined that the earth also wanted something to bear it up) but thought of this word substance, he needed not to have been at the trouble to find an elephant to support it, and a tortoise to support his elephant: the word substance would have done it effectually. And he that inquired might have taken it for as good an answer from an Indian philosopher--that substance, without knowing what it is, is that which supports the earth, as we take it for a sufficient answer and good doctrine from our European philosophers--that substance, without knowing what it is, is that which supports accidents. So that of substance, we have no idea of what it is, but only a confused, obscure one of what it does.

Chapter XXIII. *Of Our Complex Ideas of Substances*

1. The mind being, as I have declared, furnished with a great number of the simple ideas, conveyed in by the senses as they are found in exterior things, or by reflection on its own operations, takes notice also that a certain number of these simple ideas go constantly together; which being presumed to belong to one thing, and words being suited to common apprehensions, and made use of for quick dispatch, are called, so united in one subject, by one name; which, by inadvertency, we are apt afterward to talk of and consider as one simple idea, which indeed is a complication of many ideas together: because, as I have said, not imagining how these simple ideas *can* subsist by themselves, we accustom ourselves to suppose some *substratum* wherein they do subsist, and from which they do result, which therefore we call *substance*.

2. So that if any one will examine himself concerning his notion of pure substance in general, he will find he has no other idea of it at all, but only a supposition of he knows not what *support* of such qualities which are capable of producing simple ideas in us; which qualities are commonly called accidents. If any one should be asked, what is the subject wherein colour or weight inheres, he would have nothing to say, but the solid extended parts; and if he were demanded, what is it that solidity and extension adhere in, he would not be in a much better case than the Indian before mentioned who, saying that the world was supported by a great elephant, was asked what the elephant rested on; to which his answer

was--a great tortoise: but being again pressed to know what gave support to the broad-backed tortoise, replied--*something, he knew not what*. And thus here, as in all other cases where we use words without having clear and distinct ideas, we talk like children: who, being questioned what such a thing is, which they know not, readily give this satisfactory answer, that it is *something*: which in truth signifies no more, when so used, either by children or men, but that they know not what; and that the thing they pretend to know, and talk of, is what they have no distinct idea of at all, and so are perfectly ignorant of it, and in the dark. The idea then we have, to which we give the *general* name substance, being nothing but the supposed, but unknown, support of those qualities we find existing, which we imagine cannot subsist *sine re substante*, without something to support them, we call that support *substantia*; which, according to the true import of the word, is, in plain English, standing under or upholding.

3. An obscure and relative idea of *substance in general* being thus made we come to have the ideas of *particular sorts of substances*, by collecting *such* combinations of simple ideas as are, by experience and observation of men's senses, taken notice of to exist together; and are therefore supposed to flow from the particular internal constitution, or unknown essence of that substance. Thus we come to have the ideas of a man, horse, gold, water, etc.; of which substances, whether any one has any other *clear* idea, further than of certain simple ideas co-existent together, I appeal to every one's own experience. It is the ordinary qualities observable in iron, or a diamond, put together, that make the true complex idea of those substances, which a smith or a jeweler commonly knows better than a philosopher; who, whatever *substantial forms* he may talk of, has no other idea of those substances, than what is framed by a collection of those simple ideas which are to be found in them: only we must take notice, that our complex ideas of substances, besides all those simple ideas they are made up of, have always the confused idea of something to which they belong, and in which they subsist: and therefore when we speak of any sort of substance, we say it is a thing having such or such qualities; as body is a thing that is extended, figured, and capable of motion; spirit, a thing capable of thinking; and so hardness, friability, and power to draw iron, we say, are qualities to be found in a loadstone. These, and the like fashions of speaking, intimate that the substance is supposed always *something besides* the extension, figure, solidity, motion, thinking, or other observable ideas, though we know not what it is.

4. Hence, when we talk or think of any particular sort of corporeal substances, as horse, stone, etc., tough the idea we have of either of them be but the complication or collection of those several simple ideas of sensible qualities, which we used to find united in the thing called horse or stone; yet, *because we cannot conceive how they should subsist alone, nor one in another*, we suppose them existing in and supported by some common subject; which support we denote by the name substance, though it be certain we have no clear or distinct ideas of that thing we suppose a support.

Book IV. Of Knowledge and Probability

Chapter III. *Of the Extent of Human Knowledge*

1. Knowledge, as has been said, lying in the perception of the agreement or disagreement of any of our ideas, it follows from hence That, *It extends no further than we have ideas*. First, we can have knowledge no further than we have *ideas*.

2. Secondly, That we can have no knowledge further than we can have *perception* of that agreement or disagreement. Which perception being: (1) Either by *intuition*, or the immediate comparing any two ideas; or, (2) By *reason*, examining the agreement or disagreement of two ideas, by the intervention of some others; or, (3) By *sensation*, perceiving the existence of particular things: hence it also follows:

3. Thirdly, That we cannot have an *intuitive knowledge* that shall extend itself to all our ideas, and all that we would know about them; because we cannot examine and perceive all the relations they have one to another, by juxta-position, or an immediate comparison one with another. Thus, having the ideas of an obtuse and an acute angled triangle, both drawn from equal bases, and between parallels, I can, by intuitive knowledge, perceive the one not to be the other, but cannot that way know whether they be equal or no; because their agreement or disagreement in equality can never be perceived by an immediate comparing them: the difference of figure makes their parts incapable of an exact immediate application; and therefore there is need of some intervening qualities to measure them by, which is demonstration, or rational knowledge.

4. Fourthly, It follows, also, from what is above observed, that our *rational knowledge* cannot reach to the whole extent of our ideas: because between two different ideas we would examine, we cannot always find such mediums as we can connect one to another with an intuitive knowledge in all the parts of the deduction; and wherever that fails, we come short of knowledge and demonstration.

5. Fifthly, *Sensitive knowledge* reaching no further than the existence of things actually present to our senses, is yet much narrower than either of the former.

6. Sixthly, From all which it is evident, that the *extent of our knowledge* comes not only short of the reality of things, but even of the extent of our own ideas. Though our knowledge be limited to our ideas, and cannot exceed them either in extent or perfection; and though these be very narrow bounds, in respect of the extent of All-being, and far short of what we may justly imagine to be in some even created understandings, not tied down to the dull and narrow information that is to be received from some few, and not very acute, ways of perception, such as are our senses; yet it would be well with us if our knowledge were but as large as our ideas, and there were not many doubts and inquiries concerning the ideas we *have*, whereof we are not, nor I believe ever shall be in this world resolved. . . .

Name_____

Date _____

1. Where do our ideas come from, according to Locke?

2. What is a simple idea? Give examples.

3. What is a complex idea? Give examples.

4. What does Locke mean by substance? Why is it important to his theory?

5. What does Locke believe about the certainty of knowledge?

22 *Idealism; George Berkeley*

❧ BIOGRAPHY ❧

George Berkeley[a] (1685-1753) was born near Kilkenny in Ireland of English descent. He was obviously an intelligent young lad as can be seen by the fact that he was sent to Trinity College in Dublin at the age of fifteen. He received his B.A. degree three years later and in 1707 he became a fellow of that institution. Two years subsequent to that he published his first book, An Essay Towards a New Theory of Vision. *During the same year he was ordained deacon and the following year a priest in the Protestant Church. He did not, however, remain in Ireland. He not only traveled to London, but to the Continent as well where he met with such notable individuals as Addison, Swift, Pope, Steele and Malblanche.*

One of Berkeley's dreams was to establish a seminary on the Island of Bermuda which was to be funded by the British government. Subsequently he journeyed to Rhode Island to lay the groundwork for his project. However, the money was not forthcoming and he was forced to return to the motherland. In 1734 he was appointed bishop of Cloyne, Ireland. During the following year he refused the offer of the more lucrative position of Bishop of Clogher. It is apparent that he was during his priesthood primarily concerned with the economic plight of the poor of which there were many in his diocese. In 1752 he moved with his wife and family to Oxford and died in a peaceful manner the following year.

He was a man who never lost his zest for writing and publishing his ideas which ranged from the metaphysical position of idealism (immaterialism) to that of the virtues of tarwater as a panacea for all medical ailments.

[a.] Pronounced as Bark´ lay.

Idealism of the British variety, as opposed to that of the Germans, is a form of empiricism. Empiricism is that epistemological[1] school of thought which maintains that *all* our knowledge of the external world is gained through the use of our five senses. There is no doubt that the essential[2] foundation of our knowledge is so acquired. We come into this world as blank sheets from an epistemological point of view. We need at least some data to generate knowledge. This is obtained by experiencing the world and this is only done through our senses.

---

[1] *epistemology:* the division of philosophy that investigates the nature and origin of knowledge.

[2] *essential:* constituting or part of the essence of something; basic or indispensable.

The fundamental issue that dominated modern philosophy (roughly between the 17th and 19th centuries A.D.) was whether or not the use of reason when applied to this basic (sense) data could produce any knowledge which is new or unique. The empiricist said "no". The members of the competing epistemological school of thought were rationalists who maintained that the application of reason could indeed generate new and unique knowledge.

So far as the most fundamental cases of the acquisition[3] of knowledge is concerned there was no conflict between these two schools of thought. For example, there is no doubt that a child who for the first time fondles a rose bush will get his hands pricked by the thorns on the stems of those beautiful flowers. The experience provides the basis of some knowledge. Only the most untutored[4] would disagree with this claim as to the acquisition of knowledge. But such an example is very elementary. Let us consider a case slightly more complicated. How, for example, did the concept of a mermaid come about? No one has ever experienced such a creature. If so, then did not the use of reason play some role in its conception? The empiricist would typically maintain that the *idea* of a mermaid is not unique for its component parts can be traced back to the sense experience of a fish and a female *homo sapiens*[5]. All that reason (imagination, if you will) has done is reorganize the individual parts of those experiences and developed something that *appears* unique, but is really nothing other than a variation on a theme.

In all fairness to the rationalists, they would not disagree with this example. They provide other examples which support the claim that the use of reason, when applied to sense experience, produce knowledge which could not be achieved without the use of reason. However, we are not here concerned with the dispute between the rationalists and empiricists. Rather, the present issue concerns the confrontation between the (a) realists and (b) idealists, realizing at the same time that they are both members of the empiricist school of thought.

(a) Realists are the philosophical equivalent of scientists. They accept no claim about the world to be true that cannot be verified[6] by means of sense experience. There are two crucial issues at stake here. (1) Verification entails[7] objectivity. Keep in mind that we are presently concerned with claims to knowledge. If one says, "There is a white refrigerator in front of me", it must at least be *possible* for a second party to experience the same phenomenon[8] and subsequently agree with the aforesaid claim, if such a pronouncement is to be considered true. After all, if such a criterion[9] for a knowledge claim was not essential, then it would make perfect sense for someone who was hallucinating to maintain that there were, *in fact*, pink alligators running about the walls around him. The necessity of objectivity makes perfect sense so far as the realist is concerned.

This brings us to the second working principle of the realist. (2) Common sense leads us to believe that there is an external world, namely, a world which exists regardless of whether or not we perceive[10] it at any

---

3   *acquire:* to gain possession of.

4   *untutored:* unsophisticated; unrefined.

5   *homo sapiens:* the biological classification for human beings.

6   *verify:* a statement, principle, or belief considered to be established and permanent truth.

7   *entail:* to have as a necessary accompaniment or consequence.

8   *phenomenon:* any occurrence or fact that is directly perceptible by the senses.

9   *criterion:* a standard rule or test on which a judgement or decision can be based.

given moment. For example, it does not lend itself to common sense to believe that when we do not perceive the automobile in our garage that it does not exist. For sure, it is a matter of common sense to possess such a *belief*. The rock bottom epistemological issue at stake between the realists and idealists is whether we can *know* that the item in question, namely, the car or any other thing, really exists if it is unperceived. Just what (epistemological) guarantees do we have that anything unperceived exists? For the realist common sense plays a crucial role in our knowledge of the external world.

(b) Idealists are empiricists in the sense that one can only rely on one's sense experience in order to acquire knowledge. However, they are more rigorous when it comes to their commitment as to what exists *as a result* of our sense experience. Common sense is okay up to a certain point. But what do we really know for *certain*? We can say in a rather loose way that we know that the car is in the garage even though we are not perceiving it at the present moment. But what does that really mean when it comes to making a knowledge claim? It means that we *believe* that our auto is so located. And from a practical point of view such a belief is no doubt justified. But from the standpoint of knowledge, is there any guarantee that the auto *is*, in fact, in the garage? We can only determine that by going and looking. But once we cease to so perceive the object in question, what evidence do we have at our disposal to verify that the car is *really* there? The point is that our senses are all we have to rely on in order to make such a claim.

Interestingly enough, the issue of objectivity that the realists make such an issue of at this point breaks down. Pushed to the extreme, we apparently do not even have any objective criteria to determine whether or not the supposed objective second party is real or not. How do we know that the hoped for input is not a mere figment of our imagination? We may accept such an evaluation, but at the same time what evidence do we have as to whether or not such input is factual? We can be sure given such a situation that we are, in fact, getting input, but that has only to do with our perceptions, not that such input is objective. It is our own subjective evaluation that the input is objective.

The point is simply this. There is a difference between the claims that:

(a) I am having a pineapple-like perception, and
(b) There *is* a pineapple that I am perceiving, and
(c) I am having the perception that someone is verifying my perception of a pineapple, and
(d) Someone else *exists* who is verifying my perception of a pineapple.

The difference between (a) and (b) and (c) and (d) may appear to be nitpicking, but it focuses on the differences between the realist and idealist. The realist maintains that under normal circumstances statements (b) and (d) are perfectly legitimate conclusions to be drawn from the perceptions he has which are expressed by statements (a) and (c). To him, the leap from (a) and (c) to (b) and (d) is simply a matter of common sense. And indeed, under normal circumstances common sense demands that such a leap is justified. However, (a) and (c) are expressions of sense experience which can no more be doubted than the perceptions we have during dream

---

[10] *perceive:* to sense by one of our five senses.

states whereas (b) and (d) are ontological[11] claims about the external world.

From a philosophical point of view, how can one determine and consequently *know* that the perceptual circumstances surrounding any given perception are normal? What possible criteria are there for any given perceiver to determine such objectivity when he is trapped by his own perceptions? If no such criteria exist, then it seems to follow that the assertions of (b) and (d) are not knowledge claims, but only those of belief albeit[12] reasonable ones. Granted, it may appear to be a mere technicality, but from an epistemological point of view it is very important. It centers on the question as to whether we (really) have any knowledge of the external world if there are no criteria by which we can establish for certain any such knowledge.

The use of common sense is an adequate guide in most (practical) cases. But philosophers are more demanding than that. They want to know what criteria, if any, *guarantee* knowledge of the external world. Common sense is one thing, but we all know that it can be fallible[13]. As philosophers, we want infallibility, if nothing else in the area of epistemology! Hence, if common sense is no guarantee; that is, no absolutely reliable criterion from an epistemological standpoint, then it appears that there really is no logical basis for making the transition from (a) and (c) to (b) and (d) above. Regarding those claims, all we can be certain about are those perceptions we have which are expressed by the former set of statements. Those claims have, strictly speaking, nothing whatsoever to do regarding the external world. They are only perception claims and, in and of themselves, carry with them no ontological commitments other than those regarding the perceptions so stated. Our perceptions seem to be our only infallible guide regarding whether or not anything "out there" does exist. This is really the basis of idealism. Epistemologists of this school of thought simply will not accept the use of common sense at this level of the debate as a criterion for knowledge of the external world, for common sense is predicated[14] upon the prior assumption that we perceive the world under *normal circumstances*. And we simply have no way whatsoever of establishing what constitutes "normal circumstances".

The upshot of all this, so far as the idealist is concerned, is that all that we can know (for certain) is the information we obtain by one or more of our five senses. In other words, the *existence* of any given object is *dependent* upon the perception of it by any given perceiver. As Berkeley so succinctly[15] made the point, *esse est percipi*, namely, to *be* is to be perceived.

As pointed out above, we are not here concerned with knowledge in the practical sense of the term, but knowledge which is certain. How do you know for certain that those things which you believe to exist, which you are not now presently perceiving, do *in fact* exist? You don't. Why? Because there is no way of ascertaining[16] their present state of existence unless you are perceiving them *right* now. Here Berkeley is perfectly consistent with the empiricist school of thought. He relies upon (sense) perception as the guideline for knowledge. But at the same time he

---

[11] *ontology:* that branch of philosophy that deals with the nature of being, i.e., existence.

[12] *albeit:* although; even though; though; notwithstanding.

[13] *fallible:* capable of error.

[14] *predicate:* to base or establish.

[15] *succinct:* clearly expressed in few words; concise.

[16] *ascertain:* to discover through examination or experimentation; find out.

refuses to accept anything for real that he does not perceive at the present moment for, logically speaking, there is no other epistemological guideline that we can rely on as a criterion for (certain) knowledge; hence, *esse est percipi*.

Berkeley took issue with John Locke, another English empiricist of the same period. Locke was an (epistemological) realist who maintained that the objects of the external world possessed both primary and secondary qualities. The former are bulk, solidity, extension, figure and mobility. That is, objects possess these qualities regardless of whether or not anyone at any given time is perceiving them. Common sense, according to him, leads everyone to believe that there are objects that exist in the external world which possess these qualities independent of anyone's perception of them. After all, one can not reasonably maintain that the stairs one just fell down are a figment of one's imagination. They obviously possess bulk and extension, the agent's motion notwithstanding! Otherwise, why would one have tumbled down them if they did not exist independently of the agent in question? Once could claim that such an experience is tantamount[17] to a dream, but such an analysis of the experience appears somewhat vacuous[18] especially if the person in question ends up with a fractured leg. Such a situation is hardly equivalent to the *results* of a bad dream.

Given such an example, a realist such as Locke would appear to have an edge on any idealist. He maintains, however, that the manner by which we know primary qualities is through the secondary qualities such as color, taste, and sound. Such qualities are not only produced by objects in the external world, but are dependent upon our perceptions of them. As a result, secondary qualities vary from individual to individual. For example, that which appears to be warm to a person coming in from the cold will not so appear to another who has been inside the same abode[19] for an extended period of time. By drawing such a distinction, Locke is able to explain that there are objects which exist external and independent of us (via[20] their primary qualities) and at the same time account for our different perceptions of them (via secondary qualities).

However, Berkeley argues that Locke's aforesaid distinction is fallacious on the basis that one cannot separate primary and secondary qualities when it comes to perceiving the so-called "real" world. How, for example, can one separate (even intellectually) the quality of color from any given object in question. The mere notion of a colorless object, which on Locke's account must be extended by virtue of its (supposed) independent existence, is inconceivable. If such is the case, then primary qualities are as dependent upon any given individual's perception of them as are the secondary qualities he believes to exist. And this is precisely Berkeley's point. If the nature of secondary qualities is dependent upon any given perceiver at any given time and, if one cannot even intellectually separate secondary qualities from the primary ones, must it not be the case that the latter are equally dependent upon a given perceiver? Again, *esse est percipi* holds true, not only for secondary qualities, but for primary ones as well.

At this stage of the discussion, it appears that Berkeley has the advantage. From a logical point of view he is correct in saying that we can

---

[17] *tantamount:* equivalent in effect or value.

[18] *vacuous:* devoid of matter, empty.

[19] *abode:* a dwelling place or home.

[20] *via:* by way of.

never know that something in the external world exists for certain unless it is being perceived. However, there is a potential ambiguity[21] packed into such a claim. (a) It may mean that one can never know that something in the external world exists for certain unless *he* is perceiving the given object in question. (b) On the other hand, it may mean that an object in question cannot be known to exist for certain unless someone is (presently) perceiving it. (a) is a form of idealism which is known as solipsism. 'Solipsism' is derived from the Latin words *solus* (alone) and *ipse* (self). This is the most extreme form of idealism. To maintain such a position is tantamount to claiming that anything that is not presently being perceived by the perceiver in question simply does not exist. The motto of a solipsist is, "I alone exist". In other words, nothing exists unless *I* am perceiving it.

Extreme as this position may appear, it does have the advantage of resolving some epistemological problems. For example, if solipsism is the case, then there is no difficulty in resolving the ontological status of dreams and hallucinations. The issue of whether or not they are "real" becomes vacuous. That which is perceived exists on the basis that it is perceived. *Esse est percipi.* Although such a position dissipates[22] some philosophical problems, it challenges common sense. We somehow *know* that dreams are not real in the same way that actually falling down a flight of stairs is real. Such knowledge appears to be a matter of common sense. But then again, we have already ascertained that common sense is not an iron-clad guideline by which knowledge is acquired. When the chips are down, the solipsist has the edge, for there really is no *objective* criterion by which certain knowledge of the external world can be attained. All we really have to go on is our own sense perceptions of what, from a common sense point of view, seems to be real, namely, a world and all that therein is that exists external to our respective perceptions of it. But again, strictly speaking, there are no absolute guarantees that such an external world does, in fact, exist.

Berkeley, however, is not a solipsist. Rather, he opts for the second interpretation of idealism, namely, (b) that a given object in question cannot be known to exist for certain unless *someone* is (presently) perceiving it. Interestingly enough, Berkeley does have a feeling for the criterion of common sense when it comes to knowledge of the external world. It does not appear reasonable to him that when he is not presently perceiving a specific waterfall that it therefore does not exist. At the same time, he cannot relinquish[23] his fundamental principle that to be is to be perceived.

How is this epistemological principle made to square with common sense? Berkeley's answer to this dilemma[24] is that there must be some higher being who eternally perceives everything; that is, the world and all that therein is and thereby via such continual perception makes it reasonable for one to believe that there are objects in that world which continue to exist even though he is not perceiving them at any given moment. Such an almighty being, he concludes, must be God. Given Berkeley's *esse est percipi* criterion for certain knowledge of the external world together with common sense, this is the only conclusion he can derive[25]. If it does not

---

[21]   *ambiguity:* susceptible of multiple interpretation.

[22]   *dissipate:* to drive away or dispel by or as if by dispersing; rout; scatter.

[23]   *relinquish:* to surrender; renounce.

[24]   *dilemma:* a situation that requires one to choose between two equally balanced alternatives.

[25]   *derive:* to get by reasoning.

make sense for things in the external world to exist unless they are perceived by some (perceiving) agent *and* if common sense leads us to believe that things in the external world exist when we or any other human being are not perceiving them, then there *must* be some higher being who maintains a constant perceptual vigilance[26] of the world and everything in it. Otherwise, we are saddled with a dilemma which cannot be resolved.

A careful reading of Berkeley makes it evident that he rejects the notion of material substance thus ruling out Locke's theory of it. This is not to say that he rules out the existence of *things*. Admittedly, this appears somewhat strange. The point is that if there is no legitimate distinction be primary and secondary qualities, all that is perceived are ideas. To perceive is to have an idea. When we perceive color we are having a sensation. But "no sensation can be in a senseless thing". Consequently, color cannot inhere in a material thing. If not, there can be no idea of material substance, and the postulation[27] of it is gratuitous[28] and totally unnecessary. *Things*, however, need not presuppose corporeity[29] and therefore Berkeley uses the term 'idea' for what most people understand to be things for two reasons:

> ". . .first, because the term *thing*, in contradistinction to *idea*, is generally supposed to denote somewhat existing without the mind: secondly, because *thing* hath a more comprehensive signification than *idea*, including spirits or thinking things as well as ideas. Since therefore the objects of sense exist only in the mind, and are withal thoughtless and inactive, I chose to mark them by the word *idea*, which implies those properties."

If, however,

> "you agree with me that we eat and drink and are clad with the immediate objects of sense which cannot exist unperceived or without the mind: I shall readily grant it more proper or conformable to custom, that they should be called things rather than ideas."

It should now be evident that Berkeley uses the term 'idea' to signify what we perceive, namely, sensible objects and by its use he in no way intends to undermine the reality of the objects of sense-perception. Once this is understood, the above mentioned mishap with the staircase no longer presents a problem in his theory. The staircase is an idea. It simply is not *my* idea as is one of my dreams. In this manner Berkeley can account for adverse[30] experiences and remain consistent with his principle that to be is to be perceived. Presumably, I would not choose to fall down a flight of stairs. If the stairs are an idea in the mind of God, then I can account for experiences that I do not will to come to pass. But care must be taken. It is crucial to understand that what Berkeley calls ideas are not ideas *of* things: they *are* things. An idea of a thing would necessarily presuppose the idea of material substance which is unjustifiable. An act of perceiving is to perceive sensible things themselves. Hence, to be is to be perceived.

---

[26] *vigilant:* on the alert; watchful.

[27] *postulate:* to assume or claim as true, real, existent, or necessary.

[28] *gratuitous:* not called for by the circumstances; unwarranted.

[29] *corporeity:* state or quality of having or being a body; physical nature.

[30] *adverse:* in hostile opposition to one's interests.

The major problem Berkeley has is his equivocal[31] use of his fundamental principle. "To be is to be perceived" can mean either

(a) Existence is guaranteed by perception or
(b) Existence is dependent upon perception.

Few would argue over the truth of (a). If I want to guarantee the existence of my car I can go to the garage and verify its existence. However, the truth of (b) does not follow from (a). Yet Berkeley most certainly thinks (b) *is* true when he says that what we eat and drink are "immediate objects of sense which cannot exist unperceived without the mind". (b) may be true or it may be false. The problem is that we will never know which it is. Our inevitable lack of knowledge as to the truth value of (b) leaves open the possibility that it is false. Berkeley takes (b) to be true. But that is unwarranted. The falsity of (b) would not only make possible but most reasonable the existence of an external world which provides the causal basis for our perceptions of it. Such being a possibility, there is no conclusive reason to court idealism as a theory of knowledge.

Suggested Readings: Idealism; Berkeley

1. Bradley, F. H., *Appearance and Reality* (Oxford: Clarendon Press, 1930).
2. Copleston, F., *A History of Philosophy*, Vol. V, (N.Y.: Doubleday & Co., 1994), Chaps 12-13.
3. Ewing, A.C., *Idealism: A Critical Survey* (London: Methuen, 1934).
4. Hicks, G. Daves, *Berkeley* (London, 1932).
5. Hoernle, R. F. A., *Idealism as a Philosophy* (New York: Doran, 1927).
6. Leroy, A. L., *George Berkeley* (Paris, 1959).
7. Luce, A. A., *Berkeley's Immaterialism* (N.Y.: Russell & Russell, 1945).
8. Moore, G.E., "Refutation of Idealism," in *Philosophical Studies* (London: Routledge & Kegan Paul, 1922).
9. Royce, Josiah, *The Spirit of Modern Philosophy* (New York: Tudor, 1955).
10. Sillem, E. A., *George Berkeley and the Proofs for the Existence of God* (London and New York, 1957).
11. Steinkraus, Warren E. (ed.), *New Studies in Berkeley's Philosophy* (New York: Holt, Rinehart and Winston, 1966).
12. Tipton, I. C., *Berkeley* (London: Methuen, 1974).
13. Warnock, G. J., *Berkeley* (Baltimore: Penguin Books, 1953).
14. Wild, J., *George Berkeley: A Study of His Life and Philosophy* (New York, 1936, 1962).

---

[31] *equivocal:* having two or more significations; ambiguous.

Name_____

Date _____

1. What is the fundamental issue which divides the realist and idealist?

2. Explain *esse est percipi*.

3. Is Berkeley a solipsist? Explain.

4. How does Berkeley account for the continued existence of things when he is not perceiving them?

5. How does Berkeley account for the "real" difference between a dream of falling down a flight of stairs and actually falling down a flight of stairs?

Three Dialogues between Hylas and Philonous

The First Dialogue

Philonous:[1] Good morrow, Hylas: I did not expect to find you abroad so early.

Hylas:[2] It is indeed something unusual; but my thoughts were so taken up with a subject I was discoursing of last night, that finding I could not sleep, I resolved to rise and take a turn in the garden....You were represented in last night's conversation as one who maintained the most extravagant opinion that ever entered into the mind of man, to wit, that there is no such thing as *material substance* in the world.

Phil: That there is no such thing as what *philosophers* call *material substance*, I am seriously persuaded: but, if I were made to see anything absurd or skeptical in this, I should then have the same reason to renounce this, that I imagine I have now to reject the contrary opinion.

Hyl: What! Can anything be more fantastical, more repugnant to common sense, or a more manifest piece of skepticism, than to believe there is no such thing as *matter*?

Phil: Softly, good Hylas. What if it should prove that you, who hold there is, are, by virtue of that opinion, a greater sceptic, and maintain more paradoxes and repugnances to common sense, than I who believe no such thing?

Hyl: You may as soon persuade me, the part is greater than the whole, as that, in order to avoid absurdity and scepticism, I should ever be obliged to give up my opinion in this point....

Phil: What mean you by sensible things?

Hyl: Those things which are perceived by the senses. Can you imagine that I mean anything else?

Phil: Pardon me, Hylas, if I am desirous clearly to apprehend your notions, since this may much shorten our inquiry. Suffer me then to ask you this farther question. Are those things only perceived by the senses which are perceived immediately? Or may those things properly be said to be *sensible* which are perceived mediately, or not without the intervention of others?

Hyl: I do not sufficiently understand you.

---

[1] This name is derived from the Greek word for mind [editor's note].

[2] This name is derived from the Greek word for matter [editor's note].

Phil: In reading a book, what I immediately perceive are the letters; but mediately, or by means of these, are suggested to my mind the notions of God, virtue, truth, etc. Now, that the letters are truly sensible things, or perceived by sense, there is no doubt: but I would know whether you take the things suggested by them to be so too.

Hyl: No, certainly: it were absurd to think *God* or *virtue* sensible things; though they may be signified and suggested to the mind by sensible marks, with which they have an arbitrary connexion.

Phil: I seems then, that by *sensible things* you mean those only which can be perceived *immediately* by sense?

Hyl: Right.

Phil: Does it not follow from this, that though I see one part of the sky red, and another blue, and that my reason does thence evidently conclude there must be some cause of that diversity of colours, yet that cause cannot be said to be a sensible thing, or perceived by the sense of seeing?

Hyl: It does.

Phil: In like manner, though I hear variety of sounds, yet I cannot be said to hear the causes of those sounds?

Hyl: You cannot.

Phil: And when by my touch I perceive a thing to be hot and heavy, I cannot say, with any truth or propriety, that I feel the cause of its heat or weight?

Hyl: To prevent any more questions of this kind, I tell you once for all, that by *sensible things* I mean those only which are perceived by sense; and that in truth the senses perceive nothing which they do not perceive *immediately*: for they make no inferences. The deducing therefore of causes or occasions from effects and appearances, which alone are perceived by sense, entirely relates to reason.

Phil: This point then is agreed between us--that *sensible things are those only which are immediately perceived by sense.* You will farther inform me whether we immediately perceive by sight anything beside light, and colours, and figures; or by hearing, anything but sounds; by the palate, anything beside tastes; by the smell, beside odours; or by the touch, more than tangible qualities.

Hyl: We do not.

Phil: It seems, therefore, that if you take away all sensible qualities, there remains nothing sensible?

Hyl: I grant it.

Phil: Sensible things therefore are nothing else but so many sensible qualities, or combinations of sensible qualities?

Hyl: Nothing else.

Phil: Heat then is a sensible thing?

Hyl: Certainly.

Phil: Does the *reality* of sensible things consist in being perceived? Or is it something distinct from their being perceived, and that bears no relation to the mind?

Hyl: To *exist* is one thing, and to be *perceived* is another.

Phil: I speak with regard to sensible things only. And of these I ask whether by their real existence you mean a subsistence exterior to the mind and distinct from their being perceived?

Hyl: I mean a real absolute being, distinct from, and without any relation to, their being perceived.

Phil: Heat therefore, if it be allowed a real being, must exist without[3] the mind?

---

[3]   *without:* outside [editor's note].

Hyl: It must.

Phil: Tell me, Hylas, is this real existence equally compatible to all degrees of heat, which we perceive; or is there any reason why we should attribute it to some and deny it to others? And if there be, pray let me know that reason.

Hyl: Whatever degree of heat we perceive by sense, we may be sure the same exists in the object that occasions it.

Phil: What! The greatest as well as the least?

Hyl: I tell you, the reason is plainly the same in respect of both. They are both perceived by sense; nay, the greater degree of heat is more sensibly perceived; and consequently, if there is any difference, we are more certain of its real existence than we can be of the reality of a lesser degree.

Phil: But is not the most vehement and intense degree of heat a very great pain?

Hyl: No one can deny it.

Phil: And is any unperceiving thing capable of pain or pleasure?

Hyl: No, certainly.

Phil: Is your material substance a senseless being, or a being endowed with sense and perception?

Hyl: It is senseless without doubt.

Phil: It cannot therefore be the subject of pain?

Hyl: By no means.

Phil: Nor consequently of the greatest heat perceived by sense, since you acknowledge this to be no small pain?

Hyl: I grant it.

Phil: What shall we say then of your external object; is it a material substance, or no?

Hyl: It is a material substance with the sensible qualities inhering in it.

Phil: How then can a great heat exist in it, since you own it cannot in a material substance? I desire you would clear this point.

Hyl: Hold, Philonous, I fear I was out in yielding intense heat to be a pain. It should seem rather, than pain is something distinct from heat, and the consequence or effect of it.

Phil: Upon putting your hand near the fire, do you perceive one simple uniform sensation, or two distinct sensations?

Hyl: But one simple sensation.

Phil: Is not the heat immediately perceived?

Hyl: It is.

Phil: And the pain?

Hyl: True.

Phil: Seeing therefore they are both immediately perceived at the same time, and the fire affects you only with one simple or uncompounded idea, it follows that this same simple idea is both the intense heat immediately perceived, and the pain; and, consequently, that the intense heat immediately perceived is nothing distinct from a particular sort of pain.

Hyl: It seems so.

Phil: Again, try in your thoughts, Hylas, if you can conceive a vehement sensation to be without pain or pleasure.

Hyl: I cannot.

Phil: Or can you frame to yourself an idea of sensible pain or pleasure in general, abstracted from every particular idea of heat, cold, tastes, smells, etc.?

Hyl: I do not find that I can.

Phil: Does it not therefore follow, that sensible pain is nothing distinct from those sensations or ideas, in an intense degree?

Hyl: It is undeniable; and, to speak the truth, I begin to suspect a very great heat cannot exist but in a mind perceiving it.

Phil: What! Are you then in that skeptical state of suspense, between affirming and denying?

Hyl: I think I may be positive in the point. A very violent and painful heat cannot exist without the mind.

Phil: It has not therefore, according to you, any *real* being?

Hyl: I own it.

Phil: Is it therefore certain that there is no body in nature really hot?

Hyl: I have not denied there is any real heat in bodies. I only say there is no such thing as an intense real heat.

Phil: But did you not say before that all degrees of heat were equally real; or, if there was any difference, that the greater were more undoubtedly real than the lesser?

Hyl: True: but it was because I did not then consider the ground there is for distinguishing between them, which I now plainly see. And it is this: because intense heat is nothing else but a particular kind of painful sensation; and pain cannot exist but in a perceiving being; it follows that no intense heat can really exist in an unperceiving corporeal substance. But this is no reason why we should deny heat in an inferior degree to exist in such a substance.

Phil: But how shall we be able to discern those degrees of heat which exist only in the mind from those which exist without it?

Hyl: That is no difficult matter. You know the least pain cannot exist unperceived; whatever, therefore, degree of heat is a pain exists only in the mind. But as for all other degrees of heat, nothing obliges us to think the same of them.

Phil: I think you granted before that no unperceiving being was capable of pleasure, any more than of pain.

Hyl: I did.

Phil: And is not warmth, or a more gentle degree of heat than what causes uneasiness, a pleasure?

Hyl: What then?

Phil: Consequently, it cannot exist without the mind in an unperceiving substance, or body.

Hyl: So it seems.

Phil: Since, therefore, as well those degrees of heat that are not painful, as those that are, can exist only in a thinking substance; may we not conclude that external bodies are absolutely incapable of any degree of heat whatsoever?

Hyl: On second thoughts, I do not think it so evident that warmth is a pleasure as that a great degree of heat is a pain.

Phil: I do not pretend that warmth is as great a pleasure as heat is a pain. But, if you grant it to be even a small pleasure, it serves to make good my conclusion.

Hyl: I could rather call it an *indolence*. It seems to be nothing more than a privation[4] of both pain and pleasure. And that such a quality or state as this may agree to an unthinking substance, I hope you will not deny.

Phil: If you are resolved to maintain that warmth, or a gentle degree of heat, is no pleasure, I know not how to convince you otherwise than by appealing to your own sense. But what think you of cold?

---

4   *privation:* the absence of positive character or existence [editor's note].

Hyl: The same that I do of heat. An intense degree of cold is a pain; for to feel a very great cold, is to perceive a great uneasiness: it cannot therefore exist without the mind; but a lesser degree of cold may, as well as a lesser degree of heat.

Phil: Those bodies, therefore, upon whose application to our own, we perceive a moderate degree of heat, must be concluded to have a moderate degree of heat or warmth in them; and those, upon whose application we feel a like degree of cold, must be thought to have cold in them.

Hyl: They must.

Phil: Can any doctrine be true that necessarily leads a man into an absurdity?

Hyl: Without doubt it cannot.

Phil: Is it not an absurdity to think that the same thing should be at the same time both cold and warm?

Hyl: It is.

Phil: Suppose now one of your hands hot, and the other cold, and that they are both at once put into the same vessel of water, in an intermediate state; will not the water seem cold to one hand, and warm to the other?

Hyl: It will.

Phil: Ought we not therefore, by your principles, to conclude it is really both cold and warm at the same time, that is, according to your own concession, to believe an absurdity?

Hyl: I confess it seems so.

Phil: Consequently, the principles themselves are false, since you have granted that no true principle leads to an absurdity.

Hyl: But, after all, can anything be more absurd than to say, *there is no heat in the fire?*

Phil: To make the point still clearer; tell me whether, in two cases exactly alike, we ought not to make the same judgment?

Hyl: We ought.

Phil: When a pin pricks your finger, does it not rend and divide the fibres of your flesh?

Hyl: It does.

Phil: And when a coal burns your finger, does it any more?

Hyl: It does not.

Phil: Since, therefore, you neither judge the sensation itself occasioned by the pin, nor anything like it to be in the pin; you should not, conformably to what you have now granted, judge the sensation occasioned by the fire, or anything like it, to be in the fire.

Hyl: Well, since it must be so, I am content to yield this point and acknowledge that heat and cold are only sensations existing in our minds. But there still remain qualities enough to secure the reality of external things.

Phil: But what will you say, Hylas, if it shall appear that the case is the same with regard to all other sensible qualities, and that they can no more be supposed to exist without the mind, than heat and cold?

Hyl: Then indeed you will have done something to the purpose; but that is what I despair of seeing proved.

Phil: Let us examine them in order. What think you of *tastes*--do they exist without the mind, or no?

Hyl: Can any man in his senses doubt whether sugar is sweet, or wormwood bitter?

Phil: Inform me, Hylas. Is a sweet taste a particular kind of pleasure or pleasant sensation, or is it not?

Hyl: It is.

Phil: And is not bitterness some kind of uneasiness or pain?

Hyl: I grant it.

Phil: If therefore sugar and wormwood are unthinking corporeal substances existing without the mind, how can sweetness and bitterness, that is, pleasure and pain, agree to them?

Hyl: Hold, Philonous, I now see what it was deluded me all this time. You asked whether heat and cold, sweetness and bitterness, were not particular sorts of pleasure and pain; to which I answered simply, that they were. Whereas I should have thus distinguished--those qualities, as perceived by us, are pleasures or pains; but not as existing in the external objects. We must not therefore conclude absolutely, that there is no heat in the fire, or sweetness in the sugar; but only that heat or sweetness, as perceived by us, are not in the fire or sugar. What say you to this?

Phil: I say it is nothing to the purpose. Our discourse proceeded altogether concerning sensible things, which you defined to be the *things we immediately perceive by our senses.* Whatever other qualities, therefore, you speak of, as distinct from these, I know nothing of them, neither do they at all belong to the point in dispute. You may, indeed, pretend to have discovered certain qualities which you do not perceive, and assert those insensible qualities exist in fire and sugar. But what use can be made of this to your present purpose, I am at a loss to conceive. Tell me then once more, do you acknowledge that heat and cold, sweetness and bitterness (meaning those qualities which are perceived by the senses), do not exist without the mind?

Hyl: I see it is to no purpose to hold out, so I give up the cause as to those mentioned qualities. Though I profess it sounds oddly, to say that sugar is not sweet.

Phil: But, for your farther satisfaction, take this along with you: that which at other times seems sweet, shall, to a distempered palate, appear bitter. And, nothing can be plainer than that diverse persons perceive different tastes in the same food; since that which one man delights in, another abhors. And how could this be, if the taste was something really inherent in the food?

Hyl: I acknowledge I know not how....

Phil: And I hope you will make no difficulty to acknowledge the same of *colours.*

Hyl: Pardon me: the case of colours is very different. Can anything be plainer than that we see them on the objects?

Phil: The objects you speak of are, I suppose, corporeal substances existing without the mind?

Hyl: They are.

Phil: And have true and real colours inhering in them?

Hyl: Each visible object has that colour which we see in it....

Phil: What! Are then the beautiful red and purple we see on yonder clouds really in them? Or do you imagine they have in themselves any other form than that of a dark mist or vapour?

Hyl: I must own, Philonous, those colours are not really in the clouds as they seem to be at this distance. They are only apparent colours.

Phil: Apparent call you them? How shall we distinguish these apparent colours from real?

Hyl: Very easily. Those are to be thought apparent which, appearing only at a distance, vanish upon a nearer approach.

Phil: And those, I suppose, are to be thought real which are discovered by the most near and exact survey.

Hyl: Right.

Phil: Is the nearest and exactest survey made by the help of a microscope, or by the naked eye?

Hyl: By a microscope, doubtless.

Phil: But a microscope often discovers colours in an object different from those perceived by the unassisted sight. And, in case we had microscopes magnifying to any assigned degree, it is certain that no object whatsoever, viewed through them, would appear in the same colour which it exhibits to the naked eye.

Hyl: And what will you conclude from all this? You cannot argue that there are really and naturally no colours on objects: because by artificial managements they may be altered, or made to vanish.

Phil: I think it may evidently be concluded from your own concessions, that all the colours we see with our naked eyes are only apparent as those on the clouds, since they vanish upon a more close and accurate inspection which is afforded us by a microscope. Then, as to what you say by way of prevention: I ask you whether the real and natural state of an object is better discovered by a very sharp and piercing sight, or by one which is less sharp?

Hyl: By the former without doubt.

Phil: Is it not plain from dioptrics[5] that microscopes make the sight more penetrating and represent objects as they would appear to the eye in case it were naturally endowed with a most exquisite sharpness?

Hyl: It is.

Phil: Consequently the microscopical representation is to be thought that which best sets forth the real nature of the thing, or what it is in itself. The colours, therefore, by it perceived are more genuine and real than those perceived otherwise.

Hyl: I confess there is something in what you say....

Phil: ...I would fain know farther from you, what certain distance and position of the object, what peculiar texture and formation of the eye, what degree or kind of light is necessary for ascertaining that true colour, and distinguishing it from apparent ones.

Hyl: I own myself entirely satisfied that they are all equally apparent and that there is no such thing as colour really inhering in external bodies, but that it is altogether in the light. And what confirms me in this opinion is that in proportion to the light colours are still more or less vivid; and if there be no light, then are there no colours perceived. Besides, allowing there are colours on external objects, yet, how is it possible for us to perceive them? For no external body affects the mind, unless it acts first on our organs of sense. But the only action of bodies is motion; and motion cannot be communicated otherwise than by impulse. A distant object therefore cannot act on the eye; nor consequently make itself or its properties perceivable to the soul. Whence it plainly follows that it is immediately some contiguous substance, which, operating on the eye, occasions a perception of colours: and such is light.

Phil: How! Is light then a substance?

Hyl: I tell you, Philonous, external light is nothing but a thin fluid substance, whose minute particles being agitated with a brisk motion, and in various manners reflected from the different surfaces of outward objects to the eyes communicate different motions to the optic nerves; which, being propagated to the brain, cause therein various impressions; and these are attended with the sensations of red, blue, yellow, etc.

Phil: It seems then the light does no more than shake the optic nerves.

---

[5] *dioptrics:* the study of refraction of light [editor's note].

Hyl: Nothing else.

Phil: And consequent to each particular motion of the nerves, the mind is affected with a sensation, which is some particular colour.

Hyl: Right.

Phil: And these sensations have no existence without the mind.

Hyl: They have not.

Phil: How then do you affirm that colours are in the light; since by *light* you understand a corporeal substance external to the mind?

Hyl: Light and colours, as immediately perceived by us, I grant cannot exist without the mind. But in themselves they are only the motions and configurations of certain insensible particles of matter.

Phil: Colours then, in the vulgar sense, or taken for the immediate objects of sight, cannot agree to any but a perceiving substance.

Hyl: That is what I say.

Phil: Well then, since you give up the point as to those sensible qualities which are alone thought colours by all mankind beside, you may hold what you please with regard to those invisible ones of the philosophers....

Hyl: I frankly own, Philonous, that it is in vain to stand out any longer. Colours, sounds, tastes, in a word all those termed *secondary qualities*, have certainly no existence without the mind. But by this acknowledgment I must not be supposed to derogate anything from the reality of matter or external objects; seeing it is no more than several philosophers maintain, who nevertheless are the farthest imaginable from denying matter. For the clearer understanding of this, you must know sensible qualities are by philosophers divided into primary and secondary[6]. The former are extension, figure, solidity, gravity, motion, and rest; and these they hold exist really in bodies. The latter are those above enumerated; or, briefly, *all sensible qualities beside the primary*; which they assert are only so many sensations or ideas existing nowhere but in the mind. But all this, I doubt not, you are apprised of. For my part, I have been a long time sensible[7] there was such an opinion current among philosophers, but was never thoroughly convinced of its truth until now.

Phil: You are still then of opinion that *extension* and *figures* are inherent in external unthinking substances?

Hyl: I am.

Phil: But what if the same arguments which are brought against secondary qualities will hold good against these also?

Hyl: Why then I shall be obliged to think, they too exist only in the mind.

Phil: Is it your opinion the very figure and extension which you perceive by sense exist in the outward object or material substance?

Hyl: It is.

Phil: Have all other animals as good grounds to think the same of the figure and extension which they see and feel?

Hyl: Without doubt, if they have any thought at all.

Phil: Answer me, Hylas. Think you the senses were bestowed upon all animals for their preservation and well-being in life, or were they given to men alone for this end?

Hyl: I make no question but they have the same use in all other animals.

---

6 This is a reference to John Locke's theory; see Chapter 20 [editor's note].

7 *sensible:* aware [editor's note].

Phil: If so, is it not necessary they should be enabled by them to perceive their own limbs and those bodies which are capable of harming them?

Hyl: Certainly.

Phil: A mite therefore must be supposed to see his own foot, and things equal or even less than it, as bodies of some considerable dimension; though at the same time they appear to you scarce discernible, or at best as so many visible points?

Hyl: I cannot deny it

Phil: And to creatures less than the mite they will seem yet larger?

Hyl: They will.

Phil: Insomuch that what you can hardly discern will to another extremely minute animal appear as some huge mountain?

Hyl: All this I grant.

Phil: Can one and the same thing be at the same time in itself of different dimensions?

Hyl: That were absurd to imagine.

Phil: But from what you have laid down it follows that both the extension by you perceived, and that perceived by the mite itself, as likewise all those perceived by lesser animals, are each of them the true extension of the mite's foot; that is to say, by your own principles you are led into an absurdity.

Hyl: There seems to be some difficulty in the point.

Phil: Again, have you not acknowledged that no real inherent property of any object can be changed without some change in the thing itself?

Hyl: I have.

Phil: But as we approach to or recede from an object, the visible extension varies, being at one distance ten or a hundred times greater than at another. Does it not therefore follow from hence likewise that it is not really inherent in the object?

Hyl: I own I am at a loss what to think.

Phil: Your judgment will soon be determined, if you will venture to think as freely concerning this quality as you have done concerning the rest. Was it not admitted as a good argument, that neither heat nor cold was in the water, because it seemed warm to one hand and cold to the other?

Hyl: It was.

Phil: Is it not the very same reasoning to conclude, there is no extension or figure in an object, because to one eye it shall seem little, smooth, and round, when at the same time it appears to the other, great, uneven, and angular?

Hyl: The very same. But does this latter fact ever happen?

Phil: You may at any time make the experiment, by looking with one eye bare, and with the other through a microscope.

Hyl: I know not how to maintain it; and yet I am loath to give up *extension*, I see so many odd consequences following upon such a concession.

Phil: Odd, say you? After the concessions already made, I hope you will stick at nothing for its oddness....

Hyl: I acknowledge, Philonous, that, upon a fair observation of what passes in my mind, I can discover nothing else but that I am a thinking being, affected with variety of sensations; neither is it possible to conceive how a sensation should exist in an unperceiving substance. But then, on the other hand, when I look on sensible things in a different view, considering them as so many modes and qualities, I find it necessary to suppose a *material substratum*, without which they cannot be conceived to exist.

Phil: *Material substratum* call you it? Pray, by which of your senses came you acquainted with that being?

Hyl: It is not itself sensible; its modes and qualities only being perceived by the senses.

Phil: I presume then it was by reflexion and reason you obtained the idea of it?

Hyl: I do not pretend to any proper positive *idea* of it. However, I conclude it exists, because qualities cannot be conceived to exist without a support.

Phil: It seems then you have only a relative *notion* of it, or that you conceive it not otherwise than by conceiving the relation it bears to sensible qualities?

Hyl: Right.

Phil: Be pleased therefore to let me know wherein that relation consists.

Hyl: Is it not sufficiently expressed in the term *substratum*, or *substance*?

Phil: If so, the word *substratum* should import that it is spread under the sensible qualities or accidents?[8]

Hyl: True.

Phil: And consequently under extension?

Hyl: I own it.

Phil: It is therefore somewhat[9] in its own nature entirely distinct from extension?

Hyl: I tell you, extension is only a mode, and matter is something that supports modes. And is it not evident the thing supported is different from the thing supporting?

Phil: So that something distinct from, and exclusive of, extension is supposed to be the *substratum* of extension?

Hyl: Just so.

Phil: Answer me, Hylas. Can a thing be spread without extension? Or is not the idea of extension necessarily included in *spreading*?

Hyl: It is.

Phil: Whatsoever therefore you suppose spread under anything must have in itself an extension distinct from the extension of that thing under which it is spread?

Hyl: It must.

Phil: Consequently, every corporeal substance, being the sub*stratum* of extension, must have in itself another extension, by which it is qualified to be a *substratum*: and so on to infinity? And I ask whether this be not absurd in itself, and repugnant to what you granted just now, to wit, that the *substratum* was something distinct from and exclusive of extension?

Hyl: Aye but, Philonous, you take me wrong. I do not mean that matter is spread in a gross literal sense under extension. The word *substratum* is used only to express in general the same thing with *substance*.

Phil: Well then, let us examine the relation implied in the term substance. Is it not that it stands under accidents?

Hyl: The very same.

Phil: But, that one thing may stand under or support another, must it not be extended?

Hyl: It must.

---

8   *substratum* in Latin literally means "spread under" [editor's note].
9   *somewhat:* something [editor's note].

Phil: Is not therefore this supposition liable to the same absurdity with the former?

Hyl: You still take things in a strict literal sense. That is not fair, Philonous.

Phil: I am not for imposing any sense on your words: you are at liberty to explain them as you please. Only, I beseech you, make me understand something by them. You tell me matter supports or stands under accidents. How? Is it as your legs support your body?

Hyl: No; that is the literal sense.

Phil: Pray let me know any sense, literal or not literal, that you understand it in. How long must I wait for an answer, Hylas?

Hyl: I declare I know not what to say. I once thought I understood well enough what was meant by matter's supporting accidents. But now, the more I think on it the less can I comprehend it: in short I find that I know nothing of it.

Phil: It seems then you have no idea at all, neither relative nor positive, of matter; you know neither what it is in itself, nor what relation it bears to accidents?

Hyl: I acknowledge it.

Phil: And yet you asserted that you could not conceive how qualities or accidents should really exist, without conceiving at the same time a material support of them?

Hyl: I did.

Phil: That is to say, when you conceive the real existence of qualities, you do withal[10] conceive something which you cannot conceive?

Hyl: I was wrong, I own....

Phil: ...But (to pass by all that has been hitherto said and reckon it for nothing, if you will have it so) I am content to put the whole upon this issue. If you can conceive it possible for...any sensible object whatever to exist without the mind, then I will grant it actually to be so.

Hyl: If it comes to that the point will soon be decided. What is more easy than to conceive a tree or house existing by itself, independent of, and unperceived by, any mind whatsoever? I do at this present time conceive them existing after that manner.

Phil: How say you, Hylas, can you see a thing which is at the same time unseen?

Hyl: No, that were a contradiction.

Phil: Is it not as great a contradiction to talk of *conceiving* a thing which is *unconceived*?

Hyl: It is.

Phil: The tree or house therefore which you think of is conceived by you?

Hyl: How should it be otherwise?

Phil: And what is conceived is surely in the mind?

Hyl: Without question, that which is conceived is in the mind....

Phil: You acknowledge then that you cannot possibly conceive how any one corporeal sensible thing should exist otherwise than in a mind?

Hyl: I do....

The Second Dialogue

Phil: ...To me it is evident, for the reasons you allow of, that sensible things cannot exist otherwise than in a mind or spirit. Whence I conclude, not that they have no real existence, but that, seeing they depend not on

---

[10] *withal:* with that [editor's note].

my thought, and have an existence distinct from being perceived by me, *there must be some other Mind wherein they exist.* As sure, therefore, as the sensible world really exists, so sure is there an infinite omnipresent Spirit who contains and supports it.

Hyl: What! This is no more than I and all Christians hold; nay, and all others too who believe there is a God, and that He knows and comprehends all things.

Phil: Aye, but here lies the difference. Men commonly believe that all things are known or perceived by God, because they believe the being of a God; whereas I, on the other side, immediately and necessarily conclude the being of a God, because all sensible things must be perceived by Him.

Hyl: But, so long as we all believe the same thing, what matter is it how we come by that belief?

Phil: But neither do we agree in the same opinion. For philosophers, though they acknowledge all corporeal beings to be perceived by God, yet they attribute to them an absolute subsistence distinct from their being perceived by any mind whatever; which I do not. Besides, is there no difference between saying, *There is a God, therefore He perceives all things; and saying, Sensible things do really exist; and, if they really exist, they are necessarily perceived by an infinite Mind: therefore there is an infinite Mind, or God?* This furnishes you with a direct and immediate demonstration, from a most evident principle, of the *being of a God.* Divines and philosophers had proved beyond all controversy, from the beauty and usefulness of the several parts of the creation, that it was the workmanship of God. But that--setting aside all help of astronomy and natural philosophy, all contemplation of the contrivance, order, and adjustment of things--an infinite Mind should be necessarily inferred from the bare *existence of the sensible world*, is an advantage to them only who have made this easy reflexion: That the sensible world is that which we perceive by our several senses; and that nothing is perceived by the senses beside ideas; and that no idea or archetype of an idea can exist otherwise than in a mind. You may now, without any laborious search into the sciences, without any subtlety of reason, or tedious length of discourse, oppose and baffle the most strenuous advocate for atheism....It is evident that the things I perceive are my own ideas, and that no idea can exist unless it be in a mind. Nor is it less plain that these ideas or things by me perceived, either themselves or their archetypes, exist independently of my mind, since I know myself not to be their author, it being out of my power to determine at pleasure what particular ideas I shall be affected with upon opening my eyes or ears: they must therefore exist in some other Mind, whose will it is they should be exhibited to me. The things, I say, immediately perceived are ideas or sensations, call them which you will. But how can any idea or sensation exist in, or be produced by, anything but a mind or spirit? This indeed is inconceivable. And to assert that which is inconceivable is to talk nonsense: is it not?

Hyl: Without doubt.

Phil: But, on the other hand, it is very conceivable that they should exist in and be produced by a Spirit; since this is no more than I daily experience in myself, inasmuch as I perceive numberless ideas; and, by an act of my will, can form a great variety of them and raise them up in my imagination: though, it must be confessed, these creatures of the fancy are not altogether so distinct, so strong, vivid, and permanent, as those perceived by my senses--which latter are called *real things.* From all which I conclude, *there is a Mind which affects me every moment with all the sensible impressions I perceive.* And from the variety, order, and manner of these, I conclude *the Author of them to be wise, powerful, and good, beyond comprehension.*

Name_____

Date _____

1. According to Berkeley, what is it that we perceive?

2. In Berkeley's view an object cannot be separated from the sensation of it. True or false? Explain.

3. Berkeley considers it an obvious fact that things have no existence independent of minds. True or false? Explain.

4. How does Berkeley differ from Locke regarding the existence of primary qualities?

5. How does Berkeley account for the fact that I cannot will to perceive whatever I want?

381

23 Adverbial Theory; Roderick Chisholm

❧ BIOGRAPHY ❧

Roderick M. Chisholm (1916-   ) was born at North Attleboro, Massachusetts and is one of the premier epistemologists of the 20th century. He attended Brown University where he earned his B.A. degree in 1938 after which he did graduate studies at Harvard University where he was awarded his Ph.D. in 1942. He served in the U.S. Army from 1942 to 1946.

Chisholm's achievements are almost too many to be listed. He has been one of the most prolific writers on epistemology and metaphysics of this century with more than two hundred articles as well as three books to his credit. He is a unique individual in that he possesses the rare combination of excellence both as a scholar and teacher. His publication record speaks for itself. What most people are not privy to is his teaching technique which is tantamount to a mind functioning like a scalpel with respect to philosophical problems and at the same time with wit. He loves an intellectual challenge, but is not threatened by those who present them. In short, he has not inflated himself because of his success.

After the war he was Barnes Foundation Professor of Philosophy at the University of Pennsylvania; then he returned to Brown University where he served as Chairman of the Department of Philosophy from 1951-1964. Since that time he has successively held the chairs of Romeo Elton Professor of Metaphysical Philosophy and the Andrew W. Mellon Professor of the Humanities. During his tenure at Brown University, Professor Chisholm frequently visited elsewhere: Harvard University, 1950, 1960 and 1969; University of Southern California, 1955; Karl-Franzens-Universital as Fulbright Professor, 1959-60; Princeton University, 1961-62; University of California at Santa Barbara, 1964; University of Alberta at Calgary, 1965; University of Illinois at Urbana, 1966; University of Chicago, 1967; and the University of Massachusetts at Amherst, 1970.

Chisholm has also had an active involvement in professional organizations. He was President of the Eastern Division of the American Philosophical Association in 1968; President of the Metaphysical Society of America, 1972-73; Chairman of the Council for Philosophical Studies since 1972; Executive Director of the Franz Brentano Foundation since 1970; President of the Fourth Interamerican Congress of Philosophy in 1957; and Secretary of the Societal Interamericana de Filosofia, 1946-47.

The epistemological[1] adverbial theory is one based on the common sense point of view that there exists an external world, namely, a world and all its contents, independent of our perceptions of it which *causes* us to perceive[2] it in the various ways that we do. For example, a penny perceived at different angles by two or more people results in as many different perceptions of that object as there are perceivers of it. Common sense leads one to conclude that those different perceptions are of one and the same coin, but it cannot be denied that there are, nevertheless, as many different perceptions of it as there are perceivers engaged in that perceptual process. The adverbial theory is one which caters to common sense, and at the same time explains the problem of different perceptions on behalf of various perceivers of the same (supposed) thing in the external world.

How is such a difference of perception to be explained? One way to solve the problem is to argue (and not without reason) that you, the perceiver, are the only one so perceiving. Such a position is called "solipsism" which is derived from the Latin words *solus* (alone) and *ipse* (self). This epistemological position maintains that you, and *only* you, exist which entails[3] that your perceptions are the only ones which exist. If such is the case, then there is no conflict between your perceptions of the world and those of someone else's. After all, the data[4] that is in the possession of someone else is secondary, if not meaningless, because that other person is simply part of *your* perception and only that.

However, we know that individual perceptions are not concrete guidelines as to the independent existence of the world and everything in it for we have all had the experience of dreams. Hallucinations also confirm this point. Dreams and hallucinations are not by most accounts believed to be real. If the theory of solipsism is the case, then there are no criteria[5] to distinguish between the real world and the dream one. Such a solution to the problem does not square with common sense. It simply does not make sense if (a) two people perceive a car accident and one party maintains that his perception of it was the only one which was real or (b) that when one falls down a flight of stairs that the resultant leg fracture is simply a matter of one's imagination. Common sense, if nothing else, leads us to believe that there is an external world which exists independently of our perceptions of it and which provides the causal basis of such perceptions.

One of the fundamental problems with this common sense view is that it rests on the *belief* that there is an external world and all that therein is which gives rise to our individual perceptions of it. Beliefs as to the nature of the external world are not the same as knowledge of it. We know full well that there are false beliefs. After all, in the 15th century people believed that the world was flat. But they were wrong. A knowledge claim entails that what is believed is, in fact, the case. That is one of the crucial differences between knowledge and belief. Now apart from the criterion of common sense, what is there that one can rely on to tell the difference between what one believes to be the case and what one knows to be the case? If there is none, then all we have to rely on from an

[1]   *epistemology:* that branch of philosophy that deals with the nature and origins of knowledge.

[2]   *perceive:* to become aware of directly through any of the senses.

[3]   *entail:* to have as a necessary accompaniment or consequence.

[4]   *datum:* what is given; information. Data is the plural form of the word.

[5]   *criterion:* a standard, rule, or test on which a judgement or decision can be based. Criteria is the plural form of the word.

epistemological point of view is what we perceive *sans*[6] the aid of some-one else's perceptions, for they amount to nothing other than hearsay, namely, our perceptions of their evaluations of what *they* perceive. And, if this is the case, then the epistemological position of solipsism stated above must be valid[7].

In answer to this problem, epistemologists have maintained that apart from common sense, the criterion of adequate evidence is necessary to distinguish between whether one has knowledge of a given state of affairs or mere belief of it. The obvious philosophical question is, what constitutes adequate evidence, namely, what are the criteria of adequate evidence whereby one can distinguish between whether or not he possesses knowledge or mere belief of a given state of affairs? Keep in mind that one of the primary problems is to account for (a) the difference of perceptions by two or more people of presumably the same object at the same time and (b) the difference of perceptions by the same person of presumably the same object at different times.

Roderick Chisholm is the principle proponent of the adverbial theory. In a very traditional way, he maintains that there are three criteria necessary for one to make a claim to knowledge. They are that:

(1) Jones *believes* that there is a refrigerator in front of him,
(2) There *is* a refrigerator in front of Jones, and
(3) Jones has *adequate evidence* that there is a refrigerator in front of him.

The rock bottom epistemological issue concerns criterion (3). Just what constitutes adequate evidence so far as Chisholm is concerned? His adverbial theory is an attempt to answer that question. At the outset, let us make no mistake in understanding that he believes that there is an external world and it provides the causal basis of the perceptions we have of it. His goal is to account not only for the independent existence of such an external world, but at the same time explain the differences of the perceptions of it on behalf of varied and sundry perceivers. He argues that the entities of the (external) world *appear* differently to each and every perceiver of it. More accurately, each and every perceiver is appeared to by any given object in the external world in a different fashion. One might reasonably ask at this point, "What does this analysis have to do with adverbs since it is labeled the adverbial theory?" The answer is that the way in which a person or various perceivers are appeared to is expressed by the use of adverbs. For example, one is appeared to redly or brownly or largely or smoothly. Such a way of viewing the situation preserves the independent status of the objects one perceives and at the same time allows for the different perceptions each perceiver has of the object or state of affairs in question.

Someone at this stage may wonder whether or not Chisholm is simply playing with words. Just what, for example, is the difference between one perceiving an appearance of an object and being appeared to by the entity in question? Is not the difference a matter of a turn of phrase as opposed to one of ontology[8]? *Apparently,* yes! But let us not let certain characteristics about language deceive us. More often than not, especially where the English language is concerned, we employ what is known as the sub-

---

[6]   *sans:* without.

[7]   *valid:* well-grounded; sound; supportable.

[8]   *ontology:* that branch of philosophy that deals with the nature of being.

stantive form of a concept. The word 'appearance' is one such word.
When so used, it connotes[9] that there is something substantive; that is,
"real" which exists that justifies an ontological commitment to such a supposed thing. But the use of language is not an iron-clad and determining
factor as to what exists "out there" in the so-called real world. Often
times, we opt for a way of expressing an object or a state of affairs by
means of an economical use of language. Employment of the substantive
mode more often than not "fills this bill". After all, there is no doubt that
it is more economical from a linguistic point of view to say that:

(a) "there is the appearance of a red car" as opposed to the utterance that
(b) " I am presently being appeared to carly and redly".

Statement (a) carries with it the ontological commitment to an appearance. Now just what is that? Most philosophers feel uncomfortable
admitting appearances into their ontology for no other reason than that
they tend to be somewhat mysterious "entities"[10]. For example, ghosts are
a type of appearance. Because ghosts are understood to *be* appearances,
they are not (normally) accepted as real "things".[11]

The point is that the way by which we describe what we perceive is
not necessarily a word game. Appearances are indeed mysterious entities.
That there are appearances from a *substantive* point of view is most questionable. Although the ontological status of appearances may be doubtful, there nevertheless remains the issue that we are appeared to
differently by "things" which are believed to be more substantive than
mere appearances by virtue of them existing in and comprising part of an
external world. Chisholm's theory amounts to the claim that we are
appeared to directly by such (supposed) objects as opposed to us perceiving an appearance (i.e., a third whatnot) of the entity in question which
produces the appearance of the thing being perceived.

This theory does an adequate job of explaining the differences of perception of the same object on behalf of a given individual at different
times and the difference of perceptions of the same object by two or more
persons at the same time. So far, however, it has not dealt with the problem of appearances on behalf of a given individual who would not be construed[12] as being appeared to by an object in the so-called "real" world.
Namely, how does such a theory account for such appearances as dreams
and hallucinations? Such phenomena are not caused by corresponding
objects in the external world. Yet, there is no doubt that under such circumstances one is being "appeared to". In order to solve this puzzle,
Chisholm introduces criteria for adequate evidence for knowledge of the
external world. These criteria are deliberation, reflection or inference. If
one has a dream, there is no doubt that he has been appeared to in varied
and sundry ways, but upon reflection, there is a huge question mark as to
whether or not what was perceived was real. However, if one is appeared
to firely in one's backyard, then one does not deliberate, reflect or infer

---

[9]   *connote:* to suggest or imply in addition to literal meaning.

[10]   *entity:* a particular and discreet unit; an entirety.

[11]   (a) and (b) are alternative ways of expressing different perceptions. It would be tempt-
       ing to suggest (c) as less cumbersome and more to the point.
                          (c) The car appears red.
       Note, however, that (c) asserts the existence of a car which is illegitimate since all we
       know for sure is what we perceive and those perceptions vary according to the per-
       ceiver. (a) and (b) are statements of perception.

[12]   *construe:* to infer or deduce.

regarding the manner by which he is (being) appeared to. These three criteria, according to Chisholm, make it possible for one to determine the difference between appearance and reality.

However, there are some counterexamples[13] which do not conform to the above criteria. Take, for example, the person who is stranded in the desert and perceives an oasis. Chances are that he will believe, due to his deprived state, that there *really* is water ahead of him. He is being appeared to waterly, but there is no water hole to substantiate his being appeared to in such a manner. Not only that, chances are that the agent in question will not deliberate, reflect or infer that that by which he is being appeared to is something nonexistent. Hence, the issue becomes whether or not Chisholm's criteria for adequate evidence of the external world are adequate. His response to such a counterexample is that we must rely upon "normal circumstances". He would be correct if all perceptual circumstances were normal. But they are not. The point is that at a certain level, if one is to commit oneself to the existence of a world external to ourselves, then we can never at *all* times be sure that we are being appeared to by it in an accurate manner, namely, as that world actually, or factually, is. At a certain level, we must have faith that there is a world external to us whereby for the most part it is appeared to us in an accurate manner (given normal conditions) whereby at the same time recognizing that such conditions do not always exist and that we can be deceived regarding the actual nature of external world on the basis of how we are appeared to by its contents.

There is a final problem which pertains to Chisholm's theory as well as all epistemological viewpoints which employ the notion of "normal circumstances" by which the external world is evaluated; that is, judged to be the case. It is common, and more often than not, acceptable to maintain, for example, that a red light will so appear if it is illuminated under normal circumstances. But just what are the criteria that establish *normal* circumstances? The answer to that question is anybody's guess. To employ the opinion of a scientist regarding his strict laboratory qualifications does not finalize the issue, for one will discover as much controversy among scientists as to what constitutes normal conditions as with any other group of specialists. That is because packed into the notion of normal circumstances is the precondition of objectivity. This brings us straight to the heart of the matter. Objectivity with respect to the external world is, strictly speaking, unattainable because all anyone has to rely on is his own perceptions of it which are by nature subjective; that is, subject to the person doing the perceiving. That this is the case is demonstrated by the fact that (1) a perceiver throughout his lifetime does not always perceive the external world, such as is the case with dreams, and (2) even when he is perceiving he cannot be *absolutely* certain that he is perceiving it under normal circumstances and therefore whether he has *adequate* evidence that he is certain in his perceptions of it. Chisholm is faced with this problem as is any epistemologist who opts[14] for the common sense point of view that there exists an external world independent of our perceptions of it. His theory, however, surmounts many of the problems of perception other great minds in the history of Western Culture attempted to solve but did so in a less adequate manner.

One final point ought to be brought into focus. It is indeed a matter of common sense to believe that there *is* an external world and all that therein is independent of our perceptions of it. Hopefully, the above epis-

---

[13] *counterexample:* an example that refutes a claim about some subject matter.

[14] *opt:* to make a choice or decision.

temological exploration has demonstrated that the use of common sense is not a *guarantee* to the ascertainment[15] of truth concerning such a world. The point is that common sense as it is applied to that which (supposedly) goes on about us carries with it some problems and those are primarily philosophical in nature.

Suggested Readings: Adverbial Theory; Chisholm

1. Chisholm, R. M., *Perceiving: A Philosophical Study* (Cornell University Press, 1957).
2. Sellars, Wilfred, "Phenomenalism" in *Science, Perception and Reality* (London: Roulledge & Kegan Paul, 1963), esp. pp. 92-5.
3. _____, *Science and Metaphysics* (London: Routledge & Kegan Paul, 1968), esp. pp. 9-28.
4. Tye, Michael, *The Metaphysics of Mind* (Cambridge: Cambridge University Press, 1989).

---

[15] *ascertain:* to discover through examination or experimentation; find out.

Name_____

Date _____

1. How might one argue against solipsism?

2. What are the three criteria for knowledge?

3. Why is Chisholm's theory of knowledge called "adverbial"?

4. What three criteria does Chisholm give for determining the difference between appearance and reality?

5. What counterexample can be raised that creates problems for this theory?

Adverbial Theory

Roderick M. Chisholm
"Appear," "Take," and "Evident"

Chisholm, R. M., "'Appear,' 'Take,' and 'Evident'" in *The Journal of Philosophy*, Vol. LIII, No. 23 (1956), pp. 722-31. Reprinted by kind permission of R. M. Chisholm.

"Appear," "Take," and "Evident"

1. If a man looks toward the roof and *sees* that his cat is there, he is not likely to *say* "I take that to be a cat" or "I have adequate evidence for the proposition or hypothesis that that is a cat." But, I suggest, if he does see that his cat is there, he does take it to be his cat and he does have adequate evidence for the hypothesis that what he sees is his cat. And I would suggest, more generally, that the locution "There is something such that S *perceives that* it is f" may be defined as meaning: first, there is something which S takes to be f; secondly, S has adequate evidence for the proposition or hypothesis that the thing is f; and, lastly, the thing *is* f. By adding qualifications about sense organs we may formulate similar definitions of one of the more important senses of "see" and of "hear."

Such definitions will not be interesting or significant unless we can say what is meant by "take" and by "adequate evidence" without using "see," "hear," or "perceive." Let us begin, then, with the concept of *adequate evidence*.

2. "Adequate evidence" is an *epistemic* term--a term we use in appraising the epistemic, or cognitive, worth of statements, hypotheses, and beliefs. Making use of the locution, "S ought to place more confidence in h than in I," where "S" may be replaced by the name of a person and "h" and "I" by the names of propositions, beliefs, statements, or hypotheses, we may explicate some of our more important epistemic terms in the following way. "It would be *unreasonable* for S to accept h" means that S ought to place more confidence in non-h than in h; "h is *acceptable* for S" means that it would not be unreasonable for S to accept h; "h is (epistemically) *indifferent* for S" means that both h and non-h are acceptable for S; and "S has *adequate evidence* for h" means that non-h is unreasonable for S, or, in other words, that S ought to place more confidence in h than in non-h. By making use of the additional locution, "S accepts h," we may define one important use of "know" and one important use of "certain." The locution "S *knows that* h is true" could be said to mean, first, that S accepts h, secondly that S has adequate evidence for h, and, thirdly, that h is true. And "S is *certain* that h is true" could be said to mean, first, that S knows that h is true, and, secondly, that there is no proposition or hypothesis I such that S ought to place more confidence in I than in h.[1]

Our present problem is this: How are we to decide which propositions are evident? Or, more exactly: By means of what principles could our subject S *apply* the locution "S has adequate evidence for h"? In setting this problem for ourselves--the problem of "the criterion"[2] --we do not presuppose, nor should we presuppose, that there are certain principles which people actually think about, or refer to, in order to *decide* whether they have adequate evidence for their beliefs. The grammarian, similarly, may try to describe the conditions under which, say, people use the imperfect tense rather than the past perfect; but, in so doing, he does not mean to imply that, before using this tense, people think about these conditions or try to decide whether or not they apply. It is important to note that we cannot answer our question by reference solely to the logic of induction and the theory of probability. For the principles of induction and probability will not tell a man which propositions are evident unless he applies them to *premises* which are evident.[3]

In the present paper, I wish to describe and to illustrate one approach to this philosophical problem.

3. I suggest that we consider the analogue of our problem in *moral philosophy*. What do we regard as the proper way of applying our *moral* terms? To answer this question, let us ask further: How would we go about *defending* a particular application of some moral terms--say, some particular application of the term "right"?

If we say, of some particular act, that that act is *right* and if we are prepared to defend our statement, then we are prepared to appeal to some characteristic *in virtue of which* that act is right. Possibly we are prepared to show that the act is an instance of courage, or of forgiveness, or that it is motivated by a wish to decrease the amount of pain in the world. This characteristic, whatever it may be, is one such that every act to which it applies is an act which is right, or which "tends to be right." But it is not a characteristic which we need to describe or identify in distinctly *moral* or *ethical*, terms. If we wish to point out that someone is motivated by the wish to decrease the amount of pain in the world, or that he is acting courageously, we can convey what we want to convey without using "right" or "good" or "ought" or any other ethical term. Let us say, following Professor Broad, that the characteristic to which we appeal is one which is "right-making."[4]

There are three important points to be made about "right-making" characteristics. (1) A "right-making" characteristic is one which can be described and identified in ethically neutral language--without the use of ethical terms. (2) When we find out, or when we show, that a particular

---

[1]   If we wish to avoid the "true" we may replace the locution "S accepts h" by "S accepts the hypothesis that x is f" or "S accepts the hypothesis that ...", then, instead of saying " h is true," we may say "x is f" or "..." I have discussed the above concepts in more detail in "Epistemic Statements and the Ethics of Belief," *Philosophy and Phenomenological Research*, Vol. XVI (1956), pp. 447-460.

[2]   See Sextus Empiricus, *Outlines of Pyrrhonism*, Books I and II. Cardinal Mercier described the attempts to deal with this problem as works of "criteriology"; see D.J. Mercier, *Criteriologie Generale*.

[3]   Indeed, the principles of probability and induction will not tell S whether or not S has adequate evidence for a certain hypothesis h unless two epistemic conditions are fulfilled: (i) S must apply the principles to premises for which he has adequate evidence; and (ii), in doing so, S must not leave out any relevant evidence--i.e., of those hypotheses for which he has adequate evidence, his premises should include all which have a probability in relation to h. Carnap refers to this second requirement, which had been formulated by Bernoulli, as the "requirement of total evidence." See Carnap's *Logical Foundations of Probability*, pp. 211 ff., 494.

act is right, we find out, or show, that the act has some "right-making" characteristic. And (3) every act which is right is right *in virtue* of some "right-making" characteristic of the act--some characteristic such that every act which has that characteristic is right, or "tends to be right." Similar points may be made, *mutatis mutandis*[5], of such ethical terms as "wrong," "good," and "bad."

Among the traditional tasks of moral philosophy is that of describing characteristics which are "right-making," "wrong-making," "good-making," and the like. In listing such characteristics, the moral philosopher is not providing *definitions* of the ethical terms concerned. We may say, following one ancient usage, that he is providing *criteria* for applying these terms.

Our problem--the "problem of the criterion"--is that of finding similar criteria for applying our epistemic vocabulary.

4. Hobbes said, "The inn of evidence has no sign-board." But I suggest that, whenever a man has adequate evidence for some proposition or hypothesis, he is in a state which constitutes a *mark of evidence* for that proposition or hypothesis.

What, then, would be a "mark of evidence" for a proposition or hypothesis h? In asking this question, we are asking: What would be a *criterion* by means of which a particular subject S might apply our locution, "S has adequate evidence for h"?

Just as there were three points to be made about "right-making" characteristics, there are three points to be made about marks of evidence-- about "evidence-bearing" characteristics.

(1) A mark of criterion, for any subject S, that S has adequate evidence for a given proposition or hypothesis h, would be some state or condition of S which could be described without using "know," or "perceive," or "evident," or any other epistemic term. That is to say, it would be a state or condition of S which would be described in language which is "epistemically neutral."

(2) It is tempting to say that a mark for S, that S has adequate evidence for a given proposition or hypothesis h, would be some state or condition to which S appeals when he wishes to *show* that he has evidence for h--or some state or condition which he *discovers* to hold when he discovers he has adequate evidence for h. But the words "discover" and "show," in this present use, are themselves epistemic terms. To *discover* that some condition holds is, among other things, to acquire adequate evidence for believing that it does; and to *show* some other person that some condition holds is, among other things, to enable him to have adequate evidence for believing that it holds. If we are to formulate our second requirement in "epistemically neutral" language, I believe we must say something like this: A mark or criterion, for any subject S, that S has adequate evidence for a given proposition or hypothesis h would be some state or condition of S which is such that S could not make any mistake at any time about his *being* in that state or condition at that time. That is to say, S could

---

4   "Moral characteristics are always dependent upon certain other characteristics which can be described in purely neutral non-moral terms. Let us call those non-moral characteristics whose presence in anything confers rightness or goodness on it right-making or wrong-making characteristics. And let us define good-making and bad-making characteristics in a similar way." C.D. Broad, "Some of the Main Problems of Ethics," *Philosophy*, Vol. 21 (1946), p. 103. Compare *Butler's Moral Philosophy*, by A.E. Ducan-Jones, Chapter Eight, Sections 1 and 2; and R.M. Hare, *The Language of Morals*, pp. 80 ff.

5   *mutatis mutandis:* with the respective differences having been considered [editor's note].

never believe falsely at any time either that he is in that state at that time or that he is not in that state at that time.

(3) Finally, a mark or criterion, for any subject S, that S has adequate evidence for a given proposition or hypothesis h would be a state or condition such that, whenever S is in that state or condition, S has adequate evidence for h.[6]

5. Philosophers have proposed various criteria, or marks, of evidence, but in most cases their proposals fail to meet one or more of the three conditions we have formulated. We cannot be content to say, as apparently some philosophers would be, that a man has adequate evidence for any proposition which he *knows*, or *remembers*, or *sees*, or *perceives* to be true. For "see," "know," "remember," and "perceive," as here used, are epistemic terms--terms we have defined by means of our locution, "S ought to place more confidence in h than in I." Such criteria, therefore, do not meet the first of our conditions. It has been suggested that we have adequate evidence for any proposition which is accepted by "the scientists of our culture circle." It has also been suggested that we have adequate evidence for any proposition "revealed to us by God." Possibly the words "scientist" and "revealed," in these criteria, fail to conform to our first condition. In any case, both criteria fail to meet the second condition. We are all quite capable of believing falsely at any time that a given proposition is accepted by the scientists of our culture circle at that time or has been revealed to us by God at that time.

According to Descartes, we have adequate evidence for those propositions "we conceive very clearly and very distinctly." This criterion does not seem to meet our third condition. For we can conceive very clearly and very distinctly what is expressed by many statements we know to be false.

Are there *any* states or conditions which provide us with marks of evidence? I shall try to describe two such states.

6. The locution, "x appears so-and-so to S," in one of its many senses, is used to describe one mark of evidence.

Possibly the sense of "appear" I have in mind will be suggested by the following example. Let us consider the statement: "Things which are red usually appear red (look red) in ordinary light." Among the uses of "appear red" ("look red") is one such that, in that use, the statement "Things which are red usually appear red in ordinary light" is analytic. For, in this use, "appears red" may be taken to mean the same as "appears in the way that things which are red usually appear in ordinary light." But there is another use of "appears red" which is such that, in that use, the statement "Things which are red usually appear red in ordinary light" is

---

6   Cardinal Mercier formulated three requirements--those of being "internal," "objective," and "immediate"--which would be met by any adequate theory of "certitude." The first and third of his requirements, I think, may be intended to serve the purpose of the second one I have listed above. His second requirement serves the purpose of the third condition I have listed above. It may be interpreted as also ruling out the philosophical view that statements expressing theories of evidence are neither true or false. Although Mercier was sensitive to the charge of circularity, he did not formulate a requirement comparable to the first one I have listed above. And the criterion of "certitude" which he proposed does not seem to meet the first of my requirements. He said that we have certitude when the subjects and predicates of our judgements *express* or *manifest* reality; but I believe that the terms "express" and "manifest," as he intended them, are epistemic terms, the meanings of which can be conveyed only by such terms as "know," "evident," or "perceive." See D.J. Mercier, *Criteriologie Generale*, Eighth edition (Louvain, 1923), Sections 150-153, and *Manual of Modern Scholastic Philosophy*, Volume I, p. 369.

synthetic. Using "appears red" in this second way, we could say: "There is a certain way of appearing--appearing red--which, as it happens, we have found to be the way in which red things usually appear." (The word "appear" is also intended in this second way in such statements as the following, which are to be found in the writings of empirical philosophers: "We can never know that such things as apples are red unless we first know either that they sometimes appear red or that they resemble, in important respects, things which do appear red.")

In the first of these two uses, the locution "appears so-and-so" functions essentially as a *comparative* locution. When we say of anything that it "appears so-and-so," in this sense, we mean to draw a comparison between the thing and things that *are* so-and-so. We mean to say something like this: "The thing appears the way you would normally expect things that are so-and-so to appear under conditions like these (or under conditions of such-and-such a sort)." But when we use "appears so-and-so" in the second of the two ways I have tried to describe, our statements are not in the same sense comparative statements; "x appears so-and-so," in this use, does not entail any such statement as "x appears the way things that are so-and-so might normally be expected to appear." Let us say that, in this second use, the locution "x appears so-and-so" is used *non-comparatively.*

According to my suggestion, then, the locution "x appears so-and-so to S," when used *non-comparatively,* describes a condition which provides S with a mark of evidence for the proposition that x appears so-and-so to S. If something appears blue to S (in the non-comparative sense of "appears blue"), then, in being thus "appeared to," S is in a state which provides him with a mark of evidence for the proposition that something appears blue to S.[7] Let us see whether this criterion of evidence fulfills our three conditions.

First, the ways of being "appeared to" in question can be described without using "know," or "perceive," or "evidence," or any other epistemic term. And since they can be described in "epistemically neutral" language, they meet the first of our conditions.

Secondly, if a subject S is "appeared to" in one of the ways in question, then, surely, he could not believe at that time that he is not being thus "appeared to." Nor could he believe that he was being thus "appeared to" at a time when he was not being thus "appeared to." Is it possible for something to appear blue to me while I believe that nothing does, or for me to believe that something appears blue to me at a time when nothing does? (If "appears blue" were meant in its comparative sense, then we should have to say that these things are quite possible. But it is here meant in its non-comparative sense.) We could say: There are ways of appearing which are such that, for any subject S, whenever S is appeared to in one of those ways, it is false that S believes he is not being appeared to in that particular way; and whenever S is not being appeared to in one of those ways, it is false that S believes he is being appeared to in that particular way. Hence appearing may be said to satisfy the second of the conditions we have proposed for a mark of evidence.

---

[7] Strictly speaking, a mark of evidence is described, not by "x appears so-and-so to S," but by "S is appeared to so-and-so, i.e., in such-and-such a way." The victim of delirium tremons, who says of an hallucinatory elephant or lizard.,"That appears pink," may be right in using "pink" and wrong in thinking that *something* appears pink. But he couldn't go far wrong if he said only "I'm appeared pink to"--or, in more philosophical language, "I sense pink."

And surely appearing satisfies the third of our conditions. Whenever anything appears in such-and-such a way to a subject S (or, better, whenever S is appeared to in such-and-such a way), then S has adequate evidence for the proposition that something is appearing to him (or, better, that he is being appeared to) in that particular way.

To be sure, no one is ever likely to say "I have adequate evidence for the proposition that something is appearing blue to me." But a man who is thus appeared to may use this proposition as a premise in the application of probability and induction. For example, if he happens to have adequate evidence for the proposition, "Most of the things that appear blue in this light are blue," if something now appears blue to him, and if he has adequate evidence for no other proposition bearing upon the probability of "This is blue," then he has adequate evidence for the proposition "This is blue." It is in this sense that he may be said to have adequate evidence for "Something appears blue to me."

7. *Empiricism*, as an epistemological thesis, may now be defined by reference to this "appearing" criterion of evidence and to the logic of probability, or confirmation.[8] According to empiricism in its most extreme form, the "appearing" criterion, when supplemented by the logic of probability, affords us our only criterion of evidence. If a subject S has adequate evidence for some statement h, then, according to this form of empiricism, either (a) h describes one of the ways S is being appeared to, in the non-comparative sense of "appear," or (b) h is a statement which is probable in relation to such non-comparative appear statements.

I think that the philosophers who have accepted this empirical thesis, or some modification of it, have been influenced by certain facts concerning the way in which we defend, or try to justify, our beliefs. But I will not discuss these facts here. Rather, I will note what seems to be one of the limitations of empiricism, as defined, and I will try to formulate an alternative thesis.

The limitation of empiricism, as defined, is that it would seem to lead us to what Hume called "scepticism with regard to the senses." For it is very difficult to think of any proposition about the "external world" which is probably--more probable than not--in relation to any set of propositions about the way in which one is appeared to. That is to say, it is very difficult to think of a set of statements of this sort: one of them is a synthetic statement, attributing some property to a material thing; the others are statements of the form, "I am appeared to in such-and-such a way," where the expression "appeared to in such-and-such a way" has what I have called its non-comparative use; and, finally, the statement about the material thing is probably--more probable than not--in relation to the statements about appearing. If there are no such sets of statements and if the empirical thesis is true, then any synthetic proposition about a material thing would be one which, for each of us, is epistemically indifferent--no more worthy of our confidence than is its contradictory. And if all of this were true, we might well conclude, with Hume, that "it is in vain to ask, whether there be body or not?"[9]

I suggest, however, that there are other marks of evidence. One of them is described by the word "take" which occurs in our definition of "perceive." (And therefore reference to "adequate evidence" in our definition is, in a certain sense, redundant.) I shall restrict myself, in what follows, to certain comments on this additional mark of evidence.

---

[8]   I use "empiricism" in one of its traditional senses. The word has many other meanings, of course, in recent philosophy.

8. What is it for a man to *take* something to have a certain characteristic--to take something to be a cat? First of all, of course, he *believes* that the thing is a cat. Secondly, the thing is appearing to him in a certain way. Thirdly, he believes (or assumes, or "takes it for granted") with respect to one of the ways he is being appeared to, that he would not now be appeared to in just that way if the thing were not a cat. (And undoubtedly he also believes, with respect to certain ways in which he might act, that if he were now to act in those ways he would be appeared to in still other catlike ways--i.e., in ways he would not be appeared to if the thing were not a cat.) And, finally, these beliefs or assumptions were not arrived at as the result of reflection, deliberation, or inference; the man didn't weigh alternatives and then *infer* that the thing was a cat.

More generally, the locution "There is something x such that S *takes* x to be f" may be said to mean this: there is something x such that x appears in some way to S; S believes that x is f; S also believes, with respect to one of the ways he is appeared to, that he would not be appeared to in that way, under the conditions which now obtain, if x were not f; and S did not arrive at these beliefs as a result of deliberation, reflection, or inference.

If a man takes something to be a cat, then, as I have noted, he is not likely to say "I take that to be a cat." He is more likely to say "I see that that is a cat."[10] But the fact that he wouldn't say "I take that to be a cat" doesn't imply that it's false that he takes the thing to be a cat. When the King dies, his subjects do not say "Some public official has passed away." But the fact that they do not say it does not imply it's false that some public official has passed away. If taking, as thus conceived, is a mark of evidence, then it must satisfy our three conditions. And I believe that it does. For (1) we have been able to say what taking is without using any epistemic terms; our description, or definition, does not make use of "know," "evident," "see," "perceive," or any other epistemic term. (2) No one can ever be said to believe falsely, or mistakenly, either that he is, or that he is not, taking something to be a cat. Of course a man may take something falsely to be a cat; i.e., he may mistake something for a cat. And a man may believe falsely today that yesterday he took something to be a cat. But no one can believe falsely now, with respect to himself, that he is now taking something to be a cat, or that he is not now taking something to be a cat. (Instead of saying "No one can believe falsely that...," we may say, if we prefer, "It makes no sense to say of anyone that he believes falsely that....") And I suggest (3) that if a man takes something to be a cat he thereby has adequate evidence for the proposition or hypothesis that the thing is a cat.[11]

---

9   *Treatise of Human Nature,* Book I, Part IV, Section ii ("Of Scepticism with regard to the Senses"). Thomas Reid wrote as follows, with respect to the empirical thesis and its apparent skeptical consequences: "A traveler of good judgement may mistake his way, and be unawares led into a wrong track; and while the road is fair before him, he may go on without suspicion and be followed by others; but when it ends in a coal-pit, it requires no great judgement to know that he had gone wrong, nor perhaps to find out what misled him" (*An Inquiry into the Human Mind,* Chapter One, Section 8). The empiricist may be tempted at this point to accept "phenomenalism"--the view that statements about material things may be translated into statements about "appearances"--in the hope that phenomenalism provides a way out of the coal-pit. But we cannot be sure that phenomenalism would provide such a way out, for no one has ever been able to make the required translations. And therefore we have no map to examine.

10   If a second man is not sure that our perceiver sees that the thing is a cat, the second man will say "He takes it to be a cat" or--what comes to the same thing--"He thinks he sees that it's a cat."

11   H.H. Price suggests a similar view in *Perception,* p. 185.

This theory of evidence has a kind of "internal" justification. For the hypotheses and propositions for which most of us have adequate evidence, if this theory is correct, indicate that most of our "takings" are true--that most of our "takings" are *perceivings*. These hypotheses and propositions indicate, as Peirce pointed out, that human beings have a tendency to make correct guesses and that the human mind is "strongly adapted to the comprehension of the world."[12]

Some of our "takings" are false. And therefore, if what I have been saying is true, there are times when we ought to place more confidence in a false proposition than in its true contradictory. The apparent paradox involved in saying that our false "takings"--our mistakes--are a mark of evidence has its analogue in moral philosophy. It is difficult to avoid saying that occasionally the right choice--or at least the choice that is praiseworthy--leads to consequences which are worse than those which the wrong--or blameworthy--choice would have led to.

And theories of evidence ("So-and-so, but not such-and-such, is a mark of evidence") are, generally, very much like theories of morals ("So-and-so, but not such-and-such, is invariably *right*"). If there is any good reason to think that statements expressing theories of morals are neither true nor false, then, I feel certain, there is also a good reason to think that statements expressing theories of evidence are neither true nor false.

---

[12]   C.S. Peirce, *Collected Papers*, 6.417.

Name_____

Date _____

1. What is Chisholm's main concern in this selection?

2. What does Chisholm intend to show by the analogy to moral philosophy?

3. Give one reason why the word "take" works for Chisholm as a mark of evidence?

4. Why cannot one say that a man has adequate evidence for a proposition when he simply "sees" it to be true?

5. Chisholm believes that human beings have a propensity for making correct guesses about what they perceive. True or false? Explain.

24

Problems of Metaphysics

Metaphysics is that philosophical inquiry the name of which is derived from the Greek phrase, *meta ta physika* which literally means "after the things of nature". *Meta* is the Greek word for beyond. So metaphysics means beyond (the) physics. But what on earth does that mean? The most traditional sense of the word 'physics' means the study of natural science, namely, an investigation of how the world we live in functions. People involved with this discipline are concerned with the task of ascertaining[1] and, consequently, formulating the underlying working laws of the universe such as the law of conservation of energy and the law of gravity. More often than not, especially in a technological age such as we are presently experiencing, it appears that once questions as to just how the world[2] functions are answered that that is the end of the matter. After all, we sufficiently understand the workings of nature even to the extent that we can put a man on the moon!

However, it has occurred to some individuals that there is something more to the world than just the physics of it. To discover this additional "something" we must go *beyond* physics in order to arrive at a *total* understanding of how the world functions. This additional inquiry is called metaphysics, namely, that study of the universe and all that is in it which goes beyond physics. In this chapter we will examine the four most common subcategories of the study of metaphysics. They are (1) ontology, (2) the problem of causation, (3) the problem of free will vs. determinism and (4) the problem of personal identity.

(1) Ontology is that branch of metaphysics which is the study of being or what there is. It is derived from the Greek word *onto* which means being and 'ology' which is a suffix meaning "the science of". Unlike the natural sciences which are concerned with (1) ascertaining the composition of the universe (i.e., chemistry and biology) and (2) how it functions (i.e., physics), ontology is that inquiry which strives to answer the questions: (a) What *types* of things are there in the world? (b) What is the nature of those (types of) things?

Regarding (a) we are not concerned with establishing a taxonomy[3] of all the individual things that exist in the universe such as tables and chairs, cattle and sheep. The discovery of such things and the constituents[4] of them, ontologists leave to students of the natural sciences. The items just mentioned are individual in nature. They exist as separate entities[5] in and of themselves. Ontologists, on the other hand, are interested in the *types* of things that constitute the universe. When we speak of types of things we mean things that are members of some class. We know, for example, that cattle and sheep belong to the same class (of things) since both are mammals. The point is that classes (types) are more general in nature

---

[1]   *ascertain:* to discover through examination or experimentation; find out.

[2]   Throughout this explanation of metaphysics, I will use the words 'world' and 'universe' synonymously.

[3]   *taxonomy:* the science, laws, or principles of classification.

[4]   *constituent:* serving as a part of a whole; component.

[5]   *entity:* something that exists independently, not relative to other things.

than the individual things which constitute them. There is no doubt that students of the natural sciences are interested in classifying the "things" with which they are concerned. Ontologists, however, are interested in a different kind of classification of the entities of the world. One of these ontological types is predicated[6] on tangibility[7]. The members of this class are called *concrete entia*, namely, they have spatio-temporal coordinates, i.e., boundaries, and, therefore, are tangible.[8] It is in this sense that the four aforementioned items are members of the same (ontological) class.

The most untutored[9] view of the world is that *concrete entia* are its sole constituents. Here care must be taken for one need not be able to perceive[10] a given entity in order for it to qualify as concrete in nature. After all, one does not perceive the individual molecules which compose tables and chairs, cattle and sheep. But consider, such "things" as molecules must be *concrete entia*, otherwise any aggregate[11] of them could not be perceived. How, for example, could a crow be tangible if the parts which constitute it (even at the most minute level) were not also concrete in nature. Hence, students of the natural sciences direct their efforts towards understanding *concrete entia* be they of a microscopic or macroscopic[12] form. Once this is understood, it still remains the case that the vast majority of people, tutored and untutored alike, believe that the universe is composed only of *concrete entia*.

Philosophers, however, tend not to be so hasty regarding their conclusions. If one scrutinizes[13] the use of language, one will notice that many words refer to "things". The process of referring is analogous[14] to the game of pin the tail on the donkey except that in this case we use certain words to label things. Now many of those things to which words refer are *concrete entia*. However, the referents of many words, namely, those "things" which are labeled by words, do not appear at the outset to be *concrete entia*. That does not in the least (a) render[15] the use of those words meaningless or (b) lead us to believe that the referents of such words are nonexistent or unreal. Consider, for example, the statement, "The flood was a terrible event". Note that this sentence makes reference to some "thing" called an event. (1) The use of the word 'event' is certainly not meaningless. (2) By so using that word we refer to some "thing", namely, a happening, in this case a flood. But is an event concrete in nature? Is it something that one can pick up and throw around like a football? Certainly not. If it is not, then events must be members of another ontological class of things. Those "things" which are not material by nature ontologists call *nonconcrete entia*. Given a little thought, there are numerous so-called "things" we refer to (by the use of language) and which we believe to be real. Another such example is that which we refer

---

6   *predicate:* to base or establish (a concept, statement or action).

7   *tangible:* able to be perceived as materially existent.

8   The use of the term *concrete entia* does not mean an entity which is solid in the sense that rock is solid. In this sense, soft, malleable and fluid "things" are also *concrete entia*.

9   *untutored:* having no formal education or instruction.

10   *perceive:* to become aware of directly through any of the senses.

11   *aggregate:* gathered together into a mass or sum so as to constitute a whole.

12   *macroscopic:* pertaining to observations made without magnifying instruments, especially by the unaided eye.

13   *scrutinize:* to examine or observe with great care; inspect minutely or critically.

14   *analogous:* similar or comparable in certain respects.

15   *render:* to give or make available.

to by the word 'fact'. It is not uncommon to hear one say, "It is a fact that so and so". But what is a fact? Such "things" as facts certainly are not concrete in nature. Therefore, they must be members of the class of *nonconcrete entia*.

Unless we believed in the existence of *nonconcrete entia* we would not be able to explain or account for any of the *concrete entia* we believe to be real. In other words, the reality of *concrete entia* is ontologically; that is, their existence is *dependent upon* the existence of *nonconcrete entia*. For example, common sense leads us to believe that tables are real. From a macroscopic point of view, it is reasonable to believe that a given table is composed of wood. The wood is concrete. From a microscopic viewpoint, the atoms which constitute this wood are equally concrete. However, if one were to ask if the table or the wood or the molecules in question had properties, a positive answer would not be out of order. Does the table possess the property of being colored? Does the table have the property of being smooth or rough? Certainly, these questions are meaningful. Even a physicist would agree. We describe *concrete entia* by making reference to the properties they possess. Furthermore, without the belief in the existence of properties, there would be no way we could understand the make-up of *concrete entia* much less describe them. Properties constitute one of the ontological underpinnings of *concrete entia* be they microscopic or macroscopic. In other words, properties are necessary for our being able to make sense of and describe the *concrete entia* of the world. If properties are *necessary* ontological underpinnings of *concrete entia*, then they must be equally real.

The same argument applies to such *nonconcrete entia* as facts and events. *Concrete entia* not only possess spatio-temporal coordinates in and of themselves, but they also stand in relation to one another. That they do so stand is not only a fact, but it is also a fact that they stand in different relationships to one another. For example, it is a fact that Boston is north of New York City. Both cities possess spatio-temporal coordinates, but how on earth could one describe the *reality* of the relationship of the one to the other without assuming that it is a fact that they are so related? A fact is defined as the way "things" are. In this case, the two "things" in question are[16] in a given relationship to one another and hence, their *relationship* constitutes a fact. Relationships, however, are not concrete. One cannot pick up and toss around a relationship! The relationships between two or more concrete things are not necessarily static. The universe possesses the *property* of motion. Some concrete things change their relationships with one another. Changes in relationships are called events. For example, if a car wreck occurs, an event takes place.[17] Now, try to place yourself in a position of explaining such changes in the world without *necessarily* making reference to events or some equivalent notion such as a happening. I submit that it will be impossible. If it is impossible, then it *must* be the case that events are real at least so far as we are able to understand the world and the workings of it. Events, however, are nonconcrete in nature.

The point of this discussion is twofold. (a) An investigation into the issue concerning the types of things that constitute the world yields that it is not only composed of *concrete entia* but *nonconcrete entia* as well. (b) Furthermore, the belief (assumption, if you will) in the latter is absolutely necessary for our being able to understand the former and the world within which they exist. *Nonconcrete entia* constitute the underpinnings

---

[16] Note that the word 'are' is a cognate of existence (i.e., is).

[17] As such, events are a subclass of facts.

of *concrete entia*. And this is an exceedingly important point. One cannot pet a property (in the sense discussed above) as one can his dog. We can perceive the latter, but not the former *per se*[18]. To be sure, we can perceive that the dog is honey-colored and in that sense perceive that the animal in question has the property of being honey-colored. But in order for us to perceive such *a* property, property *in general must exist* in the first place. But we are incapable of perceiving the "thing" property in general which provides the ontological basis of specific properties. Consider it in this manner. Red and purple are colors. Hence, any concrete thing that possesses either one of them has the property of being colored. Now, unless color itself was something real, even though we cannot perceive color *per se*, then we could not perceive the specific colors in question. Hence, the nonconcrete entity color must exist. Since this as well as other nonconcrete entities must exist yet are not perceivable, they do indeed go beyond physics. Such general entities are not "up front" as are cattle and sheep, but hidden albeit[19] necessary in order to adequately explain the perceptible things of the world.

The *meta* aspect of metaphysics, therefore, ought not be construed in a horizontal fashion. From an ontological point of view we do not seek something beyond in the sense of "down the road" beyond, namely, something equally as concrete in order to explain that which we already know to be so constituted. This we leave to the physicist. Rather, a true rendering of the concept *meta* is vertical in nature. Stated in a symbolic way, the tree that one perceives exists above the ground. However, reason tells us that such a structure could not exist erect unless it possessed underpinnings, namely, roots. But the roots are invisible. In order to understand how the tree maintains itself, one must comprehend what lies beneath the surface. It is in this sense that the study of metaphysics is the avenue by which we understand not only the ultimate constituents of the universe but also in a very real way how it functions.

Once it is accepted that *nonconcrete entia* are here with us to stay, the philosopher becomes curious as to the nature of them. What, for example, is the nature of a relationship? They obviously are not tangible. This issue leads us one step deeper into ontology. Specifically, it involves the issue of particulars vs. universals. The former are *concrete entia*. The latter are defined as that which two or more things have in common. For example, one may perceive that the covers of the five books in front of him are colored red. If so, they all have the property of redness in common. They all have the property of *being* red. But what is the nature of that which they have in common, namely, redness above and beyond the fact of being red? Look at it this way. If it were not for the fact that there was the *nonconcrete entity* redness, it would not be possible for the books in question to possess that property. Each book is red, not redness. But since they have redness in common redness must *be* something. If so, what is the nature of it? Sure, we can categorize it as a universal, but then the question becomes "What is the nature of a universal?" In light of our example, "What is the nature of (the universal) redness?"

Let us consider another example. We all know that to which the word 'man' refers. The referents of this word can be particulars (concrete entities) for they are tangible in nature. However, we also use the word 'man' in a general way. This use of the word does not refer to any *specific* (thing) man. Hence, it does not refer to a particular. The word 'man' refers to a class of things, not to the particular entities that constitute that

---

[18] *per se:* in or by itself; intrinsically.
[19] *albeit:* although; even though; though.

class. The particulars in question all have the property of *manness* in common. By definition, then, that to which the word 'man' refers must be a universal.

The concern for understanding the nature of universals has consumed an enormous amount of intellectual energy throughout the history of Western Philosophy. That this is the case is evident once one understands what the word 'philosophy' means. It is derived from the ancient Greek words *philia* (love) and *sophia* (wisdom). Hence, a philosopher is a lover of wisdom. The concept of wisdom entails a true understanding of the nature of the universe and all that is in it. This quest for understanding leads certain individuals (known as philosophers) to probe beyond (hence *meta*) that which is immediately perceptible (i.e., concrete entities) for the purpose of understanding the nature of that which makes such things capable of being perceived in the first place. As has been demonstrated above, one cannot so understand, much less explain, the nature of particulars without making reference to and assuming that there are such "things" as *nonconcrete entia,* a subclass of which are universals. As can well be imagined, a great deal of controversy has occurred over the years as to the nature of such so-called "things".

(2) One of the nonconcrete entities referred to above was events. This notion provides the basis of the second issue of concern of metaphysics. An event is defined as the change in relationship between two or more concrete entities. We have yet to explore the notion of change. Just what is "packed into" the concept of change? For one thing, it involves causation. Events simply do not occur unless there is some cause of them. Common sense tells us that much. But what does it mean to say that, "so-and-so" *caused* "such-and-such" to happen? After all, we use the word 'cause' and cognates[20] of it most freely. Certainly, we must know or have some comprehension of that to which the word refers. If pressed to the wall, not many people will be able to offer an adequate explanation of the concept of causation. If you do not believe me, try to explain it yourself or ask a friend. Chances are the response will be along the line of "Well, you know what I mean". But obviously, the whole point in asking the question in the first place is that the meaning of the concept of causation is not clear. Sure, we perceive happenings, for example, someone throwing a rock at a bottle and consequently breaking it. We naturally conclude that the striking of the bottle by the projectile in question caused it to shatter. On the other hand, we do not normally believe that there is a causal connection between walking under a ladder and a subsequent mishap. However, let us suppose that there occurred some adversity[21] attendant to such behavior. What reason would we have to believe that the behavior in question did not cause that which happened after ambulating[22] under the runged apparatus[23]? The most common response is that there is no *consistency* between the antecedents[24] of such behavior and the consequents[25] of it. Hence, consistency seems to be one criterion of causation. From a scientific point of view this criterion constitutes the principle one. For example, if one is to establish an hypothesis, theory or law by which cer-

---

[20] *cognate:* related in origin, as certain words in different languages derived from the same root.

[21] *adversity:* a state of hardship or affliction.

[22] *ambulate:* to walk.

[23] *apparatus:* instruments, appliances or machinery designed for a particular use.

[24] *antecedent:* any occurrence or event prior to another.

[25] *consequent:* following as a natural effect; result or conclusion.

tain data[26] react, one must demonstrate that they do so repeatedly given relatively similar circumstances. However, there are two problems associated with the criterion of consistency, (a) one theoretical and (b) one practical. (a) From a theoretical standpoint, one can never be sure that the way events occurred in the past will (for certain) happen in the future. Common sense, for all practical purposes, may make it more convenient to so believe, but the events of such a belief are not guaranteed. For example, it is indeed to our advantage from a pragmatic[27] standpoint to believe that the sun will rise tomorrow predicated on our past experience, but we have no guarantee of it. After all, there is absolutely no telling what will happen in the future. Just think about that. All we really have to go on is the past. (b) From a practical point of view, we know that the notion of causation is not predicated upon the recurrence, and hence consistency, of events. One does not require a repeat of a pin being jabbed into the sole of his foot to appreciate the concept of causation. Once is enough! Somehow, one comprehends that the jabbing in question caused the pain. Not only that, one need not become so personal about the matter. If an Aborigine were thrown into the world in which we live he would no doubt conclude by his first experience of flipping on a light switch that the proximate[28] illumination was caused by his action. The notion of causation is immediate. The observation of it in such a case undermines the need for repetition. Given these practical as well as theoretical barriers, just where does that put us in our understanding of the concept of causation? In a metaphysical way, it puts us back to the starting point. Obviously, those knowledgeable of the discipline of physics offer little help in this regard for they *take for granted* the notion of causation. Such individuals are primarily concerned with how "things" happen not with what a happening (i.e., causal sequence) is *per se*. In essence[29], that is the difference between a physicist and a metaphysician. The former is primarily concerned with how the world functions in terms of the causal relationships between its constituents, whereas the latter strives for an understanding of the nature of that which makes the universe and everything in it so function. In other words, the physicist takes for granted the notion of causation and he readily employs it in order to (successfully) explain the occurrences of (natural) events. The philosopher, on the other hand, is a bit more hesitant. It appears reasonable to him that if the concept of causation is *necessary* in order to comprehend the specific nature of the specific occurrences within the world (i.e., universe) in which we live, that we ought first and foremost arrive at an adequate understanding of the concept we (necessarily) use in order to elucidate[30] the happenings in question. It should be obvious from what has been stated above that this task is not so easy. Again, ask yourself, "What is causation *per se*?" Such is a *meta*physical question. One can perceive the causal sequence of an automobile tail-ending another such vehicle. It makes perfect sense to conclude that the resultant damage was caused by two cars colliding. In fact, the destruction in question *could not be* understood much less accounted for unless the concept of causation is employed. Here, however, the emphasis is placed upon the specific event in question. In such a

---

[26]   *datum:* something that is given from being experimentally encountered; a fact. Data is the plural form of the word.

[27]   *pragmatic:* dealing with facts or actual occurrences; practical.

[28]   *proximate:* next or nearest in space, order, time, etc.

[29]   *essence:* the quality or qualities of a thing that give it its identity; the intrinsic or indispensable properties of a thing.

[30]   *elucidate:* to make intelligible; explain.

case, the philosopher is not concerned with the actual situation in question. (We leave that to lawyers!) Rather, the nature of the underlying notion in question, namely, causation (without which any given event could not be adequately understood much less explained) constitutes a central issue of concern for students of metaphysics.

(3) Another metaphysical issue concerns the relationship between free will and determinism. We normally prefer to believe that we are in control of our lives, that if any determinism is involved in the process *we* do the determining, namely, that we are agents that freely decide and hence determine what we do regardless of the complexity of the situation at hand. In short, we do what we want to do and the wants involved are *our* wants. The problem is that it is easier to cite factors over which we have no control which play a determining role in our behavior. We have, for example, no "say" regarding what we are fed when we are infants. That in itself can have a definite determining effect regarding the manner in which we subsequently develop both physically and mentally. We have no control over the fact that we are born mammals without wings and cannot fly without rather sophisticated props. Just where does our freedom lie if there *is* any meaningful sense of the term? Certainly it is a matter of free will that we choose to go to a given movie. To suggest that such a decision was determined by a force other than ourselves is ludicrous[31]. We may, in fact, be machines of a sort, but not the equivalent of computers which are programmed to do *exactly* what they do by some external force or determinant. Rather, it is generally believed by philosophers and laymen alike that *homo sapiens*[32] do, in fact, have a measure of control over that which they do. The problem with respect to this metaphysical issue is to prove that (human) freedom (of choice) does, in fact, exist. Is there a viable[33] case to be made in support of free will? There is an abundance of evidence that human action is to a great extent determined. Early behaviorists such as C. L. Hull and B. F. Skinner maintained that human beings are programmed by external stimuli in relatively the same manner in which rats can be conditioned. Approached in such a manner, it would indeed appear reasonable that the members of the species *homo sapiens* have no control over their behavior patterns. Although the above mentioned individuals would not admit it, it nevertheless remains a fact that human beings are not *mentally* the equivalent of the subjects viz., rats upon which they formulated their theory known as behaviorism. Their research is an extension of Pavlov's discoveries which demonstrated that if one rang a bell in proximity to offering a dog food that the subject in question would come to salivate[34] upon hearing the ringing bell.[35] However, scientists of this persuasion do not have as their subjects human beings. And it is highly questionable indeed that *homo sapiens* do, in fact, function in the same manner in which the experimental subjects which scientists have at their disposal act and react under a controlled environment. First of all, there is no feasible[36] way in which a *homo sapiens* can be isolated and controlled regarding his environment such as one can do with a rat. Hence, any correlation between the causes of the behavior of

[31] *ludicrous:* foolish.

[32] *homo sapiens:* the biological classification for human beings.

[33] *viable:* workable.

[34] *salivate:* to excrete fluid via the mouth.

[35] Pavlov (1849-1936) was a Russian physiologist who originated the theory of conditioned reflex via his experiments primarily with dogs.

[36] *feasible:* capable of being accomplished or brought about; practicable.

such diverse[37] beasts is purely a matter of speculation. Obviously, the motivation behind the behaviorist's theory is that any organism which possesses a central nervous system cannot think and does not have a mind. Behaviorists are basically threatened by the concept of mind. They prefer trying to demonstrate that mind does not exist rather than to address the highly probable reality of it. The notion of mind is exceedingly[38] elusive[39]. People, including scientists, tend to be not only curious but apprehensive[40] about that which they do not understand. And for sure, the nature of mind is enough to give anyone pause. Behaviorists attempted to demonstrate that there was no such "entity" rather than accept its reality and try to explain the nature of it. At this stage of the game, it has been fairly well recognized that human beings do not function in their day-to-day activities as do rats in a Skinner box.[41] This is not to say that external forces (i.e., external stimuli) do not have significant influence on people's behavior. The central issue concerns the *degree* of determinism so far as the philosophical issue is concerned. We know we are not the equivalent of conditioned rats, but we also know that we are conditioned to a certain degree; that is, determined by, for example, the diet to which we are subjected at an early age and how we are treated (i.e., trained) by our parents in the formative years. In other words, the environment plays a significant role in determining human behavior. Such a fact does not demonstrate that we are analogous to rats.

Even though the environment exerts[42] its influence upon human beings, just how much does it? Notwithstanding environmental influences such as our parents, what amount of free will do we have? At this point it is obvious that that is not an easy question to answer. It is one which scientists have not been able to resolve and one which has concerned philosophers for thousands of years.

One should note at this point that the problem of causation is not unrelated to the issue of free will vs. determinism. If there is free will regardless of its extent, then it is incumbent[43] upon us to ascertain the difference between actions which are self-caused as opposed to causal events which are not. In other words, there is a difference between me raising my arm and my arm rising. In the latter case, I exercise no power; that is, my arm may rise due to an electric shock or by someone else shoving my arm up. It is over this issue that the debate concerning free will vs. determinism has centered for the past three decades. This area of study is known as action theory and seeks to determine the difference between human action and mere bodily movement. If human action can be demonstrated to be self-caused, by virtue of oneself causing (i.e., determining) it, then one can reasonably infer that such action is free, otherwise not.

(4) Another crucial metaphysical issue concerns the problem of personal identity. It can be formulated in one of two ways.

---

[37] *diverse:* having variety in form; multiform.
[38] *exceed:* to go beyond the prior or proper limits of.
[39] *elusive:* hard to grasp or retain mentally.
[40] *apprehensive:* anxious or fearful about the future; uneasy.
[41] A Skinner box is an apparatus which is primarily designed to condition the inhabitants thereof by means of external stimuli.
[42] *exert:* to put into vigorous action.
[43] *incumbent:* resting upon as a duty or obligation.

(a) In what sense can we say that a person is the *same* at time t_1 as he is at time t_2?

(b) From an ontological point of view, what is the referent of the first person pronoun 'I'?

(a) Most people believe that they are the same person from one moment to the next. But as is the case with the problem of free will vs. determinism, there is much more evidence to demonstrate that we are not the same person from time to time. We know, for example, that our epithelial[44] cells regenerate[45] and totally replace the existing ones in seven year cycles. Hence, we cannot, strictly speaking, say from that point of view that we are the same person that we were seven years ago for we possess a completely different set of said cells. Not only that, it is obvious that people (1) change psychologically as time passes, and (2) develop a greater bank of experience by which one cannot maintain that one is (precisely) the same person he was as a child. Nevertheless, there *seems to be* some common "thread" that ties those diverse experiences together whereby it appears reasonable to claim that we are the *same* person who had them.

The central issue concerning this formulation of the problem is over the meaning of the word 'same'. Let us draw an analogy. Suppose you own a boat. Furthermore, let us suppose that you replaced one of its hatches. Now if someone were to ask you after such a modification if this is the *same* boat you purchased a year ago, the answer would be obvious. Of course it is the same boat. At the very best, it would be considered a bad joke to say, "No, it is not the same because I replaced a hatch". But technically speaking it is not the same. If it is not precisely the same boat, then in what sense is it so? The same reasoning applies to human beings. Given that there are changes regarding any given individual, in what sense is it coherent[46] to claim that he is the same person from one time to the next? Think about that. We obviously take such sameness for granted. The difference in this case between the layman[47] and the philosopher is that the latter prefers to assume nothing. He desires to know what it is about us that justifies us in claiming that there is something constant throughout our lives which makes it reasonable for us to claim that we remain the same person from time to time. The determination of the nature of that "something" is central to any solution to the problem of personal identity.

(b) We have all asked the question, "What is the *real* me?" It is an attempt to determine the referent of the word 'I'. Does your personal identity reside in your body, your mind or both? Descartes, for example, argued that one's mind was the only "thing" that one could be absolutely certain that existed.[48] One could reasonably doubt that one's body was real for he could not ascertain any criteria that absolutely distinguished dreams or hallucinations from so-called "normal" perceptions. Let's put it this way. If one dreamed 50% of the time and was awake the other 50% of it, how on earth would one know what was real so far as anything phys-

---

[44] *epithelium:* membranous tissue characteristic of the outer covering of the body of an organism, specifically *homo sapiens*.

[45] *regenerate:* to replace by formation of a new tissue.

[46] *coherent:* capable of logical, intelligible speech or thought.

[47] *layman:* one who does not have special or advanced training or skill.

[48] Descartes (1596-1650) was that philosopher designated as the father of Modern Philosophy which extends from approximately 1650 to 1850 A.D.

ical was concerned? After all, our bodies appear very real in dreams. What we do know for certain, whether or not we are dreaming or awake is that we are aware of the activity by which our bodies partake. This awareness is a characteristic of our minds. Hence, Descartes reasoned that the referent of the word 'I' is a person's mind. (He was, of course, equating the word 'mind' with that of consciousness). It has not been uncommon in the history of Western Philosophy to draw a clear-cut distinction between the mind and the body. However, the brain *per se* is not equivalent to the mind. We know that (1) both exist and (2) they are not identical for frogs have brains but not minds at least as far as we have been able to ascertain. If this is the case, then Descartes may well have a point in his favor. We cannot be absolutely certain of the "real" existence of our bodies, but we can rest assured that the *awareness* of it is real. Hence, he argues that that which constitutes personal identity, namely, that to which the word 'I' refers is consciousness qua[49] mind.

This point of view, however, raises certain difficulties. Given the fact that consciousness is intimately associated with brain activity, let us imagine a case in which we could, by sophisticated surgical means, transplant and subsequently switch two peoples' brains. How do you suppose a professional football player would react regarding his *own* identity if his brain had been surgically "hooked up" with the body of a 97-pound weakling? If we agree that one's mind is closely associated with one's brain, and that one's personal identity is tantamount[50] to mind, then the football player would have no need of worrying about a loss of identity for he would still be in possession of his mind albeit in an inferior body. However, even if such an operation were possible, it would undoubtedly do no good to try to convince the pro that he need not worry about his personal identity on the basis that the referent of the word 'I' was his mind qua brain. The likely response would be that by hence possessing a 97-pound body he could no longer *be* a professional football player and that furthermore his being such a creature was part and parcel of possessing a body that could live up to that role. So, it is not at all clear that Descartes' view concerning personal identity is satisfactory. And the more we understand from a scientific point of view the interrelationship between the workings of the brain and consciousness (qua mind) the more confusing the issue of personal identity becomes. Philosophers are not of a kind that seek to create problems. Rather, they are individuals who try to solve those which are at the basis of humanity. Everyone has at one time or another wondered what he was in terms of his individual or personal identity. Such a problem is not an ivory tower one. It is basic. We want to know what we *are*. And it is as simple as that. Furthermore, there is nothing unusual about such a concern. The difference between the layman and a philosopher is that the latter makes it his profession to seriously pursue answers to such issues. He wants to *know* (in this case) what constitutes personal identity. He is not satisfied by a plethora[51] of "You know what I mean" answers to such fundamental questions. It is in this regard that the quest[52] of the philosopher is humble. He genuinely desires to understand the basics of the universe such as the nature of causation and universals qua properties which make possible individual (i.e., particular) things existing as the (types of) things they are. He wants to know if there is a *real* differ-

---

[49]   *qua:* considered as; in the function, character, or capacity of.

[50]   *tantamount:* equivalent in effect or value.

[51]   *plethora:* superabundance; excess.

[52]   *quest:* the act or insistence of seeking or pursuing something; a search.

ence between the human machine and computers. That is, do we have free will? The philosopher wants to know what the *real* me is.

In order to answer such questions, one must go beyond physics. One must dig beneath the surface, namely, that which is apparent, "up front" or obvious and probe the recesses of one's intellectual capacity for the purpose of understanding the ultimate nature of the world. The study of metaphysics constitutes such a back to basics movement.

Suggested Readings: Metaphysics

Ontology

1. Aaron, R. I., *The Theory of Universals* (New York and London, 1967), Part II.
2. Anscombe, G. E. M., and Geach, P. T., "Aristotle," in *Three Philosophers* (Oxford and New York, 1961).
3. Aristotle, *Categories and De Interpretatione*, translated by J. L. Ackrill (Oxford and New York, 1963), especially pp. 3-11.
4. Goodman, N., "A World of Individuals," in *The Problem of Universals* (Notre Dame, Indiana, 1956).
5. Kung, G., *Ontology and the Logistic Analysis of Language* (Dordrecht, Holland, and New York, 1967).
6. Loux, M., (ed.), *Universals and Particulars* (New York, 1970).
7. Passmore, J., "The Two-Worlds Theory," in *Philosophical Reasoning* (London and New York, 1961).
8. Plato, *Parmenides*, translated with commentary by F.M. Cornford in *Plato and Parmenides* (London and New York, 1939).
9. _____, *Phaedo*.
10. Price, H. H., *Thinking and Experience* (London, 1953).
11. Quine, W.V., "On What There Is," in *From a Logical Point of View* (Cambridge, Mass., 1953).
12. Russell, Bertrand, *Problems of Philosophy* (London and New York, 1912), Chapters 9-10.
13. Schoedinger, A., (ed.), *The Problem of Universals* (Atlantic Heights, N.J.: Humanities Press International, 1992).
14. Wittgenstein, L., *Blue and Brown Books* (Oxford and New York, 1958).
15. _____, *Philosophical Investigations* (Oxford and New York, 1963).
16. Woozley, A.D., "Universals," in *Theory of Knowledge* (London and New York, 1949).

Causation

17. Berofsky, B., *Determinism* (Princeton, 1971).
18. Bunge, M., *Causality* (Cambridge, Mass., 1959).
19. Ducasse, C.J., *Causation and the Types of Necessity* (Seattle, 1924; 1969).
20. Goodman, N., *Fact, Fiction and Forecast*, 2nd ed. (Indianapolis, 1965).
21. Hart, H.L., and Honoré, A.M., *Causation and the Law* (Oxford, 1959).

22. Michotte, A., *The Perception of Causality* (New York, 1963).
23. Rescher, N., *Hypothetical Reasoning* (Amsterdam, 1964).
24. Suppes, P., *A Probabilistic Theory of Causality* (Amsterdam, 1970).
25. Von Wright, G.H., *Explanation and Understanding* (lthaca, N.Y., 1971), pp. 34-82.

Free Will vs. Determinism and Action Theory

26. Dennett, D. C., *Content and Consciousness* (N.Y.: Humanities Press, 1969).
27. Hempel, C. G., "The Logical Analysis of Psychology" in H. Feigl and W. Sellars (eds.), *Readings in Philosophical Analysis* (New York: Appleton-Century-Crofts, 1949).
28. Hook, Sidney (ed.), *The Dimensions of Mind* (New York: New York University Press, 1960),
29. Hull, C.L., *Principles of Behavior* (New York: Appleton-Century-Crofts, 1943).
30. Lange, F. A., *History of Materialism* (London: Routledge & Kegan Paul, 1925).
31. Louch, A. R., *Explanation and Human Action* (Berkeley & Los Angeles: University of California Press, 1969).
32. Meiland, J. W., *The Nature of Intention* (London: Methuen & Co., Ltd., 1970).
33. Melden, A. I., *Free Action* (London: Routledge and Kegan Paul, Ltd., 1961).
34. Price, H.H., "Image Thinking," in *Proceedings of the Aristotelian Society*, 1951-52.
35. Ryle, Gilbert, *The Concept of Mind* (London: Hutchinson, 1949).
36. Schoedinger, A., *Wants, Decisions and Human Action: A Praxeological Investigation* (Washington, D.C.: University Press of America, 1978).
37. Smart, J.J.C., "Sensations and Brain Processes" in the *Philosophical Review* (Ithaca New York, 1959).
38. Taylor, C., *The Explanation of Behavior* (London: Routledge & Kegan Paul, 1964).
39. Taylor, R., *Action and Purpose* (N.Y.: Humanities Press, 1973).
40. Tolman, E. C., *Purposive Behaviour in Animals and Men* (New York: Appleton-Century-Crofts, 1932).
41. Watson, J. B., *Psychology From the Standpoint of a Behaviorist* (Philadelphia: Lippincott, 1919).
42. _____, *Behaviourism* (New York: Norton, 1924).
43. White, A. R. (ed.), *The Philosophy of Action* (Oxford: Oxford University Press, 1968).

Personal Identity

44. Allport, Gordon, *The Person in Psychology* (Boston: Beacon Press, 1968).
45. Anderson, Alan Ross (ed.), *Minds and Machines* (Englewood Cliffs, N.J.: Prentice-Hall, Inc., 1964).

46. Armstrong, D.M., *Bodily Sensations* (London: Routledge & Kegan Paul, 1962).
47. Bartlett, Sir Frederic, *Thinking* (New York: Basic Books, 1958).
48. Bruner, J. S., Goodnow, J. J., and Austin, G. A., *A Study of Thinking* (New York: John Wiley & Sons, Inc., 1956).
49. Bruner, J. S., Oliver, R. R., and Greenfield, P. M., et. al., *Studies in Cognitive Growth* (New York: John Wiley & Sons, Inc., 1966).
50. Crosson, F.J., and Sayre, K.M. (eds.), *The Modeling of Mind* (South Bend: University of Notre Dame Press, 1963).
51. Flew, Anthony (ed.), *Body, Mind, and Death* (New York: The Macmillan Company, 1964).
52. Flugel, J. C., *Studies in Feeling and Desire* (London: Gerald Duckworth & Co., Ltd. 1955).
53. Geach, Peter, *Mental Acts* (London: Routledge & Kegan Paul, Ltd., 1957).
54. Hampshire, Stuart, *Thought and Action* (London: Chatto and Windus, Ltd., 1959).
55. Hook, Sidney (ed.), *Psychoanalysis, Scientific Method and Psychology* (Washington Square: New York University Press, 1959).
56. _____, *Dimensions of Mind* (New York: Collier Books, 1961).
57. Norbeck, E., Price-Williams, and McCord, W., *The Study of Personality* (New York: Holt, Rinehart and Winston, Inc., 1968).
58. Russell, Bertrand, *The Analysis of Mind* (London: George Allen & Unwin, Ltd. 1921)
59. Shoemaker, Sydney, *Self-Knowledge and Self-Identity* (Ithaca: Cornell University Press, 1963).
60. Vinacke, W.E., *The Psychology of Thinking* (New York: McGraw-Hill, Inc., 1952)

S T U D Y
⁊ Q U E S T I O N S ⁊

Name_____

Chapter 24:
Problems of Metaphysics

Date _____

1. Distinguish between *concrete entia* and *nonconcrete entia* and give examples.

2. What is the argument for the existence of *nonconcrete entia*?

3. Of what importance is knowledge of *nonconcrete entia*?

4. What is the importance of understanding causation?

5. Why is the behaviorist argument for determinism not persuasive?

6. Explain the difference between "human action" and "mere bodily movement."

7. What is problematic about personal identity?

8. What are three possible answers to the question: What is the referent of the first person pronoun 'I'?

9. What problem arises when we say that what is "really me" is my mind or consciousness?

25 Realism; Plato

Plato (427-347 B.C.) was born in Athens of an aristocratic family some members of which were politically prominent. Their political persuasion was anti-democratic as was Plato's. However, the democratic cause was victorious, thereby nipping in the bud any political career Plato may have wished for.

Plato became acquainted with his mentor[a] Socrates sometime during his late teenage years. Plato revered[b] Socrates as a model philosopher. The latter was a very outspoken individual on all matters. He was prone to "tell it like it is" and this eventually got him into political hot water. The power structure was sufficiently threatened by him that they condemned him for corrupting the youth of Athens and therefore Athenian society. They offered him an ultimatum; either silence yourself or leave Athens. Neither alternative appealed to Socrates, so he was condemned to death.

Given this background, it is no wonder that Plato ultimately shunned[c] any sort of political involvement in Athens. He chose instead to follow in the footsteps of his teacher. This ultimately led him to found the Academy which was similar to our concept of a university. It offered courses in mathematics, astronomy, physical sciences and philosophy. He was the head of this institution and was its primary lecturer. This does not mean, however, that Plato lost interest in the nature of politics. His attention in part focused on political philosophy which concerns the form of government which will best meet the needs of the individuals of any given society. His conclusion, in short, was that the profession of government is no different than any other professional or vocational pursuit. It requires training. Those who are trained with respect to the leadership of society are the ones who should be the cream of the crop for they must ultimately make decisions that affect the whole of society. They are the ones who should know right from wrong, good from bad. However, such concepts are ones the nature of which are the proper concern of philosophers. Hence, Plato reasoned that philosophers ought to be the rulers of society.

---

[a] *mentor:* a teacher or coach.

[b] *revere:* to regard with deep respect.

[c] *shun:* to keep away from; avoid scrupulously or consistently.

A sizeable amount of metaphysical[1] energy in the history of Western Philosophy has been expended on trying to ascertain[2] the nature of universals as opposed to particulars. The latter are individual things which most conspicuously[3] possess spatio-temporal coordinates. That is, they are tangible[4] in nature. A tree, for example, is a particular. A universal, on the other hand, is defined as a characteristic that two or more things have in common. Let us suppose that one perceives[5] five red books. What do they have in common? They obviously have at least two "things" in common, namely bookness and redness. None of these (hypothetical) books are identical to bookness or redness. That being the case, bookness and redness must be something (i.e., some "thing") other than those five particular red books. Philosophers want to know what the nature of those so-called "things" are. Bookness and redness are not tangible as are the (hypothetical) red books. Bookness and redness are universals. Many particulars have them in common, realizing, of course, that what all books have in common is bookness regardless of color and there are innumerable red particulars which are not books. Therefore, it would appear that there is no necessary link between a particular and a universal. The latter can be in many places at the same time whereas the former are bound by spatio-temporal coordinates which is to say, particulars are *concrete entia* and universals are *nonconcrete entia*. Just what are these *nonconcrete entia* called universals? That question philosophers have been trying to answer since Plato and his mentor Socrates raised the issue some 2400 years ago. Plato came to the conclusion that universals possess an independent status tantamount[6] to particulars. That is to say, universals are just as real as the individual things that we see, feel, taste, smell and hear. If being a red book is not identical to the qualities of redness and bookness, then just what is the nature of universals?

A little thought will reveal that we not only use universal words meaningfully, but that we could not adequately converse without them. All common nouns refer to universals. As Aristotle noted, "universals are predicable of many", e.g., John is a man, Max is a man and George is a man. The common noun 'man' is predicated of John, Max and George, each of whom are particulars of which there are many. Common nouns are of utmost importance because without them we do not have language. Just try to communicate without using common nouns. Given the meaningful use of common nouns as well as our necessary linguistic dependence upon them, it follows that to which they refer is very important in understanding what is (i.e., exists). Predicates determine what type of thing a particular is. The predicate man classifies John, Max and George. But man is general, not particular, by virtue of being predicable of many. What is it that 'man' refers to? It is the universal manness. But what is that? That is the problem of universals.

Realism is that metaphysical school of thought which maintains that universals exist independently of a perceiver just as much as do trees. The former may not be tangible as are the latter, but they nevertheless possess an independent status. This means that such specific universals as red-

---

[1]   *metaphysics:* the branch of philosophy that systematically investigates the nature of the conceptual foundation and therefore reality of the universe and all that is in it.

[2]   *ascertain:* to discover through examination or experimentation; find out.

[3]   *conspicuous:* easy to notice; obvious.

[4]   *tangible:* able to be perceived as materially existent.

[5]   *perceive:* to become aware of directly through any of the senses.

[6]   *tantamount:* equivalent in effect or value.

ness, largeness or bookness do not derive their existence by being perceived by anyone. If something possesses the quality of largeness in common with something else, that is a fact no matter what. Two large things can exist and the universal largeness will exist regardless of whether or not anyone perceives the fact that they partake of that universal. Such a metaphysical position is not without merit. After all, one would not normally maintain that of two trees possessing differing dimensions never perceived by a human being that one of them was not larger than the other. The assumption that such a pair of unperceived trees exists is not unwarranted[7] given that there are regions of the earth that no one has so perceived in the past or present. Such an example reasonably leads one to conclude that the universal largeness is independent of perception and must exist on its own. Generations of perceivers have come and gone and the universal largeness nevertheless remains. Such an independent status of universals provides the foundation for (metaphysical) realism. Plato was of this persuasion.

At the outset, Plato "bought into" the Heraclitean Doctrine of Flux.[8] Surprisingly enough, this analysis of the nature of the world is amazingly consistent with our modern day view of it . Heraclitus maintained that the universe is in a perpetual state of change. Nothing remains the same from one moment to the next. Whereas he did not speak in terms of free-floating atoms as we now do, it nevertheless seemed reasonable to him that nothing remained the same from one moment to the next notwithstanding that our senses indicate the contrary. It may appear to one that the staircase he ascends is the same from day to day, but the object in question does, in fact, change if nothing else than due to the wear by our footsteps. The point is that the world we live in is in a constant state of change, including ourselves. Nothing is constant. It is very important to bear in mind that Plato accepted this theory for by so doing he set the stage for a rock bottom problem regarding his own metaphysical theory. This problem can only be exposed by examining his other metaphysical commitments.

Closely associated with the notion of universals is the concept of an essence. An essence is that characteristic or set of characteristics without which a particular (thing) would not be the *type* of entity[9] that it is. Types are the same as classes, a notion which we employ in everyday discourse as much as that of universals. Any two particular human beings are unique[10] from a specific point of view. However, they are members of the same class or type of entity, namely, the class *homo sapiens*[11]. What qualifies a thing for class membership? They are characteristics such that *unless* the thing in question possesses them, they simply do not qualify for the class under consideration. Those characteristics of any given entity which are necessary for it to gain membership in some class are essential characteristics. For example, an ashtray does not qualify for membership in the class of *homo sapiens* since one of the essential (i.e., necessary) characteristics of the latter is being alive. Ashtrays, in contrast, are inani-

---

[7] *warrant:* justification or reasonable grounds for some act, course, statement or belief. Unwarranted is the negation of warrant.

[8] Heraclitus was a pre-Socratic philosopher. The exact dates of his life are unknown. His writings are traced to between 500 and 460 B.C.

[9] *entity:* a particular and discreet unit: an entirety.

[10] *unique:* being the only one of its kind.

[11] *homo sapiens:* the biological classification for human beings.

mate[12] in nature. Essential characteristics are qualities that a particular (thing) *must* possess *in order to be* a member of a certain class of things.[13]

Here some confusion may result due to the fact that two things may be members of one class and not another. A man and a woman are both members of the class *homo sapiens* whereas at the same time one is a member of the class of male *homo sapiens* and the other a member of the class of female *homo sapiens*. This demonstrates that the nature of classes is stratified. There are not only the separate classes of male and female *homo sapiens*, but the more general class of *homo sapiens* is a subclass of mammals which includes such creatures as dogs and cats. The class of mammals is, in itself, a subclass of animals which includes birds, and amphibians. It is of philosophical interest to determine the essential characteristics of a given class be it narrow or broad. At this point it may appear that such a concern falls primarily within the purview[14] of the biologist. But consider the issue in this manner. If one were to replace the forearm of a human being with that of a dog, would our sample specimen be a member of the class *homo sapiens* or a member of the class canine? Chances are we would assign the creature in question to the former class. The philosophical issue turns on just how many changes it takes for the subject in question to be considered a *homo sapiens* with canine characteristics as opposed to a canine with the characteristics of a *homo sapiens*. Just what is the breaking point? That point holds the key to the essential characteristics at stake in this example, namely, between what is necessary for one to qualify for membership in the class *homo sapiens* as opposed to the class canines. The issue of determining essential characteristics is of philosophical importance because such characteristics indicate what any given particular (thing) *is*. Either one is a human being or a dog. We as philosophers want to know what precisely makes a thing what it is. If we can get a handle on what makes an entity exactly what it *is*, then we will have acquired an understanding of reality. And this is precisely the goal of any philosophical investigation.

Plato was no exception. He begins by trying to determine the essences of some fairly abstract notions such as beauty, knowledge and that of number. Throughout his philosophical inquiry, it occurred to him that a necessary characteristic of the latter concept was that it did not change. It matters not, for example, how any given number is communicated, be it written or spoken, the concept nevertheless remains the same. After all, the notion of the number five was the same for the Bedouin sheepherder two thousand years ago as it is for us today. That is, five apples are the same as five flying carpets so far as the number five is concerned. Plato eventually came to the conclusion that *all* essences are unchanging. Put in a rather abstract manner, the essence of essences is that they do not change. Now recall that essences or essential characteristics are a guide to what particulars really are. So far as Plato was concerned, an understanding of them is the key to a comprehension of reality, namely, what *is*. Formally stated, his reasoning followed that of the syllogism[15], namely, (1) essences are real (that is, they are that which makes

---

[12]   *inanimate:* not having the qualities associated with active, living organisms.

[13]   Essential characteristics are contrasted with accidental ones, namely, characteristics which a particular (thing) may possess which are not necessary for a given class membership. For example, the characteristic blue eyes is not an essential one for membership in the class *homo sapiens*.

[14]   *purview:* the extent or range of function, power, or competence; scope.

[15]   *syllogism:* a form of deductive reasoning consisting of a major premise, a minor premise, and a conclusion.

something what it really is so far as the *type* of thing that it is); (2) reality is unchanging (namely, essential characteristics qualifying something for class membership never change), therefore, (3) essences are unchanging (in nature).

Now recall that Plato also believed in the Heraclitean Doctrine of Flux. This automatically presents a problem, for if everything in the universe is in a continual state of change, how is it that anything is *real* if that which constitutes reality is unchanging in nature? Strictly speaking, nothing in the world in which we live can *be* real given Plato's analysis of the nature of essences and his commitment to the Doctrine of Flux. He concludes that there exists two distinct worlds; the world of reality and the world of flux. Hence, he is classified as a *dualistic realist*. The world of essences and universals is the world of Form. The perceived world, the one we live in, is the world of content, of physical stuff. Form gives shape to stuff and consequently "makes" stuff, the type of stuff we identify it to be. Form brings reality, if you will, to stuff. The world of Form is the world of Reality. The world of content is the world that appears to us via[16] our five senses. The perceptual world is therefore the world of Appearance. The world of Form is really real whereas the world we live in is just "sort of" real. The latter is real for two reasons, (1) we know for sure that we, as living breathing individuals, possess an element of reality and (2) we are able to classify the things we perceive in the world in which we live. If we are capable of doing this, then we must have some inkling as to what those things, such as doghouses *are*. If we are able to classify the things we perceive, we must have at least a partial knowledge of the essential characteristics of them. Plato is literally faced with a problem of eating his cake and having it too. If he is to be consistent, he must either (a) maintain there is only one real, i.e., unchanging world, namely, that of essences and that the one we live in is unreal for it is continually changing or (b) maintain that the world in which we live is changing, but nevertheless real and that essences can change. There are simply no other options open to him.

One might inquire how he got himself into this paradox[17]. It should be noted at this point that Plato was initially concerned with determining the essences of such abstract notions as beauty, knowledge and number. He did not begin his investigation with such mundane things as doghouses. Whereas we do have some inkling as to the essential characteristics of the latter, "nailing down" those of the former is much more difficult since the subjects at hand are intangible in nature. If he had at the outset attempted to determine the essential characteristics of such "down to earth" things as doghouses, he might not have been so prone to believe that essences are unchanging. After all, is it not possible for a doghouse to lose its essence and "take on" the essence of a *pile* of wood if the former is disassembled? The constituents of both are the same, namely, wood, but the former possesses the essence of a doghouse whereas the latter has the essence of a pile of lumber. It is evident that the world changes and part of that flux includes a change in essential characteristics of the things we perceive. This we *know* for a fact. If we have knowledge of such a situation, then it cannot be otherwise (see Chapter 18).

One source of the paradox which we have been examining has already been exposed, namely, the inconsistency involved by maintaining that the real world, the world of essences, is unchanging while the one in

---

[16] *via:* by way of.

[17] *paradox:* an assertion that is essentially self-contradictory, although based on a valid deduction from acceptable premises.

423 Part V: Metaphysics

which we live is in a continual state of change. An unwillingness to "bend" in either direction on Plato's behalf precludes[18] any sort of bridge between the two. However, there is a more subtle aspect of this unsolvable dilemma[19]. Plato makes an unwitting transition from ascertaining the nature of essences to the *knowledge* of them. It involves a shift in emphasis from metaphysics to epistemology[20]. Determining the nature of essences is a metaphysical pursuit. However, an investigation into what we know regarding the world in which we live is an epistemological one. Strictly speaking, we might be able to determine the essence of, for example, a doghouse, without at the same time being able to classify anything which we perceive as *being* a doghouse. But such is only a theoretical possibility. In practice, however, we do *know* that there *are* doghouses as a result of our perceptions. If we are capable of classifying things (as a result of our perceptions of them), then we must have at least some knowledge of their essential characteristics. And this is the approach Plato takes to bridge the gap between the world of reality (i.e., the world of essences) and the world of which we possess immediate perceptual knowledge. He attempts to build this bridge in several different ways.

(1) At the outset, he argues that we are capable of *knowing* (i.e., classifying) the individual things (existing in the world in which we exist) as the entities they are because they partake[21] of their respective essence which is a member of the other world. In other words, we are able to identify those things which we call doghouses because they possess a "wee" bit of the pure form (i.e., essence) of doghouse. Such a proposed solution is unsatisfactory because it entails that the perpetually[22] changing things of the world in which we live possess a portion of the corresponding essences of them which are by nature unchanging. This results in continually changing things possessing an element of lack of change. Obviously, such a solution to the problem is unsatisfactory for it results in a contradiction. Something that always changes cannot, in any way, be something which does not change even in the slightest degree. In light of this difficulty, Plato attempted another solution

(2) He argued that the things of the world in which we live are mere copies of their real correspondents which *in toto*[23] constitute the world of essences. Instead of partaking of essences, the things which we perceive and consequently classify as the things they *are*, are mere copies of that which is real. It is as if what we perceive are imperfect photographs of the real thing in question. As a result, we only possess a rather incomplete knowledge of that which we perceive. For example, the object we identify as a doghouse has enough in common with the essence of a doghouse for us to adequately identify and classify it as such without it at the same time possessing the essence of a doghouse. At the outset, this solution to the problem of two distinct worlds appears plausible. However, the solution is only apparent. It nevertheless remains the case that we can never *know* the things which we perceive as the things they really are. All we perceive are appearances of reality. If all we perceive are appearances,

---

[18]   *preclude:* to make impossible or impracticable by previous action; prevent.

[19]   *dilemma:* a situation that requires one to choose between two equally balanced alternatives.

[20]   *epistemology:* the branch of philosophy that deals with the nature and origins of knowledge.

[21]   *partake:* to take part or have a share; participate.

[22]   *perpetual:* continuing indefinitely without interruption; constant.

[23]   *in toto:* in the whole; as a whole.

then so far as we are concerned, we may as well be living in a dream world. Knowledge of appearances is hardly a guide to a knowledge of reality. At this point, all one can say is, "Nice try Plato; close, but no cigar".

Plato attempted to resolve this problem until he went to his grave, but to no avail. He did so because he was unwilling to sacrifice his commitment to the Heraclitean Doctrine of Flux or modify his belief that essences are unchanging. Without a compromise one way or the other he is stuck with worlds of which never the twain[24] shall meet. Plato remains to this day the paradigm[25] of a dualistic realist.

Much of what has been discussed so far concerns the nature of essences and their relationship to the world in which we live. However, this chapter began with an explanation of the nature of universals. What happened to them? Nothing happened to them. They reside in the world of Forms along with essences. This is easy to understand if one compares the definition of each. First of all, both pertain to characteristics. Characteristics are either essential or accidental. Particulars possess both types of characteristics (see footnote 2). Two or more particulars may well have an accidental characteristic in common. Nevertheless, such an accidental characteristic is real by virtue of possession by the particulars in question. Furthermore, a characteristic that is accidental to one type of thing may well be essential to a different type of thing. For example, it is an accidental characteristic that a chair be greenish-yellow, but that is an essential characteristic of bile, that viscid[26] fluid secreted by the liver. Hence, so far as Plato is concerned, universals reside in the same world as do essences, namely, the world of Forms, the "really" real world as opposed to the "sort of real" world in which we live.

Suggested Readings: Realism; Plato

1. Allen, R.E., ed. *Studies in Plato's Metaphysics* (London, 1965).
2. Banbrough, Renford, ed., *New Essays on Plato and Aristotle* (London, 1965).
3. Bluck, R.S., *Plato's Life and Thought* (London, 1949).
4. Cherniss, H.F., *Aristotle's Criticism of Plato and the Academy* (Baltimore, 1944).
5. Copleston, F., *A History of Philosophy*, Vol. I (N.Y.: Doubleday & Co., 1994) Chapter 20.
6. Field, G. C., *The Philosophy of Plato* (Oxford, 1949).
7. Grube, G.M.A., *Plato's Thought* (London, 1935).
8. Merlan, Philip, *From Platonism to Neoplatonism* (The Hague, 1953).
9. Murphy, N.R., *The Interpretation of Plato's Republic* (Oxford, 1951).
10. Ross, W.D., *Plato's Theory of Ideas* (Oxford, 1953).
11. Shorey, Paul, *What Plato Said* (Chicago, 1933).
12. Taylor, A.E., *Plato: The Man and His Work* (London, 1926).

---

[24] *twain:* two.

[25] *paradigm:* an example or model.

[26] *viscid:* sticky.

Name_____

Date _____

1. What is Plato's argument for why philosophers should be the rulers of society?

2. What are universals? Give examples.

3. What position does Plato hold regarding the existence of universals?

4. What aspect of Plato's metaphysical view came from Heraclitus?

5. Explain what is meant by "Plato is a dualistic realistic"?

From *The Dialogues of Plato*, translated by B. Jowett, Vol. I (N.Y.: Random House, 1937), pp. 770-794.

The Republic

Book VI

Now, that which imparts truth to the known and the power of knowing to the knower is what I would have you term the idea of good, and this you will deem to be the cause of science, and of truth in so far as the latter becomes the subject of knowledge; beautiful too, as are both truth and knowledge, you will be right in esteeming this other nature as more beautiful than either; and, as in the previous instance, light and sight may be truly said to be like the sun, and yet not to be the sun, so in this other sphere, science and truth may be deemed to be like the good, but not the good; the good has a place of honour yet higher.

What a wonder of beauty that must be, he said, which is the author of science and truth, and yet surpasses them in beauty; for you surely cannot mean to say that pleasure in the good?

God forbid, I replied; but may I ask you to consider the image in another point of view?

In what point of view?

You would say, would you not, that the sun is not only the author if visibility in all visible things, but of generation and nourishment and growth, though he himself is not generation?

Certainly.

In like manner the good may be said to be not only the author of knowledge to all things known, but of their being and essence, and yet the good is not essence, but far exceeds essence in dignity and power.

Glaucon said, with a ludicrous earnestness: By the light of heaven, how amazing!

Yes, I said, and the exaggeration may be set down to you; for you made me utter my fancies.

And pray continue to utter them; at any rate let us hear if there is anything more to be said about the similitude[1] of the sun.

Yes, I said, there is a great deal more.

Then omit nothing, however slight.

---

[1] *similitude:* similarity; likeness, resemblance [editor's note].

I will do my best, I said; but I should think that a great deal will have to be omitted.

You have to imagine, then, that there are two ruling powers, and that one of them is set over the intellectual world, the other over the visible. I do not say heaven, lest you should fancy that I am playing upon the name (ουρανοζορατοζ) . May I suppose that you have this distinction of the visible and intelligible fixed in your mind?

I have.

Now take a line which has been cut into two unequal parts, and divide each of them again in the same proportion, and suppose the two main divisions to answer, one to the visible and the other to the intelligible, and then compare the subdivisions in respect of their clearness and want of clearness, and you will find that the first section in the sphere of the visible consists of images. And by images I mean, in the first place, shadows, and in the second place, reflections in water and in solid, smooth and polished bodies and the like: Do you understand?

Yes, I understand.

Imagine, now, the other section, of which this is only the resemblance, to include the animals which we see, and everything that grows or is made.

Very good.

Would you not admit that both the sections of this division have different degrees of truth, and that the copy is to the original as the sphere of opinion is to the sphere of knowledge?

Most undoubtedly.

Next proceed to consider the manner in which the sphere of the intellectual is to be divided[2].

In what manner?

Thus--There are two subdivisions, in the lower of which the soul uses the figures given by the former division as images; the enquiry can only be hypothetical, and instead of going upwards to a principle descends to the other end; in the higher of the two, the soul passes out of hypotheses, and goes up to a principle which is above hypotheses, making no use of images as in the former case, but proceeding only in and through the ideas themselves.

---

[2]   What follows in the text is Plato's analogy of the line by which we can better understand the four stages of cognition. The analogy is thus diagramed.

Objects	States of Mind
The Good	Reason and
Forms	Intelligence
INTELLIGIBLE WORLD	
Mathematical objects	Understanding and Thinking
Visible things	Faith or Belief
WORLD OF APPEARANCE	
Images	Perception of Shadows or Imagining

This analogy is immediately followed (in Book VII) by the allegory of the Cave which is an alternative way of making the same point [editor's note].

I do not quite understand your meaning, he said.

Then I will try again; you will understand me better when I have made some preliminary remarks. You are aware that students of geometry, arithmetic, and the kindred sciences assume the odd and the even and the figures and three kinds of angles and the like in their several branches of science; these are their hypotheses, which they and every body are supposed to know, and therefore they do not deign[3] to give any account of them either to themselves or others; but they begin with them, and go on until they arrive at last, and in a consistent manner, at their conclusion?

Yes, he said, I know.

And do you not know also that although they make use of the visible forms and reason about them, they are thinking not of these, but of the ideals which they resemble; not of the figures which they draw, but of the absolute square and the absolute diameter, and so on--the forms which they draw or make, and which have shadows and reflections in water of their own, are converted by them into images, but they are really seeking to behold the things themselves, which can only be seen with the eye of the mind?

That is true.

And of this kind I spoke as the intelligible, although in the search after it the soul is compelled to use hypotheses; not ascending to a first principle, because she is unable to rise above the region of hypothesis, but employing the objects of which the shadows below are resemblances in their turn as images, they having in relation to the shadows and reflections of them a greater distinctness, and therefore a higher value.

I understand, he said, that you are speaking of the province of geometry and the sister arts.

And when I speak of the other division of the intelligible, you will understand me to speak of that other sort of knowledge which reason herself attains by the power of dialectic[4], using the hypotheses not as first principles, but only as hypotheses--that is to say, as steps and points of departure into a world which is above hypotheses, in order that she may soar beyond them to the first principle of the whole; and clinging to this and then to that which depends on this, by successive steps she descends again without the aid of any sensible object, from ideas, through ideas, and in ideas she ends.

I understand you, he replied; not perfectly, for you seem to me to be describing a task which is really tremendous; but, at any rate, I understand you to say that knowledge and being, which the science of dialectic contemplates, are clearer than the notions of the arts, as they are termed, which proceed from hypotheses only: these are also contemplated by the understanding, and not by the senses: yet, because they start from hypotheses and do not ascend to a principle, those who contemplate them appear to you not to exercise the higher reason upon them, although when a first principle is added to them they are cognizable by the higher reason. And the habit which is concerned with geometry and the cognate sciences I suppose that you would term understanding and not reason, as being intermediate between opinion and reason.

You have quite conceived my meaning, I said; and now, corresponding to these four divisions, let there be four faculties in the soul--reason answering to the highest, understanding to the second, faith (or conviction) to the third, and perception of shadows to the last--and let there be a

---

[3] *deign:* to deem worthy [editor's note].

[4] *dialectic:* the art or practice of examining opinions or ideas logically by the method of question and answer so as to determine their truth or validity [editor's note].

scale of them, and let us suppose that the several faculties have clearness in the same degree that their objects have truth.

I understand, he replied, and give my assent, and accept your arrangement.

Book VII

And now, I said, let me show in a figure how far our nature is enlightened or unenlightened--Behold! human beings living in an underground den, which has a mouth open towards the light and reaching all along the den; here they have been from their childhood, and have their legs and necks chained so that they cannot move, and can only see before them, being prevented by the chains from turning round their heads. Above and behind them a fire is blazing at a distance, and between the fire and the prisoners there is a raised way; and you will see, if you look, a low wall built along the way, like the screen which marionette players have in front of them, over which they show the puppets.

I see.

And do you see, I said, men passing along the wall carrying all sorts of vessels, and statues and figures of animals made of wood and stone and various materials, which appear over the wall? Some of them are talking, others silent.

You have shown me a strange image, and they are strange prisoners.

Like ourselves, I replied; and they see only their own shadows, or the shadows of one another, which the fire throws on the opposite wall of the cave?

True, he said; how could they see anything but the shadows if they were never allowed to move their heads?

And of the objects which are being carried in like manner they would only see the shadows?

Yes, he said.

And if they were able to converse with one another, would they not suppose that they were naming what was actually before them?

Very true.

And suppose further that the prison had an echo which came from the other side, would they not be sure to fancy when one of the passers-by spoke that the voice which they heard came from the passing shadow?

No question, he replied.

To them, I said, the truth would be literally nothing but the shadows of the images.

That is certain.

And now look again, and see what will naturally follow if the prisoners are released and disabused of their error. At first, when any of them is liberated and compelled suddenly to stand up and turn his neck round and walk and look towards the light, he will suffer sharp pains; the glare will distress him, and he will be unable to see the realities of which in his former state he had seen the shadows; and then conceive some one saying to him, that what he saw before was an illusion, but that now, when he is approaching nearer to being and his eye is turned towards more real existence, he has a clearer vision--what will be his reply? And you may further imagine that his instructor is pointing to the objects as they pass and requiring him to name them--will he not be perplexed? Will he not fancy that the shadows which he formerly saw are truer than the objects which are now shown to him?

Far truer.

And if he is compelled to look straight at the light, will he not have a pain in his eyes which will make him turn away to take refuge in the objects of vision which he can see, and which he will conceive to be in reality clearer than the things which are now being shown to him?

True, he said.

And suppose once more, that he is reluctantly dragged up a steep and rugged ascent, and held fast until he is forced into the presence of the sun himself, is he not likely to be pained and irritated? When he approaches the light his eyes will be dazzled, and he will not be able to see anything at all of what are now called realities.

Not all in a moment, he said.

He will require to grow accustomed to the sight of the upper world. And first he will see the shadows best, next the reflections of men and other objects in the water, and then the objects themselves; then he will gaze upon the light of the moon and the stars and the spangled heaven; and he will see the sky and the stars by night better than the sun or the light of the sun by day?

Certainly.

Last of all he will be able to see the sun, and not mere reflections of him in the water, but he will see him in his own proper place, and not in another; and he will contemplate him as he is.

Certainly.

He will then proceed to argue that this is he who gives the season and the years, and is the guardian of all that is in the visible world, and in a certain way the cause of all things which he and his fellows have been accustomed to behold?

Clearly, he said, he would first see the sun and then reason about him.

And when he remembered his old habitation, and the wisdom of the den and his fellow-prisoners, do you not suppose that he would felicitate[5] himself on the change, and pity them?

Certainly, he would.

And if they were in the habit of conferring honours among themselves on those who were quickest to observe the passing shadows and to remark which of them went before, and which followed after, and which were together; and who were therefore best able to draw conclusions as to the future, do you think that he would care for such honours and glories, or envy the possessors of them? Would he not say with Homer,

> 'Better to be the poor servant of a poor master,'

and to endure anything, rather than think as they do and live after their manner?

Yes, he said, I think that he would rather suffer anything than entertain these false notions and live in this miserable manner.

Imagine once more, I said, such an one coming suddenly out of the sun to be replaced in his old situation; would he not be certain to have his eyes full of darkness?

To be sure, he said.

And if there were a contest, and he had to compete in measuring the shadows with the prisoners who had never moved out of the den, while his sight was still weak, and before his eyes had become steady (and the time which would be needed to acquire this new habit of sight might be very considerable), would he not be ridiculous? Men would say of him that up he went and down he came without his eyes; and that it was better not even to think of ascending; and if any one tried to loose another and

---

[5]   *felicitate:* to make happy [editor's note].

lead him up to the light, let them only catch the offender, and they would put him to death.

No question, he said.

This entire allegory, I said, you may now append, dear Glaucon, to the previous argument; the prison-house is the world of sight, the light of the fire is the sun, and you will not misapprehend me if you interpret the journey upwards to be the ascent of the soul into the intellectual world according to my poor belief, which, at your desire, I have expressed--whether rightly or wrongly God knows. But, whether true or false, my opinion is that in the world of knowledge the idea of good appears last of all, and is seen only with an effort; and, when seen, is also inferred to be the universal author of all things beautiful and right, parent of light and of the lord of light in this visible world, and the immediate source of reason and truth in the intellectual; and that this is the power upon which he who would act rationally either in public or private life must have his eye fixed.

I agree, he said, as far as I am able to understand you.

Moreover, I said, you must not wonder that those who attain to this beatific[6] vision are unwilling to descend to human affairs; for their souls are ever hastening into the upper world where they desire to dwell; which desire of theirs is very natural, if our allegory may be trusted.

Yes, very natural

And is there anything surprising in one who passes from divine contemplations to the evil state of man, misbehaving himself in a ridiculous manner; if, whole his eyes are blinking and before he has become accustomed to the surrounding darkness, he is compelled to fight in courts of law, or in other places, about the images or the shadows of images of justice, and is endeavoring to meet the conceptions of those who have never yet seen absolute justice?

Anything but surprising, he replied.

Any one who has common sense will remember that the bewilderment of the eyes are of two kinds, and arise from two causes, either from coming out of the light or from going into the light, which is true of the mind's eye, quite as much as of the bodily eye; and he who remembers this when he sees any one whose vision is perplexed and weak, will not be too ready to laugh; he will first ask whether that soul of man has come out of the brighter life, and is unable to see because unaccustomed to the dark, or having turned from darkness to the day is dazzled by excess of light. And he will count the one happy in his condition and state of being, and he will pity the other; or, if he have a mind to laugh at the soul which comes from below into the light, there will be more reason in this than in the laugh which greets him who returns from above out of the light into the den.

That, he said, is a very just distinction.

But then, if I am right, certain professors of education must be wrong when they say that they can put a knowledge into the soul which was not there before, like sight into blind eyes.

They undoubtedly say this, he replied.

Whereas, our argument shows that the power and capacity of learning exists in the soul already; and that just as the eye was unable to turn from darkness to light without the whole body, so too the instrument of knowledge can only by the movement of the whole soul be turned from the world of becoming into that of being, and learn by degrees to endure the sight of being, and of the brightest and best of being, or in other words, of the good.

---

6   *beatific:* blissful [editor's note].

Very true.

And must there not be some art which will effect conversion in the easiest and quickest manner; not implanting the faculty of sight, for that exists already, but has been turned in the wrong direction, and is looking away from the truth?

Yes, he said, such an art may be presumed.

And whereas the other so-called virtues of the soul seem to be akin to bodily qualities, for even when they are not originally innate they can be implanted later by habit and exercise, the virtue of wisdom more than anything else contains a divine element which always remains, and by this conversion is rendered useful and profitable; or, on the other hand, hurtful and useless. Did you never observe the narrow intelligence flashing from the keen eye of a clever rogue--how eager he is, how clearly his paltry soul sees the way to his end; he is the reverse of blind, but his keen eyesight is forced into the service of evil, and he is mischievous in proportion to his cleverness?

Very true, he said.

But what if there had been a circumcision of such natures in the days of their youth; and they had been severed from those sensual pleasures, such as eating and drinking, which, like leaden weights, were attached to them at their birth, and which drag them down and turn the vision of their souls upon the things that are below--if, I say, they had been released from these impediments and turned in the opposite direction, the very same faculty in them would have seen the truth as keenly as they see what their eyes are turned to now.

Very likely.

Yes, I said; and there is another thing which is likely, or rather a necessary inference from what has preceded, that neither the uneducated and uninformed of the truth, nor yet those who never make an end of their education, will be able ministers of State; not the former, because they have no single aim of duty which is the rule of all their actions, private as well as public; nor the latter, because they will not act at all except upon compulsion, fancying that they are already dwelling apart in the islands of the blest.

Very true, he replied.

Then, I said, the business of us who are the founders of the State will be to compel the best minds to attain that knowledge which we have already shown to be the greatest of all--they must continue to ascend until they arrive at the good; but when they have ascended and seen enough we must not allow them to do as they do now.

What do you mean?

I mean that they remain in the upper world: but this must not be allowed; they must be made to descend again among the prisoners in the den, and partake of their labours and honours, whether they are worth having or not.

But is not this unjust? he said; ought we to give them a worse life, when they might have a better?

You have again forgotten, my friend, I said, the intention of the legislator, who did not aim at making any one class in the State happy above the rest; the happiness was to be in the whole State, and he held the citizens together by persuasion and necessity, making them benefactors of the State, and therefore benefactors of one another; to this end he created them, not to please themselves, but to be his instruments in binding up the State.

True, he said, I had forgotten.

Observe, Glaucon, that there will be no injustice in compelling our philosophers to have a care and providence[7] of others; we shall explain to them that in other States, men of their class are not obliged to share in the toils of politics: and this is reasonable, for they grow up at their own sweet will, and the government would rather not have them. Being self-taught, they cannot be expected to show any gratitude for a culture which they have never received. But we have brought you into the world to be rulers of the hive, kings of yourselves and of the other citizens, and have educated you far better and more perfectly than they have been educated, and you are better able to share in the double duty. Wherefore each of you, when his turn comes, must go down to the general underground abode, and get the habit of seeing in the dark. When you have acquired the habit, you will see ten thousand times better than the inhabitants of the den, and you will know what the several images are, and what they represent, because you have seen the beautiful and just and good in their truth. And thus our State which is also yours will be a reality, and not a dream only, and will be administered in a spirit unlike that of other States, in which men fight with one another about shadows only and are distracted in the struggle for power, which in their eyes is a great good. Whereas the truth is that the State in which the rulers are most reluctant to govern is always the best and most quietly governed, and the State in which they are most eager, the worst.

Quite true, he replied.

And will our pupils, when they hear this, refuse to take their turn at the toils of State, when they are allowed to spend the greater part of their time with one another in the heavenly light?

Impossible, he answered; for they are just men, and the commands which we impose upon them are just; there can be no doubt that every one of them will take office as a stern necessity, and not after the fashion of our present rulers of State.

Yes, my friend, I said; and there lies the point. You must contrive for your future rulers another and a better life than that of a ruler, and then you may have a well-ordered State; for only in the State which offers this, will they rule who are truly rich, not in silver and gold, but in virtue and wisdom, which are the true blessings of life. Whereas if they go to the administration of public affairs, poor and hungering after their own private advantage, thinking that hence they are to snatch the chief good, order there can never be; for they will be fighting about office, and the civil and domestic broils which thus arise will be the ruin of the rulers themselves and of the whole State.

Most true, he replied.

And the only life which looks down upon the life of political ambition is that of true philosophy. Do you know of any other?

Indeed, I do not, he said.

And those who govern ought not to be lovers of the task? For, if they are, there will be rival lovers, and they will fight.

No question.

Who then are those whom we shall compel to be guardians? Surely they will be the men who are wisest about affairs of State, and by whom the State is best administered, and who at the same time have other honours and another and a better life than that of politics?

They are the men, and I will choose them, he replied.

---

[7]   providence: a looking to, or preparation for, the future; provision [editor's note].

And now shall we consider in what way such guardians will be produced, and how they are to be brought from darkness to light--as some are said to have ascended from the world below to the gods?

By all means, he replied.

The process, I said, is not the turning over of an oyster-shell, but the turning round of a soul passing from a day which is little better than night to the true day of being, that is, the ascent from below, which we affirm to be true philosophy?

Quite so.

And should we not enquire what sort of knowledge has the power of effecting such a change?

Certainly.

What sort of knowledge is there which would draw the soul from becoming to being? And another consideration has just occurred to me: you will remember that our young men are to be warrior athletes?

Yes, that was said.

Then this new kind of knowledge must have an additional quality?

What quality?

Usefulness in war.

Yes, if possible.

There were two parts in our former scheme of education, were there not?

Just so.

There was gymnastic which presided over the growth and decay of the body, and may therefore be regarded as having to do with generation and corruption?

True.

Then that is not the knowledge which we are seeking to discover?

No.

But what do you say of music, what also entered to a certain extent into our former scheme?

Music, he said, as you will remember, was the counterpart of gymnastic, and trained the guardians by the influences of habit, by harmony making them harmonious, by rhythm rhythmical, but not giving them science; and the words, whether fabulous or possibly true, had kindred elements of rhythm and harmony in them. But in music there was nothing which tended to that good which you are now seeking.

You are most accurate, I said, in your recollection; in music there certainly was nothing of the kind. But what branch of knowledge is there, my dear Glaucon, which is of the desired nature; since all the useful arts were reckoned mean by us?

Undoubtedly; and yet if music and gymnastic are excluded, and the arts are also excluded, what remains?

Well, I said, there may be nothing left of our special subjects; and then we shall have to take something which is not special, but of universal application.

What may that be?

A something which all arts and sciences and intelligences use in common, and which every one first has to learn among the elements of education.

What is that?

The little matter of distinguishing one, two, and three--in a word, number and calculation--do not all arts and sciences necessarily partake of them?

Yes.

Then the art of war partakes of them?

To be sure.

Then Palamedes, whenever he appears in tragedy, proves Agamemnon ridiculously unfit to be a general. Did you never remark how he declares that he had invented number, and had numbered the ships and set in array the ranks of the army at Troy; which implies that they had never been numbered before, and Agamemnon must be supposed literally to have been incapable of counting his own feet--how could he if he was ignorant of number? And if that is true, what sort of general must he have been?

I should say a very strange one, if this was as you say.

Can we deny that a warrior should have a knowledge of arithmetic?

Certainly he should, if he is to have the smallest understanding of military tactics, or indeed, I should rather say, if he is to be a man at all.

I should like to know whether you have the same notion which I have of this study?

What is your notion?

It appears to me to be a study of the kind which we are seeking, and which leads naturally to reflection, but never to have been rightly used; for the true use of it is simply to draw the soul towards being.

Will you explain your meaning? he said.

I will try, I said; and I wish you would share the enquiry with me, and say 'yes' or 'no' when I attempt to distinguish in my own mind what branches of knowledge have this attracting power, in order that we may have clearer proof that arithmetic is, as I suspect, one of them.

Explain, he said.

I mean to say that objects of sense are of two kinds; some of them do not invite thought because the sense is an adequate judge of them; while in the case of other objects sense is so untrustworthy that further enquiry is imperatively demanded.

You are clearly referring, he said, to the manner in which the senses are imposed upon by distance, and by painting in light and shade.

No, I said, that is not at all my meaning.

Then what is your meaning?

When speaking of uninviting objects, I mean those which do not pass from one sensation to the opposite; inviting objects are those which do; in this latter case the sense coming upon the object, whether at a distance or near, gives no more vivid idea of anything in particular than of its opposite. An illustration will make my meaning clearer--here are three fingers--a little finger, a second finger, and a middle finger.

Very good.

You may suppose that they are seen quite close: And here comes the point.

What is it?

Each of them equally appears a finger, whether seen in the middle or at the extremity, whether white or black, or thick or thin--it makes no difference; a finger is a finger all the same. In these cases a man is not compelled to ask of thought the question what is a finger? for the sight never intimates to the mind that a finger is other than a finger.

True.

And therefore, I said, as we might expect, there is nothing here which invites or excites intelligence.

There is not, he said.

But is this equally true of the greatness and smallness of the fingers? Can sight adequately perceive them? and is no difference made by the circumstance that one of the fingers is in the middle and another at the extremity? And in like manner does the touch adequately perceive the qualities of thickness or thinness, of softness or hardness? And so of the other senses; do they give perfect intimations of such matters? Is not their mode of operation on this wise--the sense which is concerned with the quality of hardness is necessarily concerned also with the quality of softness, and only intimates to the soul that the same thing is felt to be both hard and soft?

You are quite right, he said.

And must not the soul be perplexed at this intimation which the sense gives of a hard which is also soft? What, again, is the meaning of light and heavy, if that which is light is also heavy, and and that which is heavy, light?

Yes, he said, these intimations which the soul receives are very curious and require to be explained.

Yes, I said, and in these perplexities the soul naturally summons to her aid calculation and intelligence, that she may see whether the several objects announced to her are one or two.

True.

And if they turn out to be two, is not each of them one and different?

Certainly.

And if each is one, and both are two, she will conceive the two as in a state of division, for if they were undivided they could only be conceived of as one?

True.

The eye certainly did see both small and great, but only in a confused manner; they were not distinguished.

Yes.

Whereas the thinking mind, intending to light up the chaos, was compelled to reverse the process, and look at small and great as separate and not confused.

Very true.

Was not this the beginning of the enquiry 'What is great?' and 'What is small?'

Exactly so.

And thus arose the distinction of the visible and the intelligible.

Most true.

This was what I meant when I spoke of impressions which invited the intellect, or the reverse--those which are simultaneous with opposite impressions, invite thought; those which are not simultaneous do not.

I understand, he said, and agree with you.

And to which class do unity and number belong?

I do not know, he replied.

Think a little and you will see that what has preceded will supply the answer; for if simple unity could be adequately perceived by the sight or by any other sense, then, as we were saying in the case of the finger, there would be nothing to attract towards being; but when there is some contradiction always present, and one is the reverse of one and involves the conception of plurality, then thought begins to be aroused within us, and the soul perplexed and wanting to arrive at a decision asks 'What is absolute unity?' This is the way in which the study of the one has a power of drawing and converting the mind to the contemplation of true being.

And surely, he said, this occurs notably in the case of one; for we see the same thing to be both one and infinite in multitude?

Yes, I said; and this being true of one must be equally true of all number?

Certainly.

And all arithmetic and calculation have to do with number?

Yes.

And they appear to lead the mind towards truth?

Yes, in a very remarkable manner.

Then this is knowledge of the kind for which we are seeking, having a double use, military and philosophical; for the man of war must learn to art of number or he will not know how to array his troops, and the philosopher also, because he has to rise out of the sea of change and lay hold of true being, and therefore he must be an arithmetician.

That is true,

And our guardian is both warrior and philosopher?

Certainly.

Then this is a kind of knowledge which legislation may fitly prescribe; and we must endeavour to persuade those who are to be the principal men of our State to do and learn arithmetic, not as amateurs, but they must carry on the study until they see the nature of numbers with the mind only; nor again, like merchants or retail-traders, with a view to buying or selling, but for the sake of their military use, and of the soul herself; and because this will be the easiest way for her to pass from becoming to truth and being.

That is excellent, he said.

Yes, I said, and now having spoken of it, I must add how charming the science is! and in how many ways it conduces to our desired end, if pursued in the spirit of a philosopher, and not of a shopkeeper!

How do you mean?

I mean, as I was saying, that arithmetic has a very great and elevating effect, compelling the soul to reason about abstract number, and rebelling against the introduction of visible or tangible objects into the argument. You know how steadily the masters of the art repel and ridicule any one who attempts to divide absolute unity when he is calculating, and if you divide, they multiply, taking care that one shall continue one and not become lost in fractions.

That is very true.

Now, suppose a person were to say to them: O my friends, what are these wonderful numbers about which you are reasoning, in which, as you say, there is a unity such as you demand, and each unit is equal, invariable, indivisible--what would they answer?

They would answer, as I should conceive, that they were speaking of those numbers which can only be realized in thought.

Then you see that this knowledge may be truly called necessary, necessitating as it clearly does the use of the pure intelligence in the attainment of pure truth?

Yes; that is a marked characteristic of it.

And have you further observed, that those who have a natural talent for calculation are generally quick at every other kind of knowledge; and even the dull, if they have had an arithmetical training, although they may derive no other advantage from it, always become much quicker than they would otherwise have been.

Very true, he said.

And indeed, you will not easily find a more difficult study, and not many as difficult.

You will not.

And, for all these reasons, arithmetic is a kind of knowledge in which the best natures should be trained, and which must not be given up.

I agree.

Let this then be made one of our subjects of education. And next, shall we enquire whether the kindred science also concerns us?

You mean geometry?

Exactly so.

Clearly, he said, we are concerned with that part of geometry which relates to war; for in pitching a camp, or taking up a position, or closing or extending the lines of an army, or any other military manoeuvre, whether in actual battle or on a march, it will make all the difference whether a general is or is not a geometrician.

Yes, I said, but for that purpose a very little of either geometry or calculation will be enough; the question relates rather to the greater and more advanced part of geometry--whether that tends in any degree to make more easy the vision of the idea of good: and thither, as I was saying, all things tend which compel the soul to turn her gaze towards that place, where is the full perfection of being, which she ought, by all means, to behold.

True, he said.

Then if geometry compels us to view being, it concerns us; if becoming only, it does not concern us?

Yes, that is what we assert.

Yet anybody who has the least acquaintance with geometry will not deny that such a conception of the science is in flat contradiction to the ordinary language of geometricians.

How so?

They have in view practice only, and are always speaking, in a narrow and ridiculous manner, of squaring and extending and applying and the like--they confuse the necessities of geometry with those of daily life; whereas knowledge is the real object of the whole science.

Certainly, he said.

Then must not a further admission be made?

What admission?

That the knowledge at which geometry aims is knowledge of the eternal, and not of aught[8] perishing and transient.

That, he replied, may be readily allowed, and is true.

Then, my noble friend, geometry will draw the soul towards truth, and create the spirit of philosophy, and raise up that which is now unhappily allowed to fall down.

Nothing will be more likely to have such an effect.

Then nothing should be more sternly laid down than that the inhabitants of your fair city should by all means learn geometry. Moreover the science has indirect effects, which are not small.

Of what kind? he said.

There are the military advantages of which you spoke, I said; and in all departments of knowledge, as experience proves, any one who has studied geometry is infinitely quicker of apprehension than one who has not.

Yes indeed, he said, there is an infinite difference between them.

Then shall we propose this as a second branch of knowledge which our youth will study?

Let us do so, he replied.

And suppose we make astronomy the third--what do you say?

I am strongly inclined to it, he said; the observation of the seasons and of months and years is as essential to the general as it is to the farmer or sailor.

I am amused, I said, at your fear of the world, which makes you guard against the appearance of insisting upon useless studies; and I quite admit

---

[8] *aught:* anything whatever [editor's note].

the difficulty of believing that in every man there is an eye of the soul which, when by other pursuits lost and dimmed, is by these purified and re-illumined; and is more precious far than ten thousand bodily eyes, for by it alone is truth seen. Now there are two classes of persons: one class of those who will agree with you and will take your words as a revelation; another class to whom they will be utterly unmeaning, and who will naturally deem them to be idle tales, for they see no sort of profit which is to be obtained from them. And therefore you had better decide at once with which of the two you are proposing to argue. You will very likely say with neither, and that your chief aim in carrying on the argument is your own improvement; at the same time you do not grudge to others any benefit which they may receive.

I think that I should prefer to carry on the argument mainly on my own behalf.

Then take a step backward, for we have gone wrong in the order of the sciences.

What was the mistake? he said.

After plane geometry, I said, we proceeded at once to solids in revolution, instead of taking solids in themselves; whereas after the second dimension the third, which is concerned with cubes and dimensions of depth, ought to have followed.

That is true, Socrates; but so little seems to be known as yet about these subjects.

Why, yes, I said, and for two reasons:--in the first place, no government patronizes them; this leads to a want of energy in the pursuit of them, and they are difficult; in the second place, students cannot learn them unless they have a director. But then a director can hardly be found, and even if he could, as matters now stand, the students, who are very conceited, would not attend to him. That, however, would be otherwise if the whole State became the director of these studies and give honour to them; then disciples would want to come, and there would be continuous and earnest search, and discoveries would be made; since even now, disregarded as they are by the world, and maimed of their fair proportions, and although none of their votaries[9] can tell the use of them, still these studies force their way by their natural charm, and very likely, if they had the help of the State, they would some day emerge into light.

Yes, he said, there is a remarkable charm in them. But I do not clearly understand the change in the order. First you began with a geometry of plane surfaces?

Yes, I said.

And you placed astronomy next, and then you made a step backward?

Yes, and I have delayed you by my hurry; the ludicrous state of solid geometry, which, in natural order, should have followed, made me pass over this branch and go on to astronomy, or motion of solids.

True, he said.

Then assuming that the science now omitted would come into existence if encouraged by the State, let us go on to astronomy, which will be fourth.

The right order, he replied. And now, Socrates, as you rebuked the vulgar manner in which I praised astronomy before, my praise shall be given in your own spirit. For every one, as I think, must see that astronomy compels the soul to look upwards and leads us from this world to another.

---

[9] *votary:* a person who is devoted to any game, study or pursuit [editor's note].

Every one but myself, I said; to every one else this may be clear, but not to me.

And what then would you say?

I should rather say that those who elevate astronomy into philosophy appear to me to make us look downwards and not upwards.

What do you mean? he asked.

You, I replied, have in your mind a truly sublime conception of our knowledge of the things above. And I dare say that if a person were to throw his head back and study the fretted ceiling, you would still think that his mind was the percipient, and not his eyes. And you are very likely right, and I may be a simpleton: but, in my opinion, that knowledge only which is of being and of the unseen can make the soul look upwards, and whether a man gapes at the heavens or blinks on the ground, seeking to learn some particular of sense, I would deny that he can learn, for nothing of that sort is matter of science; his soul is looking downwards, not upwards, whether his way to knowledge is by water or by land, whether he floats, or only lies on his back.

I acknowledge, he said, the justice of your rebuke. Still, I should like to ascertain how astronomy can be learned in any manner more conducive to that knowledge of which we are speaking?

I will tell you, I said: The starry heaven which we behold is wrought upon a visible ground, and therefore, although the fairest and most perfect of visible things, must necessarily be deemed inferior far to the true motions of absolute swiftness and absolute slowness, which are relative to each other, and carry with them that which is contained in them, in the true number and in every true figure. Now, these are to be apprehended by reason and intelligence, but not by sight.

True, he replied.

The spangled heavens should be used as a pattern and with a view to that higher knowledge; their beauty is like the beauty of figures or pictures excellently wrought by the hand of Daedalus, or some other great artist, which we may chance to behold; any geometrician who saw them would appreciate the exquisiteness of their workmanship, but he would never dream of thinking that in them he could find the true equal or the true double, or the truth of any other proportion.

No, he replied, such an idea would be ridiculous.

And will not a true astronomer have the same feeling when he looks at the movements of the stars? Will he not think that heaven and the things in heaven are framed by the Creator of them in the most perfect manner? But he will never imagine that the proportions of night and day, or of both to the month, or of the month to the year, or of the stars to these and to one another, and any other things that are material and visible can also be eternal and subject to no deviation--that would be absurd; and it is equally absurd to take so much pains in investigating their exact truth.

I quite agree, though I never thought of this before.

Then, I said, in astronomy, as in geometry, we should employ problems, and let the heavens alone if we would approach the subject in the right way and so make the natural gift of reason to be of any real use.

That, he said, is a work infinitely beyond our present astronomers.

Yes, I said; and there are many other things which must also have a similar extension given to them, if our legislation is to be of any value. But can you tell me of any other suitable study?

No, he said, not without thinking.

Motion, I said, has many forms, and not one only; two of them are obvious enough even to wits no better than ours; and there are others, as I imagine, which may be left to wiser persons.

But where are the two?

There is a second, I said, which is the counterpart of the one already named.

And what may that be?

The second, I said, would seem relatively to the ears to be what the first is to the eyes; for I conceive that as the eyes are designed to look up at the stars, so are the ears to hear harmonious motions; and these are sister sciences--as the Pythagoreans say, and we, Glaucon, agree with them?

Yes, he replied.

But this, I said, is a laborious study, and therefore we had better go and learn of them; and they will tell us whether there are any other applications of these sciences. At the same time, we must not lose sight of our own higher object.

What is that?

There is a perfection which all knowledge ought to reach, and which our pupils ought also to attain, and not to fall short of, as I was saying that they did in astronomy. For in the science of harmony, as you probably know, the same thing happens. The teachers of harmony compare the sounds and consonances which are heard only, and their labour, like that of the astronomers, is in vain.

Yes, by heaven! he said; and 'tis as good as a play to hear them talking about their condensed notes, as they call them; they put their ears close alongside of the strings like persons catching a sound from their neighbour's wall--one set of them declaring that they distinguish an intermediate note and have found the least interval which should be the unit of measurement; the others insisting that the two sounds have passed into the same--either party setting their ears before their understanding.

You mean, I said, those gentlemen who tease and torture the strings and rack them on the pegs of the instrument: I might carry on the metaphor and speak after their manner of the blows which the plectrum[10] gives, and make accusations against the strings, both of backwardness and forwardness to sound; but this would be tedious, and therefore I will only say that these are not the men, and that I am referring to the Pythagoreans, of whom I was just now proposing to enquire about harmony. For they too are in error, like the astronomers; they investigate the numbers of the harmonies which are heard, but they never attain to problems--that is to say, they never reach the natural harmonies of number, or reflect why some numbers are harmonious and others not.

That, he said, is a thing of more than mortal knowledge.

A thing, I replied, which I would rather call useful; that is, if sought after with a view to the beautiful and good; but if pursued in any other spirit, useless.

Very true, he said.

Now, when all these studies reach the point of inter-communion and connection with one another, and come to be considered in their mutual affinities, then, I think, but not till then, will the pursuit of them have a value for their objects; otherwise there is no profit in them.

I suspect so; but you are speaking, Socrates, of a vast work.

What do you mean? I said; the prelude or what? Do you not know that all this is but the prelude to the actual strain which we have to learn? For you surely would not regard the skilled mathematician as a dialectician?

---

[10]   *plectrum*: a thin piece of metal, bone, plastic, etc., used for plucking the strings of a lyre, guitar, mandolin, etc. [editor's note].

Assuredly not, he said; I have hardly ever known a mathematician who was capable of reasoning.

But do you imagine that men who are unable to give and take a reason will have the knowledge which we require of them?

Neither can this be supposed.

And so, Glaucon, I said, we have at last arrived at the hymn of dialectic. This is that strain which is of the intellect only, but which the faculty of sight will nevertheless be found to imitate; for sight, as you may remember, was imagined by us after a while to behold the real animals and stars, and last of all the sun himself. And so with dialectic; when a person starts on the discovery of the absolute by the light of reason only, and without any assistance of sense, and perseveres until by pure intelligence he arrives at the perception of the absolute good, he at last finds himself at the end of the intellectual world, as in the case of sight at the end of the visible.

Exactly, he said.

Then this is the progress which you call dialectic?

True.

But the release of the prisoners from chains, and their translation from the shadows to the images and to the light, and the ascent from the underground den to the sun, while in his presence they are vainly trying to look on animals and plants and the light of the sun, but are able to perceive even with their weak eyes the images in the water [which are divine], and are the shadows of true existence (not shadows of images cast by a light of fire, which compared with the sun is only an image)--this power of elevating the highest principle in the soul to the contemplation of that which is best in existence, with which we may compare the raising of that faculty which is the very light of the body to the sight of that which is brightest in the material and visible world--this power is given, as I was saying, by all that study and pursuit of the arts which has been described.

I agree in what you are saying, he replied, which may be hard to believe, yet, from another point of view, is harder still to deny. This however is not a theme to be treated of in passing only, but will have to be discussed again and again. And so, whether our conclusion be true or false, let us assume all this, and proceed at once from the prelude or preamble to the chief strain, and describe that in like manner. Say, then, what is the nature and what are the divisions of dialectic, and what are the paths which lead thither; for these paths will also lead to our final rest.

Dear Glaucon, I said, you will not be able to follow me here, though I would do my best, and you should behold not an image only but the absolute truth, according to my notion. Whether what I told you would or would not have been a reality I cannot venture to say; but you would have seen something like reality; of that I am confident.

Doubtless, he replied.

But I must also remind you, that the power of dialectic alone can reveal this, and only to one who is a disciple of the previous sciences.

Of that assertion you may be as confident as of the last.

And assuredly no one will argue that there is any other method of comprehending by any regular process all true existence or of ascertaining what each thing is in its own nature; for the arts in general are concerned with the desires or opinions of men, or are cultivated with a view to production and construction, or for the preservation of such productions and constructions; and as to the mathematical sciences which, as we were saying, have some apprehension of true being--geometry and the like--they only dream about being, but never can they behold the waking reality so long as they leave the hypotheses which they use unexamined, and are unable to give an account of them. For when a man knows not his own first principle, and when the conclusion and intermediate steps are also constructed out of he knows not what, how can he imagine that such a fabric of convention can ever become science?

Impossible, he said.

Then dialectic, and dialectic alone, goes directly to the first principle and is the only science which does away with hypotheses in order to make her ground secure; the eye of the soul, which is literally buried in an outlandish slough, is by her gentle aid lifted upwards; and she uses as handmaids and helpers in the work of conversion, the sciences which we have been discussing. Custom terms them sciences, but they ought to have some other name, implying greater clearness than opinion and less clearness than science: and this, in our previous sketch, was called understanding. But why should we dispute about names when we have realities of such importance to consider?

Why indeed, he said, when any name will do which expresses the thought of the mind with clearness?

At any rate, we are satisfied, as before, to have four divisions; two for intellect and two for opinion, and to call the first division science, the second understanding, the third belief, and the fourth perception of shadows, opinion being concerned with becoming, and intellect with being; and so to make a proportion--

> As being is to becoming, so is pure intellect to opinion
> And as intellect is to opinion, so is science to belief, and understanding
>   to the perception of shadows.

But let us defer the further correlation and subdivision of the subjects of opinion and of intellect, for it will be a long enquiry, many times longer than this has been.

As far as I understand, he said, I agree.

And do you also agree, I said, in describing the dialectician as one who attains a conception of the essence of each thing? And he who does not possess and is therefore unable to impart this conception, in whatever degree he fails, may in that degree also be said to fail in intelligence? Will you admit so much?

Yes, he said; how can I deny it?

And you would say the same of the conception of the good? Until the person is able to abstract and define rationally the idea of good, and unless he can run the gauntlet of all objections, and is ready to disprove them, not by appeals to opinion, but to absolute truth, never faltering at any step of the argument--unless he can do all this, you would say that he knows neither the idea of good nor any other good; he apprehends only a shadow, if anything at all, which is given by opinion and not by science--dreaming and slumbering in this life, before he is well awake here, he arrives at the world below, and has his final quietus[11].

In all that I should most certainly agree with you.

---

[11]   *quietus:* discharge or release from life; death [editor's note].

Name_____

Date _____

1. Plato's allegory about the prisoners symbolizes his metaphysical views. In the allegory, what does the prison (den) represent? To what is the world outside analogous? What do the weights that chain the prisoners represent?

2. Plato's allegory is also considered a parable regarding education. What is Plato's view regarding how knowledge is attained? (Can it be "put into" the soul? What would the role of the teacher be?)

3. What are the duties of philosophers?

4. Why does Plato put so much emphasis on the importance of studying arithmetic?

5. What is the final goal of education?

26 *Conceptualism; John Locke*

❦ **B I O G R A P H Y** ❦
_____

(see Chapter 11)

One of the most important subcategories of metaphysics is that of ontology. Ontology is derived from the Greek word *onto* (being) and 'ology' (the science of). The science of being is that (intellectual) pursuit which attempts to determine in a rational; that is, consistent manner just exactly what sorts of things (beings) constitute[1] the universe. From a philosophical point of view, we are not interested in the different kinds of *particular* entities[2] that clutter our world such as tables and chairs. Such items are important, but constitute only one *kind* of thing, namely, they are members of the class of *concrete entia*; that is, things which are tangible[3] in nature. But if you think about it for a while, it will become evident that *concrete entia* are not the only types of things that go to make up our universe. For example, we readily admit of the existence of events. Are they tangible? Of course not. One cannot pick up and toss around an event the way one can a football (something concrete). Events are non-concrete in nature and therefore, belong to a different *class* of things. Ontology is that field of study that attempts to determine as accurately as possible the various types (classes) of things that go to make up the world (universe). People interested in this area of philosophical inquiry are akin to a store manager taking inventory. What is of utmost importance is accuracy regarding the store's contents. It will do the manager no good if he counts more or less than what resides in his store. He desires an exact account. So, too, with respect to the ontologist. He does not desire his ontology to be cluttered with unnecessary things, entities which appear to constitute a class by themselves but which can be reasonably explained as or subsumed by some other (necessary) class of things. Nor does he want to conclude his investigation with fewer types of things than is necessary to adequately explain the universe.

Regarding this endeavor[4], an important distinction has been made by ontologists, namely, between particulars and universals. The former are normally identified as *concrete entia*. The latter are defined as that which two or more things have in common. Consider, two or more green automobiles. They have at the very outset two things in common, namely, they are green and they are cars. Aside from the fact that the things in question possess these properties, the philosopher wants to know what is the nature of that which they have in common. They have greenness and carness in common. But is greenness and carness the same as a given

---
[1] *constitute*: to be the element or part of; make up; compose.

[2] *entity*: something that exists independently; not relative to other things.

[3] *tangible*: able to be perceived as materially existent.

[4] *endeavor*: a conscientious or concerned effort toward a given end.

entity *being* a green automobile? It would appear not. The effort of attempting to reduce the universals e.g., the commonalities of greenness and carness to that of particular entities possessing those qualities appears fruitless. Try such a reduction process yourself. I think that you will discover that such an endeavor is impossible, which means that we simply cannot do without universals when it comes to taking an inventory of the constituents of the world (universe). There are two conclusions which we can draw at this point. (1) Universals are indispensable if we desire to offer an adequate explanation (inventory) of the universe. (2) Universals are intangible in nature, namely, they are members of the class of *nonconcrete entia*. Whereas one can see the color green as a property of some concrete entity, one cannot touch or see that color by itself, unattached to some (concrete) thing.[5] Hence, the universal greenness must be something which is nonconcrete in nature. It is at this point that we come to the essential[6] issue in this chapter. It can be construed[7] in the time-honored context of which came first, the chicken or the egg? That is, do universals exist prior to and independently of those concrete things which have them in common, or are universals mental constructs formed by perceivers *after* they have had the sense experience of two or more concrete things that possess the same property?[8] Realists such as Plato argued that the first alternative is the case. He maintained that there must be some ontological foundation that provides the basis for the commonality between two or more concrete entities. On the other hand, conceptualists such as Locke argue that universals are nothing other than abstract mental concepts. This is a very important ontological issue. It is crucial because, if the realists are correct in their analysis, then universals exist as independent constituents of the world regardless of any conception of them. In other words, they existed before *homo sapiens*[9] came on the scene and they will survive that species' extinction. If, on the other hand, the conceptualists are on target, then universals are not everlasting "things" which are part of the inventory of the world's so called store. If such be the case, universals are abstract mental tools which human beings generate for the purpose of more easily understanding the environment in which they live. If so, then how are universals conceived?   Not surprisingly, the answer varies from conceptualist to conceptualist.

John Locke's theory is based on the distinction between essential and accidental characteristics. An essential characteristic is a characteristic without which a thing (i.e., particular) would not be the type of thing that it is. For example, an essential characteristic of pigs is that they are vertebrates. In other words, a given particular could not *be* a pig unless it possessed a spinal column. Accidental characteristics, however, are such that a thing (i.e., particular) can be the type of thing that it is (e.g., pig) without possessing such characteristics. That is, a (particular) pig need not have a broad dark colored band across its back in order to be a member of the class (i.e., type) pig. A conceptualist such as Locke gets his start by arguing that no two pigs (or anything else, for that matter) are identical. As

---

[5]   One might claim that he has often had a vision of green and therefore that he has perceived the universal greeness by itself. However, such a vision is not one of pure green, for that which one perceives is always something akin to a blotch or patch of green.

[6]   *essential*: of or constituting the intrinsic, fundamental nature of something.

[7]   *construe*: to discover and apply the meaning of; interpret.

[8]   Anything that is experienced by one or more of our five senses is called sense experience in philosophical lingo and is synonymous to perception.

[9]   *homo sapiens*: the biological classification of human beings.

Joseph Butler (1694-1752), another British philosopher observed, "Everything is what it is and not another thing". In other words, each particular (that is, thing) is indeed particular. No two of them are identical since each particular is a unique combination of essential and accidental characteristics. Consequently, universals do not exist in the world of particulars, for that is a world of uniqueness thus undermining the commonality essential to universals. Nevertheless, certain particulars are pigs and others are horses. The former are members of one distinct class and thus have that (i.e., pigness) in common and so too with regard to all particular horses. They have horseness in common. That which two or more particulars have in common is the definition of a universal. So if universals do not "reside" in the world of particulars, where are they? They must exist somewhere since we know that all pigs have something in common as do all horses. Locke argues that what we perceive[10] are particulars. On the basis of a perceptual instance of a horse we can subsequently form a mental image of a horse. In other words, you can imagine a horse in your mind's eye. Now your mental image of a horse need not correspond to any given particular horse you have previously perceived. The mental image you form may be unique in that it may well possess certain characteristics of several horses you have perceived. In such a case, the image is general in that it is an amalgam[11] of numerous particular horses, yet your mental image is nevertheless of *a* horse. As such, this image cannot be the universal horse since it is a particular amalgam horse. The universal horse is an abstract mental image the content of which consists only of essential horse characteristics. In other words, the universal horse is a concept formed by the mental image of a pure horse. It is pure since it lacks any and all accidental characteristics possessed by particular horses. Human beings have this power of abstraction whereby they can recognize and subsequently intellectually separate the essential characteristics from the accidental ones relative to classes. It is the essential characteristics which, if you will, define a class and therefore what is required for class membership. A universal is an abstract mental concept (i.e., mental image) which is pure by virtue of not being tainted by any accidental characteristics. As concepts, universals reside not in the world external to us (i.e., the world we perceive). Rather, they are the "things" which we conceive and reside in the conceptual world of our imagination qua[12] mental images. Therefore, universals have no independent ontological status.[13] They are concepts, the products of human abstraction and therefore ontologically dependent upon that abstracting process.

Suggested Readings: Conceptualism; Locke

1. Aaron, R.I., "Locke's Theory of Universals," *Proceedings of the Aristotelian Society*, Vol. 33 (1932-33).
2. Cassirer, Ernst, *Substance and Function*, (Dover Books).
3. Copleston, F., *A History of Philosophy*, Vol. V (N.Y.: Doubleday &

---

[10] *perceive*: to become aware of directly through any of the senses.

[11] *amalgam*: a combination or mixture; blend.

[12] *qua*: in the function, character or capacity of.

[13] Compare this analysis to that of Plato who argued that universals do possess an independent ontological status by virtue of constituting a world of their own. The world of Forms is independent of human conception or understanding.

Co., 1994), Chapter 5.

4. Cranston, M., "Men and Ideas; John Locke," *Encounter*, Vol. 7 (1956).

5. James, William, *Some Problems of Philosophy* (Peter Smith, Pub.).

Name_____

Date _____

1. What is the basic difference between Locke and Plato regarding universals?

2. What is the difference between accidental and essential characteristics?

3. Why do universals not exist "in the world" according to Locke's view?

4. What does Locke claim that universals are?

5. "Everything is what it is and not another thing." Explain.

Book III Of Words

Chapter II: Of the Signification of Words

1. Man, though he have great variety of thoughts, and such from which others as well as himself might receive profit and delight; yet they are all within his own breast, invisible and hidden from others, nor can of themselves be made to appear. The comfort and advantage of society not being to be had without communication of thoughts, it was necessary that man should find out some external sensible signs, whereof those invisible ideas, which his thoughts are made up of, might be made known to others. For this purpose nothing was so fit, either for plenty or quickness, as those articulate sounds, which with so much ease and variety he found himself able to make. Thus we may conceive how *words,* which were by nature so well adapted to that purpose, came to be made use of by men as the signs of their ideas; not by any natural connexion that there is between particular articulate sounds and certain ideas, for then there would be but one language amongst all men; but by a voluntary imposition, whereby such a word is made arbitrarily the mark of such an idea. The use, then, of words, is to be sensible marks of ideas; and the ideas they stand for are their proper and immediate signification.

2. The use men have of these marks being either to record their own thoughts, for the assistance of their own memory; or, as it were, to bring out their ideas, and lay them before the view of others: words, in their primary or immediate signification, stand for nothing but *the ideas in the mind of him that uses them*, how imperfectly soever or carelessly those ideas are collected from the things which they are supposed to represent. When a man speaks to another, it is that he may be understood: and the end of speech is, that those sounds, as marks, may make known his ideas to the hearer. That then which words are the marks of are the ideas of the speaker: nor can any one apply them as marks, immediately, to anything else but the ideas that he himself hath: for this would be to make them signs of his own conceptions, and yet apply them to other ideas; which would be to make them signs and not signs of his ideas at the same time; and so in effect to have no signification at all. Words being voluntary signs, they cannot be voluntary signs imposed by him on things he knows not. That would be to make them signs of nothing, sounds without signification. A man cannot make his words the signs either of qualities in

things, or of conceptions in the mind of another, whereof he has none in his own. Till he has some ideas of his own, he cannot suppose them to correspond with the conceptions of another man; nor can he use any signs for them: for thus they would be the signs of he knows not what, which is in truth to be the signs of nothing. But when he represents to himself other men's ideas by some of his own, if he consent to give them the same names that other men do, it is still to his own ideas; to ideas that he has, and not to ideas that he has not.

3. This is so necessary in the use of language, that in this respect the knowing and the ignorant, the learned and the unlearned, use the words they speak (with any meaning) all alike. They, in every man's mouth, stand for the ideas he has, and which he would express by them. A child having taken notice of nothing in the metal he hears called *gold*, but the bright shining yellow colour, he applies the word gold only to his own idea of that colour, and nothing else; and therefore calls the same colour in a peacock's tail gold. Another that hath better observed, adds to shining yellow great weight: and then the sound gold, when he uses it, stands for a complex idea of a shining yellow and a very weighty substance. Another adds to those qualities fusibility: and then the word gold signifies to him a body, bright, yellow, fusible, and very heavy. Another adds malleability. Each of these uses equally the word gold, when they have occasion to express the idea which they have applied it to: but it is evident that each can apply it only to his own idea; nor can he make it stand as a sign of such a complex idea as he has not.

4. But though words, as they are used by men, can properly and immediately signify nothing but the ideas that are in the mind of the speaker; yet they in their thoughts give them a secret reference to two other things.

First, *They suppose their words to be marks of the ideas in the minds also of other men, with whom they communicate*: for else they should talk in vain, and could not be understood, if the sounds they applied to one idea were such as by the hearer were applied to another, which is to speak two languages. But in this men stand not usually to examine, whether the idea they, and those they discourse with have in their minds be the same: but think it enough that they use the word, as they imagine, in the common acceptation of that language; in which they suppose that the idea they make it a sign of is precisely the same to which the understanding men of that country apply that name.

5. Secondly, because men would not be thought to talk barely of their own imagination, but of things as really they are; therefore they often suppose the *words to stand also for the reality of things*. But this relating more particularly to substances and their names, as perhaps the former does to simple ideas and modes, we shall speak of these two different ways of applying words more at large, when we come to treat of the names of mixed modes and substances in particular: though give me leave here to say, that it is a perverting the use of words, and brings unavoidable obscurity and confusion into their signification, whenever we make them stand for anything but those ideas we have in our own minds.

6. Concerning words, also, it is further to be considered:

First, that they being immediately the signs of men's ideas, and by that means the instruments whereby men communicate their conceptions, and express to one another those thoughts and imaginations they have within their own breasts; there comes, by constant use, to be such a connexion between certain sounds and the ideas they stand for, that the names heard, almost as readily excite certain ideas as if the objects themselves, which are apt to produce them, did actually affect the senses. Which is manifestly so in all obvious sensible qualities, and in all substances that frequently and familiarly occur to us.

7. Secondly, that though the proper and immediate signification of words are ideas in the mind of the speaker, yet, because by familiar use from our cradles, we come to learn certain articulate sounds very perfectly, and have them readily on our tongues, and always at hand in our memories, but yet are not always careful to examine or settle their significations perfectly; it often happens that men, even when they would apply themselves to an attentive consideration, do set their thoughts more on words than things. Nay, because words are many of them learned before the ideas are known for which they stand: therefore some, not only children but men, speak several words no otherwise than parrots do, only because they have learned them, and have been accustomed to those sounds. But so far as words are of use and signification, so far is there a constant connexion between the sound and the idea, and a designation that the one stands for the other; without which application of them, they are nothing but so much insignificant noise.

8. Words, by long and familiar use, as has been said, come to excite in men certain ideas so constantly and readily, that they are apt to suppose a natural connexion between them. But that they signify only men's peculiar ideas, and that *by a perfect arbitrary imposition*, is evident, in that they often fail to excite in others (even that use the same language) the same ideas we take them to be signs of: and every man has so inviolable a liberty to make words stand for what ideas he pleases, that no one hath the power to make others have the same ideas in their minds that he has, when they use the same words that he does. And therefore the great Augustus himself, in the possession of that power which ruled the world, acknowledged he could not make a new Latin word: which was as much as to say, that he could not arbitrarily appoint what idea any sound should be a sign of, in the mouths and common language of his subjects. It is true, common use, by a tacit consent, appropriates certain sounds to certain ideas in all languages, which so far limits the signification of that sound, that unless a man applies it to the same idea, he does not speak properly: and let me add, that unless a man's words excite the same ideas in the hearer which he makes them stand for in speaking, he does not speak intelligibly. But whatever be the consequence of any man's using of words differently, either from their general meaning, or the particular sense of the person to whom he addresses them; this is certain, their signification, in his use of them, is limited to his ideas, and they can be signs of nothing else.

Chapter III: Of General Terms

1. All things that exist being particulars, it may perhaps be thought reasonable that words, which ought to be conformed to things, should be so too--I mean in their signification: but yet we find quite the contrary. The far greatest part of words that make all languages are general terms: which has not been the effect of neglect or chance, but of reason and necessity.

2. First, It is impossible that every particular thing should have a distinct peculiar name. For, the signification and use of words depending on that connexion which the mind makes between its ideas and the sounds it uses as signs of them, it is necessary, in the application of names to things, that the mind should have distinct ideas of the things, and retain also the particular name that belongs to every one, with its peculiar appropriation

to that idea. But it is beyond the power of human capacity to frame and retain distinct ideas of all the particular things we meet with: every bird and beast men saw; every tree and plant that affected the senses, could not find a place in the most capacious understanding. If it be looked on as an instance of a prodigious memory, that some generals have been able to call every soldier in their army by his proper name, we may easily find a reason why men have never attempted to give names to each sheep in their flock, or crow that flies over their heads; much less to call every leaf of plants, or grain of sand that came in their way, by a peculiar name.

3. Secondly, If it were possible, it would yet be useless; because it would not serve to the chief end of language. Men would in vain heap up names of particular things that would not serve them to communicate their thoughts. Men learn names, and use them in talk with others, only that they may be understood: which is then only done when, by use or consent, the sound I make by the organs of speech, excites in another man's mind who hears it, the idea I apply it to in mine, when I speak it. This cannot be done by names applied to particular things; whereof I alone having the ideas in my mind, the names of them could not be significant or intelligible to another, who was not acquainted with all those very particular things which had fallen under my notice.

4. Thirdly, But yet, granting this also feasible, (which I think is not,) yet a distinct name for every particular thing would not be of any great use for the improvement of knowledge: which, though founded in particular things, enlarges itself by general views; to which things reduced into sorts, under general names, are properly subservient. . . .

6. The next thing to be considered is--How general words come to be made. For, since all things that exist are only particulars, how come we by general terms; or where find we those general natures they are supposed to stand for? Words become general by being made the signs of general ideas: and ideas become general, by separating from them the circumstances of time and place, and any other ideas that may determine them to this or that particular existence. By this way of abstraction they are made capable of representing more individuals than one; each of which having in it a conformity to that abstract idea, is (as we call it) of that sort.

7. But, to deduce this a little more distinctly, it will not perhaps be amiss to trace our notions and names from their beginning, and observe by what degrees we proceed, and by what steps we enlarge our ideas from our first infancy. There is nothing more evident, than that the ideas of the persons children converse with (to instance in them alone) are, like the persons themselves, only particular. The ideas of the nurse and the mother are well framed in their minds; and, like pictures of them there, represent only those individuals. The names they first gave to them are confined to those individuals; and the names of *nurse* and *mamma*, the child uses, determine themselves to those persons. Afterwards, when time and a larger acquaintance have made them observe that there are a great many other things in the world, that in some common agreements of shape, and several other qualities, resemble their father and mother, and those persons they have been used to, they frame an idea, which they find those many particulars do partake in; and to that they give, with others, the name *man*, for example. And thus they come to have a general name, and a general idea. Wherein they make nothing new; but only leave out of the complex idea they had of Peter and James, Mary and Jane, that which is peculiar to each, and retain only what is common to them all.

9. That this is the way whereby men first formed general ideas, and general names to them, I think is so evident, that there needs no other proof of it but the considering of a man's self, or others, and the ordinary proceedings of their minds in knowledge. And he that thinks *general natures* or *notions* are anything else but such abstract and partial ideas of more complex ones, taken at first from particular existences, will, I fear, be at a loss where to find them. For let any one effect, and then tell me, wherein does his idea of *man* differ from that of *Peter* and *Paul*, or his idea of *horse* from that of *Bucephalus*, but in the leaving out something that is peculiar to each individual, and retaining so much of those particular complex ideas in several particular existences as they are found to agree in? Of the complex ideas signified by the names *man* and *horse*, leaving out but those particulars wherein they differ, and retaining only those wherein they agree, and of those making a new distinct complex idea, and giving the name *animal* to it, one has a more general term, that comprehends with man several other creatures. Leave out of the idea of *animal*, sense and spontaneous motion, and the remaining complex idea, made up of the remaining simple ones of body, life, and nourishment, becomes a more general one, under the more comprehensive term, *vivens*.
. . .

11. To return to general words: it is plain, by what has been said, that *general* and *universal* belong not to the real existence of things; but are the inventions and creatures of the understanding, made by it for its own use, and concern only signs, whether words or ideas. Words are general, as has been said, when used for signs of general ideas, and so are applicable indifferently to many particular things; and ideas are general when they are set up as the representatives of many particular things: but universality belongs not to things themselves, which are all of them particular in their existence, even those words and ideas which in their signification are general. When therefore we quit particulars, the generals that rest are only creatures of our own making; their general nature being nothing but the capacity they are put into, by the understanding, of signifying or representing many particulars. For the signification they have is nothing but a relation that, by the mind of man, is added to them.

12. The next thing therefore to be considered is, What kind of signification it is that general words have. For, as it is evident that they do not signify barely one particular thing; for then they would not be general terms, but proper names, so, on the other side, it is as evident they do not signify a plurality; for *man* and *men* would then signify the same; and the distinction of numbers (as the grammarians call them) would be superfluous and useless. That then which general words signify is a *sort* of things; and each of them does that, by being a sign of an abstract idea in the mind; to which idea, as things existing are found to agree, so they come to be ranked under that name, or, which is all one, be of that sort. Whereby it is evident that the *essences* of the sorts, or, if the Latin word pleases better, *species* of things, are nothing else but these abstract ideas. For the having the essence of any species, being that which makes anything to be of that species; and the conformity to the idea to which the name is annexed being that which gives a right to that name; the having the essence, and the having that conformity, must needs be the same thing: since to be of any species, and to have a right to the name of that species, is all one. As, for example, to be a man, or of the *species* man and to have right to the *name* man is the same thing. Again, to be a man, or of the species man, and have the *essence* of a man, is the same thing. Now, since nothing can be a man or have a right to the name man, but what has a con-

formity to the abstract idea the name man stands for, nor anything be a man, or have a right to the species man, but what has the essence of that species; it follows, that the abstract idea for which the name stands, and the essence of the species, is one and the same. From whence it is easy to observe, that the essences of the sorts of things, and, consequently, the sorting of things, is the workmanship of the understanding that abstracts and makes those general ideas.

Name_____

Date _____

1. Words are signs of _____.

2. Do we arbitrarily assign words to ideas?

3. Why are there far more general terms in a language than particular ones?

4. Why are general terms necessary for the advancement of knowledge?

5. How do general terms come to be made?

6. General terms do not apply to the real existence of things. True or false? Explain.

27 *Nominalism; George Berkeley*

<table>
<tr><td>

⁊ BIOGRAPHY ⁊

(see Chapter 22)

</td></tr>
</table>

A subcategory of metaphysics centers on what might be labeled cosmic inventory taking. It is called ontology. Strictly speaking, ontology means the science of being. But that definition in and of itself is not very enlightening. The word *onto* is the Greek for being. The science of being is that intellectual pursuit the goal of which is to ascertain[1] as precisely as possible the different *types* of things which occupy the universe. It is not uncommon for one to believe that the only constituents of the world[2] are concrete in nature, namely, things which possess spatio-temporal coordinates such as tables and chairs. However, a little reflection will demonstrate that such tangibles[3] do not nor cannot stand alone as the only things in the inventory of the store of the universe. For example, we often speak of events. Two automobiles colliding constitutes[4] an event. Tangible entities[5] without doubt play a role in such an occurrence, but they are not identical to it. The event as a result of the two misguided tangible objects is nonconcrete in nature. One cannot dent an event such as one can a car. Yet think about how difficult it would be to think about the world in which we live and how it functions without the presupposition of such so-called "things" as events.

Concrete entia constitute only one type of "thing" in the inventory of the universe. The philosopher is interested in not only determining the number of types of "things" that occupy the universe, but the *nature* of those different types of "things" as well. Things possessing spatio-temporal coordinates are called *particulars* by philosophers. Particulars are physical in nature. The ultimate nature of these things primarily concerns the physicist. He desires a knowledge of the physical characteristics of such entities.

On the other hand, the essence[6] of the nontangible constituents of the world is of primary interest to the philosopher qua[7] ontologist. For example, he wants to know what are the criteria[8] that make an event an event.

---

[1] *ascertain*: to find out with certainty; determine.

[2] I shall use the terms 'world' and 'universe' synonymously.

[3] *tangible*: able to be perceived as materially existent.

[4] *constitute*: to be the elements or parts of; make up; compose.

[5] *entity*: something that exists independently; not relative to other things.

[6] *essence*: the quality or qualities of a thing that give it its identity; the intrinsic or indispensable properties of a thing.

[7] *qua*: in the function or capacity of.

[8] *criterion*: a standard, rule, or test on which a judgment or decision can be based. Criteria is the plural form of the word.

Events, however, are not the only members of the class *nonconcrete entia*. Consider the thing which two or more particulars have in common. Take, for example, five green automobiles. They have at the very outset one thing in common. They are all green. That is something that cannot be denied. If it cannot be doubted, then it must be the case that that which they have in common, namely, greenness, is some "thing". Now the question is, what is the nature of that common "thing"? Philosophers call it a *universal*. Universals obviously are nonconcrete in nature for one cannot fondle greenness even though one can caress a green automobile. That which the five objects in question have in common is obviously not identical to any one of the green cars. This point is apparent by the fact that five green shirts also participate in or share the universal greenness. It follows, therefore, that universals are not identical to the concrete objects which possess them as characteristics. They appear to be "things" which *can be* characteristics of any given concrete object, but at the same time possess some sort of independent status from those concrete objects that so possess them. At the outset, universals seem to reside in an ontological never-never land. When they (universals) are (intellectually) divorced from those things which possess them, their (true) nature becomes opaque[9]. And we know that they can be so separated from the things that possess them as the car and shirt examples above demonstrate.

If universals are "things" *not* identical to the concrete objects which exemplify[10] them, then just exactly what is their true nature? The answer to this question is of primary importance to the ontologist. Let us regroup for a moment. We know that (a) the universe possesses an inventory of more than one *type* of thing. There are within that inventory at the very least nonconcrete things as well as concrete entities. (b) We also know that of the class of *nonconcrete entia* there exist universals. However, we do not yet know what the nature of a universal is. To so determine is our present concern.[11] So far all that we have ascertained[12] is that universals are things which reside in a never-never land of some sort. One manner by which we can determine the nature of them is to zero in on the nature of this rather opaque abode[13] in which they (supposedly) reside. There are several options. Universals may be such that they exist independently not only of the objects that possess them, but separate from human conception as well. That is, greenness, for example, just might be something that exists regardless of green automobiles *and* those perceiving[14] human creatures which make the association between two or more green things. After all, it is not inconceivable that dinosaurs possessed green scales at a time when there were no *homo sapiens*[15] to perceive the commonality of their greenness. Those philosophers who argue for the independent and self-sufficient status of universals are called (ontological) realists.

On the other hand, there are those philosophers who are eager to point out that were it not for the powers of human conception, the notion of universals would be rendered[16] vacuous[17]. They argue that the existence of

---

[9]   *opaque*: obscure or unintelligible.

[10] *exemplify*: to show by example; serve as an example of.

[11] Such a claim is not to be construed as the only important issue confronting the philosopher as ontologist.

[12] *ascertain*: to discover through examination or experimentation; find out.

[13] *abode*: a place where one lives or stays; home; residence.

[14] *perceive*: to become aware of directly through any of the five senses.

[15] *homo sapiens*: the biological classification of human beings.

[16] *render*: to cause to be or become; make.

[17] *vacuous*: devoid of substance or meaning, inane.

universals is the result of and, therefore, dependent upon the innate[18] capacity of thinking creatures to abstract. The *ability* to abstract provides the basis for the existence of universals. That is, if it were not for the existence of creatures who had the capacity to engage in abstract thinking, the notion of universals would never arise in the first place. Hence, it must be the case that universals are nothing other than abstract mental concepts.

The position that the conceptualist promotes presents some rather tacky difficulties. It is predicated[19] upon the assumption that human beings have the ability to intellectually separate the accidental and essential characteristics of an object which they perceive *and* generate a *concept* comprised only of the essential characteristics of the perceived particular thing in question so that an association can be made with other particular things of the same type. Here some clarification is necessary. Accidental characteristics are those which an object possesses which it can do without and still remain a member of the class of things to which it belongs. For example, the characteristic of blue eyes is not an attribute[20] necessary in order for a human being to legitimately be considered a member of the class *homo sapiens*. However, the possession of two eyes, whether or not one or both are blue and/or dysfunctional, *is* necessary for one to qualify as a member of that type of creature called human being. In other words, an *essential* characteristic is one without which a thing would not be the type of thing that it is.[21]

The conceptualist argues that human beings possess the intellectual powers to separate the accidental and essential characteristics of objects and universals are those concepts which are conceptions comprised solely of the essential characteristics of any given class of objects. The expression of concepts is accomplished by the use of *general* words in our vocabulary. For instance, the word 'dog' is a common noun, namely, a general word whereas the word 'Rover' is a word that signifies a *particular* dog. We simply could not possess and subsequently demonstrate such language use unless we, as human beings, could conceptualize in the first place. Hence, conceptualists conclude that universals are conceptual in nature.

It is at this point that the nominalist enters this ontological debate. His argument begins at a fundamental level. That is, we as human beings only perceive *individual* things (i.e., particulars). He also recognizes that it is commonplace for us to employ general words, such as 'dog', in our vocabulary. He questions, however, that the use of such words indicates that there are concepts qua *universals* possessed by language users that *correspond* to common words (i.e., common nouns). What evidence do we have other than language use to support the claim that universals are concepts? Apparently, none. If pressed to the wall, the conceptualist cannot provide a description of an idea (concept) that comprises only the essential characteristics of *any* type of object other than a general term, namely, a common noun. It is at this point that the nominalist goes on the attack. And he uses the weapons of his adversary[22] to his advantage. The

---

[18] *innate*: possessed by birth; inborn.

[19] *predicate*: to base or establish (a concept, statement or action).

[20] *attribute*: a characteristic or quality of a person or thing.

[21] That a person is born or becomes blind is irrelevant to this discussion concerning the essential characteristics of *homo sapiens*. The point is that if a creature were born with only one eye, say in the middle of his forehead, he would not be considered to be one possessing the characteristics necessary for him to qualify as a member of the class of *homo sapiens*.

conceptualist supports his position by claiming that the generation of general terms, manifested by language use, is the key indicator that the users of language possess concepts otherwise they (namely, concepts) would not be manifested by their (human) use. The nominalist, on the other hand, argues that even though human beings have the ability to abstract, it does not follow from such activity that such creatures possess separate and identifiable ideas or concepts as universals in their heads that precisely correspond to or are expressed by the general words that they use. Since the only criterion that we possess for the existence of concepts is language use, it appears reasonable for the nominalist to claim that universals reside in the general words which we use to express them. In other words, universals *are*, in fact, the general words (i.e., common nouns) which are linguistic expressions of the *essential* characteristics of the particular things (of the same type) which we perceive. Nominalism means that the universal "lies" within the word. Philosophers of this persuasion have a good point. They say, "Let us look at the language being used at a given moment". Since it is the case that a given language user cannot offer criteria other than language to explain the common characteristics of two or more things, it must, therefore, be the case that language is that realm wherein universals are to be found. Since a universal is that which two or more things have in common, it follows that the nature of a universal is purely linguistic, namely, they are such that the nature of a universal is solely linguistic. Universals *are* general words, nothing more, nothing less. This, however, is a rather crude expression of the doctrine and is called naive nominalism. If a universal is nothing more than a common noun, then there would be two separate universals expressed by the words 'horse' and 'cheval' since those are two distinct words yet they mean the same thing.

George Berkeley was a nominalist who supported the above line of reasoning, but in a more subtle[23] way. He begins by attacking John Locke's doctrine of abstract general ideas. Abstract general ideas are not to be confused with general ideas. Locke states that "ideas become general by separating from them the circumstances of time, and place, and any other ideas, that may determine them to this or that particular existence. By this way of abstraction they are made capable of representing more individuals than one. . . ." For example, one may have the idea (i.e. mental image) of a particular triangle. That idea is made general by removing it from the context within which it is that particular triangle (such as the one I recall perceiving five minutes ago). My idea becomes general by it becoming an image of some scalene triangle or other. However, that general idea becomes an abstract general idea when its content consists solely of the essential characteristics of triangularity *sans*[24] all accidental characteristics possessed by particular triangles (such as the prime measurements of their sides). Although Berkeley is prepared to admit general ideas in some sense, he flatly denounced the existence of *abstract* general ideas. His rejection begins with introspection. Introspection is as if one rolled his eyeballs 180° and peered into himself. Berkeley looks into his mind in search of an abstract general idea and determines that whatever mental image he "focuses upon" is of some particular or other. He is incapable of coming across the mental image of, for example, an abstract general (i.e., universal) horse.

²² *adversary*: an opponent; enemy.

²³ *subtle*: capable of making or noticing fine distinctions in meaning.

²⁴ *sans*: without.

If all of our mental images are of particulars, how can any of them be general ideas? He says, "if we will...speak only of what we can conceive, I believe that we shall acknowledge that idea which, considered in itself, is particular, becomes general by being made to represent or stand for all other particular ideas of the same sort". Universality does not, therefore, consist "in the absolute positive nature or conception of anything, but in the relation it bears to the particulars signified or represented by it." From this it does not follow that we possess no powers of abstraction if we mean by 'abstraction' attending to or concentrating on a given feature of a particular. "It must be acknowledged that a man may consider a figure merely as a triangular, without attending to the particular qualities of the angles, or relations of the sides. ...In like manner we may consider Peter so far forth as a man, or so far forth as animal..." In other words, the idea of Peter is made general if one utilizes that idea as standing for all men or all animals. There is no universal man or universal animal which is the content of a mental image Locke calls an abstract general idea. The content of all ideas is particular in nature.

Universality, then, turns out to be a matter of function or use. This is a proxy function of letting one's idea of a particular stand for all other particulars of the same kind. This function is successfully communicated to others by the use of general words. As Berkeley states: "a word becomes general by being made a sign, not of an abstract idea, but of several particular ideas, any one of which it indifferently suggests to the mind". There are no such "things" as universals. Universality is a function. The linguistic expression of that function is by means of general words most notably in the form of common nouns. It should be obvious that Berkeley is no naive nominalist. Universals do not reside "in" general words because there are no universals *per se*[25]. Rather, general words are the vehicles by which the function of universalizing is linguistically conveyed from one person to another.

Suggested Readings: Nominalism; Berkeley

1. Copleston, F., *A History of Philosophy*, Vol. V (N.Y.: Doubleday & Co., 1994), Chapter 12.
2. Goodman, N., "A World of Individuals," *The Problems of Universals* (Notre Dame, Indiana: University of Notre Dame Press, 1956).

---

[25] *per se*: by (or in) itself.

Name_____

Date _____

1. How do ontological realists and conceptualists differ in their beliefs about the nature of universals?

2. What is meant by accidental characteristics of an object?

3. Nominalism means that the universal "lies" within _____.

4. Universals are _____according to naive nominalism.

5. Why is Berkeley not a naive nominalist?

Introduction

1. Philosophy being nothing else but the study of wisdom and truth, it may with reason be expected that those who have spent most time and pains in it should enjoy a greater calm and serenity of mind, a greater clearness and evidence of knowledge, and be less disturbed with doubts and difficulties than other men. Yet so it is, we see the illiterate bulk of mankind that walk the high road of plain common sense, and are governed by the dictates of nature, for the most part easy and undisturbed. To them nothing that is familiar appears unaccountable or difficult to comprehend. They complain not of any want of evidence in their senses, and are out of all danger of becoming skeptics. But no sooner do we depart from sense and instinct to follow the light of a superior principle, to reason, meditate, and reflect on the nature of things, but a thousand scruples spring up in our minds concerning those things which before we seemed fully to comprehend. Prejudices and errors of sense do from all parts discover themselves to our view; and, endeavouring to correct these by reason, we are insensibly drawn into uncouth paradoxes, difficulties, and inconsistencies, which multiply and grow upon us as we advance in speculation, till at length, having wandered through many intricate mazes, we find ourselves just where we were, or, which is worse, sit down in a forlorn skepticism.

2. The cause of this is thought to be the obscurity of things, or the natural weakness and imperfection of our understandings. It is said, the faculties we have are few, and those designed by nature for the support and comfort of life, and not to penetrate into the inward essence and constitution of things. Besides, the mind of man being finite, when it treats of things which partake of infinity, it is not to be wondered at if it run into absurdities and contradictions, out of which it is impossible it should ever extricate itself, it being of the nature of infinite not to be comprehended by that which is finite.

3. But perhaps we may be too partial to ourselves in placing the fault originally in our faculties, and not rather in the wrong use we make of them. It is a hard thing to suppose that right deductions from true principles should ever end in consequences which cannot be maintained or made consistent. Upon the whole, I am inclined to think that the far greater part, if not all, of those difficulties which have hitherto amused philosophers, and blocked up the way to knowledge, are entirely owing to ourselves--that we have first raised a dust and then complain we cannot see.

4. My purpose therefore is, to try if I can discover what those principles are which have introduced all that doubtfulness and uncertainty, those absurdities and contradictions, into the several sects of philosophy; insomuch that the wisest men have thought our ignorance incurable, conceiving it to arise from the natural dullness and limitation of our faculties. And surely it is a work well deserving our pains to make a strict inquiry concerning the first principles of human knowledge, to sift and examine them on all sides, especially since there may be some grounds to suspect that those lets[1] and difficulties, which stay and embarrass the mind in its search after truth, do not spring from any darkness and intricacy in the objects, or natural defect in the understanding, so much as from false principles which have been insisted on, and might have been avoided.

6. In order to prepare the mind of the reader for the easier conceiving what follows, it is proper to premise somewhat, by way of introduction, concerning the nature and abuse of language. But the unraveling this matter leads me in some measure to anticipate my design, by taking notice of what seems to have had a chief part in rendering speculation intricate and perplexed, and to have occasioned innumerable errors and difficulties in almost all parts of knowledge. And that is the opinion that the mind hath a power of framing *abstract ideas*[2] or notions of things. He who is not a perfect stranger to the writings and disputes of philosophers must needs acknowledge that no small part of them are spent about abstract ideas. These are in a more especial manner thought to be the object of those sciences which go by the name of logic and metaphysics, and of all that which passes under the notion of the most abstracted and sublime learning, in all which one shall scarce find any question handled in such a manner as does not suppose their existence in the mind, and that it is well acquainted with them.

7. It is agreed on all hands that the qualities or modes of things do never really exist each of them apart by itself, and separated from all others, but are mixed, as it were, and blended together, several in the same object. But, we are told, the mind being able to consider each quality singly, or abstracted from those other qualities with which it is united, does by that means frame to itself abstract ideas. For example, there is perceived by sight an object extended, coloured, and moved: this mixed or compound idea the mind resolving into its simple, constituent parts, and viewing each by itself, exclusive of the rest, does frame the abstract ideas of extension, colour, and motion. Not that it is possible for colour or motion to exist without extension; but only that the mind can frame to itself by *abstraction* the idea of colour exclusive of extension, and of motion exclusive of both colour and extension.

8. Again, the mind having observed that in the particular extensions perceived by sense there is something common and alike in all, and some other things peculiar, as this or that figure or magnitude, which distinguish them one from another; it considers apart or singles out by itself that which is common, making thereof a most abstract idea of extension which is neither line, surface, nor solid, nor has any figure or magnitude, but is an idea entirely prescinded from all these. So likewise the mind, by leaving out of the particular colours perceived by sense that which distinguishes them one from another, and retaining that only which is common to all, makes an idea of colour in abstract which is neither red, nor blue, nor white, nor any other determinate colour. And, in like manner, by con-

---

[1]   *let*: something that prevents or impedes; obstruction [editor's note].
[2]   This is a clear reference to John Locke [editor's note].

sidering motion abstractedly not only from the body moved, but likewise from the figure it describes, and all particular directions and velocities, the abstract idea of motion is framed; which equally corresponds to all particular motions whatsoever that may be perceived by sense.

9. And as the mind frames to itself abstract ideas of qualities or modes, so does it, by the same precision or mental separation, attain abstract ideas of the more compounded beings which include several coexistent qualities. For example, the mind having observed that Peter, James, and John resemble each other in certain common agreements of shape and other qualities, leaves out of the complex or compounded idea it has of Peter, James, and any other particular man that which is peculiar to each, retaining only what is common to all, and so makes an abstract idea wherein all the particulars equally partake; abstracting entirely from and cutting off all those circumstances and differences which might determine it to any particular existence. And after this manner it is said we come by the abstract idea of man, or, if you please, humanity, or human nature; wherein it is true there is included colour, because there is no man but has some colour, but then it can be neither white, nor black, nor any particular colour, because there is no one particular colour wherein all men partake. So likewise there is included stature, but then it is neither tall stature, nor low stature, nor yet middle stature, but something abstracted from all these. And so of the rest. Moreover, their being a great variety of other creatures that partake in some parts, but not all, of the complex idea of man, the mind, leaving out those parts which are peculiar to men, and retaining those only which are common to all the living creatures, frames the idea of *animal*, which abstracts not only from all particular men, but also all birds, beasts, fishes, and insects. The constituent parts of the abstract idea of animal are body, life, sense, and spontaneous motion. By *body* is meant body without any particular shape or figure, there being no one shape or figure common to all animals, without covering, either of hair, or feathers, or scales, etc., nor yet naked: hair, feathers, scales and nakedness being the distinguishing properties of particular animals, and for that reason left out of the *abstract idea*. Upon the same account the spontaneous motion must be neither walking, nor flying, nor creeping; it is nevertheless a motion, but what that motion is it is not easy to conceive.

10. Whether others have this wonderful faculty of abstracting their ideas, they best can tell; for myself, I find indeed I have a faculty of imagining, or representing to myself, the ideas of those particular things I have perceived, and of variously compounding and dividing them. I can imagine a man with two heads, or the upper parts of a man joined to the body of a horse. I can consider the hand, the eye, the nose, each by itself abstracted or separated from the rest of the body. But then whatever hand or eye I imagine, it must have some particular shape and colour. Likewise the idea of man that I frame to myself must be either of a white, or a black, or a tawny, a straight, or a crooked, a tall, or a low, or a middle-sized man. I cannot by any effort of thought conceive the abstract idea above described. And it is equally impossible for me to form the abstract idea of motion distinct from the body moving, and which is neither swift nor slow, curvilinear nor rectilinear; and the like may be said of all other abstract general ideas whatsoever. To be plain, I own myself able to abstract in one sense, as when I consider some particular parts or qualities separated from others, with which, though they are united in some object, yet it is possible they may really exist without them. But I deny that I can abstract from one another, or conceive separately, those qualities which it is impossible should exist so separated; or that I can frame a general

notion, by abstracting from particulars in the manner aforesaid--which last are the two proper acceptations of "abstraction." And there are grounds to think most men will acknowledge themselves to be in my case. The generality of men which are simple and illiterate never pretend to abstract notions. It is said they are difficult and not to be attained without pains and study; we may therefore reasonably conclude that, if such there be, they are confined only to the learned.

11. I proceed to examine what can be alleged in defense of the doctrine of abstraction, and try if I can discover what it is that inclines the men of speculation to embrace an opinion so remote from common sense as that seems to be. There has been a late deservedly esteemed philosopher who, no doubt, has given it very much countenance, by seeming to think the having abstract general ideas is what puts the widest difference in point of understanding betwixt man and beast.

> The having of general ideas, [saith he] is that which puts a perfect distinction betwixt man and brutes, and is an excellency which the faculties of brutes do by no means attain unto. For, it is evident we observe no footsteps in them of making use of general signs for universal ideas; from which we have reason to imagine that they have not the faculty of abstracting, or making general ideas, since they have no use of words or any other general signs.

And a little after:

> Therefore, I think, we may suppose that it is in this that the species of brutes are discriminated from men, and it is that proper difference wherein they are wholly separated, and which at last widens to so wide a distance. For, if they have any ideas at all, and are not bare machines (as some would have them), we cannot deny them to have some reason. It seems as evident to me that they do, some of them, in certain instances reason as that they have sense; but it is only in particular ideas, just as they receive them from their senses. They are the best of them tied up within those narrow bounds, and have not (as I think) the faculty to enlarge them by any kind of abstraction.--John Locke, *Essay on Human Understanding*, Bk. II, chap. XI, secs. 10, 11.

I readily agree with this learned author, that the faculties of brutes can by no means attain to abstraction. But then if this be made the distinguishing property of that sort of animals, I fear a great many of those that pass for men must be reckoned into their number. The reason that is here assigned why we have no grounds to think brutes have abstract general ideas is, that we observe in them no use of words or any other general signs; which is built on this supposition--that the making use of words implies the having general ideas. From which it follows that men who use language are able to abstract or generalize their ideas. That this is the sense and arguing of the author will further appear by his answering the question he in another place puts: "Since all things that exist are only particulars, how come we by general terms?" His answer is: "Words become general by being made the signs of general ideas." (*Essay on Human Understanding*, Bk. III, chap. III, sec. 6) But it seems that a word becomes general by being made the sign, not of an abstract general idea, but of several particular ideas, any one of which it indifferently suggests to the mind. For example, when it is said "the change of motion is proportional to the impressed force," or that "whatever has extension is divisible," these propositions are to be understood of motion and extension in general; and nevertheless it will not follow that they suggest to my thoughts an idea of motion without a body moved, or any determinate direction and velocity, or that I must conceive an abstract general idea of extension, which is neither line, surface, nor solid, neither great nor small, black, white, nor red, nor of any other determinate colour. It is only implied that whatever particular motion I consider, whether it be swift or slow, perpendicular, horizontal, or oblique, or in whatever object, the axiom concerning it holds equally true. As does the other of every particular extension, it matters not whether line, surface, or solid, whether of this or that magnitude or figure.

12. By observing how ideas become general we may the better judge how words are made so. And here it is to be noted that I do not deny absolutely there are general ideas, but only that there are any *abstract* general ideas; for, in the passages we have quoted wherein there is mention of general ideas, it is always supposed that they are formed by abstraction, after the manner set forth in sections 8 and 9. Now, if we will annex a meaning to our words, and speak only of what we can conceive, I believe we shall acknowledge that an idea which, considered in itself, is particular, becomes general by being made to represent or stand for all other particular ideas of the same sort. To make this plain by an example, suppose a geometrician is demonstrating the method of cutting a line in two equal parts. He draws, for instance, a black line of an inch in length: this, which in itself is a particular line, is nevertheless with regard to its signification general, since, as it is there used, it represents all particular lines whatsoever; so that what is demonstrated of it is demonstrated of all lines, or, in other words, of a line in general. And, as that *particular* line becomes general by being made a sign, so the *name* 'line,' which taken absolutely is particular, by being a sign is made general. And as the former owes its generality not to its being the sign of an abstract or general line, but of all particular right lines that may possibly exist, so the latter must be thought to derive its generality from the same cause, namely, the various particular lines which it indifferently denotes.

13. To give the reader a yet clearer view of the nature of abstract ideas, and the uses they are thought necessary to, I shall add one more passage out of the *Essay on Human Understanding*, which is as follows:

> *Abstract ideas* are not so obvious or easy to children or the yet unexercised mind as particular ones. If they seem so to grown men it is only because by constant and familiar use they are made so. For, when we nicely reflect upon them, we shall find that general ideas are fictions and contrivances of the mind, that carry difficulty with them, and do not so easily offer themselves as we are apt to imagine. For example, does it not require some pains and skill to form the general idea of a triangle (which is yet none of the most abstract, comprehensive, and difficult); for it must be neither oblique nor rectangle, neither equilateral, equicrural, nor scalenon, but *all and none* of these at once? In effect, it is something imperfect that cannot exist, an idea wherein some parts of several different and *inconsistent* ideas are put together. It is true the mind in this imperfect state has need of such ideas, and makes all the haste to them it can, for the conveniency of communication and enlargement of knowledge, to both which it is naturally very much inclined. But yet one has reason to suspect such ideas are marks of our imperfection. At least this is enough to show that the most abstract and general ideas are not those that the mind is first and most easily acquainted with, nor such as its earliest knowledge is conversant about.--Bk. IV, chap. VII, sec. 9.

If any man has the faculty of framing in his mind such an idea of a triangle as is here described, it is in vain to pretend to dispute him out of it, nor would I go about it. All I desire is that the reader would fully and certainly inform himself whether he has such an idea or no. And this, methinks, can be no hard task for anyone to perform. What more easy than for anyone to look a little into his own thoughts, and there try whether he has, or can attain to have, an idea that shall correspond with the description that is here given of the general idea of a triangle, which is "neither oblique nor rectangle, equilateral, equicrural nor scalenon, but all and none of these at once?"

14. Much is here said of the difficulty that abstract ideas carry with them, and the pains and skill requisite to the forming them. And it is on all hands agreed that there is need of great toil and labor of the mind, to emancipate our thoughts from particular objects, and raise them to those sublime speculations that are conversant about abstract ideas. From all which the natural consequence should seem to be, that so difficult a thing as the forming abstract ideas was not necessary for *communication*, which is so easy and familiar to all sorts of men. But, we are told, if they seem obvious and easy to grown men, it is only because by constant and familiar use they are made so. Now, I would fain know at what time it is men are employed in surmounting that difficulty, and furnishing themselves with those necessary helps for discourse. It cannot be when they are grown up, for then it seems they are not conscious of any such painstaking; it remains therefore to be the business of their childhood. And surely the great and multiplied labour of framing abstract notions will be found a hard task for that tender age. Is it not a hard thing to imagine that a couple of children cannot prate[3] together of their sugar plums and rattles and the rest of their little trinkets, till they have first tacked together numberless inconsistencies, and so framed in their minds abstract general ideas, and annexed them to every common name they make use of?

15. Nor do I think them a whit more needful for the *enlargement of knowledge* than for *communication*. It is, I know, a point much insisted on, that all knowledge and demonstration are about universal notions, to which I fully agree: but then it doth not appear to me that those notions are formed by abstraction in the manner premised; *universality*, so far as I can comprehend, not consisting in the absolute, positive nature or conception of anything, but in the relation it bears to the particulars signified or represented by it; by virtue whereof it is that things, names, or notions, being in their own nature *particular*, are rendered *universal*. Thus, when I demonstrate any proposition concerning triangles, it is to be supposed that I have in view the universal idea of a triangle; which ought not to be understood as if I could frame an idea of a triangle which was neither equilateral, nor scalenon, nor equicrural; but only that the particular triangle I consider, whether of this or that sort it matters not, doth equally stand for and represent all rectilinear triangles whatsoever, and is in that sense *universal*. All which seems very plain and not to include any difficulty in it.

18. I come now to consider the *source* of this prevailing notion, and that seems to me to be language. And surely nothing of less extent than reason itself could have been the source of an opinion so universally received. The truth of this appears, as from other reasons, so also from the plain confession of the ablest patrons of abstract ideas, who acknowledge that they are made in order to naming; from which it is a clear consequence that if there had been no such thing as speech or universal signs there never had been any thought of abstraction. See Bk. III, chap. VI, sec.

---

3   *prate*: to talk much and foolishly; chatter [editor's note].

39, and elsewhere of the *Essay on Human Understanding*. Let us examine the manner wherein words have contributed to the origin of that mistake: First, then, it is thought that every name has, or ought to have, one only precise and settled signification, which inclines men to think there are certain abstract, determinate ideas that constitute the true and only immediate signification of each general name; and that it is by the mediation of these abstract ideas that a general name comes to signify any particular thing. Whereas, in truth, there is no such thing as one precise and definite signification annexed to any general name, they all signifying indifferently a great number of particular ideas. All which doth evidently follow from what has been already said, and will clearly appear to anyone by a little reflection. To this it will be objected that every name that has a definition is thereby restrained to one certain signification. For example, a "triangle" is defined to be "a plain surface comprehended by three right lines," by which that name is limited to denote one certain idea and no other. To which I answer, that in the definition it is not said whether the surface be great or small, black or white, nor whether the sides are long or short, equal or unequal, nor with what angles they are inclined to each other; in all which there may be great variety, and consequently there is no one settled idea which limits the signification of the word "triangle." It is one thing for to keep a name constantly to the same definition, and another to make it stand everywhere for the same idea; the one is necessary, the other useless and impracticable.

19. But to give a farther account how words came to produce the doctrine of abstract ideas, it must be observed that it is a received opinion that language has no other end but the communicating our ideas and that every significant name stands for an idea. This being so, and being withal certain that names which yet are not thought altogether insignificant do not always mark out particular conceivable ideas, it is straightway concluded that they stand for abstract notions. That there are many names in use amongst speculative men which do not always suggest others determinate, particular ideas, or in truth anything at all, is what nobody will deny. And a little attention will discover that it is not necessary (even in the strictest reasonings) significant names which stand for ideas should, every time they are used, excite in the understanding the ideas they are made to stand for: in reading and discoursing, names being for the most part used as letters are in algebra, in which, though a particular quantity be marked by each letter, yet to proceed right it is not requisite that in every step each letter suggest to your thoughts that particular quantity it was appointed to stand for.

20. Besides, the communicating of ideas marked by words is not the chief and only end of language, as is commonly supposed. There are other ends, as the raising of some passion, the exciting to or deterring from an action, the putting the mind in some particular disposition; to which the former is in many cases barely subservient, and sometimes entirely omitted, when these can be obtained without it, as I think does not unfrequently happen in the familiar use of language. I entreat the reader to reflect with himself, and see if it doth not often happen, either in hearing or reading a discourse, that the passions of fear, love, hatred, admiration, disdain, and the like, arise immediately in his mind upon the perception of certain words, without any ideas coming between. At first, indeed, the words might have occasioned ideas that were fitting to produce those emotions; but, if I mistake not, it will be found that, when language is once grown familiar, the hearing of the sounds or sight of the characters is oft immediately attended with those passions which at first were wont to be produced by the intervention of ideas that are now quite

omitted. May we not, for example, be affected with the promise of a *good thing*, though we have not an idea of what it is? Or is not the being threatened with danger sufficient to excite a dread, though we think not of any particular evil likely to befall us, nor yet frame to ourselves an idea of danger in abstract? If anyone shall join ever so little reflection of his own to what has been said, I believe that it will evidently appear to him that general names are often used in the propriety of language without the speaker's designing them for marks of ideas in his own, which he would have them raise in the mind of the hearer. Even proper names themselves do not seem always spoken with a design to bring into our view the ideas of those individuals that are supposed to be marked by them. For example, when a schoolman tells me, "Aristotle hath said it," all I conceive he means by it is to dispose me to embrace his opinion with the deference and submission which custom has annexed to that name. And this effect is often so instantly produced in the minds of those who are accustomed to resign their judgment to authority of that philosopher, as it is impossible any idea either of his person, writings, or reputation should go before. Innumerable examples of this kind may be given, but why should I insist on those things which every one's experience will, I doubt not, plentifully suggest unto him?

21. We have, I think, shown the impossibility of abstract ideas. We have considered what has been said for them by their ablest patrons, and endeavored to show they are of no use for those ends to which they are thought necessary. And lastly, we have traced them to the source from whence they flow, which appears evidently to be language. It cannot be denied that words are of excellent use, in that by their means all that stock of knowledge which has been purchased by the joint labors of inquisitive men in all ages and nations may be drawn into the view and made the possession of one single person. But at the same time it must be owned that most parts of knowledge have been strangely perplexed and darkened by the abuse of words, and general ways of speech wherein they are delivered. Since therefore words are so apt to impose on the understanding, whatever ideas I consider, I shall endeavor to take them bare and naked into my view, keeping out of my thoughts so far as I am able, those names which long and constant use hath so strictly united with them; from which I may expect to derive the following advantages--

22. *First*, I shall be sure to get clear of all controversies purely verbal; the springing up of which weeds in almost all the sciences has been a main hindrance to the growth of true and sound knowledge. *Secondly*, this seems to be a sure way to extricate myself out of that fine and subtle[4] net of *abstract ideas* which has so miserably perplexed and entangled the minds of men; and that with this peculiar circumstance, that by how much the finer and more curious was the wit of any man, by so much the deeper was he likely to be ensnared and faster held therein. *Thirdly*, so long as I confine my thoughts to my own ideas divested of words, I do not see how I can easily be mistaken. The objects I consider, I clearly and adequately know. I cannot be deceived in thinking I have an idea which I have not. It is not possible for me to imagine that any of my own ideas are alike or unlike that are not truly so. To discern the agreements or disagreements there are between my ideas, to see what ideas are included in any compound idea and what not, there is nothing more requisite than an attentive perception of what passes in my own understanding.

23. But the attainment of all these advantages doth presuppose an entire deliverance from the deception of words, which I dare hardly prom-

---

[4]   *subtle*: able to make fine distinction; keen [editor's note]

ise myself; so difficult a thing it is to dissolve an union so early begun, and confirmed by so long a habit as that betwixt words and ideas. Which difficulty seems to have been very much increased by the doctrine of *abstraction*. For, so long as men thought abstract ideas were annexed to their words, it doth not seem strange that they should use words for ideas; it being found an impracticable thing to lay aside the word, and retain the *abstract* idea in the mind, which in itself was perfectly inconceivable. This seems to me the principal cause why those men who have so emphatically recommended to others the laying aside all use of words in their meditations, and contemplating their bare ideas, have yet failed to perform it themselves. Of late many have been very sensible of the absurd opinions and insignificant disputes which grow out of the abuse of words. And, in order to remedy these evils, they advise well, that we attend to the ideas signified, and draw off our attention from the words which signify them. But, how good so ever this advice may be they have given others, it is plain they could not have a due regard to it themselves, so long as they thought the only immediate use of words was to signify ideas, and that the immediate signification of every general name was a determinate abstract idea.

24. But, these being known to be mistakes, a man may with greater ease prevent his being imposed on by words. He that knows he has no other than *particular* ideas, will not puzzle himself in vain to find out and conceive the *abstract* idea annexed to any name. And he that knows names do not always stand for ideas will spare himself the labor of looking for ideas where there are none to be had. It were, therefore, to be wished that everyone would use his utmost endeavors to obtain a clear view of the ideas he would consider, separating from them all that dress and incumbrance of words which so much contribute to blind the judgment and divide the attention. In vain do we extend our view into the heavens and pry into the entrails of the earth, in vain do we consult the writings of learned men and trace the dark footsteps of antiquity; we need only draw the curtain of words, to hold the fairest tree of knowledge, whose fruit is excellent and within the reach of our hand.

25. Unless we take care to clear the first principles of knowledge from the embarrassment and delusion of words, we may make infinite reasonings upon them to no purpose: we may draw consequences from consequences, and be never the wiser. The farther we go, we shall only lose ourselves the more irrecoverably, and be the deeper entangled in difficulties and mistakes. Whoever therefore designs to read the following sheets, I entreat him to make my words the occasion of his own thinking, and endeavour to attain the same train of thoughts in reading that I had in writing them. By this means it will be easy for him to discover the truth or falsity of what I say. He will be out of all danger of being deceived by my words, and I do not see how he can be led into an error by considering his own naked, undisguised ideas.

Name_____

Date _____

1. How are abstract ideas thought to be formed? Give examples.

2. Why does Berkeley deny that there are abstract ideas?

3. What kind of ideas do we have according to Berkeley?

4. Why has the doctrine of abstract ideas been embraced in the past?

5. What examples does Berkeley give of the use of words for reasons other than communicating ideas?

28 *Ordinary Language Analysis; Ludwig Wittgenstein*

[a.] *argue*: to give evidence of.

[b.] *constituent*: component.

[c.] *empirical:* relying or based solely on experiment and observation.

[d.] The Greek word for beyond is *meta*; hence, metaphysics; that is, that which is beyond physics.

[e.] *fictitious*: not real; pretended; imaginary.

At the outbreak of World War I, Wittgenstein enlisted in the Austrian Army. This did not deter him from his philosophical writings. Myth or no, it is commonly believed that he was taken prisoner by the Italian Army while working on the Tractatus *in a fox-hole!*

During the years immediately after the war, Wittgenstein did not devote his time to the pursuit of philosophy. Rather he became a teacher of children nine to ten years of age in the village of Trattenback, Austria. He became disenchanted with this when he was informed by his superiors that he was altogether too rigorous.

After a period of floundering, he returned to Cambridge with a fellowship. He lectured there from 1930 to 1936 during which time he frequented his cottage in Norway. It was during this period that he began to realize certain flaws in his first book and began to correct them. He shifted his emphasis from the tenability[a] of an ideal language to the importance of analyzing ordinary language, the language that the man in the street uses and the games *we play with respect to our discourse. Given his analysis, we all play linguistic games. Philosophical problems arise if we do not appreciate the linguistic game rules that we are playing from moment to moment. There is the beauty linguistic game. There is the God linguistic game. Such linguistic games do not mean that the use of the words requisite to such (linguistic) games are meaningless (viz. such words as 'beauty' and 'God'). Philosophical confusion arises by unwittingly applying the rules of one linguistic game to that of another. This analysis of language use is made apparent in* The Blue and Brown Books, *a compilation of lecture notes on behalf of Wittgenstein's students, his* Philosophical Investigations *and his* Zettel, *a compilation of Wittgenstein's personal notes.*

Throughout his life, Wittgenstein was a tormented individual. He was a perfectionist regardless of the nature of the discipline he pursued. By applying his standards of rigor plus innovation to the discipline of philosophy he provided an insight to his chosen field of inquiry that very few individuals have accomplished.

[a]   *tenable*: that can be held, defended or maintained.

One primary concern in the area of metaphysics is that of ontology. 'Ology' means 'the science of'. *Onto* is the Greek word which means being. Hence, the word 'ontology' means the science of being. However, that definition of ontology is not very enlightening. The notion of being is more complex than meets the eye. Believe it or not, there are several types of so-called "things" that exist; that is, that are in the world (i.e., universe)[1] as well as the manner in which they exist. There are things which exist as concrete entities, namely, those with spatio-temporal coordinates. Such things are tangible[2]. On the other hand, there are "things" which are nonconcrete in nature such as events. Think about that for a moment. Is it possible to pick up an event and toss it around as one can a football? Of course not. Hence, it appears to be the case that there are both nonconcrete as well as concrete "things" that comprise the universe.

[1]   Throughout this chapter, I will use the words 'world' and 'universe' synonymously.
[2]   *tangible*: able to be perceived as materially existent.

Alternatively, there are ways in which the same type of thing can exist. Something can exist either as an object dependent upon an act of thought or independent of such an act. A unicorn, for example, is some *thing* that does not exist independent of some person (or other) thinking about such a creature. Unicorns simply do not exist (i.e., be) on their own. We know that as a matter of fact. But by the fact that unicorns are thought about gives such a thing some sort of status of existence. This type of existence is termed by philosophers unexemplified existence. It also happens to be the case that there are things which exist, or possess their being, independently of an act of thought such as a dishwasher. Common sense tells us that such a machine exists when we are not thinking about it. The entities that possess this type of being exist in an exemplified way.

It is clear that there are some so-called "things" which are nonconcrete in nature which exist in an exemplified manner. As pointed out above, events so qualify. After all, one cannot fondle an event, but at the same time one cannot reasonably deny that they occur independently of an act of thought. If such nontangible "things" are real; that is, possess existence independently of our thoughts, just what sort of ontological status do they possess? That is a very good question. It is at this point that the plot thickens somewhat. Talk about intangible but perceivable qualities of specific events is fairly elemental. There are other "things", however, that so qualify that are a bit more elusive[3] in nature. Philosophers also make the distinction between the accidental and essential properties that any given "thing" possesses. The former refers to any characteristic that a thing possesses, be it concrete or otherwise, that it can conceivably do without and nevertheless remain the *type* of thing that it is. For example, a *homo sapiens*[4] can lack blue eyes and still be a human being. An essential property, on the other hand, is one without which a thing *cannot* be the type of thing that it is. Essential characteristics allow one to classify any given thing as the *type* of thing that it is. This issue tends to be a very complicated one; one with which both the scientist and the philosopher are concerned. However, the scientist approaches the problem from an entirely different point of view than does the philosopher. The latter views the nature of essential characteristics not simply as a means to classify diverse (individual) entities, but as what constitutes reality. After all, if one can determine the essential characteristics of some "thing", then one has within his grasp the nature of reality, namely what something really is.[5] So, it turns out that the ontologist is one who is in search of a knowledge of the essential characteristics of any given thing, whether it be exemplified or unexemplified. Just what is it that makes some *thing* what it is? That which makes a thing what it *is* is due to that thing's possession of essential characteristics. It is the type of thing that it is *because*[6] of the essential characteristics which it possesses. But what is an essential characteristic aside from a mere definition of it? More specifically, what is the nature of an essence? Such a question is the source of a tremendous amount of philosophical debate which has extended over many centuries.

In order to achieve a proper perspective of Wittgenstein's analysis of the nature of essences, it is necessary to understand some alternative points of view. (1) Realists argue that essences constitute[7] a separate cat-

---

[3] *elusive*: hard to grasp or retain mentally.

[4] *homo sapiens*: the biological classification for human beings.

[5] Note that the word 'is' is a cognate of existence or being.

[6] Note that the word 'because' literally means the cause of being.

[7] *constitute*: to be the elements or parts of; make up; compose.

egory of existence, the nature of which is intangible but only perceivable via[8] some tangible entity[9]. The consequence of such a philosophical position is that essences could exist (in an exemplified manner) independently of human existence. Essences stand on their own, independent of human thought. (See Plato, Chapter 24.) Universals are akin to essences in that a universal is a characteristic which two or more particulars have in common. Consequently, a universal characteristic need not be an essential one since, for example, two people may share the common characteristic of blue eyes although possessing blue eyes is not an essential characteristic of human beings. Clearly, however, essential characteristics manifest commonality.

(2) Conceptualists maintain that whereas essential characteristics account for particulars (i.e., individual things) being the types of things they are, universals are the products of human abstraction. For example, when one is considering only one characteristic of a particular, the emphasis is on the way in which the object is viewed, not the way in which it really exists (viz. as a combination of several characteristics). The act of conceiving universals, therefore, always involves a process of abstraction. It is a partial view of many particulars. The activity of thought isolates features that are common to a number of particular objects and attends to them as separate entities. These "entities" (e.g., whiteness or pigness) are genuine aspects of discrete[10] objects perceived by the senses. But they are not forms of being distinct from objects. They are simply concepts.

(3) Nominalists are philosophers who ascertain[11] some difficulties with both aforementioned philosophical positions. On the one hand, it is very difficult to accept the fact that essences and universals can float around unattached to particular entities. On the other hand, the nominalist foresees some complications attendant to the conceptualists point of view. Notwithstanding the human ability to abstract, it is nevertheless quite difficult, if not impossible, to thoroughly describe the nature of a concept. It is not very enlightening to simply maintain that concepts are simply concepts without any further description of them. Hence, the nominalist argues that universals reside in the meanings of common nouns we use to express the class membership of the individual (particular) things that we perceive[12]. For example, when one views a herd of cattle, he is able to notice certain similarities among them. It is not the case, according to the nominalist, that those characteristics (which make it possible for each member of the herd to be classified as cattle) possess a status independent of all those beasts. Rather, the essential characteristics by which we identify an animal as a cow or bull is in the meanings of the common words we use, namely, 'cow', 'bull', 'cattle' and the like. Universals literally lie within the language we use to express those characteristics.

Wittgenstein was not satisfied with any of the above analyses of the nature of essences and universals. He simply could not "buy in" on the realist's point of view. This is made very clear in those passages of his *Philosophical Investigations* where he examines the nature of games. He suggests that we attempt to discover some set of essential characteristics

---

[8]   *via*: by way of.

[9]   *entity*: a particular and discrete unit; an entirety.

[10]   *discrete:* separate and distinct; not attached to others; unrelated.

[11]   *ascertain*: to discover through examination or experimentation; find out.

[12]   *perceive*: to become aware of through sight, hearing, touch, taste or smell.

which *all* games possess. Indeed, there are similarities between some games, such as ball games *or* board games. But what do ball *and* board games have in common other than the fact that they simply *are* games. One cannot even reasonably maintain that all games have rules in common since there are some games that have no rules at all, such as a child who plays the game of willy-nilly, tossing a ball into the air. The closest we can come to establishing essential characteristics of a class of things is what Wittgenstein called family resemblances. This means that some games have some characteristics in common and some do not. One can view the situation as a rope with fibers. Some of the fibers overlap and in that sense have something in common. However, the individual fibers (i.e., games) do not run the entire length of the rope so that a fiber at one end does not overlap with a fiber at the other end and in that sense they have nothing in common. Nevertheless both of these fibers are part of the same rope. In the same way, some games have nothing in common with other games save for the fact that they simply *are* games. Renford Bambrough makes the point most succinctly[13].

> The nominalist says that games have nothing in common except that they are called games. The realist says that games must have something in common, and he means by this that they must have something in common other than that they are games. Wittgenstein says that games have nothing in common except that they are games. He asserts at one and the same time the realist's claim that there is an objective justification for the application of the word "game" to games and the nominalist's claim that there is no element that is common to all games.[14]

The net effect of Wittgenstein's analysis of universals is that there are none. Games simply are games. Because of this, we would be going on a philosophical wild goose chase were we to suppose that there is some "thing" additional to particular games that all such games have in common; that is, a universal. All that two (or more) particulars have in common is similarity; that is, resemblance. In the strict sense of the term, each particular (object) is unique.

One of the reasons why Wittgenstein argues that there is no such thing as a universal independent of things that are identifiable as the things they are is because (a) many natural; that is, self-sufficient things are classified differently by different groups of people. Such differences of classification are predicated[15] upon the different needs of the group of people doing the classifying. For example, Eskimos have more than twenty different classifications for snow. That is because their needs are different than ours. (b) Many so-called things are the result of human design and development. These "things" run the gamut from institutions to hardware. For example, it is humans that developed the institution called marriage. They did so as a result of some need. Due to this fact, it appears absurd to Wittgenstein to ask the question, "What is the universal of marriage?" Marriage is simply marriage! In a similar vein[16], it is human beings that designed and developed the rockets that put man on the moon. Those things did not exist prior to man as did, say, snow. Conse-

---

[13] *succinct*: clearly expressed in few words; concise.

[14] Renford Bambrough, "Universals and Family Resemblances," *Proceedings of the Aristotelian Society*, 60 (1960-61), pp.217-218.

[15] *predicate*: to base or establish (a concept, statement, or action). Used with "on" or "upon".

[16] *vein*: course or tenor of thought.

quently, to Wittgenstein's way of thinking, it is somewhat frivolous[17] to concern oneself with a search for the universal of rockets which, according to some realists, must have existed prior to the exemplification of rockets. Human beings built them in response to some need and they; that is, rockets simply are what they are. As the noted 18th century philosopher Joseph Butler observed, "Everything is what it is and not another thing". In other words, no two things are, strictly speaking, identical. Every individual thing is unique. If such is the case, then the distinction between essential and accidental characteristics collapses. All that remains is similarity or resemblance between particulars. Not surprisingly, this view is known as particularism. Wittgenstein was a particularist. This position entails that only things capable of being perceived exist (which includes such nonconcrete "things" as facts). What is capable of being perceived is within the realm of physics. Anything that goes beyond the realm of physics simply does not exist. Therefore, philosophy as a discipline concerned solely with metaphysical issues is ca-put. So far as Wittgenstein is concerned, the only legitimate role philosophers play is in dispelling the confusions generated by applying the rules of one language-game to another. This is called ordinary language analysis. Beyond that, philosophy, strictly speaking, does not exist. The sole concern of philosophical analysis is to root out the *source* of philosophical confusion. Once it is understood that that source is one of confused use of language, then it becomes apparent that there is no (and are no) philosophical (which means metaphysical) problems concerning any "thing" in "this here" world.

It is not just the case that philosophy qua[18] metaphysics is dead. Wittgenstein's view is that metaphysics is nonexistent. Given the fact that metaphysics, in the ultimate sense of the word, is synonymous with philosophy, there is no such thing as philosophy. The only and proper role of one who claims to be a philosopher is analyzing ordinary language; that is, the pursuit of exposing so-called philosophical problems as what they genuinely are, namely, confusions concerning language use. The role of the philosopher is to "let the fly out of the fly-bottle". In other words, the role of the philosopher is not to create problems but to rid himself, as well as the rest of humanity, of them. To think that to go beyond physics qua metaphysics provides the answer to, or is going to provide a solution to, everyday "so-called" philosophical human questions or concerns is not only naive but philosophically unsound. Metaphysics simply does not exist. Consequently, a question as to the nature of universals is vacuous[19].

Wittgenstein has had a tremendous effect upon the philosophical world during the 20th century. While at Cambridge University he developed a loyal following of students so dedicated to his views they functioned as disciples of the prophet. The works of Wittgenstein are notoriously difficult reading. His writings appear to be an extended string of most often unrelated or disjointed pensés[20]. Consequently, the editor has chosen a reading by Renford Bambrough to express Wittgenstein's views concerning the issue of essences and universals.

[17] *frivolous*: unworthy of serious attention; insignificant; trivial.
[18] *qua*: considered as; in the function, character, or capacity of.
[19] *vacuous*: senseless; inane.
[20] *pensé*: an undeveloped thought.

Suggested Readings: Ordinary Language Analysis; Wittgenstein

1. Austin, J. L., *How To Do Things With Words* (N.Y.: Oxford University Press, 1972).
2. Brown, Roger, *Words and Things* (Glencoe, Ill.: The Free Press, 1958).
3. Cohen, Jonathan L., *The Diversity of Meaning* (London: Methuen & Co., Ltd., 1962).
4. Katz, Jerold J., *The Philosophy of Language* (New York: Harper & Row, Publishers, 1966).
5. Lehrer, Adrienne & Keith, *Theory of Meaning* (Englewood Cliffs, N.J.: Prentice-Hall, Inc., 1970).
6. Rorty, Richard, ed., *The Linguistic Turn* (Chicago: University of Chicago Press,1967).
7. Salomon, Louis B., *Semantics and Common Sense* (New York: Holt, Rinehart & Winston, Inc., 1966).
8. Wittgenstein, L., *Philosophical Investigations*, G.E.M. Anscombe, trans. (N.Y.: The MacMillan Co., 1953).
9. _____, *The Blue and Brown Books* (N.Y.: Harper Torchbooks, Harper and Row, Publishers, 1958).
10. _____, *Zettel*, G.E.M. Anscombe, trans. (Berkeley & Los Angeles: University of California Press, 1967).

Name_____

Date _____

1. According to Wittgenstein what is it that types of things have in common?

2. What does Wittgenstein mean by "family resemblances"?

3. Regarding the existence of universals, Wittgenstein believes there are none. True or false? What are the reasons Wittgenstein gives for his view?

4. What is particularism?

5. What is the role of philosophy according to Wittgenstein?

6. Metaphysics, in Wittgenstein's view, does not exist. True or false? Explain.

❦ **R E A D I N G S** ❦

___

Ordinary Language Analysis

___

Ludwig Wittgenstein
Universals & Family
Resemblances
by Renford Bambrough

Universals and Family Resemblances

. . .If I ask you what these three books have in common, or what those four chairs have in common, you will look to see if the books are all on the same subject or by the same author or published by the same firm; to see if the chairs are all Chippendale or all three-legged or all marked "Not to be removed from this room." It will never occur to you to say that the books have in common that they are books or the chairs that they are chairs. And if you find after close inspection that the chairs or the books do not have in common any of the features I have mentioned, and if you cannot see any other specific feature that they have in common, you will say that as far as you can see they have nothing in common. You will perhaps add that you suppose from the form of my question that I must know of something that they have in common. I may then tell you that all the books once belonged to John Locke or that all the chairs came from Ten Rillington Place. But it would be a poor sort of joke for me to say that the chairs were all chairs or that the books were all books.

If I ask you what *all* chairs have in common, or what *all* books have in common, you may again try to find a feature like those you would look for in the case of *these three* books or *those four* chairs; and you may again think that it is a poor sort of joke for me to say that what all books have in common is that they are books and that what all chairs have in common is that they are chairs. And yet this time it is not a joke but an important philosophical truth.

Because the normal case where we ask "What have all *these* chairs, books or games in common?" is one in which we are not concerned with their all being chairs, books or games, we are liable to overlook the extreme peculiarity of the philosophical question that is asked with the words "What do *all* chairs, *all* books, *all* games have in common?" For of course games *do* have something in common. They *must* have something in common, and yet when we look for what they have in common we cannot find it. When we try to say what they have in common we always fail. And this is not because what we are looking for lies deeply hidden, but because it is too obvious to be seen; not because what we are trying to say is too subtle and complicated to be said, but because it is too easy and too simple to be worth saying: and so we say something more dramatic, but something false, instead. The simple truth is that what games have in common is that they are games. The nominalist is obscurely aware of this, and by rejecting the realist's talk of transcendent, immanent or subsistent forms or universals he shows his awareness. But by his own insistence that games have nothing in common except that they are called games he shows the obscurity of his awareness. The realist too is obscurely aware of it. By his talk of transcendent, immanent or subsistent forms or universals he shows the obscurity of his awareness. But by his hostility to the nominalist's insistence that games have nothing in common except that they are called games he shows his awareness.

All this can be usefully explained by the application of what I will call "Ramsey's Maxim." F. P. Ramsey, after mapping the course of an inconclusive dispute between Russell and W. E. Johnson, writes as follows:

> Evidently, however, none of these arguments are really decisive, and the position is extremely unsatisfactory to any one with real curiosity about such a fundamental question. In such cases it is a heuristic[1] maxim that the truth lies not in one of the two disputed views but in some third possibility which has not yet been thought of, which we can only discover by rejecting something assumed as obvious by both the disputants. (*The Foundations of Mathematics*, pp. 115-116.)

It is assumed as obvious by both the nominalist and the realist that there can be no objective justification for the application of a general term to its instances unless its instances have something in common over and above their having in common that they are its instances. The nominalist rightly holds that there is no such additional common element, and he therefore wrongly concludes that there is no objective justification for the application of any general term. The realist rightly holds that there is an objective justification for the application of general terms, and he therefore wrongly concludes that there *must* be some additional common element.

Wittgenstein denied the assumption that is common to nominalism and realism, and that is why I say that he solved the problem of universals. For if we deny the mistaken premiss that is common to the realist's argument and the nominalist's argument then we can deny the realist's mistaken conclusion and deny the nominalist's mistaken conclusion; and that is another way of saying that we can affirm the true premiss of the nominalist's argument and can also affirm the true premiss of the realist's argument.

The nominalist says that games have nothing in common except that they are called games.

The realist says that games must have something in common, and he means by this that they must have something in common other than that they are games.

Wittgenstein says that games have nothing in common except that they are games.

Wittgenstein thus denies at one and the same time the nominalist's claim that games have nothing in common except that they are called games and the realist's claim that games have something in common other than that they are games. He asserts at one and the same time the realist's claim that there is an objective justification for the application of the word "game" to games and the nominalist's claim that there is no element that

---

[1]   *heuristic*: helping to discover or learn [editor's note].

is common to all games. And he is able to do all this because he denies the joint claim of the nominalist and the realist that there cannot be an objective justification for the application of the word "game" to games unless there is an element that is common to all games (*universalia in rebus*) or a common relation that all games bear to something that is not a game (*universalia ante res*).

Wittgenstein is easily confused with the nominalist because he denies what the realist asserts: that games have something in common other than that they are games.

When we see that Wittgenstein is not a nominalist we may easily confuse him with the realist because he denies what the nominalist asserts: that games have nothing in common except that they are called games.

But we can now see that Wittgenstein is neither a realist nor a nominalist: he asserts the simple truth that they both deny and he also asserts the two simple truths of which each of them asserts one and denies the other.

I will now try to put some flesh on to these bare bones.

The value and the limitations of the nominalist's claim that things which are called by the same name have nothing in common except that they are called by the same name can be seen if we look at a case where a set of objects literally and undeniably have nothing in common except that they are called by the same name. If I choose to give the name "alpha" to each of a number of miscellaneous objects (the star Sirius, my fountain-pen, the Parthenon, the colour red, the number five, and the letter Z) then I may well succeed in choosing the objects so *arbitrarily* that I shall succeed in preventing them from having any feature in common, other than that I call them by the name "alpha." But this imaginary case, to which the nominalist likens the use of all general words, has only to be described to be sharply contrasted with the typical case in which I apply a general word, say "chair", to a number of the instances to which it applies. In the first place the *arbitrariness* of my selection of alphas is not paralleled in the case in which I apply the word "chair" successively to the chair in which I am now sitting, the Speaker's Chair in the House of Commons, the chair used at Bisley for carrying the winner of the Queen's Prize, and one of the deck chairs on the beach at Brighton. In giving a list of chairs I cannot just mention anything that happens to come into my head, while this is exactly what I do in giving my list of alphas. The second point is that the class of alphas is a *closed* class. Once I have given my list I have referred to every single alpha in the universe, actual and possible. Although I *might* have included or excluded any actual or possible object whatsoever when I was drawing up my list, once I have in fact made my arbitrary choice, no further application can be given to the word "alpha" according to the use that I have prescribed. For if I later add an object that I excluded from my list, or remove an object that I included in it, then I am making a different use of the word "alpha." With the word "chair" the position is quite different. There are an infinite number of actual and possible chairs. I cannot aspire to complete the enumeration of all chairs, as I can arbitrarily and at any point complete the enumeration of all alphas, and the word "chair," unlike the word "alpha", can be applied to an infinite number of instances without suffering any change of use.

These two points lead to a third and decisive point. I cannot teach the use of the word "alpha" except by specifically attaching it to each of the objects in my arbitrarily chosen list. No observer can conclude anything from watching me attach the label to this, that, or the other object, or to any number of objects however large, about the nature of the object or objects, if any, to which I shall later attach it. The use of the word "alpha" cannot be learned or taught as the use of a general word can be learned or taught. In teaching the use of a general word we may and must refer to characteristics of the objects to which it applies, and of the objects to which it does not apply, and indicate which of these characteristics count for the application of the word and which count against it. A pupil does not have to consult us on every separate occasion on which he encounters a new object, and if he did consult us every time we should have to say that he was not *learning* the use of the word. The reference that we make to a finite number of objects to which the word applies, and to a finite number of objects to which the word does not apply, is capable of equipping the pupil with a capacity for correctly applying or withholding the word to or from an infinite number of objects to which we have made no reference.

All this remains true in the case where it is not I alone, but a large number of people, or all of us, who use the word "alpha" in the way that I suggest. Even if everybody always called a particular set of objects by the same name, that would be insufficient to ensure that the name was a general name, and the claim of the name to be a general name would be defeated by just that necessity for reference to the arbitrary choices of the users of the name that the nominalist mistakenly claims to find in the case of a genuinely general name. For the nominalist is right in thinking that if we always had to make such a reference then there would be no general names as they are understood by the realist.

The nominalist is also right in the stress that he puts on the role of human interests and human purposes in determining our choice of principles of classification. How this insistence on the role of human purposes may be reconciled with the realist's proper insistence on the objectivity of the similarities and dissimilarities on which any genuine classification is based can be seen by considering an imaginary tribe of South Sea Islanders.

Let us suppose that trees are of great importance in the life and work of the South Sea Islanders, and that they have a rich and highly developed language in which they speak of the trees with which their island is thickly clad. But they do not have names for the species and genera of trees as they are recognized by our botanists. As we walk round the island with some of its inhabitants we can easily pick out orange-trees, date-palms and cedars. Our hosts are puzzled that we should call by the same name trees which appear to them to have nothing in common. They in turn surprise us by giving the same name to each of the trees in what is from our point of view a very mixed plantation. They point out to us what they called a mixed plantation, and we see that it is in our terms a clump of trees of the same species. Each party comes to recognize that its own classifications are as puzzling to the other as the other's are puzzling to itself.

This looks like the sort of situation that gives aid and comfort to the nominalist in his battle against the realist. But if we look at it more closely we see that it cannot help him. We know already that our own classification is based on similarities and differences between the trees, similarities and differences which we can point out to the islanders in an attempt to teach them our language. Of course we may fail, but if we do it will not be because we *must* fail.

Now *either* (a) The islanders have means of teaching us their classifications, by pointing out similarities and differences which we had not noticed, or in which we had not been interested, in which case *both* classifications are genuine, and no rivalry between them, of a kind that can help the nominalist, could ever arise;

or (b) Their classification is arbitrary in the sense in which my use of the word "alpha" was arbitrary, in which case it is not a genuine classification.

It may be that the islanders classify trees as "boat-building trees", "house-building trees," etc., and that they are more concerned with the height, thickness and maturity of the trees than they are with the distinctions of species that interest us.

In a particular case of *prima facie*[2] conflict of classifications, we may not in fact be able to discover whether what appears to be a rival classification really *is* a classification. But we can be sure that *if* it is a classification *then* it is backed by objective similarities and differences, and that if it is *not* backed by objective similarities and differences then it is merely an arbitrary system of names. In no case will it appear that we must choose between rival systems of genuine classification of a set of objects in such a sense that one of them is to be recognized as *the* classification for all purposes.

There is no limit to the number of possible classifications of objects. (The nominalist is right about this.)[3]

There is no classification of any set of objects which is not objectively based on genuine similarities and differences. (The realist is right about this.)

The nominalist is so impressed by the infinite diversity of possible classifications that he is blinded to their objectivity.

The realist is so impressed by the objectivity of all genuine classifications that he underestimates their diversity.

Of course we may if we like say that there is one complete system of classification which marks all the similarities and all the differences. (This is the realist's summing up of what we can learn by giving critical attention to the realist and the nominalist in turn.) Or we may say that there are only similarities and differences, from which we may choose according to our purposes and interests. (This is the nominalist's summing up.)

In talking of genuine or objective similarities and differences we must not forget that we are concerned with similarities and differences between *possible* cases as well as between actual cases, and indeed that we are concerned with the actual cases only because they are themselves a selection of the possible cases.

Because the nominalist and the realist are both right and both wrong, each is driven into the other's arms when he tries to be both consistent and faithful to our language, knowledge and experience. The nominalist talks of resemblances until he is pressed into a corner where he must acknowledge that resemblance is unintelligible except as a resemblance *in a respect*, and to specify the respect in which objects resemble one another is to indicate a *quality* or *property.* The realist talks of properties and qualities until, when properties and qualities have been explained in terms of other properties and other qualities, he can at last do nothing but point

---

[2]   *prima facie:* at first sight; before further examination [editor's note].

[3]   Here one may think of Wittgenstein's remark that "Every application of every work is arbitrary," which emphasizes that we can always find some distinction between any pair of objects, however closely similar they may be. What might be called the principle of the diversity of discernables guarantees that we can never be forced to apply the same word to two different things.

to the *resemblances* between the objects that are said to be characterized by such and such a property or quality.

The question "Are resemblances ultimate or are properties ultimate?" is a perverse question if it is meant as one to which there must be a simple, *single* answer. They are both ultimate, or neither is ultimate. The craving for a single answer is the logically unsatisfiable craving for something that will be the ultimate terminus of explanation and will yet itself be explained.

Name_____

Date _____

1. How does Wittgenstein differ from both a nominalist and a realist? (Hint: ". . . he asserts the simple truth that they both deny and he also asserts the two simple truths of which each of them asserts one and denies the other.")

2. Why cannot a term (i.e., word) used to refer to an arbitrarily chosen group of particulars be a genuine general name (i.e., common noun)?

3. Can there be more than one legitimate means of classifying the same set of nonarbitrarily chosen particulars? Explain.

4. Do you believe that Wittgenstein solved the problem of universals? Why or why not?